Product Liability

Product Liability

Jane Stapleton
Fellow, Balliol College, Oxford

Butterworths
London, Boston, Dublin, Edinburgh, Kuala Lumpur,
San Juan, Singapore, Sydney, Toronto, Wellington
1994

United Kingdom	Butterworth & Co (Publishers) Ltd, 88 Kingsway, LONDON WC2B 6AB and 4 Hill Street, EDINBURGH EH2 3JZ
Australia	Butterworths, SYDNEY, MELBOURNE, BRISBANE, ADELAIDE, PERTH, CANBERRA and HOBART
Canada	Butterworths Canada Ltd, TORONTO and VANCOUVER
Ireland	Butterworth (Ireland) Ltd, DUBLIN
Malaysia	Malayan Law Journal Sdn Bhd, KUALA LUMPUR
New Zealand	Butterworths of New Zealand Ltd, WELLINGTON and AUCKLAND
Puerto Rico	Butterworth of Puerto Rico, Inc, SAN JUAN
Singapore	Butterworths Asia, SINGAPORE
USA	Butterworth Legal Publishers, CARLSBAD, California; and SALEM, New Hampshire

A CIP Catalogue record for this book is available from the British Library.

ISBN 0 406 03503 2

Typeset by Goodfellow & Egan Phototypesetting Ltd, Cambridge
Printed and bound in Great Britain by Latimer Trend & Company Ltd, Plymouth

Preface

ABOUT THE BOOK

This book concerns the most important new statutory liability in the post-war era in the UK. This liability was created by Part I of the Consumer Protection Act 1987, which implements a European Community (EC) Directive (85/374/EEC), itself roughly modelled on s 402A of the Restatement of Torts (Second) of the United States. The book is arranged in three Parts – History, Theory and Stability – but within these divisions I have pursued a number of connected aims and themes. These are set out in detail in Chapter 1 and range from an account of the doctrinal evolution of the new product liabilities in both the US and EC, through an evaluation of the theoretical background to the product liability debate on both sides of the Atlantic, to an analysis of the workability of limited regimes of this sort. I also cover practical issues such as the present and future impact of the new EC law on who is sued, claims rates, success rates and insurance premiums, as well as its possible future impact on doctrine and legal reasoning. Nonetheless one of my principal aims, and probably the most unusual, is to use the study of product liability as a vantage point from which to consider important general topics in civil liability. Examples include the impact of EC Membership (from Part 1); the strengths and weaknesses of modern theories of civil liability as evaluated from the perspective of a tort lawyer concerned with real detailed legal rules (from Part 2); and the sources of instability in legal regimes, not just those limited in the way product liability rules are but also broader liabilities such as negligence. In short, I have tried to draw out of the product liability story issues which are important for the wider context of civil liability. This often produces a structure and emphasis which is unconventional but I hope it presents readers with a discussion that concentrates at an appropriate level of detail on the most stimulating problems and ideas thrown up for consideration by the new products law.

The final typescript was delivered to Butterworths on 20 July 1993 but it has been possible to include some developments up to 24 November 1993.

Jane Stapleton
Balliol, 24 November 1993

Acknowledgments

My principal intellectual debt is owed to Patrick Atiyah and John Fleming whose work first fired my interest in tort law in general and whose later encouragement led me to study Anglo-American legal problems in particular.

In writing this book I have been helped with advice and assistance from a number of people, all of whom I gratefully thank. Leigh Gibson from the Consumers in the European Community Group and Gareth Johnston of the Northern Ireland Civil Service were especially helpful on matters relating to the EC bureaucracy. Friedrich Kretschmer (Bundesverband der deutschen Industrie e V) and my father Colin Stapleton have been invaluable sources of information on continental and Australian legal developments respectively. The staff of the Bodleian Law Library have solved many difficulties for me and on a number of occasions I have relied upon the good-will of the Balliol College Office staff for which I am continually grateful. Shirley Enoch turned my poor handwriting into manuscript form and I am particularly thankful for the high quality of her work.

In many places the ideas in this book have grown out of the work of other schol-ars and I hope that I have acknowledged this accurately – but I apologize in advance if I have inadvertently missed out an appropriate citation. In thinking about and then writing this book I have enjoyed the intellectual stimulus and support of my Oxford students and colleagues. To them warm thanks and the hope that the cooperative spirit which a collegiate academic environment fosters so well can be preserved in the future. In particular, I want to thank my fellow lawyers at Balliol – Paul Davies, Donald Harris and Joseph Raz – for their strong support and encouragement on which I have relied heavily over the past few years. Finally, I owe a particular debt of gratitude to C J Miller and my husband Peter Cane who both read the book in manuscript form and gave careful and constructive criticism.

By far my greatest personal debt is owed to my wonderful and patient family. I dedicate the book to my two golden apples, Daniel and Lucy, and to Peter their devoted father for whom, happily for all of us, equity starts at home.

Contents

List of figures

Abbreviations

Law Coms

The Law Commission and the Scottish Law Commission, *Liability for Defective Products* (June 1977) Cmnd 6831.

Strasbourg Convention

Strasbourg Convention on Products Liability in Regard to Personal Injury and Death, Council of Europe, 27.1.77.

Pearson Com

Royal Commission on Civil Liability and Compensation for Personal Injury (ch Lord Pearson) (March 1978) Cmnd 7054 Vol I, Chapter 22.

draft Directive

EEC Draft Directive on products liability, O J No C 241, 14.10.76 (first draft), O J No C 271, 26.10.79 (second draft).

initial reformers

Law Coms, Strasbourg Convention, Pearson Com, EEC Draft Directive

the Directive

Council Directive on the approximation of the laws, regulations and administrative provisions of the Member States concerning liability for defective products, 25.7.85; O J No L 210/29, 7.8.85. See Appendix 1.

CPA

Consumer Protection Act 1987 (UK). See Appendix 2.

'defect-free' strict liability

A regime of strict product liability without a requirement that the product be defective, an example of which is full strict liability defined and described in Chapter 6, under heading 4.

EEC

European Economic Community (one of the three European Communities), in 1993 renamed European Community (EC) by the Treaty on European Union (TEU), also known as the Maastricht Treaty.

Table of statutes

References in this Table to *Statutes* are to Halsbury's Statutes of England (Fourth Edition) showing the volume and page at which the annotated text of the Act may be found.

Page references printed in **bold** type indicate where the Act/Directive is set out in part or in full.

List of cases

History

CHAPTER 1

Product liability law reform

1 PURPOSES

British and Commonwealth tort lawyers of my generation have witnessed an extraordinary turn-about over the last two decades. At law school we were initiated into the field at the time a wide consensus held that – at least in the area of personal injuries – tort law was a bankrupt system to be swept aside in favour of a more rational needs-based system of comprehensive compensation. The sort of tinkering with separate limited areas of liability which the Pearson Royal Commission recommended in 1978 was widely attacked as at best ignoring the real issues, and at worst exacerbating the anomalies and injustices said to be inherent in the tort system. Yet now in our middle age, we look back to find not only the eclipse of the comprehensive entitlement movement but also that the only product of this reform fervour is a stark example of the sort of piecemeal law reform which we had been led to believe was destructive of the development of the law along broad rational lines.

At one level, then, the purpose of this book is to explore the origins, theoretical context and stability of this new limited law – the 1985 European Economic Community (EEC) Directive on product liability, implemented in Britain in Part I of the Consumer Protection Act 1987 – to see how limited regimes of this sort emerge, and how they can be justified or at least made to work in a convincing way.[1] The notion of 'product liability' may be definable in terms of, say, the responsibility which the law places on those who supply products for the losses caused by their condition, but the fact that product liability can be defined as a distinct legal category does not itself establish the wisdom of separating it out from the general organisation of civil obligations.

At another level the study uses product liability as a vantage point from which to investigate important general topics in civil liability. Not all the areas which might be illuminated in this way can be covered in one book,[2] but I hope those which have been pursued here are the ones of the most general interest. For example, the fact that the history of the new product rule in the Directive is embedded in earlier

---

1 In this sense it is complementary to other studies on the new law's domestic and comparative impact across Member States such as *European Product Liability* ed P Kelly and R Altree (London, Butterworths, 1992); G Howells *Comparative Product Liability* (Aldershot, Dartmouth, 1993); A Geddes *Product and Service Liability in the EEC* (London, Sweet and Maxwell, 1992); J Finsinger and J Simon *The Harmonization of Product Liability Laws in Britain and Germany* (London, Anglo-German Foundation, 1992).

2 For example, conflicts of law problems are not dealt with as these are thoroughly examined elsewhere: P Kaye *Private International Law of Tort and Product Liability* (Aldershot, Dartmouth, 1991).

developments in the United States allows an examination of the contrasting social and legal culture of the US in some detail (Part 1). Similarly, looking eastward, the products Directive opens up important general questions about the impact of EC membership on the political and legislative freedom of Member States. Next, one of the purposes of the extensive investigation in the middle section of the book of possible theoretical foundations of the new product rule is to provide an approach to the current vigorous debates about the foundations of civil liability which is not that of legal philosophy but of mainstream tort scholarship. One value this book may therefore have is to introduce mainstream tort lawyers to the important elements in these debates, using real and familiar legal rules to anchor the discussion. It may also help legal philosophers to understand the concerns of tort lawyers. Finally, at this general level, the investigation in the Third Part of the stability of the product rule allows important conclusions to be made about the sources of instability in legal rules, particularly those rules limited in their application to certain specific enterprises, and those which, in their application to individual cases, can potentially have such a wide socio-economic impact that the separation of powers doctrine might appear to be breached.

In this book I have tried not only to describe and evaluate these issues but to venture positive suggestions; and I hope that where these value judgments occur, they do so openly. There has been a large shift from the optimistic 'comprehensive reform' outlook of tort lawyers twenty years ago to today's somewhat bewildered agnosticism about the direction and fate of tort law. This study aims to help understanding of how that shift happened and what it can tell us about future options for the law of civil obligations.

2   THEMES

It is useful at the outset to introduce some of the themes of the study. One immediately apparent concern is with the products regime in the United States. The history of the Directive is linked directly to the earlier common law development in the US of a liability imposed on those who supply a product in the course of a business. That doctrine, crystallizing around 1960 and set out in s 402A of the Second Restatement of Torts, is widely regarded in the US as the 'most prominent feature of modern civil jurisprudence'.[3] Yet although it inspired and served as a model for the proponents of reform at both the national UK and European levels, the processes by which the US and EC rules became law contrast sharply, providing the best modern illustration of the divergence of legal culture between the US and the process of reform now preferred in the UK and EC. On the other hand, the US experience in the three decades since the adoption of the rule in s 402A may exert considerable influence in the future on EC practitioners and judges dealing with the Directive – not least in the UK where the language and cultural barriers to continental European materials should not be underestimated. Nor will this simply be as a source of possible fact situations giving rise to claims. Specialists in European comparative law predict that where the European Court of Justice (ECJ) is forced to decide an issue

---

3 G Priest 'Product Liability Law and the Accident Rate' in *Liability: Perspectives and Policy* ed R Litan and C Winston (Washington, Brookings Inst, 1988) 184.

under the Directive it will adopt the approach of flexible substantive reasoning used by US courts rather than the more formalistic approach traditionally adopted by British courts.[4] The ECJ will at some time be asked to determine whether a worker injured by the product he or she was making had been injured by a product 'put into circulation in the course of a business'; and whether software, maps and other designs are a 'product'. If the US approach *is* followed, the answer to these questions will be determined not by past technical precedents as to the abstract meaning of words such as 'put into circulation' and 'product' but by the policy concerns and objectives said to underlie the Directive. The implications for the related areas of UK law – especially the law of sales – which have hitherto been interpreted in a formalistic way could be great. A word or concept might mean one thing under the Sale of Goods Act and be given a different meaning under the Directive by the ECJ. A close examination of the US experience helps illuminate the sites of such potential infection of larger fields.

There has been little detailed study in the UK and Europe of US product liability experience[5] but this has not prevented its rhetorical deployment in arguments about the Directive, about the inclusion of the development risk defence and about the review of this defence, due to be held in 1995. Yet the importance of the US experience of the products rule in s 402A is matched by the need for caution in its use. This is because it is moulded, as was its history, by an amalgam of factors unique to the social, legal and economic culture of the US. Central to this is the relative paralysis of the US legislative process and the parallel activism of US courts reflected in their embrace of substantive rather than formalistic arguments to flesh out the rule and increase its ambit. Since substantive reasoning can generate widely differing results, there is a bewildering array of conflicting case law across the 51 US jurisdictions.[6] Institutional factors, such as the use of juries, the contingency fee system and the lack of an equivalent to the National Health Service, combine with a generous availability of punitive damages to produce apparently huge awards. Accidents of history have also been important in shaping the consciousness of US courts and commentators in this area in a way fundamentally different from that of their European counterparts. While modern European reformers were forced by the Thalidomide tragedy of the 1960s to put unforeseeable losses and injuries to 'bystanders' (ie victims who are neither buyers nor users of the product) at the centre of their analysis, the US had no equivalent of the Thalidomide tragedy during the years of doctrinal development (Thalidomide was not released generally in the US). In the US early formative causes célèbres in the products field typically involved foreseeable risks to those who bought or used or worked with the relevant product, so the focus of doctrinal development and the attendant theoretical debate was quite different from that in Europe.

Another important theme is how theory has a useful role in any evaluative study of legal rules. Finding a reason why a particular plaintiff might deserve

---

4 S Whittaker 'European Product Liability and Intellectual Products' (1989) 105 LQR 125, 132. On the distinction between substantive and formalistic reasoning see P Atiyah and R Summers *Form and Substance in Anglo-American Law* (Clarendon Press, Oxford, 1987).

5 A notable exception is the work of W Felstiner and R Dingwall, eg, *Asbestos Litigation in the UK; An Interim Report* (Centre for Socio-Legal Studies, Oxford, 1989).

6 The jurisdictions comprise the 50 states plus the federal admiralty jurisdiction – federal courts have no power to create a federal common law. On these general points see Atiyah and Summers op cit 58–60 and generally.

compensation is not difficult but it is insufficient, as are reasons why a particular defendant should be penalised. These sorts of reasons fail to justify the basic fact that the plaintiff receives only what the defendant is obliged to pay. The rationale for both elements must, therefore, be coextensive. In the demanding task of finding such a rationale it becomes vitally important to distinguish the effects of a rule from its possible goals, to identify the points at which a theorist is making ideological choices, and to consider how perspectives can be shifted depending on whether it is the distributional effects of a rule which are focused upon or the way in which the award of damages 'corrects' the injury done by the defendant to the plaintiff.[7]

In terms of theory it might at first be thought that what had happened to the 1960s and 1970s movement for a comprehensive approach to personal injuries compensation was that it met and was defeated by the force of a great counter-idea in support of civil liability. Certainly in the US (but for different reasons) there has been a flowering of ambitious abstract theories, economic and moral, in defence of tort liability; and it is symptomatic of the importance of the US product rule both politically – for it is responsible for vast numbers of claims – and doctrinally – being allegedly a hybrid of tort and contract ideas – that a product sale and injury is often the paradigm case to which a particular theory is applied. One theme of the theoretical discussion in this book is, therefore, to see how important the gap is between these abstract 'ideal type' theories popular in North America which address only a few of the constituents of a cause of action – typically causation and the standard of conduct of the parties – and the complex content of real rules such as those in the Directive with its requirements of 'defect', 'product', 'put into circulation', etc.

A central problem with the theoretical debate is the looseness with which many key terms are used. Notions of 'risk spreading' are often merged with the quite distinct idea of 'risk distribution'. 'Enterprise liability' is used synonymously with ideas as diverse as 'market-share liability' (a causation doctrine concerned with identification of defendants) and a 'policy imposing the social costs of an enterprise on those who benefit directly from it'.[8] Terms such as 'corrective (or commutative) justice' and 'distributive justice' are often used in opposition to each other even though arguably they are more plausibly seen as merely different perspectives on a broader issue.[9] Most worrying in the context of a search for rationales to support the alleged shift to stricter liability for products is the ambiguity with which the term 'strict liability' is often used. No longer does it retain a universal meaning of a liability for which reasonable care is no answer. At one extreme it is wrongly used synonymously with the concept of 'absolute liability'; at the other it is also used to describe the liability set out in s 402A of the Second Restatement of Torts and the EEC products Directive, even though the availability of a development risk defence for unforeseeable losses under both regimes means that manufacturer liability is arguably analogous to negligence (albeit perhaps allowing the imposition of a very high standard of care). It is true that s 402A and the Directive do impose, overall, a stricter liability *regime*, but this is only because on the periphery of the core liability

---

7 This point about the distributive justice and corrective justice perspectives is developed in more detail in Chapter 8, under heading 3.

8 See respectively the influential Comment (by Sheiner) 'DES: A Proposed Theory of Enterprise Liability' (1978) 48 Fordham LR 963; R Cunningham 'Apportionment Between Partmakers and Assemblers in Strict Liability' (1982) 49 U Chi LR 544, 558.

9 J Finnis *Natural Law and Natural Rights* (Clarendon Press, Oxford, 1980) 179, 'the distinction between distributive and commutative justice is no more than an analytical convenience'.

of manufacturers, a strict liability is imposed on some innocent suppliers of the product ... importers, retailers, etc. Two major themes of Part 2, therefore, are the clarification of the relevant debased terminology in which the alleged policies and principles of civil liability theory have been couched, and then the determination of the extent to which pure theory can provide a basis for such a richly textured and multilayered liability as that set out in the EEC Directive and s 402A.

The search for the theoretical foundations for the Directive and s 402A pin-points weaknesses and anomalies within the product regimes themselves. In itself this is not very interesting – law without any anomaly is an impossible ideal and, in any case, law with certain anomalies can still be stable. But close evaluation allows us to distinguish those areas of uncertainty and instability in the Directive and s 402A which are inherent generally in civil liabilities based on balancing standards and causal requirements, from those which are particular to the product rules and there-fore especially threaten their integrity. Two sources of such latter instability are noteworthy. First, the substantive reasoning of the ECJ presupposes and will be dependent on those reasons which are seen as justifying the creation of a new law in the Directive. Unless we have an adequate rationale for how, where and why we have drawn boundaries around such a limited civil liability, we may be unable to hold those boundaries stable in the face of the onslaught of substantive reasoning – a result that not only broadens the specific liability but destabilizes the associated areas of law on which it impinges. But this potential instability may be limited, for there is only so much the expanding pressure of substantive reasoning can achieve in the face of express legislative provisions.

A greater potential instability lies in the problem of 'overlapping enterprises'. If a convincing explanation cannot be found for singling out producers of products for special treatment by the rules of civil liability, those enterprises will have a genuine grievance. This is because in the real world, injuries are typically the result of a combination of interacting or 'overlapping' activities and enterprises, only one of which may be product-related. Take as an example the passenger who is injured because, when a carelessly driven bus skids on a carelessly banked road, she is un-able to reach one of the few safety bars provided in the design of the bus. In theory, the enterprises not only of the bus manufacturer and designer are implicated but also those of the bus operator and local authority responsible for road design and con-struction. However, even if the Directive provides no doctrinal advantage in suing the product manufacturer the new law may in time generate a sufficiently higher consciousness among legal advisers that in such multiple causation contexts claims are channelled to enterprises engaged in the manufacture and supply of the impli-cated product. In turn this could generate pressure from these enterprises for the lia-bility in the Directive either to be abolished or at least converted into a more general liability to fall on all those who, say, act in the course of a business. Of course, it would be some considerable time before such instability would be precipitated: in the UK successful claims involving products, including those at work and those also involving services, are so few – the Pearson Commission estimated only 2,000 claims per year[10] – that even though the doctrinal focus of the Directive on product manufacturers may seem strikingly unjust relative to other business defendants, it may be that the cost of increased claims to product businesses may still be tolerable to them relative to their other costs. But for lawyers interested in the development of

10 Pearson Com para 1202 (early 1970s figures).

the law along broad rational lines, the Directive should not be accepted complacently. Its obstructive position between the law of contract and tort raises fundamental questions about the appropriate spheres and rationales of those fields.

Within this larger picture of the law of civil obligations generally, the post-war
developments in the area of product liability in both the EC and the US can be seen
as part of a larger, albeit uncoordinated, movement within the law this century to
come to terms with modern circumstances. These include the phenomena of large
distant enterprises, mass marketing and a dramatic increase in scientific and economic understanding of the interdependence of much human activity. In this environment the contract/tort polarity of individual free contracts and injuries between
strangers is no longer adequate to deal with much of the experience of the community. Such developments have not only led to the withering of our confidence in traditional contract principles and assumptions, but have also brought the role of tort
law and its relationship and overlap with other spheres of law under sharp scrutiny.
A quarter of a century ago Grant Gilmore noted that to isolate product liability for
separate analysis would falsify and distort debate.[11] The final theme of this study is
to identify those aspects in the story of product liability reform which have larger
significance and some of which may suggest the direction in which the law of civil
obligations might better develop to respond sensibly and sensitively to the forces
now pressing upon it.

11 G Gilmore 'Product Liability: A Commentary' (1970) 38 U Chi LR 103, 116.

CHAPTER 2

Evolution of product liability doctrine in the US

1 'PRODUCT LIABILITY'

The scope of 'product liability' is not self-evident. At its most general it denotes the responsibility which the law places on those concerned with the supply of products for the losses caused by the condition of those products. As the term is commonly used in the UK, however, it refers to the *tortious* liability of a commercial supplier of products for certain injuries caused by those products: for example, the liability of a manufacturer to the consumer of its contaminated ginger beer. Even though the history and substance of the two forms of liability are closely intertwined, in Britain and the rest of Europe the term tends not to include liabilities in contract. Even within the field of tortious liability, the modern European notion of 'product liability' is considerably narrower than, say, 'liability arising out of product-caused injury'. It excludes, for example, injuries by products which have not yet been commercially supplied. Since these boundaries lack adequate modern justification, it will be one of the objectives of this study to show that 'product liability' does not constitute a satisfactorily coherent field of legal organization. For the present, though, we can usefully adopt a broad definition and aim principally to analyse the history, substance and operation of 'liability for goods which have been supplied commercially'. At the turn of the twentieth century, liability for product injuries in both the UK and US was dominated by the form of contract law developed by courts during the nineteenth century. Liability in tort was subservient to and derivative of such contractual liability, so a useful starting point for this study is nineteenth century contract law.

2 CONTRACT LIABILITY FOR PRODUCT INJURIES UNTIL 1913

Tracing the substance of the common law before the nineteenth century is difficult. Reasons for this include the fact that the cost of litigation took it out of the reach of most potential claimants so that the number of claims was low and probably unrepresentative of grievances. Furthermore, the reporting of judgments may often have been inaccurate; but, even if accurate, the general practice of judges was to focus narrowly on the case in hand rather than engage in wider syntheses of earlier case law. In the case of contractual complaints about the quality of goods, the pre-nineteenth century common law attitude remains a matter of debate.[1] While in related

---

1 For recent accounts see J Gordley *The Philosophical Origins of Modern Contract Doctrine* (Oxford, Clarendon Press, 1991) esp 159, and D Ibbetson 'Sale of Goods in the Fourteenth Century' (1991) 107 LQR 480.

areas there is case law evidence of interventionist (perhaps even paternalistic) judicial attitudes towards those in contractual relation to one another, the case law from this period relating to the quality of goods is very small. Atiyah suggests that this may have been because of the generally low value of goods relative to litigation costs; the tradition and adequacy of inspection as a way of discovering defects; the general adequacy of regulatory statutes to protect consumers from hard-to-discover defects such as adulterated food; and cultural inhibitions in conceding that one had been outwitted in a typical face-to-face market transaction.[2] Whatever the reasons for the low incidence of case law on the quality of goods, Atiyah concludes that it meant that 'the protection for the buyer against shoddy or defective goods does not seem to have been a common law tradition'.[3]

The common law was forced to take up a position on the issue during the the economic expansion of the nineteenth century. The volume of transactions exploded and transactions which previously had been relatively uncommon – such as between distant parties – became commonplace. By the middle of the nineteenth century, the volume of litigation on matters of fitness and quality of goods sold had become huge, and a tussle had developed between two starkly contrasting judicial approaches. On the one hand, there were judges who had been converted to the new economic theories of laissez-faire with their corollary in the law of sales of caveat emptor – 'let the buyer beware' – and, in the absence of an express agreement to the contrary, let the buyer bear the risk of quality defects. This contract doctrine was said to rest, inter alia, on the desirability of certainty about the terms of the agreement and diminution of litigation.[4] It allowed the seller to remain silent about defects in the goods/realty whether he knew or should have known of them or not. Such contract ideas still survive and have recently emerged as a powerful influence on the product liability debate.

Opposed to these views were a cluster of British judges who, adhering to the previous interventionism of the eighteenth century, appreciated that the dynamics of the new markets often increased the barriers to truly consensual agreements, an effect of the free market which earlier experience had shown could occur. The hostility of these judges to the laissez-faire obsession with express agreements and caveat emptor was forcefully put and in terms still relevant to the 'back to contract' fashion in the US today by Sir John Byles writing in 1845 on the topic of public regulation:

> ... perfect freedom in contracts ... is specious and seducing, from its simplicity. It is easily understood and easily applied. Men congratulate themselves on their superior wisdom, and look down with a smile of contempt on the antiquated and barbarous rubbish of public regulations. The painful duty of investigating details, and judging by experience of the applicability of the principles to particular classes of cases is superseded.[5]

---

2 P Atiyah *The Rise and Fall of Freedom of Contract* (Oxford, Clarendon Press, 1979) 179–180.

3 Atiyah, op cit, 179.

4 Law Commission *Caveat Emptor in Sales of Land*, a Consultative Paper from the Conveyancing Standing Committee of the Law Commission (Law Commission, London, 1988) para 2.1; Mercantile Law Commission 1855, 2nd Report, p 10 (18 Official Report (3rd series) col 657). See also Law Commission *Civil Liability of Vendors and Lessors for Defective Premises* (Law Commission, London, No 40, 1970) para 15.

5 J Byles *Observations on the Usury Laws* (London, S Sweet, 1845) 54. On these general points see Atiyah, op cit, 180, 472, 474 ff.

These judges proceeded to construct solutions to the new wave of disputes about goods by the implication of terms in the sale contract, for example by holding that in general a seller of a good must be taken implicitly to warrant his title. The two such implied terms of most importance later in the context of product liability were the implied warranty of merchantability and, where a particular purpose had been made known to the seller, the implied warranty of fitness for that particular purpose. Comparable developments occurred in the US where there is also evidence of an earlier eighteenth century judicial interest in intervening to construct fair bargains.[6]

What were the market phenomena which provoked this interventionist approach? Probably the most important factor was that, as the industrial revolution accelerated, there was an increased incidence of sales of new goods where reasonable opportunities for inspection of the goods by the buyer were not feasible for one of a number of reasons. Sometimes the nature of the new types of good made inspection difficult or impossible at least without expert technical advice, which was often in short supply. Even if the intrinsic nature of the good did not produce this situation, the volume of transactions and the new forms in which products were packaged and delivered often did. But most importantly of all, inspection was often rendered difficult if not impossible – at least for commercial buyers in the chain – by the increasing number of contracts formed between parties acting at a distance, in some cases before the relevant goods had come into existence, and the speed at which goods were passed down the lengthening commercial chain. In such circumstances these traditionally-minded judges seemed impressed by the reality of the buyer's reliance on the superior knowledge and commercial integrity of the seller and perhaps on the apparently increased reliability and safety of goods. They saw it as the common law's duty to construct a fair bargain to protect such reliance of those 'necessarily ignorant' of the quality of the goods they bought for a price which had presumably been accepted on the basis of this reliance.[7] To modern minds this seems common sense. As Prosser noted in 1943, 'it cannot reasonably be thought that the buyer is willing to pay good money for whatever the seller will give him and remain completely at the seller's mercy'.[8] In any case, the implied terms as to quality also seemed to be in line with sellers' increasing appreciation of the value of goodwill and their correspondingly increased acceptance of responsibility for quality – a point supported by the fact that by the 1860s much of the vast trade in Indian cotton was conducted on an express standard term of merchantability.[9]

Although the tussle between the new laissez-faire contract ideas and those of the traditionalists continued for some decades, the latter's view eventually came to predominate so that by 1893 Chambers had no difficulty in formulating the implied warranties of merchantability and fitness for purpose as the accepted common law position.[10] As Atiyah sums it up:

---

6 See, eg, *Timrod* v *Shoolbred*, 1 SCL (1 Bay) 325 (SC, 1793). Also, see W Prosser 'The Implied Warranty of Merchantable Quality' (1943) 27 Minnesota LR 117, 146–8, 155–6.

7 Atiyah, op cit, 479.

8 Prosser, op cit, 159.

9 A W B Simpson 'The Origins of Futures Trading in the Liverpool Cotton Market' in *Essays for Patrick Atiyah*, ed P Cane and J Stapleton (Oxford, Clarendon Press, 1991) 179, 185, n 35. On goodwill see also: K Llewelyn quoted by J Chait, 'Continuing the Common Law Response to the New Industrial State' (1974) 22 UCLALR 401, 405 fn 15; Prosser, op cit, 122; Atiyah, op cit, 475, 479.

10 M Chalmers *The Sale of Goods* (London, William Clowes & Sons, 1890) pp 20–3.

The truth is ... that the early nineteenth century saw little more than a brief flirtation with the doctrine *caveat emptor*; from the beginning this flirtation had to contend with serious opposition from judges who still believed that it was part of the job of the Courts to see that contracts were fair; and by the 1860s, at least in contracts of sale of goods, these judges had won out, and the flirtation was over. The common law had, in large part, returned to the traditions of eighteenth century Equity when the fairness of a contractual exchange was still an all-important part of contract law.[11]

What were the important features of these implied warranties of quality? First, by the time they were being developed, the warranty concept was seen as contractually based. Yet it had only been with the rise of non-interventionist contract ideas such as caveat emptor that it had become necessary to separate out the spheres of contract and interventionist tort.[12] The interest in fair bargains of those courts which created the implied warranties harked back to the earlier interest in fairness which had shown 'remarkable tenacity over the centuries' and had influenced *both* forms of civil liability.[13] Indeed, all warranties implied by law had had a hybrid origin, owing more to tortious ideas than contractual ones.[14] Another aspect of these liabilities which has proved important in the current product liability debate is that they can be seen as consistent with modern ideas of economic efficiency. Put into this jargon they can be treated as recognizing that nineteenth century commercial buyers of goods, often buying from a geographically distant seller, typically faced considerable market defects. These included informational asymmetries, high information costs,[15] and the irrational or at least mistaken assumption that the seller was, in part, selling information about the quality of the product and that that was reflected in the 'fair' price. In such cases, so modern economic theory goes, forced internalization to the seller, and through the sellers' chain, to the cheapest cost avoider, usually the manufacturer, may be justified (Chapter 5).

   Perhaps the most important technical feature of these warranties in terms of their impact on the course of product liability reform was that, not only were they regarded as imposing a contractual obligation, but an obligation which was strict in nature; that is, an obligation which could be breached despite the seller's use of all reasonable care.[16] It could apply, for example, to undiscoverable defects in quality. There is nothing self-evident about this: indeed, as we will see, when modern US courts created a parallel warranty of quality in the realty sector the standard was only one of reasonable care (Chapter 12, under heading 1). But there is no clear explanation why the implied warranties – especially the implied warranty of merchantability – were formulated as strict obligations. Explanations for the strictness of the warranty of merchantability in terms of the buyer's problems in proving

---

11 Atiyah, op cit, 479.
12 J McLaren 'The Convergence of Tort and Contract: A Return to More Venerable Wisdom?' (1989) 68 Can BR 30.
13 McLaren, op cit, 43. See also Gordley, op cit, 105–7, 159–160, but contrast H Collins *The Law of Contract* (London, Weidenfeld & Nicolson, 1986) who seems to assume this is a modern concern, 121–3, 130.
14 Prosser, op cit, 118; McLaren, op cit, 37.
15 The seller often knew more about the quality of the good and considerable costs were involved in the buyer acquiring comparable information or bargaining about the issue.
16 See, eg, *Frost v Aylesbury Dairy Co Ltd* [1905] 1 KB 608.

negligence[17] seem, in the absence of evidence of explicit judicial reasoning, merely ex post rationalizations. So too, explanations based on price levels are dubious.[18] It is one thing to say that prices today may reflect the allocation to the seller of the risk of defects not discoverable by reasonable means. But it is quite another to imply that the warranty of merchantable quality was imposed because the relevant judges thought that early nineteenth century prices of goods already reflected this allocation. It seems equally plausible that many merchant sellers either did not consider the risk or placed their faith in caveat emptor. Either way, the risk would not have been reflected in their prices. Certainly judges sometimes asserted that prices paid for goods 'may be assumed to represent (the) value'[19] which the buyer had bargained for and was therefore entitled to receive. But this is simply to assert the conclusion that losses associated with poor quality were to fall on the seller, for no such correlation between price paid and strict entitlement to corresponding value – the 'fair bargain' idea – was seen to be dictated in other contexts such as realty sales where, despite the buyer's payment of a substantial price, the seller was not held to a strict obligation to transfer property of corresponding value or even to take reasonable care to do so. In this context, caveat emptor was upheld.

If we speculate about the reasons for the strict standard, one possibility is the influence of property rights on contractual rights in general. Earlier cases on sales of goods had established that on agreement property passed, so that the buyer's rights at the time of agreement overlapped with his rights as owner[20] such as the right to possession which was protected by strict obligations. When agreement began to precede delivery, such rights survived and perhaps set a pattern of strict obligations which later influenced the obligations relating to the nature and quality of the goods which courts read into the agreement. A possibility limited to the warranty of merchantable quality is that this was implicitly treated as a sub-species of the implied warranty of correspondence with description which was being developed simultaneously. In cases of sale by description – say of peas – it was not acceptable to argue that all the seller was promising to do was to take all reasonable care that what he delivered was peas rather than beans. He had to deliver peas.[21] Inasmuch as the idea of implied agreement formed the basis of this warranty, a *strict* obligation reflected market sense. In cases where the goods met the contract description but suffered from a substantial defect in quality, the analogy with the strict obligation relating to description probably seemed strong, and certainly the two warranties were often run together in the early cases.[22] Perhaps in the early stages of the development of the warranty of merchantability it was simply assumed that reasonable care by a supplier would have revealed the defect. Certainly from a modern perspective, the terminology of nineteenth century case law appears confused and vague in the deployment of negligence and strict liability

17 Such as those of Williston, see F Kessler 'The Protection of the Consumer Under Modern Sales Law: Part I' (1964) 74 Yale LJ 262, 272–3.
18 See, eg, G Treitel *Remedies for Breach of Contract* (Oxford, Clarendon Press, 1988) 21.
19 *Readhead* v *Midland Rly Co* (1869) LR 4 QB 379, 386.
20 D Ibbetson 'Sale of Goods in the Fourteenth Century' (1991) 107 LQR 480.
21 *Bowes* v *Shand* (1877) 2 App Cas 455, 480 (per Lord Blackburn); *Chanter* v *Hopkins* (1838) 4 M & W 399, 404 (Lord Abinger).
22 See *Randall* v *Newson* (1877) 2 QBD 102, 109 (Brett J A) and cases cited in Chapter 9, n 13. See also *Benjamin's Sale of Goods*, 4th edn (London, Sweet & Maxwell, 1992) ss 11.002–11.003 (F M B Reynolds); S Stoljar 'Conditions, Warranties and Descriptions of Quality in Sale of Goods – I' (1952) 15 MLR 425, 435–6.

concepts.[23] Whatever the origin of the seller's strict obligation with respect to the merchantability of goods, it has been the single most potent aspect of the developing law of product liability. It made commercial sellers accustomed to strict obligations with respect to quality long before they were exposed to a fault standard in tort in this regard, and long before pressures developed to convert that standard into a strict standard. This acclimatization helps explain how stricter liability was able to infect US *tort* law in the gradual and almost unremarked fashion that it did (Chapter 2, under heading 4).

The next important characteristic of the implied warranty of merchantability was that it was a *dealer's* liability; that is, it only attached to commercial sales by dealers in goods of the relevant description. This limitation may have simply been a function of the size of transactions which would make it worthwhile for the buyer to sue, but it is more likely to have been seen as a necessary element in recognizing those sales of goods in which the implied term was justified. When a buyer bought from a dealer in a particular type of good, the buyer's reliance was predictable and a defensible level of expectations could be defined: 'merchantability', that is, acceptability *in that market*. Another boundary of the implied warranty of merchantability was that it was limited to sales of goods. Corresponding strict obligations were not developed in respect of services and realty.

A final important point is that judicial concern centred on transactions where inspection of the goods was *impossible*. This became a pre-condition of the implied warranty of merchantability at common law.[24] The focus on non-inspectability helps to explain the exclusion of realty and of services transactions from the reach of the warranty.[25] More importantly, since consumer transactions[26] were usually still carried out in face-to-face dealings with sellers so that inspection was still theoretically feasible, it is striking that the warranty which later proved to be of most importance to consumers developed in response to the needs of the business community and operated initially as a remedy for *commercial buyers* rather than the consumer-buyer at the end of the chain. This character of being a 'businessman's remedy' was dramatically changed in 1893 when Parliament, in purporting to codify the common law of sales, radically amended the relevant clause concerning the quality of goods. It enacted the rule that commercial sellers of goods owed the implied warranty of merchantability *unless* inspection by the buyer had actually taken place *and* such inspection should reasonably have revealed the defect.[27] As had already been the law under the wider form of warranty implied by Scottish courts,[28] the risk of undiscoverable defects in goods was now to fall on the seller. The reason for this dramatic change is unclear. Assimilation of the laws of England and Scotland is not a sufficient answer, for the statutory provision is wider than the Scots law had been. In

---

23 On which see G Schwartz 'The Character of Early American Tort Law' (1989) 36 UCLA LR 641 and M Horwitz *The Transformation of American Law 1780–1860* (Cambridge, Harvard University Press, 1977) 86–8.

24 See, eg, *Jones* v *Just* (1868) LR 3 QB 197; M Chalmers *The Sale of Goods* (London, William Clowes & Sons, 1890), 20–3. Contrast Gordley, op cit, 159–160.

25 Realty and the work done by a service-provider could usually still be inspected easily.

26 Here 'consumer transaction' means one in which one party (the 'consumer') does not make the contract in the course of a business and the other party does. See Unfair Contract Terms Act 1977, s 12(1)(a) and (b).

27 Sale of Goods Act 1893, 56 & 57 Vict, ch 71, s 14(2); M Chalmers *The Sale of Goods Act 1893* (London, William Clowes & Sons, 1894), 30. Now see Sale of Goods Act 1979 (C 54), s 14(2)(b).

28 Mercantile Law Commission, op cit, 10.

any case, this would simply beg the question of what was the reason for the earlier Scottish rule?

Whatever its Parliamentary origin, the new law converted the common law warranty originally constructed to protect the economic interests of a commercial buyer who had received poor quality goods into a remedy of great potential for protection of consumers. Before 1894 merchantability and fitness for purpose claims usually revolved around the economic loss the commercial buyer would typically suffer by receiving defective goods. There were occasions, however, when the defect in the received good caused physical injury to the 'other property' already owned by the commercial buyer, and so the implied warranty claim was for physical loss.[29] After 1894 and the formal extension of the implied warranty of merchantability to typical consumer contexts, this form of the implied warranty claim assumed great importance. This was because there is a greater possibility of physical injury being caused to the ultimate buyer of consumer goods such as food and of classes of goods that were now being bought in large numbers such as automobiles, cosmetics and medicines. By the early decades of the twentieth century it was not unusual for consumers to bring personal injury claims based on the implied warranty of merchantability particularly in respect of impure food and drink.[30] Comparable developments occurred in the US where the common law 'codification' in the 1906 Uniform Sales Act (eventually adopted by two-thirds of the states) also extended the reach of the warranty to consumer contexts in the same way as the British legislation had done.

Important though the remedy given by the merchantability warranty was – and being a strict obligation against the seller the plaintiff actually dealt with, and one that covers both physical and economic loss, it remains a powerful and convenient remedy for the buyer – it was firmly characterized as a remedy in contract. This meant that the development of the warranty liability was severely restricted when late nineteenth century contract law adopted an inflexible notion of privity – an idea that it was somehow contrary to the nature of a contract that it should be capable of conferring enforceable rights on a third party. The rigid doctrine of privity was allowed to freeze out more equitable responses to the emerging problem of ever-lengthening middle party chains, responses which might have included the idea that, for instance, the warranty ran with the goods to the benefit of the ultimate buyer (or even user) suffering the loss. That contract was allowed to develop in this way was no doubt helped by the fact that the problems of the private buyer, let alone the injured non-buyer, were not commonly being presented to courts in the mid- to late-nineteenth century, at least not as warranty claims; and by the fact that contract doctrine was assuming a monolithic form in which no distinction was made between different contract types – for example, between sales to private individuals and sales to merchants in the course of their business. By the time warranty claims by the former class became common, that is after 1893, the privity doctrine had acquired an irresistible and universal force.

In the context of the warranty of merchantable quality the effect of the privity doctrine was to render the warranty available only to those victims of defective goods who were in privity with the seller being sued. The privity requirement barred

---

29 Early examples under the fitness for purpose warranty are *Smith* v *Green* (1875) 1 CPD 92; *Randall* v *Newson* (1877) 2 QBD 102.
30 For an early example, see *Wren* v *Holt* [1903] 1 KB 610.

two different classes of claim. First, it barred claims by the buyer against someone, for example the manufacturer, who was higher up the chain than the immediate seller. Today such buyers who are within the distribution chain of contract but who did not buy directly from the target-defendant are termed 'vertical non-privy plaintiffs'. This bar operated even though, in the absence of exclusion clauses, there is little to object to in allowing a claim between parties who are not in privity with one another: the defendant is held to no greater liability than he already faced under the warranty in *his* sales contract and the plaintiff is given no greater rights than he already had against the middle party – a point French law has recognized in the 'actione contractuelle directe'. But at least such buyers could usually sue their immediate seller. The second and more dramatic effect of the privity rule was that it barred any warranty claim by a non-buyer injured by using the product herself (a 'mere user' or 'horizontal non-privy plaintiff') or by someone else's use of the product (the 'bystander' plaintiff). The limitation of the classes of individual to whom sellers could be liable for breach of the warranty would not have constituted such an important barrier to product claims as it did, if those not in privity with the defendant had had another basis on which to sue. Here, however, they ran into the infamous 'privity fallacy'.

3 TORT AND THE PRIVITY BAR

The developing idea of privity had an impact outside the law of contract by dramatically inhibiting the development of parallel remedies in the emerging tort of negligence. In the mid- to late-nineteenth century tort notions had to struggle with the fact that under the laissez-faire approach to contract 'a right to due care was still largely seen as something for which a man had to pay'.[31] Reported claims between strangers were rare. Most physical injury claims arose in 'relational contexts', that is where there had been a pre-existing relationship between the parties, for example of employment, carriage or occupier and entrant of land. The rarity of stranger cases can be illustrated by an important comment in a case concerning a claim in tort against the lessor of a carriage by the servant of the carriage's lessee. In *Winterbottom* v *Wright* (1842) Lord Abinger observed that there seemed to be no precedent for such an action[32] and the court went on to decide against liability. The court did not address the issue of whether the plaintiff was owed any tort obligation independent of contract but seems simply to have assumed that no such *independent* tort action should lie. The judges then went on to base their decision on a much narrower ground: that an action in tort could not be derived or *generated* solely on the basis that the defendant's conduct constituted a breach of some contract. This reasoning was based on the quite valid fear of generating a multiplicity of tort claims based on each breach of contract (which we might call 'dependent' tort claims). But this left unanalysed the question of whether an independent tort duty *should* exist here.

---

31 Atiyah, op cit, 501.
32 *Winterbottom* v *Wright* (1842) 10 M & W 109; 152 ER 402, 404. Probably a correct view of the precedents as they stood in 1842, the claim not arising from status, public calling or the like, see V Palmer 'Why Privity Entered Tort – An Historical Re-examination of *Winterbottom* v *Wright*' (1983) 27 Am JLH 85, 87–8, 94.

Later, however, and in particular once the concept of privity had solidified as a central tenet of contract doctrine, the decision in *Winterbottom* v *Wright* was taken in both the UK and US to have laid down a general rule against *independent* tort actions in cases where the defendant's relevant conduct constituted a breach of contract. This rule, later described as the 'privity fallacy', meant that a plaintiff who was a third party to a contract could not base a claim in tort – ie claim the benefit of an *independent* tort duty – if the defendant's conduct which was identified as the tort also happened to constitute a breach of the contract. Thus in future cases a lessor who had been under a contractual obligation to a lessee to keep the carriage in good repair would be held to owe no independent tort obligation to the victim-employee.

Winterbottom v *Wright* was not what we might today describe as a mainstream product liability case because it did not involve the condition of a product produced by manufacture, but a negligent omission adequately to *repair* something by a defendant who had *undertaken a contractual obligation* to do so. Indeed, so long as caveat emptor prevailed, the making and/or selling of defective goods would not by itself have constituted a breach of contract to the buyer and so would not have brought the actual decision in *Winterbottom* into play. But the case was quickly used to bar claims in tort based on the defectiveness of products sold. In particular, it was used to protect manufacturers from liability in tort to the ultimate victims of their negligently-made products.[33] This extension appears to have been achieved via two elaborations of the principle which *Winterbottom* came to stand for, both of which have important modern analogues in areas such as economic loss claims and realty transactions. First, it was argued the buyer should not be allowed to bring a claim *in tort* against his seller or against the distant manufacturer so as to impose on such defendants risks which they *had not undertaken* in their respective contracts of sale. Similarly, the non-buyer victim was to be allowed no better claim than the buyer had. Of course, it may be sensible to prevent the buyer using tort to circumvent the positive risk allocations made in contract. Contracts for the sale of goods were typically silent about the relevant risk, and so long as caveat emptor prevailed courts construed that silence as a *positive* allocation of the risk to the buyer. In this context the shielding of the immediate seller and distant manufacturer from both contract and tort claims made some sort of sense. Once courts and then Parliament recognized the contractual liability of sellers for the defective quality of goods via the implication of implied warranties of quality in substitution for caveat emptor, the problem of a claim by a buyer circumventing a positive contractual allocation of risk disappeared because the seller was now taken to have routinely undertaken the obligation with respect to quality. In retrospect, this should have opened up the possibility of the recognition of an independent tort duty to consumer buyers, users and bystanders.[34] But at the turn of the century the privity fallacy had taken on an authority of its own and still survived to bar tort claims for defective products by most victims.

Why judges adhered to the privity fallacy is unclear. Perhaps it was simply the power of stare decisis. Certainly there seems to be no evidence that this was due to the crude self-interest of judges investing in the commercial sector, since what little evidence there is suggests nineteenth century judges much preferred to invest in

---

33 See *Longmeid* v *Holliday* (1851) 6 Exch 761; 155 ER 752.

34 In this sense modern liability in the tort of negligence for product injuries was dependent on this development in contract law, see J Stapleton 'Duty of Care and Economic Loss: A Wider Agenda' (1991) 107 LQR 249.

public activities than in private enterprise.[35] Nor can it neatly be ascribed to a more abstract public policy of protecting emerging industry. Recent research sharply questions this earlier 'subsidy to enterprise' theory of judicial attitudes to tort in the nineteenth century. Moreover, it seems unlikely that the growth of liability for negligence replaced widespread strict liability: judged by the reported case law, liability for physical injury was rarely imposed except in a few relational contexts, where it tended to be strict.[36] In analyzing Anglo-American case law from the period Gary Schwartz discovered that in many areas negligence was used to generate an 'abundant source of liability' which was vigorously applied to private capital.[37] In this light the rise of negligence as a basis of recovery in the mid- to late-nineteenth century could be read as a growing trend towards rather than against victim protection, even if some argue that the adoption of fault rather than strict liability to do this reveals a recognition of and support for entrepreneurial interests.[38] The important point here is that these growth areas of liability tended to be in contexts where, although the defendant may have been acting in performance of a contract with a third party, this was ignored or not noticed. Thus, as a small but increasing stream of such claims between 'strangers' reached the courts, the negligence doctrine could be developed and applied without the fetter of precedent or the need to accommodate it within contractual ideas. There seems, for example, to have been little difficulty in holding railways liable in negligence to those injured at level-crossings, possibly the single largest cause of accidental death in the US at the turn of the century.[39]

Nonetheless, the majority of reported cases about physical loss in this period still arose in contexts perceived as relational, such as the liability of employers to employees, of product sellers to those injured by goods sold and of occupiers of land to entrants. This may well have been because there were fewer non-legal barriers to the pursuit of a claim in such contexts; but it is still relevant that once a claim was perceived as having a contractual context, courts became concerned to allow the contract to regulate the parties' liability. Thus in *Winterbottom* v *Wright* the court concentrated on the limits of the defendant's commitments under the contract and used the circular argument – which would defeat any new liability – that to recognize the plaintiff's claim would upset the defendant's expectations as to his potential liability which he had thought would be solely regulated by the contract. Even after the recognition of implied warranties of quality demolished this argument in cases of claims by consumer buyers, it still could be, and was, used against other non-privy plaintiffs in these relational contexts. The buyer could sue on the contractual warranty but other victims had no contractual or tortious claim. Injecting duties into contracts via implied terms can at most help plaintiffs in privity with the defendant. But if non-privy plaintiffs had been allowed to make claims simply on the basis of

---

35 D Duman *The Judicial Bench in England 1727–1875: The Reshaping of a Professional Elite* (London, Royal Historical Society, 1982), 139.

36 R Rabin 'The Historical Development of the Fault Principle: A Reinterpretation' (1981) 15 Georgia LR 925; G Schwartz 'Tort Law and the Economy in Nineteenth-Century America: A Reinterpretation' (1981) 90 Yale LJ 1717; G Schwartz 'The Character of Early American Tort Law' (1989) 36 UCLA LR 641. But contrast D Kretzmer 'Transformation of Tort Liability in the Nineteenth Century: The Visible Hand' (1986) 4 OJLS 46.

37 Schwartz (1981) op cit, 1770.

38 R Abel 'A Critique of American Tort Law' (1981) 8 Br J Law Soc 199, 211–212. Rabin, op cit, also points out the failure to recognize negligence claims in areas such as nervous shock and economic loss.

39 See Schwartz, (1981) op cit, 1765–6 and Abel, op cit, 212, n 5.

the defendant's breach of a contract with a third party, there was a real danger that contract would have been swallowed up and the laissez-faire ideal of the centrality of contract shattered. However, from the plaintiff's point of view the fact that the defendant was in a contractual relationship with a third party should have been irrelevant. At heart, then, the privity fallacy seems to have been more a child of contract theory than a direct socio-economic tool or the outcome of a judicial theory about the independent role of tort. Its ascendancy mirrored the rise of certain notions about the nature and the dominance of contract. This in turn produced a lop-sided, incoherent theory of negligence – a phenomenon which the modern 'back to contract' theories tend to ignore (see Chapter 6, under heading 3 and Chapter 8, under heading 5). Real coherence in negligence doctrine was delayed until well into the twentieth century when such thinking had been put into retreat and the privity fallacy could be confidently jettisoned.

There were already signs of this outcome in the later nineteenth century. A tension developed between the classical contract-centred approach and the approach in those negligence cases in which the contractual relationship of the defendant with a third party was ignored or not noticed and which were dealt with on the basis that the case was one between strangers. The *Winterbottom* v *Wright* objection that the plaintiff was using tort in a way which 'upset' the expected limits of the plaintiff's contractual rights and/or the defendant's contractual obligations was often overlooked. In *Heaven* v *Pender* (1883),[40] for example, the court imposed on the supplier of goods a tort duty of care to a non-privy plaintiff with respect to defects in the goods of which the defendant actually knew. In *Indermaur* v *Dames* (1866)[41] the plaintiff who successfully sued in tort was an entrant who was injured on the defendant's premises where he had gone as a result of his employment by a third party. The court *could* have seen the *Winterbottom* analogy and asked whether the plaintiff was entitled to warnings of dangers when he had no contract with the occupier himself. It did not. One of the first important areas in which the realities of the situation were confronted was injuries to railway passengers.[42] The market practice of pooling resources on the railways had meant that a passenger might have paid railway company X for her ticket but have been carried on and injured by railway company Y. The contractual context could not be ignored. After struggling to construct an artificial contract-based remedy, the courts recognized in 1880 the liability of Y to the victim, despite the absence of a contract between them and despite the contractual relations each had with other third parties.

The shift had started. By the early years of the twentieth century reliance solely on contract to protect from the losses of physical injury in these relational contexts was being jettisoned in favour of a view dramatically opposed to such ideas. No longer were such victims to be left to whatever contractual rights they had (or, more typically, had not) bargained for. The new focus was the recognition of a legally imposed obligation to take care to avoid physical loss by affirmative negligent conduct, owed even to those who had no contract with the defendant. Under this slowly emerging counter-idea, the defendant was to take care to avoid such loss, not because it had a bargain with the plaintiff to do so, but because it was thought fair

---

40 (1883) 11 QBD 503.
41 (1866) LR 1 CP 274.
42 Atiyah, op cit, 503–504. Contrast the relative ease with which US railway passengers recovered in the period (ie up to 1860) studied by Schwartz (1981) op cit.

that it should reach such a level of conduct. On both sides of the Atlantic the attractions of the new idea produced pockets of tort liability recognized to be exceptions to the privity rule.[43] Two important pockets in relation to products were, first, where a supplier of goods might be held liable in tort where it actually knew of the defect and failed to warn of it; and secondly where the defendant had manufactured an inherently dangerous product. But the privity bar remained intact over a wide area, especially in the products field. This reflected itself in the volume of claims. For example, in California, one of the most vigorous centres of modern products litigation, there was in the nineteenth century only one claim by a non-privy plaintiff against a product seller and even that revolved around the special circumstance of an express warranty.[44] In both the UK and US, there was no significant volume of tort-based product claims until the rejection of the privity bar, in 1932 and 1915 respectively.

Relevant social theories and values were not standing still in the late nineteenth century. In addition to the gathering strength of the tort-based counter-idea just discussed, even more radical ideas about liability for injury were emerging in fields related to products. In particular, an incompletely formed notion of 'enterprise liability', which had seemed to underlie the doctrine of vicarious liability, was being adapted and extended to ground fairness and deterrence rationales for employer's strict liability for work-related injuries to his employees, and these bore fruit in the workers' compensation schemes dating from 1897. As we will see in Chapter 8, the notion that 'the cost of the product should bear the blood of the workman'[45] is not so very different from the slogans used to promote stricter tort liability for product injuries in the late twentieth century.

4   *MAZETTI* (1913) AND ITS AFTERMATH: DIVERGENCE OF ANGLO-AMERICAN PRODUCT LAWS BEGINS

Dissatisfaction with the privity bar grew as mass markets developed, middle-parties became more common and the incidence of product injuries to non-privy victims, especially from motor vehicles, increased. This led in 1915 to the decision of *MacPherson* v *Buick Motor Co* (1916) in the US.[46] Here the manufacturer of a defective car whose wheel collapsed was sued in the tort of negligence for personal injuries suffered by the plaintiff who had bought it from a retailer. In allowing this claim the New York Court of Appeals led by Judge Cardozo expanded the 'inherently dangerous' exception to the privity rule to such an extent that it came to be accepted in later cases that the rule itself had been swallowed up. The equivalent development was to occur in the UK in *Donoghue* v *Stevenson* (House of Lords, 1932).[47] Henceforth, in both countries negligence claims could be made by non-

43 Set out in *Huset* v *JI Case Threshing Machine Co* 120 F 865 (1903). An earlier unsuccessful attempt to generalize the duty had been made in the UK by Brett M R in *Heaven* v *Pender* (1883) 11 QBD 503, 509.

44 *Lewis* v *Terry* 111 Cal 39; 43 P 398 (1896); see Schwartz, (1981) op cit, 1766.

45 Quoted by W Prosser *Handbook of the Law of Torts*, 5th edn (St Paul, West Publishing Co, 1984) 573.

46 *MacPherson* v *Buick Motor Co* 111 NE 1050 (1916); see W Prosser *Handbook of the Law of Torts*, op cit, 682–3.

47 [1932] AC 562.

privy plaintiffs (including mere bystanders) arising out of both the design of the product and manufacturing errors. The defendant could no longer use the limits of its contractual obligations to construct an immunity from tort liability to a third party who had suffered physical loss because of its negligence conduct. Despite the burgeoning of the tort of negligence after the defeat of *Winterbottom* and its eventual application to every aspect of the manufacture and distribution of products, *MacPherson* was, in fact, not the crucial development giving US and later EC products laws their modern distinguishing characteristics. Rather the source of the special status given to *product* injuries in modern US tort law dates from a relatively obscure development in the contractual field of implied warranty. The Trojan horse by which stricter obligations were smuggled into the tort domain was the abandonment of the privity requirement in claims based on the implied warranty of merchantability.

By the time nineteenth century judges began to imply warranties of quality into sales of goods, warranty had taken on a fully contractual flavour. Once the privity doctrine had taken root by the end of the century it became a settled part of what might loosely be called 'classical' warranty law that the only party to whom such protection was available was the party in contractual privity with the defendant seller. In the US this concept began to break down in the twentieth century to produce a form of 'aclassical warranty' which dispensed with privity and later with other attributes of a 'classical' warranty claim. Such developments remain virtually unknown in Britain where warranty claims retain their traditional or 'classical' requirements including privity. Prosser dates this US development from the Washington state case of *Mazetti* v *Armour & Co* (1913)[48] where a vertical non-privy plaintiff (ultimate buyer) was allowed to leapfrog the retailer and sue the manufacturer of impure food under implied warranty. *Mazetti* had been decided at a time of national agitation over food standards. Its lead was followed quickly in a small number of comparable food/drink cases which justified the abandonment of the privity requirement by a wide variety of devices which included the attractive and popular idea thought up by a Mississippi court in 1927 that the implied warranty 'ran' with the product from the manufacturer to user just as obligations under covenant could run with land to non-privy beneficiaries.[49] In *Baxter* v *Ford Motor Co* (1934)[50] the benefit of manufacturers' *express* warranties was extended to ultimate buyers.

The early evolution of aclassical warranty did not go unresisted. Only seven years after it had demolished the privity bar in negligence claims in *MacPherson*, the New York Court of Appeals, including Judge Cardozo, rejected such an implied warranty claim by a non-privy plaintiff, loyally applying the classical requirement of privity.[51] But the doctrinal significance of the developments signalled by *Mazetti* – the violation of the citadel of privity – was not widely appreciated or emphasised. Prosser,

---

48 135 P 633 (1913) (recovering pure economic loss); Prosser *Handbook of the Law of Torts*, op cit, 690.
49 These devices were listed by C Gillam 'Product Liability in a Nutshell' (1957) 37 Ore LR 119, 153–5; and D Noel 'Manufacturers of Products – The Drift Toward Strict Liability' (1957) 24 Tenn LR 963, 985–8. Defeat of the realty right by a bona fide purchaser shows the analogy in the specific device discussed is not exact.
50 12 P 2d 409; 15 P 2d 1118 (1932), 35 P 2d 1090 (1934).
51 *Chysky* v *Drake Bros Co* 139 NE 576 (1923).

later to be the leading popularizer of stricter product liability to non-privy victims, seemed pre-occupied at this time with promoting the benefits of classical warranty claims to plaintiffs in privity. In an exhaustive article in 1943 on the implied warranty of merchantability, he mentions the privity issue and *Mazetti* only once and in passing.[52] On the other hand, Prosser did acknowledge elsewhere at this time that stricter liability to non-privy plaintiffs may be 'the law of the future' to be imposed in tort as a matter of public policy.[53] So too in his 1941 draft text of the Uniform Commercial Code, Llewellyn tried unsuccessfully to convince the other drafters to allow jurisdictions the option of dropping the privity requirement in certain claims based on the merchantability warranty.[54]

But in retrospect the most important recognition of the doctrinal significance of the abandonment of privity was that by Justice Traynor in a 1944 Californian case, *Escola* v *Coca-Cola Bottling Co of Fresno*.[55] In that case a waitress injured by an exploding coke bottle successfully sued the manufacturer in negligence, the case turning on the doctrine of res ipsa loquitur. Traynor argued obiter, however, that plaintiffs such as the waitress should be able to sue in tort on the basis of the strict liability of the manufacturer. The 'intricacies of the law of sales' such as privity should be abandoned and the underlying public policy of the implied warranty of merchantability used to construct an independent and coherent strict liability for products in tort.

The flow of cases allowing aclassical warranty claims by non-privy plaintiffs seemed to slow down in the 1930s and 1940s, but during the 1950s their greater potential as compared with *MacPherson*-type negligence claims became more widely appreciated. While *MacPherson* had removed the privity barrier for a large number of claims, the flood of negligence claims which then followed highlighted in turn the widespread problems of proving negligence-in-fact in modern complex manufacturing processes. Surreptitiously raising the standard of care and generous use of res ipsa loquitur could make the defendant's life harder in many cases and, where successful, these tactics sufficiently raised the expectations of certain defendants that imposition of the strict liability represented by aclassical warranty liability came to appear less of a revolution (especially since all sellers had been long accustomed to strict obligations with respect to quality under the ordinary 'classical' warranty liability). But there were still a significant number of cases in which proof of negligence-in-fact was an intractable problem. The attractions of a shift to aclassical warranty were consequently great and courts began to apply the idea beyond food and drink cases to products used for intimate external bodily use (cosmetics, hair dyes, etc). It had also, by this time, become routine for the warranty concept to be applied to complaints not just about manufacturing errors, but about the design of the product itself, and such claims were also arising in negligence.[56]

---

52 Prosser (1943), op cit, 119.
53 W Prosser, *Handbook of the Law of Torts*, 1st edn (St Paul, West Publishing Co, 1941) 692.
54 J Clutterbuck 'Karl Llewellyn and the Intellectual Foundations of Enterprise Liability' (1988) 97 Yale LJ 1131, 1147; G Priest 'The Invention of Enterprise Liability: A Critical History of the Intellectual Foundations of Modern Tort Law' (1985) 14 J Leg Studs 461, 497–8.
55 150 P 2d 436 (1944).
56 G Schwartz 'New Products, Old Products, Evolving Law, Retroactive Law' (1983) 58 NYULR 796, 802; 'Forward: Understanding Products Liability' (1979) 67 Calif LR 435, 438.

5   *HENNINGSEN* (1960), *GREENMAN* (1963) AND S 402A OF THE SECOND RESTATEMENT OF TORTS

At the same time, there was an increase in academic interest in replacing the artificial rationales for aclassical warranty claims by a more general rule. In 1960 Prosser published an article – 'The Assault Upon the Citadel (Strict Liability to the Consumer)' – which was to prove highly influential in later case law and theoretical debate.[57] In it he described, and to some extent exaggerated, the case law history of the abandonment of privity in implied warranty claims. He emphasized the hybrid origin of warranty claims in tort and contract, deducing that 'if warranty is a matter of tort as well as contract ... then it should need no contract.'[58] He highlighted the advantages of allowing recovery in such cases and concluded that it would be sensible to recognize the 'policy basis' of the liability and hence to recognize an independent and generalized strict liability in tort for product injuries, dropping altogether the pretence of a warranty basis to such claims. The weight and coherence of Prosser's 'policy basis' were in fact quite poor – which was understandable given that his goal was the limited tidying up of an already well-settled area (warranty) and that his focus was on the relatively unproblematic area of manufacturing errors.

But in a dramatic coincidence, the New Jersey Supreme Court was independently deciding the case of *Henningsen* v *Bloomfield Motors Inc* (1960)[59] in which it allowed a car manufacturer and retailer to be sued under the implied warranty of merchantability by a mere user of the car who had suffered personal injuries. The extension of aclassical warranty to all classes of goods had thereby effectively been made. The court also refused to uphold the manufacturer's disclaimer, a significant development given the rise of warranty disclaimers. Confirmation of these developments was reflected in the 1962 version of the Uniform Commercial Code where a provision along the lines of the earlier Llewellyn draft was included to authorize courts to abandon the privity requirement in warranty claims brought by certain foreseeable horizontal non-privy plaintiffs (ie mere users) who had suffered personal injuries, and preventing defendants disclaiming the operation of that provision. The provision was not limited to claims concerning special classes of product such as food.[60] The Code later (1966) introduced wider alternatives on the privity issue, but because in all cases the Code explicitly does not bar further case law and legislative relaxation of its suggested rules, it has played neither a controlling nor pace-setting role here, and each jurisdiction has developed its own, often complex, rules on the privity issue in warranty claims.[61]

---

57 (1960) 69 Yale LJ 1099. The influence of this article is undisputed, although opinions conflict on the relative historical importance of various academic sources of reform ideas: see G Priest 'Strict Products Liability: The Original Intent' (1989) 10 Cardozo LR 2301 partially revising his earlier ideas in 'The Invention of Enterprise Liability: A Critical History of the Intellectual Foundations of Modern Tort Law' (1985) 14 J Leg Studs 461; D Owen 'The Intellectual Development of Modern Products Liability Law' (1985) 14 J Leg Studs 529; G Schwartz 'Directions in Contemporary Product Liability Scholarship' (1985) 14 J Leg Studs 763, 767–9 and 'The Beginning and the Possible End of the Rise of Modern American Tort Law' (1992) 26 Georgia LR 601; Clutterbuck, op cit.

58 Prosser, op cit (1960) 1127; see also Prosser *Handbook of the Law of Torts*, 1st edn (1941) 690.

59 161 A 2d 69 (1960).

60 See s 2–318, silent on vertical non-privy and bystander plaintiffs. This now forms Alternative A of the current s 2–318.

61 Under the revised s 2–318, the new alternatives allowed claims by foreseeable victims including bystanders who had suffered personal injury (alternative B) or foreseeable victims suffering any injury (alternative C). Both prevent defendants excluding the relaxation of privity to such classes.

The significance of *Henningsen* was immediately apparent. No longer was 'aclassical' warranty to be thought an oddity limited to a few sub-classes of goods. It could be applied generally. Moreover, other incidents of the classical warranty besides privity, such as the defendant's right to disclaim, were seen as potentially dispensable 'intricacies' of sales law. If courts were to interfere to this extent in the relations between, say, a manufacturer and a mere user, then the idea that the manufacturer's obligations with respect to physical loss had a contractual basis had to go. It was becoming clear that aclassical warranty was simply a device by which courts could interfere to regulate the relevant relationship on public policy grounds and, if necessary, in a manner contrary to any express agreement between the parties such as a disclaimer. In this sense, it represented a radically different form of judicial intervention on the basis of 'fairness' to that which had underlain the original implication of classical warranties of quality: that particular forced loss allocation had always been treated by courts (and later in sales legislation) as rebuttable by express agreement. If there were policy arguments which could defeat not only privity requirements but express disclaimers as well, the substance of the liability became nakedly tortious, even if it imposed strict liability, which was atypical of tort. Judicial recognition of the independently tortious nature of this apparently strict liability for product injuries came in the 1963 case of *Greenman* v *Yuba Power Products Inc*[62] when the Californian Supreme Court was faced with an implied warranty claim against a power tool manufacturer by the mere user who had suffered personal injuries due to the defective condition of the tool. Not only was the plaintiff a horizontal non-privy party, but he had failed to comply with another of the requirements of classical warranty claims, namely giving the defendant timely notice of the claim of breach. Justice Traynor led the court in abandoning not just the privity requirement but also all the other 'intricacies' of the classical law of sales[63] including the notice requirement, and in recognizing, as an alternative finding, that the basis of recovery was an independent 'strict' liability in tort for defective products.

These developments strengthened Prosser's hand as the Reporter to American Law Institute which was at this time drafting the Second Restatement of Torts (formally a non-binding but highly influential attempt to distil common-law principles as operated by the courts at that time). He was able, again with some exaggeration of the breadth of case law developments,[64] to extend his original draft section setting out the new liability from food (1961 draft), to things used for intimate bodily use (1962 draft) to all products (final 1964 draft). The accompanying comments emphasized that the basis of the liability was not warranty in the traditional or 'classical' sense, but tort.[65] The new section, 402A, was adopted in 1964 and published in 1965. It reads:

402A Special Liability of Seller of Product for Physical Harm to User or Consumer.

(1)   One who sells any product in a defective condition unreasonably dangerous to the user or consumer or to his property is subject to liability for physical harm thereby caused to the ultimate user or consumer, or to his property, if

---

62 377 P 2d 897 (1963).
63 On these privity, disclaimability, notice and limitation rules, see UCC s 2–318; 2–316, 2–302, 2–719(3); 2–607(3)(a); 2–725, respectively.
64 Priest, op cit (1985) 512–8.
65 See American Law Institute *Restatement of the Law: Second: Torts 2d* (St Paul, West Publ Co, 1965) s 402A, comment m.

(a) the seller is engaged in the business of selling such a product, and
(b) it is expected to and does reach the user or consumer without substantial change in the condition in which it is sold.
(2) The rule stated in Subsection (1) applies although
(a) the seller has exercised all possible care in the preparation and sale of his product, and
(b) the user or consumer has not bought the product from or entered into any contractual relation with the seller.

Jurisdictions rapidly adopted a *Greenman* or s 402A type of rule, the latter being the more popular. By the end of 1970, 'strict' tort liability for products in general was firmly adopted in more than half (28) US jurisdictions. The figure had risen to 41 by 1976, and today nearly all jurisdictions have or have had some variant of the rule in place.

There is still vigorous debate in the US about the precise origins of these developments. But what was certain was that inasmuch as the new rule created strict liabilities it was conceptually novel because strict tort liability was not otherwise a common phenomenon in the modern era. But in the way US courts came to apply it, did the new rule create strict or stricter liability? The answer to this question depends on which class of defendants is considered. Despite the rhetoric, under s 402A courts imposed no stricter standard of liability than before on manufacturers (see Chapter 10). Under negligence prior to the 1960s they had been held to a fault standard with regard to design defects and a covert strict standard with regard to most manufacturing errors. With regard to manufacturers, the historical record suggests that the principal aim of the judicial and academic formulators of the new rule was merely to make uniform and explicit the strict standard *for manufacturing errors*.[66] The issue of design defects was not faced squarely until later when courts – having tried to apply the 'strict' liability of the new rule to defective design claims against manufacturers – began to concede openly that only a fault standard was appropriate in such design cases (albeit one that had now become more demanding under the rhetorical pressure of s 402A), and that there should be no liability for unforeseeable risks (see Chapter 10). After initial confusion, then, the new rule was not taken to impose *stricter* liability on manufacturers, although it contained an element (but not a new element) of strict liability (ie the liability applied to manufacturing errors).[67]

Overall, however, the rule could be said to have imposed a new stricter liability *regime* because of its impact on other parties. This is why it is legitimate, if a little dangerous, to describe it as 'strict tort liability'. New strict liabilities were indisputably created because the rule applies to all sellers down the commercial chain *regardless of their personal fault*. In this way it does expose certain parties to a strict liability they would not otherwise have faced. Thus, while beforehand a retailer may have been under a strict classical warranty obligation, this had only been owed to one party, the immediate buyer. So long as the retailer had been reasonably careful with respect to the product, this was his sole liability in tort or contract arising out of losses due to its defective condition. Following *Greenman*/s 402A, the early

---

66 G Priest 'Strict Products Liability: The Original Intent' (1989) 10 Cardozo LR 2301; J Fleming *The American Tort Process* (Oxford, Clarendon Press, 1988) 62.

67 A state of affairs confirmed by current summaries of agreed doctrinal propositions: J Henderson and A Twerski 'A Proposed Revision of Section 402A of the Restatement (Second) of Torts' (1992) 77 Cornell LR 1512.

Californian cases of *Vandermack* (1964), *Canifax* (1965) and *Santor* (1965) showed that innocent retailers, wholesalers and distributors, respectively, could be made strictly liable in tort for the defective products they supplied to a wide category of non-privy plaintiffs.[68] Similarly, following *Cintrone* (New Jersey, 1965), courts rapidly extended the s 402A/*Greenman* rule to certain lessors of products such as self-drive vehicles.[69] The non-negligent non-manufacturing middle party certainly now faced a major new source of liability which was strict because their reasonable conduct did not protect them (see also Chapter 10, under heading 4).

Although proponents of the rule championed its conceptual importance in exuberant language, they believed its practical importance in terms of outcomes would be small. Prosser, for example, thought that, at most, one in 100 cases might be affected; and the general belief that the volume of consumer product injuries was not a substantial problem for society was reflected in the failure of manufacturers seriously to oppose the change in the law.[70] This complacency was understandable given the early focus on manufacturing errors – on which the Comments concentrate almost exclusively – where the standard to which the product would be held appeared obvious, namely that of the correctly constructed product. This led to a neglect of the theoretical and practical difficulties in justifying and defining the concept of 'defect'. Instead it seemed to be assumed that 'defect' was little different from the notion of 'unmerchantability' or 'unreasonable' condition. Prosser himself thought 'the substance of the seller's undertaking remains unaffected'.[71] If this were so, and if middle parties who were held liable could pass the new liability up the chain to the manufacturer responsible for the product's condition, then it seemed the ultimate allocation of loss would be little different from that which existed under the demanding negligence standard which had effectively already subjected most manufacturing errors to a strict standard by the combined effects of res ipsa loquitur and vicarious liability. While such manufacturing errors remained the focus of attention, the new rule could simply be seen as saving non-privy plaintiffs the complex and costly hassle of trying to prove such negligence against a manufacturer, while giving them a variety of defendants on which the liability could fall in the first instance. The result was remarkably little concern about design defects or about the potentially disruptive flow-on effects into other fields of tort liability. Inasmuch as design defects cases (and the subset of failure to warn cases) were addressed by commentators at all, the consensus was that they should and would continue to be dealt with under a fault standard.[72] Overall the general view was that the reform was a fast, interesting, but basically modest, adjustment to the liability rules governing the sale of goods.

That the change was identified more as an amendment of sales rules than as a recognition of independent tort obligations is reflected in the scope of the rule itself.

68 *Vandermack* v *Ford Motor Co* 391 P 2d 168 (1964); *Canifax* v *Hercules Powder Co* 46 Cal Rpt 552 (1965); *Santor* v *A & M Karagheusian Inc* 207 A 2d 305 (1965).

69 *Cintrone* v *Hertz Truck Leasing* 212 A 2d 769 (1965).

70 Prosser, op cit 'Assault' (1960) 1114; Priest, op cit 'Strict Products Liability: The Original Intent' (1989) 2317 and n 69 therein; M Horowitz 'Symposium Discussion' (1989) 10 Cardozo LR 2329, 2335. See also Schwartz, op cit 'Directions' (1985), 769; Schwartz, op cit 'New Products' (1983) 802–5; N Terry 'Stricter Products Liability' (1987) 52 Miss LR 1, 7–8.

71 W Prosser 'The Fall of the Citadel (Strict Liability to the Consumer)' (1966) 50 Minn LR 791, 804–5.

72 Priest, op cit 'Strict Products Liability: The Original Intent' (1989), 2303.

Here the sales legacy is clear in its limitation to goods, thereby excluding the services and realty sectors, and its limitation to goods sold by a commercial seller in the course of business. From the perspective of the European reforms, one of the most obvious indications of the sales ghost in US products law is the early neglect of the bystander issue. What should happen if a defective good causes injury to a party who neither bought nor used nor consumed it? US courts soon found it relatively easy to relax certain elements in the s 402A/*Greenman* rule, such as extending its obligations to lessors, but they found it much more problematic to extend the protection of the rule to bystanders. So, too, the authorization to relax the privity requirement in the warranty claims under the 1962 version of the Uniform Commercial Code had not extended to claims by bystanders. The Restatement itself had expressed caution about claims by such parties (caveat 1 and comment o), and even in 1966 Prosser himself was still ambivalent about the issue, which he thought raised a special but unspecified 'fundamental question of policy'.[73]

The origin of this reluctance to allow the new rules to embrace bystanders is not hard to see. Claims by consumer buyers could be seen as unremarkable because such victims were at least within the contractual chain and consequently had comparable rights against the immediate seller. Even mere users for whom goods were bought, could be seen as third party beneficiaries of the contract of sale whom classical contract had failed, and to whom the protection given to the buyer by virtue of the sale might modestly be extended. But bystanders fell outside the classes of claimant who could easily be associated with the sale. They had, for example, not been misled by representations of safety. Here, predicating the claim under s 402A/*Greenman* on the prior sale of the good would raise basic issues about why the sale element mattered at all. The US courts slowly came to accept bystander claims, perhaps helped by the later development of theoretical justifications for s 402A/*Greenman* which apply as forcefully, if not more forcefully, to bystander claims as to others. Today some of the most notorious litigation – such as that by the children of mothers who took the drug diethylstilbestrol (DES) when pregnant – are based on the acceptance of bystander claims. Even so, the bystander issue is often neglected or marginalized by US commentators when analyzing the current regime, a clever tactic for those who want to reassert the predominance of 'classical' contract solutions (Chapter 6, under heading 3). By contrast, in Europe the focus on the bystander victims of Thalidomide created a more open debate and a more tenacious focus on these issues.

Another and more striking feature which confirms that the new tort liability was not created afresh, is that it failed to make any distinction between types of physical loss. Personal injuries and property damage were treated equivalently. Little, if any, thought was given to the question of whether the allegedly new independent tort liability should be limited to personal injuries on public policy grounds, even though the early landmark cases – the aclassical warranty food cases, *Henningsen* and *Greenman* – all concerned this type of loss. Today most commentators and the US Supreme Court itself concedes that personal injury grounds the paradigm product liability claim,[74] but no serious attempt was or is made to see if policy justifies limiting

---

73 Prosser, op cit 'The Fall' (1965), 819.
74 *East River SS Corpn* v *Transamerica Delaval Inc* 106 S Ct 2295, 2300 (1986). See also G Schwartz 'Economic Loss in American Tort Law: The Examples of J'Aire and of Products Liability' (1986) 23 San Diego LR 37, 51 and reservations of Justice Holman in *Brown* v *Western Farmers Association* 521 P 2d 537, 544 (1974).

the regime to such claims. The new tort liability was extended to claims for physical damage to other property already owned by the plaintiff on the unimaginative basis that 'physical injury to property is so akin to personal injury that there is no reason for distinguishing them'.[75] Despite the irrelevance of 'consumer-protection' arguments and in sharp contrast to the European reforms, the US liability was also applied to interests in commercial property, ie where the 'other' property had been used in the course of a business; and economic loss consequential on physical damage to the plaintiff's other property is also widely allowed. The legacy of traditional warranty, under which all such classes of loss were equally recoverable, is clear.

It is not that the type of loss went unremarked in the US. For, once the privity and other boundaries of classical warranty had been pierced and the s 402A/*Greenman* rule had been created, defenders of the new rule had to address the issue of how to keep warranty law distinct from, and not swallowed by, their new creation. The underlying concern was to keep the spheres of consensual relations separate from relationships regulated or imposed by public policy: a problem perceived as one relating to the preservation of the contract/tort boundary. As we will see, a critical element in this strategy is often thought to be a distinction about the type of loss complained about. In particular, tort is traditionally hostile to claims about pure economic loss, while from its inception the implied warranty of merchantability covered such loss – indeed, while it remained in effect a commercial buyer's remedy this was the standard basis of complaint. To prevent the new tort rule swallowing the implied warranty, the solution was clear. The s 402A/*Greenman* rule had initially been expressed in terms only of physical loss, so as early as 1966, in *Seely* v *White Motor Co* (California),[76] Justice Traynor forcefully rejected the idea that the new rule could be extended to pure economic loss claims. Pure economic loss at least was to be kept exclusively within the province of warranty, which was seen as providing an adequate remedy. But defining pure economic loss to be the legitimate and exclusive province of warranty not tort required defenders of the new rule in tort to confine 'warranty' again to a traditional contract base. Although *Mazetti* itself had been an aclassical warranty claim for pure economic loss, such claims now had to be refused if the line between tort and contract was to retain its formal integrity. Fortunately the UCC had by this stage provided such flexibility with respect to the privity issue that it could be read as allowing aclassical warranty claims for some heads of loss (such as personal injuries) but not for others. The result was that advocates of allowing strict liability claims by non-privy plaintiffs in physical loss cases, such as Prosser and Traynor, became strong advocates of exercising that flexibility in a *restrictive* way to maintain the privity requirement in warranty claims for pure economic loss; and their earlier emphasis on the hybrid nature of warranty was replaced by the admission that this had been an artificial 'device' to justify stricter tort liability to the consumer.[77] In the economic loss area warranty was to be accorded its former status as an exclusive remedy, one lying in contract with its accompanying requirement of privity. The *Seely* view has prevailed in most jurisdictions so that not only is the stricter tort liability not applied

---

75 *Seely* v *White Motor Co* 403 P 2d 145, 152 (1965) (per Traynor C J); Prosser, op cit 'The Assault' (1960), 1143.

76 403 P 2d 145 (1965).

77 E Rabin and J Grossman 'Defective Products or Realty Causing Economic Loss: Toward a Unified Theory of Recovery' (1981) 12 Southwestern ULR 4, 19. Prosser *Handbook of the Law of Torts*, 4th edn (St Paul, West Publ Co, 1971) 656.

to pure economic loss claims, but even when the claim is in 'warranty', privity is required.

An important effect of this move to maintain a coherent contract/tort boundary has been to complicate greatly the implied warranty field. Once liability for physical loss to non-privy plaintiffs had been duplicated in tort under the rule in s 402A, the courts could have rationalized the situation by restricting the term 'warranty' to claims by those in privity with the defendant and who could satisfy the other incidents of classical warranty such as notice. However, they did not do this but continued to use the term 'warranty' to cover both classical and aclassical warranties and to allow 'warranty' claims by non-privy plaintiffs. The result is that today, within any one US jurisdiction, when a 'warranty' claim is brought, sometimes privity will be required, sometimes not; sometimes disclaimers will be enforced, sometimes not; and sometimes the other Code defences, such as notice and limitation requirements, will be allowed to operate, while sometimes they are highly attenuated. The complexity of this situation alone creates significant problems of uncertainty for potential defendants and insurers who typically operate in the markets of many jurisdictions. But there will also in any given case be the strong possibility of accompanying claims in negligence and 'strict' tort – and in some special cases even express warranty may be argued. In all of these, significant local variations can occur on a number of issues. Because the arguments for relaxing traditional requirements in a warranty claim on any particular issue (privity, disclaimers, etc) are comparable to those justifying 'strict' tort liability, the potential for wasteful duplication and complication is enormous. Nonetheless, at the end of the 1960s this was not well appreciated. Those within the US system were generally proud and satisfied with developments in the products field. Outsiders envied their robust and apparently successful tackling of law reform in the area.

6   THE 1970S TO THE PRESENT

Unforeseen by its proponents, the new rule in s 402A/*Greenman* was to become much more important than a tidying up of sales law. Despite the attempt in *Seely* to keep the rule within limits, courts found numerous ways in which to increase its reach beyond the apparent contemplation of its drafters. Thus, for example, New Jersey quickly allowed the rule to apply to claims of non-commercial plaintiffs for pure economic loss (*Santor* (1965)).[78] Similarly, during the 1970s, the *Greenman*-derived rule in California diverged sharply from that reflected in s 402A: California had been willing to apply only the notion of 'defect' and had refused to require that the defect also be 'unreasonably dangerous' as stated in s 402A. Moreover, during the 1970s the Californian Supreme Court elaborated the notion of defect in a way extremely generous to plaintiffs.[79] Also during this decade allowing 'defect' to be shown by a patent danger or by a failure to withstand foreseeable misuse became common (Chapter 10, under heading 7), and rules on defences as well as causation and identification of defendants became more and more generous to plaintiffs (see

---

78 *Santor* v *A & M Karagheusian Inc* 207 A 2d 305 (1965).
79 *Cronin* v *J B E Olson Corpn* 501 P 2d 1153 (1972); *Barker* v *Lull Engineering Co* 573 P 2d 443 (1978).

Chapter 11).[80] From 1970, courts increased the range of transactions to which the rule could apply so that the new liability began to infect settled areas of liability such as realty sales, landlord and tenant, occupiers' liability and workers' compensation (see Chapter 12).[81] Under the pressure of product claims the attitude to punitive damages also developed in pro-plaintiff directions.

Most important was that during the late 1960s and 1970s courts were increasingly faced with defective design claims, and since the early 1980s these have formed the overwhelming bulk of US product lawsuits. Early proponents of the rule had neglected this type of claim and it was not until the late 1960s that a careful analytical separation of manufacturing and design defect was made.[82] Design claims gave rise to academic concern about the imponderables involved in adjudications on such an open-ended concept as 'defect' and about the wide potential ramifications of a finding that a product line was defective. But by the early 1970s US courts were routinely accepting that allegations of defective design were worthy of being put to the jury, and there was nothing in the s 402A/*Greenman* rule or the ideas associated with it which precluded the doctrine's application in this way. More than anything else it was this unintended application of s 402A to the design context that gave the new product liability in the US its explosive character – it underlay, for example, the high volume, high profile asbestos, DES (diethylstilbestrol), Dalkon Shield and Agent Orange litigation – even though, as we see in Chapter 10, it was a legal time-bomb which had also lain at the heart of other civil liabilities such as warranty and negligence. Despite these developments, the original proponents of the rule were, ironically, accurate in thinking that it represented little doctrinal novelty. The modern doctrine of negligence is capable of adopting identical rules in relation to negligent design, burden of proof, comparative negligence, volenti, etc, as those prompted by the new rule, and thereby delivering results just as favourable to plaintiffs (see Chapter 10, under heading 7). On the other hand, far from fulfilling Prosser's desire to simplify litigation, these doctrinal developments in the rule itself have made many products claims much more complex and costly to mount.

Ironically it was just at this time when the rise of design claims was making the problems of duplication of causes of action and the internal complexity of the 'strict' tort rule more apparent, that the field of product liability attracted added political respectability and academic brilliance. The late 1960s and early 1970s had been marked by high-profile federal consumer legislation on product safety in general and vehicle safety in particular which had attracted a wide pro-consumer consensus in the product field.[83] Meanwhile, new theories, such as that set out by Calabresi in *The Costs of Accidents* (1970),[84] emerged to underpin and justify stricter liability, in particular for product injuries; and these economic and moral theories seemed, in turn, to exert an expansionary pressure on doctrine or, at least, on doctrinal rhetoric. Alongside developments in doctrine and theory, even more

80 See eg *Daly* v *General Motors Corpn* 575 P 2d 1162 (1978); *Sindell* v *Abbott Laboratories* 607 P 2d 924 (1980), respectively.
81 *Schipper* v *Levitt & Sons Ltd* 207 A 2d 314 (1965); *Kreigler* v *Eichler Homes Inc* 74 Cal Rptr 749 (1969); *Becker* v *IRM Corpn* 698 P 2d 116 (1985); *Garcia* v *Halsett* 82 Cal Rptr 420 (1970); *Bell* v *Industrial Vangas Inc* 637 P 2d 266 (1981).
82 Priest, op cit 'Strict Products Liability: The Original Intent' (1989), 2330.
83 G Schwartz 'The Beginning and the Possible End of the Rise of Modern American Tort Law' (1992) 26 Ga LR 601, 612–17.
84 G Calabresi *The Costs of Accidents* (New Haven, Yale UP, 1970).

striking was the acceleration from the early 1970s in the rate of litigation. Whether the great increase in claims was principally triggered by real changes in liability rules or by other reasons of legal culture (see Chapter 4, under heading 8), it had a number of dramatic effects. First, it eventually led many theorists to re-evaluate the policies said to underlie stricter tort liability for products in order to see, for example, whether inadequate weight had been given to the administrative burdens which rules can generate. Secondly, it led in some dramatic cases to the bankruptcy or take-over of particular corporations, leading to developments in the separate fields of insolvency and successor liability law. Thirdly, the rise in litigation was identified as the cause for the 1975–6 'product liability insurance crisis'. Having remained constant from 1963 until 1975, the cost of liability insurance, as a per-centage of sales revenue, suddenly increased. In fact, this 'crisis' may have been due to any of a number of factors. It may have been due to changes in doctrine in the preceding years which insurers were suddenly taking into account in setting rates. It may have been due to the increasing uncertainty in liability outcomes gen-erated by the duplication of causes of action and the apparently wide variation in rules between jurisdictions, and even to the internal incomprehensibility of such standards. It may have been merely due to an unforecast increase in the volume of product litigation, independently of whether the stricter tort rule for products had increased the scope of the liability of the relevant class of potential defendants and hence the success rate of claims. There is also the strong possibility that the insur-ance crisis had little to do with any of these matters but had most to do with the imperfections and dynamics of the insurance market itself – a conclusion bolstered by the suddenness of the 'crisis' and evidence of similar cyclical 'crises' in non-product liability fields of insurance.

Whatever its origin, the perceived cause of the difficulties in obtaining insurance in certain product areas led to a rash of ad-hoc state legislation which attempted to tinker with peripheral rules by, for example, placing caps on damages for non-eco-nomic losses. These were widely regarded as inadequate. A Federal Interagency Task Force was appointed to look into product law reform.[85] Reporting in 1977, it concluded that there were two key problems. First, some insurers were increasing premiums erratically and this was felt particularly acutely by small business. The Task Force's comments on this issue led in 1981 to the federal enactment of the Risk Retention Act,[86] which pre-empts restrictive state insurance regulations which had prevented businesses pooling their product liability risks. Allowing self-insurance cooperatives and insurance-purchasing groups alleviated the insurance problems of small business but did not address the second and more fundamental problem identi-fied by the Task Force: the nation-wide diversity and consequent uncertainty of the legal standards to be applied in products cases, specifically in design and failure to warn complaints. Not only did this phenomenon present problems of high adjudi-cation costs and forum shopping, it multiplied the cost and inaccuracies in rate-making by insurers who often operate in national markets. It was also widely suspected that unpredictable and difficult to understand liability standards were not

---

85 *Interagency Task Force on Product Liability Final Report* (Springfield, National Technical Info Service, 1977).
86 Risk Retention Act of 1981, PL 97–45, 15 USC §3901 et seq. See also Risk Retention Act of 1986, PL 99–563, which amends original statute to allow groups other than product manufacturers to pur-chase liability insurance via risk retention groups.

only dampening research and development initiatives and other prevention incentives, but resulting in the failure to release useful products – such as swine-flu vaccine which producers withheld in 1976 until government acted to protect them from liability.[87] The eventual result of these concerns was the Model Uniform Product Liability Act 1979 (MUPLA),[88] which it was hoped would be adopted by a large majority of states, creating the uniformity of approach needed to stabilize insurance rates and create certainty in incentives.

Quite apart from the increasing interest in creating uniformity of product rules, a growing body of opinion during the 1970s had argued that the scope of substantive liability itself was getting out of hand. Design and failure to warn cases were identified as a major source of uncertainty and unacceptable expansion of liability. The imposition of liability on non-manufacturing middle-parties was portrayed as a wasteful, unfair and purposeless exercise. Punitive damages awards by juries were seen as a source of anomalous and outrageous outcomes. The drafters of MUPLA within the Department of Commerce reflected this disillusioned view in their text. The cost and confusion of multiple causes of action was to be replaced by a single product liability action under which all product defect claims for physical loss were to be made. This could take any of four forms, but only in cases of breach of express warranty and of manufacturing defects would the strict liability standard be preserved. In design and failure to warn cases a negligence standard was to be openly recognized. Non-manufacturing sellers were to be liable only if negligent or if the relevant manufacturer was judgment-proof. Criteria for the award of punitive damages were set out, and the issue of quantum was to be for the judge. Other provisions addressed issues such as limitation periods and ceilings on damages. Except for the initiative on middle-party liability, limiting or even removing what had arguably been the only significantly new strict liability created by the s 402A/*Greenman* rule, MUPLA's ideas were not widely adopted. This was not surprising: middle parties are typically sued in their home state; but since more than 70% of products are shipped outside the state of origin,[89] home state producers would not derive much benefit from isolated home state legislative reform, especially as their insurance premiums may be set on a nation-wide market basis. Unilaterally restricting the remedies of local consumers would also be unpopular with voters. Even where there was partial adoption of MUPLA or some other state reform, local variations were very wide.

More impressive was the reaction to public concern caused by the 1986 liability insurance 'crisis' which was not restricted to product liability and which had led to the sudden withdrawal or jump in price of certain goods and services.[90] The large majority of states rapidly legislated to confine tort recoveries. These laws, however, applied to all tort claims and nearly all only addressed peripheral issues by, for example, imposing caps on pain and suffering awards, eliminating or modifying joint and several liability (from which 'deep-pocket' public defendants were suffering) and the collateral source rule, and by controlling punitive damages awards.

---

87 M Franklin and J Mais 'Tort Law and Mass Immunization Programs: Lessons from the Polio and Flu Episodes' (1977) 65 Calif LR 754.

88 Model Uniform Product Liability Act, 44 Fed Reg 62, 714 (1979).

89 V Schwartz and L Mahshigian 'A Permanent Solution for Product Liability Crises: Uniform Federal Tort Law Standards' (1988) 64 Den LR 685, 694.

90 G Priest 'The Current Insurance Crisis and Modern Tort Law' (1987) 96 Yale LJ 1521; G Priest 'Modern Tort Law and Its Reform' (1987) 22 Valparaiso ULR 1.

With a few noteworthy exceptions such as the 1987 New Jersey statute,[91] they left intact the basic framework of tort rules, in particular, stricter tort liability for products, so that, if anything, this late 1980s flurry of state legislative reform left the law applicable to product claims in an even more diverse and confusing state than before. This, plus the earlier failure of MUPLA, has led to the current consensus that if uniform products reform is needed, it will only be successful if approached by a federal law which preempts state law. From the early 1980s many such federal Bills have been presented to Congress, ranging from those which substantially follow MUPLA in content to those which adopt a radical approach based upon creating incentives for the parties to settle claims.[92]

The reform debate has been fuelled by the publicity surrounding the vast sums of money set aside by product manufacturers to meet tort liability: for example, $2.5 billion by one asbestos company, $3 billion by another, $2.4 billion by the manufacturer of the Dalkon Shield and $4.75 billion by suppliers of silicone breast implants.[93] Earlier academic enthusiasm for, and confidence in, stricter tort liability for products has given way in many cases to a pessimism about both the theory and practice of the rule. Many scholars have swung back to a much greater reliance on market, that is, contract-centred solutions (see Chapter 8, under heading 5). Even mainstream academic discussion has revealed itself uncommitted to real *strict* liability on manufacturers: when the New Jersey Supreme Court held that reasonable care was no answer to a s 402A claim in *Beshada* v *Johns-Manville Products Corpn* (1982),[94] it met with virtually unanimous academic disapproval, and virtually all eminent scholars now agree that liability for design and warning cases is and should be fault-based. Many US courts seem also to have lost confidence in the earlier direction of doctrinal development. Although since the late 1970s the focus for the disillusioned has been the possibility of state or federal legislative narrowing of product liability, case law seems to have turned in this direction. High-profile courts have begun to sound cautious notes. In the mid-1980s New Jersey effectively retracted *Beshada* (in *Feldman* v *Lederle Laboratories* (1984)),[95] and changed its once generous attitude to economic loss claims under s 402A (in *Spring Motors Distrib Inc* v *Ford Motors Co* (1985)).[96] The United States Supreme Court, when at last faced in its admiralty jurisdiction with the issue of economic loss recovery under the product rule, chose to approve the more conservative line of *Seely* (in *East River SS Corpn* v *Transamerica Delaval Inc* (1986)).[97] The California Supreme Court, its expansionist tendencies having been checked by the electoral defeat of most of its leading liberal judges, has removed whole classes of product from the reach of the *Greenman* rule and seems to have begun an assault on the subjugation of mere suppliers to strict liability under that rule, a critical move as

---

91 NJ Stat Ann 2A: 58C-1 to -7 (West 1987), on which see W Dreier 'Analysis: 1987 Products Liability Act' (1989) 41 Rutgers LR 1279.

92 See eg former Senator Kasten's series of Bills (the latest being s 640) and the original Senate Bill 1999 of Senator Danforth based on Professor O'Connell's elective no-fault schemes, on which see J O'Connell, 'Balanced Proposals for Product Liability Reform' (1987) 48 Ohio State L J 317 and S Sugarman 'Taking Advantage of the Torts Crisis' (1987) 48 Ohio St LJ 329.

93 See: [July 1990] Prod Liab Int 108, the Manville Trust; [March 1990] Prod Liab Int 40, the Robbins Trust [Oct 1993] Prod Liab Int 156.

94 447 A 2d 539 (1982). On the general point see Chapter 10, under heading 6.

95 479 A 2d 374 (1984).

96 489 A 2d 660 (1985).

97 476 US 858; 106 S Ct 2295 (1986).

this was the principal novelty introduced by the rule.[98] More generally, since the early to mid-1980s a 'quiet revolution' seems to have occurred at the trial court level with a pro-defendant shift in judicial decisions on doctrinal issues away from extending the boundaries of product liability and towards the stabilization and mild retrenchment of plaintiffs' rights to recover, a development which some commentators attribute both to external negative feedback to judges about the liability and legal costs burden on business from earlier expansionary decisions, and to the perceived 'inherent limits of the judicial process' as it grapples with design defect cases.[99]

Moves to narrow the special product rule and liability in other tort contexts are still resisted by an alliance of organized interests; labour, consumers and plaintiffs' lawyers. Such interests claim that industry is flourishing, that there is little or no evidence that (apart from the special case of drugs) R and D is more deterred in the US than elsewhere, nor that the US liability regimes render unmarketable designs that can profitably be marketed elsewhere.[100] The insurance 'crises' are, it is argued, but a product of the dynamics of the insurance market itself and of the practices of its players: they are not crises created by liability rules. Like those of industry, the profits of insurance companies in the early 1990s were 'soaring'. Moreover, far from plunging the civil justice system into crisis, 'strict' tort liability for products has provided, it is argued, a necessary tool of consumer protection in the face of regulatory impotence. Bulges in the *rate* of litigation only represent the processing of a few 'problem products' in mass markets, and do not provide the evidence for the widespread litigation crisis defence interests suggest.

Independent studies by the Rand Corporation have, to some extent, supported this 'non-crisis' view.[101] Although 97% of claims are litigated in state courts, the most reliable data on the filing of product claims for the period 1973–1986 are filings in federal courts. Rand analyzed these and found that, although in these 85,694 suits 19,456 different lead defendants had been named, there were dramatic differences in distribution. Thousands of defendants were named only once or twice, while a tiny number of defendants were named in thousands of suits. The latter were themselves concentrated in only a few sectors: asbestos, pharmaceuticals and motor vehicles. One of the most dramatic examples within these sectors was in pharmaceuticals, where two companies alone accounted for almost 7,000 of the 11,000-plus suits filed in that sector – bulges which represented the passage through the legal system in the relevant period of the 'problem products' of the Dalkon Shield and Bendectin. Even more stunning was the finding that once the rapid growth in filings for a few

---

98 *Brown* v *Superior Court (Abbot Laboratories)* 751 P 2d 470 (1988) (prescription drugs); *Anderson* v *Owens-Corning Fiberglass Corpn* 810 P 2d 549 (1991) (asbestos). See Chapter 10, under heading 7 (v). On mere suppliers see *Mexicali Rose* v *Superior Court* 822 P 2d 1292 (1992) (a natural impurity food case: chicken bone in enchilada) and *Murphy* v *E R Squibb & Sons Ltd* 710 P 2d 247 (1985) (pharmacist dispensing prescription drugs).

99 J Henderson and T Eisenberg 'The Quiet Revolution in Products Liability: An Empirical Study of Legal Change' (1990) 37 UCLA 479, 481. See also 'Inside the Quiet Revolution in Products Liability' (1992) 39 UCLA 731 by the same authors. Compare G Schwartz 'The Beginning and the Possible End of the Rise of Modern American Tort Law' (1992) 26 Ga LR 601.

100 See eg F Vandall 'Our Product Liability System: An Efficient Solution to a Complex Problem' (1988) 64 Den ULR 703, 716, and Ralph Nader 'The Assault on Injured Victims' Rights' (1988) 64 Den ULR 625, 628–9.

101 T Dungworth *Product Liability and the Business Sector* (Santa Monica, Rand Corpn, 1988) R-3668-ICJ.

problem products such as asbestos was subtracted from the total, the underlying growth in filing rates for product claims – some growth being expected from population growth – was not much greater than the figure for non-product-liability torts, and was substantially less than the rate for all other private civil suits. In an even more impressive study by Henderson and Eisenberg, the authors found that for the period 1985 to 1990 there had actually been a dramatic *decline* in non-asbestos product filings in federal courts.[102] These studies on filings plus the evidence of a quiet conservative 'revolution' in application of doctrine suggest that one view of the current product liability situation in the US is, first, of a system with a 'normal' rate of claims and, secondly, of a system where liability rules and success rates are acceptable and, if anything, contracting under judicial and legislative pressure. This would help explain the alleged buoyancy of industry and insurance company profits. On the other hand, considerable academic and political hostility to the status quo continues.

At one level Europe has little to learn from this domestic debate about the appropriateness of US product liability rules. It hinges not just on ideological preferences but also often on an interpretation of what is going on in the market place. Are the *success* rates of product claims (as distinct from the Rand criteria of claims rates) different from those of other civil claims? Are domestic US firms really being deterred from R & D in some substantial way? Do they suffer competitive disadvantage in international markets? In the absence of Rand-type studies, such 'arguments' reduce to speculation and rhetoric. The internal complexity of market dynamics would make any such future studies very difficult to do and their conclusions would probably carry little weight when applied to another legal and economic system where, for example, claims rates are much lower, tax policy is different, and public provision in areas such as health care is much more generous. But at another level the US debates of the 1980s and early 1990s *do* have a lesson for Europe, in that disillusionment with product liability has in some quarters evolved into or merged with a new and wider disillusionment with the US tort system itself. Equally applicable to the general area of tort liability were seen to be complaints about high personal injury awards, the targeting of deep pocket (often public) defendants, uncertain and uneven application of liability rules, punitive damages, insurability problems and the deterrence of 'useful' conduct. Major factors identified as causing legal 'crisis' were seen as attributes not specifically of the *product liability* regime but of the *tort* liability regime in general, not just of the process of product litigation but of the torts process itself.

This perspective appears to inform, for example, two massive studies, one by a special Committee of the American Bar Association *Towards a Jurisprudence of Injury* (1984) and the other *Enterprise Responsibility for Personal Injury* (1991), a report for the American Law Institute.[103] The content and fate of the latter is particularly interesting because it is likely to influence the parameters of the reform debate for some time. The study – which sought to assess the way the tort system handles personal injuries resulting from modern technology and enterprise – analysed product injuries together with environmental, workplace and medical injuries. Its report champions the allegedly indispensable value of the private model

---

102 Henderson and Eisenberg, op cit, 518–522.
103 *Towards a Jurisprudence of Injury* (Reporter M Shapo) (Am Bar AJ 1984); American Law Institute
    Reporters' Study: Enterprise Responsibility for Personal Injuries (Philadelphia, ALI, 1991).

of civil justice in securing compensation for and effective prevention of personal injuries; but, reflecting the newer 'no crisis' view, it is relatively sanguine about necessary reforms. Its proposals leave central doctrines intact, recommending neither an expansion nor contraction of the standard of liability. Rather, it proposes peripheral reforms to the rules and procedures governing the assessment of tort damages (eg scales for pain and suffering, controls on punitive damages, reform of the collateral source rule and separate treatment for 'reasonable legal fees') and reforms to facilitate toxic tort claims. The Report suggests a new realization of the incoherence of treating product injuries separately from others. Were this perspective to take hold in the US then, although European jurisdictions with very different legal cultures have little in detail to learn from the US products reform debate, the acknowledgement that 'product liability' has nothing to justify its separate treatment within the wider field of civil liability, would be a valuable lesson for the EC to take now from the US. But it is a lesson which may rapidly be lost sight of: the principal outcome of the ALI report so far has been in the re-presentation of the products rule rather than its reabsorption into a wider liability doctrine: an ALI group was appointed in 1992 to re-draft s 402A in a 3rd Restatement.[104]

US commentators often lament the blindness of the EC adoption of a products Directive at a time when the US products rule had fallen into considerable disrepute locally. But the US products debate has been equally blind. It focuses on the problems of litigation boom, insurability and vague standards and fails to see that these are not unique to that doctrine but would infect alternative rules such as negligence (see Chapter 10). What *is* problematic, both conceptually and practically, about s 402A and the Directive alike is the attempt to treat product injuries separately. The incoherence of this strategy has particularly grave consequences in the EC context where, by locking themselves into the artificiality of a 'product liability' reform, Member States have pre-empted a more rational organization of liability or its replacement in the personal injuries field by a comprehensive system of compensation, if that ever finds political favour (see Chapter 3).

---

104 J Henderson and A Twerski 'A Proposed Revision of Section 402A of the Restatement (Second) of Torts' (1992) 77 Cornell LR 1512.

Evolution of UK product liability doctrine and the 1985 EEC Directive

1 THE RELEVANT LAW IN THE UK UNTIL 1962

Little changed in the relevant UK common law from the removal of the privity barrier to tort claims for physical loss in *Donoghue* v *Stevenson* (1932) until the turn of the 1960s. If the victim had bought the defective product she could sue the commercial seller for her physical loss caused by the product under the strict obligations as to quality set out in the warranties implied under the Sale of Goods Act. But British courts remained loyal to the 'classical' contract requirement of privity and were reluctant to tackle its neglect of the impact of contracts on third parties. Those who were not in privity with the defendant were not allowed to sue under these warranties, whether they were mere bystanders, or the victims increasingly favoured by developing US doctrine, namely consumer buyers and mere users.[1] Of course, for the consumer buyer, her warranty claim against the retailer was usually a simple and convenient remedy because the relevant retailer was readily identifiable and local. But what if the claim against the retailer was impossible or unattractive, eg because the latter was judgment-proof for some reason? Since buyers could sue a party if it had made an express undertaking with respect to the quality of the product, such an 'express warranty' claim could not only be made against a party with whom the sale contract had been made, the retailer, but others higher up the chain of contracts of sale. Thus in theory it would enable some buyers to leapfrog up that chain to sue a manufacturer on the basis that the latter had made an express warranty and was in breach of that strict obligation under a collateral contract with the buyer. The buyer's purchase from the intermediate retailer in reliance on the express warranty would form the consideration for this collateral contract.[2] But British courts have been demanding here: they will accept the argument in relation to *specific* assertions of quality directed to the *individual* buyer; but unlike US courts, they refuse to perceive in normal advertising claims by manufacturers a sufficiently unambiguous promise to constitute the express warranty and/or the necessary intention to create legal relations to form the collateral contract.[3] British courts have held to this view despite trenchant academic criticism, legislative reform in the case of negligent mis-statements, and the early extension of the benefit of such 'express warranties' to non-privy plaintiffs in the US in *Baxter* v *Ford Motor Co*

---

1 See eg *Daniels and Daniels* v *R White & Sons Ltd and Tarbard* [1938] 4 All ER 258.
2 See eg *Wells (Merstham) Ltd* v *Buckland Sand and Silica Co Ltd* [1965] 2 QB 170; *Shanklin Pier Ltd* v *Detel Products Ltd* [1951] 2 KB 854.
3 A rare but famous example of the argument's success is *Carlill* v *Carbolic Smoke Ball Co* [1893] 1 QB 256.

(1934).[4] In contrast, undertakings set out in manufacturers' guarantees – commonly printed on swing-tags affixed to the product – are often both clearly promissory and unambiguous. If entry into the contract of sale with a middle party was induced by *these* undertakings, UK courts do concede that they could form the basis of a collateral contract claim. The problem for the buyer suffering physical loss is that almost invariably the undertaking in the guarantee is not one as to quality but is limited to an undertaking to repair or replace a faulty good.

Even had British courts been more generous in their construction of advertising statements, the collateral contract device would probably not have yielded the results in their hands now seen in the US for two reasons. First, in the UK those few occasions on which UK courts have accepted the device have been confined to cases where there is some *express* commitment by the manufacturer to the buyer. Technically it *was* open to British courts to allow the collateral contract to be based on an *implied* undertaking and to see in the very activity of manufacture and sale the necessary sort of implied undertaking as to minimum (merchantable?) quality. Certainly elsewhere UK courts recognize the desirability of ensuring that liability is channelled to the causally responsible party: rights of indemnity are seen explicitly to provide a justification for the strict obligations imposed on the innocent supplier in contracts for work and materials.[5] But British courts seem content to rely on the domino effect of such warranty litigation up the chain to achieve the goal of internalization to the manufacturer rather than to develop generous doctrines to allow leapfrogging of the sales chain. Perhaps the vulnerability of this strategy to chain breakage (eg by a chain member going out of business or losing its record of who its own supplier had been) is accepted as the preferable alternative to the problems of duplication and evasion involved in the construction of collateral contracts implied from conduct.

Recognition of contractual claims by which the buyer could leapfrog the sales chain (using his entry into the contract of sale as consideration) would still not have brought about the dramatic expansion of liability of US doctrine because it would not have assisted those outside the sales chain altogether. It would not have given a warranty claim to anyone who did not already have one against *some* party in the chain. Mere users do not give consideration for any express or implied undertaking, and extension of the benefit of such undertakings to them would have been seen as too great a break with orthodox contract doctrine.[6] Even the current Law Commission proposals to abandon privity in certain contracts for the benefit of third parties would not reach the majority of product users since the proposals are limited to contracts intended by *both* parties (here the product supplier and buyer) to create *legal obligations* enforceable by the user: a rare case indeed in the retail context.[7] Even if there were to be a reformed contract-centred approach

---

4　12 P 2d 409 (1932), 35 P 2d 1090 (1934); the theory at first instance being express warranty but on the second appeal this shifted to one of strict liability in the nature of deceit for innocent misrepresentation, see W Prosser *Handbook of the Law of Torts* 4th edn (St Paul, West Publishing Co 1971) p 651.

5　See eg *Young & Marten Ltd* v *McManus Childs Ltd* [1969] 1 AC 454, 475 (Lord Upjohn); *Simaan General Contracting Co* v *Pilkington Glass Ltd (No 2)* [1988] 1 All ER 791, 804 (Bingham LJ). As a justification for liability of innocent suppliers under the Directive, see Chapter 11, under heading 8.

6　As it did eg when the Australian government extended express and implied sales warranties to vertically non-privy plaintiffs but not to those outside the sales chain – see below under heading 7.

7　The Law Commission *Privity of Contract: Contracts for the Benefit of Third Parties*, Consultation Paper No 12 (London, HMSO, 1991).

which assisted such third parties who merely benefited from the sale agreement, as there has been in some EC countries, it would not address the problem that was to become the modern focus of British and European concerns, namely that of the injured bystander. Bystanders neither give consideration, nor rely on implications of quality, nor benefit from the product's supply. They cannot be helped by contract thinking.

Until the late 1950s the way this inflexible contract orthodoxy operated in the product field did not meet with widespread criticism. In any case, in tort there was widespread confidence after *Donoghue* v *Stevenson* that the negligence cause of action provided adequate, indeed highly adaptable, solutions to a wide variety of physical injury situations. Where a party suffered loss because of a defective product, he could recover if he showed that the defendant, typically the manufacturer, had been careless in its construction, design, marketing, instructions or warnings, and at least in cases of personal injury or physical damage to property already owned by the plaintiff, it would not matter if the plaintiff was the buyer, a mere user or a bystander, nor would it matter if the careless defendant was the manufacturer, the supplier or repairer of goods. This confidence was then badly shaken by developments in the early 1960s.

2   THE 1960s: THE LEGISLATURE REMOULDS CONTRACT

During the 1960s the rise in public concern about consumer protection across a wide range of situations, brought controversy and change in important areas of British law relating to product injury. On the one hand, sales law was subjected to vigorous law reform review in the light of modern mass marketing practices and was reshaped to an extraordinary degree by Parliament bent on protecting the consuming public. Meanwhile, the Thalidomide drug disaster fuelled popular and academic disquiet about the way tort was operating from the perspective of providing compensation to those suffering personal injuries. To a surprising extent these two concerns proceeded in parallel in the 1960s rather than merging as they had begun to do in the US after *Henningsen* (1960).

One of the central concerns of the nascent consumer movement in the late 1950s and early 1960s was the ease and increasing frequency with which manufacturers and sellers of goods were excluding – often under the guise of 'guarantees' – the statutory sales warranties with respect to quality. Although from the start these statutory warranties had been excludable,[8] both the Molony Committee (1962) and Law Commission (1969) recommended that the statutory sales warranties be made non-excludable by a business as against a person dealing as a 'consumer'.[9] They did so on the basis that such buyers find it virtually impossible

---

8 Sale of Goods Act 1893, s 55.

9 A concept requiring, inter alia, that the good be of a type ordinarily supplied for private use or consumption (see now Unfair Contract Terms Act 1977, s 12(1)(c)). See *Final Report of the Committee on Consumer Protection* ('Molony Committee') (1962) Cmnd1781; *First Report of the Law Commission on Exemption Clauses in Contracts* (Amendments to Sale of Goods Act 1893), Law Com No 24 (1969).

to gauge the quality of many complex modern products, often standardized and pre-packaged, and to appreciate the implications of disclaimers.[10] Those few who did appreciate their meaning were often faced with standard-form disclaimer terms across the market in the good but, being in a small minority, had insufficient bargaining power to compel modification of terms either by the ousting of the disclaimer or reduction in the price charged. The vulnerability of the majority who believed that they were paying for a quality which because of a disclaimer they were not in fact entitled to, was seen to justify intervention to render disclaimers generally unenforceable. The fact that the legislation does not allow individual consumers to accept a disclaimer in return for a lower price might be attacked by libertarians on the ground that a buyer should be free to choose to bear a risk. But this argument lacks force if the dynamics of the mass market make it possible, and perhaps the most efficient and therefore arguably non-abusive[11] tactic, for the seller to use a standard-form disclaimer and to resist tailoring the bargain to individual buyers who choose a different distribution of risk. The dynamics of the mass market and the resultant standard market terms prevent 'free bargains'[12] whether or not the use of disclaimers is controlled (see Chapter 5, under heading 7).

In 1973 Parliament enacted the Law Commission's recommendations which had gone somewhat further than the Molony Committee by suggesting that attempts to exclude sale warranties otherwise available to *commercial* buyers of goods should also be controlled, albeit only by subjecting them to a reasonableness test.[13] The same controls were used when later legislation implied, as against a business, parallel warranties into all contracts for the supply of goods, not just sale contracts: these warranties were declared non-excludable against a buyer acting as a consumer and subject to a test of reasonableness in other cases.[14] In 1976 it was made an offence to include such void exclusion terms relating to product quality in consumer transactions.[15] The motivation behind these moves echoed the fairness concerns of the nineteenth century creators of these warranties – a recognition that the law had a legitimate role in overcoming the natural inequalities which a complex free market often throws up. But the concern of nineteenth century reformists had been limited

10 Molony Committee op cit paras 411, 426–7, 435; Law Com No 24 op cit paras 65,72. In US see eg *Seely* v *White Motor Co* 403 P 2d 145 (1965), 157 (per Peters J); F Kessler 'Contracts of Adhesion – Some Thoughts about Freedom of Contract' (1943) 43 Col LR 629; the signal theory discussed by G Priest 'A Theory of the Consumer Product Warranty' (1981) 90 Yale LJ 1297, esp at 1344.

11 D Yates *Exclusion Clauses in Contracts* 2nd edn (London, Sweet & Maxwell, 1982) 269. Contrast Kessler, op cit (that standardized terms are exploitative).

12 On the general issue see Lord Reid in *Suisse Atlantique Société d'Armement Maritime SA* v *Rotterdamsche Kolen Centrale NV* [1966] 2 All ER 61 at 76, 'Freedom to contract must surely imply some choice or room for bargaining'. More recently see Lord Templeman in *Smith* v *Eric S Bush* [1989] 2 All ER 514, 520 ('consumers who have need of manufactured articles and services are not in a position to bargain') and 523 ('... standard form exclusion clauses which individual members of the public are obliged to accept.')

13 Supply of Goods (Implied Terms) Act 1973 (c 13), s 4, now see Unfair Contract Terms Act 1977 (c 50), s 6(2) and (3). This creates difficulties for retailers who are bound by the manufacturer's 'reasonable' exclusion clause, see Yates, op cit. 80–1. Contrast Directive on Unfair Terms in Consumer Contracts (93/13/EEC), OJ No L 95/29, 21.4.93.

14 Supply of Goods and Services Act 1982 (c 29), ss 4 and 9, following *Report on Implied Terms in Contracts for the Supply of Goods* Law Com No 95 (1979). Note Unfair Contract Terms Act 1977, ss 7(2), (3).

15 The Consumer Transactions (Restrictions on Statements) Order 1976, SI 1976 No 1813.

to the inequality of information commercial buyers faced in modern mass marketing conditions. Other forms of inequality of bargaining powers were ignored and
this is reflected in the original rebuttability by express terms of the warranties of
quality. The moves by Parliament in the 1970s and 1980s to make these warranties
non-excludable in consumer sales reflect a much wider concern with, and willingness to intervene to correct, market inequalities. The outcome was that in cases of
business supply of goods acquired for private use by a person who subsequently
suffered loss as a result of the unmerchantable condition of the good, the buyer was
given a remarkable remedy by Parliament. Although contractual in form and in
some minor incidents, such as limitation period, it was, in other respects, at least as
good as the benefit of a parallel strict tort duty. Indeed, in covering pure economic
loss claims it was significantly better, since tort is extremely reluctant to cover such
claims. As concerns private contracting parties complaining about product quality
or safety, this was almost as far as the remodelling of contract could or needed to
go.[16] But for others suffering injury the citadel of privity still stood as a barrier to
such remedies.

By the time the Law Commissioners were making their first recommendations on
exemption clauses in contracts in 1969, the novel US products rule had begun to
exert an influence on interested observers in Britain. The Law Commissioners themselves seemed impressed by the aclassical warranty device used in the US to extend
the benefits of warranty to vertical and horizontal non-privy plaintiffs suffering
physical loss due to products. After consultation, however, they felt that such dramatic change to contract theory should only be introduced after a detailed survey of
the contract and tort aspects of product liability.[17]

3   THE 1970s: CONCERN MOUNTS TO COMPENSATE PERSONAL INJURIES

The issue of privity was, therefore, on hold at the beginning of the 1970s. Neither
the Molony Committee nor the Law Commissions in their first report on exemption
clauses were centrally concerned with personal injury compensation. In terms of the
adjustments recommended and subsequently made to sales and contract law in general in the 1960s and 1970s, the moral force of the reform argument derived from a
desire to control unfair bargains involving 'consumers' (defined narrowly as a 'purchaser for private use') and unscrupulous dealing, not from the plight of crippled
children and lives ruined by inadequate compensation.

A shift is, however, discernible between the working paper (1971) and final report
(1975) at the next stage of the Law Commissions' enquiry into exclusion clauses[18] –
an enquiry focusing principally on attempts to exclude liability for negligence and
the awkward and inadequate attempts of the common law to control them. In the
working paper the concern continues to be to prevent unscrupulous manufacturers

16 Only the final rationalization, now allowed in France, was not taken: allowing the consumer buyer to
   leap-frog the retailer to sue the manufacturer directly in warranty.
17 Law Com. No 24, op cit 62–3.
18 *The Exclusion of Liability for Negligence in the Sale of Goods*, Law Com Working Paper No 39
   (1971); *Exemption Clauses: Second Report* Law Com No 69 (1975).

ousting their tort liability to ultimate buyers of goods who, due to one of a variety of reasons, may not have had a satisfactory claim against the intermediate seller and were therefore forced to try and leapfrog up the chain using a tort claim. The final report takes a much more general approach to the 'serious social evil', the 'abuse of freedom of contract' which exemptions from negligence liability can present. While reciting the problems private individuals have in recognizing, understanding and bargaining around exemption claims, the Law Commission now stresses the special place of personal injuries:

> a civilized society should attach greater importance to the human person than to property ... there was a prima facie case for an outright ban on claims totally excluding liability for death or personal injury due to negligence ... the case for (this) is in essence that persons injured ... as a result of another's negligence must always be entitled to full compensation from him or his insurer.[19]

The Law Commission did not accept this argument in all contexts. They took into account cases where one party was not in such a comparatively weak bargaining position and did not place such a high degree of reliance for his safety on the care of another so as to justify a total ban. But Parliament later adopted a more radical position and in the Unfair Contract Terms Act 1977 banned all clauses purporting to exclude liability for personal injuries arising in the course of a business.[20] In respect of negligence claims relating to property and economic loss, exemption clauses were controlled only by a reasonableness standard, but one which was to be applied in light of the relative bargaining power of the parties.[21]

In the reform of sales and negligence law, then, personal injuries were belatedly being given a priority status. The issue was cropping up in other areas too. In 1969 Parliament had created a special pocket of vicarious liability of employers in relation to personal injuries caused to employees in the course of employment by defective work equipment.[22] Where had sensitivity to this issue come from? In parallel to these developments, tort liability for personal injuries had acquired considerable notoriety in the mid to late 1960s. In 1961 it was first recognized that the pregnancy drug Thalidomide caused birth defects in the children of some users. Of the 8,000 affected children spread over 30 countries, 450 were in the UK. The difficulties experienced by the deformed children in obtaining tort compensation focused media and academic interest in the 'lottery' of obtaining compensation for personal injuries via the slow, costly and uncertain process of a claim in tort for negligence. Considerable public emotion was generated in favour of the Thalidomide victims by the campaign of *The Sunday Times*. The vigour of this campaign owed much in its later stages to the freedom of the press aspects it had acquired rather than the paper's concern with humiliating the producers into a more generous settlement figure. An interesting contrast can be drawn between this example and subsequent media campaigns such as that concerning the arthritis drug Opren on the one hand, and on the other, media disinterest in product disasters such as the

---

19 Law Com No 69, op cit paras 72, 74. See also paras 11, 44 and 50.
20 Unfair Contract Terms Act 1977, s 2(1). Contrast Law Com No 69, op cit para 74.
21 See Unfair Contract Terms Act 1977, s 2(2); Law Com No 69, para 188 suggesting factors relevant to reasonableness; *Smith* v *Eric S Bush* [1989] 2 All ER 514, 531, Lord Griffiths, with whom the other Law Lords agreed on the point.
22 Employer's Liability (Defective Equipment Act) 1969 (c 37).

estimated 3,500 excess deaths of asthmatics in England and Wales in the period 1961–7 which had probably been caused by the use of pressurized aerosols.[23]

Importantly for the shape of subsequent reforms, the Thalidomide episode concerned the supply of drugs. In the UK 80% of pharmaceuticals are supplied by the NHS under a statutory duty not under a contract of sale; so injured NHS drug users have no contract claim. More importantly, the risks posed by Thalidomide happened not to be faced by consumer buyers or mere users but by 'mere bystanders'. Even the acclaimed and envied aclassical warranty theories being deployed in the US which would have reached non-privy *users* would not have assisted such victims. Their remedy had to lie, if at all, in tort. Since for only a very few personal injury victims is a claim for breach of statutory duty a possibility,[24] for the Thalidomide children and for the overwhelming majority of product victims the relevant tort remains negligence. Negligence consequently became the focus of those who had become interested in compensating personal injuries in general and the Thalidomide children in particular.

It was condemned as a wholly inadequate avenue on two bases. First there were the problems plaintiffs faced in establishing proof of carelessness under complex modern manufacturing and marketing conditions where the relevant facts were usually within the exclusive control of the defendant. The plaintiff would have to prove not only that the risk was foreseeable, but that taking that risk was unreasonable. In a limited number of cases – typically those involving a manufacturing error in a product such as leaving residual excess sulphates in woollen pants[25] – the plaintiff was in the particularly strong position of being able to argue either on the basis of res ipsa loquitur that the producer's quality control system was inadequate, or that the operation of that system by the producer's workforce, for whom it was vicariously liable, was careless. But the producer could escape liability by showing that the defect was unforeseeable and not reasonably discoverable while under his control, or that the defect might have arisen after leaving his control.[26] Where the injury was due to the design of the product itself, as in the case of Thalidomide, the only option for plaintiffs was to allege negligent design or negligent failure to warn of a foreseeable risk. The threshold task of proving that risks were foreseeable in these design cases can be a very costly and difficult one, as is shown indirectly by the fact that even now, late 1993, no pharmaceutical producer has yet been held liable for drug-related injury by an English court (although there have been notable out-of-court settlements).

The other basis of criticism of the tort of negligence was more fundamental and involved a growing disillusionment with the fault principle on which the tort rested.

---

23 W Inman and A Adelstein 'Rise and Fall of Asthma Mortality in England and Wales in Relation to Use of Pressurized Aerosols' [1969] 2 Lancet 279; W Inman 'Role of Drug-Reaction Monitoring in the Investigation of Thrombosis and the Pill' (1970) 26 British Med Bull 248.

24 In a series of statutory provisions (in the Consumer Protection Act 1961 (c 40), s 3(1), replaced by the Consumer Safety Act 1978 (c 38), s 6(1), replaced by Part II of the Consumer Protection Act 1987 (c 43) s 41(1)), it was provided that a person injured because of a defendant's breach of a specific safety regulation made under the statute, could claim for breach of statutory duty. But note, no such claim can be based on breach of the general safety requirement in Part II, s 10 of the Consumer Protection Act 1987 (s 41(2)).

25 *Grant* v *Australian Knitting Mills Ltd* [1936] AC 85.

26 See eg, *Evans* v *Triplex Safety Glass Co Ltd* [1936] 1 All ER 283; *Duncan* v *Cammell Laird & Co Ltd* [1943] 2 All ER 621, appealed on other grounds [1944] 2 All ER 159, CA affd [1946] 1 All ER 420n, HL.

Sometimes these two strains were confusingly run together when the tort of negligence was criticized for imposing on the plaintiff the difficult requirement of proving fault! But beneath criticism of the *operation* of negligence principles was discernible a separate and more radical objection to compensating personal injuries on the basis of cause and fault. Two academic treatises, Ison's *The Forensic Lottery* (1967) and Atiyah's *Accidents, Compensation and the Law* (1970), became highly influential in focusing interest in reform of the area. This concern with personal injuries as a distinct public policy issue had a clear modern pedigree. It had arisen indirectly in the special context of industrial injuries and gathered political and intellectual force by being placed at the centre of one branch of his welfare state plan laid out in the early 1940s by Lord Beveridge.[27] Beveridge's idea was of community responsibility to ensure support for victims of personal injuries on the basis of need rather than differential treatment according to the cause of injury. In the 1970s this was an intellectually appealing approach to rationalists who despaired of the operation of tort ever being made acceptably workable, yet who saw the social argument for some sort of support for those disabled by personal injuries. This view was later summed up by Patrick Atiyah,

> All the disabled are entitled to equal sympathy and equal support from the State and ad hoc treatment of special groups can only lead to the abandonment of all rationality in policy.[28]

On this basis, even if the fault principle could be made to operate respectably and efficiently, it should be rejected as setting up unacceptable divisions between the compensated victims of fault and the uncompensated majority. Although this approach leaves unanswered the question of why personal injuries should be thought of as a significantly distinct form of misfortune, there can be no doubt that in the modern era it is so regarded. The common law has not been able adequately to reflect this – the law of tort and contract do not formally distinguish types of physical loss – so it was to be expected that other avenues would be sought.

Unlike in the United States, collectivist solutions attract wider support in the UK and Commonwealth, so it was no surprise that British and Commonwealth critics of tort rejected the possible reform of making tort liability stricter and embraced limited or, more commonly, comprehensive proposals for a no-fault scheme of compensation to replace tort in the field of personal injury. In the area of traumatically caused injuries to the person, such a scheme was achieved in New Zealand in 1972, and a full disability scheme was to be adopted by the Whitlam government in Australia, but fell with the defeat of that government in 1975. In Britain a Royal Commission under Lord Pearson was appointed in 1973 to look specifically into the issue of the reform of compensation mechanisms for personal injuries.

---

27 J Stapleton *Disease and the Compensation Debate* (Oxford, Clarendon Press, 1986) Chapter 7.
28 P Atiyah *Accidents Compensation and the Law* 3rd edn (London, Weidenfeld & Nicolson, 1980) 431. See also P Atiyah 'No Fault Compensation: A Question that Will Not Go Away' (1980) 54 Tulane LR 271.

4   MOVES TO COMPREHENSIVE REFORM STALL

Three developments in the 1970s led to the shelving of these moves for comprehensive personal injuries reform; UK entry into the EC; the worsening economic climate; and the election in 1979 of a Conservative government which championed the free-market, preferred individualistic solutions rather than collectivist welfare programmes, and specifically regarded 'the law of tort ... (as) part of the fabric of our society depending as it does on the philosophy of duty and personal responsibility.'[29]

During the early 1970s there developed in Europe wide interest in emulating the apparent rationalization of US sales law. It seemed to offer a specific solution to the problems of the Thalidomide claimants which had also arisen in continental legal systems, especially in West Germany where approximately 5,000 Thalidomide children had been born. The United Kingdom had joined the European Community in 1972. In 1976 the European Commission presented a draft Directive to the EC Council of Ministers and in 1977 the Council of Europe, of which the UK was also a member, published a Convention on Product liability (the 'Strasbourg Convention'), both attempting to create an obligation akin to the strict sales obligation of quality which could benefit non-privy victims of personal injuries.[30] When in 1977 the Law Commissions came to do their promised review of product liability, their proposals were roughly comparable. Significantly, they rejected the aclassical warranty path as involving too much distortion of settled contract law, in favour of the apparently open fields of tort law.[31] By the time of these developments, the concern with personal injuries had become pronounced in the UK and Europe so that these initial proposals displayed a hybrid origin, intellectually derived from a US-influenced concern with the commercial sale and supply of goods but emotionally committed to dealing with personal injuries as a matter of priority, in particular as suffered by the type of bystander in the Thalidomide incident. On the one hand, therefore, the proposals were concerned with injuries caused by *products* only after they had been *supplied* in the course of *business*, but on the other hand they did not require the victim to have any connection with the chain of supply contracts. Both the Strasbourg Convention and the Law Commissions' proposals were also explicitly limited to personal injury claims – as were the parallel proposals of the Pearson Commission Report in 1978 (and predictably so given its terms of reference).[32] The draft Directive alone sought to include claims relating to physical damage to property. All four reports of what I shall call these 'initial reformers' rejected the development risk defence but embraced the then orthodox position concerning pure economic loss: that pure economic loss due to product defects was only to be recoverable in contract and not under tort.

Meanwhile in the UK the higher profile move toward comprehensive reform for personal injury compensation had begun to lose its way. Understandably, the Law

---

29 Minister for Consumer Affairs, Rt Hon Sally Oppenheim, discussing the draft Directive: 991 HC Official Report (6th series) col 1110.
30 See OJ No C 241, 14.10.1976 (also Bull of EC Supp 11/79) see opinions of European Parliament, OJ No C 127, 21.5.79 and of ECSOC, OJ No C 114, 7.5.79; European Convention on Product Liability in Regard to Personal Injury and Death (Strasbourg, 27 January 1977), both reproduced in the Law Com report No 82 (1977) with their accompanying memoranda.
31 *Liability for Defective Products* Law Com No 82 (1977) paras 32–3.
32 *Royal Commission on Civil Liability and Compensation for Person Injury* Cmnd 7054 (1978) (hereafter 'Pearson') Chapter 22 (vol 1).

Commissions' 1977 products report passed the buck on the comprehensive option to the mammoth Pearson Commission enquiry which seemed to have terms of reference well-suited to its consideration. But subsequently the majority of observers – including presumably the English and Scottish Law Commissions – were staggered by the Pearson Commission's decision not to consider that option at all. It triggered a despairing avalanche of criticism from the scholars and others who had lost confidence in the tort system and who – with an eye to the apparently successful implementation of the personal injuries scheme in New Zealand – saw a non-tort no-fault compensation system for all accidents as a more rational and just use of resources for accident victims. The strategy adopted unanimously by the Pearson Commission was to select categories based on the cause of injury – one being defective products – and to make reform suggestions for each category in turn. It was a decision that cannot simply be explained as the product of unanimous timorous souls because there was quite clearly a number of conflicting schools of thought among the members of the Commission itself. It seems likely that when the 'collectivists' realized that conservative pro-tort Commissioners [who defended tort as 'a safeguard against a system of total dependence on the state'[33]] would not approve the comprehensive option, they chose to compromise in the hope that a unanimous report would achieve *some* advance in the improvement of compensation prospects, at least for some accident victims. With hindsight, however, the absence from the report of a strong, well-argued minority report in favour of radical comprehensive reform seems substantially to have contributed to the loss of momentum for reform. For, once a conservative government was elected the following year (1979), any support of government for a comprehensive reform, already weakened by the deteriorating economic situation, evaporated altogether. By failing to set out the case for such reform – let alone a minority report supporting it – the Pearson Commissioners helped smother the public debate on the issue. The new government was hostile even to the very limited no-fault reforms suggested by Pearson, and it seems it will be a long time before a government will be willing to repeat the expensive exercise of a similar enquiry.

In frustrated reaction to these developments, academic interest in general personal injury reform subsided. Electoral and media interest also continued to dissipate in the late 1970s and 1980s as other priorities attracted attention. The anomaly of the no-fault benefits under the 1979 Vaccine Damage Payments Act was accepted on the basis of the specific public health issues involved, while mass product disasters such as Opren and the contamination of blood products by the AIDS virus were now being treated by the media, politicians and many academics as one-off disasters, provoking little renewed interest in comprehensive reform of personal injuries compensation. The few left who were interested in reform looked elsewhere – inter alia to the European Communities where, as we have seen, one project for reform was still alive.

---

33 Pearson para 1716. Compare para 1713.

5   EC ACTS ON PRODUCTS

One of the arguments used to win domestic electoral support for UK entry into the European Community (1972) was its consumer protection programme.[34] Within this programme initiated by the Heads of Government meeting in Paris in 1972 and set out in a Council of Ministers Resolution in 1975,[35] one of the most glamorous angles was the harmonization and improvement of avenues of compensation for consumers suffering losses caused by the market, in particular by moving civil liability for defective goods towards the stricter regime operating in the US. As we have seen, a draft Directive on the topic was published in 1976.

(a)   The negotiation period 1979–1985

There proved to be deep divisions within the Member States on the detail of the new proposed liability. Despite the presentation in 1979 to the Council by the Commission of a second compromise draft,[36] the Member States continued to disagree on a common formula. Business in some states such as France, Belgium and Luxembourg, had already been forced to adapt to civil liability more rigorous than simple fault, as adventurous courts tried to develop better consumer remedies by the development of tort doctrine and the relaxation of the equivalent of the privity doctrine in contract. In the 'chicken-pest' case of 1968, for example, the West German Supreme Court had reversed the burden of proof of negligence in product cases, while the continued aftermath of the Thalidomide tragedy, which had struck West Germany particularly badly, culminated in the statutory subjection of the pharmaceutical industry in 1976 to outright strict liability, albeit with financial ceilings on claims in recognition of the mass tort potential of drug disasters.[37] On the other hand, in other Member States, such as Italy, Spain and Portugal, business faced a comparatively undemanding fault-based regime. The progress of EC reform was surprisingly not slowed by a growing and informed academic concern that far from being an enviable model, the operation of the US product liability regime provided strong reasons for caution. In fact, no concerted effort seems to have been made in the EC to analyze and learn from the dramatic US experience. Instead, the pace of reform was slowed down by increasing objections from business groups wary of the effects of economic recession; by the insistence of some Member States (Germany and

---

34 Part of the EC's 'human face': A Dashwood 'The EEC Commission's Proposal on Product Liability' [1977] JBL 202; G Borrie, *The Development of Consumer Law and Policy – Bold Spirits and Timorous Souls* (London, Stevens, 1984) 99, 101–2. On the history of consumer protection in the EC in general see the Commission publication, ISEC/B2/93, 1.1.93 and E Lawlor, *Individual Choice and Higher Growth*, 2nd edn (Luxembourg, Com of EC, 1989).

35 OJ No C 92, 25.4.1975. In general see G Close 'The Legal Basis for the Consumer Protection Programme of the EEC and Priorities for Action' (1983) 8 Eur LR 221.

36 OJ No C 271, 26.10.1979.

37 'Chicken-pest' case: Judgment of 26 Nov, 1968, Fed SC in Civil Matters (Bundesgerichtshof), W Ger, 51 Official Reporter [BGHZ] 91 (1969); s 84 of the Drug Act (Arzneimittelgesetz), Bundesgesetzblatt, Teil I [BGBI I] 2445. On domestic Member State rules relating to manufacturers' (etc) liability, see N Reich and H Micklitz *Consumer Legislation in the EC Countries* (London, Van Nostrand Reinhold Co, 1980) 94–100; M Whincup *Product Liability Law* (London, Gower, 1985) 140–151; Law Com, *Privity of Contract*, op cit paras, 24–9; I Awford 'Strict Product Liability – A Revolutionary Change?' [June 1991] Prod Liab Internat 90.

Denmark) that there be financial limits on liability to ensure it could be insured against; and by the fluctuating attitudes of Member States as governments within them changed. The most important example of the latter was the election in 1979 of a Tory government in the UK committed, despite the opposition of the Bar, the Law Society and consumer groups, to the inclusion of the development risk defence (for unforeseeable risks) to protect business.

Nonetheless, the internal dynamics of the EC as well as the possible domestic political advantage to be gained from consumer protection measures, ensured that negotiations about the draft Directive continued. One of the most important of these internal dynamics is that, in a quasi-federalized system such as the EC where central laws prevail over inconsistent 'state' laws, there are, quite apart from any legal constraints, political pressures acting as a brake on the enactment of consumer protection measures by individual Member States. Even in the absence of any relevant EC law an individual Member State would be reluctant to take a unilateral consumer protective measure which it feared would result in a flight of business (and jobs) to low-protection Member States who have not taken such a measure. In such a climate of fear no action may appear politically feasible unless it is by the EC: EC action, by being mandatory throughout the Community, would not generate such a relocation of business within the Community. This dynamic, then, discourages domestic reform even where central measures have not yet been taken. It can simultaneously fuel the EC reform process because it appears the only realistic reform avenue; although, as we shall see, it is a process which can ironically produce a legal ceiling of protection to the detriment of consumers.

Events in the negotiation period 1979–85 also illustrate a wider problem in the EC politico-legal system, namely that the EC's legislative process is relatively unreceptive to democratic input. Once the second draft Directive entered the secretive maze of European negotiations in 1979, political bargaining, largely behind closed doors, seemed to take over. Little effective non-governmental lobbying on issues of principle seemed to occur. Such UK input as there was seems to have come mostly from UK-government representatives and appointees rather than from MEPs, committees or MPs of the Westminster Parliament, unions, or consumer lobby groups.[38] Similarly, in terms of the reporting back of the progress of the negotiations to interested parties in the Member States who were outside the relevant government circles, very few public documents were produced for this purpose over the entire nine-year period from first- to final-draft stages of the Directive. Moreover, it seems to have taken a considerable time for hard-copy notification of the very existence of such documents to reach, say, the major law libraries of the UK.[39] This last phenomenon, which originates in the Commission policy not officially to distribute EC

---

38 A subcommittee of the Economic and Social Committee of the EC, ECSOC (which consists of about 200 members nominated by Member States made up of representatives of employers, workers, and other interest groups), had reported on the first draft Directive on 3 February 1978, and its later opinion on it dated 13 July 1978 was published *a year later* in OJ No C 114, 7.5.1979. However, the origin, size (only 15 members spread across all Member States), and obscurity of this subcommittee suggest that it did not provide anything like as efficient a conduit for the communication of the concerns of domestic-interest groups as the relevant bodies and avenues in the UK law-reform process.

39 In 1993 the monthly listing of relevant EC documents (including ECSOC Opinions), *Documents* (ISSN 0256–0976) was taking eight months to appear in the Bodleian Library in Oxford. But now see Communication, Openness in the Community: COM (93)258, 2/6/93.

documents until translated into all nine official EC languages, helps to frustrate the activities of individual citizens concerned with current reforms such as the proposed Directives on liability for services and on unfair contract terms. What is more, it operates positively to advantage those – such as businesses – who can afford liaison with specialist advisers and lobbyists based in Brussels where the Commission regularly circulates documents in their original French or English well ahead of the official circulation. With the modern rise of pressure group politics[40] this obstructed and unequal access to information creates a clear problem in establishing the democratic legitimacy of laws emanating from the EC.

(b) The 1985 Directive

Eventually, by allowing Member States to derogate from the Directive on three issues, a somewhat reluctant consensus was achieved in 1985 and a final Directive was adopted by the Council of Ministers.[41] Broadly, this provides that where a person can prove that her person or private property has been physically injured by the defective condition of a product which had been put into circulation in the course of business, she can sue its manufacturer, importer, 'own-brand' supplier or, unless he can name his own supplier, a mere supplier, without having to prove negligence against any specific party or that the defendant caused the defect. There are special time limits for claims, and contributory negligence is a defence, but the new claim does not replace existing remedies, and it is non-excludable. Member States can choose to depart from the provisions of the Directive by imposing financial limits on claims, by including game and unprocessed agricultural produce and/or by excluding its development risk defence. The Directive does not have direct effect in the UK[42] – claims must be brought under the local statute which implements the Directive in local law – although it is convenient shorthand to refer hereafter to 'claims made under the Directive'. The state of implementation at the time of writing is shown in Figure 3.1 a and b.[43]

To allow any form of a development risk defence based on the level of safety which was achievable at the relevant date of a defendant's conduct is a fundamental derogation from the principles embraced by the initial reformers, all of whom had rejected the defence and predicated liability solely on causation by a defective product. The Directive's wording of the defence probably reintroduces a fault standard by which to judge the product – albeit one with the burden of proof now on the defendant (see Chapter 10). If this is true, then the Directive would not have introduced into the UK system any added liability on those, nearly always manufacturers, whose responsibility it was for the condition of the product. It may well be that in *practice*,

---

40 C Harlow 'A Community of Interests? Making the Most of European Law' (1992) 55 MLR 331, 349.

41 OJ No L210, 7.8.1985, p 29.

42 On the possibility of direct effect in jurisdictions which were late in implementing or which have yet to do so, see G Howells 'Implications of the Implementation and Non-Implementation of the EC Product Liability Directive' (1990) 41 NI LQ 22.

43 See J Stapleton 'A Personal Evaluation of the Implementation of the EEC Directive (85/374/EEC) on Product Liability' (1993) 1 Torts LJ 90 which notes English commentaries of foreign language implementations, and see also *European Product Liability*, ed P Kelly and R Attree (London, Butterworths, 1992). Judgment against France for non-implementation was handed down by the ECJ in early 1993: OJ No C 35/9, 9.2.93.

Figure 3.1a: Implementation of product liability Directive (85/374/EEC) as at 24.11.93

Country	Form	Commencement Date	Is development risk defence available	Are game and unprocessed agricultural produce excluded?	Is there a financial ceiling of ECU 70 million?	European Commission action?	Separate Scheme for Pharmaceuticals?
UK	Consumer Protection Act 1987	March 1988	Yes	Yes	No	Yes	
Greece	Common Decision of Ministers (dubious constitutional validity) confirmed by legislation in December 1991	July 1988	Yes	Yes	Yes (ECU 43 million)		
Italy	Presidential Decree No. 224 of 24.5.88	July 1988	Yes	Yes	No	Yes	
MANDATORY IMPLEMENTATION DATE (31.7.88)							
Luxembourg*	Act of 21.4.89	April 1989	No	No	No		
Denmark	Act No. 371 of 7.6.89	June 1989	Yes	Yes	No		
Portugal	Decreto-Lei No 383/89 of 6.11.89	November 1989	Yes	Yes	Yes (10,000 m Escudos) £40 m approx		
Germany	Product Liability Act (15.12.89) 1989	January 1990	Yes	Yes	Yes (DM 160 m) £50 m approx		Yes (statutory)
Netherlands	New articles 1407a et seq of the Civil Code	November 1990	Yes	Yes	No		
Belgium*	Statute	February 1991	Yes	Yes	No		
Ireland	The Liability for Defective Products Act 1991	December 1991	Yes	Yes	No		
France*						Yes	
Spain							

*signatories of the Strasbourg Convention on Product Liability

Figure 3.1b: Non-EC developments (legislation 'shadowing' Directive) 85/374/EEC

	Form	Commencement Date	Is development risk defence available	Are game and unprocessed agricultural produce excluded?	Is there a financial ceiling	Separate Scheme for Pharmaceuticals?
Austria*†	Federal Act of 21.1.88	July 1988	Yes	Yes	No	
Norway†	Product Liability Act (Act No 104) 1988	Jan 1989 (Chapters 1 & 2); July 1989 (Chapter 3)	No	No	No (except for pharmaceuticals)	Yes (statutory)
Finland†	Products Liability Act 1990	Sept 1991	No	No	No	Yes (voluntary)
Sweden†	Statute	Jan 1992	Yes	No	No	Yes (voluntary)
Iceland†	Statute	Jan 1992	Yes	No	Yes	
Switzerland†	Statute of 18.6.93	Jan 1994	Yes	Yes	No	
Liechtenstein†	Statute of 12.12.92, to be activated when EEA becomes applicable to Liechtenstein		Yes	Yes	No	
Hungary	Statute	Jan 1994	Yes	Yes	No	
Australia	Trade Practices Amendment Act 1992 (Cth.) inserting Part VA in the Trade Practices Act 1974 (Cth.)	July 1992	Yes	No	No	
Japan	PENDING					Yes (statutory)

*signatories of the Strasbourg Convention on Product Liability
†EFTA countries

exposure will be greater because under the Directive the defendant bears the burden of proof on matters such as whether the product was defective when it was circulated, but doctrinally the Directive could only claim to be a stricter regime by virtue of its *incidental* imposition of liability on parties who would not be held responsible under today's negligence regime in the UK, eg importers, conglomerate producers (where the defect is in a component made by another), 'own-brand' suppliers, and mere suppliers (who cannot name their own supplier), where in all cases the defect is not reasonably discoverable by that party. The Directive's principal doctrinal novelty, as that of s 402A/*Greenman*, lies in this incidental form of strict, probably 'vicarious' liability (see Chapter 10, under heading 3).

Courts may interpret the Directive's development risk defence narrowly with the effect of greatly raising the duty of care resting on manufacturers; they would then *in practice* be exposed to harsher liability by the Directive. The UK government tried to evade even this possibility in its implementing statute, the Consumer Protection Act 1987 (Part I) by providing an unequivocally generous form of the defence (see Chapter 10), but the European Commission initiated legal proceedings against the UK in 1990 to force it to amend this aspect of its law to come into line with the perceived principles of the Directive. In any case UK courts are obliged by the European Communities Act 1972 and by s 1(1) of the CPA to read the latter in a way consistent with the Directive, so it is the interpretation of the Directive's wording which will prove crucial.

6   PREEMPTION OF MORE RADICAL NATIONAL REFORM

One eminent continental scholar has speculated that preemption of local reform was a specific goal of the products Directive: 'a European harmonization of product liability rules ... was intended to stifle too far-reaching Member States' initiatives based upon the US model'.[44] Of more general importance is the fact that the acceptance and implementation by the UK of the Directive not only defused what little domestic impetus there had been for *comprehensive* personal injuries reform, but introduced a significant new barrier to such change. In their 1977 report on product liability the Law Commissions had strongly opposed the draft Directive on the grounds that it might legally preclude the UK moving to a more broadly based personal injuries compensation scheme which did away with distinctions based on the cause of injury.[45] The National Consumer Council and Director-General of Fair Trading raised similar concerns.[46] If such a new scheme were to abolish other forms of redress including that under the Directive – as virtually any comprehensive proposals would do – it would be incompatible with any obligation which may be implied under the Directive[47] to provide product victims with exactly the redress

---

44 N Reich 'Product Safety and Product Liability' (1986) 9 J Consumer Policy 133, 136.

45 Law Com op cit, para 138. A result acknowledged by the European Commission: Com of EC, Answer to Written Question No 506/77 (from Mr Calewaert), 22.11.77.

46 G Borrie *The Development of Consumer Law and Policy – Bold Spirits and Timorous Souls* (London, Stevens, 1984) 117–8.

47 But which is explicit under Article 10 of the Strasbourg Convention on Product Liability which forbids contracting States from adopting rules derogating from the Convention '*even if these rules are more favourable to the victim*'.

established by it, and would expose the UK to infringement proceedings by the European Commission before the European Court of Justice. In other words, if the Directive is valid and guarantees its exact form of redress, a Member State would be prevented from embracing the trade-off, which is the political and financial key to a New Zealand-type reform, whereby future product victims are denied the remote chance of tort-level damages in exchange for lower but guaranteed support following disablement. A Member State would probably also be precluded from adopting a limited or comprehensive no-fault scheme even if it retained the liability set out in the Directive if the ECJ regarded such a move as upsetting the necessary 'level playing-field' of the common market by disturbing the balance of consumer/producer interests fixed by the Directive.[48] If this is the nature of the Directive and if it is valid, not only does it fail significantly to improve the position of consumers, but the very phenomenon of European Community action in this area will prevent Member States either liberalizing their product liability laws further or replacing them in favour of a more comprehensive scheme for the compensation of victims of personal injuries.

(a)   Legality of the Directive

A future reformist government in the UK intent on instituting a New Zealand-type comprehensive compensation scheme could avoid these paralyzing effects of the Directive by arguing that the Directive is ultra vires and therefore no impediment to local developments in the product liability or wider compensation fields. But would such a legal challenge succeed?[49] As its legal basis the Preamble of the Directive refers to Article 100 of that Treaty which allows the Council of Ministers to issue Directives for the approximation of laws which directly affect the establishment and functioning of the common market. The Preamble then asserts that the Directive is necessary 'because the existing divergences [in producer liability for defective products] may distort competition and affect the movement of goods within the common market and entail a differing degree of protection of the consumer ...' (bracketed words added).

(i) The 'no harmonization' argument   The first argument that the Directive has an insufficient legal basis in the Treaty of Rome is that since the Directive at best achieves no harmonization of laws and at worst increases diversity of rules on

---

48 On the general point of level playing-fields see Case 120/78: [1979] ECR 649 (the '*Cassis de Dijon*' case), Article 30 of the Treaty of Rome and Postscript to this chapter. The controversial 'barrier' to such reform allegedly presented by Article 13 – on which see N Reich 'The Product Liability Debate – Continued' (1991) 14 J Consumer Policy 1, 5 is less troublesome: reformers need only decouple the reforms to avoid the *Directive* affecting existing domestic rules.

49 Presumably the 'cleanest' way of making such a challenge would be to repeal Part I of the Consumer Protection Act 1987 and await non-implementation proceedings under Article 169 of the Treaty of Rome. Direct challenge to the legal basis of the Directive by a Member State under Article 173 is now time-barred (time limit is two months), and collateral challenge via Article 177 would be awkward technically if taken by the Member State itself. There is not a great deal of discussion of the legality point but see Close, op cit; S Whittaker 'The EEC Directive on Product Liability' (1985) 5 Yearbook of European Law 233. I am assuming here that a political settlement – whereby the other Member States allow the reformist government to derogate completely and permanently from the Directive – proves impossible to secure.

product liability between Member States, it is ultra vires. Perhaps the strongest factor supporting this argument is the fact that – unlike the Model Uniform Product Liability Act in the US – the liability set up by the Directive is in addition to, not in substitution for, the domestic laws of the Member States, including existing statutory liabilities such as that under the German pharmaceutical legislation of 1976 (Article 13). Adding a new liability to disparate civil liabilities is an odd way to attempt 'harmonization'. Similarly it is hard to see how allowing Member States to depart from the Directive in three major areas helps harmonization. The Directive itself creates yet further divergences. Firstly there is the problem created by the phenomenon of nine official languages in the Community. Laws are promulgated in these different languages and, translations being inexact, substantially different meanings can creep in. The main example of this in the product Directive is in the area of what are called the 'financial thresholds'. Article 9 of the Directive sets out what 'damage' is *actionable* 'damage' for the purposes of a claim under it, and for damage to private property it sets a so-called 'threshold' of 500 ECU. But the different official language versions of the Directive make different provision on this issue. The English language version speaks of a 'lower threshold of 500 ECU' which suggests a person could recover nothing if the defective product ruined a TV set costing 400 ECU but could recover it in full if the TV set cost 600 ECU. The Dutch and Greek versions suggested this interpretation too. But the French, German and Italian language versions of the Directive suggest that *all* property loss claims would be subject to a 500 ECU deduction.

More important divergences are created by the various domestic acts of implementation of the product Directive because each displays a whole series of minor variations from the Directive's actual terms. For example, in the UK's implementation in Part I of the Consumer Protection Act 1987 there are at least five points at which the UK law seems an inadequate implementation of the Directive – creating differences between the UK law and what is, or should be, the law in other Member States. *Firstly*, there is the now notorious problem with the Consumer Protection Act version of the development risk defence (Chapter 10, under heading 3). *Secondly*, the Directive excludes agriculture produce which has not yet undergone 'initial processing' but the CPA lengthens the protection until the produce has undergone something called 'industrial processing', which seems to be a much later stage of processing (Chapter 12, under heading 1(a)). This leads to a *third* divergence: under the CPA, once the product has undergone whatever the necessary processing must be, the liability falls on the processor, not on the farmer as required by the Directive, even though the defect may well have been created by the farmer's activities, as is the case with salmonella in eggs (Chapter 12, under heading 1(a)). A *fourth* divergence is that the CPA does not allow a claim to be made for property damage which a defective component causes to a conglomerate product in which it is supplied, yet under the Directive it seems that the private owner of such a conglomerate product should be able to recover by designating the 'defective product' as the component, as is allowed by the definition of 'product' in Article 2 (Chapter 11, under heading 2(b)). *Finally* there are problems with the CPA's definition of crucial terms. In the Directive the notion of 'product' is defined as a 'movable' but the CPA's term is 'goods', and this seems narrower (Chapter 4, heading 11, Chapter 12, heading 1). Similarly the term 'put into circulation' in the Directive is vital to three defences, but the CPA uses the term 'supply' which seems considerably narrower, giving business wider defences than anticipated by the Directive (Chapter 12, heading 4(d)) (see Chapter 4, heading 11 on interpretation).

The Directive also creates divergences by omission. It leaves large doctrinal gaps to be filled by varying local rules and local interpretation. These matters include: causation;[50] remoteness of damage; standard of proof; contributory negligence; procedural and discovery rules; rules relating to the possible suspension or interruption of the limitation period (Article 10(2)); laws governing rights of recourse (Article 5) which are notoriously variable across the Member States;[51] and assessment rules governing set-offs and so-called 'non-material damage' (Article 9). The contrast between the UK and Germany on this last point is instructive. Under the CPA the plaintiff can claim for personal injuries and it is assumed – as with other statutory creations of tortious liability such as the Occupiers' Liability Acts – that this will enable a claim under the CPA to include not only heads of pecuniary loss, such as loss of wages, but also heads of non-pecuniary loss, such as pain and suffering and loss of amenity. In contrast, in the German implementation of the Directive, non-material damage is excluded, just as it is under the German pharmaceutical legislation of 1976, so that a victim would need a parallel claim under traditional German negligence principles if he or she wanted to recover non-pecuniary damage related to a product injury. Even between Member States which do allow such recovery under the liability in the Directive, there is a notorious variation between approaches as to quantum in this area.

Finally, there is a large potential for variation in the way local law courts interpret key concepts left undefined by the Directive such as 'movable' and 'put into circulation'. Is software a 'product'? What does 'processing' mean? Has a laundromat machine been 'put into circulation'? It is quite conceivable that UK, German and Greek courts will differ in answering these questions, and indeed they could well differ on the key value judgment in the Directive's definition of 'defectiveness', namely what a victim is 'entitled to expect' in the way of safety. The technical authority of the ECJ to harmonize such issues of interpretation depends in practice on how often issues under the Directive come before it. And it also depends on whether the ECJ wants to risk rocking the Community boat by disagreeing with a domestic interpretation when it can easily retreat behind the assertion that such matters are ones of fact and not appropriate for appeal, thereby preserving an appearance of harmonization which is merely superficial. It is true that divergences such as these allow states, in areas where they are hostile to particular aspects of European action, to 'do in practice what they were already doing or perhaps wished to do apart from any European intervention';[52] and it is also true that while the policies of each of the governments of Member States remain consistent with the Directive, challenges to its legality will not arise. But this temporary political acceptance in itself will not be sufficient to establish the Directive's validity under the Treaty of Rome if the Directive *did* face a challenge by a future reformist Member State.

(ii) The 'no impact on competition and free movement' argument　An alternative or additional ground for challenge by such a government would be to argue that a

---

50 Compare, eg, German courts' flexible attitude to causation: B Markesinis 'Litigation-mania in England, Germany and the USA: Are we so very different?' (1990) 49 CLJ 233, 248–9.

51 T Weir 'Torts', Vol XI of *International Encyclopedia of Comparative Law* (The Hague, Mouton, 1976) 57.

52 Whittaker, op cit 236.

measure to harmonize *product liability laws*, no matter how detailed and free of derogation such a measure was, has itself no legal basis in the Treaty of Rome. To take two of the three justifications cited in the Preamble: it is clear that enhanced competition and free movement of goods are advantages to the market. That a firm's exposure to local product liability rules is reflected in its cost structures is also clear. What is not clear is that the variation in these rules between Member States results in such significant variation in costs relative to other factors affecting costs, such as local taxation or the cost of fuel and insurance, that competition and free movement of goods within the market are significantly affected. Competition and free movement *could* be affected if, for example, the local liability rules were so swingeing that they acted as an informal deterrent or customs barrier to other Member States' producers because they either chose never to enter the local market, or felt it necessary to adapt their products and quality control systems. But where was the evidence of this?

Early questioners of the legal basis of the proposed Directive, including the European Parliament's Legal Affairs Committee, its Committee on Economic and Monetary Affairs and the UK Parliament's House of Lords Select Committee on the European Communities,[53] noted that in the formulation and text of the Directive it was merely asserted that domestic liability rules relating to products *may* distort competition/free movement. But a nexus to constitutional power cannot usually be established by mere assertion or by the mere possibility that the condition giving occasion for the exercise of power exists. In federal constitutions, for example, it is not sufficient for the federal legislature to assert that a matter comes within its enunciated heads of legislative power. It must actually do so, even if a generous interpretative attitude is otherwise taken to the limits of central power. This has been the approach of the European Court of Justice to the interpretation of those Treaty of Rome provisions which define the Community's law-making power in terms of subject-matter, such as 'vocational training' under Article 128.[54] The position is different, however, where the law-making power is defined[55] in terms of a socio-economic effect. Sometimes here, as in Articles 85 and 86 of the Treaty of Rome (the competition powers), evidence of actual effect is clearly not necessary as the power is couched in terms of provisions which '*may* affect trade between Member States' (emphasis added). But in contrast to this, the relevant Article for the products Directive, Article 100, authorizes the harmonization of laws which 'directly affect' the common market. Certainly, if the ECJ were to deduce that in the latter case, actual evidence of the relevant effect was needed to establish the legality of the

53 1978–1979 European Parliament Working Doc (DOC no 246/78)(1978), paras 3, 12 (Legal Affairs Committee) and Appendix V, para 3 (Committee on Economic and Monetary Affairs), but this report was sent back by the European Parliament for reconsideration and a compromise was reached whereby the constitutionality issue was dropped, see 1979–1980 European Parliament Doc (DOC No 71/79)(1979); even so some Conservative MEPs continued to raise the constitutional point, see 'Europe' 27.4.79, p 8; 'Liability for Defective Products', House of Lords Select Committee on the European Communities, Session 1979–80, 50th Report, HC (236) para 10. See also G Borrie 'Product Liability in the EEC' (1987) 9 Dublin ULJ 82, 89. See also G Borrie (1984), op cit 118–120.

54 See eg Case 242/87: *EC Commission* v *Council of the European Communities* [1989] ECR 1425 (that 'vocational training' does not include 'scientific research').

55 The same questions arise where the source document states the relevant power in terms of subject-matter, but this is then judicially interpreted to authorize not only laws on that subject-matter but laws which affect that subject-matter: a noted example was the United States Supreme Court upholding federal civil-rights laws under the commerce power.

measure, the 1985 Directive would, as critics allege, be vulnerable on these grounds. There was no evidence adduced that such laws do *directly* affect the functioning of the market to a significant extent relative to other sources of distortion. There was no evidence, for example, that there had been a flight of players in the pharmaceutical market from Germany after the introduction of strict liability in 1976, nor was there evidence that German pharmaceutical companies had thereafter found it significantly more difficult to compete in other Member States. Nor was there any positive evidence adduced that the Directive would result in enhancement of competition and free movement of goods.

But such evidence is unlikely to be called for by the ECJ, which would probably (and rightly) perceive the extraordinary difficulties in adjudicating coherently on such issues. If the Directive is to be held intra vires the power in Article 100 it will not be, as some optimists suggest,[56] because the European Court of Justice would simply want to uphold the validity of a Council Directive duly (indeed, unanimously) agreed between Member States. Such optimism overlooks the fact that governments change. There may well be later national governments who will want to do more to protect consumers than the earlier agreement and more than the majority of Member States will agree to do. If the ECJ is to hold the Directive to be within Article 100, a more likely consideration will be the recognition that Article 100 provides no obvious avenue by which the court could hold ultra vires harmonization measures in fields which conceivably but not demonstrably touch on the common market. Certainly this has been the ECJ approach in the area of environmental protection.[57]

But there are two problems with the timid approach of the ECJ to the validity issue. The first is that it can clash with another timid ECJ characteristic – the strong tendency to respect existing local *judge-made* law. Thus in *Alsthom Atlantique* v *Sulzer* (1991)[58] the ECJ came close to demolishing the argument that local liability rules are disruptive to trade and competition. The facts in the case were simple: when S supplied marine engines to A which proved to harbour a latent defect, A sued S for repair costs. The French Court of Cassation had previously interpreted Article 1643 of the French Civil Code as establishing a presumption (which cannot be rebutted except in the case of contractual relations with a person engaged in the same specialized field) that a person supplying goods by way of trade is aware of any defects in the goods sold. But S argued that in no other Member State did there exist equivalent case law, and that therefore such case law was liable to distort competition and impede the free movement of goods contrary to provisions of the Treaty of Rome. The ECJ stated, inter alia, that the Treaty of Rome did not preclude the application of such case law of a Member State because it 'applied without distinction to commercial relations governed by French law and did not aim *or have the effect* of specifically restricting trade flows and thereby favour national production or the domestic market' (emphasis added). It is hard to see how the ECJ can have it both ways: if the fact that local liability rules apply to all competitors supports the conclusion that they do not restrict trade or competition, then how can the

---

56 Whittaker, op cit 235.
57 Cases 91 and 92/79, *EC Commission* v *Italy* [1980] ECR 1099 and 1115; see P Sands 'European Community Environmental Law: Legislation, the European Court of Justice and Common-Interest Groups' (1990) 53 MLR 685. Compare Case 155/93.
58 Case C-339/89: [1991] ECR I-107.

harmonization of liability rules (as attempted in the 1985 Directive) be justified in terms of the removal of their distorting effect on trade and competition?

The timid approach of the ECJ on the validity issue is also in danger of provoking serious political frustration. The wider the ECJ interprets Community power to be under Treaty of Rome provisions, such as Article 100, the more limited will be the room for manoeuvre by later dissenting governments where community action is interpreted as intended to create a level economic playing-field across the market by fixing a mandatory balance of competing interests. Since a domestic law which seeks to give more protection upsets this balance, it is vulnerable to attack for disturbing the 'level playing-field' of the Community. The more often Community action is seen as aimed at striking such a mandatory balance, the more often will Member States find that their ability to respond to perceived social evils is fettered. At a political level, it is now becoming appreciated that continued enthusiasm by Member States for the Community depends on the clear designation of secure and generous areas in which national governments are free to act without being tied to the community consensus about how to deal with the particular social evil and the trade-offs attendant on any solution. A weak manifestation of this is the restraining doctrine of 'subsidiarity', that is, that the primary responsibility and decision-making competence should rest with the lowest possible level of authority in the political hierarchy, and that therefore the Commission should not propose binding EC measures unless they were absolutely appropriate or more effective at the Community level. Inserted into the Treaty of Rome[59] by the Treaty on European Union (Article 3(b)), this 'doctrine' does not seem sufficiently precise to be justiciable so it provides no real security for a dissenting government, nor in itself generates legal boundaries of law-making competence.

The stronger manifestation of these concerns is the call for an explicit constitutional settlement by which EC measures would be *legally* confined within designated realms, so that the validity of measures could be judged not by their acceptance by Member State governments at the time of enactment, but by an external, explicit division of powers under which Member States retained substantial and prevailing authority over, for example, social welfare provision of which a comprehensive approach to compensation for personal injuries and disabilities in general would be part.

Given these concerns it is not clear that the ECJ will accept that there are no problems in the legal basis of the product liability Directive as it is stated in the Preamble, simply because it met with approval by Member State governments at the time. After all – as we have seen – there was a considerable body of contemporary critics of its legal basis both within the European and Westminster parliaments, as well as outside. The ECJ might try to respond to the recent political concern with 'states' rights' by developing new doctrines to restrain Community law-making. For example, by emphasizing the word 'directly' in Article 100, it might hold that, since liability rules could not have a sufficiently *direct* effect on the common market, the Directive had no legal basis in that Article.

(iii) The argument that 'consumer protection was ultra vires'   If a future dissenting Member State could establish that the asserted effects on competition and move-

---

59 The source of legitimacy of all EC measures: F Vibert 'Europe's Constitutional Deficit' in *Europe's Constitutional Future* (London, Institute of Economic Affairs, 1990) 69, 79–80.

ment of goods provided no legal basis for the Directive, it would also have to convince the ECJ that the third justification cited in the Preamble to the Directive, namely the purported consumer-protection goal, was not authorized by the Treaty of Rome. Again, 'nationalists' or 'States'-rights advocates' would note that the 1957 Treaty of Rome – concluded in an era when commercial rather than consumer concerns were dominant – scarcely mentions 'consumer' (it does so only twice), let alone a consumer protection programme or policy. It might be difficult to argue that consumer protection was seen as an essential implied attribute of the concept of a 'common market', especially one authorizing a harmonization measure consisting of a 'levelling-up' of liability which, if anything, would make the market a more onerous place to carry on one's business.[60] Yet in its Explanatory Memorandum to the 1976 draft Directive, the Commission noted that domestic rules offering differing degrees of protection to consumers is 'not compatible with a common market for all consumers'.[61] This idea was part of a wider vision that the 'common market' had a social dimension, and it underlay the initial political decision for a consumer protection programme in the EC taken at the Paris meeting of Heads of Government in 1972 where Article 235 of the Treaty of Rome was cited as a possible legal basis for action. That Article allows measures designed to obtain one of the objects of the Community in cases where the Treaty has not expressly provided the necessary power. But if the concept of the 'common market' cannot legitimately be seen directly to have the social dimension reflected in consumer protection measures, consumer protection would not by itself be an object of the Community which could trigger Article 235.

However sound earlier doubts about the legal basis of the Directive may have been, developments starting in the mid 1980s will probably frustrate future challenges to its validity. Firstly, in 1985 the ECJ asserted that the parallel field of environmental protection, about which the Treaty of Rome was silent, was 'one of the Community's essential objectives' supporting the argument that the EC had an implicit social dimension authorizing legislation such as the 1985 Directive.[62] Secondly, in 1986 a new Article 100a of the Treaty of Rome was added by the Single European Act (SEA).[63] This provides for the adoption of harmonization measures which have as their object the establishment and functioning of the internal market, and it requires that the Commission, in its proposals for such measures which concern consumer protection, take as a base a high level of protection to ensure consumer confidence in the functioning of the market; and it introduces qualified majority voting in this field. These references to consumer protection went a considerable way to supporting the view that the Treaty of Rome did – or at least after the SEA did – authorize a consumer protection programme as an *independent* 'object' of the Treaty. Such a 3-year plan was launched by a Council Resolution in

---

60 On the arguments that a free market necessarily requires consumer protection, see Lawlor, op cit 8–9. But see eg criticism by the Danish Government discussed by Close, op cit 222–3; and Borrie (1984), op cit 104, who seems to regard product liability as an issue with no real Community dimension.

61 See Law Com, op cit 82. The 1976 Memo is reproduced at the end of the report of the Law Commissions.

62 Case 240/83: *Procureur de la République* v *Association de Défense des Brûleurs d'Huiles Usagées* [1985] ECR 531.

63 Suppl 2/86 of Bull of EC The SEA also explicitly amended the Treaty of Rome to encompass environmental issues: Article 130r to 130t, on which also see L Kramer *Focus on European Environmental Law* (London, Sweet & Maxwell, 1992) Chapter 12.

1989 giving particular prominence to moves on unfair contract terms and access to justice.[64] Even more difficulty for a future challenge to the Directive's validity is now presented by the Treaty on European Union (the Maastricht Treaty) which amends the Treaty of Rome inter alia to confirm EC competence over, or extend it to, consumer protection (Article 129A). A Member State is now unlikely to challenge the validity of the 1985 Directive, for even if the ECJ were to accept the argument that as things stood in 1985 the Directive could *not* derive authority from any of the three asserted goals in the Preamble, it would nevertheless be a pyrrhic victory: other Member States could now, by majority vote under the Single European Act, restore the Directive by basing it on this new independent head of legislative competence in the TEU and perhaps even do so with retrospective effect.

The only remaining strategy a Member State could hope to use to extricate itself from the products Directive would be to argue that, even if technically within a subject-matter of legislative competence ('consumer protection'), this particular piece of legislation fell foul of the subsidiarity doctrine: that is, its specific goal of better consumer remedies was better attempted at local level. It is, however, wholly unclear how the doctrine might operate in a challenge to validity (see above), and a Member State would be better advised to pursue a more positive argument that even if intra vires the Directive only lays down minimum requirements for a product liability regime. It is to such an argument that we now turn.

(b)   Economic and social goals in conflict: The nature of the Directive: maximum and minimum Directives

It is important to know what restraints, legal and practical, a Directive places on the law reform capacity of Member States, a capacity which is acknowledged in the subsidiarity doctrine. This is particularly important in the consumer protection field where, despite the rhetoric of the Commission and politicians, there seems little genuine commitment in the Council of Ministers and Commission. As the umbrella organization for UK consumer groups notes, 'EC support for consumer affairs at present is pathetic ... for every one ECU the Community intends to spend on consumer protection ... it will spend 325 ECU on tobacco support. This is indefensible.'[65] The pressure on and dynamics within the Commission also suggest there is little likelihood that rethinking in the products field is on the EC agenda – the attitude seems to be, 'We have our Directive on that, we have done the job'. Nor could a future radical government take much comfort from the content of that Directive for, as we have seen, in the (pre-Single European Act) negotiations, the necessity for unanimity ensured that the text of the Directive reflected the lowest common denominator of reform and contained relatively insignificant advances for most UK consumers. This levelling down dynamic of the Community was later confirmed by the choices of Member States on the three options: for example, of those who have

---

64 OJ No C294, 22.11.1989, p 1. A second 3-year plan is proposed: COM (93) 378. For earlier Resolutions on the EC consumer protection programme see OJ No C92, 25.4.1975 (First Programme), p 2; OJ No C133, 3.6.1981 (Second Programme), p 1; OJ No C167, 5.7.1986 (Third Programme), p 1.
65 Consumers in the EC Group *The Participation of Consumers in National and European Community Policy-Making in the Run-up to 1992 and Thereafter* (London, CECG, 1989) p 8.

so far implemented, all except one has adopted the development risk defence even though many had earlier opposed its inclusion in the Directive (see Figure 3.1 above).

This question of what legal or political restraints the Directive now places on domestic reform turns on what is the underlying vision of the EC. Here the new interest in social issues has created a strategic dilemma for reformist governments because there are now *two* relevant but potentially antagonistic Community objectives, and they have different implications for a Member State's ability to legislate in the relevant field. First, if the relevant Community object behind the Directive is seen as an *economic* one, an important criterion is that the Directive promotes or maintains a 'level playing-field' for business. If a Community law is judged to rest on this economic goal, it is likely to be read as setting *the* appropriate balance between whatever competing interests are involved, and as preventing later departures from that balance by a Member State wanting to give greater protection to one such interest. What this means is that when the Community is viewed principally as an economic union with economic goals, even EC measures which appear to set a floor of protection, for example for consumers, *in practice* also set a ceiling of protection. Sometimes a Community measure makes this explicit as in Directives concerning cigarettes which provide that a Member State may not prohibit or restrict the sale of imported products which comply with the Directives' de facto levels.[66] This measure sets a legal minimum standard but it can also set it as a maximum, although Member States may be free to impose stricter rules on local producers, they may not want to subject their own producers to such requirements when EC imports would be free of them.

Even if a Community law does not make it explicit that inter-Member State trade must not be affected by a local law, this would still be the effect if the object of the law was held to be the creation of the 'level playing-field'. This must seem odd to the citizens of the UK especially in the consumer field: in areas where the UK might well have accorded more protection to the individual, membership of the EC has *limited* the protection the citizen might otherwise have had, contrary to the apparent promises on entry to the EC and contrary to the promises of enhanced consumer protection in the Single European Act. Advocates of community law might argue that such effects are simply the price to be paid for advances on other fronts, but this argument becomes proportionately weaker the greater the field in which Community law paralyzes local initiatives.

This is just the case with the products Directive of 1985. Most commentators regard this as fixing the position of consumers and suppliers to ensure a level playing-field for business.[67] If it is implicitly such a 'maximum Directive', one from which Member States are prevented from departing at all, it would prevent more pro-victim measures such as the expansion of the types of loss actionable under the Directive to include damage to commercial property or the unequivocal extension of the protection of the new law to the producer's workforce by the abolition of the defence in Article 7 that the defendant 'did not put the product into circulation'. So

---

66 Directive on tar yield of cigarettes, OJ No L137/36, 30.5.90, Article 7. See also the tobacco labelling Directive discussed in the Postscript to this chapter. Compare EC rules on bus seat belts, Independent 12/11/93.
67 See, eg, A Geddes 'The Incoming Tide: The Impact of EEC Law' [1991] NLJ 1330, 1337, and G Dehn 'Opren – Problems, Solutions and More Problems' (1989) 12 J Consumer Policy 397, 413.

too it would prevent more pro-supplier measures such as wider defences – a reading supported by the current infringement proceedings brought by the European Commission against the UK for providing in its implementing legislation a development-risk defence wider than that in the 1985 Directive. If, then, the products Directive is seen as based solely on the economic goal of a 'level playing-field', it would preempt not only such limited products reforms in a Member State but any comprehensive reorganization of compensation/liability systems which affected the balance set by that measure.

But there is now a second vision of the Community, that of a social union with explicit emphasis on consumer protection, and with it we now have a second competing formal object of the Community. The tension between the two objectives will be relevant to the way the ECJ interprets the often vague wording of EC laws, but it will also be relevant to the threshold question of the legality of those laws since a Community law purporting to promote a permitted social object may, at least now after the TEU, be intra vires even though the connection with trade is tenuous. Importantly, it is assumed that a social objective can encompass Community provisions which provide a *floor* of protection for citizens, above which a Member State is free to enact a higher level of protection locally.[68] Certainly this is the explicit form of measures such as the 1987 Directive on lead content in petrol, the 1990 Directive on package holidays and the 1993 Directive on unfair terms in consumer contracts.[69] So too consumer groups, stung by the legal and political paralysis which maximum Directives can have on domestic consumer protection initiatives, have begun to lobby to ensure that proposed Directives are amended to make them explicitly 'minimum Directives', which enable a Member State to apply more comprehensive legislation or to introduce stricter rules if it wants.[70]

Might not then a future reformist government in the UK argue that, even if supported by a valid object of the Community, the product liability Directive does not preclude a Member State providing citizens with even better protection? In other words, could it be argued that the 1985 Directive was *implicitly* a minimum Directive? The first problem with this tactic is that the actual wording of the Preamble of the 1985 Directive suggests that it is concerned to *remove* differing degrees of consumer protection between Member States. Secondly, even if a Directive *is* a minimum Directive the Member State will want to apply its higher domestic standard of, say, product liability, to both domestic *and* imported goods – a goal which runs directly counter to the goal of eliminating barriers to trade between States (see Postscript). This illustrates a profound dilemma surrounding EC legislative competence and preemptive effect: where EC laws have been or can be portrayed as having both economic and socially protective *effects*, who is to know (before the ECJ decides)

---

68 For example Article 118A(3) of the Treaty of Rome now provides: 'The provisions adopted pursuant to this Article shall not prevent any Member State from maintaining or introducing more stringent measures for the protection of working conditions compatible with this Treaty.'

69 See respectively OJ No L158/9, 23.6.90, Article 8; OJ No L225/33, 13.8.87, Article 1; OJ No L 95/29, 21.4.93, Article 8.

70 See, eg, Consumers in the European Community Group, *Unfair Terms in Consumer Contracts* (London, CECG, 1990), CECG 90/27 Rev 2; Consumers in the European Community Group *Liability for the Supply of Services* (London, CECG, 1991) CECG 91/11. See also European Consumer Law Group 'Response to the EC Proposed Directive on Liability for Services' (1992) 14 J Consumer Policy 431, 438.

which of these effects is the goal of a particular EC law and how? Consider Article 8 of the 1993 Directive on unfair terms in consumer contracts which reads 'Member States may adopt or retain the most stringent provisions compatible with the Treaty in the area covered by this Directive, to ensure a maximum degree of protection for the consumer'. This explicitly suggests that it is the consumer protection effect which is the goal, but even so do not the words 'compatible with the Treaty' re-introduce the 'economic level playing field' goal and hence a bar on such local initiatives applying to traders of other Member States? Certainly the Preamble explicitly argues – as the products Directive Preamble argued – that the Directive is justified because disparities between existing local rules may distort competition. A Member State needs answers to these questions before it can determine the degree to which, if at all, the EC law legally inhibits local initiatives, and before it can determine the potency of any subsidiarity argument it considers raising, if not against the validity of such a law, at least against its political wisdom.

Even if the products Directive allowed a Member State to provide 'better protection' for its citizens across the board, whether a comprehensive personal injuries system would be regarded in this way would depend on the level of benefits it offered relative to the systems it replaced and the weight given to the fact, if it were so, that those few who at present have rights to tort-level damages would be worse off under such a system. If an analogy can be drawn with its attitude to local environmental measures which allegedly affect trade (albeit in the absence of a relevant EC measure),[71] the ECJ might also be expected to apply a principle of proportionality, attempting to weigh the speculative impact on trade against the advantages of such a scheme to injured citizens. However these questions are resolved in the future, the uncertainties surrounding the legal status and nature of the barrier to domestic reform represented by the product liability Directive will tend to have a paralysing effect on the political will of reforming governments.[72] Internal reform of civil liability and/or of a more radical comprehensive reform of personal injury compensation will appear more intractable than ever.

The fact that the product liability Directive has severely put back the cause of personal injuries reform is little appreciated. Those few UK advocates of radical reform of personal injuries compensation who remained active in the 1980s not only swallowed the increased anomalies the Directive generated between victims of personal injuries, but failed adequately to grasp the pre-emption dangers of EC action, even though the parallel problem in the regulatory field was evident, and in some cases they actively embraced the Directive on the grounds that some reform is better than none. The principal new lobby-group of the late 1980s – the Citizen Compensation Campaign (Citcom) set up in 1988 under the presidency of Lord Scarman – adopted an agenda of reforms which accepted the basic premise of liability-based compensation and concentrated on limited doctrinal and procedural reforms rather than setting its sights on a comprehensive compensation system. Ironically, other astute UK campaigners, such as the Consumers' Association,

---

71 Case 302/86: *EC Commission* v *Denmark* [1988] ECR 4607. See also Sands, op cit. Note, there are comparable problems in the pursuit of a level playing field by the GATT agreement: PE 163–773/ fin, pp 42–3.

72 A similar legal and/or political freezing of domestic reform occurs in the regulatory field: see the 'regulatory gap' problem discussed by T Bourgoignie and D Trubeck *Consumer Law, Common Markets and Federalism in Europe and the United States* (Berlin, Walter de Gruyter, 1987) 3, 13–14.

appreciated that little real expansion of liability was involved in the Directive, but thought the symbolic recognition of a 'strict' producers' responsibility, plus the potential increase in the claims consciousness of the public and solicitors, were sufficient reasons to embrace the reform.[73] Unlike other interests groups,[74] consumer groups failed to ensure that Member States clearly retained the option of providing better protection, whether in the form simply of better remedies for product victims (by, for example, the abolition of certain defences) or, more importantly, in the form of comprehensive entitlement to compensation regardless of cause of injury. When weighed against the potential long-term pre-emption of substantive product liability reform and of wider compensation options, support for the Directive may prove to have been a grave strategic mistake and one with significantly wider lessons for those who value the freedom of Member States to experiment locally with fresh ideas and radical law reform.

7   DEVELOPMENTS OUTSIDE THE US AND THE EC

Since the mid-1970s, EC developments proceeded without significant influence from what was happening to product laws in outside jurisdictions. During the 1980s not a lot was happening. In 1980, in response to the proposed Directive, Israel created a new cause of action in relation to product-caused personal injury which purports to impose strict liability on producers, but the 1979 Ontario Law Reform Commission's proposal for a new additional principle of strict liability on business suppliers of defective products which cause personal injury or damage to non-business property stalled.[75] Australia used federal legislation in 1978 to introduce a type of aclassical warranty: imposing liability for express and implied supply warranties on manufacturing corporations in favour of the consumer buyer and, in the case of merchantable quality, to any consumer deriving title through that buyer.[76] However, the move was designed only to help consumers *economically* disappointed with their bargain[77] rather than to compensate for physical losses, so it only extended the benefit of the strict liability to those in the ownership chain and did not assist mere users or bystanders.

After 1985 the Directive itself prompted reform elsewhere. In 1989 the Australian Law Reform Commission recommended reform of the whole area of product-caused losses by the creation of a new superseding liability for such losses based on mere causation – 'the way goods acted' – but with a development risk defence – proposals which were eventually dropped in favour of a federal measure enacted in 1992 which parallels the final Directive and includes a development risk

---

73 See, eg, the views of David Tench of the Consumers' Association reported in Product Liability International (Sept 1985) 139.
74 For example, those involved in lobbying for Article 118A(3) of the Treaty of Rome; see fn 68 above.
75 See respectively Defective Products (Liability Law), 5740–1980, D More *Product Liability: Israel* (London, Oceana Pubs Inc, 1987) 3, and S Waddams 'The Law of Product Liability in the Consumer Law Province of Canada' in C Miller (ed), *Comparative Product Liability* (London, British Institute Int & Comp Law, 1986) 161.
76 Trade Practices Act 1978, ss 74A–74L.
77 D Harland 'The Liability to Consumers of Manufacturers of Defective Goods – An Australian Perspective' [1981–3], J Consumer Policy 212, 225.

defence.[78] Most of the seven EFTA (European Free Trade Association) countries have also subsequently adopted legislation parallel to the Directive (see Figure 3.1 above) and this will become obligatory under the 1993 agreement between the EC and six EFTA countries (not Switzerland) to form a European Economic Area. Finally, proposals for parallel legislation are now pending in a number of other countries in the South-East Asia region such as Taiwan, South Korea and, in particular, Japan where reform is likely in the very near future.

POSTSCRIPT TO HEADING 6

An illuminating recent case before the ECJ concerned a 1989 Directive which requires mandatory health warnings on tobacco products to cover 'at least 4%' of surface area.[79] The implementing UK Regulation required domestic production to conform to an 'at least 6%' standard. Tobacco companies and Advocate General Lenz argued that the level playing field goal also applied to domestic markets and so required full harmonization which necessarily implied that the minimum 4% standard also had to be a maximum legal requirement which a local law could not disturb. But the UK successfully argued that the level playing field only relates to inter-Member State trade, that the Directive was a minimum Directive and in the light of such incomplete harmonization a Member State was free to impose higher standards on domestic production because this did not erect barriers to trade between States. This shows that even if a Directive *is* held to set only a minimum standard this is insufficient to enable a State to provide higher consumer protection for its citizens across the *entire* domestic market place. The latter requires the measure to be held justified *despite* the barriers to trade between States it represents, yet the occasions where the ECJ has preferred defence of the consumer here over inter-Member State trade are rare and haphazardly reasoned.[80] That such a justification argument is simply pre-exempted by explicit provisions in both the cigarette tar and labelling Directives where domestic public health interest is pronounced suggests that in today's EC the level playing field argument will prevail over comprehensive protection initiatives of a State. This merely leaves the possibility of a future formal repatriation of consumer protection competence in accord with 'subsidiarity' but this is already resisted by elements of EC institutions.[81]

78 See respectively Australian Law Reform Commission *Report No 51: Product Liability* (Canberra, AGPS, 1989) and Trade Practices Amendment Act 1992 which added Part VA to the Trade Practices Act 1974 (Cth), on which see J Kellam *Australian Product Liability* (Sydney, CCH, 1992), and I Malkin and E J Wright 'Product Liability under the Trade Practices Act – Adequately Compensating for Personal Injury?' (1993) 1 Torts LJ 63.

79 *R* v *Secretary of State for Health, ex p Gallagher* (1993) Times, 28 June, Case C-11/92 judgement of 22 June 1993. (See also Case C-222/91 of same date.) Directive 89/622/EEC, OJ No L 359, 8.12.89 amended by 92/41/EEC, OJ No L 158, 11.6.92.

80 *European Community Law* (3rd edn), eds D Wyatt and A Dashwood (London, Sweet & Maxwell, 1993) 229–231, 364–7. Contract *Sulzer*'s case, n 58 above.

81 See PE A3 – 0380/92 on subsidiarity and consumer protection.

CHAPTER 4

Lessons and limits of the US experience

1   USEFULNESS OF THE US EXPERIENCE

What does a comparison of the US and EC product liability 'systems' tell us? First, despite a common origin in sales warranties, technical differences clearly exist. The EC law is more pro-plaintiff in that:

(1) Once the plaintiff has proven cause and defect the burden of proof on most other issues shifts to the defendant. The plaintiff need not prove, for example, that the defect existed when the product left the defendant's control, in contrast to negligence claims in the UK and to all versions of product liability in the US.
(2) In Member States where a development risk defence is not allowed, the plaintiff can, as in warranty-based claims, recover for injuries due to undiscoverable defects (in contrast to negligence and s 402A/*Greenman* claims).

On the other hand, the Directive is more pro-defendant in that:

(1) Liability is channelled to a limited number of suppliers of the defective product (in contrast to s 402A/*Greenman* claims).
(2) Monetary ceilings and exclusion of unprocessed primary produce may be imposed.
(3) There is no liability for damage done to the plaintiff's commercial property nor for pure economic loss (in contrast to the s 402A/*Greenman* rule under which the former is routinely allowed and, in some jurisdictions, the latter).
(4) The burden of proof of defectiveness is on the plaintiff (in contrast to some US jurisdictions, notably California, which may have imposed it on the defendant).

Apart from identifying these relatively small doctrinal divergences, the contrasting development and the diverse case law of US product liability also helps to flag the sort of problems the EC product law will have to grapple with – for example, the difficulties inherent in a 'crashworthiness' claim concerning an allegedly defective vehicle. At a more general level, the comparison of the development of the special liability rules on both sides of the Atlantic well illustrates common and contrasting factors influencing the reform of legal rules.

2   ACCIDENT, COMPROMISE, MUDDLE AND MOMENTUM

First, it is important to acknowledge that, despite the rhetoric of law reformers after the event, accident, compromise, muddle and momentum often play important roles in law reform, and the history of product liability in both the US and UK is certainly rich with examples. Take, for example, the sales warranties of quality developed in the nineteenth century from which the current special tort rules relating to product-caused losses in both the US and UK originated. While certain limits on these warranties can be rationally explained by particular historical conditions relating to the dynamics of new types of transaction between businesses (eg the limit to goods, the limit to goods already put into commercial circulation), the origin and justifications of certain other features of this warranty – the strict standard, the extension to cover the common consumer context of face-to-face dealings in the Sale of Goods Act 1893 – are something of a mystery. Yet each of these boundaries, frozen by that statute, took on their own momentum, so that by the time twentieth-century concern with personal injuries was aroused, the anomaly was seen not as the strict standard to which suppliers of goods were held to their contractual partners but the poorer negligence-based remedies available to mere users and bystanders suffering personal injury caused by goods. Although the way the product rules remove this anomaly creates another anomaly, now between those injured by products and other injured plaintiffs, no convincing explanation is given. Yet is it clear why the former anomaly based on the privity issue is more objectionable than this new anomaly? If privity is not a respectable distinction to make between victims of injuries caused by goods, why do we now distinguish injuries caused before and after the goods are put into commercial circulation?

Historical accident helped to obscure these central questions. The early cases in which the warranty of merchantability was developed did not happen to involve factual situations in which the court would have been forced squarely to address the question of whether the warranty should be strict. Such factual situations are where the relevant risk was unequivocally unforeseeable, or cases where the defendant was clearly regarded as having used all reasonable care, because here a result for the plaintiff could only be reached by the application of a liability which was strict. By the time courts were faced with such cases, the warranty had been mysteriously and without elaboration assumed to be strict. Similarly, the fact that a warranty claim could yield compensation for personal injuries, and consequently the potentially 'anomalous' parallel of warranty with the other emerging remedy for such injury – negligence – only emerged when claims of this type happened to be brought and reported in the early decades of this century.

In the US the accident of a nationwide food quality controversy helped precipitate the birth of aclassical warranty in *Mazetti* and perhaps also to mask its potential to flow on to fields of much broader doctrinal importance. In the late 1950s and early 1960s the apparent lack in the US of mass *design* disasters, or at least of litigation based on such disasters, reinforced the judicial and academic assumption that the emerging new tort liability for product injuries was concerned with manufacturing errors, thereby masking the explosive potential of the rule in relation to design cases. The same can be said of the US neglect of bystander issues which allowed reformers to maintain a warranty outlook on the problem and adopt warranty-derived boundaries to liability.

In Europe, by contrast, Thalidomide provided what the Americans had lacked: a notorious paradigm case of product injury which galvanized wide public attention (perhaps fortuitously since it became linked by the media to wider issues of freedom of speech – see Chapter 3, under heading 3) and focused it not just on the problem of fault-based remedies in general, but on design issues, bystanders and unforeseeable risks. Since coverage of unforeseeable risks can only occur under a strict liability rule, this ensured that the issue of a truly strict liability on manufacturers was at centre-stage of European thinking as it had never been in the US. So, too, the focus on bystanders ensured that warranty-based proposals for reform were swiftly rejected in Europe. Nor should the fact that the Thalidomide injuries happened to have involved innocent new-born babies being injured by a *product* supplied in the course of business be underestimated: presumably the identification of where the law's inadequacies lay might well have been different had the babies' injuries been caused by, say, industrial effluent polluting water supplies. Reformers might instead have focused on environmental liability (as the Japanese did after the Minimata pollution injuries) and have constructed a more wide-ranging liability on enterprises, not limited to supplied products or products at all.

The chance timing of the Thalidomide disaster was also influential in Europe. At this stage – the early to mid 1960s – s 402A had already 'swept' the United States but had not yet revealed its worst dangers. During the relatively prosperous period from that time until the mid-1970s, when news of trouble in the US product liability regime first began to be heard widely in Europe, the US rule seemed to be an affordable, highly successful, popular law reform model which would fill the apparent gap in remedies revealed by the Thalidomide tragedy. The initial and continued neglect in the US of design, bystander and unforeseeable risk issues allowed Europeans to assume that these presented no particular difficulties under the US rule. In the UK and Europe in the uncritically pro-compensation atmosphere of the 1970s, the initial reformers – the Pearson Commission, the Law Commissions, EC Commission and Strasbourg Convention drafters – could blithely adopt an approach of giving justifications *for* liability within the broad parameters of s 402A (give or take a few issues such as the development risk defence and channelling), while failing to advance reasons why injuries outside these bounds should not be given the added protection which s 402A provided. By the time US critics began to allege that product claims, especially design claims, were precipitating a crisis in the courts, in business and in the insurance markets, the draft Directive had already entered the maze of EC negotiations into which little principled, as opposed to bargaining, input seemed to go.

3   THE LIMITS OF PREDICTION

The US's head start of a quarter century in stricter product liability might hold important clues as to the impact the Directive will have in the UK and other EC Member States. But the institutional and cultural settings of product liability systems in the US and Member States are very different making specific extrapolation, let alone prediction, from the US experience a dangerous approach. The most obvious problem with the 'US experience' is that it is overwhelmingly anecdotal: very few broadly-based empirical studies on the impact of US product laws are available. Apart from evidence from very small market sectors – such as the impact of projected liability on the availability of vaccines[1] – the studies on filing rates (Chapter 2, under heading 6), and on the comparative real value of awards, there is surprisingly little to go on. There is, for example, little evidence across *wide* market sectors and over time about the following: the success rate of product claims; the

---

1 See J Fleming *The American Tort Process* (Oxford, Clarendon Press, 1988) 15. See also W Viscusi 'The Performance of Liability Insurance in States with Different Products-Liability Statutes' (1990) 19 JLS 809.

settlement rate; the availability of insurance; the level of insurance premiums; product-caused injury rates; the level of product prices; the impact on research and development; the reduction or elimination of supply of types of good (apart from a few notorious examples such as childhood vaccines, asbestos and IUDs); the bankruptcy rate among manufacturers; and the international competitiveness of firms exposed to stricter product liability.

Apart from these primary variables, one might also want to consider secondary effects. For example, to the extent that product-related claims are doctrinally and/or institutionally more attractive to US plaintiffs, one might expect to have seen a siphoning-off of claims from defendants who were not caught by the s 402A/*Greenman* liability, such as mere service-providers. Thus a person who falls and is injured when a bus brakes sharply and is unable to reach a restraint bar in time, might prefer to sue the manufacturers of the bus for defective design rather than the bus operator. In practical terms, this should mean a reduction in liability exposure in such sectors, perhaps with flow-on effects in insurance, prices, safety incentives, etc. Such secondary effects have also not been the subject of broadly-based empirical research. Nor has an associated line of enquiry been carefully evaluated – that of the indirect shielding of the victim's employer. In the US under the sole remedy rule, employees injured at work can only obtain low workers' compensation from their employer. As a result, workers injured by, say, unguarded plant machinery routinely sue the product manufacturer – indeed, it has been estimated that between 11% and 30% of product liability claims are for work-related injuries, accounting for 50% of the total product liability payouts by insurers.[2] The over-internalization to manufacturers and the over-externalization from employers have not been evaluated empirically.

Studies which have been done on the primary or secondary impact of US products doctrine are either too narrowly based to be of general usefulness, or have not been adequately corrected for obvious distortions – a special problem with studies of insurance prices, the dependency of which on factors such as the economic cycle rather than those identified by theories of liability exposure, is notorious. Yet even if broadly-based and statistically significant data existed on such variables as outlay on quality control, the problems in assessing their relationship to US products doctrine are compounded, firstly, by the large number of other forces influencing the variable besides the state of liability doctrine and, secondly, by the special complexities in identifying and characterizing doctrinal content and change in a nation with such diverse legal environments as the US. As we will see, this problem is itself exacerbated by the tendency towards vagueness in American law.

The absence of monitoring data from the US on its product regime, where it has long been the centre of academic and political controversy, does itself have a lesson for Europeans because it suggests that gauging the impact of a new liability rule such as that in the product liability Directive may be a prohibitively costly and complex task. Anecdotal and impressionistic evidence may be the best we can expect when dealing with law reform of this nature, but it must be recognized that even the impressions of unbiased observers may be ill-founded. Where limited tests of impressions of civil liability have been carefully examined, the 'common wisdom' has often been shown to be surprisingly at odds with reality. For example, the impression that liability rules crudely follow attributions of fault conflicts with empirical

2 Fleming, op cit 26; P Atiyah 'No-Fault Compensation: A Question That Will Not Go Away' (1980) 54 Tulane LR 271, 286.

evidence that an accident victim's attribution of fault is heavily influenced by advice as to who is likely to be held liable.[3] Similarly, the common view that damages awards in the US are very substantially more generous in real terms than in the UK has not been borne out by careful comparisons of asbestos awards.[4] In the medical malpractice area the common idea that doctors' day-to-day behaviour is influenced by liability rules has been questioned by empirical studies, as has the idea that US law in this area is now so pro-plaintiff that 'innocent' doctors are being held liable.[5]

Extrapolation to the UK and Europe from the US experience is not only dangerous because that experience is poorly understood. It is also risky because of the vast institutional and cultural differences between the US and EC Member States. As John Fleming puts it,

> what makes American tort law so peculiarly different from that of other countries ... is not ... substantive doctrinal content so much as the institutional framework in which it operates.[6]

4   THE INSTITUTIONAL SETTING OF DOCTRINE IN THE UNITED STATES

From the point when their doctrinal approaches diverged in the early decades of the twentieth century, the British and American histories of product liability show contrasting judicial attitudes to precedent and doctrinal integrity. In giving birth to aclassical warranty in *Mazetti*, for example, the court simply asserted 'if there is no authority for this remedy, it is high time for such an authority'.[7] This willingness of US courts to abandon the privity requirement in order to launch the idea of a separate tort liability for products illustrates more general characteristics of the attitude of the twentieth century US judiciary to legal rules and legal change. Atiyah and Summers have described how, relative to the formal reasoning adopted by twentieth century UK judges and earlier followed by many US courts, US legal reasoning is now highly 'substantive', that is, it is strongly influenced by reasons of a moral, economic, political, institutional or other social nature.[8] The substantivism of US judges and the American legal system in general bears a complex relationship to the specific history, institutions and culture of that country. The twentieth century embrace of substantive reasoning, for example, coincided with a rejection of positivist legal theories which emphasized the literal interpretation of statutes and the adherence to earlier case law (precedent) as rules, in favour of an instrumentalist approach to decision-making. It also coincided with an increasing awareness of the difficulty of achieving law reform by the legislative process in the US.

---

3 S Lloyd-Bostock 'Common Sense Morality and Accident Compensation' [1980] Ins LJ 331, 338, 344.

4 W Felstiner and R Dingwall *Asbestos Litigation in the United Kingdom* (Oxford, ABF & Centre for Socio-Legal Studies, 1988).

5 D Harris 'Evaluating the Goals of Personal Injuries Law: Some Empirical Evidence' in *Essays for Patrick Atiyah*, ed P Cane and J Stapleton (Oxford, Clarendon Press, 1991) 289, 298–302.

6 Fleming, op cit (v), see also 31.

7 *Mazetti* v *Armour & Co* 135, P 633, 636 (1913).

8 P Atiyah and R Summers *Form and Substance in Anglo-American Law* (Oxford, Clarendon Press, 1987) 1.

Atiyah and Summers date the instrumentalist revolution in American legal theory to the turn of the century when Oliver Wendell Holmes wrote that law is 'what the courts will do in fact' and that should be 'to bring about a social end which we desire'.[9] The judges' task was to decipher the social 'ends which the ... rules seek to accomplish, the reason why the ends are desired, what is given up to gain them, and whether they are worth the price'.[10] The new view matched the emergence of important wider cultural perceptions, for example, that law was the outward expression of a country's sense of justice and that change was likely to be beneficial. Central to this new approach was the attempt to determine the real and projected impact of legal rules to see if the relevant ends were being or could be expected to be achieved in practice. As we have seen, monitoring such impact is hard enough, but deciding the threshold question of what are the social ends law should be serving is a 'nightmare'[11] into which instrumentalism leads.

The instrumentalist revolution legitimized a judicial approach which is startling to the British lawyer: which British judge, for example, would have approved the $125 million Agent Orange settlement in the terms of Chief Judge Weinstein: that whether the plaintiffs' hurt could be traced to the defendants' chemical 'was beside the point in the broader context of the nation's obligations to Vietnam veterans and their families'?[12] More generally, US courts openly embrace a level of judicial lawmaking and looseness towards precedent which is unheard of in the UK. Whereas 'most American lawyers tend to think of a case-law rule as in some sense ... incorporating its underlying reasons, so that it tends to be a mere guide to decision making',[13] British lawyers distinguish a rule from the reasons for it. The history of US products law is rich in illustrations of the substantive approach. *Mazetti* is an early example of the new judicial activism, as is the attitude taken in *Henningsen* to exclusion clauses and recognition in *Greenman* of a separate tort cause of action. Indeed the separate tort rule for products is often cited as one of the most dramatic examples of US judicial activism and treatment of rules of law as 'tentative working rules' in the area of civil obligations.[14]

The twentieth century activism of US judges was fuelled and supported by institutional factors, including their constitutional position which is much more openly subject to the political process than in the UK, and the difficulty in securing reform of, inter alia, the law of obligations via federal or state legislation. Even the recent wave of US tort and product liability reform statutes supports this observation, being principally confined to peripheral issues. Legislative paralysis produces an expectation that courts will fill the gap left by legislative inaction by creating new law more openly than would be acceptable in the UK where the legislature's supremacy is revered and where Parliament is regarded as more likely to enact reforms regarded as necessary; and such judicial activity is regarded as legitimate. But in areas such as civil obligations, US legislative paralysis creates a particularly

---

9 O Holmes 'The Path of the Law' (1897) 10 Harv. LR 457, 461; O Holmes, 'Law in Science and Science in Law' (1899) 12 Harv LR 443, 460.

10 O Holmes, op cit 'The Path of the Law' 476.

11 Atiyah and Summers, op cit 262.

12 *Re 'Agent Orange' Product Liability Litigation* 597 F Suppl 740, 862 (1984) (per Chief Judge Weinstein).

13 Atiyah and Summers, op cit 418.

14 See eg F Kessler 'The Protection of the Consumer under Modern Sales Law: Part I, A Comparative Study' (1964) 74 Yale LJ 262; Atiyah and Summers, op cit 136; Fleming, op cit 56.

dangerous cycle. The substantive approach to legal reasoning tends to produce a certain vagueness of rules and extension of their scope of application which is particularly acute in open-ended areas such as tort. Yet retreat to more formal reasoning is difficult and unlikely in the US context, so the only route to more hard-edged rules or 'brighter lines' would be the legislative process. Yet it was the failure of this process which itself fuelled and legitimized judicial activism in the first place.

The history of US products law also illustrates how, even where the legislature has spoken, US courts may take a significantly more robust attitude to its words than would be acceptable in the UK. To British (and some US[15]) eyes it might seem that the creation of a classical warranty and later stricter tort liability were examples of this, and were unacceptable evasions of the legislative authority of sales legislation. The basis of this argument is that these common law developments allowed plaintiffs to launch what were in fact warranty claims without meeting the requirements of privity and other 'intricacies' of sales law such as prompt notice of claim, limitation rules, etc, while depriving the defendant of his freedom to attempt to exclude or limit such liability.

At other points the history of product liability shows a similar attitude to statute: courts have attacked the limited state product liability and tort reform statutes of the late 1970s and 1980s using reasoning which has ranged from 'sleight of hand' to respectable constitutional argument.[16] Claims by injured workers provide a particularly unequivocal example of the judicial evasion of statute: driven by a desire to treat worker injuries no differently from other injuries, post-war courts allowed employees to pursue product claims arising from work-related injuries. Under the statutory scheme of workers' compensation – benefits for which had become wholly out of line with damages in tort for comparable injury – the rule was that workers' compensation was to be the exclusive remedy against the employer for work-related injury, and this might well have been taken to imply that it was also to be the employee's sole remedy against *anyone* for such injury. Allowing claims by employees against third party manufacturers of machines or tools certainly offends the latter idea. But whatever may be implied into the rule, the further attempt by some courts to allow tort claims against a victim's own employer, either by allowing a recourse action by the sued product manufacturer or by allowing a direct product claim by the employee against the employer, is an evasion of a statutory intention which is clear.[17]

The history and content of US products law is also marked by a characteristically flexible attitude to linguistic precision. In the twentieth century, for example, the term 'warranty' was first said by some such as Prosser to denote a privity requirement, later to represent a hybrid tort/contract idea which did not necessarily require privity and then, in order to deal with the problem of pure economic loss claims (Chapter 2, under heading 5), to require privity after all. This loose attitude to terms is reflected in the form of s 402A which contained no definitional subsection. In subsequent case law, adventurous courts, preferring to analyse and be guided by what they understood to be the substantive basis of the rule, found no rational reason

---

15 See *Heaven* v *Uniroyal Inc* 305 A 2d 412 (1973), 427; J Wade 'Strict Tort Liability for Products: Past, Present and Future' (1984) 13 Cap ULR 335, 344; M Shanker 'A Re-examination of Prosser's Product Liability Crossword Game' (1979) 29 Case W Res LR 550, 552–4.

16 Fleming, op cit 69.

17 Even if it borders on the obsolete given the respective levels of damages of the two remedies, see G Calabresi *A Common Law for the Age of Statutes* (Cambridge, Harvard UP, 1982) 143.

why that rule should be limited to the terminology of the Restatement – which was, after all, intended only as a statement of the common law precedents as they stood at the time of drafting. For example, despite the fact that s 402A was limited to 'sellers', liability under it was quickly extended to 'hirers'; and the 'definition' of 'product' now seems dependent on the overall conclusion courts reach as to whether, on policy grounds, the liability *should* apply (see Chapter 12, under heading 4(c)).[18]

The preference of US courts for being guided by the substantive reasons for the rule rather than the words of the Restatement, inevitably led some to develop the rule much farther than its original champions envisaged because the available theories about the basis of the rule failed to provide it with hard borders. When theory is vague, contradictory or in dispute, reasonable judges can, and invariably do, differ on its application, so that the way s 402A was expanded was neither predictable nor uniform. The attempt to base substantive reasoning on confused theory can also produce unexpected flow-on effects in other areas of liability. This has happened with case law on the separate product rule in tort which has influenced other areas such as occupier's liability, landlord and tenant, successor corporation liability; and by provoking some jurisdictions to allow recovery for economic loss to non-privy plaintiffs, it has exerted pressure on the traditional tort/contract boundary itself.

The most striking example of US courts' interpretation of what the rule reflected in s 402A of the Restatement should embrace is, strangely, a conservative example. We have seen that courts were happy to relax the notion of 'seller' in s 402A and to apply it to truck lessors. Yet when faced with claims arising out of defects in products supplied under, say, contracts for work and materials – the so-called 'sales/service hybrid' cases – courts generally refused to allow them. The reason often given was that the product had not been the subject of a contract of *sale* as, it was argued, was required by the s 402A limitation to 'sellers' (see Chapter 12, under heading 4). This seems bizarrely inconsistent with the flexible attitude to 'seller' taken in the lessor cases. Of course, the inconsistency might be resolved by substituting a broader-based reason, for example, that the word 'seller' implies a contract for the *supply* of a good in which that supply is the sole or at least dominant subject-matter of the contract. But this is the very sort of artificial, formalistic and, from a substantive viewpoint, incoherent distinction US courts typically avoid. The point to be made here is that the general acceptance of these eccentric sales/service decisions owes a great deal to the general incoherence into which s 402A case law has fallen in the absence of clear sound bases for substantive reasoning and shows how eccentricity can be masked by the general confusion as to aims and purposes.

5   THE SOCIAL INSURANCE EFFECT AND OTHER EXPANSIONARY PRESSURES

Instrumentalism depends for its efficacy on the existence of clear arguments which motivate and justify judicial law-making. In the history of product liability a large array of these arguments have surfaced and the following chapters evaluate them. Some deserve special mention here, however, because they are especially closely related to the institutional and cultural framework within which US product rules

18 J Maloney 'What is or is not a product within the meaning of s 402A?' (1974) 57 Marq LR 625, 627.

developed. First, the historical expansion of liability for products in the US during the twentieth century up until the early 1980s was marked by a general judicial approval, if not outright promotion, of the social insurance *effect* of a holding of liability against a manufacturer. If the loss is shifted from the back of the individual victim and via the manufacturer's liability not only to those who benefit from its enterprise – its shareholders, workforce and customers – but via the manufacturer's insurance to an even wider pool of interested parties, two effects follow: the victim is compensated and a wide (hopefully relevant) part of the community pays. The attraction of such effects was great in a society which, relative to other post-war Western democracies, provides less public assistance for the payment of health care costs and less income support.[19] In such an environment and especially in the economic boom time of the 1950s and 1960s, it was understandable that judges began thinking instrumentally of tort less as a mechanism for resolving disputes between two parties and more as part of a social programme of relief for injury. The advance of product liability in particular at this time may also have been assisted by post-war confidence in the perfectability of technology.

The shifting of focus to community welfare goals, however, carried with it a great destabilizing danger, for judges seemed happier in recognizing such benefits of liability than in addressing its financial and doctrinal costs. In the years following *Greenman* and s 402A when the plaintiffs' bar began to argue for the application of the new products rule to design and failure to warn cases, judges felt little, if any, reluctance in accepting the argument. Later the same judicial welcome often met arguments for the relaxation of other rules such as of causation. Under this welfarist pressure the doctrinal boundaries of potential liability appeared rapidly to expand outwards and the volume of tort claims in general and product claims in particular appeared to burgeon.

The plaintiffs' bar

Ironically, while judges were being strongly influenced by the desirability of community goals such as social insurance and later deterrence, they were being invited to expand liability by an increasingly specialized plaintiffs' bar motivated by a highly individualist ideology. For these lawyers the vindication of a plaintiff's rights, public accounting from and disapproval of the individual wrongdoer, and retribution were central functions of tort claims, which it was the duty of an entrepreneurial plaintiffs' bar to champion. Despite their overt discomfort with wider, apparently collectivist, notions of loss-distribution, and so on, many of the plaintiffs' bar's principal arguments depend on the wider impact of liability beyond the two parties to a claim. For example, the defeat of a defendant is valued not only for its deterrence of the individual, but for its warning to others. Some members of the plaintiffs' bar see claims in respect of a particular type of defective product (IUDs, asbestos, machine tools, recreational equipment, etc) as one way in which tort law can and should control the relevant industry in the face of regulatory inefficiency. Far from seeing pharmaceutical companies, for example, as noble health care

---

19 In *Liability: Perspectives and Policy*, ed. R Litan and C Winston (Washington DC, Brookings Inst, 1988) see P Danzon 'Medical Malpractice Liability' 101, 125 (17% of US population has no health insurance). On the general point, see G Schwartz 'The Beginning and the Possible End of the Rise of Modern American Tort Law' (1992) 26 Georgia LR 601, 616–619.

providers to be nurtured and protected from ruinous liability exposure, they see them as multinational profit-making entities who are not adequately regulated by the Federal Drug Administration (FDA). Nor is linking the defendant's profit-making and its liability such a fanciful idea: it may well have had an unrecognized influence in the development of substantial areas of civil liability (Chapter 8, under heading 1). In any case ideological perspectives of the plaintiffs' bar have been an important source for the creative arguments US judges have adopted in the development of US product liability. Associated with the phenomenon of the specialist, aggressive plaintiff's bar is the contingency fee system which itself encourages speculative argument in favour of the expansion of liability, at least if the plaintiff is likely to secure a large award against a defendant with a sufficiently deep pocket to meet judgment.

Juries and doctrine

A third force favouring the expansion of US tort doctrine is the jury system. One of the most important ways by which the more pro-plaintiff attitude of US tort judges was reflected was their progressive abandoning of control over juries.[20] Substantive judicial reasoning need not, but in the open-textured civil liability area often does, lead to vaguer or more relaxed standards by which to assess whether or not an issue is to go to the jury. In US jurisdictions where juries are, if not routinely pro-plaintiff, at least sufficiently varied and volatile to produce the occasionally radically pro-plaintiff result, the legal outcomes available *in practice* are often a significant advance on what had been thought hitherto on the basis of the 'law in books' to be the limits of recovery. The usefulness of juries in masking or justifying extension of liability is particularly clear in design cases. It is hard to know on what criteria to judge design compromises: it is often an issue on which reasonable minds could reasonably differ (see Chapter 10). The judicial acceptance that the rule reflected in s 402A should cover such claims raised the embarrassing prospect of a judiciary struggling vainly to lay down and to justify, necessarily with written reasons, the impossible: a clear coherent standard for design choices and compromises. By increasingly leaving important issues relevant to design cases to the jury, judges were able to evade this danger and, superficially at least, to protect the legitimacy of the adjudication process in such cases.

6 CLAIMS vs DOCTRINE: THE UNREPRESENTATIVE 'RIM' OF LIABILITY

The judicial activism of US tort judges has advantages and disadvantages. It can be seen as a necessary source of innovation and invigoration of the law, keeping it in pace with social developments. The handling of the problem of exclusion clauses in mass markets and the attempt to overcome the limitation and causation problems in non-traumatic latent physical damage cases are good examples here. On the other

---

20 Fleming, op cit 131, 134–5. See also 114–6. Recent important empirical work suggests a complex relationship exists between plaintiffs' success rates and choice of judge or jury trial: K Clermont and T Eisenberg 'Trial by Judge or Jury: Transcending Empiricism' (1992) 77 Cornell LR 1124.

hand, it tends to threaten doctrinal coherence. As tort doctrine seemed to expand in the post-war period, the rate of civil claims boomed. By 1990 the cost of the US tort system was 2.6% of gross national product compared to 0.4–0.6% for European Community countries.[21] As a result, tort law became a prominent item on the political agenda, at least of political rhetoric. But what has in fact been happening to tort doctrine and product liability doctrine in particular? What can be observed in the post-war period are a few striking decisions on liability, a boom in claims and an increasing insurance burden on potential defendants. But these phenomena do not necessarily indicate that liability doctrine was really advancing substantially. Even if the rate of *success* of, say, product claims had remained constant, an increase in the number of claims would increase the insurance burden as successful claims increased from, say, 1 in 10 to 10 in 100 and defence costs would also rise ten-fold. So the question is, has the *rate of success* changed? Detailed empirical work on US case law is needed to answer such a question because of a phenomenon we might call the 'unrepresentative rim of liability' in systems such as the US.

In a unitary hierarchical system of formal reasoning and relatively strict precedent, the outer rim of liability formed by the most pro-plaintiff case law decisions represents the true boundary of potential liability. There is little, if any, scope for a court faced with a set of facts within that rim to deny the plaintiff's claim. On the other hand, in a system where substantive reasoning is adopted, the bonds of precedent are much looser. Even where a case is decided in favour of one plaintiff's novel argument (on either doctrine or procedure) – hence pushing out the rim of potential liability for future cases – later courts even within the same jurisdiction may evaluate the substantive policies differently and reach an opposite pro-defendant conclusion – a process illustrated by the *Beshada* and *Feldman* cases in New Jersey (see Chapter 2, under heading 6). This means the rim represents only the apparent boundary of liability in that jurisdiction. Within it plaintiffs may still lose. In areas such as product liability where the US Supreme Court exercises very little unifying influence on the development of doctrine and procedure, the result nationwide is often great difficulty in describing or predicting outcomes in individual cases. This tendency towards vagueness in doctrine, characteristic of systems of substantive reasoning, is particularly well illustrated by the warranty and separate tort rules of US liability for product-caused loss. While some novel decisions, such as the extension of the s 402A/*Greenman* rule from sellers to vehicle-hirers in *Cintrone* (1965), were rapidly and uniformly accepted both within the home jurisdiction and elsewhere, other landmark pro-plaintiff cases concerning that rule, such as cases imposing liability for unforeseeable risks or pure economic loss, received a much more mixed reception.

It was the rim of potential or apparent liability in the products field which steadily widened throughout the 1960s and 1970s as more pro-plaintiff outcomes occurred. Some of this apparent expansion may simply have been due to rhetoric: for example, despite numerous judicial avowals that this was what was happening, manufacturers were not being held strictly liable for conditions attributable to the design of the product (see Chapter 10). Nonetheless, whatever the truth is about what happened to the *success rate* of claims – whether doctrinal advance was real or only apparent, gradual or intermittent – the appearance of ever-expanding liability generated by the high-profile rim cases, plus the often sensational publicity given to

21 Product Liability International [January 1990] p 8.

particularly large awards (especially inflated by punitive damages), clearly had a profound impact on the claims consciousness of victims and their lawyers in the tort area in general and the products area in particular. This probably also had a feedback effect on juries' general ideas about responsibility – after all we already know that aggrieved individuals are strongly influenced in their attribution of responsibility by their perception of what the law on the issue is (see above under heading 3) and there is reason to think juries are similarly influenced by the apparent reach of legal liability. The fact that the outcome of a case cannot be predicted simply on the basis that it falls within the apparent rim of liability, plus the way high profile rim cases can heighten claims consciousness helps explain why, in systems of substantive reasoning, it is hard to identify real doctrinal change and to distinguish the question of legal change from the volume-of-claims issue. It also helps explain why, when some judicial caution began to emerge in the products field in the early to mid 1980s, pro-defendant outcomes at first went relatively unnoticed until the work of Henderson and Eisenberg (see Chapter 2, under heading 6). There were, after all, still plenty of high-profile pro-plaintiff outcomes to maintain the impression that product liability was continuing to expand.

7   UNCERTAINTY AND EQUAL TREATMENT

The vagueness and unpredictability of US product liability doctrine has helped stir considerable academic and judicial interest in the cost and efficiency of the US tort process, and this has had effects on the discussion of liability rules. For example, strict liability for manufacturing errors is now often justified on the ground that the costs of adjudication under a strict liability rule are less than under a negligence rule. Such concentration on issues of cost and efficiency is less likely to occur in a less litigious jurisdiction in which courts adopt more formalistic modes of reasoning. In the US, however, there is surprisingly little interest in another result of the vagueness of product liability law: the danger of unequal treatment. Even within the same jurisdiction closely similar cases can be resolved within a short period of time in opposite ways either by conflicting findings of law (eg on whether electricity is capable of being a 'product') or by jury evaluation of issues including defectiveness and quantum of damages. The phenomenon, reproduced across all 51 jurisdictions, is striking in particular cases.[22] The effect should not be overstated: eg a report by the US General Accounting Office in 1989[23] concluded that, in general, product liability *award levels* across five states were not as erratic as claimed by defence interests. But the potential for individual variation in result between certain like cases is widely accepted: one expert, in assessing the damages awards for deaths caused by the crash of an aeroplane, estimated that for victims of identical age and background awards could vary between States from $10,000 to $2m.[24]

22 Contrast *Hill* v *Searle Laboratories* 884 F 2d 1064 (8th Circ, 1989), 1070 and *Lacy* v *G D Searle & Co* 567 A 2d 398 (Del 1989) (on whether Searle could raise the 'learned intermediary' defence with regard to the CU-7 intrauterine device); *Brawner* v *Liberty Industries Inc* 573 SW 2d 376 (1978) and *Keller* v *Welles Department Store of Racine* 276 NW 2d 319 (1978).
23 US General Accounting Office *Product Liability: Verdicts and Case Resolution in Five States* (September 1989).
24 M Shapo, Reporter *Towards a Jurisprudence of Injury* (American Bar Association, 1984) 2–26.

Yet the real or potential variability in result between like cases does not generate the sort of anxious arguments about fairness to plaintiffs which it would in the UK. As John Fleming put it: 'consistency and uniformity, as ideals of equal justice are not valued to the same degree in America as they are in England ...'.[25] Nor could they afford to be in a system characterized by substantive judicial reasoning, loose control over juries, resultant volatile and vague rules, and a commitment to the local development of law (tort law at least) as a reflection of the sense of justice of the local community. In such a legal environment diversity of result is not only expected but can be positively valued as a sign of the vigour of this grassroots idea of justice: variations between states reflecting geographical variations in social values, variations within a jurisdiction reflecting the pluralism of values within local communities. In any case, in certain fields different results are probably a more justifiable, or at least a more realistic answer to certain questions since they are issues on which reasonable minds can differ. Indeed, the explosive impact of the post-war development of product liability lay in its revelation that product design was one such issue (see Chapter 10).

8   THE US DEFENDANT'S PROBLEMS: UNCERTAINTY, PUNITIVE DAMAGES, THE PLAINTIFFS' BAR, etc

The uncertainty surrounding US products law has not been strongly criticized by plaintiffs' interests, but it has been attacked for the problems it causes defence interests. Firstly, there is the alleged waste it causes as plaintiffs' lawyers resist settlement in the hope that the case will turn out to produce a ground-breaking pro-plaintiff outcome which pushes out the rim of potential liability either in terms of grounds of liability or quantum. Secondly, it creates incentives for costly forum shopping between jurisdictions. Thirdly, problems are created for defendants and their insurers when their future liability exposure is clouded in uncertainty both because the current liability position is unclear and because of the possibility of unpredictable future changes in doctrine. The latter problem is, of course, particularly acute in the context of long life products or products which might cause latent physical loss. Defendants' interests are therefore to be found urging reform of the law on, inter alia, the grounds of certainty while plaintiffs' interests tolerant of uncertainty in outcome coalesce to resist it.

Potential defendants have other reasons for wanting reform of tort law in general and product liability in particular. Relative to defendants in the UK and most EC countries, US defendants face the added disadvantage of a more extensive pre-trial discovery process. There is also the real prospect of an award of punitive damages being made by a sympathetic jury, a problem compounded by the high publicity given to the initial award of such damages and the relative under-reporting of the later reduction in quantum which commonly occurs when the case is appealed. It is a reasonable guess that large initial awards such as that against Ford Motor Company in the notorious Pinto case ($125m, later reduced on appeal to $3.5m) fuel the expectations of some later claimants and their legal representatives while also affecting jury sensibilities. Another problem for potential defendants is the US rule

---

25 Fleming, op cit 125. See also 116–7.

on costs – each party pays their own. The incentive on defendants to settle small claims even if hopeless is, therefore, great. The same dynamic can also operate towards the larger end of the spectrum: the $125m Agent Orange settlement, for example, has been ascribed to such forces.

The prospect of a specialist plaintiffs' bar which cooperates – or 'networks' – by the exchange of relevant information is a further problem US defence interests face. In product design claims in particular, even though formal class actions are relatively rare, this cooperation can give a powerful tactical advantage by the informal coordination of claims. In contrast, in the UK where class actions are not allowed, and the volume of claims is much lower, the equivalent development is at a much more primitive stage.[26] The Law Society's recent decision to vet personal injuries lawyers' competence and its role in helping co-ordinate mass trauma claims may encourage specialization and cooperation in the field, but the state of specialized legal representation for plaintiffs in UK and Europe still lags a long way behind that in the US. In the US it is not uncommon for an individual lawyer to specialize in product claims relating to one type of product, say, pharmaceuticals, or even in some cases one particular product line (eg the Dalkon Shield, etc). In contrast, only very recently (1990) has a UK equivalent of the powerful US plaintiffs' bar grouping, the American Trial Lawyers Association, been formed[27] and, outside a dozen cities, the chances are slim of a UK victim finding locally a product liability specialist, let alone a pharmaceutical specialist. The contrast between US and UK levels of legal specialization is linked both to the contingency fee system and the value of claims. Specialization is (or is perceived to be) a more lucrative approach to the organization of legal practice in the US. Furthermore, as we have seen, some US plaintiffs' lawyers seem to regard their role as more than just the facilitation of compensation to their individual client. Their rhetoric sometimes suggests a belief that tort law serves other valuable social goals such as the vindication of rights, publicizing of wrongdoing and deterrence of future injury. Such an 'ideological' view of their role would seem to have some sort of supportive inter-relationship with specialization.

Finally, potential defendants in the US have to contend with the phenomenon of claims volume. The rate of claims made and then of actual lawsuits filed in the US is considerably greater than the rate in the UK, even when adjustment is made for population differences. This is particularly the case in the products field where, using mid 1970s figures, it has been calculated that for every 700 US product-related lawsuits *filed*, there were only two in the UK.[28] The origin of the differences is unclear but seems to be the complex result of a number of cultural and institutional factors. The contingency fee system plus the rule that the loser does not pay the costs of the winner makes access to the tort system relatively easy for many US claimants. Most product claims seem to be for personal injuries and the contingency fee system makes this a particularly lucrative area of specialization for plaintiffs' lawyers; and this specialization would itself tend to facilitate claims. Similarly, the more generous

---

26 See, for example, W McBryde and C Barker 'Solicitors' Groups in Mass Disaster Claims' *NL J* 12.4.91, 484.

27 Note the membership of the Association of Personal Injury Lawyers was 1,160 on 15 November 1993 (ATLA has approx 70,000 members).

28 P Atiyah 'Tort Law and the Alternatives: Some Anglo-American Comparisons' (1987) 198 Duke LJ 1002, 1013. Compare B Markesinis, 'Litigation-Mania in England, Germany and the USA: Are we so very different?' [1990] Camb LJ 233.

discovery rules and the more volatile position of doctrine under the dual threat of substantive judicial reasoning and jury adjudication tend to make some initially borderline and/or speculative cases more worth pursuing in the US.

At least with respect to personal injuries, the injured would also seem to have more motivations to claim in tort in the US. First, the alternative avenues of support and compensation are not as well-developed nor as widely perceived as being adequate as they are in the UK where state and private insurance benefits usually cover at least health care costs (see heading 5, above). Secondly, because tort claims by employees against their employers are barred by US workers' compensation law, and because levels of workers' compensation are inadequate, employees have a strong incentive to sue product manufacturers in tort; and this is reflected in the high rate of product liability claims relative to other tort claims in the US. Thirdly, claims arising out of the death of a person with no dependants (a large percentage of potential victims: under-age children, senior citizens, etc) can result in substantial awards of damages in the US while in the UK a very low statutory cap applies (currently £7,500) to claims by non-dependent relatives. So, too, under US rules, those already being compensated from other 'collateral' sources, are much less likely to have such sums set-off against their tort damages than in the UK. Finally, one might also speculate that certain Americans are more litigious because of greater awareness that what has happened to them may provide the basis of a legal complaint and because of the cultural importance given to law and the legal system as a way of vindicating a person's interests. Even if true, this itself might be a mere function of a system which makes access to justice so much easier and more commonplace than in the UK. This would not, however, explain dated but intriguing data suggesting that there are huge geographical variations in the number of product suits brought in the US.[29] An explanation for the variations *and* for the relatively greater total of claims per capita in the US would be that there was a direct link between physical and social mobility and propensity to sue (more US citizens being mobile in these senses than UK citizens). This suggestion is to some extent confirmed by empirical studies which show that settled US rural residents sue less and tend to regard making civil claims as an 'attempt to escape responsibility'.[30]

Even though the Rand studies discussed in Chapter 2, under heading 6 suggest that the rate of product filings is no greater than the level of other civil filings in the US, the latter rate is, for whatever reasons, considerably higher than in the UK. If we assume that no lower proportion of *claims* end up being *filed* in the US than in the UK (a not unreasonable assumption given the relatively strong incentives in the US to pursue defendants) and even if the legal liability rules were identical so that the *success rate* per product claim were identical in the US and UK, defendants in the US indisputably face considerably heavier liability and defence cost burdens because of the volume of claims.

---

29 Atiyah 'Tort Law and the Alternatives' op cit 1014 fn 51. One possible partial explanation may be that since a large proportion of US product claims involve design complaints, geographical concentrations may centre on head-office centres (at least for those atypical 'bulge' claims identified by Rand).

30 D Engel 'The Oven Bird's Song: Insiders, Outsiders and Personal Injuries in an American Community' (1984) 18 Law & Soc Rev 551, 559.

9   POLITICAL POLARIZATION OF THE REFORM DEBATE

Even if the post-war developments in products doctrine had not substantially increased the individual plaintiff's chance of success, it is now clear that defendants would still have had significant reasons for urging reform. The product liability debate between the defendants' interests and plaintiffs' interests has become highly polarized, reflecting deep constitutional and ideological tensions. Plaintiffs' interests use the 'states' rights' argument to resist federal reform of products law (and tort in general), claiming that individuals' private claims should be judged by community, ie local, values. On the other hand, in order to promote national reform, it is defendants' interests who emphasize national community values: the need for, and the requirements and benefits of, a set of nationwide market rules. But potential defendants and their insurers want more than uniform rules. They want to confine liability more narrowly and they have strong rational arguments about community interest in their favour.

The plaintiffs' bar use the individualistic rhetoric of corrective justice and pursue their individual plaintiffs' rights by a remedy, tort, designed to vindicate such rights. Yet in doing so they must appeal to the underlying judicial interest in social insurance which approves of tort performing a communal support function. Defendants' interests can argue with reason that, because the rationale of tort law was historically seen to be one of individual redress, its forms render it an inefficient technique by which to pursue welfarist goals. They can also claim that such pursuit is in conflict with deeply held ideas about the individualistic basis of civil liability. It is one thing to shape doctrine rooted in a corrective justice rationale *incidentally* to promote certain social welfare effects, but another to elevate such effects to the status of goals so that the traditionally understood rationale is gravely undermined. A thin line exists between adapting law to new social needs and distorting law beyond its capacity to retain wide legitimacy. For example, the erosion of the causal rules for identification of the two individual parties to the tort dispute has probably caused such distortion (see Chapter 11).

The boom in product and tort claims in the 1960s and onwards, due to the apparent relaxation of the doctrinal boundaries of recovery, raised the stakes for both sides of the argument. Both are highly organized and their respective campaigns have ensured that product and tort law reform generally has become a highly visible, highly politicized issue in the US. Given the structure of the 1970s debate in the UK about the future of tort, the principal irony in this conflict in the US is that those representing the victims are highly individualistic in approach and do not campaign for more comprehensive rational reform; indeed, they reject any government intervention at all, while the opposing forces of business emphasize the disarray of legal rules and process in order to urge intervention by government through law reform. Moreover, the current paralysis and incompleteness of the reform process reveals an interesting clash of American values. In the post-war period there has not only been a growth in consumers' consciousness of 'rights', but also what Fleming describes as a 'spectacular rise in American values of "entitlement"' (ie welfare rights) evidenced by a 'marked shift of resources to social welfare expectations in response to heightened public expectations of entitlement'.[31] Yet for complex socio-political reasons, there has not been, nor is there likely soon to be, any working through of

---

31 Fleming, op cit 4–5.

these developments into a public programme of accident compensation. Collectivism in this sense is not yet ideologically acceptable in the US, it seems. The willingness of the judiciary to fill the gap by turning tort into a generous source of such compensation – some say a virtual welfare system in itself – seemed to satisfy these pressures, even if haphazardly. At the same time, the expansion of tort and specifically of product liability as an avenue for compensation was able to masquerade as conforming to the other American ideals such as vindication of individual rights within a corrective justice model of two party litigation and as preserving the goal of keeping government off the back of enterprise, the responsibilities of which should be to the individual not to the collective. So long as welfarist pressures collide with ideological resistance to collectivist solutions, the inevitable pressure on US judges and juries to fill the gap with tort damages will be substantial. The arguments for confining this avenue of compensation must have a different basis, such as that tort is over-deterring research and development.

10   THE INSTITUTIONAL SETTING OF PRODUCTS DOCTRINE IN THE UK

The development of products law in the US heavily influenced European attitudes but its influence – all one way and at times pronounced – was not always a coherent and constructive one. The European envy of and later concern about the US product liability regime was often ill-considered, unresearched and lacking in a sensitive consideration of the problems involved. For example, the reports by UK and European reformers scarcely touch on the controversial issues which conscious design choices raise for adjudication. Nor was there any sophisticated analysis of the contrasting legal culture in which the US rule was operating. Yet, as we have just seen, in the twentieth century the cultural and institutional setting of product liability rules in the UK is vastly different from that in the United States, and different again from that in other Member States.[32] This not only helps explain the divergent histories of those rules on the two sides of the Atlantic but should temper expectations that we can extrapolate from US experience to predict the impact of the Directive in any one Member State.

For example, the volume of tort claims in the UK is much smaller than in the US. Claims consciousness and claims motivation seem to be much lower both on the part of victims and legal representatives who tend to be much less specialized and coordinated, and less attracted to the low prestige field of personal injury practice than in the US, where such practice can be seen as a noble fight for the underdog. In the UK, and generally in the EC, claimants in tort (except for defamation) have neither access to jury trial[33] nor (effectively) to punitive damages, so that the sort of high profile awards which might raise claims consciousness do not often appear. The absence of the contingency fee system,[34] the rule that the loser pays the costs of both sides and the fact that legal aid is not widely available are major disincentives to claims in the UK where access to justice is not traditionally given a high

---

32 See eg the impressive study by Markesinis, op cit.
33 On which see *H v Ministry of Defence* [1991] 2 QB 103, CA.
34 Contrast the 'conditional fee' previewed in the Courts and Legal Services Act 1990, s 58.

priority. Culturally, litigation is seen as an abnormal and somewhat distasteful process. Non-litigious forms of support to those suffering personal injuries are more highly developed than in the US and more widely regarded as adequate in many cases.

In the UK there is a single jurisdiction, there is no problem of juries applying liability rules in an unpredictable way, and there are relatively few appellate level judges, which means that leave to appeal is not given freely. Although the House of Lords may depart from its earlier precedents, even there the influence of precedent is today very strong. The judicial strategy is to pursue certainty with only incremental change. In the US the society's success is widely regarded as owing much to its ability to adapt quickly to new circumstances, typically by entrepreneurial creativity. In such a context where the wealth and ultimate security of the nation is seen to be wrapped up with its ability to change, judicial creativity is less likely to be feared. In the UK, by contrast, the cultural consensus has been that the wealth and security of the community rests on the stability of its economic and social arrangements. As a result it is thought that social and legal change, when necessary, should be cautious and slow. Modern UK judges embrace this view. Their adherence to precedent and an incremental approach to the development of the common law superficially provides this necessary stability, even though it can often make law more complex and uncertain.[35] If the development of the common law should proceed only 'incrementally and by analogy with established categories',[36] judicial activism will not be regarded as the proper route for substantial legal change, especially when this is perceived as but part of a comprehensive reform of the law. This means that, in the UK, judicial perception that a case in hand is but one of a more generally defined category, triggers not a bold wide-ranging development based on principle relevant to that wide category, but referral to the avenue seen as the legitimate one for substantial legal change, that is the superior legislature. Typical of this style is Lord Bridge who in a recent case concluded:

> As a matter of legal principle ... I can discover no basis on which it is open to the court to embody this policy in the law without the assistance of the legislative and it is ... a dangerous course for the common law to embark on the adoption of novel policies which it sees as instruments of social justice but to which, unlike the legislature, it is unable to set carefully defined limitations.[37]

The supreme legislature with its democratic mandate has the ability to direct full investigations into the socio-economic implications and necessary compromises of proposed change. Unlike the US, there is confidence (partially justified) that such enquiry will be made and needed reforms enacted.

The history of UK products laws reflects these general traits. Leading figures, such as the Director of Fair Trading, argued that it was not feasible for courts to act as a substitute for Parliament in developing stricter liability for defective products – the impact on research and development alone was an issue outside the capacity

---

35 P Atiyah *Pragmatism and Theory in English Law* (London, Stevens, 1987) 159–161. In the area of economic loss, for example, see J Stapleton 'Duty of Care and Economic Loss: A Wider Agenda' (1991) 107 LQR 249.

36 The often approved dictum of Justice Brennan in *Sutherland Shire Council* v *Heyman* (1985) 60 ALR 1, 43–4.

37 *D & F Estates Ltd* v *Church Comrs for England* [1988] 2 All ER 992, 1009. See also *Jones* v *Secretary of State for Social Services* [1972] AC 944, 1026 per Lord Simon.

and legitimate role of judges.[38] Mid- to late-twentieth century UK case law in the field is characterized by a cautious preference for adherence to precedent rather than bold legal change. Unlike US courts, British courts were unwilling to make inroads into the citadel of privity by developing aclassical warranty ideas, or to offend the formal idea of freedom of contract by striking down exemption clauses on the grounds that they were unfair and not really agreed to because of the inequality of the parties' bargaining power. In the twentieth century concern has arisen particularly about the safety of dwellings, about personal injuries and about the phenomenon of inequality of bargaining power in the profit-making context. While in the hands of its creative judiciary, US common law has been able to develop some specialized rules in an attempt to tackle each of these concerns – the rule reflected in s 402A being a prime example – UK common law has remained too frozen by precedent to respond to them: the response has been almost wholly legislative: the Defective Premises Act 1972; Limitation Act 1963; the Employer's Liability (Defective Equipment) Act 1969; and the Unfair Contract Terms Act 1977. It was therefore typical of a much wider phenomenon of the legal culture that post-war concern with consumer issues was dealt with by legislation. Such consumer protection legislation imposed administrative and criminal controls and rarely gave rise to civil liability. This was also typical of a legal culture in which there is a high level of (justified) mistrust of using civil liability as a tool of social engineering, either as an important regulator of behaviour or as a major and reliable source of support for those suffering loss. In this sense Part I of the Consumer Protection Act 1987, which creates civil liability, is a striking exception in the field of consumer protection.

Who makes law reform?

In the UK the relevant influences in the process of law reform also contrast with those in the US. In the US when it became more likely that judges would listen to novel substantive arguments, the role of academics in legal change was elevated. It was then possible for a relatively few individuals – both academics such as Prosser and Llewellyn and activist judges such as Traynor – to define a problem and select its solution. For example, Prosser's initial interest in sales warranties led him to see the 'problem' as one of the privity barrier to suits against manufacturers by buyers and users and to see its abandonment as simply a limited 'tidying up' of sales law. Section 402A itself represented the culmination of activity by a relatively few intellectuals – it was not the product of public concern about the volume or severity of personal injuries caused by products nor was it shaped by political compromise. In the UK, by contrast, the political pressure for change in liability for defective products came, at least initially, less from judges, academics and the legal representatives of those injured by such products, and more from the unfocused attention of the media on selected cases, especially Thalidomide. Later, the preponderance of academic opinion at the time of the initial product reform proposals was in favour of something far more radical than tinkering with civil liability. One result of this mismatch was that it led to a gap in theoretical writing in the UK about the foundations of civil liability in general and about stricter product laws in particular. This

---

38 G Borrie *The Development of Consumer Law and Policy – Bold Spirits and Timorous Souls* (London, Stevens, 1984) 33–4, 124.

then helped mislead reformers, politicians and consumer groups into their uncritical admiration of the US rule and later their relatively benign attitude to the EC Directive.

11 THE LIKELY LONG-TERM IMPACT OF THE DIRECTIVE IN THE UK

While some description of the short-term impact of the Directive is possible (see Chapter 13, under heading 6), the great institutional differences between the US and the UK swamp any hope that detailed extrapolation might be possible from the US experience in order to predict the long-term impact of the new product liability in the UK. But speculation is possible. The publicity given to the Act might be expected to cause claims consciousness eventually to rise among both victims and their legal advisers, and with it the volume of claims relating to product-caused loss; although because of cultural and institutional barriers this will never be as explosive a rise as it was in the US. Even if the success rate of such product claims is no greater than at present under other heads of liability (eg under negligence or supply of goods legislation), the overall burden of liability costs on business would rise with the claims rate, and so some marginal effect in prices may be expected. Whether there will be any long-term effect on prevention incentives and hence on injury rates is more problematic. Gordon Borrie has noted that even legislation which merely consolidates or codifies existing law, like the Sale of Goods Act 1979 and the Supply of Goods and Services Act 1982, has an educative value for traders, often prompting them to reassess their quality control systems and insurance cover.[39] On the other hand, even if the reach of liability *has* formally and substantially expanded, so that in theory both injury rates and insurance premium levels should be affected, it is well known that these are areas in which other factors can swamp the effects of changes in liability rates. But liability has not expanded substantially. The contexts in which a plaintiff will be able to succeed under the CPA, where before she would have failed under alternative causes of action, will be very few. Liability of importers and suppliers of anonymous or otherwise untraceable goods has expanded, although overall these will be uncommon claims – most claims will be taken against the manufacturer and with regard to it liability exposure has not significantly changed. In a few marginal cases the shifting of the burden of proof on key issues will, however, improve the prospects of success.

Another long-term effect of the Directive (and CPA) may be that as people become more aware of the possibility of suing product manufacturers, claims which might have been made against other parties (such as the bus operator in the example given under heading 3, above) will be made against manufacturers. This re-channelling of claims towards manufacturers could have flow-on effects. Politically it may be significant if it generates in manufacturers a sense of injustice which results in pressure to reform the new rule. It may also have flow-on effects in other areas of liability such as the distribution of claims in the tort of negligence which makes no distinction between service givers and goods manufacturers.

39 Ibid 36.

Even if we ignore possible distortions in other areas of liability, the degree to which any 'harmonization' of laws would enhance community trade itself depends on two factors. First, it would require that before the Directive, manufacturing and trading decisions within the EC were significantly influenced by the existing and contrasting liability regimes between Member States so that the new uniformity of laws would eliminate significant differentials. There is no evidence that decisions were influenced in this way. Secondly, it would require that surviving local differences in both the institutional setting[40] and doctrinal implementation of the Directive (on which see Chapter 3, under heading 6(a)(i)) are of insignificant importance. Intuitively this seems unlikely: if the operation of relatively similar rules in the US and UK can differ markedly because of different institutional and cultural settings, potential variations within a group of twelve, which includes socio-legal communities as diverse as the UK and Greece, seem significant. With respect to doctrinal implementation, it would not be surprising if the local judicial determination of the level of safety citizens are entitled to expect (Article 6) varied between the poorer southern Member States and the much more prosperous northern States. Even between Britain and Germany comparative studies have found divergent judicial approaches to parallel pre-Directive product claims: whereas British courts tend to focus on consumer expectations, German courts are more sensitive to the ability of and cost to the manufacturer of avoiding a product risk.[41]

Finally, the Directive may have long-term effects in the way UK lawyers think about doctrine. Given the cultural preference for formalist and incremental legal change, UK lawyers are trained to address the sophisticated minutiae of existing legal rules with relatively little emphasis on broad social policy argument. There is no point in marshalling socio-economic arguments for the abandonment of privity if there is no real or perceived chance judges will feel free to abandon it. But in exercising its role as ultimate arbiter of legal issues arising under the Directive, the European Court of Justice will take a far more substantive non-literal view of its provisions than UK lawyers are used to. Section 1 of the CPA provides that 'this Part shall have effect for the purpose of making such provision as is necessary in order to comply with the product liability Directive and shall be construed accordingly'. This is in line with earlier decisions of the ECJ where it emphasized the duty of national courts to construe the provisions of a national law implementing a Directive 'in the light of the working and the purpose of the Directive'.[42] This has obvious implications in cases where there appears a clear difference between the substance of the Directive and the domestic law implementing it (on these see Chapter 3, under heading 6(a)(i)). But these are not too troublesome: under the Treaty of Rome and the European Communities Act 1972 UK courts are obliged and have so far been willing to distort traditional approaches to statutory interpretation so that domestic law conforms to the UK's community obligations.[43] More

---

40 For example, the level of legal costs, availability of state legal aid, the sufficiency of alternative sources of support, even the differences between an adversarial rather than an inquisitorial procedure.

41 J Finsinger and J Simon *The Harmonisation of Product Liability Laws in Britain and German* (London, Anglo-German Foundation, 1992) 284.

42 See eg Case 14/83: *Von Colson v Land Nordrhein-Westfalen* [1984] ECR 1891.

43 See in general J Steiner 'Coming to Terms with EEC Directives' (1990) 106 LQR 144. And this will be assisted by the recent House of Lords decision in *Pepper (Inspector of Taxes) v Hart* [1993] 1 All ER 42 which held that henceforth when courts are confronted by domestic legislation which is ambi-

difficult problems will arise when the ECJ evaluates the terms of the Directive from a purposive perspective. This is an approach very foreign to most UK lawyers. Take, for example, the concept of 'product' which is used interchangeably with the idea of 'goods' in the Treaty of Rome.[44] UK lawyers will probably be tempted to read 'product' effectively to mean 'goods' (as the CPA does) and may also then fall into the trap of reading 'goods' to have a meaning equivalent to its meaning in the Sales of Goods legislation. But this latter concept is considerably narrower than the meaning the ECJ has already given to that term in Article 169 proceedings: that 'goods' means something capable of money valuation and of being the object of commercial transactions.[45] When faced with questions such as whether software (a non-good under UK sales law) is a 'good'/'product' under the Directive, the ECJ's evaluation of the purpose of that Directive may well produce an affirmative decision. The ECJ may interpret the concept of 'put into circulation' in the Directive to cover more situations than are covered by the parallel concept of 'supply' under the CPA (see in general Chapter 12).

The ECJ's substantive approach could produce an expansionary tendency similar to that experienced in the US – borderline cases being brought within the ambit of the Directive both because the object of legal harmonization seems to justify it and, as in the US, because other purported purposes of the law, such as deterrence, do not justify the boundaries which a literal interpretation of the text of the Directive would set down. If, as European comparativists predict, the ECJ will use the doctrinal experience of the US in interpeting and applying the Directive,[46] UK lawyers will have to make significant adjustments to their approach, becoming familiar with the approach of, say, the New Jersey Supreme Court. Substantivism leads to a diversity of possible outcomes – as the US experience itself shows – and the art of distinguishing 'soft' precedents with the aid of substantive arguments is one at which UK lawyers, steeped in formalism and linguistic precision, are not well-skilled. One prediction, then, of what the impact will be of Directives such as the products Directive on local legal culture is that it will give lawyers an incentive to acquire such skills and to familiarize themselves with Community and, in the case of product liability, US precedents. This experience may also put pressure on related areas. For example, the recognition of software as a 'good' for the purposes of the Directive would create anomalies with domestic laws which utilize a narrower concept of 'good'. Similarly, the development of design liability under the Directive may well prompt analogous 'negligent design' claims. In the very long term, the greater familiarity with substantive argument which EC laws such as the Directive necessitate, may also subtly erode the confidence of UK lawyers in formalism itself.

guous or obscure or the literal meaning of which leads to an absurdity, they may refer to clear Parliamentary statements of a Minister or other promoter of the Bill in order to construe its terms. This is because such statements often make clear the basis on which the Parliamentary drafters argue that the statutory language does adequately capture the spirit of the terms in, say, the Directive the Bill seeks to implement. For examples of such statements concerning Part I of the CPA (where the relevant promoters were the Lord Advocate, Lord Cameron of Lochbroom; and the Parliamentary Under-Secretaries of State for Trade and Industry, Lord Lucas of Chilworth and Mr Michael Howard) see 483 HL Official Report (5th series) cols 840ff, 851–3 and 487 HL Official Report (5th series) cols 784–5 (development risk defence); 483 HL Official Report (5th series) cols 737, 759–760; 830–2 (on meaning of 'initial processing'); and 483 HL Official Report (5th series) cols 879, 868–70 (exclusion of damage done by defective component to final conglomerate product).

44 J Steiner *Textbook on EEC Law*, 3rd edn (London, Blackstone Press, 1992) 70.

45 7/68 *EC Commission* v *Italy* [1968] ECR 423.

46 S Whittaker 'European Product Liability and Intellectual Products' (1989) 105 LQR 125, 132.

PART TWO

Theory

CHAPTER 5

Liability as an economic strategy

1 INTRODUCTION

In Part 2 we lay aside the suspicion arising from Part 1 that the development of
special product rules in both the US and the European Community was due more to
historical accident than to the emergence of a coherent new principle of civil
liability. Law reform should be a purposive enterprise and there is a communal
expectation that changes to the law are made in order to pursue rational goals. Perhaps the rule of law itself requires not just that we have rules but that they are based
on purposes which are open to public debate.[1] Also it is only once the purported purposes of a law and their relative weight are identified that we can evaluate whether
they were internally consistent goals, whether the detail of the new law is a way of
achieving those goals in a consistent and coherent way, whether the law has successfully achieved its goals, how hard cases may be decided under the purposive interpretative approach and whether the current doctrinal position is a stable one viewed
in the longer term. Examination of theory is also a necessary preliminary to the
normative questions of whether different goals and different legal arrangements
would be preferable.

In the British and EC reform documents of the mid-1970s the treatment of the
arguments in favour of the Directive and the reallocation of resources it potentially
involved was surprisingly superficial. What should be made of this and of the dearth
of UK and EC theoretical academic writing in the area? By the time these documents were written in the mid-1970s a wealth of theoretical material *had* emerged
from the US where the dramatically swift adoption of the new rule in the early
1960s had later been followed by academics postulating much more sophisticated
rationales for the new civil liability rule than the incoherent amalgam of ideas used
by the reforming courts and earlier academic proponents of the US rule. These
reformers had considered the rule represented by s 402A as a limited tidying up of
sales law, intellectually neat and attractive but of relatively little practical importance (see Chapter 2, under heading 5); this was an understandable attitude given
their preoccupation with manufacturing errors. Understandable, too, was the poverty
and half-heartedness of their efforts to provide theoretical justifications for the
change – after all, sales law was a firmly established, well-accepted area, the limited
rationalization of which hardly seemed to need a vast new theory of liability. Lip
service *was* paid, in Prosser's articles and in the key judgments, to the fashionable
intellectual ideas of the time – 'risk-distribution', 'cost-internalization', 'compensation', 'deterrence', 'inequality of bargaining power' – but in ways which failed to
provide a rigorous basis for and explicit limitation to the scope of the new liability.

---

1 P Atiyah *Pragmatism and Theory* (London, Stevens & Sons, 1987) 144.

The unquestioning focus on manufacturing errors allowed s 402A and, more importantly, its Comments to be drafted in a way which did not carefully confine its scope to such cases. As the explosive potential of s 402A was later being realized in a flood of difficult design defect cases, defenders of the rule – now revealed as a much more extensive rule than its originators had foreseen – turned to more elaborate conceptual ideas. Some of these were sophisticated developments of those earlier intellectual enthusiasms, others were novel and breathtakingly broad theories of civil liability, notably from the law and economics school.

The historical process by which these ideas emerged and interacted is complex and not of direct interest here. What is important is that against the background and availability of these theories the shallowness of the UK and European reformers' analysis is striking. No coherent principle of civil liability emerges from the UK and European reform documents, nor does even a convincing set of pragmatic considerations and compromises favouring the reform. Instead, like US courts uncertain of the original reasons for s 402A, yet wary of adopting one of the later more sophisticated rationales to the exclusion of others, European reformers gave us a plethora of rationales,[2] some of which are internally inconsistent, and with no indication of the weight and priority to be given to each. Among the short-term implications of this is that, when faced with difficult boundary issues under the Directive, courts will have little clear guidance on where and why to draw the line of liability. Similarly, monitoring the success of the Directive will be confounded by the confusion as to its goals: should we be looking for a rise in the number of claims to vindicate a goal of facilitation of claims, or should we hope to see fewer claims as the deterrent force of the Directive bites? More broadly, the ragbag of reasons formally given in support of the Directive frustrates internal analysis as criticism of one aspect of the law, in terms of its counterproductive effect in terms of one goal, can be met with the reply that it nevertheless promotes another goal. With no ranking of the importance of these goals the critic's target is always moving. Judged overall the British and European reform documents displayed an extraordinary neglect of theoretical issues, of the dangerous confusion into which the US rule fell because *its* framers had inadequately thought out its rationale, and of the difficulty of controlling the use of a rule after its inauguration unless a relatively clear doctrinal analysis is available to courts. To some extent these problems are less pressing under the EC rule than under s 402A because the former operates on a statutory basis, not as a fluid common law rule open to judicial 'development', and because liability is 'channelled' only to some product suppliers. But in the long term even such a rule, if based on artificial and inadequately justified boundaries, is likely to prove unstable.

2 SUBORDINATE CONSIDERATIONS

What, then, are the ideas on which the Directive was or might be based? It is convenient first to look at 'subordinate considerations' such as facilitating compensation which, though commonly mentioned in US case law, US academic writing

2 See, eg, Law Coms para 23; 1976 Draft Directive, Preamble. *Escola* v *Coca-Cola Bottling Co of Frésno* 150 P 2d 436 (1944), 440–1 (J Traynor).

and in the UK and EC reform documents, cannot alone provide convincing bases of civil liability because they cannot justify the shape and location of the boundaries of relevant rules. A common mistake is to confuse the effects of a rule with its possible goals. An effect of a rule *may* also have been the rule's goal, but this does not *necessarily* follow. Facilitating compensation may be an effect produced by a change in the law such as the Directive – and an effect we find attractive – but to provide a convincing justification for a rule of civil liability a rationale must be sufficiently detailed to explain its boundaries, and the simple facilitation of compensation argument does not do this. This is not to say that these factors had no influence historically in the development of the new product rules on both sides of the Atlantic, for they have an important rhetorical appeal; and the key US case law which transformed warranty claims for physical loss into a new form of tort claim clearly relied upon them for this effect. Nevertheless, even in those judgments, ideas of compensation, loss-spreading and the like were deployed simply as add-on support for what was seen as a self-evidently justified rationalization of existing principles, while the view that all that was happening was a minor development of an already well-settled area of liability (warranty) enabled the US courts to shirk the task of synthesising a coherent theory to explain the shape of the new liability.

(a)   The anomaly argument

Reformers in the US and EC agreed that it was anomalous that the injured buyer of a defective good should have a better avenue of compensation than the injured user. UK and European reformers used the case of *Daniels and Daniels*[3] to illustrate the phenomenon: in the same action the injured buyer of poisonous lemonade was able to sue the seller for breach of contract despite the absence of negligence on the seller's part (ie on the basis of a strict warranty liability) while the injured user, forced to rely on the tort of negligence and finding no-one in the chain of manufacture and distribution who had been careless, failed. Although the elimination of anomaly could be sound justification for legal change, the anomaly argument in favour of the Directive is only superficially attractive. It could be argued that tort, being flexible in responding to community values, reflects the appropriate standard to apply to claims for physical loss, that is fault. From this perspective the anomaly might better have been identified as the *strict* standard of the warranty of merchantability on which physically injured buyers were able to sue. Not only is the origin of this standard obscure, but its application in warranty claims for physical losses might be regretted from today's perspective towards physical losses.[4] So long as the law persists in seeing contractual arrangements as appropriately calling forth a different standard of obligation from that underlying obligations in the tort of negligence, anomalies are inevitable. In short, were the law to be feeling its way to a consistent approach to claims for physical injury, it is not self-evident that the strict standard would be regarded as the appropriate one. In any case, the Directive does

---

3 *Daniels and Daniels* v *R White & Sons Ltd and Tarbard* [1938] 4 All ER 258. See Law Coms paras 25–28. Contrast *Hill* v *James Crowe (Cases) Ltd* [1978] 1 All ER 812.

4 At least personal injuries: 'an allegation of negligence is in general essential to the relevancy of an action of reparation for personal injuries', *Read* v *J Lyons & Co Ltd* [1947] AC 156, 170–1 (Lord Macmillan).

not remove anomaly. At best it simply shifts the line of anomaly from between buyers of goods and others to a point between those injured by goods and those injured in other ways. At worst it multiplies anomalies by adding yet another, but limited, avenue of compensation for physical losses (see also Chapter 13, under heading 7).

(b) The efficient administration of justice

In its list of its main considerations of policy, the Law Commission cited the discouragement of unnecessary litigation and the removal of procedural or evidentiary difficulties which impede rather than assist the course of justice. Recent US theorists, exasperated by the theoretical confusion and litigious morass into which the US products rule has now fallen, also stress the importance of the efficiency of the legal system as a factor in the light of which the first order demands of theory might have to give way. Certainly, the efficient administration of justice is an uncontroversial goal and in efficiency terms a legal system is best served by consistent, certain and predictable rules which provide a clear framework within which parties can settle their disputes without trial and at low cost. A moment's thought, however, will show that this can rarely be more than a subordinate concern which qualifies and supports legal change based on other grounds. For were it to be a principal concern and goal, the most logical rule for it to produce in the products field is the 'bright-line' of no liability at all. Of course, concern with lowering administrative costs and delay, and therefore with the simplification of the fact-finding process, often *does* exert pressure to simplify substantive and evidentiary rules. This concern alone, however, does not dictate or explain the direction in which that legal reform moves. Finally, even if it were true that the cause of action in the Directive is simpler and cheaper to administer than other causes of action, this would only have improved administrative matters if it had *replaced* de iure or de facto more costly-to-administer causes of action. This it did not do: it is an additional cause of action and one which plaintiffs will be best advised to plead in addition to, not in place of, other claims (see Chapter 13, under heading 6).

(c) Facilitating compensation: loss-spreading, deep pockets, insurance

One of the most pervasive fallacies in the product liability field is that the new product rules in the US and EC can be explained and justified in terms of the goal of facilitating the compensation of the injured. When put baldly in this way, the contention is easily exploded for not only does it fail to explain defences to a *liability*, but 'if compensation were the only goal, then by far the most effective and efficient method of accomplishing it would be through a system of general *social insurance*.'[5] (emphasis added). Marginally more sophisticated versions of the idea are the 'deep-pocket' and loss-spreading arguments. The first of these emphasises that certain potential defendants are more likely to have sufficient financial reserves to cushion the loss associated with the relevant injury and that there is social value in shifting the loss from the individual victim for whom the concentration of the loss

---

5 G Calabresi 'The Decision for Accidents: An Approach to No-Fault Allocation of Costs' (1965) 78 Harv LR 713, 744.

can prove catastrophic to the 'deep-pocket' defendant for whom the loss will be far less disruptive. A related idea is the concern to provide the victim with a range of potential defendants so that, were one to prove untraceable, bankrupt, or otherwise bad for judgment, the victim will still have someone to sue. While the 'blunderbuss' of the US rule, which exposes all sellers in the chain of manufacture and distribution to the liability, meets this concern, and the Law Commission used it intermittently to support certain of its recommendations (see Chapter 11, under headings 7 and 8), it both cuts across other asserted concerns which favour the focusing of liability on one party (eg to avoid the pyramiding of insurance and to focus deterrence incentives) and does not explain the choice of civil liability rather than social insurance.

Often associated with the deep-pocket idea is that of 'loss-spreading'. In *Becker* v *IRM Corpn* (1985)[6] the majority of the Supreme Court of California described this as the 'paramount' policy of the products rule. This idea is that liability should be shifted from the victim to those (often, but not necessarily, deep pockets) who have a better capacity to spread the loss over many parties, thereby diluting the social impact of the loss. It is not clear whether the common version of this idea – to look for the best insurer, ie the party who had or could have bought insurance cover against the relevant risk most cheaply – is based on moral or economic arguments.[7] The moral justification that in the relevant circumstances an undifferentiated social *group* should pay is hardly one which the relevant UK government negotiating the products Directive (the Thatcher administration) would have embraced: loss-spreading simpliciter smacks of socialism and the welfare state. The economic justification is similarly problematic because although economic analysts of law can explain the economic advantages of the loss-spreading effect of, say, insurance (in terms of reduction of disutility in the form of disruption costs), the reality of insurance in practice is to dilute another economic effect of liability, deterrence incentives.

As with the crude compensation goal, the weightiest objection to arguments that a liability is or should be based on deep-pocket, loss-spreading and best-insurer goals is simple: they do not identify the class of defendants from which the deep-pocket, best loss-spreader or cheapest insurer is to be selected nor why only particular forms and instances of loss are to be spread, etc. More importantly, as Calabresi's argument implies, the deepest pocket, best loss-spreader and cheapest insurer is the Exchequer so that logical pursuit of such goals would produce a formal system of social insurance. The *boundaries* of civil liability show that its goal cannot be loss-spreading, etc, and clear judicial confirmation of this exists in UK and Commonwealth appellate judgments.[8] Even when these ideas are subjugated to some other principle which *does* select a subset of potential defendants – say a principle which selects only those but for whose conduct the injury would not have occurred – pursuit of them does not necessarily point, in the area of product injuries, to the party selected by the Directive as the principal target of liability, the manufacturer of the

---

6 698 P 2d 116 (1985), 123. On 'risk-spreading' see also W Prosser 'The Assault Upon the Citadel (Strict Liability to the Consumer)' (1960) 69 Yale LJ 1099, 1120.

7 See, eg, the confusion of R Posner: 'Strict Liability: A Comment' (1973) 2 J Legal Studies 205, 210, n 11; 'The Concept of Corrective Justice in Recent Theories of Tort Law' (1981) 10 J Legal Studies 187, n 3. On this theme see Law Coms para 23(c). Note both the social insurance (compensation) and 'best/convenient insurer' themes are distinct from the argument that the goal of liability is to provide the plaintiff with insurance – see Chapter 8, under heading 4.

8 See, eg, *Caltex Oil (Australia) Pty Ltd* v *Diedge Willemstad* (1976) 136 CLR 529, 580: 'the task of the court remains that of loss-fixing rather than loss-spreading' (Stephen J).

product. In many fields such 'goals' would select the retailer. The food retailer 'Sainsbury's' has a deeper pocket than most of its suppliers of small food items and arguably is in a better position to insure and spread the loss.

Despite their incoherence as rationales for civil liability, loss-spreading and deep-pocket considerations were also not unimportant in the historical development and operation of the product rules. First, as we have seen, the early US proponents of the US rule referred to the social insurance advantages it would entail. Later, US courts were encouraged by these ideas to allow applications of the rule far outside that foreseen by its originators. The expansionary pressure they exerted on substantive doctrine was probably matched in importance by their influence in practice on juries. Social scientists[9] suggest that ordinary people tend to allocate responsibility according to where they think compensation will be forthcoming. It is not hard to imagine that juries would tend to regard corporate defendants as deep-pockets who can 'afford' the relevant loss, that this introduced a pro-liability bias in the outcome of jury deliberations, and that such outcomes may have exerted expansionary pressure on substantive doctrine such as the concept of 'defect'. While the absence of juries in the relevant EC trials will prevent this latter effect, we can expect the former effect, that is that the desire to facilitate compensation, be it via deep pockets or cheap insurers, will exert strong expansionary pressures on the boundaries of the Directive. To contain these pressures towards covert social insurance, the ECJ and other EC courts will need a clear and coherent theory which justifies both the Directive's liability and its boundaries.

3 SUBSTANTIVE THEORIES

In the US the abandonment of privity in warranty actions produced a common law rule which rendered all who had previously owed the warranty obligation – all commercial suppliers down the chain of manufacture and distribution – liable to the eventual victim in tort – a result justified at the time by crude social insurance ideas of loss-spreading and deep pockets. But once in operation, the open-endedness of this rationale and the litigation crisis which developed forced supporters of the rule to suggest more justifications for it, justifications antagonistic to the goal of social insurance, and supportive of a limited system of civil liability. At a crude level European reformers seem to have been aware of and attracted by these new ideas, if only as a potential route around the problems to which that open-ended rationale had led. Certainly in Europe a heavy emphasis was from the start put on the desirability of *focusing* liability to the party responsible for the condition of the product, thereby cutting across ideas of, say, supplying the victim with a large range of potential defendants from which to choose the deepest pocket, etc. But what precisely did theory have to offer the Europeans?

(a) The role of theory

What does a theory need to be able satisfactorily to do? It is not sufficient for a theory to be able to accommodate the core of a liability – to explain, for example,

9 See S Lloyd-Bostock 'Common Sense Morality and Accident Compensation' [1980] Ins LJ 331.

why a negligent driver must pay damages to a pedestrian he or she runs down. It must also be able to explain where all the boundaries of the rule lie and why they need to be there. This is no mean task given the many dimensions a rule may have. For example, a theory which, it is claimed, supports a civil liability such as that set out in s 402A of the Second Restatement of Torts or the final Directive on product liability must first explain the two-party nature of such a civil claim: it must not only explain why and to what extent the relevant victim should be compensated, and why and to what extent the particular defendant(s) should pay, but why these amounts coincide and why payment is made by defendant to plaintiff. There may be strong moral or economic arguments for the compensation of the plaintiff, or for the financial penalization of the defendant. But these are irrelevant here because they are inadequate to the task of providing a justification for the two-party model of civil liability with which we are faced. With respect to the selection of parties – who can sue, who can be sued – a sophisticated theory should also be clear about the extent to which the inevitable dilution of its goals through the operation of insurance is relevant and/or to be tolerated.

A civil liability is also predicated on a particular invasion of the plaintiff's interests – the 'gist' of the complaint or cause of action. Theory must, therefore, be capable of explaining why certain invasions of interest are actionable and some are not: why, for example, the plaintiff's suffering of cancer may be actionable but a plaintiff's exposure to an increased risk of cancer may not be; or why physical injury to the plaintiff's already owned property is actionable but not pure economic loss. Typically, a civil liability rule is also bounded by causal requirements, for example, that the defendant caused (or, in a more attenuated form of causal connection, 'provided the opportunity' for someone else to cause) the damage of which the plaintiff is complaining and, where this is so, any satisfactory theory of the liability must be able to explain them. The product rules reflected in s 402A and the Directive also have particular boundaries such as the limitation to injuries caused by *products* (apparently excluding those caused by realty and services), the limitation to products which have been put into circulation (excluding, for example, injuries to the production workforce), the limitation to products supplied *in the course of a business* and a limitation to personal injuries and, in the Directive, physical damage to non-commercial property (excluding pure economic losses and physical damage to commercial property). All these many boundaries need to be supported and explained by a satisfactory theory, as does the Directive's ban on any exclusion of its liability (Article 12).

Here lies the principal cause for complaint tort lawyers should have with the current surge in tort theory: it tends to be concerned with just one boundary of liability, namely that which relates to the defendant's behaviour, often described as the 'standard' of liability. This issue is certainly an issue which fascinates philosophers (and most tort theorists these days are more philosophers than tort lawyers).[10] It is also an important one. It was, after all, a desire to raise the standard of liability which provided the rhetorical thrust of calls for product liability reform. But as we will see throughout Part 2, the complex debates on the standard of liability fail to address the issue which is arguably much more important to the lawyer both

10 See, eg, I Englard *The Philosophy of Tort Law* (Aldershot, Dartmouth, 1993); J Coleman *Risks and Wrongs* (Cambridge, Cambridge University Press, 1992). Contrast the work of Tony Honoré which is more alive to the complexity of real tort rules.

historically and in practical terms: the question of a rationale for a rule of tort liability *limited* to products (be it fault based or strict).

Within the standard of liability issue, the two most important parameters are the foreseeability of a risk and the utility of running that risk. These generate four basic options for the standard of a liability, and these are set out in Figure 5.1. Although an accurate definition of a strict liability is liability against which the defendant's reasonable care is no answer, often a more useful talisman of whether a defendant is being exposed to a strict liability is whether he is vulnerable to liability for unforeseeable risks. This is because under a fault-based rule – that is, where reasonable care is a defence – a court could nearly always raise the standard of care in such a way as to support the conclusion that the defendant had failed to take reasonable preventative measures in relation to a foreseeable risk, even if such measures would require the defendant not to engage in the foreseeably risky activity at all. But this tactic is not possible with unforeseeable risks because it cannot be said that a defendant failed to take adequate care with respect to a risk which could not have been foreseen by him. *Only under a strict liability rule can liability for unforeseeable risks be achieved.*

Figure 5.1: Standards of non-dependent liability*
(also discussed in Chapter 6, under heading 4 and Chapter 9, under heading 3)

	otherwise covers all risks	covers only a subset of risks
covers foreseeable and unforeseeable risks	FULL STRICT LIABILITY	LIMITED HINDSIGHT STRICT LIABILITY – eg warranty of merchantability (limited by 'merchantability' concept) – eg hindsight cost-benefit[†] strict liability (limited by 'defect' requirement)
covers foreseeable risks only	FORESIGHT STRICT LIABILITY	FAULT/NEGLIGENCE – eg where standard of care is limited by notions of 'reasonableness' (*Donoghue* v *Stevenson*, *McPherson* v *Buick*, etc) – eg where standard of care is limited by notions of 'custom'

*   Vicarious liability is the principal dependent liability.
†   Either or both assessed with hindsight see Chapter 10, under headings 3 and 5.

According to this criterion it is possible to confirm that the warranty of merchantability and the initial proposals for reform in the UK and Europe (the Pearson Commission, Law Commissions, Strasbourg Convention and 1976 Draft Directive) imposed a strict liability on all defendants since for no defendant was reasonable care a defence, and liability for (at least some) unforeseeable risks was imposed. In contrast, the product regimes in s 402A and the final Directive of 1985 allow a 'development risk defence' by which defendants can escape liability where the risk was not discoverable at the time the product was supplied. In practice this reduces the rule to one in which producers are subject to a liability virtually identical with that in negligence (albeit with significantly increased burdens of proof), while the liability of others assumes more the character of a new 'vicarious liability' (see Chapter 10).

The second parameter relevant to the issue of defendants' behaviour is whether the defendant is to be held liable for all risks or only for some, for example, those where the costs of the risk-taking outweigh its benefits. The implied warranty of merchantability, although a strict liability because it encompasses unforeseeable risks, is restricted in such a way: a supplier of goods is liable only if the condition of the goods renders them unmerchantable. Similarly, all the initial proposals in the UK and the rest of Europe, as well as the final Directive and US product rule, are predicated on the relevant product being 'defective'.

In short, then, an adequate theory of the standard of liability issue must explain its handling of unforeseeable risks, whether and why the utility, etc, of the risk-taking is relevant, and any differential standards of behaviour applied to different defendants. There is inevitably a large gap between the simplistic 'ideal types' of rule suggested by the theories of liability which will be discussed hereafter, and the complex rules which actually exist and with which they need to be compared. No theory of civil liability has yet, for example, been able adequately to explain the two-layered liability involved in the vicarious liability of employers whereby the strict liability of the latter is dependent on the tortious (usually fault-based) liability of the employee. But evaluation of theories said to be relevant to a shift towards stricter product liability is essential in determining whether the existing law is complex because it is incoherently fragmented and in need of fundamental repair in the direction of one of these 'ideal types', or whether it is a regime which is richly structured because it is a rational response to the complex needs of the relevant area of social interaction. The process should, in other words, help identify where multi-dimensional product rules are desirable, and where they produce anomalous results and threaten weakness and instability in the legal regime.

Finally, the theoretical analysis helpfully exposes that truism of law reform: whether intentionally or not, law reform serves the interests of some at the expense of the interests of others. By pinpointing who these groups are and the nature and extent to which a legal change shifts entitlements, we should be able to formulate with greater precision those political trade-offs fuelling and counteracting moves to change legal rules. Sometimes in the market place, for example, we allow business to exploit its informational, organizational and financial superiority over private consumers in order to generate profits, and sometimes we do not. As we shall see, the issues of where and why we draw this line lies at the heart of the product liability debate.

(b)   The economic/non-economic divide

There are two broad types of theory advanced to support the product rules: the instrumentalist arguments of the economist-lawyers concerning how legal rules can be set to produce incentives to behaviour in order to achieve certain specified consequences (here the 'efficient' level of 'deterrence' of product injuries); and arguments based on justice and fairness both between plaintiff and defendant (corrective or commutative justice) and between classes (distributive justice). A convenient way to get an overview of these theories is to separate the economic (Chapters 5 and 6) from the moral arguments (Chapters 7, 8 and 9) and then within each to examine the arguments for the conclusion that internalization of the initial victim's loss to a certain party should occur. There are two aspects of this. Firstly, *what* should be internalized (eg all accident costs, only those of foreseeable accidents, only those where the costs of the product outweigh its benefits), and *to whom* (eg to just one party or to anyone in the chain). Secondly, given that such internalization of costs is desirable, do social arrangements need to be altered to effect this, and if so, how? The complexity of the theoretical debate in the US is due not simply to a common failure in judgments and some academic work to keep separate distinct substantive arguments, for example to distinguish the economic arguments from the moral. It is also due to the ambiguity within the arguments as to the form of internalization needed and the route it should take. This leads both to odd alliances across ideological camps, and to fierce disagreements within ideological camps. Certain advocates of greater consumer protection, for example, find themselves in agreement with certain law and economic analysts that stricter liability is justified. The law and economics camp is itself split three ways between favouring strict liability, negligence or market (contract) solutions. Moralists are split between favouring stricter liability, negligence or the sweeping away of civil liability as a vehicle for compensation of personal injuries. The theoretical debate has also beeen complicated by changes of opinion: since the draft Directive was issued there has been a shift in the writings of both prominent moralists and advocates of an efficiency approach, for example, from support for a robust strict liability regime in tort to the severe containment of this paternalistic device with much greater reliance placed on contractual protection. My aim is not to chronicle the historical development and interplay of these ideas, but to show that a search through the major themes of the theoretical debate suggests that the liability set out in the Directive has no coherent justification, to ask why this is so, and to discover the implications this may have for the future of tort liability.

4   WEALTH MAXIMIZATION ARGUMENTS FOR INTERNALIZATION

(a)   Some preliminaries

The economic approach to law usefully emphasises that any law has economic consequences because it affects the use of resources. It forces us to realize that law reform has costs and benefits which should be appreciated even if, for other reasons, we choose not to follow the cheapest overall solution. Wealth maximization theorists start from the premise that there are no other such reasons and that the only relevant social goal is financial wealth maximization. They then proceed to determine the most efficient use of resources whereby wealth can be maximized. Were this optimal state to exist, accidents, for example, would still occur but their rate would be optimal, ie the cost of one more accident would be just matched by the cost of avoiding it. While this perfect state is unattainable, if wealth maximization were our only goal we would seek changes in our social arrangements which produced a state closer to this optimum.

It is important at the outset to acknowledge that these ideas are ones we *all* intuitively accept in broad outline in much of our lives. We could substantially reduce the road toll by the precaution of lowering the speed limit to 10 mph, but the cost of this move in terms of economic and social dislocation is such that we do not do it. We accept that the cost of these precautions is too great relative to the cost of the accidents we would prevent. On the other hand, there are real difficulties with the efficiency theory. The central *internal* problem is that, even if we accept its assumption that efficiency is the only acceptable social goal, the theory purports to be able to *fine-tune* social arrangements to achieve this goal in areas in which the appropriate costings are simply unavailable. The key *external* criticism is that, even if available, such costings may well be regarded as a morally distasteful and intolerable criterion by which many social arrangements should be judged.

(b)   The basic theory and its terminology

In the decades since the Second Restatement of Torts (1965), 'economic' or 'efficiency' theory has emerged in the US as the dominant academic technique by which to evaluate products law and law reform in general. This centrality of economic theory is understandable given that its application relates to the deterrence of accidents, and the relevant US case law, academic commentaries, EC reform documents and final Directive all espouse deterrence as a central policy goal of the reform.[11] The normative economic theory of the allocation of losses associated with the condition of products evolved from work by Calabresi in the 1960s and later came to be dominated by the Chicago lawyer-economists led by Posner. In terms of the various schools of economic thought these approaches fall into the neoclassical camp which rests on various assumptions – about rationality, the importance of individual preferences and maximizing behaviour; and that groups behave as simple aggregates of individuals which enable simplified models of the world to be constructed and from which normative conclusions may then be derived. The aim is to rank alternative economic arrangements – ie different allocations of scarce resources – in terms of their ability or *efficiency* to enhance or *maximize* a particular goal. This technique of ranking solutions according to their '*allocative efficiency*' can then suggest changes which might be made to current arrangements including legal entitlements (eg entitlements to sue for a particular loss) if maximization of the goal designated at the outset is desired. Thus it may be found that a change to legal liability rules would produce shifts in economic incentives in such a way that in future rational parties affected by those rules would change their behaviour in a way which would maximize that goal.

The criterion of efficiency used by Calabresi and Posner is the *Kaldor-Hicks criterion* which states that if, in a proposed legal change, all the potential gainers of the relevant resource would have been willing under the previous regime in principle to compensate the losers for their losses and still regard themselves as better off than before the change, then the change improves efficiency: it is a 'Kaldor-Hicks efficient move'. The resource should be allocated to those gainers. It is sometimes said

---

11 See, eg, *Escola* v *Coca-Cola Bottling Co of Fresno* 150 P 2d 436 (1944), 440; W Prosser 'Assault Upon the Citadel (Strict Liability) to the Consumer' (1960) 69 Yale LJ 1099, 1122–3; Law Coms para 23; Pearson Com, para 1234.

that under Kaldor-Hicks there is no need for the compensation to be made as this is merely a distributional move between the parties, but there are problems with this proposition which we need not pursue here.

'Maximization' and 'allocative efficiency' have no meaning except in relation to a stated goal. For each different goal a different allocation of resources would be optimal. However, these terms, along with the even more bland 'efficiency', have come to be used as short-hand for one particular goal – *wealth-maximization* – and its associated strategy of legal arrangements. While Calabresi merely worked out sophisticated and elegant strategies available *if* maximization of financial wealth were the sole goal of the relevant area of law, Posner and his followers actively advocated this as the desirable goal of many legal arrangements. There are clearly large ethical assumptions here and we later look at the criticism to which they have given rise (in Chapter 6, under heading 6). The important point to keep in mind at this stage is that where the goal *is* financial wealth, the Kaldor-Hicks calculation is revealed as a question of willingness (and hence ability) to pay for a resource. With respect to the goal of maximization of wealth, the optimal allocation of resources is reached when all relevant resources are in the hands of those who value them the most (in the sense of being willing and able to pay more for them than anyone else).

Applied to the context of the quality of products, the wealth maximization criterion states that the point of optimal efficiency is the allocation of resources (here the quality of products, their volume of production, etc) which minimizes the social costs flowing from the condition of those products – social costs being judged by the willingness of the relevant parties to pay money to avoid them. If we take into account the administrative costs of the social arrangements needed to promote the trade-off between the costs of accidents and the costs of their avoidance, this strategy of achieving the wealth maximization goal can be stated as the minimization of the sum of precaution, accident and administrative costs. Since the strategy is often put in terms of deterring accidents so as to reduce the rate of accidents to the point where the sum of these costs is minimized, it is often described as the theory of '*economic deterrence*' or simply '*deterrence theory*'.

Finally, if all those interested in a resource were free to bargain (at no cost) for them, this efficient allocation of resources would result. Resources would reach the hands of those who valued them the most. The optimal level of accidents would be reached. As we will see, in 1960 Coase showed that in such conditions where there were 'zero transaction costs' this would happen even if the law initially assigned the entitlement to the resource to some other party.[12] The party who was willing to pay more would bargain with ('bribe') that party to get it.

(c)   Pigou, transaction costs and price deterrence

In the real world not all those interested in (in the sense of being willing and able to pay for) a resource, including safety, *do* bargain. One important reason why this may be so is that bargaining costs may be prohibitive. This creates inefficiencies. For example, say two firms produce toothpaste. The producers of toothpaste A employ a method which produces factory effluent which is harmless. The producers of toothpaste B employ a process producing toxic effluent which pollutes surrounding water

12 R Coase 'The Problem of Social Cost' (1960) 3 J Law & Econ 1.

supplies resulting in, say, one death per million tubes of toothpaste produced. If the social cost in lost resources represented by these deaths is not internalized to the price structure of firm B, there are 'externalities'. Pigou noted that these arise inter alia 'where one person ... in the course of rendering some service, for which payment is made, to a second person, incidentally also renders ... disservices to other persons ... of such a sort that compensation (cannot) be enforced on behalf of the injured parties.'[13] Externalities produce inefficiencies.

Pigou, writing in 1932, had noted that before market transactions could produce the efficient allocation of resources, the external social costs of, say, producing toothpaste B must be internalized to that activity so that the prices of competing toothpastes reflected their relative social cost in resources. He recommended the manipulation of liability rules to do this. As the price of toothpaste B rises to a level reflecting the 'true social cost' of the product, some consumers will switch to the cheaper (because socially safer) substitutes such as toothpaste A or, if these do not exist, cease to buy toothpaste B. In this way the activity generating excessive social costs declines to a level closer to the optimal level. This is then reflected in the rate of injury, here in the rate of pollution deaths.

The externalities perspective laid central stress on the price mechanism as a technique for deterring inefficient activities and the inefficient allocation of resources this implies. It had, in other words, a focus on *price deterrence* – its strategy of deterring inefficiency being built on the operation of the price mechanism. An important element of the price deterrence logic, and one vital to the product liability debate, is that only if *all* social costs of an activity are internalized to it will optimal efficiency be achieved. That is, the strategy requires that not only foreseeable and avoidable risks be internalized but also unforeseeable (and hence unpreventable) risks and risks the overall costs of which are outweighed by benefits (where prevention is undesirable).

This was the perspective with which in 1961 Calabresi began his series of papers on economics and law. 'Costs should be borne by the activity which causes them'[14] and the function of prices, he argued, is to reflect the actual costs of competing goods and thus enable buyers to cast an informed vote in making their purchases. But although price deterrence has since then been seen as one of the policy goals behind product liability reform, at least in the US,[15] the Pigovian approach has certain problems. In particular, it tends to assume that it will be clear to which particular activity a particular social cost should be internalized. This is often not the case – a problem we might term that of 'overlapping enterprises'. Often the particular social cost in question would not have been suffered 'but for' a number of activities. After all, but for the neighbours being near toothpaste B factory and drinking the water, they would not have been poisoned by its effluent. Are the effluent deaths appropriately seen as a cost of the factory's activities or as a cost of living nearby? Is it less wasteful of society's resources in general to affect the price of toothpaste B or of houses in the vicinity? And even if we can say it is the former, who in the chain of distribution and supply of toothpaste should have to bear the social costs if both retailer and manufacturer, etc, could reflect it in the price of toothpaste B?

13 A Pigou *The Economics of Welfare*, 4th edn (London, Macmillan, 1932) 183.
14 G Calabresi 'Some Thoughts on Risk Distribution and the Law of Torts' (1961) 70 Yale LJ 499, 533.
15 *Cipollone* v *Liggett Group Inc* 644 F Suppl 283, 288 (1987).

(d)   Calabresi, prevention and cheapest cost avoiders; Posner

In 1960 Coase had exposed this 'what is the cost of what' dilemma; yet at the same time he had noted that it would not matter on which activity the loss initially rested in cases of low transaction costs because here bargaining 'around the rules' would ultimately achieve the efficient allocation of resources anyway. But Calabresi was keen to work out an economic approach for situations where transaction costs were *prohibitive*, such as the pollution cases, so this observation of Coase did not assist him, and he was forced to devise a fresh mechanism by which not only the appropriate activity but also the appropriate party within it was selected to bear the social cost. Here the lawyers' perspective made a significant contribution in pinpointing *within* an activity the appropriate party to bear the cost. For tort lawyers are, thanks to the dominance of the tort of negligence, keenly aware of foreseeable and hence avoidable risks. They are, therefore, more used to thinking of the economic incentives which internalization of costs (eg as exemplified in liability burdens) bring in terms of incentives to take *preventative* action in future rather than in terms of its impact on the price of the activity which is the perspective economists tend to take. It may be that from a price deterrence perspective there is little to distinguish internalizing the social costs of drug injuries to the manufacturer from internalizing them to the retailer: either is in a position to reflect the cost in the price to the public. But the prevention perspective allows us to see why internalizing to the manufacturer of drugs is likely to produce greater improvements in overall efficiency.

To see this, begin with the simplest scenario, where the product activity is clearly the only relevant one and the accident is 'unilateral', that is where the actions of the victim cannot affect the probability or severity of the accident loss. A clear example is the Thalidomide case. Here a prevention perspective selects the party in the best position to detect the risk as the one to make the cost/benefit analysis between accident costs and accident avoidance costs and to act on that analysis, for example by taking cost-justified precautions, so that accidents which are not cost-effective (ie the social costs of which exceed the benefits of not taking precautions) do not occur in the future. It was in this way that Calabresi in his well-known *market deterrence* strategy was able to add to the strategy of using legal rules to internalize the relevant social cost, when there were high transaction costs (see under heading 5, below), guidance as to whom that strategy might designate as defendants. Internalization was not simply to 'the activity' but to the 'cheapest cost avoider'[16] (the 'cca') within the activity, the definition of whom included an amalgam of abilities but gave central importance to the ability to prevent the risk arising in the future.

There are internal problems with the concept of this 'cheapest cost avoider', (Chapter 6, under heading 5(b)) but putting these aside for the moment, Calabresi's theory does explain why in simple unilateral product accident cases, the best party to bear the loss may well be the one in the production and distribution chain due to whose behaviour, or during whose period of control, the relevant dangerous condition was created in the product. Thus, if cough syrup sold by the mass retailer Sainsbury's is discovered to have mercury in it, the relevant party from the prevention perspective is probably not the injured consumer, nor the deep-pocketed Sainsbury's, but the independent producer of the cough syrup who could most cheaply

---

16 G Calabresi and J Hirschoff 'Towards a Test for Strict Liability in Torts' (1972) 81 Yale LJ 1054, 1060.

check the quality of the product. The more economic pressure is focused on this party, the more likely it will translate efficiently into the correct degree of altered behaviour. The more it is deflected on to others, the more diffuse become the incentives, and although private transactions might occur to relocate the incentive to the appropriate party, the cost of these transactions will result in dilution of the incentive. This, as we will see, leads on to conclusions about the role of insurance and about the appropriate attitude to joint injurers. Here the important point is simply that the prevention perspective suggested not only coherent reasons for seeking to locate certain product losses on producers, but also – unlike the subordinate considerations discussed earlier (under heading 2, above) – why others ought *not* to have costs internalized to them even if they were deep pockets etc. It went a good way to providing that essential explanation of why, in what direction, and to what extent, arrangements should be reformed to improve the efficient allocation of resources (assuming a wealth maximization goal).

But if the strength of the Calabresian theory was that it explained how channelling social costs to particular parties within an activity could improve efficiency, one of its most striking weaknesses was its difficulty in predicting who this 'cheapest cost avoider' might be in other than simple unilateral situations where the only causally relevant fact was the condition of a product. The theory might be simple: in cases of high transaction costs a legal entitlement must be created giving victims the right to sue the cheapest cost avoider for damages (under heading 5, below). But how was it possible to decide which party in a complex interaction was the cheapest cost avoider? While in a Thalidomide or a 'mercury in cough syrup' case the theory may clearly point to the manufacture and distribution of the product as the relevant activity and within that activity to the manufacturer as being a cheaper cost avoider than a retailer (and hence being the preferable target for the imposition of liability), it is still not easy to see which is the relevant activity and who is the cheapest cost avoider in cases of overlapping activities, such as the polluting toothpaste factory and neighbours: is it cheaper in terms of resources to deter the pollution, or to pollute and move the population? Even if we accept it is cheaper to require childproof lids on toxic pharmaceuticals than to oblige individual supervision of children, we intuitively know that there will be some product contexts where childproof devices are not the cheapest solution, and that it will be cheaper to rely on the activities of intermediaries. The question is, when? Even more problematic for efficiency theory is how to justify a *limited* liability rule addressed only to certain defendants – as s 402A and the Directive are – because there may be no good reason to limit one's search for the cca to this limited class (see Chapter 6, under heading 5(f)).

The Posnerian school of economics and law appears at first to sidestep this dilemma of how to decide where, in cases of high transaction costs, the legal entitlement should be placed to optimize efficiency. Posner argued that in cases of high transaction costs the law should simply mimic the bargains those involved would have reached but for transaction costs. Thus if a victim would, but for those costs, have been willing and able to bribe another to take precautions against the relevant risk which threatened and eventually injured the victim, then the law should assign to the victim an entitlement to sue that party. In this way incentives are generated for cost-justified, but only cost-justified, precautions. Certainly viewed from the perspective of precaution incentives alone, this outcome is optimal and it is an outcome which Posner argues is achieved by a system of negligence. In fact, Posner had not solved the 'what is a cost of what' problem of overlapping enterprises – he had simply asserted, in effect, that one could rely on the plaintiff's own choice of defendants within the wide range allowed by negligence and traditional devices such as duty, remoteness, etc, to ensure that those defendants (which he claims are) relevant to an optimal efficiency strategy, were selected. We see later (Chapter 6, under heading 5(f)) that, in the context of the product liability debate, this is not a convincing argument.

Nevertheless, Posner's normative prescription that liability should be based on negligence neatly dovetailed with his descriptive thesis that wealth maximization was already embedded in civil liability, most notably in its handling of accidents on the basis of fault, which he discerned as a covert cost-benefit calculation. The neatness of this dual theory, as well as Posner's provocative ethical assertions, attracted wide attention. The more Calabresi perceived a need for and got bogged down in the fine-tuning of his theory of the cheapest cost avoider to deal with complex real world situations, the more the simplistic Posnerian approach became the focal economic theory. The eclipse of the Calabresian theory in favour of Posner is very important for tort theory in general and product liability theories in particular. This is because the cheapest cost avoider approach encompasses both prevention and price-deterrence strategies, and in so doing supports a liability rule extending to, and internalizing to defendants, losses associated with unforeseeable risks. Since only strict liabilities can cover such risks – a fault-based rule cannot cover them since it is impossible to be careless with regard to an unforeseeable risk – the Calabresian approach points to strict liabilities being the more efficient device for internalization. In contrast, Posner argues for the efficiency of negligence. Since the key debate in the product field has been on the issue of whether liability should be strict or fault-based, the rise of the pro-negligence school of economic analysis of law has had profound implications historically, as we shall see. The Posnerian approach seriously neglects price deterrence, however; so it is the Calabresian theory which is used in the following discussion to illustrate the economic rationale of stricter product liability rules.

5 THE COASE THEOREM AND THE JUSTIFICATION FOR INTERVENTION VIA CHANGES IN LEGAL ENTITLEMENTS/LIABILITY

Before an economic theorist can propose changes in legal rules or can rationalize past legal changes such as s 402A and the Directive as ways of creating incentives towards a more efficient allocation of resources, he or she must take account of the Coase theorem. This is because it states that where transaction costs are zero – ie where all relevant parties have or can costlessly acquire perfect information, and can costlessly bargain and enforce that bargain with all others – legal intervention will not be necessary (or effective) in improving the efficient allocation of resources. If bargaining about rights to resources is costless, they will be transferred to those who value them the most, and the efficient allocation of resources will be achieved. In the context of accidents this means that the efficient level of accident losses will be produced *anyway* because all relevant costs will be internalized to the appropriate activity by market forces: costs associated with foreseeable risks by the willingness-to-bribe of potential victims; and costs of unforeseeable risks via price deterrence. This can be expressed in Calabresi's terms of 'cheapest cost avoider'. The Theorem states that whenever accident costs exceed the cheapest cost avoider's prevention costs, *all* those who would initially bear the costs of the activity will bribe the cheapest cost avoider to prevent the accident (up to a value of their individual private loss). Let us make the major and important assumption (for argument's sake) that the economic and physical victims of an activity are not, at the outset, entitled under any legal rule to compensation, and that therefore they initially bear the costs of the activity. The effect of the initial victims' willingness-to-bribe is to exert an economic pressure equivalent to the aggregate of their private losses on the cca and this pressure operates whether or not the latter accepts the bribe. If he does, the precautions are taken and/or the price adjustments made. If he resists, the same pressure occurs but now in the form of lost bribes. Let us look more carefully at this in the product context. Assume the cca is the producer of a product with a foreseeable preventable defect. According to the Coase theorem, those endangered by it will, in the absence of transaction costs, pay the cca to prevent the defect. For those in a supply relationship with the producer this bribe may be reflected in signalling willingness to pay more for a defectless product. If the cca rejects the bribe and continues to market the defective product, he is in effect incurring a cost to the extent of the foregone bribe. This exerts pressure on him to rethink his position.

In a setting of zero transaction costs, market forces will internalize the net private costs of the risk-taking activity to the cca, regardless of the initial distribution of legal rights. Changes to liability rules would not be needed to achieve internalization and optimal efficiency. Law reform would change the distribution of rights (and therefore wealth), but not whether the efficient point was reached. Indeed it would be preferable to avoid the additional expense of (the administration of) a liability rule and to allow losses to lie where they fall. In such circumstances and with wealth maximization as the only goal (ie with no other goal of, say, the redistribution of wealth), the desirable efficient approach would be one which leaves losses where they lie. But transaction costs are never nil. In particular, it typically costs money to acquire all relevant information, and then to negotiate and enforce a bargain. Even so, if transaction costs are low, the more efficient solution might still be to let losses lie where they fall. Sometimes, a 1:1 deal between commercial parties conforms to this description. If, however, transaction costs are high enough it may become cheaper to use a liability rule to impose the allocation of costs which the parties would have reached in the absence of transaction costs. Of course, where this arrangement would have left the loss on the initial victim – because he or she was the cheapest cost avoider – no liability rule is needed (for efficiency reasons) even when transaction costs are prohibitively high. This is mirrored in the common sense approach the law takes to cases where, say, an adult recklessly drinks bleach for fun. Such a person is denied a civil remedy and cannot shift the injury costs to someone else. This is consistent with our intuitive appreciation that the victim is the person most cheaply able to avoid that loss. For other parties such as the manufacturer or retailer of the bleach, the cost of preventing the risk of this misuse would be prohibitive. Fortuitously there is no clash here between the strategy required by wealth maximization theory and that generated by moral theories of corrective justice based on causation of past events (see Chapters 7, 8 and 9): both require a denial of a remedy. The way a legal system may deliver this common sense result varies, ranging from the denial of a causal connection between the manufacturer's activities and the loss, to arguing that the victim had willingly accepted the risk. However it is packaged, the result is clearly right.

But if we return to our assumption of a *unilateral* situation where the victim is clearly not the cca and also assume the high transaction costs typical of bystander cases like Thalidomide, the wealth maximization theory recommends that law intervene and a rule be imposed which focuses the relevant loss on the cheapest cost avoider of it.[17] It is important to note two points here. First, if we start from a world where losses lie where they fall, such a rule will have an impact on (ie reflect a shift in) the distribution of legal rights, ie entitlements, and this will consequently shift wealth (see Chapter 6, heading 6(iv)). Secondly, there are various techniques by which focusing can be done by means of a liability rule. The choice depends, as we will see, on the nature of the perceived transaction costs. For example, in cases where the victim and cca are contractually linked (eg via a sales contract), the law might choose to replace the caveat emptor position of letting losses lie where they fall with a warranty obligation (a term 'implied by law') on the cca (let us assume the seller) and either ban altogether attempts to disclaim that obligation or limit their effectiveness; or it might forbid the limitation of any parallel voluntary obligation apparently expressly warranted by the cca, or subject such attempts to proof by the cca that in the particular context the transaction costs were sufficiently low to allow real bargaining. If it were not known in advance whether the parties would be contractually linked, the tactic could be either extension of the above warranty regime to non-privy victims (the aclassical warranty device) with possible control of disclaimers as described; or imposition of a comparable tort obligation on the cca, again with the necessary level of control of disclaimers. These devices can achieve roughly the same thing – hence the ease of the historical transition from one to another in the *Henningsen* to *Greenman* development.

In terms of wealth maximization theory, therefore, a great deal depends in unilateral cases on the question of whether the transaction costs between the victim and the cca are more than the administration costs of the potential corrective legal device. Since we have no clear empirical evidence on this, analysts are forced to guess. Inevitably these guesses will be influenced by the guesser's general beliefs and confidence in how smoothly (cheaply) markets operate and how well the legal system works. Such beliefs in turn can reflect much wider ideological and cultural attitudes. Relative to Europe, there is a greater confidence in market solutions in the US which helps explain the deep divisions that have arisen between adherents of wealth maximization goals: some regard product liability as justified; but others, now perhaps the majority, allege bargaining is a cheaper route to internalization than the baroque and costly system of rules which the products field produced from the early 1970s. Some even argue for a return to caveat emptor. We now need to look a little more deeply at this conflict and the qualifications it produced in the recommendations of the lawyer-economists for product liability rules.

---

17 And/or on someone in a position to bargain sufficiently cheaply with the cca. For example, even if the manufacturer is the cca, it may not be much less efficient to impose liability on the retailer if the latter's ability to bargain with the manufacturer is good. Reliance on this domino effect back up existing chains of bargains may even be the most efficient strategy once other costs are taken into account.

6   WHY LEGAL INTERVENTION MIGHT BE CALLED FOR IN THE PRODUCTS CONTEXT: INFORMATIONAL BARRIERS

In the products field the market imperfection which dominates the debate among economists is that of informational asymmetry. Before a potential victim of a risk can bribe the cca to prevent the risk occurring, he must know of the relevant risk, be able to quantify its likelihood, and assess its likely cost were he to fall victim to it. As we have seen (Chapter 2, under heading 2), even in non-mass markets a form of informational imperfection can be a problem: as transactions in goods in the nineteenth century became more commonly conducted at a distance, commercial buyers became less able to inform themselves of quality matters relating to the goods they were buying. Their concern was simply the threat of economic loss this presented to them. By defeating the rival approach of caveat emptor, the new general warranty of merchantability forced the matter to the attention of both parties. Thereafter, if the seller wanted to escape the risk that his goods were unmerchantable, he either had to undertake preventative action or signal his unwillingness to bear the risk by disclaiming and by acceptance of the consequently lower price offered by the buyer. The more reliable the quality of a seller's goods, the less reduction in price he needed to accept in order to disclaim.

But in *mass-markets* buyers can still face information problems even if the transaction is face to face. First, now that the injury-causing potential of goods has become more appreciated, the relevant risk is no longer seen as just a risk of economic loss, but includes all the costs which the condition of the good might inflict on the buyer, user or bystander. In modern mass-markets where complex and diverse goods abound, the problem of imperfect information about this range of risks among acquirers (even commercial acquirers), users and bystanders is commonplace. This is an asymmetrical phenomenon because goods manufacturers typically acquire much greater knowledge of the quality and risks of their products through their design, research and development, testing and inspection, and by monitoring their performance after sale. Informational superiority is one reason why, at least in unilateral products cases, the manufacturer would appear to be the cca. On the other hand, even though a user might not know exactly how a motor vehicle engine works or in what way it presents a risk (and hence how to go about prevention), he might in theory still be in a position to appreciate the level of risk he faces, and hence be motivated to bribe the manufacturer to take preventative action. So the fact that the manufacturer is the cca does not necessarily imply that internalisation ought to be ensured via liability rules. This depends on the height of the transaction costs barrier to such bribe transactions, and economic analysts disagree on this key question even in consumer contexts.

Posner and Calabresi are generally associated with a pro-liability approach because of their sensitivity to the transactional difficulties of potential victims, at least consumer victims; while analysts such as Danzon argue that the ability of the less informed victims to bargain for safety with the cca (or cheaply with an intermediary) is sufficiently good to make the bargaining route to internalisation often cheaper than that of a loss-shifting liability rule.[18] The latter's argument that repeat

---

18 Compare W Landes and R Posner *The Economic Structure of Tort Law* (Cambridge, Harvard University Press, 1987) 180–1 with P Danzon 'Comments on Landes and Posner: A Positive Economic Analysis of Product Liability' (1985) 14 J Legal Studies 569. For more recent pro-market analysis see A Schwartz 'The Case Against Strict Liability' (1992) 60 Fordham LR 819.

purchasing allows consumers to learn, only works for relatively low price items. For high price goods, such as cars, major electrical goods, the frequency of repeat purchases is low relative to the changes in product models. From the Posnerian/Calabresian perspective, even those potential victims of mass produced goods who are in a bargaining relationship (privity) with, or in a bargaining chain leading to, the cca, can typically face prohibitive informational barriers to bargaining about the risk. Intuitively this seems undeniable: the circumstances of many such purchases (even by commercial users, say, of electrical office heaters) tend to be such that the buyer cannot, or cannot without prohibitive cost, acquire sufficient information to inform himself of relevant risks presented by the product about which he should bargain with the cca if the efficient solution is to be attained.

The fact that car purchase is a major transaction for most consumers, yet 'lemons' are still bought, attests to this. The fact that virtually all contracts made are on standard terms about which no bargaining occurs is not the problem (see below). An efficient solution could still be reached if, for example, the buyer has a sufficient choice of contractual offers from which to choose, including an offer which satisfied his or her requirements. The buyer *does*, however, have to be able to grasp what exactly *is* on offer from the various sources. Here is the first problem, for in mass-markets our intuition and experience suggests that it is typically not easy or even worth the buyer's while to read whatever information accompanies the offer, especially when it relates to remote risks attaching to the myriad of low priced goods encountered every year.

Price signals

What about the argument that where the cca is in the chain of manufacture and supply it can in theory use *price differentials* between goods to *signal* information about differing levels of safety and so enable buyers to distinguish between substitutes on this basis? Even in theory this argument is only convincing if inter alia all other variables relating to price (such as the cost of design, production and transport) were identical between the substitutes. But substitutable goods vary widely in these respects. Differentials in price attributable to safety and durability can be swamped by differentials due to other factors. For example, a stylish Volvo car costs more than a Mini Metro, even though the former has more safety features. More importantly, even if faced with two otherwise identical items, say toasters, a consumer may have good reason in real markets to deduce that one reason a cheap toaster is cheap is because it is *less* safe. In other words, in real markets consumers often and rationally read into price differentials the opposite message from that which economic theory suggests.

These points are illustrated in Figure 5.2.[19] Following the Coase theorem, *in perfect conditions* the safer product will be cheaper regardless of liability rules. In a world where losses are left to lie where they fall (Fig 5.2a), the cca who accepts the bribes to take precautions will be able not only to pay for the precautions out of the

19 Figure 5.2 represents mean values for product liability injury 'costs' and hence 'bribes'. In fact each buyer's potential losses would be different (eg different level of potential loss of wages), so whether a buyer would choose to bribe the cca to take precautions would vary. The result is that the market produces goods of a range of quality, ie a range of precautions taken. Note A and C reflect the degree of price deterrence in perfect conditions.

Figure 5.2: Pricing signals

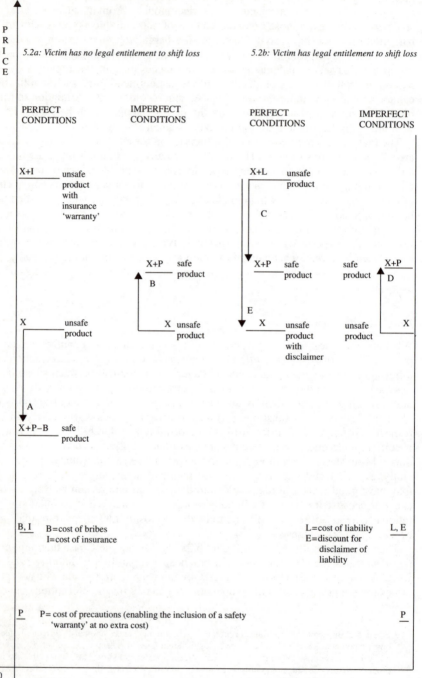

bribe, but also to lower his price marginally below that of unbribed competitors (since by definition bribes only occur if they are greater than the cost of precautions by the cca). This is shown as A in Figure 5.2a. The cca can then reinforce this signal by including a safety 'warranty' at no extra cost. *In the real world*, however, the relative price position of safe and less safe products can be reversed, again regardless of liability rules: in many *real* regimes where the losses are left to lie where they fall, potential victims cannot (because, for example, they do not see the need to) bargain with the cca, and so the producer who takes precautions to make his product safer will not be able to subsidise his price with bribes. This is shown as B. The same phenomenon occurs in a regime where the victim has a legal entitlement to shift the loss to the cca (see Figure 5.2b). In perfect conditions the safe product is cheaper than the unsafe one which bears liability costs (an effect shown as C), while in real conditions where, for example, the legal process does not efficiently internalise all the costs of the unsafe product to it, the price of the unsafe product can fall below that of the safer substitute (see D). Indeed, it is a sign of how externalised are the costs of defective goods today that we tend to expect to have to pay higher prices for safer goods; we do not expect safety precautions to more than pay for themselves in the way economic theory describes will happen in perfect systems.

One reason why economic theory predicts results which do not occur is because it makes the unreal assumption that the buyer knows which legal regime of entitlements (Figure 5.2a or 5.2b) is operating. But how many buyers know whether it is a caveat emptor or a warranty regime which is in place? How many bystanders know if the loss must lie where it falls or can be shifted by tort liability? In a regime, for example, where the law implies a warranty (that is it gives the victim a legal entitlement to shift the loss) a consumer may not know this and as a result may be misled into paying more for an express 'warranty' which is worthless because it duplicates the protection provided by the legally implied warranty. More dangerously, she may not appreciate that a 'warranty' she gratefully accepts is in fact a *partial disclaimer* of the warranty implied by law because it is narrower and 'replaces other warranties'. Empirical evidence also fails to support the signalling theory which would seem to predict variation in, say, the terms relating to quality offered by suppliers. In fact, little variation appears in real consumer markets.

The pricing signal is additionally, probably fatally, confused by the ambiguity of the notion of warranty. The practice of offering extra 'warranties' *for a price* can be read as in fact signalling not *safer* goods but a form of self-insurance against risks posed by the unsafe product (see Chapter 8, under headings 4–5). How is the buyer to know whether the 'warranty' attached to a product signals its superior safety over the competition (the safety 'warranty' which might accompany the safe product) or by contrast signals a level of safety equivalent to the unsafe competition but also the offer of insurance cover against loss resulting from the product (the 'insurance warranty' in Figure 5.2a)? What is more, most products cannot be made 100% free from a relevant defect, so the price of even a relatively very safe good can be treated as having a certain element of insurance. In other words, the warranty accompanying such a good can be read as carrying *both* a promise of safety *and* a promise that in case loss is caused by the product the victim will be compensated. Of course, the safer the good, the lower the insurance element in the 'warranty' can be. But what is clear is that the idea that price signals relative risks of different products to the consumer, ignorant of the risks, is hopelessly compromised if a buyer first needs to know the relative likelihood of the risks eventuating in order to know the degree to which the 'warranty' entails a promise of safety and the degree to which it offers insurance!

A parallel problem exists in regimes where the victim has a legal entitlement to shift the loss to the cca (see Figure 5.2b). In theory here the only role of a 'warranty' would be to signal that the product was safe. A 'warranty' signalling insurance would be at best a nonsense and at worst misleading, because buyers do not need insurance if they have the legal entitlement. In the real world a buyer might not know of her entitlement and so she may believe that the 'warranty' indicated that the product came with a level of safety or insurance to which she would not otherwise be entitled, and so that it was a warranty which was worth paying extra for. This confusion is compounded by the possibility (still allowed in some jurisdictions) that the pricing party uses a term to disclaim the initial obligation – a move which should result in a price discount (see E in Figure 5.2b) – but does so in a way which is not only unclear to the buyer but suggests that the pricer is offering the buyer an *additional* entitlement for which the consumer might again think it worth paying more! Examples here include a 'guarantee' which is in fact only co-extensive with the entitlement which the buyer already has in law or which is narrower.[20] Of course, this indecipherable amalgam of signals in prices would not matter if we could assume buyers were indifferent to whether the risk eventuated or not (ie indifferent between safety and insurance), but this is highly unlikely especially in personal injuries contexts.

There are good reasons, therefore, in mass-markets for being sceptical about the capacity of the pricing device to signal sufficient information to buyers to enable the efficient solution to result without legal intervention. Nor did we need, in getting to this conclusion, to resort to emotive charges of manipulative and oppressive pricing and terms. In high volume markets it may well not be economical to bargain individually with customers; the efficient bargaining channel may well be a standard form contract (including a standard price) that the buyer is forced to take or leave. The natural dynamics of a mass-market alone, even without oppressive conduct by sellers, provide justification for not relying on the aggregation of individual bribes by potential victims to get the cca to undertake precautions and so on. It is the natural dynamics of the mass-market which necessitate the use of liability rules to effect the necessary internalization: the initial victim being given in advance the entitlement to be compensated by the cca It is important to concede that in regimes where the cca is, in theory, legally obligated in this way (Figure 5.2b) the legal system's failure *in practice* to internalize costs appropriately to unsafe products (because, for example, of difficulty of access to justice for the poor) may be just as possible an explanation for pricing distortion as oppressive market practices.

Quite apart from the potential inverting effect on prices of the dynamics of the mass-market and the externalities involved in relying on internalisation via a liability rule (compare C and D in Figure 5.2), there are other problems with the theory of price signals. Let us assume a car market in which prices do reflect factors like safety in the way theory predicts: safer cars are cheaper. But, as we saw, price reflects a number of factors. The signal theory requires that the proportion of the price reflecting these different factors be separately identified. That means that the price of an unsafe car must be broken down so that the buyer can see what

---

20 For proposals to help consumers distinguish a good guarantee from a worthless one, see National Consumer Council *The Consumer Guarantee* (London, NCC, 1989).

proportion of the price is referable to the safety of the car and what proportion to other factors such as design and transport costs. But in the real world this process is rarely administratively economical for the pricer, especially in relation to low price goods; hence the rarity of such price analysis. Even if a price were to be internally itemized, there are still problems in the conveyance of accurate information by this technique.[21] Suppose that in a caveat emptor regime, the cca sells direct to potential victims and offers to the latter a warranty allegedly indicating separately the level of risk in the product. The pricer will have an incentive to divide the price misleadingly: to underprice the warranty in order to signal that the product is of higher quality than it is. More importantly, there will be problems in complex products with many safety and quality dimensions (in the case of cars, for example, front, side and rear crash worthiness, fuel tank security, steering wheel and dashboard design, durability). Even granted that the separate pricing of a safety warranty informs the potential victim of the total risks of the product, how can this then enable that party to exert his bargaining power when he may have quite different attitudes to different risks; for example, indifferent to steering wheel risks, but willing to pay for the warranty *if* it mostly reflects a high level of crashworthiness?

The next problem is that even if potential victims of the relevant risk *could* be given the necessary information about it, there is evidence that in certain cases the human ability to perceive and assess risk (especially low probability risk) accurately is poor. There is considerable psychological evidence, for example, that perception of the risk of personal injury is erratic, at times resulting in gross overestimates, at others gross underestimates. This alone goes a long way to explaining and justifying the interventions of the law in the area of liability risks for personal injuries. Similarly, even economists now appreciate the phenomenon of 'bounded rationality', that is, the cognitive limits of individuals to deal comprehensively with complex decisions they have to make, given constraints on time, attention and cognitive capacity. Clearly, this last human failing afflicts both potential injurer and potential victims in the product context. But its distorting effect is likely to be greatest if the decision about the risks lies on a potential victim, for whom it is simply a peripheral issue among many in life (how many finely printed grocery labels is it realistic to expect a consumer to analyse?) rather than on the injurer whose raison d'etre is the making of commercial profit from this very sort of risk-taking. It is realistic to expect considerably more rational risk-evaluation from commercial enterprises whose profitability hinges on their ability accurately to pay systematic attention to the costs of their risk-taking activities, than from individual victims.[22] In addition, to bargain rationally about even a known and accurately perceived product risk – to be able to judge, for example, the significance of the price and 'warranty' signals – the parties must not only be able rationally to evaluate that risk, but also to be aware of and rationally to analyse the applicable legal regime (see above) in which it operates. Even if potential victims have and know of their entitlement, they may undervalue it because of their aversion to the prospect of legal action. This analysis suggests that, as between producers and consumers, the

---

21 M Geistfeld 'Imperfect Information, the Pricing Mechanism and Product Liability' (1988) 88 Col LR 1057. Compare the unreal assumptions of perfect knowledge by G Priest 'A Theory of the Consumer Product Warranty' (1987) 90 Yale LJ 1297, 1307.

22 H Latin 'Problem-Solving Behaviour and Theories of Tort Liability' (1985) 73 Calif LR 677, 695. See also on general point M Spence 'Consumer Misperception, Product Failure and Product Liability' (1978) 44 Rev Econ Studs 561.

former would be the cheaper cost avoiders; but also that in relation to most mass produced products it is unrealistic to expect that we can rely on mere price signals to enable individual consumers rationally to bargain in respect of the myriad product risks they encounter.

7   NON-INFORMATIONAL TRANSACTION COSTS IN MASS PRODUCT MARKETS; EXCLUSION CLAUSES; TYPES OF LOSS

Even though economic analysts of product rules tend to focus on informational asymmetries, this is not the only relevant distortion in modern product markets, as judges and others have emphasized for decades (see Chapter 3, under heading 2). There are also the problems produced by market concentration (be it monopoly or cartelisation). If we assume that in a unilateral context some potential victims of a product condition *do* acquire sufficient information about the risks and accurately evaluate their weight, the dynamic of mass-markets may still prevent this group organising sufficiently cheaply and exerting sufficient economic pressure to compel, for example, the modification of standard terms. This may not be a problem: stand-ard term contracts which account for virtually all contracts now made, may well be administratively the cheapest form of relationship for both parties and hence *not necessarily* abusive. For similar reasons it may be that all relevant competitors have identical (not necessarily abusive) terms so that even the aware potential victim can exert little pressure on the potential injurer short of doing without the type of good altogether. But the prohibitive cost of tailoring individual bargains in mass-markets per se provides no economic reason for the law's intervention. For if the contents of the standard form are that which informed potential victims would bargain for, the result is efficient. Care has to be taken, in other words, in drawing conclusions from the pattern of terms found in real markets: uniform terms do not *necessarily* imply abusive conduct, contrary to the assertions of some critics.[23] It is only once the *content* of the standard form departs significantly from the bargain that informed poten-tial victims would have made that the argument for intervention becomes greater, as does the moral force of allegations of abusive conduct. An example of this – con-ceded to be quintessentially exploitative by commentators otherwise critical of product rules favouring consumers – are attempts completely to disclaim the warranty of merchantability for new goods, since it is highly likely that informed buyers would not accept such a term.

In monopolized, cartelized or otherwise poorly competitive markets, the buyer who is aware that the standard terms are not what he or she wants may have nowhere else to go. The less able potential victims are to dissent from the standard offer by choosing an alternative offer, the stronger the position of the standard offerer who thereby has an economic incentive to shift its terms even more in its favour in order to exploit this market advantage. We have already come across one manifestation of this: 'guarantees' which mislead consumers into thinking they offer more than the consumer is otherwise entitled to when in fact they offer no more, and

---

23 Although nor does the fact that uniformity occurs across suppliers of different market power support the assertion that abusive conduct is therefore not occurring. Contrast Priest 'A Theory of the Con-sumer Product Warranty', op cit 1320.

in some cases less, than that entitlement.[24] It is important to appreciate that this phenomenon can operate against commercial as well as private buyers. In some contexts, then – such as the explicitly cartelized background to the *Henningsen* case[25] – legal intervention to ensure internalisation of costs can be economically justified solely on the basis of non-informational barriers to bargaining.

Much more commonly, however, a buyer's informational weakness makes cartelization unnecessary. Informational asymmetries are a neutral problem: a supplier can also face prohibitively high barriers to conveying adequate information to potential buyers in order to make his offer look different from and superior to another.[26] The natural fall-back position of such suppliers in such circumstances is not to compete on terms such as warranty (if operating in a 'let losses lie where they fall' regime such as caveat emptor) or the narrowness of disclaimers (in an imposed warranty regime) but to offer terms in relation to quality which are the most favourable to the supplier. Competitors hence fall into line with each other on virtually all terms relating to quality and rely on competition via other variables such as price. But since even price is an inadequate signal of information (see above), legal intervention to assist internalisation can be justified across virtually all mass markets even if there is no evidence of market concentration.

Exclusion clauses/disclaimers

Finally, this discussion of the nature of the transaction costs which may justify legal intervention also gives us an indication of what form and *degree* of legal intervention might be appropriate. In particular it tells us something about the crucial role of exclusion clauses and the way they re-distribute risk and loss relative to the initial distribution of entitlements. If, for example, there are high transaction costs in the form of informational asymmetry between victims and the defendant class who are usually the cca of a particular form of loss suffered by the victim, the appropriate internalisation rule requires *only* that the initial entitlement to compensation be placed on the victim. If, apart from his ignorance about the relevant risk, he can still bargain individually, then if a specific cca attempts to shift the loss back via an exclusion clause the victim will have had the issue of quality brought to mind and can in theory demand a lower price or shift to another competitor of the defendant. Thus in efficiency terms the implication of a *rebuttable* warranty of merchantability in commercial contracts for the supply of goods in the nineteenth century was the appropriate legal response to the identification of the information problems of commercial buyers who were thought otherwise to be able to bargain adequately.

If, however, the potential victim is not only in an informationally vulnerable position but *also* would find it difficult or impossible to resist a market-wide standard term disclaimer of the relevant risk, the appropriate internalisation under economic theory would be not only to place the initial entitlement on the potential victim but also to freeze it there by striking down disclaimers which seek to shift it without the compensation which economic theory requires to be given to generate deterrent

---

24 Unless market apologists (such as Priest, op cit) can show that the inclusion of terms such as the latter – 'limitation of warranty' clauses – result in price discounts, their unproven assumption of a sensitive and competitive price mechanism is as dubious as their opponents' intuitive belief about the exploitative tendencies of enterprises.

25 *Henningsen v Bloomfield Motors Inc* 161 A 2d 69 (NJ, 1960), 86.

26 W Landes and R Posner *The Economic Sturcture of Tort Law*, op cit 281–2.

incentives on the cheapest cost avoider. *Rendering exclusion clauses void can be as necessary a part of the efficiency strategy as the initial liability rule.*[27]

Economic theory is therefore consistent with a legal attitude to disclaimers which separates them according, inter alia, to the type of market. If we make the general assumption that commercial supply of goods to private parties take place in contexts where buyers are not in a position to bargain around an exclusion clause even if they were able fully to appreciate the risk information it relates to, not only should the law grant the initial entitlement to the victim in relation to types of loss for which others are typically the cca (as when it implies a warranty of merchantability) but any exclusion clause in relation to such types of loss should be rendered void. This is what now happens in the UK to purported exclusions of the warranty of merchantability against consumer buyers. Some sales to commercial buyers are like sales to consumers (for example, a small plumbing firm buying tools/van/office heater/office typewriter), while in others the buyer is able genuinely to bargain about disclaimers (to get a satisfying price for trading his entitlement) so case by case evaluation of this class of disclaimers (eg by subjecting them, as happens under the Unfair Contract Terms Act 1977, to a requirement of reasonableness in the light of the underlying market) might be necessary for an efficiency-oriented strategy.

It is important not to get this issue about bargaining potential mixed up with the issue of uncertainty about who is the cheapest cost avoider. Bargaining potential is a function of market structure and is appropriately handled by the attitude to exclusion clauses. Where bargaining *is* possible, the law should not intervene to disrupt exclusion clauses because they provide, at least in theory, a technique for re-allocating the loss to the cheapest cost avoider despite the law's initial allocation of entitlement. In particular, courts and legislatures, in regulating exclusion clauses, should not allow the plaintiff to circumvent a *real* agreement or understanding as to the allocation of risk.[28] If the Directive covers any such cases the provision therein which renders void purported exclusions of its liability would be unsupported by efficiency theory.

The attitude to exclusion clauses is an all or nothing issue: if the market conditions are such that the relevant parties *could not* bargain, then that would apply to *all* relevant types of loss. Yet the defendant may only be the cca for some of the relevant types of loss (eg for personal injuries but not pure loss of profits), so there needs to be a way of subjecting him to liability for these while allowing him to be free of liability for the other types. This might seem to create a dilemma for the efficiency strategist. While barriers to bargaining support control of exclusion clauses, they do not support a control which distinguishes between exclusion clauses according to the type of loss to which they relate. The inability to bargain, which is the justification of the control of exclusion clauses, does not vary according to the type of loss.[29] Nonetheless, the necessary fine-tuning *can* occur by formulating the *initial liability* to exclude from its reach those cases where it is sufficiently clear that the defendant

27 Hence the reason the law imposes immutable/irrebuttable rules on parties to a contract need not be parentalism. Contrast I Ayres and R Gertner 'Filling Gaps in Incomplete Contracts: An Economic Theory of Default Rules' (1989) 99 Yale LJ 87, 88.

28 Consistency in the attitude to exclusion clauses is necessary to prevent the use of tort to evade contract. Comparable care is needed in the recognition of the initial entitlement, be it in the form of the protection of a tort obligation or its analogue in the privity context, namely a term implied by law: J Stapleton 'Duty of Care and Economic Loss: A Wider Agenda' (1991) 107 LQR 249.

29 Even if one makes the provocative assumption that liability is merely a device for self-insurance (for criticism of which see Chapter 8, under heading 4), the analysis here still applies.

is not the cca (eg pure loss of profits claims) and by operation on a case-by-case basis of doctrinal values such as causation, product misuse and defences based on victim behaviour to take account of less certain cases.

Types of loss

This important last point deserves amplification: an efficient strategy towards the goal of wealth maximization requires the internalization to the defendant of those costs, but only those costs, in relation to which he is the cheapest cost avoider, and legal intervention is required only where transaction costs with respect to those losses are high. It may be that while transaction costs are prohibitively high for all losses experienced by the victim, only for some of them is someone else the cheapest cost avoider. If the issue was clear, the efficiency strategy would limit legal intervention to the internalization of losses of this latter type; in other words, the product liability rule would from the outset only relate to such losses. But if, as is the case in the real world, it was unclear who would be the cheapest cost avoider for a particular type of loss, it might be appropriate prima facie to extend liability to those losses but to allow bargaining (disclaimers) or to develop some legal device to exclude, on a case-by-case basis, claims for that particular type of loss where the plaintiff is the cheapest cost avoider. In commercial sales where (apart from informational asymmetries which can be dealt with by the initial entitlement distribution) there *is* a capacity for bargaining, the parties should be left to decide how losses such as pure loss of profits should be distributed between them, and any resultant disclaimers relating to such loss should be upheld. However, in other contexts where transaction costs are prohibitive, purported disclaimers will have to be ignored (see above). As we saw, it is an all or nothing issue. The bargaining costs facing a victim with respect to physical losses are the same as for other sorts of loss. This means that the initial rule will have to make more careful provision about which types of loss should be internalized by the rule. For example, with the type of loss called pure loss of profits there is the strong possibility that the victim is the cca (see Chapter 6, under heading 5(a)). Here it makes sense, in classes of relationship where there is no possibility of real bargaining around the rule by the victim, to exclude from the rule's coverage at the outset lost profit claims. On the other hand, as between strong commercial parties it may be efficient to place on the seller a warranty of merchantability which covers pure lost profits and, if it proves inefficient in an individual case, to leave the parties to bargain around the rule by use of a disclaimer.

Since the Directive only deals with contexts where real bargaining around the rule is likely to be rare *and* to a class of loss (physical loss) for which the victim is often not the cca, it reduces the risk of the inefficiency which the outlawing of exclusion clauses at first seemed to threaten (see above). As we will see later (Chapter 6, under heading 5(d)), however, this is at the expense of *not* attempting to cover the hard cases where the victim is a commercial enterprise which cannot form real bargains with the cca and cases where types of loss other than physical loss should be shifted from the victim. The inefficiency lies in what is omitted from the reach of the Directive.

CHAPTER 6

Critique of wealth maximization

1 MARKET APOLOGISTS

From within the law and economics camp most critics of the Posner/Calabresi justification for legal intervention in the product area see the market as a much better
informed and cheaper forum than the courts in which to allocate product losses.
They argue that for many consumer products the phenomenon of repeat purchase
and the value of goodwill undermine the argument that it is not rational for consumers to consider low probability events.[1] But to European eyes such justifications for
the market can at times appear wilfully insensitive to the market distortions which
were slowly appreciated during the nineteenth and twentieth century, and as a rather
crude use of the Coase theorem to provide a rationale for laissez-faire ideology.
Even the mass repeat purchase of a bag of mixed groceries from Sainsbury's every
Saturday hardly overcomes the obvious logistical and psychological difficulties in
obtaining and processing information about their attendant risks. And if we make
the reasonable assumption that relatively more injuries occur, not through groceries,
but through objects such as sports equipment, electrical appliances, furniture and
automobiles, the repeat purchase arguments fall. A key weakness, then, in the
market proponent's argument that consumers can inform themselves and so enter
relatively efficient bargains about product risk, is that daily experience runs counter
to this picture of the world.

A second sophistication to the pro-market argument, however, is that because of
the costs and informational difficulties involved in using liability rules to achieve
internalisation, the operation of the market, even if quite imperfect, is allocatively
superior. Certainly the more vague a liability rule is, the greater the costs of its operation because, for example, more claims will be brought to trial; and the greater the
opportunity for over- and under-internalisation to occur. Indeed, as we saw in
Chapter 4, a tendency to vagueness in rules and volatile or contradictory jury outcomes can be seen as a price the US pays for a legal culture which values substantivism in doctrinal issues and decentralised lay fact-finding. Even in the legal systems
of the EC countries which are less vague and volatile, we will see that there is an
inherent uncertainty in cost-benefit and perhaps causal adjudication; and this can
produce costs, for example, where cause or defectiveness is the matter of opinion
(see Chapter 10, under heading 8).

But simply referring to the legal system's cost is not sufficient. Before we resort

---

1 See eg P Danzon 'Comments on Landes and Posner: A Positive Economic Analysis of Product Liability' (1985) 14 J Legal Studies 569, 572; R Epstein 'The Unintended Revolution in Product Liability Law' (1989) 10 Cardozo LR 2193, 2204; A Schwartz 'Proposals for Product Liability Reform'
(1988) 97 Yale LJ 353, 372, 379 and 'The Case Against Strict Liability' (1992) 60 Fordham LR 819.

to the market solution (eg reverting to caveat emptor or upholding all disclaimers of the implied warranties of quality) we must be convinced of the claim that such 'legal system' costs out-weigh the extraordinary costs involved in informing consumers about product risks. Intuition – which is all we have in the absence of substantial empirical evidence – suggests we should be sceptical about this claim, and leads us to suspect that the market solution is urged for reasons other than allocative efficiency. Support for these intuitions comes from the emphasis placed by advocates of the market on the adjudicatory problems created for courts, producers and insurers by cost-benefit-based rules designed to solve the consumer information problem. Under such rules adjudication problems certainly do exist, even though in a subset of cases they can be bypassed, albeit artificially, by using a mechanical standard, as is done in the manufacturing error cases (adopting 'departure from the product line norm' as sufficient to establish defectiveness). But market analysts tend to ignore the fact that the choice of liability rule can itself eliminate many of the remaining adjudicatory costs; for example, by choosing a 'defect-free' strict liability regime (that is, a strict liability regime without a defect requirement such as 'full strict liability' (see under heading 4, below)). That economic opponents of internalisation via liability choose to focus their attention and attack on cost-benefit liability rules and the problems they present to the fact-finder, and to ignore arguably less costly rules such as full strict liability, suggests a hostility to legal intervention *regardless* of how cheap to administer it could be made by the choice of rule. The suspicion arises that some market proponents use the rhetoric of efficiency analysis to attack the current cost-benefit-based liability regime which they oppose, not for efficiency reasons, but because of its distributional effects. This would explain their preference for a shift back to the market solution, which would re-distribute wealth to producers, and also their neglect of the option of a shift to a 'defect-free' strict liability which would redistribute wealth away from them.

2   VICTIM AS A COST AVOIDER: THE CAUSATION PROBLEM FOR EFFICIENCY ANALYSIS

Market proponents do, however, expose the flaw in assuming *generally* that only one party is the cca and specifically that the victim cannot affect the probability or gravity of the product risk eventuating. If the victim is the *cheapest* cost avoider then the efficiency strategy requires the loss to lie where it falls, a no-liability position, even if transaction costs between victim and others are prohibitive. What is more, the assertion that victims may be the cheapest cost avoiders is supported by common sense. The powerfully emotive idea that consumers of defective products are 'powerless to protect themselves'[2] seems at best circular (is a product only defective if the victim cannot protect herself?), and at worst blind to the cases of reckless misuse of goods such as the earlier example of someone drinking bleach (Chapter 5, under heading 5).

But it is not obvious that raising the issue of victim's behaviour provides a fatal argument against the efficiency justification of a general liability rule aimed at internalizing costs. It simply requires appropriate legal devices by which victim

2 *Greenman* v *Yuba Power Products Inc* 377 P 2d 897, 901 (1963).

behaviour (and the possibility of parties other than the producer being *equally* cheap cost avoiders) can be taken into account.[3] We saw, for example, that the bleach example can be dealt with either in causal terms or via a volenti defence. Such techniques and their adequacy now need to be addressed in detail, and in doing so a much deeper problem with efficiency theory is highlighted: how to achieve its requirements under the existing conceptual devices of common law liability. The principal problem here is the traditional requirement of causation. To explain why this is so, we must make a detour into some causal theory.

Traditionally in those torts where damage is the gist of the action, for example negligence, there is a requirement that the defendant's conduct actually *caused* that damage. This traditional requirement is consistent with a corrective justice model of liability – a model which looks back into past events and seeks to shift losses in order to correct the disruption due to a 'wrong' that has occurred in the particular case. In contrast, the efficiency strategy sees past losses as sunk and the purpose of liability is to affect future behaviour only. Thus efficiency theory requires us to search for and impose liability on the cheapest cost avoider. This need not be the causer of the losses, the pressure of which has brought the plaintiff to court. The law's job is to select the cheapest cost avoider, and so efficiency theory would seem not to have a place for the traditional causation requirement.[4] Posner and Landes go as far as to say that the defendant will be *deemed* to have 'caused' the injury when making him liable would promote efficiency or when, in Calabresi's terms, he is the cheapest cost avoider.[5] This irrelevance of causation for economic theory has created severe problems for positive economic theory (ie the theory that seeks to rationalise past common law decisions in terms of promotion of efficiency), given the traditional vitality of the causation requirement. But it is no less of a problem for the normative theory in which we are interested as a possible rationale for the Directive: how does one construct the appropriate allocative liability rule which isolates and renders liable the cheapest cost avoider defendant? How should such a liability rule be expressed? Is the Directive consistent with this?

There are three ways an economic theorist might try to get round the problem of the traditional causation requirement of liability. First, the theorist might openly remove cause from the requirements of liability on the grounds that it is irrelevant. This is what the theory seems to demand anyway. It is, however, an approach which is unlikely to be acceptable in the short term, so entrenched are current expectations that civil liability relates in some way to causal relevance (for reasons we touch on in later chapters). The second way is to assert that by virtue of being the cheapest cost avoider, the relevant party *will be said to be* the cause. This is the Posner and Landes position. The third strategy is to argue that the causal enquiry sufficiently often identifies the cheapest cost avoider as the cause that the traditional causation requirement is an acceptable vehicle for achieving efficiency. Calabresi's attempt to argue this point relying on the idea of 'probabilistic linkage' or 'probabilistic

---

3 See eg G Calabresi and K Bass 'Right Approach, Wrong Implications: A Critique of McKean on Product Liability' (1970) 38 U Ch LR 74, 82–8.

4 R Wright 'The Efficiency Theory of Causation and Responsibility: Unscientific Formalism and False Semantics' (1987) 63 Ch-K LR 553. Of course, efficiency theory still requires and retains the other traditional causal requirement: that, on the balance of probabilities, it was *this* product which caused the loss of which the plaintiff complains.

5 W Landes and R Posner 'Causation in Tort Law: An Economic Approach' (1983) 12 J Legal Studies 109, 110.

causation'[6] was centrally flawed. This is because it required the identification of those but-for factors which 'increase the probability of an event occurring'; but since all such factors are *necessary* for the outcome, relative to what can one factor be said to have increased the chance of harm once it has occurred? The idea failed adequately to acknowledge that causal judgments *of outcomes*[7] are made with hindsight. So even if before the outcome occurs, factor X seems to increase the risk of the outcome (as the fact that stairs are unlit would seem to increase the risk of a fall), after the event we may know enough to discard X completely as a cause of the outcome (because, eg, we know the person who fell had an epileptic fit unrelated to the lighting of the stairs).

Although Calabresi failed to accommodate convincingly the causal requirement within his efficiency strategy because of his confusing introduction of the probabilistic causation concept, there is a tenable apology for the retention of the causal requirement in product liability rules supported by an efficiency argument. It is worth showing why, and in doing so why a regime of full strict liability based solely on causation might be a workable option as the form of internalization called for by efficiency theory.

(a) What is a cause?: routes by which a but-for factor may emerge as a cause

When a law requires that the defendant be a cause of the damage of which the plaintiff complains, how do courts approach this issue – known by the misleadingly scientific-sounding term, 'factual causation'? Hart and Honoré have shown that, rather than adopting the metaphysical approach of philosophers, a pragmatic approach following the ordinary use of causal language tends to be followed.[8] Such use is not arbitrary, and one of its most important features, recently confirmed in the Court of Appeal,[9] is that, while to be regarded as a 'cause' a factor must at least satisfy a 'but-for' relationship to the relevant subject-matter of the causal enquiry, this is not sufficient. But for the presence of oxygen, a forest fire would not start, but no-one would ordinarily describe this factor as a 'cause' of the fire. Only some but-for factors are regarded in ordinary use of language as 'causes' since only some but-for factors – because, for example, of their abnormality – help to explain why the outcome happened; and the core aim of causal language and enquiry, at least for lawyers, is explanation. Thus while the Thalidomide children's own existence in their mother's womb was a but-for factor leading to their deformity, they, like oxygen in the forest fire example, would clearly not be identified by ordinary language as a 'cause' of it since their existence in utero was not abnormal in the context and did not help explain their abnormalities.

6 G Calabresi 'Concerning Cause and the Law of Torts: An Essay for Harry Kalven Jr' (1975) U Chi LR 69, 87; Calabresi and A Klevorick 'Four Tests for Liability in Torts' (1985) 14 J Legal Studies 585, 598–9. See Wright, op cit for criticism.

7 Calabresi neglected the necessary threshold question of what forms (and should be allowed to form) the gist of the plaintiff's complaint – the outcome itself or only exposure to the risk? Only once this is known can the causal enquiry have any subject-matter: J Stapleton 'The Gist of Negligence: Part II' (1988) 104 LQR 389. See below under headings 5(g), (h) and 6.

8 H Hart and T Honoré *Causation in the Law*, 2nd edn (Oxford, Clarendon Press, 1985). For the contrasting metaphysical approach see J Thomson 'Causality and Rights: Some Preliminaries' (1987) 63 Chi-K LR 471.

9 *Wright* v *Lodge and Shepherd* [1992] NLJR 1269, 1270 (Straughton LJ).

Hart and Honoré also successfully showed that what leads to the elevation of certain but-for factors to the status of 'a cause' in ordinary language need not rest on evaluative or 'policy' choices. They were less successful in stressing the *variety* of routes by which such elevation occurs and that while sometimes the route was non-evaluative, sometimes it was. 'Factual causation' is in fact neither always dependent on policy choices nor always free of them. Included among the plurality of avenues by which certain but-for factors are elevated to the status of a cause are: by use of what we already know about the objective physical world; or about past behaviour (and our expectations of its continuation); or about moral expectations; or about legal expectations. Let us go through these four different routes. *Firstly*, an old tree decays and falls to the ground, crushing a wild orchid. But for gravity, the crushing would not have occurred, but gravity is of no explanatory force in relation to the outcome. If we know already that rotting trees weaken, we would select decay as the cause of the crash. Note that we can select an explanatory cause without moral or legal input, and this simple example also shows that there may be little controversy in arriving at an answer to the causal enquiry.

Secondly, say X has gratuitously always watered her neighbour's prize orchids. X stops doing this and the orchids die during a heatwave. Although X's conduct in failing to water the orchids is identical conduct to that of other neighbours, X's omission can be selected as a cause of the plants' death because her past behaviour provides part of the backdrop against which we ask for an explanation of the outcome. In the light of past behaviour her omission, but not that of the other neighbours, provides an explanation for the death of the orchids. Again we should note that we can select a cause from the array of but-for factors without making evaluations of X's conduct of a legal or moral kind. This is not to say that different people might not give different weight to past behaviour. In the opinion of some, the fact that X has watered my plants for only a week might not justify calling failure thereafter to water them a cause of their death. People may have different *opinions* about when something should be called a cause.

Thirdly, suppose Z's dog is bitten by an insect and as a result contracts an eye disease. Z ignores it and the dog loses its sight. Here we would *probably* regard Z's conduct as a cause of the blindness because against the backdrop of Z's ownership of the dog we expect Z to have acted, not because of expectations generated by past conduct but for moral reasons. Since the relevant moral expectations are not uniform – different people would attach different moral expectations of care to the ownership of animals – one can only say 'probably'; but the example is sufficient to show that it is not always true to say that 'causal relation is a neutral issue blind to right and wrong'.[10] Also embedded in this avenue to causal status are ideas of legitimate autonomy: but for the car passenger being asleep and failing to keep a look out, a car accident may not have occurred, but we do not usually identify this conduct as a 'cause of the accident'. Note how these examples again show that we can select a cause without reference to legal rules but also how this route to the selection of a cause is often very dependent on opinion.

Fourthly, we may elevate a but-for factor to the status of 'a cause', even though there is no relevant past behaviour or any expectations generated by moral reasons. This can be illustrated by the following example: say a law is enacted which reverses the side of the road on which one is to drive. Q forgets and drives on the

10 L Green 'The Causal Relation Issue in Negligence Law' (1962) 60 Mich LR 543, 549.

wrong side and collides with a car conforming to the new rule. We have no difficulty saying Q is a cause of the accident. What helped us select a cause has been the change in the legal background to the enquiry. This example shows how a legal rule can itself provide a route by which but-for factors are selected as causes. But legal rules can also provide a filter eliminating or suppressing factors which might otherwise be identified as causes. Take the facts of the decayed tree example. If a legal rule had placed a duty of tree inspection on a park ranger who had then failed to inspect the relevant tree, this omission would not only be a but-for factor of the crash, but would transcend the decay as a factor explaining the crash. *Against the background of the legal duty to act, another factor* (here the decay) *may lose its causal relevance*. But just because we can see that a legal rule *may* affect the background against which we describe and understand an event so that it may help elevate a but-for factor to a cause, does not mean that a legal rule can *dictate* a causal attribution in the way Posner and Landes argue that a legal rule (eg putting liability on the cheapest cost avoider) can dictate a causal attribution. For example, a legal rule may attach liability to mere status: we could have a rule which said the aunt of any car accident victim should be liable. Yet this does not make the aunt a *cause* of the loss. Whatever the policy behind such an 'aunt' rule it cannot be achieved even partially by use of the traditional category of causation.

(b) Cause: the temporal dimension

But would the concept of cause sufficiently often identify the cca so that we could use it to achieve the goal of efficient loss allocation? This question cannot be answered negatively simply because we know that the identity of the cca is affected by, say, developments in technology. This is because the question of what is a cause is also similarly relative to time and developments in the state of the art. This is an inescapable and crucial feature of causation which any theory of it must accommodate. What determines causation is determined by what constitutes the background of the enquiry, and this can change. We have just seen it can change as the legal rule changes over time but it can also change with other developments over time, for example scientific discovery (eg knowledge about decay in trees) and technological advances (eg the development of childproof lids, see below). Similarly time influences our expectations drawn from past behaviour and our moral attitudes to behaviour shifts over time. *What is seen as relevant to explain an event changes.*

 Let us put this in a product context. Suppose that in 1940 a child gets to a medical cabinet, swallows a number of tablets and is made ill. There is an infinite number of but-for factors here. We could, for example, always say that but for the omission of local authorities to inspect the security of all domestic medical cabinets, the illness of the child would not have happened. But in 1940 we would not have elevated this but-for factor to causal status because it would not have explained the event to us given our background, understanding and expectations generated from past behaviour, moral expectations, legal obligations, etc. The same can be said about the manufacturer's omission to fix a child-proof lid on the tablet container. In 1940 this would not have been identified as a but-for factor having causal relevance. It was a possibility no-one would have thought of, given the state of the art. Here, however, the *later* development of such devices could mean that, on identical facts in 1995, some of us might well identify such an omission by the manufacturer as a cause of the child's illness because our expectation might be that such a cheap precaution *if available* would be taken. Moreover, our expectations may have nothing to do with which legal regime of liability is operating.

On the other hand, legal duties *to take care* often provide the context in which we are asked to identify conduct as a relevant cause; but it is important to appreciate that the conclusion that conduct was a cause does not establish that the conduct was in *breach* of the fault-based liability rule. Thus in the 1995 example we might say that the omission of the child-proof lid was *a cause* of the illness but that, given other factors, it was not a *careless* piece of conduct (perhaps the tablets were for heart attack or arthritis sufferers so that easy access by the patient was essential). It is useful if we reserve the idea of legal 'responsibility' for the conclusion that a person will be liable because *all* requirements of the legal rule are satisfied, not only the causal requirement. If we do this we can then see clearly that the defendant may have caused the relevant damage but not be legally responsible for it. Similarly, the defendant may have caused the damage but for legal reasons (policies) it is regarded as unjust that he be held responsible for the full consequences, which are then described as too remote or not proximate.

It can now be seen how even under a strict liability rule, ie a rule under which reasonable care by the defendant is no answer, the state of the art can affect the issue of causation. Suppose that there is, for some reason, a rule that holds drug manufacturers strictly liable for all personal injuries they *cause* (ie 'full strict liability', see under heading 4, below). The manufacturer's omission to put a child-proof cap on a medicine bottle in 1940 would not have been regarded *in 1940* as causing the child's illness, but identical conduct in 1995 would be regarded, at least by some, as a cause of the child's illness *in 1995*. It is vital to remember that even in a strict liability regime, the issue of causation is a fluid one, taking into consideration developing expectations, etc. It is also vital to the understanding of how a causation requirement can operate in a strict liability context to appreciate how a party may be said to have caused a loss even though that party was unable to foresee the risk which later produced the loss. Let us assume a product risk which was unforeseeable and therefore unpreventable, for example a hidden adverse drug reaction. We might still argue that although both the manufacturer's activity and the victim's presence were but-for factors, it was the manufacturer's behaviour in creating, manufacturing and marketing the drug which explain the deleterious result better than the victim's behaviour. This is certainly the case in the Thalidomide situation, because some people, if not all, find it meaningful to talk about the 'cause' of a Thalidomide injury as being the drug, the outcome of the manufacturer's activity, even if the risk of that injury was unforeseeable at the time of such action.[11]

In order to arrive at this result there is no need for courts to resort to devices such as saying that it was the defendant-manufacturer's failure to warn of the unforeseeable risk which caused the injury – clearly a silly idea which no common-sense version of causation could accommodate. Lack of warning is not what caused the injury, but it can still be said that the product caused the injury or, more accurately, that the manufacturing and marketing of the drug by the manufacturer did. This

---

11 For those unhappy with describing M's behaviour as a 'cause', it may yet be possible coherently to isolate it as more than a but-for factor in 'providing an opportunity' for the product to cause harm; on such attenuated forms of causal connection see Hart & Honoré, op cit 202 and Chapter 7, under heading 3 and Chapter 8, under heading 1.

shows how knowledge gained between the accident and trial (eg the medical discovery of a link between foetal abnormalities and a pregnancy drug) can help us elevate a but-for factor to the level of a cause in a way impossible at the time of the injury. It also shows that even under a regime where liability does not hinge on a 'causation plus fault' requirement but only on causation, hindsight can change the background against which we seek a causal explanation. Hindsight can help to identify the defendant's conduct as a cause and hence to impose liability on him, even though at the time he acted he would not have been regarded as a cause and despite the fact that, even with hindsight, he is not seen to have acted with fault.

In some strict liability contexts the but-for factor of greatest explanatory force may be the victim not the manufacturer. Suppose that, unforeseen to the manufacturer, a human shampoo, if fed to household cats, generates the AIDS virus in the cat after ten years. Although we can say that but for the manufacturing etc of the manufacturer the victim's cat would not have got AIDS, it may be thought that in this context, in contrast to the Thalidomide-type of case, the dominant explanatory factor of the result was the householder's grossly abnormal behaviour in using the product in this way. This absurd departure from expected behaviour explains the outcome better than does the marketing of the dangerous product, or at least explains it equally well. The clearest way to describe this conclusion is to say the householder's behaviour is the cause because it broke the chain of causation otherwise running from the manufacturer's conduct, even though the relevant risk was not foreseeable to anyone and so no-one could be *volens* to it; or that the householder's behaviour was a co-cause. Similarly, if the risk is foreseeable, in some cases the manufacturer's activity may remain the most powerful explanatory factor as in the case, for example, of the known but random adverse reactions associated with aspirin, hepatitis in blood etc. In other cases, the victim's activity will be the best explanation: for example, where a victim knows of his susceptibility to penicillin but who takes the drug anyway. It is a matter of degree whether they are called co-causes or whether, in the first case the manufacturer's, and in the second case the victim's, behaviour is identified as the sole cause. Either way, both cases can easily be accommodated within a fault-free liability regime. These are all vital points which rebut the oft-stated assertion that strict liabilities are unworkable unless some extra limiting factor is included. It may be that a rule with a bare causal criterion generates *too much* liability (see Chapter 8, under heading 1), but it is not true that it is any more unworkable than as a component of, say, a 'causation plus fault' rule.

(c)   Cause as a sufficient approximation to cca

The relationship between the concept of a cause and efficiency theory can now be made clear. The economic rationale of a special product liability rule is that, in the relevant context, transaction costs are high and that in general the manufacturer (and, perhaps, a middle party like the retailer) rather than the victim is the cca. Internalisation to the cca via a legal rule is therefore appropriate. Now, while it is true that the behaviour of the manufacturer, and indeed the retailer, bears a but-for relation to the condition of the product (and hence to the damage it produces), would they be the parties selected by traditional causal theory so that the search for the cca approximates to this traditional causal search? What makes a cca is the finding that the cca's behaviour could in the future most cheaply make a difference to the incidence of the relevant losses. Usually there will be a strong correlation between this determination and the determination of what made the difference, or explains the occurrence of the relevant loss in the past, that is the determination of the causes of that loss. The problem is that there may be cases where the party whose conduct can be identified as a past cause of loss may not, in the future, be the cca of that loss. For example, suppose that a drug is found to cause adverse reactions in some of those who take it, and that those reactions were unforeseeable before their first occurrence. We have already seen (see (b) above) that in such a case the manufacturer can be considered to be a cause of the adverse reactions. Suppose further, however, that investigation of these reactions before trial of any claim arising out of them establishes that such reactions are only suffered by a precisely identifiable group of users, such as red-haired males. We might still want to say that the manufacturer of the drug was *a* cause of those reactions. But because we now know more about them, we may not identify the manufacturer as the cheapest cost avoider of such reactions in the future. Moreover, although we would not identify behaviour of the past red-haired victims of such reactions as in any sense their cause, we may well identify red-haired males as the cheapest cost avoiders in the future. This shows that, in some cases, the concept of cause will not identify the cca, and in theory, therefore, the type of case just described presents a very serious problem for the efficiency strategy.

In practice, however, the problem is less acute because the incidence of cases like this is very low. In most cases the future cca will have been identified as a past cause of the injury, so that the traditional causal requirement will be an acceptable vehicle through which to pursue the search for the cca. The working assumption can be made that the factor which in the past made the difference (the cause) will do so in the future (cheapest cost avoider). If there is more than one factor which made a difference in the past we can still fit the two approaches roughly together by saying that such co-causes may be equally-cheap-cost-avoiders in the future, and this allows us to use the concepts of joint tortfeasors in pursuit of the efficiency strategy.

If cause *is* an acceptable approximation to the cca, we should pause a moment to ask if the Directive's attitude to victims and its selection of potential defendants is consistent with the efficiency goal. In nearly all cases under the Directive[12] the victim is only relevant to liability if her past behaviour was causally relevant to her injury (eg if she acted abnormally, she may be regarded as having broken the chain of causation; if her behaviour was careless this is relevant to the contributory negligence defence). When it comes to potential defendants, however, some odd reasoning needs to be employed if the Directive is to be justified in efficiency terms because the liability is not even directed to the party causally responsible for the condition of the product which injured the victim. Instead, only a sub-set of potentially relevant causes is selected (manufacturer, component manufacturer, omitting, for example, up-stream designer of product and down-stream retailer of it), along with parties such as the importer and own-brand supplier who have little or no causal relevance to the injury nor are plausible candidates as cheapest cost avoiders. We will see in Chapter 11 that the fact that the Directive does not impose liability on

---

12 Article 8 extends apportionment beyond cases of contributory negligence to cases where the damage is caused by the defective product and 'any person for whom the injured person is responsible' but it will rarely cover cases in which it could not be argued that the victim's failure to control the relevant conduct of that person was a cause of the damage. The CPA fails to implement the extension.

all parties who cause the relevant condition of the product, coupled with inadequate recourse rules, means that there is a considerable potential for the dilution of the economic incentives which an efficiency justification for the Directive would require. Here it is enough to point out that, along with the imposition of a form of vicarious liability on those such as own-brand suppliers, these features of the Directive seem to be more important departures from the efficiency strategy than the use of causal ideas in the product liability rules.

3   THE BYSTANDER

While efficiency theory can point to the informational and non-informational transaction costs in mass markets as a ground for legal intervention to assist injured buyers, in fact it is the phenomenon of 'bystander injuries', that is injuries to a victim who neither bought nor used the product, which provides the most powerful argument for a liability rule to shift the loss off the victim. Here all the complex and subtle arguments of market apologists about price signals, consensual norms and consumer sovereignty fall. It is unrealistic to expect unborn children to bargain in advance about the risks of drugs taken during pregnancy, or to expect pedestrians to negotiate with every vehicle manufacturer and driver to allocate the relevant product risks efficiently. Where the bystander was not the cheapest cost avoider, the high transaction costs by which they are typically confronted provide a classic example of the economic ground for legal intervention. The alternative hypothetical market simply and indisputably does not exist. Faced with such cases, market apologists who want to claim the intellectual respectability, or at least the glamour, of the efficiency analysis are forced not only to play down the transaction costs between members of the chain of supply and buyers but to down-play the incidence of bystander injuries. By portraying the 'real' product liability debate as one about the relevant transaction costs between members of the chain and the *buyer* they hope to convince us that the market, that is the contract of supply, is a viable and indeed preferable alternative to the protection of tort liability. An extraordinary feature of US tort scholarship is that this profoundly loaded assumption that the relevant consumer is a buyer (or at least that bystander injuries are rare) is commonplace among leading US scholars, not just market apologists.[13] US legal history may seem to lend a hand here since the emergence of s 402A from the implied warranty of merchantability and its late application to bystander injuries superficially suggests that injuries to bystanders are a peripheral issue. But history has to be kept separate from the normative issue. While the historical emphasis on the buyer and the delay in the extension of the US rule to bystanders are explainable and not at all mysterious to those

---

13 See eg G Schwartz 'The Vitality of Negligence and the Ethics of Strict Liability' (1981) 15 Georgia LR 963, 980; M Rizzo and F Arnold 'Causal Apportionment in the Law of Torts: An Economic Theory' (1980) 80 Col LR 1399, 1400, n 5; G Fletcher 'Fairness and Utility in Tort Theory' (1972) 85 Harv LR 537, 544, n 24; A Schwartz 'Proposals for Product Liability Reform: A Theoretical Synthesis' (1988) 97 Yale LJ 353, 357, n 4; G Calabresi 'Product Liability: Curse or Bulwark of Free Enterprise?' (1978) 27 Cleve St LR 313, 315; R Epstein 'The Legal and Insurance Dynamics of Mass Tort Litigation' (1984) 13 J Legal Studies 475, 506 and 'Causation in Context: An Afterword' (1987) 63 Chi-K LR 653, 675; R Posner 'A Positive Economic Analysis of Product Liability' (1985) 14 J Legal Studies 537; J Coleman *Risks and Wrongs* (Cambridge, Cambridge University Press, 1992) 415.

who appreciate the haphazard origin of that rule, they should have no bearing on the normative issue.

In addition, market apologists have tried to reduce the bystander problem by asserting that most victims *could have* made suitable bargains, and through chains of these hypothetical bargains the appropriate loss internalization would be feasible if matters were left to the market. But is this convincing? Take the case of a person visiting premises where a defective coffee grinder explodes, injuring the visitor. If we want to argue for a market route to internalisation here we have to argue on the basis of some chain of agreements stretching from the victim to the cheapest cost avoider – presumably some sort of contract between visitor and occupier and then between occupier back to the cheapest cost avoider, probably the manufacturer. One of the many problems here is that the incentive this seems to give the occupier is to take out insurance, not to bargain with the manufacturer of products which happen to have found their way on to his or her premises, perhaps by way of gift.

In the end attempts to recast most cases as consensual or potentially consensual relationships – thereby helping to attract both efficiency and libertarian arguments for the non-intervention of liability rules – fail to convince. It is true that with some amendment of the privity rule we could, as some other jurisdictions have done, widen the reach of contractual protection to the third party beneficiary of a contract, but that only helps users such as Mrs Donoghue.[14] It does not reach the coffee grinder victim, let alone the Thalidomide child. The assumptions needed to justify an argument that such victims have a potentially consensual relationship with a relevant party seem bizarrely unreal. Intuitively we know that the cost is high of finding and bargaining with the relevant parties in connection with risks to safety inherent in our various environments. Think of how many places we go every day in a social non-contractual capacity. Would we have to bargain each time we visited a friend's house that someone would pay if we were injured by a defective product therein? What about all the occasions in which the defective product on the premises had got there by gift so that the occupier had no contractual relationship with the manufacturer or retailer? The costs for the occupier of bargaining with the manufacturer or retailer would be very high. Because situations such as this are increasingly common, potential victims would need to spend more and more time bargaining. It seems intuitively the case, contrary to the assertions of market apologists, that the class of bystander cases where there is not nor could be a relevant bargaining relationship is significant and getting larger. In such cases where the victim is not the cca, it is vital for the efficiency strategy that legal intervention ensures losses are shifted off the victim and on to the cca to prevent inefficient incentives, for example, for the plaintiff to take excessive precautions.

A second problem with attempts by market apologists crudely to divide cases into consensual/potentially consensual relationships and others is the perhaps accidental, but still inappropriate, association of this distinction with the tort/contract divide (see also Chapter 13, under heading 5). It is true that it is efficient to refuse the protection of an initial legal entitlement, for example rights in tort, to those who had an appropriate alternative avenue of protection eg obtaining an express contractual term with the appropriate party. Such a principle is easily supportable on other

---

14 And perhaps not even her ... the proposals in the UK seem much more limited: Law Commission *Privity of Contract: Contracts for the Benefit of Third Parties* (London, HMSO, 1991) Consultation Paper No 121.

grounds too.[15] But even if we reserve the protective assistance of the law to victims who had no appropriate avenue of protection by an express contractual term, that still requires us to judge who such parties might be and not to prejudge the issue on the crude basis of privity. This entails being sensitive to the real costs of bargaining *even within a formal contractual relationship with the relevant party.* In other words, just as we might refuse a tort remedy to a commercial user of a defective product who had no contractual connection with the chain of supply contracts on the basis that it had sufficient bargaining strength to create that relationship and to bargain with and bribe a relevant party for the protection, we may conversely want to protect a person who, although in a contractual relationship with the relevant party, is unable to extract the desired protection because of lack of information, for example. Indeed, terms implied by law – the contractual analogue of the protection given by tort duties between strangers – such as that relating to the merchantability of goods, were created to adjust appropriately the apparently consensual relationships between certain parties. From the point of view of efficiency arguments for legal intervention, the important divide is therefore not between tort and contract, but between those victims who satisfy the prerequisites of intervention, such as inability to bargain for relevant protection, and those who do not. Only if these prerequisites are satisfied might we, in the case where the parties are already linked by contract, get to the separate issue of the form such protection should take: terms implied by law or concurrent tort protection.[16]

It is because market apologists grossly underestimate the real bargaining costs in actual or proposed bargaining relationships and consequently neglect bystander injuries, that their views clash with European sensitivities in the post-Thalidomide world and lead to a suspicion that market apologists – despite their efficiency rhetoric – are really guided towards market solutions for other ideological reasons.

4 THE CONTENT OF THE ENTITLEMENT: HOW AND WHY NORMATIVE ECONOMIC DEBATE CENTRES ON A COST/BENEFIT RULE

If we assume European reformers gave priority to economic efficiency, and they certainly nod in its direction, their clear sensitivity to transaction costs and bystander injuries would have provided the key reasons for their recommending legal intervention in the market. What is more, given the inability of any form of liability other than tort to deal with bystander injuries, their decision in favour of tort liability was a natural corollary of this. But what particular form of liability would the efficiency analysis recommend? Even if we confine our attention for the moment to the issue of the standard of liability, from what we have seen of the Calabresian analysis we might have expected the content of the new regime to be sharply different from either the proposals of the initial European reformers or that finally adopted in the Directive. An examination of five different liability options demonstrates weaknesses in any economic rationale for the initial reform proposals or the Directive. It

15 See eg J Stapleton 'Duty of Care and Economic Loss: A Wider Agenda' (1991) 107 LQR 249.
16 See generally Stapleton 'Duty of Care and Economic Loss' op cit.

also helps to highlight how the dynamics of US scholarship have left a critical gap in normative theory: is the defect requirement justified?

Five potential techniques for internalising accident costs via a tort liability rule should be mentioned, four of which were illustrated in Figure 5.1 (page 97). The first rule (not illustrated) would internalise all accident costs, on the basis of a simple causal rule, even if the risk was unforeseeable or unavoidable or was outweighed by the product's benefits to the defendant. This would be justified by the assumption, reasonable in unilateral cases, that the cheapest cost avoider tends to be the party who would be found to have *caused* the accident. Since such liability would be imposed in the absence of fault on the part of the defendant, it would be a strict liability; but since it would allow no defences, it would be that form of strict liability which the Pearson Commission called an *absolute liability*.[17] Such a liability is clearly inefficient in those non-unilateral situations where the victim could also have avoided the accident with due care. It is so clear that the incidence of such cases is high that no analyst seriously proposes such a form of legal intervention.

The second form of liability, full strict liability allowing defences of both contributory negligence and volenti, which I will call *'full strict liability (with CN/V)'*, would internalise all accident costs to the defendant where it alone is the cheapest cost avoider. But it also would apportion costs where optimum cost avoidance requires this, for example by dealing with cases where there is more than one cheapest cost avoider by the contributory negligence defence and recourse rules between tortfeasors. Finally it would externalise costs when the victim is the cheapest cost avoider; that is, it would deal with cases where she is the sole cheapest cost avoider by the use of causal rules or a volenti defence. If, in the products context, we could assume that the only potent forces were the victim's behaviour and the condition of the product – that is, that there were no potential overlapping enterprises (see Chapter 13, under heading 1) – this approach would produce a rule of strict liability with defences of contributory negligence and volenti on producers of the final product, since he is the *cheapest* cost avoider out of those in the chain in most cases (see Chapter 11, under heading 7). It is very important to remember that such a rule would *not* cover every fall from a ladder or every cut by a knife. The requirement of a *causal* connection between the condition of the product and the injury *and* the availability of defences based on victim behaviour prevent this absurd result. The misconception that full strict liability covering all risks produces such results is widespread and was an important flaw infecting the reasoning of the Law Commissions' Report on product liability in 1977 (see below and Chapter 9, under heading 2(c)).

The major theorist to argue that efficiency requires a full strict liability rule, that is one without a defect requirement, is Calabresi.[18] Note that the rule is capable of internalizing all accident losses, not just those which are foreseeable and not just those resulting from accidents, the costs of which outweigh the benefits. In theory the cost/benefit analysis will still occur but it will be conducted by the party on whom the rule places the loss, for example a manufacturer in a unilateral situation or

---

17 Pearson Com p 515.
18 G Calabresi and J Hirschoff 'Towards a Test for Strict Liability in Torts' (1972) 81 Yale LJ 1055. See also M Rizzo 'Law Amid Flux: The Economics of Negligence and Strict Liability in Tort' (1980) 9 J Legal Studies 291, 317. Other proposals include J Hanson 'What Liability Crisis?' (1991) 8 Yale J on Reg 1, 8 and J Diamond 'Eliminating the "Defect" in Design Strict Product Liability Theory' (1983) 34 Hastings LJ 529, 531.

the victim in the earlier bleach example. Under such a regime any party on whom the loss lies and who is a repeat player will have an incentive not only (a) to take cost-justified *precautions* next time but (b) to carry out *research and development* into ways of detecting and controlling unforeseeable risks, and of discovering techniques by which known but unavoidable risks may be averted. Where such a party also charges a price for its risk-taking activity – as a manufacturer does – price deterrence will operate to give him an incentive (c) to *review the level of risk-creating activity* and to adjust it to a more optimum level. It is true that in bilateral cases the result of full strict liability is suboptimal because the plaintiff is held only to a care standard, that is, he only has an incentive to do (a), that is to take the precautions which seem cost-justified at the time he acts. He has no incentive for R & D, or to review his level of activity. But this result seems inescapable.[19]

A general attraction of full strict liability is that the cca is better equipped than the court to evaluate what is a cost-justified precaution (a), whether enough R & D has been done (b), and whether the activity is being pursued at an appropriate level (c). Even in complex situations, they are better answered by the cca than the court. On the other hand, if full strict liability is not to be a liability applying to all contexts but only to some – and for reasons discussed later it seems unacceptable that it should be universal in application (see Chapter 7, under headings 4 and 5, and Chapter 8, under heading 1) – any limited full strict liability rule implies a guess as to who is most likely to be the cheapest cost avoider, that is the limited class of parties which it specifies as potential defendants. Finally, it is worth noting that an existing and well-known example of full strict liability is the regime to which manufacturing errors are subjected *in practice*. The manufacturer is nearly always the cca of losses attributable to manufacturing errors, and so such cases attract strong arguments for not relying on market forces but on a liability rule to internalise the losses to the manufacturer. This is what happens covertly in negligence and, interestingly, even critics of s 402A concede that imposing full strict liability in such areas is not an inefficient interference with market forces but fully justified.

The third liability rule is like the second and would cover only foreseeable risks: foresight strict liability (see Figure 5.1). Although rights-theorists have recommended a strict liability rule along these lines, no major economic writer has advocated it, and it is best left for discussion in the following chapter concerned with non-economic rationales (see Chapter 9, under heading 3).

The fourth liability rule, 'limited hindsight strict liability' is like the second in that no distinction would be made between foreseeable and unforeseeable risks. But it is narrower because only a subset of risks would be covered. A long-standing example of this is the warranty of merchantability which only internalizes to the seller losses resulting from the unmerchantable condition of the goods, although regardless of whether this condition was foreseeable by the defendant. In the modern product liability reform debate another form of this type of liability was recommended by the Pearson Commission, Law Commissions, Strasbourg Convention and 1976 draft EC Directive: namely, liability for risks regardless of foreseeability; but the risks for which liability was to be imposed were only that subset of risks arising out of 'defective' products. Under this regime, only those risks, the costs of which outweigh the benefits, are shifted by the rule. Unlike the first three rules, this rule requires the court itself to perform the cost/benefit calculation. This is expensive,

19 S Shavell 'Strict Liability versus Negligence' (1980) 9 J Legal Studies 1, 7.

especially in the adversarial context, and reflects at least a minimal confidence that courts are able to do this calculation. Because, however, the rule addresses all product costs and benefits, not just those apparent at the time the defendant acted, it is still a *strict* liability since an argument based on reasonable care or what was known at the time of defendant action would be irrelevant. At trial, hindsight is used to discover the product's costs or its benefits (see Chapter 10, under headings 3 and 5). This means, for example, that costs of unforeseeable adverse drug reactions such as those associated with Thalidomide are put in the cost/benefit balance. So too are newly-discovered benefits of the product. It is therefore useful to describe this form of the fourth liability type as *hindsight cost/benefit strict liability*.[20]

The fifth candidate for a liability rule is not a strict liability rule. Under it the defendant would only be held liable when the costs of the product outweighed its perceived benefits at the time of the relevant risk-taking by the defendant. If we make the assumption discussed earlier that the defendant is both the cause of the injury and the cheapest cost avoider, and if carelessness is seen as incurring risks even when the costs are seen at the time to outweigh the benefits therefrom, this form of liability rule is appropriately, albeit approximately, tagged *'negligence'*. Under this rule, as under the others, the potential defendant (and plaintiff) have an incentive to take precautions which seemed cost-justified at the time, but while the rules are equivalent if only prevention incentives are taken into account, it is important to remember that the efficiency strategy operates on other fronts as well. In particular, price deterrence requires the internalization of the costs even of unforeseeable risks. (This is how incentives (b) and (c) are generated.) While full strict liability (with CN/V) internalizes these fully, and hindsight cost/benefit strict liability does so partially, under the fifth rule the costs of unforeseeable risks are not internalized at all because under the rule liability does not arise for unforeseeable risks. Unforeseeable risks therefore provide the litmus test for the divide between this rule and those varieties of strict liability under which liability for unforeseeable risks can arise, namely all the others except 'foresight strict liability'.

Under the fifth rule the defendant only receives prevention incentive (a). No-one is under an incentive to carry out research and development (b) or to review its level of activity (c). Moreover, as with the fourth rule, the burden of the cost/benefit analysis falls on courts, which are not best suited to this task. For these reasons the second rule, *full strict liability (with CN/V), would seem to emerge clearly as theoretically the best form of liability by which to internalise accident costs to promote efficiency (wealth maximization)*. Why then has this option not figured centrally in recent US scholarship, let alone in the European reform documents, and why is the 'defect' boundary simply assumed to be necessary?

'Defect'

As we have seen, of economic analysts of US tort law two stand out. Beginning in the 1960s, Calabresi wrote careful but increasingly complex analyses in which the simple ideas of internalisation to the cca by a liability rule were overlaid with beautifully worked through, but seemingly endless, qualifications. He showed elegantly that the second liability rule, full strict liability (with CN/V), was the one

---

20 G Calabresi and A Klevorick refer to this as 'ex-post Learned Hand' liability: 'Four Tests for Liability in Torts' (1985) 14 J Legal Studies 585.

which application of simple economic theory would dictate. However, he then went on to examine further complications and imperfections (for example the cost of adjudication, the gross externalisation caused by insurance, the problems where the amalgam of optimal characteristics identifying the cca were split between two or more parties) so extensively that the force of the earlier point was defused by the possibility that, taking them into account, almost any other rule might prove more efficient in particular circumstances. The impossibility of weighing these second-order factors, let alone generalising them, prevented a clear general rule emerging from his later efficiency analysis.

In contrast, Posner presented a greatly simplified economic approach (see Chapter 5, under heading 4(d)). His unreal assumptions proved attractive targets for critics from both within and outside the efficiency camp, as did his extravagant claims about the moral value of the efficiency criterion in public policy and about its historical influence on common law developments. In fact, the dominant claim of Posner's wealth maximization theory has been that it successfully rationalizes the negligence norm in tort law. In order to expound this 'positive' economic theory, Posner had to focus heavily on the prevention limb of the efficiency strategy. This is because the price deterrence limb of the efficiency strategy gives a full strict liability regime an edge over negligence in terms of efficiency. In order to argue that the negligence principle was consistent with efficient pursuit of the wealth maximization goal, Posner had to downplay or ignore these deterrence advantages of a strict liability rule, so that a negligence rule would be perceived as being roughly as efficient as a strict liability rule.

Posner was forced to assert[21] that whatever apparent administrative savings are made by reason of the fact that simpler strict liabilities seemed to avoid the need to ascertain the state of the art or reasonable level of care at the time the defendant acted, these were probably balanced by the cost of resolving causal disputes to which the focus of litigation would shift. Other tactics were to portray the rival 'strict liability' advocated by the early writings of Calabresi as one without a contributory negligence defence which, as we have seen, can easily be shown to be more inefficient than negligence in all except simple unilateral cases; and to argue that R & D incentives exist not only under strict liability but in negligence where victims bear the incentive concerning unavoidable accidents, an argument which simply ignores the much greater costs to a consumer of carrying out such research.[22] Although Posner grudgingly came to concede that, were a strict liability regime to incorporate a contributory negligence defence, it would be as efficient as negligence, his analysis never convincingly explains why the price deterrence advantages of a strict liability do not give it the edge in efficiency terms over negligence. In the product liability context, the most important result of Posner's attempt to legitimate the negligence standard in efficiency terms was his focus on the adjudication by courts of costs and benefits and his related sidelining of the option of full strict liability in which the court does not have this role (except in relation to the contributory negligence defence).

The usual way the cost/benefit standard is described in the product context is by saying that where a product's costs outweigh its benefits, that product is 'defective'.

21 R Posner 'Strict Liability: A Comment' (1973) 2 J Legal Studies 205, 209.
22 W Landes and R Posner *The Economic Structure of Tort Law* (Cambridge, Harvard University Press, 1987) 280; Posner 'Strict Liability: A Comment' (1973) 2 J Legal Studies 205, 208–9.

Thus, in arguing that the negligence standard was efficient, Posner was saying that the *defect* concept in s 402A was economically efficient: that a liability rule which *only* internalized costs where these outweighed benefits was the efficient strategy.

Due to the relative simplicity and provocativeness of Posner's wealth maximization theory, and his later claim that it had a moral basis, his became the dominant version of the normative economic theory in debate, and the Calabresian strategy of full strict liability with contributory negligence/volenti defences was submerged. The normative debate in the product field soon revolved principally around the alleged efficiency justification for defect-based regimes such as hindsight cost-benefit strict liability and negligence (examples of rules 4 and 5 above, respectively). Little attention was paid to the Calabresian liability rule which was 'defect-free', in the sense that the costs and benefits of the defendant's risk-taking were not a matter for costly adjudication by courts, and which carried price deterrence advantages, at least in theory. On the few occasions such a full strict liability (with contributory negligence/volenti defences) rule was noted, it was most often merged and confused with a bizarre type of liability in which defendants would be liable, even if the product's condition bore only a 'but-for' relation to the plaintiff's harm[23] – eg for every cut from a knife, every fall from a ladder – which is a liability easy to dismiss in efficiency terms (see Chapter 9, under heading 2(c)). This, for example, was the way the Law Commissions dealt with full strict liability. As the earlier causation discussion sought to make clear (see under heading 2, above) the mistake here is to assume there is no half-way house between a rule limited by a but-for requirement only, and one which incorporates a dual requirement that a *defect cause* injury. This overlooks the possibility of a 'defect-free rule' which has a causal requirement, such as full strict liability, and fails to note that this causal requirement has the power to filter out most but-for factors. It would eliminate, for example, the condition of the knife (or the ladder) if that but-for factor did not help explain the accident (see under heading 2, above). Unless it did so it would not be a 'cause' and the defendant responsible for the condition of the product would not be liable.[24]

It is true that causal determinations may change over time, with the state of the art and with legal or moral expectations, and so they are inherently 'soft'. It is not possible to say, for example, that a full strict liability rule would always impose (or not impose) liability in cases of misuse: sometimes a manufacturer would be regarded as a cause of an injury incurred through misuse (eg by failure in 1995 to

23 See eg H Klemme 'The Enterprise Liability Theory of Torts' (1976) 47 U Colo LR 153, 174; *Caterpillar Tractor Co* v *Beck* 593 P 2d 871, 879, 889 (1979); *Cochran* v *Brooke* 409 P 2d 904, 906 (1966); S Stoljar, 'Concerning Strict Liability' in *Essays on Torts* ed P Finn (Sydney, Law Book Co, 1989) 267, 276; R Epstein 'The Unintended Revolution in Product Liability Law' (1989) 10 Cardozo LR 2193, 2207 and 'Product Liability: The Search for the Middle Ground' (1978) 56 NCL Rev 643, 648; G Schwartz 'Understanding Product Liability' (1979) 67 Calif LR 435, 444–5 and 'The Myths of the Ford Pinto Case' (1991) 43 Rutgers LR, 1013, 1064; D More 'Re-examining Strict Product Liability's Goals and Justifications' (1989) 9 Tel Aviv Univ Studies in Law 165, 168–9; and J Henderson and A Twerski 'Closing the American Product Liability Frontier: The Rejection of Liability Without Defect' (1991) 66 NYULR 1263, 1279 ff.

24 Note: (1) There is a complex overlap between factors relevant to cause and those relevant to 'defect' but it does not follow that if a product condition is a cause of an injury it is defective even if the latter issue is judged with hindsight (see penicillin example). (2) It is not true that a factor cannot be a cause in relation to unforeseeable risks – see under heading 2, above. (3) Under full strict liability the state of the art is not relevant to show the defendant acted reasonably – because this itself is irrelevant – but it is relevant to whether that conduct was a cause of the relevant loss.

use childproof lids on drugs); sometimes not (eg where the adult victim drank bleach for fun). But as we see in greater detail later (Chapter 7, under heading 3(b)), the softness of the causal determination and the necessity to apply it afresh on a case-by-case basis 'with almost no guidance from the law'[25] is inevitable, and provides no more sound a basis for attacking a full strict liability rule than it does for attacking a rule of negligence which also requires resolution of causal issues. There may be fatal difficulties with full strict liability as a general rule (see Chapter 7 under headings 4 and 5, and Chapter 8 under heading 1) but the workability of the causal requirement is not one of them.

Finally, the channelling of the normative debate towards the 'defect'-based Posner model from the early 1970s onwards was helped by the fact that the rules from which s 402A had evolved were also limited: under the strict liability of warranty, although both foreseeable and unforeseeable risks are covered, the unmerchantability requirement serves roughly the same limiting role as a cost-benefit or 'defect' requirement; negligence is similarly limited. This may well have bolstered the assumption that a defect requirement was a natural and necessary element of a product rule.

In such an intellectual context it is easier to see how the European reformers, even if they had been alive to the intricacies of the efficiency rationale for law reform in the products field, could so completely neglect its most convincing strategy, a 'defect-free' system of full strict liability. But this neglect has profound implications. As shown in Figure 5.1, the only advance on negligence which the hindsight cost-benefit regime has is that it covers unforeseeable risks. This is an advantage which, by a judicious expansion of the notion of foreseeability in negligence, can be reduced to a small one. The advance full strict liability has over both negligence and a hindsight cost-benefit rule is more dramatic, for it would encompass not only the unforeseeable risks of, say, a drug like Thalidomide, but all losses caused by the condition of a product even if the product's utility clearly outweighed its costs. Thus, even though aspirin is a product of overwhelming benefits, full strict liability would internalize to its cost structure the few losses it unavoidably causes to a few unsuspecting users by the precipation of stomach bleeding. This class of loss is much more common than the class of absolutely unforeseeable loss so, in terms of deterrence as well as the compensation of victims, a shift to full strict liability and *the abandonment of the 'defect' requirement*, would have greater potential impact on the defendant's incentives and price structures than a shift from negligence to a hindsight cost-benefit rule.

In short, even if we assumed European reformers were dedicatedly pursuing the deterrence goals they purported to be pursuing amongst others, Posner's concern to rationalize the cost/benefit requirements of existing rules in efficiency terms plus the influence of the warranty/negligence background of the reform, would provide convincing explanations of their rather unquestioning embrace of the 'defect' requirement. It is doubly ironic that this move dramatically limited the compensatory potential of the reform, and that it was not dictated by efficiency theory. A final irony in the development of the European reform was the adoption in the final Directive of the 'development risk defence'. Of defect-based regimes, reformers in the UK and Europe had initially chosen to support the hindsight cost/benefit rule on the basis that it improved the delivery of compensation to product victims who ought not to be allowed to remain, in the words of the drafters of the Council of Europe's Strasbourg

25 Henderson and Twerski, op cit 1281.

Convention, the 'guinea pigs' for products' unforeseeable risks.[26] Not only did such a rule have greater support from efficiency theory, it was comparable to the contractual warranty of merchantability in that both were forms of limited hindsight strict liability, and so did much to remove the anomaly that the buyer had greater protection than the bystander. *In practical politics* the Law Commissions' recommendation of a shift to a hindsight cost/benefit rule looked dramatic and attractive because under it the Thalidomide children would not have had difficulty proving their case: they would not have had to show foreseeability of risks, and it was clear with hindsight that the costs of that drug outweighed its benefits. It should also have had, in theory, efficiency advantages over the existing negligence rules. In the final Directive, however, even this advance was eschewed, for Member States could provide a development risk defence to take unforeseeable risks outside the ambit of its liability.

Despite the claim that s 402A imposed 'strict liability' on manufacturers, the important issue of liability for unforeseeable losses had been generally ignored in the US until the 1980s, and the fact that this was possible supports the assertion that few risks are incapable of being portrayed as foreseeable by pro-plaintiff courts. The 'strict liability' of s 402A certainly bewildered courts, provoking some profound effects at the trial level; for example, it led some courts to refuse to allow manufacturers to argue that their specific conduct had been reasonable, and forcing them to mask this argument in terms of the available state of the art or equivalent objective-sounding devices. But there were scarcely any cases where liability was imposed on a manufacturer whom the court clearly believed had acted carefully. In sharp contrast with European writers focused on the Thalidomide issue, few US analysts addressed the issue of unforeseeable risks until 1983 when, in *Beshada* v *Johns-Manville Products Corpn*, the New Jersey Supreme Court bravely applied the hindsight cost/benefit form of strict liability apparently implicit in the wording of s 402A.[27] Here the defendant was held liable for unforeseeable risks, the 'strict liability' of s 402A ensuring that reasonable care was no defence. The subsequent virtually unanimous condemnation of the decision in the US suggests, first, that the common idea that US manufacturers are exposed to 'strict liability' under s 402A is incorrect; the reception given to the decision shows that whatever the local variations on other points, the US regime is, for manufacturers, based on foresight and is therefore close, if not doctrinally identical, to negligence (see Chapter 10, under heading 6). Secondly, if, as Posner argues, the differences between negligence and a hindsight cost/benefit strict liability regime are negligible from an efficiency perspective once second-order effects are taken into account, efficiency-minded commentators ought to have been indifferent to the result in *Beshada*, and yet many espousing that strategy were not. Thirdly, an analyst who disagreed with Posner and preferred the efficiency advantages of a strict liability regime, even one limited to cases where costs outweigh benefits, should have hailed *Beshada* as more efficient than the negligence rule based on foresight which was being applied elsewhere.

The *Beshada* controversy and the widespread rejection of a hindsight test in the US suggest that, in practice, values other than wealth maximization are in general circulation in the products field. Before we look at what these may be, and how those other non-economic values may have influenced the European reformers, it is important to examine the internal problems with the efficiency theory and strategy.

---

26 Strasbourg Convention's Explanatory Report, reproduced in Law Coms, op cit at 59, 66.
27 *Beshada* v *Johns-Manville Products Corpn* 447 A 2d 539 (1982).

If these prove severe, then the departures from optimal efficiency represented by the initial European reform proposals and by the final Directive may be explainable not in terms of the simple rejection of wealth maximization as a primary goal of law reform, but in terms of its unworkability. In other words, even a reformer or court keen on optimal deterrence of product losses may yet be forced to resort to other considerations if the internal problems with the efficiency theory make it too indeterminate in practice to be workable.

5   INTERNAL CRITICISMS OF WEALTH MAXIMIZATION

Earlier we saw how Posner used certain second-order complications to argue that in practice negligence was as efficient as cost/benefit strict liability or 'defect-free' strict liability. But these are not the only complications. There are a large number of reasons why normative economic theory as a whole does not yield sufficiently clear recommendations in practice to justify the selection of one liability rule from another. Nor can it provide anything more than a very crude indication of what economic implications a certain liability rule may have. The following is a selection of the more important internal difficulties with the economic rationale for a liability regime such as that in the Directive.

(a)   Why pay the victim?/Do enough victims sue?

While economic theory explains why accident costs might appropriately be imposed on a cca, it does not explain why the payments extracted from the cca should be paid over to the victim. The efficiency rationale of liability is forward-looking. It seeks to influence future conduct by internalization of costs. Since this could be done by a system of fines just as well as by using the extracted payment to compensate the victim, an economic rationale of liability has to depend on empirical assumptions about the administrative efficiency of the tort system relative to, say, a central administrative mechanism of fines. One would need to postulate that paying compensation to victims significantly reduces the dislocation or secondary accident costs incurred when loss is concentrated on an individual; that civil action is a relatively efficient way of internalizing costs to ccas; and that it removes a significant incentive, otherwise present, for the plaintiff to take cost-inefficient precautions himself.[28]

Quite apart from the fact that, even if these postulates are true, they do not show why the amount the defendant pays should be the *very same* amount the plaintiff gets, and the fact that they are unsupported by empirical results, there is much empirical support for the proposition that tort law is in fact a poor technique for internalizing costs. The non-legal barriers to private individuals launching and pursuing meritorious claims in the UK have become notorious, and mounting evidence suggests significant barriers of this type in the US too.[29] Even under a negligence

---

28 R Posner *Economic Analysis of Law*, 3rd edn (Boston, Little Brown & Co, 1986) 176–7.

29 These barriers include ignorance of the law, fear of the litigation process and (in the absence of contingency fees) costs: in general in UK see the Pearson Commission and *Atiyah's Accidents Compensation and the Law*, 4th edn (ed P Cane) (London, Weidenfeld & Nicolson, 1993); in US see D Hensler et al *Compensation for Accidental Injuries in the US* (Rand Institute for Civil Justice, 1991) and A Russell Localio et al 'Relation Between Malpractice Claims and Adverse Events due to Negligence' (1991) 325 N Eng J of Med 245.

regime there is strong evidence that tort over-compensates (ie over-internalizes) small claims because of their nuisance value to defendants and insurers, while in respect of larger claims the unwillingness of plaintiffs to incur the risks of litigation leads them to accept settlement offers which are too low. On the second assumption – that tort is the preferable economic vehicle for internalization because it reduces dislocation costs – this is scarcely convincing given the long delays between seriously dislocating accident and the recovery of tort damages which our 1:1 system of liability justice involves.

(b)   Difficulties in the 'cheapest cost avoider' concept

There are problems in the concept of the cheapest cost avoider.[30] It is an amalgam of abilities to foresee, accurately weigh and control a risk better than others and to reflect the costs of that risk-taking most accurately in the price of the activity. But what if one party is clearly better able to detect a foreseeable risk, another is best at evaluating costs and benefits and yet another is clearly better at taking cost-justified precautions, etc? What if one party is best at controlling the known risks of a product, but another is best at carrying out the research and development necessary to discover as yet undiscoverable ones, or most cheaply to reflect the cost of unforeseeable risks in the cost structure of the product? What, in short, is the relative importance of the various elements in the compound concept of the cca? Whom should a defendant join as a co-tortfeasor and how would a court apportion loss?

(c)   Valuation

Another central premise of economic theory is that a cca is able to put a value on the benefits of an activity and its costs. In the product sale setting it might be alleged that valuation of benefits is crudely possible via the price mechanism. Even if, as here, we ignore wealth effects (see under heading 6, below) and bystanders, it is still true that a person might value and therefore be willing to pay for many characteristics of a good: its aesthetic appeal, durability, safety, country of origin, etc. We saw earlier how impossible it often is for either side of the product bargain to glean accurate signals about more than one factor from a compound price (Chapter 5, under heading 6). Even in a cost-benefit liability regime seeking to internalize net social costs we require the court to put such a valuation on the benefits of an activity. But how can this be done without detailed assessment of accident rates pertaining to substitutes available at the relevant time since the benefits of any particular product are dependent on this factor?

There are also problems for a theory of liability which requires the court to put a valuation on the *losses* of which the victim is complaining and for which the defendant is held to be liable. Even if we take the simplest type of claim where the plaintiff is complaining of, say, a leg broken by the defendant's defective product, there is a central dilemma in putting money values to the relevant losses. While in one sense society clearly 'values' things like bodily security, it does not, for moral reasons, permit all of them to be the subject-matter of a market, ie of an exchange

---

30 See eg critique by Posner 'Strict Liability: A Comment' op cit 213–5.

relationship. In the US and EC we ban slavery even among consenting adults. In the broken leg case we may be roughly able to quantify the medical bills, lost wages, etc, but how do we quantify the value the victim would put on avoiding the pain and suffering involved in the trauma, and would not this depend on whether she was asked this before or after the event? While courts can and do 'compensate' for a damaged or lost kidney, what the court is doing is not reflecting the exchange or fictitious exchange value of the kidney – indeed, UK society explicitly bans such exchanges. How are valuations, therefore, to be made? Moreover, it seems a fair guess that even if a potential victim was given in advance an amount representing the cost of all medical bills, lost wages, etc, she would still not be indifferent to having her leg broken.

Normative economic theory of liability does not adequately explain how non-market values such as security, avoidance of pain, friendship and loyalty could be accommodated in the assessment of the damages to be paid by the cca. Even if we limit legal intervention to the goal of achieving the efficient level of physical losses produced by products, we cannot assess their undeniable non-market social costs, reflected for example in the public outrage over incidents like the Thalidomide deformities. The clearest example of the dilemma this poses efficiency theory is provided by its inability to explain assessment of damages rules which make it substantially cheaper to kill a child or injure a pensioner than to injure a robust earning adult with dependants, and cheaper to cause the latter's death, or at least render him unconscious, than merely to cripple him. It is because such assessment of damages rules only poorly and erratically internalize the non-market costs of product injuries that the incentives deducible from them appear so unacceptable.

(d) What is a cost of what?: the problem of types of loss

A major assumption of the wealth maximization rationale for product liability rules is that the rule, its boundaries and its assessment of damages rules will be able correctly to judge 'what is a cost of what'. There are a number of aspects to this. One is whether the social costs of, say, mercury found in cough syrup is a cost of the retailer's enterprise, the manufacturer's enterprise, the quality control engineer's enterprise, etc. We saw, in theory, how Calabresi's cheapest cost avoider concept provided a powerful tool for preferring internalization to the manufacturer as a more efficient arrangement than internalization to the retailer. A second aspect of the 'what is a cost of what' issue arises where risk-creating activities interact: suppose that a bus driver carelessly brakes on a poorly banked road and a passenger, unable to reach one of the few handles, falls and breaks a leg. Here the fact that potential cheapest cost avoiders (the local authority, driver, bus manufacturer) are involved in diverse enterprises presents an implicit barrier to an economic rationale of a liability rule limited to certain types of defendant. This is discussed below (see under heading (f)). A third aspect of the 'what is a cost of what' problem is 'for which losses is someone other than V, the cheapest cost avoider?' The question is best illustrated by a series of simple factual situations: V_1 buys a new television but it simply fails to work; V_2's new television shortcircuits, ruining its internal circuitry; V_3's new television explodes damaging V_3's carpet; V_4's new television explodes injuring V_4's unique old oil painting; V_5's new television explodes injuring V_5's hands; V_6, who is a self-employed publicity agent, buys a new television which explodes, damaging her desk-top publishing equipment which is put out of action for a month during which V_6 does not earn any profits.

Although it is fairly clear that the condition of the television bears a but-for relation to the losses suffered by V in all cases, and that the manufacturer is the cheapest cost avoider of that *condition*, it does *not* follow that the manufacturer is the cca of all the *losses* suffered by V. This is important. Economic theory does not distinguish between types of loss. For example, it treats physical damage in the same way as pure economic loss. Rather, it requires that each type of loss be analyzed separately to see who is the cca *with respect to that type of loss*. The efficiency-minded reformer who is faced with high transaction costs should construct a liability rule which only internalizes those types of losses for which the defendant is the cca (see Chapter 5, under heading 7). If there is some doubt on the issue, for example, whether a potential defendant is the cca of damage to property, liability could be imposed for it so long as appropriate doctrinal techniques were available to allow the defendant to escape liability (eg defences or reviewable disclaimers) in those cases, but only in those cases, where he was not the cca.

Although economic theory makes this task necessary, few economic analysts have tackled its most problematic aspects. While *non-economic* principles of liability can be found to justify different patterns of recovery for different types of loss, economic analysis is striking in its failure to provide an adequate application of its principles to different types of loss in general and to economic loss in particular.[31] It is possible, however, to sketch out the relevant questions an efficiency-minded reformer of products rules would have to address. Before doing this, we should note a general principle, to be discussed in full later. This is that in looking to see if the victim (or some other party) was the cheapest cost avoider, it is inappropriate to ask whether that person has or could have obtained insurance cheaply for that loss. This is because in the real world insurance cuts across the deterrence incentives generated by a loss. In efficiency terms, the more a party is cushioned by insurance from a loss it would otherwise bear, the less incentive that party has to take cost-justified precautions etc (see under heading (i), below). Moreover, even if it is true that a potential victim of, say, personal injuries is best able to gauge the level of lost wages the risk of a broken leg would generate (and hence best able to purchase the correct level of protection via first party insurance), this does not make that person the cheapest cost *avoider* of the social loss reflected by that loss.

---

31 For non-economic reasons for treating different types of loss differently see J Stapleton 'Duty of Care and Economic Loss: A Wider Agenda' (1991) 107 LQR 249 (pure economic loss); Chapter 8, under heading 2(b) (personal injuries). Among economist-lawyers only W Bishop and R Rabin have attempted substantial analysis on the point. Even here they have inexplicably only dealt with one form of economic loss (where non-privity plaintiffs have suffered pure loss of profits because they relied to make these profits on the integrity of property owned by a third party) and failed to devise either a positive economic theory to explain the complex and conflicting existing case law or to arrive at a clear normative synthesis of the diverse contexts in which pure economic loss is caused to an individual: see eg R Rabin 'Tort Recovery for Negligently Inflicted Economic Loss: A Reassessment' (1985) 37 Stan LR 1513; W Bishop 'Economic Loss: Economic Theory and Emerging Doctrine' in *The Law of Tort* ed M Furmston (London, Duckworth, 1986) 73, 77 ('a really convincing explanation still eludes us').

(i) Repair/replacement costs of physical damage to person or already-owned ('other') property

If we start with the personal injuries suffered by V_5, we can easily conclude that the television manufacturer is a cheaper cost avoider of the medical costs ('repair' costs) than V_5, so that in high transaction costs situations efficiency would support a liability rule internalizing such costs to the cca. Can the same be said of the costs of repairing the property owned by V_3, that is the carpet? The cost of home-owners testing electrical equipment away from any damageable property for an adequate length of time would be prohibitive, so we can conclude V_3 is not the cca of such losses and that they should also be covered by a liability rule where transaction costs are high.

The loss associated with the damage to V_4's unique old painting is more problematic. The cost of ensuring that abnormally valuable chattels are not placed near sources of risk is relatively low, there being few such chattels by definition. The possibility of V_4 being the cca of this loss therefore arises. It is arguable, however, that such cases could be accommodated within a rule which prima facie allowed recovery of repair/replacement costs to property already owned by the plaintiff but allowed the defendant to argue that the victim's siting of the property was a, or the, cause of the loss.

(ii) Economic loss (lost profits) consequential on physical damage to the person or already-owned property of V

V_5 may also want to claim for her lost income (lost profits) for the period while she is being rehabilitated (repaired!). As there is nothing V_5 could reasonably do to avoid her loss, no question arises that she is the cca. The cheapest cost avoider (say, the manufacturer) should be liable for this head of loss even in the relatively unforeseen circumstance that V_5 is a renowned professional pianist and so her lost income is abnormally high. Even unforeseeable or indeterminate losses should be candidates for possible internalization according to the price deterrence arm of efficiency strategy.

In V_6's case there is the added complication that V_6 may have been able at low cost to avoid her loss of profits by alternative equipment. Suppose that what the TV damaged were her data disks. If, at low cost, V_6 could have copied her data and kept the library copy in a different, safer environment, she may be the cca of her own loss of profits, so that the appropriate liability rule would be one which denied her claim for such a head of loss – eg by upholding a disclaimer of liability for such losses (a common commercial practice). A comparable argument about back-up systems may apply strongly in contexts, including consumer contexts, where one party has suffered (the pure economic loss?) associated with loss of goods when, for example, a security product such as a security gate alarm or lock fails and goods are stolen.[32]

---

32 On which compare *Lobianco* v *Property Protection Inc* 437 A 2d 417 (1981) and *Dove* v *Banhams Patent Locks Ltd* [1983] 1 WLR 1436 (albeit a case of negligent *installation*). On the 'classification of loss' point see Chapter 11, under heading 2. Another example would be the disclaimer made by photo-developers with respect to any damage beyond physical damage to customers' film.

(iii)   Economic loss (lost profits) consequential on physical damage to person or property of third party

There are many situations where a party suffers loss of profits because that party has relied in earning those profits on the physical integrity of the person or property of a third party which has been physically damaged by the conduct of X. For example, say V_7's income-earning asset (a factory) cannot function unless the property of a third party, say the cable of the electrical or telecommunications company which supplies the factory, is intact and functioning properly. X severs the cable. If V_7 had been able to avoid the loss which would otherwise be caused by the severance of the cable by installing a back-up generator, etc, at a lower cost than the precautions X would have had to take to avoid severing the cable, V_7 will presumably be the cca and a liability rule shifting the loss off his shoulders would be inappropriate, even if the relevant transaction costs were high. But in some cases it will be clear that the victim could not have provided a back-up at low cost, nor bargained with the cca at low cost. Take, for example, the reliance we all place on the physical integrity of other vehicles on the road. Suppose that, due to a manufacturing defect, a lorry breaks down in the Dartford or Brooklyn Tunnel. This delays other vehicles in delivering goods, which causes loss of profits to the owners of these vehicles. Prima facie economic theory would seem to require the internalization of such pure economic losses to the cca, presumably here the manufacturer: an extraordinary result for descriptive economic theory, given that in no US or EC jurisdiction does civil liability seem to arise in such cases in or outside the special product rules. To explain the pattern of real rules, it seems resort has to be made to ideas outside the realm of efficiency theory, for example the fairness idea implicit in the resistance to a liability for 'an indeterminate amount for an indeterminate time to an indeterminate class'.[33]

(iv)   Repair/replacement costs of property acquired

A particular focus for litigation in the UK during the 1970s and 1980s was 'quality' claims, that is claims for pure economic loss associated with the acquisition of property below the quality expected given the circumstances, such as price. The loss suffered by V_1 and V_2 fits into this class. Of course, if the relevant transaction costs are low, efficiency does not justify any liability rule because whatever the initial legal entitlement, the parties will transact around it. Thus, for example, between commercial parties of equal market strength an efficient arrangement concerning the loss would have been reached. But if transaction costs are high – a possibility, which as we know, can exist even if the acquirer is in privity with the creator of the relevant condition and even if the acquirer is a commercial party – the question arises of who is the cca of such a loss? Since this is the party who can price the goods most realistically, given their actual quality, it is usually the manufacturer, so efficiency requires the liability rule to extend to such repair/replacement losses.

With respect to the supply of goods, the warranty of merchantability already goes some way to achieving the appropriate internalization of this head of loss. The victim of such loss is nearly always the buyer and, as we have seen, it is the informational asymmetry of such transactions which led nineteenth century judges to award

---

33 *Ultramares Corpn* v *Touche* 174 NE 441, 444 (1931) (Cardozo CL). For a more extensive discussion see Stapleton 'Duty of Care and Economic Loss' op cit 254.

the initial entitlement (in the form of a warranty) to the victim for foreseeable *and unforeseeable* departures from the merchantable quality standard. The cca *of such losses*, either the seller or someone higher up the chain, is therefore appropriately made liable. This means that there is a good argument for *excluding* from product rules recovery for this head in cases covered by warranty, since it would represent a costly doctrinal duplication – at least if one ignores the possibility of the warranty claim collapsing because the immediate seller is unavailable to be sued.

(v)   Consequential economic loss (lost profits) due to the acquisition of property

Where acquired property is to be used to generate profits for the buyer (almost invariably limited to certain acquisitions for commercial purposes), the question arises whether loss of profits consequential on the unexpectedly poor quality of the acquired property should be the subject of an internalizing liability rule. If transaction costs between the buyer (B) and possible cheaper cost avoiders are low, there should be no liability.[34] If they are high, the question is whether B is the cca, and if not, who is? One has to be careful not to deduce from the presence, in a commercial contract for the supply of property, of a term locating such losses on the buyer that he is the cca of them. Unless we deduce *independently* that such a term (be it in the form of a disclaimer or limitation of a warranty) was the product of a true bargain, efficiency may require us to invalidate it (see Chapter 5, under heading 7). It is simply too crude and inefficient a generalization to say that commercial buyers of equipment usually have sufficient strength to get the allocation of risks which they see as most efficient.

The identity of the cca of such losses depends, as in (ii) and (iii), on the cost to B of C establishing back-up systems, etc, but this is an issue about which generalizations seem impossible to make, and a case-by-case determination seems to challenge the capacity of courts. At best economic theory seems to tell us that some, but not all, such losses of profits should be the subject of a liability rule, but is incapable of providing an appropriate rule to identify such losses or to control exclusion clauses when this is justified.[35] At the very least it fails to explain the pattern of product rules in the US and EC under which no pure economic loss claims such as those described in (iii) are covered. These types of economic loss also provide a striking illustration of a serious flaw in economic theory of liability: its failure to accommodate social gains.

(e)   Net private losses of plaintiffs not necessarily a reflection of net social losses

Economic theory requires that in cases of high transaction costs, internalization of the net social costs of an activity to the cheapest cost avoider should occur. We have already seen the difficulty in fitting these requirements within the traditional

---

34 On this argument the recovery of loss of profits in *Rivtow Marine Ltd* v *Washington Ironworks* [1974] SCR 1189 should not have been allowed. See Stapleton 'Duty of Care and Economic Loss', op cit 285.

35 In 'Concerning Cause ...' op cit (n 6, above) 91 ff, Calabresi attempts a reconciliation of remoteness case law and his economic theory of deterrence, but is unable to formulate a *normative* approach.

conceptual apparatus of civil liability such as the causation requirement, but a much graver reason exists why two party litigation cannot well achieve the economic goal. This is *not* because common law litigation cannot accommodate all relevant losses. One can, in theory, simply define the liability rule sufficiently broadly so that any-one whose loss should be internalized to the defendant-cca would have a claim (eg motorists who suffer pure economic loss associated with the tunnel blockage example, or the National Health Service in the UK in personal injury cases).[36] The problem lies in the fact that the traditional law of civil obligations has yet to develop a sufficiently refined technique by which countervailing *gains* can be taken into account.

Efficiency theory demands internalization only of *net* social losses. But net social losses cannot be identified and quantified unless we also take account of gains from the relevant occasion (say, a physical accident). This can be illustrated by a simple example. Suppose that a town lies south of a river crossed by only one bridge. Most people use the supermarket north of the bridge and some work in the town's princi-pal factory which also lies north of the bridge. Due to a blind spot caused by defec-tive design of a ship's bow, the ship collides with and demolishes the river bridge. While it is true that the supermarket suffers huge loss of profits (as townspeople turn to local shops south of the river), these private losses will be somewhat offset by the private gains to these other shops. Here simply allowing those suffering private losses (the supermarket) to recover all those losses from the cca (the ship designer) would over-deter the cca.[37] If net private losses are exactly balanced by private gains, efficiency would require no internalization *of the supermarket losses* to the cca. There has been no waste of resources, just a shift of wealth from the northern supermarket to southern shops, and efficiency theory is said not to be interested in distributional issues such as this. Real world examples are nothing like as simple as this, and it certainly cannot be assumed that where one party has lost profits as a result, say, of its reliance on the integrity of property owned by a third party, no net social costs are generated.[38] The lost profits of the northern factory and the work-force's lost wages, for example, may well *not* be matched by equivalent private

---

36 Although in practice the transaction costs involved in the pursuit of such numerous claims would make it very difficult to ensure this internalization actually occurred.

37 S Shavell *Economic Analysis of Accident Law* (Cambridge, Harv University Press, 1987) 137, unless the cca was given a cause of action to recoup the social gains of his action from the southerly shops (so that at the end of the day the cca only bore the *net* social cost of his conduct). Yet it is not feasible to see the current law of restitution assisting here since it is predicated on ideas of *unjust* enrichment, see W Bishop 'Economic Loss: Economic Theory and Emerging Doctrine' op cit 77–8, 81. Compare example in text with *Canadian National Rly Co* v *Norsk Pacific SS Co* (1992) 91 DLR (4th) 289.

38 Bishop's assumptions on this point have been strongly criticized. Compare W Bishop 'Economic Loss: Economic Theory and Emerging Doctrine' op cit 74 with M Rizzo 'The Economic Loss Prob-lem: A Comment on Bishop' (1982) 2 OJLS 197; R Rabin 'Tort Recovery for Negligently Inflicted Economic Loss: A Reassessment' op cit 1535, n 72; D Harris and C Veljanovski, 'Liability for Eco-nomic Loss in Tort' in *The Law of Tort* ed M Furmston, op cit 48–9. Moreover, there may be cases where there are no net social costs but a no-liability rule would result in the plaintiff (whose actions are governed by his private losses not net social costs) taking available but inefficient precautions to such an extent that it is more efficient to allow the plaintiff to recover from the defendant: Harris and Veljanovski, op cit 50, 66. Where such inefficient precautions are unavailable (as in *Weller & Co* v *Foot and Mouth Disease Research Institute* [1966] 1 QB 569) the 'no social costs, no liability' logic remains. Since the distinction between these two types of zero social cost case depends on complex assessments of the relative avoidance costs of defendant and plaintiff beyond the capacity of courts, they raise the same unanswered challenge for economic theory as the positive social cost cases.

gains. Even our earlier examples of an owner's losses associated with physical damage, (i)–(iii), can now be revealed as involving very crude approximations: in personal injury cases, for example, the victim's loss of wages may be almost matched
by a gain in wages by someone, hitherto unemployed, who is engaged to fill V's
place. Similarly, if what was damaged was the victim's income-earning asset, such
as V_6's data discs, the loss of profits to that victim may be balanced by the increased
profits of her competitors. In such cases only that economic loss consequential on
the physical damage (for which the defendant is the cca) which is *not* matched by
private gains to others should be internalized – for it is only *net* social losses which
should rest on the cca. But economic analysis has so far failed to construct a legal
rule by which such a result can be achieved.

Even in the simplest physical injury cases one cannot assume that the total private
losses of victims roughly represent the net social cost of the accident. It is true that
the *repair* costs of physical damage (eg medical bills in personal injury cases) may
not be matched by private gains, but a liability rule directed *only* at such losses
would not only raise moral objections, but even from an efficiency perspective it
would be a wholly inadequate application of the theory. This is because although we
might not be able to tell in any particular case whether private losses suffered represent net social losses, we can be certain that in some cases – perhaps, for example,
where a person is permanently scarred – there are net social losses. A rule which
fails to internalize the latter guarantees substantial externalization of social costs
with subsequent distortion of the deterrence incentives.

Although economic analysts admit that 'outside relatively stylized models, the
determination of [net] social cost is beset with virtually insurmountable difficulties'[39] which are certainly beyond the court's capacity on a case-by-case basis, economic analysis fails to give us even *a rough guide* as to when to truncate liability for
pure or consequential economic loss. Faced with the obvious diversity of situations
in which such losses occur, and the evident, but idiosyncratic, ripple effect of profits
by third party 'gainers', the theory seems to collapse into paralysis. Certainly it cannot be used to rationalize important aspects of the existing Directive: according to
efficiency theory it should but does not internalize, say, the repair costs of commercial vehicles damaged by the defective brakes of another vehicle on the road; and
yet be cautious of allowing, as it does, the full recovery of the lost wages of those
personally injured. More importantly, efficiency theory fails to tell us enough about
how to handle the problem of third party gainers to guide us how to amend the
Directive to promote efficiency. In general, economic analysis of the question of
type of losses in general, and social gains in the context of economic loss in particular, is extraordinarily thin, and this strongly supports the suspicion that here is the
point at which the theory is internally most vulnerable.

(f)   What is a cost of what?: the problem of overlapping enterprises

The most well-known normative economic theories of product liability break down
when faced with the common multilateral occurrences of everyday life. An example
given earlier was the case where a bus driver carelessly brakes on a poorly banked

---

39 Rizzo 'The Economic Loss Problem: A Comment on Bishop' op cit 199 (see also 207). Bishop is
also sceptical: 'Economic Loss: Economic Theory and Emerging Doctrine' op cit 81.

road injuring a passenger who was unable in time to reach one of the few handles available in the bus. Another is that of the polluting toothpaste factory discussed in Chapter 5 (under headings 4(a) and (d)). There are two aspects to this problem. First, even under a general liability rule there may seem to be a problem in determining the criteria for selecting who the defendants should be, given that, as Coase showed, many but-for factors could be implicated in an injurious event. The technique traditionally used by the law is to ask which factors/activities/enterprises were 'causes' of the loss and to rely on causal language, as well as eliminating devices such as volenti, to take into account the complex variety of grounds on which we separate out the elements which explain the result and hence point to the enterprise(s) to which the loss should be attributed. We saw how, with a little approximation, this technique can be used for the efficiency strategy too (under heading 2, above).

But the second problem of overlapping enterprises is how to justify a *limited* rule such as the products rule which *pre-selects* certain factors and eliminates others. How can the separation out for special treatment of only those product-related factors from the complex interaction of causal factors be justified? Calabresi noted the problem,[40] but did not resolve it in his normative strategy for a special *products* rule limited to certain defendants. The Posnerian approach is similarly unable to justify a liability rule limited in this way, but Posner's approach *appears* less troublesome because of his advocacy of a negligence standard – a standard identical to that already operating generally. If negligence is accepted as the appropriate standard of liability for manufacturers, then a 'special' products rule would not, in theory, be so problematic because the plaintiff would still have as much incentive and opportunity to sue those parties not covered by it as those who were covered by the rule (product suppliers). Where product and non-product enterprises overlapped, they would face similar liabilities based on negligence. Faith would then be placed in the plaintiff's own selection of defendant(s) and the court's use of doctrinal mechanisms to produce an outcome which mimicked the protection the victim would have bargained for in the absence of transaction costs. In contrast, Calabresi was keen to deploy both prevention *and* price deterrence strategies, which suggested coverage of unforeseeable risks and full strict liability as the most efficient standard of liability. Technically the problem here of determining who was the cheapest cost avoider in the absence of transaction costs in a case of overlapping enterprises is more difficult because the range of potential defendants includes careless and careful parties alike. But it is still of the same order of magnitude and might in most cases be as manageable as in negligence. The real problem for Calabresi was that *general* strict liability is widely rejected as too oppressive on potential defendants (see Chapter 7, under headings 4 and 5, and Chapter 8, under heading 1). Yet to advocate full strict liability for only some defendants (eg product suppliers) clearly required an economic rationale for targeting them in this way and not other defendants who conducted overlapping enterprises; for example, in the bus example it is not at all clear that the cheapest cost avoider would be one of the product-related defendants. Thus for Calabresi the inability of efficiency theory to generate any justifications for a *separate* product rule is a more glaring flaw – even though it infects the Posnerian theory too.

---

40 G Calabresi *The Cost of Accidents* (New Haven, Yale University Press, 1970) 138; 'Some Thoughts on Risk Distribution and the Law of Torts' (1961) 70 Yale LJ 499, 530. Compare his call in 'Four Tests for Liability in Torts' op cit 626–7 for separating out ('disaggregating') sub-classes of cases, which runs headlong into this quagmire of overlapping activities and enterprises.

Ironically not only is efficiency theory unable to explain adequately the limitation of the special products rules to the enterprise of the manufacture and supply of new products, but also it allows us to expose the distortions in efficiency terms such a limitation is likely to produce in practice. Let us take the bus example and focus on, say, the medical bills associated with the passenger's broken leg (to avoid the social gain problem). Calabresi's efficiency theory tells us that unless the transaction costs between the passenger and the cca of such losses are low, internalization of these bills to the cca should be effected by a liability rule. But the possible ccas seem to include the local authority responsible for the banking of the road, the driver, his employer, and the designer/manufacturer of the bus. It is not self-evident that the manufacturer of the bus is the cca. Putting it another way: the loss here, like many in real life, is one which is not readily assignable a priori to some specific activity such as the production of goods. Yet a special liability rule limited, as s 402A and the Directive are, to one particular sub-class of potential cheapest cost avoiders (here suppliers of goods) may severely prejudice the issue of who is the cca (see Chapter 13, under heading 1). Even if there were no doctrinal advantages because, for example, the standard of liability was merely fault, unless it remains the case that there is a clear and efficient recourse rule, the law will seem to provide a smoother path to claim against one set of potential cheapest cost avoiders than others. What is more, the separate rule is also likely to raise consciousness among potential claimants making it more likely such 'product' defendants are sued.

This is no doubt a powerful reason why, while other targets of tort litigation such as doctors and drivers may accept and even campaign for limited no-fault non-tort regimes, product suppliers would fight such a plan limited to products. Compared to road and medical spheres, there is in the product context a very high risk of overlapping activities and that a special products regime will end up channelling a wide range of accident costs to product suppliers. This is the doctrinal equivalent of the deep pocket phenomenon. The latter manifests itself under the negligence regime when a potential plaintiff, faced with a number of negligent potential defendants, chooses to sue the one with the deepest pocket. The real or apparent advantages of suing under the special product rules will generate at least some of the same distorting effects. Whereas the EC bus passenger might formerly have sued the bus company for its driver's operation of the vehicle, he or she may well in years to come 'channel' the claim to the bus manufacturer, the final allocation of incentives being relegated to the vagaries of domestic rules of recourse between tortfeasors – a notoriously difficult area of law (see Chapter 11, under heading 8).

Efficiency theory may be able to tolerate a separate products rule in those contexts where the pool of potential cheapest cost avoiders only includes the victim and members of the chain of supply – for example, in the exploding TV (under heading 5(d), above) and 'mercury in cough syrup' (Chapter 5, under heading 4) examples – because here we can, without loss of efficiency, limit the class of potential defendants. But such contexts cannot typically be identified in advance and separated from those such as the bus example where, although the condition of a product bore a but-for relation to the loss, so too did the activities of those entirely outside the enterprise covered by the product rule. At the level of causes, the condition of the product may be judged to be only one of a number of relevant *causes*. Even where the condition of the product could be isolated from other factors and identified as the sole cause of the loss – as may be the case in the context of adverse reactions to pharmaceuticals – the economic 'theory of the second best' (see (k) below) suggests that a shift to a limited pocket of strict liability for such cases might still be an inefficient move.[41]

Efficiency theory, then, far from providing a justification for imposing separate liability on these within the chain of supply of products, as s 402A and the Directive do, provides its own positive arguments *against* treating product-associated losses as special because a substantial distortion of deterrence incentives seems guaranteed by any attempt to achieve efficiency goals by means of a liability rule limited to certain potential cheapest cost avoiders.

(g)   What is the gist constituting the necessary 'damage'? (see also Chapter 11, heading 2)

The Directive covers 'personal injuries', but at least according to current British common law this is not constituted merely by exposure to the risk of, say, cancer. 'Personal injuries' denotes at least physical *changes* in the body even if undiscoverable.[42] What this means in practice is that those who have been exposed, say, to a faulty X-ray machine have to wait until medical tests reveal the first physical evidence of radiation cancer before they can sue. They are not entitled to sue merely for the risk of physical changes such as cancer or, to put it another way, for the 'loss of a chance of avoiding cancer' even if the epidemiological data makes it more likely than not that cancer will develop, or even that it is almost certain. Nor, in the UK, can exposed people sue for their present fear of future deleterious physical changes such as cancer, nor for the present economic consequences of others' fear (eg haemophiliacs exposed to the AIDS virus in blood being sacked or refused insurance), nor for the medical surveillance costs which their own fear and reasonable caution precipitates.

The omission of such present losses from the coverage of the Directive is not a priori an error from the efficiency perspective because the efficiency rationale of liability does not dictate what people should be entitled to sue for (see under heading 6, below). It is only able to indicate that, if the efficiency goal is adopted *with respect to the relevant loss*, then in cases of high transaction costs the loss should be shifted from the initial victim by a liability rule placing it on the cheapest cost avoider. This allows us to draw interesting conclusions; for example, that viewed from the efficiency viewpoint, the Directive does not seek to generate the optimal level of mere exposure to risk of personal injury and its associated costs such as the cost of present medical surveillance; and this seems odd given that the Directive allows property damage claims, for example. On the other hand, the silence of efficiency theory on the issue of what can form the gist of a complaint under a liability rule is itself one of its most striking flaws as a general justification of liability.

(h)   Latency

There is a group of problems for the efficiency approach raised by the phenomenon of the latency of loss. One obvious problem here is that if a cosmetic, for example,

---

41 See eg J Henderson 'Extending the Boundaries of Strict Product Liability: Implications of the Theory of the Second Best' (1980) 128 U Penn LR 1036. See also J Stapleton *Disease and the Compensation Debate* (Oxford, Clarendon Press, 1987) 93.

42 Here and in following text see generally J Stapleton 'The Gist of Negligence' (1988) 104 LQR 213, 'Part 2' 389.

produces an unforeseen cancer in users 10 to 20 years after use, it may well never be identified as the source of the cancer. Even if a connection is spotted, the cosmetic may only be identifiable as one *possible* cause because the numbers of those exposed and the information about them is too limited to provide statistically significant epidemiological data. In such cases not only can the product not be shown to have been a legally relevant cause of the cancer, but the question of who is the cheapest cost avoider cannot be answered correctly. Even if the epidemiological data is sufficient to establish that 40% of later cancers in those exposed to the cosmetic were caused by it, none of the costs associated with those cosmetic-caused cancers will (under current attitudes to causation and to the issue of what can form the gist of an action) be 'internalizable', because no cancerous plaintiff will be able to prove on the balance of probability that her cancer was one caused by the cosmetic.[43] Corresponding to this under-deterrence is the over-deterrence which would occur if the data suggested that 60% were due to the cosmetic – since here *all* would be able to establish the causal nexus on the balance of probabilities.

Another problem with latency of unforeseen risks is that even if ten years after the relevant product was marketed, it can be linked to the emergence of cancers in those exposed to the product, there are obvious difficulties with the theory that imposing liability *then* will have the appropriate deterrent impact on hazards associated with that product. In a large proportion of the cases where products have caused long-latent injuries, the hazardous product model is no longer being marketed by the time defendants are held liable. Thalidomide is a good example of this. In theory, of course, premiums should have been extracted at the relevant time of risk-taking (eg the marketing of the product) to cover future losses, but the problems of forecasting the level of future liability with respect to latent risks are horrendous. The accuracy of risk evaluation in such cases of 'long-tail liability' is very poor, and despite its being in contravention of good accountancy principles, insurers rely on future increases in premiums to cover past losses.[44] Under this practice, not only will it be impossible to target the correct product so that losses caused by it are minimized (both by preventative action and price deterrence), but when liability is imposed the internalized costs will have to be accommodated in other ways, often by distorting the cost structures of current product lines. A third problem is that, even if a latent risk is known or suspected at the time of marketing, corporate managers and their insurers tend to mis-assess long-term risks because they are unable, for example, to predict the number and severity of future injuries, the percentage of victims likely to claim, and so on; they also tend to mis-assess long-term benefits, to discount too heavily the present value of future losses, and to ignore the problems facing the next generation of corporate officials.[45]

---

43 This 'indeterminate' plaintiff problem must be distinguished from the 'indeterminate defendant' problem where there is no doubt the plaintiff was injured by a particular product (such as the drug DES, diethylstilbestrol) but there is uncertainty about which DES manufacturer was involved, see Chapter 11.

44 Stapleton *Disease and the Compensation Debate*, op cit 131.

45 Estimate of the number of injuries will depend on estimates of future market success: estimates of severity may be vague because of insufficient epidemiological data; estimates of claims rates depend on assessment of the future doctrinal and socio-legal environment including, for example, the availability of Legal Aid. On corporate behaviour see W Felstiner and P Siegelman 'Neoclassical Difficulties: Tort Deterrence for Latent Injuries' (1989) 11 Law and Policy 309; J Henderson 'Product Liability and the Passage of Time: The Imprisonment of Corporate Rationality' (1983) 58 NYULR 765; S Sugarman, 'Doing Away With Tort Law' (1985) 73 Calif LR 555, 569.

There can also be distortions running the other way, that is towards over-deterrence. Especially when experiencing a period of high litigiousness, risk-averse insurers may respond to their inability to forecast accurately the rate and success rate of future claims by setting overly cautious premiums. The US experience during the sudden spurt of product litigation in the 1970s and 1980s is characterized both by under-deterrence in the years preceding the litigation boom when insurers failed to foresee the liability costs associated with the latent diseases caused by products such as asbestos, and by over-deterrence, especially of research and development, during the boom years as premiums shot up to cover the claims associated with those earlier risks.

Faced with these difficulties, the most prominent proponents of the efficiency rationale for liability, Landes and Posner, suggest that liability rules *can* be adapted to cope with the phenomenon of latency: the gist of the action would no longer be the outcome (eg the cancer) but exposure to the risk of the outcome.[46] All those who had been exposed to the risk of the deleterious outcome would be able to sue for the degree of risk of, say, future medical bills. But this is no answer to the latency problem. Firstly, there are no private or social costs involved in the *mere* exposure to the risk of future losses (as opposed to, say, present surveillance costs or anxiety costs – see above under heading (g)). To award money at this point in relation to *future* costs cuts across the theory of internalizing only net social costs. Secondly, inasmuch as economic theory seeks to rationalize the payment of compensation to plaintiffs, rather than a system of fines, by reference to its effect in ameliorating the secondary accident costs generated by the disruptive force of concentrated losses (under heading (a), above), then why should the damages associated with the social losses due to the cancer outcomes be distributed throughout the class of those merely exposed to risk? Surely only by reserving such compensation for those who actually suffer the disruptive outcome can the goal of secondary cost avoidance be achieved. Thirdly, in nearly all cases where products cause substantial latent injuries, the deleterious outome was either unforeseen at the time of exposure or poorly perceived. This means that allowing claims merely on the basis of exposure to risk would have little real-world effect because potential claimants would not know that they had been exposed to a risk, or would receive damages the quantum of which was very poorly related to what would later be realized as the true level and gravity of risk.

(i)   Insurance

Insurance is a characteristic product of an imperfect market. In the real world it perpetuates imperfection and can generate its own. Lawyer-economists such as Landes and Posner, who promote a normative theory of liability based on an efficiency strategy towards a wealth maximization goal, fail adequately to address both these aspects of insurance and, in so doing, over-estimate the accuracy of the incentives which internalization via liability can achieve.

The Chicago lawyer-economists make large assumptions about the rationality and risk neutrality of the important players in the product liability context. The follow-

---

46 W Landes and R Posner *The Economic Structure of Tort Law* (Cambridge, Harv University Press, 1987) 263 ff. Compare Calabresi's failure to reformulate the damage forming the gist of the action, n 7 above.

ing section addresses the problems inherent in such assumptions as they relate to suppliers, while in this section we concentrate on insurers. Contrary to these assumptions, individual victims threatened by product losses tend to be risk averse, especially when personal injuries are threatened. More importantly, in the real market place, business-people who are the potential defendants and insurers under s 402A and the Directive are, and admit to being, risk averse. A classic manifestation of risk averseness is insurance. In the product liability context this takes two important forms – liability insurance taken out by potential defendants and first party insurance sometimes taken out by potential victims; but the argument which follows principally uses the former type as the example.

Insurance is a reflection of imperfection. In a market of perfect knowledge and risk neutrality, an 'insurance' market would in fact be no more than a savings/loan market. This is because entrants would only join an 'insurance' pool which consisted of those facing identical risks, and this would allow claim rates and premium rates to be identical and predictable. Taking out 'insurance' here would be equivalent to paying at a steady rate towards what in the long term would be a regular, if infrequent, pay-out. It would function simply to smooth the liability loss out over time. In the absence of administrative costs, the number in the pool would be irrelevant. The deterrence incentives on the individual insured who had been held liable would be *undiluted* by his membership of the pool, the advantage of which would be simply that of a savings/loan relationship.

In a market of imperfect knowledge about the relevant risk, however, insurance actually operates as a buffer between the insured and the liability, diluting the deterrence incentives for some, while intensifying them for others. This is because, in such real markets, insurance pools consist of parties who have different risk rates. Because the pool contains parties with a range of risks, the effect is not simply to smooth the impact of a party's loss over time, but to shift pool resources from below-average risk creators to above-average risk creators. To the extent that each risk creator is charged the same premium, each experiences the same deterrent effect, even though some are responsible for more social costs than others. To the extent insurers are unable to distinguish between insureds on the basis of the different risks they present, the presence of insurance *increases* the degree of externalization. The insurance buffer *dulls* the differential impact of liability. Some activities are over-deterred, others under-deterred.

The less insurers know about the risks presented by insureds, the larger the insurance pool is likely to be because one of the ways to acquire more reliable information about the probability of the insured event is to take a large sample. Yet since collecting, analyzing and acting on claims experience with a view to altering insurance pools and premiums is difficult and expensive, there comes a point when further subdivision in reliance on such information no longer appears financially warranted to the insurer – who is guided, after all, *not* by the goal of avoidance of the loss-making event, but in terms of competition for premium payers and profit.[47] In much of the product area it seems that these forces, including the extremely cautious premium-setting practices of insurers, make further sub-categorization of insurance categories unattractive at an early stage so that product risk pools tend to remain large.

---

47 A point supported by the low interest insurers take in direct pressure on insureds to take precautions. On this and the other points in the text see Stapleton *Disease and the Compensation Debate* 128–9; Sugarman 'Doing Away With Tort Law' op cit 573 ff.

Moreover, the nature of the competition in product insurance markets tends to produce *insurance packages* where the insurer charges a single premium for liability insurance in respect of a number or all of the client's products without bothering to itemize the premium or to tell the client how it was arrived at so that the latter can see what fraction of the premium is attributable to which of its products. Yet optimal efficiency requires that, say, a vehicle manufacturer is able to gauge the future liability costs arising from each of its different models, so that it can make the relevant adjustments in its preventative effort in relation to each, and reflect residual costs in the pricing structure of each model. The costs involved in sub-categorization usually make fine-tuning of this sort uneconomic for insurers. Indeed, it seems common in some sectors for premiums to be set not according to the claims record relating to a specific product, nor even to the client's total product claims record, but according to the claims record across all the producers of a certain product.

The more pronounced these features of premium-setting are, the less do the incentives created for potential defendants by the threat of liability become like the deterrence incentives which efficiency strategy requires. They become more like incentives to take out a competitively priced insurance package; while the large size of insurance pools produces a high degree of externalization from the person identified by efficiency theory as the appropriate bearer of the relevant liability costs. It is a strong possibility, therefore, that insurance not only perpetuates that degree of over-externalization generated by our current imperfect knowledge about risk levels, medical causation, etc, but also exacerbates it. Calabresi made some attempt to accommodate the phenomenon of insurance within his normative model of liability, suggesting that the search should be for the 'feasible insurance category which can deter accident costs most cheaply (which sub-categorizes as much as possible) rather than looking for a hypothetical individual cheapest cost avoider and hoping that charging him will result in the best insurance category.'[48] But this simply describes the problem rather than tells us how a legal rule can best be designed to avoid this source of considerable externalization.

The efficiency strategy is also undermined by that other phenomenon of risk-averseness, the *pyramiding of insurance*. Not only must the risk averseness of potential cheapest cost avoiders and their consequent tendency to insure against risk be taken into account, but so must the risk averseness of others who fear they may end up bearing the loss. For example, the potential initial victim of a product risk may also take out insurance to cover the risk even though, if he or she is in the chain of sale, he or she will be paying some price increment to reflect the merchantability warranty imposed on the commercial seller. This inefficient duplication of protection may be compounded if each seller up the chain takes out insurance to cover the risk that the loss will come to rest on them because, for example, they are sued and are then unable or unwilling to sue their own supplier in turn. When risk-averse parties other than the cca insure against the loss in this way, price increments imposed down the chain to cover insurance premiums accumulate and will result, even in optimally sub-categorized risk markets, in the over-deterrence of the relevant risk associated with the product.

Conversely, the efficiency strategy can be assisted by aspects of the operation of insurance in the real world, for example when insurance provides risk-averse actors

---

48 G Calabresi 'Does the Fault System Optimally Control Primary Accident Costs?' (1968) 33 Law & Contemp Probs 429, 443–4.

with confidence to engage in activities to which liability might attach.[49] It is also assisted by the phenomenon of the 'unravelling' of insurance markets. This can occur in periods where risk-averse insurers faced with uncertainties – such as the imponderables associated with latent risks or the volatile outcome of existing legal rules, or potential changes in claims rates, success rates and legal rules – substantially raise the premiums of an insurance pool. Even though risk-averse, some pool members will regard it as no longer worthwhile to remain in the pool because they perceive their own risk as substantially lower than the pool average as reflected in the new premium level. The flight from the pool of lower risk members leads the risk-averse insurer to increase the premium for the pool yet again. This in turn can herald another cycle of flight and yet more premium increases. The pool shrinks or 'unravels' as the premium spirals, leaving those perceived as the highest risk clients to pay huge premiums or be denied coverage at all. This phenomenon is not a problem for the efficiency strategy. Indeed, it assists it because, so long as the insurer continues to offer cover to high risk parties,[50] the fact that low-risk parties have left the pool will reduce the degree of subsidization received by the former and so improve the internalization of costs to the high-risk group. Moreover, we have seen that to the extent that insurers are worse than the client at evaluating the costs and benefits of a client's risk-taking, the presence of insurance increases the level of externalization above that made inevitable by imponderables such as latent risks. Thus one might argue, as some nineteenth century proponents of workers' compensation did, that an ideal efficiency strategy would be one where the appropriate liability rule was coupled with a ban on liability insurance, forcing the cca to 'go bare' and deal with the impact of liability directly.[51] Another way of putting this is that, contrary to the popular version of 'deterrence' theory, the preferable strategy, when faced with two otherwise equally 'cheap cost avoiders', is to select as target for the loss the party which is *less* able to insure against it.

But both the unravelling of insurance and the resultant withdrawal of insurance cover for certain enterprises constitute one of the major anxieties among critics of the product regime in the US. Some of these anxieties *can* be expressed in efficiency terms. For example, self-insurance is best achieved by larger enterprises so that reduced availability of external insurance might encourage to an inefficient degree the amalgamation of enterprises for the purpose of making self-insurance viable.[52] But most of the anxiety stems from the impact on what the risk-averse enterprises *do* when faced with spiralling premiums and insurability problems. Perception of an 'insurance crisis' seems directly to result at the margin in an unwillingness to take uninsurable risks, the inhibition of research and development (R & D) and refusal to release new products. An early and classic example of this was the refusal of vaccine manufacturers to release onto the market the swine-flu vaccine necessary for a government immunization programme until they had been guaranteed adequate

---

49 G Schwartz 'The Ethics and the Economics of Tort Liability Insurance' (1990) 75 Cornell LR 313, 364.
50 M Geistfeld 'Imperfect Information, the Pricing Mechanism and Product liability' (1988) 88 Col LR 1057, 1067.
51 P Bartrip and S Burman *The Wounded Soldiers of Industry* (Oxford, Clarendon Press, 1983) 168–9. The idea met with amused contempt before the Pearson Commission: N Marsh 'The Pearson Report' (1979) 95 LQR 513, 526. See also G Schwartz 'The Ethics and the Economics of Tort Liability Insurance' (1990) 75 Cornell LR 313, 314.
52 Sugarman 'Doing Away With Tort Law' op cit 573, n 67.

cover by the government effectively assuming sole defendant status, and other examples have been described by Priest.[53] While many of these examples can be traced to specific time periods during which, for whatever reason, defendants and insurers were unusually risk-averse, there is evidence that some permanent inhibition of risk-taking occurs in response to such periodic insurance phenomena.

In a world where there is inefficient risk-taking, premium increases and this suppressing effect on R & D, etc, may be just what an efficiency strategy would aim for. So why is the inhibition of risk-taking due to the unravelling of insurance markets so unpopular especially among pro-market commentators? Firstly, there is the argument that the resultant inhibition on R & D etc is not sufficiently finely tuned and that it is not just cost-unjustified risk-taking that is being inhibited. This is really an argument based on the supposed sub-optimal level of sub-categorization possible in the relevant markets, and cannot be empirically verified. Secondly, there is the possibility that even if, say, the liability costs associated with unsupervised climbing frames for children in public parks turn out to be high, their removal by risk-averse local authorities unable to obtain insurance is distasteful because the value we put on such risk-taking is not being adequately taken into account. This argument is essentially a dual complaint: that efficiency theory cannot adequately incorporate social gains; and that some values cannot be expressed in pecuniary terms. As we see later, it is this argument on which pro-market opponents of current products rules really rely (see Chapter 9, under heading 5).

(j)   Distortion from other influences on behaviour

The efficiency strategy produced by the neo-classical Chicago school is based on modification of individuals' behaviour. But it not only tends to underplay the risk averseness of the relevant parties; it also tends to make other large assumptions about the nature of the 'rationality' by which decision makers are guided. Inasmuch as institutional behaviour is relevant, it is approached in terms of the aggregation of individuals' decisions. In contrast, institutional economists stress the institutional and group environments in which decisions are made, how institutions may not only limit but mould decisions, and the diverse human motivations which may be brought to bear on these decisions, including many which run counter to the wealth maximizing assumptions of the Chicago school of lawyer-economists. Some of these motivations are rational: it is rational, for example, to withdraw a product where, despite the manufacturer's accurate assessment that it is a cost-justified product, the bad publicity generated by unproven legal claims against the product is badly damaging the wider corporate image across a wide range of its products and activities. Similarly, in the real world the threat of product liability affects enterprises in perverse ways. Firstly, it encourages the taking out and the minimization of the costs of insurance; it does not just encourage the reduction of product losses directly. Only to the extent (limited, as we have seen) that insurance costs can be minimized by direct product loss reduction is the potential defendant motivated to take action to prevent the relevant product condition causing the loss. The more often the relevant enterprise is encouraged to insure rather than to take precautions,

---

53 See respectively R Epstein 'Product Liability: The Gathering Storm' (Sept/Oct 1977) Regulation 15; G Priest 'The Current Insurance Crisis and Modern Tort Law' (1987) 96 Yale LJ 1521.

the less efficient the system appears to be. Secondly, the threat of product liability encourages relevant parties to use their superior economic power to extract settlement agreements at levels below that warranted by the doctrinal merits of the case. Thirdly, if liability (ie insurance) costs are a negligible part of the total price of a product, and especially if demand is relatively inelastic, the potential defendant will be discouraged from taking cost-justified precautions and be encouraged to pass on all the amount to buyers in conditions where, by definition, price deterrence, which requires elasticity of demand, could not be relied on to operate well. Fourthly, the threat of liability encourages secrecy, not least among enterprises vis-à-vis their insurers, and may even provoke the rearrangement of business structure and activities in a way which restrains the generation of damaging information about product dangers. Fifthly, in a legal system where non-legal barriers inhibit claims and the 'law in books' is not reflected in the expected number of verdicts for plaintiffs, a potential defendant is rational to discount substantially the size of the liability losses it faces.

The response of relevant individuals within the organizations threatened with liability costs is also influenced by other complex factors which inhibit accurate long-term cost/benefit calculations and distort their translation into effective current management strategy. We have already touched on the psychological barriers to the accurate assessment of risks posed by the product and the risk of liability for such risks, and the tendency of individuals to pursue personal career goals and to neglect the liability problems which the organization will face after the individual has left its employ.[54] But studies have also shown that, even were such assessments to be made, organizations by their structure often inhibit the generation of *coherent* in-house safety instructions and their translation into effective shop-floor practice.[55] Moreover, the impact of these forces is erratic, sometimes encouraging greater risk-taking than is cost-justified given the state of the art; while at other times risk-averseness, perhaps coupled with organizational aversion to investment in long-term R & D,[56] produces a greater inhibition of risk-taking than is warranted.

Business people may be strongly influenced by moral constraints, self-esteem and status, the stability of long-term relationships, and the threat of bad publicity however undeserved and haphazard in its incidence. In complex modern markets commercial decision-makers are swamped not only by information relevant to liability exposure but with information relating to other concerns. Dealing with regulatory obligations, taxation planning and economic forecasting requires time and money, and full rationality with respect to all such issues may well be too expensive, giving rise to short-cuts based on 'bounded rationality' such as were described earlier. The neo-classical economics of the law and economics school fail adequately to accommodate these and other phenomena of individual and group behaviour.[57] They fail to capture well the dynamic nature of markets (the possibility, for example, that rational choices may not be stable over time), the lack of competitive pressures in

---

54 See works on corporate behaviour cited above in n 45 and discussion of 'bounded rationality' in Chapter 5, under heading 6.
55 See G Eads and P Reuter *Designing Safer Products in Corporate Responses to Product Liability Law and Regulation* (Santa Monica, Rand Corporation, 1983); Sugarman 'Doing Away With Tort Law' op cit 566–9.
56 Felstiner and Siegelman 'Neoclassical Difficulties' op cit 310.
57 See eg R Ellickson 'Bringing Culture and Human Frailty to Rational Actors: A Critique of Classical Law and Economics' (1989) 65 Chi-Kent LR 23, 25.

certain sectors, and the 'opportunism' (a lack of candour in dealings) to which the latter gives rise.

Finally, the key neo-classical idea of the price signal is flawed first by the assumption that the buyer's behaviour is informed by an awareness of which legal regime is operating (and hence whether it is necessary to pay more for a 'warranty': see Figure 5.2 and accompanying discussion), and secondly by the assumption that producers can easily reflect production costs in the relevant prices, an assumption which rarely holds true in sectors with high R & D costs, such as pharmaceuticals.

(k)   The theory of the second best

The foregoing discussion suggests that a wide margin of error infects the efficiency rationale of liability rules and that it is a theory which cannot provide a sufficiently finely tuned strategy to enable us to rank one form of liability as superior in efficiency terms to another. Economic theory itself supports this disappointing conclusion because its 'theory of the second best' states that even if the distortions produced by inadequacies in the theory are small, they can have a large impact on what strategy would be optimal from an efficiency perspective. For example, if one relaxes the initial assumption about rationality only slightly, this can threaten substantial changes to what then will constitute the point of efficient allocation of resources.[58] Furthermore, in the products field there is the intractable problem of overlapping activities and vague recourse rules through which economic incentives 'leak' in an unpredictable fashion: so intertwined are product and non-product activities, as the bus example showed, that it is simply not possible to ignore the legal regime applying to non-product fields in deciding what the product rules should be. Inefficiency in these sectors can influence what the efficient approach to the product sector would be. The attempt to rationalize the sort of fine-tuned *limited* liability rule represented by s 402A and the Directive in terms of the efficient promotion of wealth maximization, seems doomed because of this problem alone.

Summary

The incompleteness of efficiency theory and its delicacy in the face of complex real world phenomena, destroys its normative claims. *Firstly*, in regard to the boundary issue which is of almost exclusive interest to analysts, the standard of liability (see Chapter 5, under heading 3, and Figure 5.1), it is unable to rank in fine gradations the different possible liability rules in terms of their efficiency in maximizing wealth. In particular, it cannot provide the basis for preferring the standard of liability in the product liability regime recommended by the initial European reformers, the one set out in the final EC Directive or the one in s 402A over that which was already in existence or over various other reform proposals made by Calabresi and others. *Secondly*, it is unable to justify other important boundaries of limited product rules such as the requirement of commercial supply and the very limitation to products. In practice, this flaw is most obviously damaging to efficiency strategies of full

---

58 G Ackerhoff and W Dickens 'The Economic Consequences of Cognitive Dissonance' (1982) 72 Am Econ Rev 307. On this see also Felstiner and Siegelman, op cit 321, n 2 and S Williams 'Second Best: The Soft Underbelly of Deterrence Theory in Tort' (1993) 106 Harv LR 932.

strict liability because such a standard of liability seems unacceptable as a rule of general application (see Chapter 7, under headings 4 and 5 and Chapter 8, under heading 1). Although a principal ground suggested for this unacceptability – that a bald causal requirement is unworkable – does not stand up to scrutiny (see under heading 4, above), we will see in following chapters that there *are* coherent reasons for this hostility (see Chapter 7, under headings 4 and 5, and Chapter 8, under heading 1). To avoid criticism on these grounds, efficiency-minded proponents of full strict liability must limit the ambit of their proposal, for example by limiting it to product injuries, but efficiency theory is unable to explain any proposal limited in such a way.[59]

Nevertheless, efficiency theory has proved useful in other ways. It provides the salutory reminders that how we arrange things does have costs and benefits; that legal regimes in particular do have deterrent and incentive effects, however unpredictable and erratic these may be; and that changes in legal rules brought about for whatever reason will have an impact on these matters. At the crudest level, for example, it suggests that if we are at all concerned about the current level of product-related losses, we should not exempt manufacturers completely from liability, leaving potential victims to bargain for protection via contracts. The analysis of transaction costs and the limitations on bargaining show us that across a large field such protection could not be obtained, and that as a result such a shift to a regime in which neither the buyer can sue (caveat emptor) nor can anyone else (as under the privity fallacy), would be likely to increase the number of shoddy goods and hence the number of injuries caused by products. The theory may not be able to gauge accurately the *extent* of the control generated by the threat of liability, but its assertion that such economic incentives currently exercise *some* restraint on potential defendants rings true and is an important corrective to the recent enthusiasm for reliance on contract in the product as well as other fields.

6 EXTERNAL CRITICISMS OF WEALTH MAXIMIZATION

It is convenient now to note a final set of criticisms of the efficiency theory since they illuminate the basis on which the competing moral rationales of tort liability we are to discuss in Chapters 7–9 proceed. These criticisms attack not so much the internal inadequacies of the neo-classical model, such as its assumption of rationality, but its root idea that the goal towards which resources should be efficiently organized is wealth maximization. There are various levels of criticism.

(a) The value in 'process' etc

First, the 'market approach' tends to treat marketable goods and services as the only resources relevant to the allocative efficiency strategy. Value is judged by exchange

---

59 In Chapters 8 and 9 we find that a non-economic theory of liability may be able to justify a strict liability limited to those acting in the course of business but again not one with the 'supplied' 'product' boundaries of the product rule. Moreover, the problem of overlapping enterprises and the ranking of different causes of action remains problematic here (see Chapter 9, under heading 6).

value. This is what is to be maximized. But people may well value (even in the sense of being willing to pay for) other aspects of social arrangement besides goods and services. For example, the process or way in which things are done – such as consultation of affected parties or the vindication of 'having one's day in court' – may be valued in this way and should enter the efficiency calculation. If a law is valued *in itself* because it is regarded as just, one cannot merely evaluate its 'efficiency' in terms of a cost/benefit impact study limited to the exchange value of the goods and services to which it relates.[60] The benefits or value of 'just' law must somehow be evaluated and taken into account.

(b)   Wealth effects: where we go from here

Next, the way the Posner approach judges allocative efficiency is by a Kaldor-Hicks criterion which ignores wealth effects.[61] That is, the analysis proceeds as if a pound(£) is 'worth' the same to a rich person as it is to a poor person. Costs and benefits are judged not by willingness to pay but by ability to pay. Thus A and B might be equally willing to hand over their entire week's income for the resource in question, but because Posner's approach ignores interpersonal comparisons – that is, the fact that a pound has 'diminishing marginal utility' the richer a person is – their bids will not be valued equally but according to the level of weekly income. The richer person – the person with the greater initial wealth entitlement – will win in the strategy to maximize wealth. While we clearly allow some resources to be allocated according to this wealth maximization criterion of highest bidder – for example, international travel and other 'luxury' resources, such as accommodation in elite hotels – it is certainly not universally agreed that all other valued resources should be allocated in a way which merely seeks to enhance this goal of wealth maximization. Life-saving medical assistance and police protection are just two examples where this is not the case. Indeed, as the institutional economist Samuels points out, it is the very propriety of allowing existing rights and the market to govern the allocation of a resource which is the key issue in any law reform debate.[62]

The reason we may baulk at allocating certain scarce resources to the highest bidder is that in a democratic state social arrangements should, and to some extent do, vindicate other non-market values. By seizing on wealth maximization as his sole goal, Posner excludes goals such as a compensation goal to which the efficiency strategy could equally well be directed. These other goals by which the market is properly limited include the collectivist protection of the weak or injured as reflected, for example, in the way the standard of care in the tort of negligence, far from being in proportion to the value to society of the victim, tends to be higher for certain less productive but more vulnerable victims such as children, the elderly and infirm. But these goals also include the protection of individual liberty. For example, in protecting autonomy society rationally allows an individual to use his property in a non-economic way, even where another was willing and able to make better use of it. It allows passengers to doze without being condemned as

60 C Veljanovski *The New Law and Economics* (Oxford Centre for Socio-Legal Studies, 1982) 139–40.
61 See in general R Markowitz 'Legal Analysis and the Economic Analysis of Allocative Efficiency' (1980) 8 Hofstra LR 811.
62 W Samuels 'The Coase Theorem and the Study of Law and Economics' (1974) 14 Nat Res J 1, 11.

contributorily negligent even though a relatively modest effort to stay alert would reduce the probability of road accidents. There is a distinct qualitative difference between having the right to walk down streets at will ab initio, and being assigned such a right subject to a balancing of interests.[63] Indeed, at the very outset of constructing a civil liability, some theory about the appropriate trade-off point between coercion and autonomy is necessary to tell us whether we should allow the essential 'gist' of the complaint to be constituted by mere exposure to a risk of, say, physical harm, or whether the physical outcome itself should be the gist, and economic theory cannot do this for us.[64]

Here, then, is the principal danger of the wealth maximization form of economic analysis of law: while appearing 'scientific' and value-free, it in fact champions one value at the expense of all others. In short, even if we all accept the current distribution of wealth and other entitlements as just, it does not follow that we agree that *where we want to go* in terms of the allocation of resources in the future should be linked to that distribution. *Why* should wealth maximization be our sole goal? Dworkin points out that it is not obvious why a society which maximizes its financial wealth would be 'better off', 'happier' or 'more just' than one with less wealth.[65] Titmus, for example, described Britain as a better society than the US because of its greater altruism, at least as manifested by the voluntary donation of blood,[66] and the recent statutory outlawing of the market in human kidneys for transplant was widely regarded as an improvement in the UK's social arrangements.

(c) The initial distribution of entitlements: how do we decide this?

Even in a world of zero transaction costs, for every different initial distribution of wealth, there will be a different pattern of demand, a different set of prices and different allocative decisions, and so the point at which the allocation of resources is optimally efficient relative to a chosen goal (eg wealth maximization) will be different. It follows that since this 'efficient state' will be different according to the initial distribution of entitlements, 'efficiency' per se is meaningless not only without regard to a stated goal but also without specifying the initial distribution of entitlement. This means that even if we ignored other goals, a normative economic theory aimed at wealth maximization cannot *by itself* be used to justify, say, the creation of the new liability in the EC Directive. It is incomplete. It must be accompanied by, indeed preceded by, a separate theory of distributive justice which determines the initial distribution of entitlements on which the 'efficiency' strategy depends. When forced to address this problem of how initial entitlements should be distributed, Posner could only suggest the somewhat circular and, to many commentators, distasteful criterion that rights should be assigned to those who value them highest, that

---

63 Veljanovski *The New Law and Economics*, op cit 139.
64 On which see under headings 5(g) and (h), above. On the link between autonomy and the common requirement of causing harm rather than merely exposing to the risk of it, see H Hart and T Honoré *Causation in the Law*, 2nd edn (Oxford, Clarendon Press, 1985) lxxix.
65 R Dworkin 'Is Wealth a Value?' (1980) 9 J Legal Studies 191. For the debate on this point see the Symposium reported in (1980) 8 Hofstra LR.
66 R Titmus *The Gift Relationship: From Human Blood to Social Policy* (London, Allen and Unwin, 1970).

is, who are willing and able to pay most for them.[67] In the case of high transaction costs, legal intervention is warranted to achieve the risk distribution which a market in those risks would have produced given the *current* distribution of wealth. This in effect assumes the latter is just.

Thus it is only if we are willing to base our product laws on the goal of wealth maximization alone (to the exclusion of other goals such as compensation, protection of the poor etc) *and* are happy to gauge optimality in terms of the *current* distribution of wealth, that the efficiency strategy elaborated earlier will be appropriate. That is Posner's dual ethical position, but it is one European reformers seem implicitly to reject. As we will see, their initial proposals and the final Directive are more consistent with a concern to vindicate other concerns in addition to the minimization of accident losses.

(d)   Transaction costs, wealth and the impact of legal intervention

The dependency of the point of 'efficiency' or 'optimal allocation of resources' on the distribution of entitlements highlights a central problem for the wealth maximizers. This is that, in order to justify legal intervention, lawyer-economists must both assume the justice of the distribution of wealth existing at the time of the intervention and yet also be indifferent to changes in the distribution of wealth which can be caused by giving someone a legal entitlement, which is a form of wealth. But it is only in terms of a particular distribution of wealth that the allocation of resources most efficient for wealth maximization can be determined, yet in intervening to reach that goal we can alter the distribution of wealth and hence the position of the point of optimal efficiency.

Furthermore, in real markets, legal intervention can *systematically* enrich one group. For example, let us imagine (as we did in Chapter 5, under heading 5) a world where the economic and physical losses associated with the condition of a product rest on the initial victim, or in other words that the victim has no entitlement to compensation from another. Now suppose that the potential victim of a product's defect is willing to bribe the cheapest cost avoider £30 to take a precaution against the risk, and that this precaution costs £20. If there are no transaction costs the bribe will be accepted and the precaution taken. This is the 'efficient state' in Kaldor-Hicks terms and achieves the optimal allocation of resources given a goal of wealth maximization. The cca is incidentally enriched by £10. But what if transaction costs, such as the cost of communications, prevent the bribe being given, as happens, for example, with the potential bribe by a pedestrian threatened by the unsafe car? The wealth maximizers argue that a liability rule entitling the potential victim to sue the cca is called for. The incentives thus created should result in the relevant precaution being taken and the identical efficient state in terms of the allocation of resources being reached. The market should be efficiently 'mimicked'. Relative to the position before the creation of the liability rule, however, the potential victims have been enriched because they no longer have to expend the bribe in order for the

---

67   R Posner 'The Ethical and Political Basis of the Efficiency Norm in Common Law Adjudication'
(1980) 8 Hofstra LR 487. It is circular because it states that the person who is entitled to resources
will be the person already entitled to other resources, but why *was* he so already entitled? For critics
see Dworkin op cit and other contributors to the 8 Hofstra LR symposium.

precautions to be taken. Unless legal changes are random in their impact, one section of society can be systematically enriched and, as the distribution of wealth changes, the point which represents the 'efficient state' will change.

Thus we can see how the rise of the tort of negligence in cases such as *Donoghue* v *Stevenson*, entitling more potential victims of certain losses to sue others, had a considerable redistributive effect from the class of potential systematic injurers (eg business enterprises) to the class of victims. The larger the range of claims for which the plaintiff becomes entitled to sue, the greater the potential redistributional impact of the legal change. Thus, with respect to the type of loss suffered by the victim, a reform which entitles plaintiffs to sue only for personal injuries (as was the case in the Law Commissions and Pearson Commission proposals) is less redistributive than one which also covers property damage (the Directive) or even pure economic loss as well. Similarly, in terms of the standard of liability, a new right of action that covers only foreseeable cost-unjustified risks (negligence, the Directive, etc) is less redistributive than one which covers all cost-unjustified risks (the hindsight cost-benefit initial proposals of the European reformers), which in turn is less redistributive than a reform which extends to all risks, foreseeable and unforeseeable, cost-unjustified or not (eg full strict liability).

It is true that where the relevant parties are in a position to bargain (at least at low cost) the redistributive impact of legal change may be softened. In fact, in theory, in a world of *no* transaction costs, the shift from, say a caveat emptor rule to an implied warranty of merchantability may have *no* redistributive effect. This is because after the change, the seller would simply raise prices to cover the risk which the new liability entitled the buyer to force the seller to bear. Instead of falling on the buyer, the risk of, say, unforeseeable losses would fall on the seller, but that would already have been compensated for by the seller charging the buyer for it by raising prices. But in the real world, transaction costs are present. Indeed, their very existence provides the justification for legal intervention even in relation to bargaining relationships. To the extent that remaining transaction costs prevent the move from caveat emptor to the implied warranty of merchantability being exactly compensated for in price changes, such a legal change would make one side of the bargain better off and would shift the point representing the 'efficient state'.

Another illustration of the difficulty which efficiency theory has with initial wealth distribution is its attitude to the wealth implications of transaction costs. Take informational asymmetry. Information is itself a form of wealth. If a consumer through ignorance buys a sub-standard product, and the legal regime is one in which *caveat emptor*, then the producer will be enriched.[68] Therefore, any legal interven-

---

68 Such bargains and the resultant distribution of resources are efficient in the 'Pareto' sense of being the best arrangements we can have in regard to any goal without injuring someone, given the full initial entitlements of the parties and (or more accurately, *including*) their protection by or vulnerability to transaction costs such as informational asymmetries (see G Calabresi 'The Pointlessness of Pareto' (1991) 100 Yale LJ 1211.) In this sense the caveat emptor regime can be described as an efficient allocation of resources, protecting values such as the autonomy of a merchant to offer goods which he knows to be shoddy or dangerous or which carry an unforeseeable risk of these conditions, and thereby to profit by the buyer's ignorance. Of course, if we select a wealth maximization strategy, we are choosing to define our goal solely in terms of overall social financial well-being and, hence in the products context, in terms of the minimization of accident costs. In such Kaldor-Hicks' terms it may well be more efficient to impose a liability rule on the more knowledgeable party involving, say, a duty to warn, but in so doing we take the risk that the disentitling of this party will not in practice be compensated by free exchange. This could happen, for example, where the party

tion designed to make good the consumer's ignorance will systematically alter the distribution of wealth to the detriment of the producers. Of course, we may be indifferent to the fact that law reform systematically disadvantages a particular group. For example, people may have been indifferent to the increased overheads of goods suppliers after caveat emptor was replaced by the implied warranty of merchantability, and of manufacturers after *Donoghue* v *Stevenson*, not all of which overheads could be passed back to those benefiting from the legal changes.[69]

But, as we have seen, such indifference to who wins and who loses as a result of law reform is itself a value judgment. Indifference to the fate of the commercial losers created by the past evolution of modern product liability laws may have resulted from an appreciation, however crude, that the relevant legal changes seemed to help efficiently reduce accident costs, a phenomenon to which no society can be indifferent. By contrast, the fact that the standard of liability under the Directive is lower than that which wealth maximization theory seems to call for may, as we are to see in later chapters, be explicable in terms of a concern for values other than wealth maximization such as the autonomy of the consumer and the profitability of product suppliers.

But while wealth maximization theory has failed to provide a convincing justification for s 402A, the Directive and their boundaries, it is valuable in forcing the critics of wealth maximization to clarify the alternative value judgments they are making. It reveals the trade-offs inherent in legal arrangements and that pursuit of any social goal has costs and losers. In particular, it shows us that both criticism and advocacy of a particular legal regime has distributional implications. So while our detailed examination of the wealth maximization argument in the product field shows it fails as a precision instrument of law reform, it confirms its broad claim to illuminate key dimensions of that process.

---

entitled by the move is a distant bystander with no pre-existing bargaining relationship. In a limited reform – as product liability is – the change is likely systematically to enrich one class at the expense of another class.

69 Even if we are not indifferent to the potential redistributional effects of a reform of the law we might still put the reform into effect but try to reverse its redistributional effects by general taxation or welfare benefits or in some other way, see Calabresi 'The Pointlessness of Pareto' op cit 1224, n 36.

CHAPTER 7

Non-economic theories of liability

1 OVER-VIEW OF CHAPTERS 7, 8 AND 9

This and the following two chapters look in detail at whether non-economic or 'moral' theories of civil liability can provide a basis for the move within the products reforms towards a regime of stricter liability. Again there are two aspects of this enquiry: whether moral theories can be found to support a standard of liability stricter than negligence; and whether such theories can be found to justify the other boundaries of the product rules relating, for example, to the types of actionable loss, to the inclusion of only product injuries and to the coverage of only those products which have been both supplied and supplied in the course of a business. As with economic theorists, moral theorists focus virtually entirely on the 'standard of liability' issue. The examination begins with the most well-known recent defence of a general strict liability – that of Epstein. Although we will find that this theory is open to criticism, such criticism does not support the conclusion that a *limited* strict liability regime is either unworkable or incoherent with a corrective/commutative justice model of civil liability.

A critique of a more recent moral defence of limited strict liability – that of Honoré – is then used as a basis for the construction in Chapter 8 of a new theory of 'moral enterprise liability' which justifies stricter liability on profit-seeking enterprises. In assessing whether this moral theory supports the other boundaries of modern product rules, the question of which defendants are appropriately targeted is raised, and this leads to a discussion of distributive justice, autonomy, the role of insurance and the availability of exclusion clauses. Central to this discussion is the work of pro-contract writers in the 'back to contract' school, whose work has recently been highly influential in the US, particularly in the context of criticism of existing product rules. Its charges of collectivism and paternalism are analyzed before the discussion turns in Chapter 9 to consideration of original EC reform proposals for a hindsight cost/benefit rule, falling between the existing negligence regime and the full strict liability supported by Calabresi and others, and by one form of moral enterprise liability. Although no independent moral rationale was offered for this 'defect' limited regime, it will be found to be accommodatable within a modified form of moral enterprise liability. Finally, the arguments surrounding the late adoption of the development risk defence are evaluated in the light of this Part's concern with theory.

2   WEALTH MAXIMIZATION AND OTHER GOALS

It is odd that lawyer-economists devote so much energy to working out the fine detail of a wealth maximization strategy when real world distortions render such detail insupportable. It is especially surprising in the case of Calabresi, who had early on conceded the reality of *mixed* social goals in this context and that:

> since in practice we will never want pure general deterrence it is not worthwhile discussing at length which forms or methods are most likely to accomplish it.[1]

There are two points here. Firstly, wealth maximization may well support a regime of full strict liability, and we may retain a preference for this even in the face of real world distortions of the efficiency theory, but if we *combine* wealth maximization with other concerns – especially amorphous paternalistic goals or, say, concern to protect the profitability of domestic product markets (see under heading 5, below) – such a preference becomes more like guesswork than the outcome of rational analysis.

Secondly, unlike other critics of wealth maximization as a *sole* goal of liability in the products context – such as 'rights theorists' who attempt to construct theories of tort liability which are independent of, or only marginally influenced by, utility considerations – Calabresi insists that wealth maximization can be and should be combined with other social goals. This is sound: that wealth maximization *is* a relevant consideration can be shown by the fact that society regards it as 'just' to allocate some scarce resources according to ability to pay. In the product context this point can be illustrated by considering abnormally high quality products: if you want vehicle tyres which will last twice as long as average you must arrange that bargain yourself and pay for it. Neither terms implied by law nor any current or proposed tort regime will interfere to allocate this resource to you. On the other hand, in other contexts society is clearly concerned with different goals to the general exclusion of wealth maximization and the allocation of resources to the highest bidder. For example, there are some contexts in which society may embrace compensation as its only goal. One example is combat injuries to service people. Another from the product context is the special compensation provision made for victims of public vaccination programmes. Efficiency theory can here be used to rank possible social arrangements of resources to determine which best enhances the delivery of such compensation without regard to issues such as deterrence.

We have already seen (see Chapter 5, under heading 2(c)) that the goal of compensation cannot be used to justify a liability regime of limited scope such as a product regime: compensation as a goal logically leads to programmes designed to deliver financial support to victims who are beyond the limits of civil causes of action. We also saw (see Chapter 3, under heading 3) that in the 1970s interest in compensation as a goal was substantial, often mixed with a concern to retain some deterrent incentives via either a central system of fines, levies (as in the New Zealand scheme) or public regulation. Not unexpectedly, then, *both* compensatory and deterrence goals were policies explicitly cited in the relevant reform documents leading up to the Directive. Other concerns, too, were made explicit. One – the concern for the profitability of potential defendants (see Chapter 9, under heading 5) – unlike the compensation goal, recommends the narrowing of liability; but like the

---

1 G Calabresi *The Costs of Accidents* (New Haven, Yale University Press, 1970) 161.

compensation goal it provides no justification for the boundaries of the liability regime adopted.

The fact that along with the wealth maximization goal of optimal deterrence of product losses, European reformers espoused a mixture of other goals, raises the question of whether there exist *coherent* non-economic justifications for their proposals and the Directive. Despite assertions by these reformers that reform was guided by 'ideas of morality and justice as well as considerations relating to insurance, economics and administrative convenience',[2] the moral foundation for the British and EC reform proposals was never made clear. Could a consideration of the competing moral theories of civil liability provide a clear basis for reform and for preferring one reform option over another? This may be quite important in practice: it may be that product liability reform is better justified, understood and interpreted by courts, not in efficiency or pro-market terms, but on ethical grounds which do not rely on social consequences for their force. What do such non-economic, non-consequentialist theories of justice suggest should be the entitlements in this field? From the following investigation of the internal problems of some of the major theories, an important general conclusion about current theory will emerge: that, although unitary theories of responsibility are now fashionable, they will always fail adequately to provide a rationale for rules which are both limited (for example, a rule limited to products) and multi-layered (for example, including, as the Directive does, fault, strict liability and vicarious liability). Finally, we will see that a non-unitary theory *can* be found which provides a much stronger support for stricter liability, even if it does not satisfactorily justify a reform *limited* to products.

3   A LIBERTARIAN'S ARGUMENT FOR STRICT LIABILITY

Economic theories of law ignore the blameworthiness of what the defendant has done and do not link liability to any concept of moral responsibility. To many people this seems unjust. Within a civil liability system the fact that the individual defendant pays exactly what the individual plaintiff receives seems to call for a rationale based, at least in part, on the individuals' relationships to one another rather than being explained on the basis merely of promoting desirable wider social consequences. In other words, the fact that the plaintiff receives exactly what the defendant is required to pay adds weight and form to those rationales for liability which can be expressed in terms of why it is just that *this* defendant is called upon to make good or 'correct' the complaint of *this* plaintiff. In the counter-attack to the law and economics movement, considerable energy has been devoted in North America to finding a unified theory of 'corrective' justice relevant to tort law, and for which products cases usually act as a paradigm as they do for economic theories. The principal focus of these theories is also the standard of liability, and since one of the key issues in the products reform debate was whether to adopt a form of strict liability, the best starting point here is to look for a moral argument that justifies such a liability. The threshold problem here is that, at first sight, it is not obvious what ethical reasons there could be for imposing strict liability on a defendant in circumstances where a reasonable person acting reasonably would have done the same thing.

2 Law Coms para 21.

The libertarian, Richard Epstein,[3] tried to provide these reasons and his defence of a general form of full strict liability has probably been the most influential theory of general strict liability in the 1970s and 1980s. According to Epstein, the central concerns of tort law should not be efficiency and wealth maximization – since, he argues, considerations of social utility represent invasions of individual autonomy in the name of the public good. Rather the focus of tort law should be the moral concept of liberty from interference and the correction of such interferences. Epstein argues that the sanctity of the person and her property require that the party who caused the loss flowing from invasion of those interests should pay compensation regardless of whether that party was at fault in causing the loss, ie that 'causing harm' should be a necessary and *sufficient* condition of tort liability. In arriving at this position, Epstein was strongly influenced by Hart and Honoré's elegant demonstration that common-sense notions of causation as reflected in the ordinary use of causal language were more focused than the mere relationship of sine qua non, and that the elevation of a 'but-for' factor to the status of a 'cause' need not depend on policy choices but be determined by independent factors such as the abnormality of the but-for factor. Epstein, however, elevated this insight into a theory of *legal* responsibility: if it can be said that X caused Y's loss, X should be legally obliged to compensate Y.

(a)   Epstein's idea of cause and its flaws

Central to Epstein's theory is the concept of causation. Following Hart and Honoré,[4] he correctly rejects the idea of the 'causal minimalists' that the but-for requirement exhausts neutral causal principles. As we have seen, the simplest example can be used to show that while the but-for characteristic is (nearly always) a necessary requirement before a factor is identified as a cause, it is not a sufficient one (see Chapter 6, under heading 2). No matter what the variation in ordinary usage of causal language may be in some contexts, no-one seeking an explanation of the event and using ordinary common usage would say that the existence of the Thalidomide children was a 'cause' of their injury, even though it clearly bore a but-for relationship to it. Nor in reaching this conclusion do we need to resort to policy considerations and choices hinging on theories of responsibility. This suggests that there is reason to believe that embedded in the ordinary use of causal language are non-controversial, non-normative grounds – *albeit not necessarily the only grounds* – for rejecting as 'causes' certain but-for factors. It is not, therefore, an adequate criticism of a unitary general theory of liability hinging on the causal requirement that it fails to perform such a necessary filtering function. Nonetheless, the Epstein theory has flaws. The first relates to the way in which he goes on to elaborate the causal doctrine. He does this by means of four causal paradigms of the proposition 'A caused B harm', based on the notions of force, fright, compulsion and the creation of dangerous conditions. Epstein fails to explain why he departs from the Hart and Honoré

---

3 See principally R Epstein 'A Theory of Strict Liability' (1973) 2 J Legal Studies 151. G Fletcher refrained from expounding his strict liability theory of non-reciprocal rights in the products context because, it seems, he mistakenly saw that as a context of consensual dealings: 'Fairness and Utility in Tort Theory' (1972) 85 Harv LR 537, 544, n 24.

4 H Hart and T Honoré *Causation in the Law*, 2nd edn (Oxford, Clarendon Press, 1985) lxxiii.

approach, or of what use his paradigms are, given that he concedes that they are not exhaustive of the causation concept derived from ordinary language.[5] The suspicion arises that when faced with the inevitable 'softness' and the 'indeterminacy' of the outcomes of Hart and Honoré's causal analysis in certain cases, Epstein retreats behind the apparently more mechanical and hard-edged certainty of particular and easy examples of causal relationship. In finding this simplified and simplistic causal analysis attractive he is not alone, but it left him open to the fatal charge of incompleteness and of dodging the real problems.

The paradigms focus on the easy cases of affirmative acts by defendants such as 'A hits B'. Indeed, at one point Epstein refers to the 'act requirement in the law of tort',[6] a wholly misleading over-view of the law of tort which in fact covers certain omissions as well as certain acts. Even when analyzing omissions Epstein focuses on the easy case of a stranger's failure to rescue which is not covered by his paradigms and for which he says liability is not appropriate. Thus, the chosen causal paradigms neatly protect the defendant's sphere of liberty. But this neatness depends on ignoring hard cases, in particular those cases where an omission is regarded in ordinary language as a 'cause' of an outcome because of the context in which the outcome occurs. Earlier (see Chapter 6, under heading 2(b)) we saw that an infinite number of omissions could be stated which would satisfy the 'but-for' requirement in relation to an outcome. Whether such an omission would be identified as a 'cause' of the event depended on the background against which the enquiry was made. The relevant background may consist merely of neutral scientific knowledge (eg that rot weakens trees), or neutral expectations of consistency of behaviour based on past observation (eg that a neighbour will continue to water plants), or expectations of behaviour based on moral values or notions of fairness, or on legal rules. 'Cause' is neither *always* neutral and non-evaluative nor *always* a morally infected concept. In addition, the outcome of causal determinations can change *over time* as changes occur in scientific knowledge, in behaviour, in moral values and in legal rules.

By failing adequately to acknowledge the subtle and powerful influence context can have on causal determinations, how changes in that background context can alter those determinations over time, and how they may be a matter of opinion, Epstein propounds an approach to causation which is easy to attack for its crudeness and gaps. Two examples, vital in the product context, are enough to illustrate this. First: defective design. We will see in Chapter 10 that in many cases in which the design of a product bears a but-for relation to the plaintiff's injury, it can uncontroversially be said that the design is also a 'cause' of the injury; this is true, for example, of a product which fails to perform a function all agree it should perform: a television with no sound or which explodes when it is turned on; a chair whose design cannot withstand the weight of a very light person. It is no surprise to find that Epstein adverts to easy cases such as these and is able to demonstrate that his paradigms, specifically the fourth, encompass them. In discussing the fourth paradigm – the creation of a dangerous condition that results in harm to either person or property – he says that it is possible to divide instances of dangerous conditions into

5 R Epstein 'Defences and Subsequent Pleas in a System of Strict Liability' (1974) 3 J Legal Studies 165, 168, n 10; on which see Hart and Honoré, op cit lxxiv, lxxvi.
6 R Epstein 'A Theory of Strict Liability' (1973) 2 J Legal Studies 151, 194. E Weinrib makes the same wrong assumption about 'the requirement of an act': 'Understanding Tort Law' (1989) 23 Val UL Rev 485, 516.

three classes: creation of things inherently dangerous; placing a thing not dangerous in itself in a dangerous position; creation of a product or other thing dangerous because 'defective', a term he relates to a 'condition that causes harm when subject to the stress that it was designed to receive when used in its intended manner.'[7] But this ignores the fact that most design disputes relate to the questions of what stress a product was designed to withstand and what *was* the 'intended manner' of its use. How crash-worthy should a car be? How much side or rear impact should it be able to withstand? When does its failure to withstand such stress elevate the car design from a mere but-for factor of the collision injuries to one of their causes? Causal paradigms like Epstein's, which do not even purport to provide answers to such hard cases, cannot provide the general theory of liability Epstein asserts that they do.

The second example from the product field is similar. Epstein's theory fails to accommodate the phenomenon that in ordinary speech it is possible for us to say that a product's condition was a 'cause' of an injury suffered as a result of its *misuse*. We saw earlier in one of the examples in Chapter 6, under heading 2 that not fitting child-proof lids on medicines may well, *in the appropriate context*, be regarded as one of the causes of a child's injury consequent on ingestion of the medicine. Moreover, as we saw, this does not necessarily import a moral judgment about the omission. It is simply that one reason we may perceive a causal connection between conduct and injury is that we have learnt that if D acts in a certain way, it will prevent an opportunity for misuse by another. Such expectations that precautions against misuse will be taken can and do develop, yet Epstein's theory fails to acknowledge this.

In short, by defining his paradigms to exclude them, Epstein avoided those contexts in which expectations of behaviour derived from and changing with the social context determine causal judgments. This laid him open to the charge that he had inverted the relationship between cause and responsibility because, in fact, causation is ascribed on the basis of moral responsibility, at least on some occasions.[8] Epstein was forced to retreat. By 1979 he was conceding that he could only continue to neglect the importance and ambiguity of context if he narrowed the initial basic intuition derived from causal language against causing harm 'into the more limited prohibition against the use of force' between strangers.[9] He was forced, in other words, to abandon his key reliance on causal language and admit that his paradigms were not a comprehensive set of rules on which a principle of causal liability could rest.

(b)   The workability of a causal criterion

Epstein's failure is important because it raises the question of whether an adequate, sufficiently wide theory of causation *could* be found. Epstein's critics had concluded that the concept of cause is an unsuitable one for assigning liability. By emphasising the problem cases Epstein evades, and the often indeterminate answers ordinary language may give to the causal question, they allege that a full strict liability

---

7 R Epstein 'A Theory of Strict Liability' (1973) 2 J Legal Studies 151, 177–8.
8 J Borgo 'Causal Paradigms in Tort Law' (1979) 8 J Legal Studies 419.
9 R Epstein 'Causation and Corrective Justice: A Reply to Two Critics' (1979) 8 J Legal Studies 477, 481.

regime is *unworkable*. Yet earlier we noted that such claims of unworkability were not convincing (Chapter 6, under heading 4), and since a moral defence to the move towards stricter liability for products requires at the least such workability, it is important to examine this charge now in more detail.

The argument from indeterminacy is both stronger and weaker than critics appreciate. It is stronger because critics fail to expose the elements of opinion in many, perhaps all, causal determinations and the consequently inevitable disagreements over whether a particular factor should be regarded as a cause or not. So tempting is the idea of causation being a scientifically neutral concept that it is difficult – even for those who appreciate its evaluative aspects – to accommodate the fact that people can differ widely in their evaluations. Take, for example, the attitude of Borgo in analyzing Epstein's example of Y suffering fright as a result of a distant person X raising his hand to mop his brow.[10] The problem here for Epstein is that even if ordinary people would unanimously say X 'caused' the fright, making X liable seems morally distasteful. Borgo highlights this dilemma for Epstein, but resolves the issue simply by asserting that X would not be said to be a cause, and asserting that Y's susceptibility was the cause as if this was self-evident. But surely whether it is appropriate to use the term 'cause' here to describe X's act is a matter of opinion. Indeed, it may well be an issue about which the same person's opinion may differ according to how the issue is presented. Thus a juror may well say 'yes' to the question 'Was X a cause of the fright?', but 'no' to the question 'Given the plaintiff's abnormal susceptibility, was X a cause of the fright?' Even if only the second question is put, people may still disagree on whether it is appropriate to describe X's conduct as a 'cause'. The central ambiguity in relying on the ordinary use of language here is that the notion of 'cause' is dependent not only on the external context but also on the observer's subjective application of the idea to it: we simply do not always agree on the application of the causal idea to a particular set of facts.

The argument from indeterminacy is also weaker than at first appears. Let us abandon for the moment Epstein's causal paradigms and imagine a rule based simply on a requirement that the defendant's conduct be a 'cause' of the plaintiff's injury. It is true that ordinary use of causal terms can be indeterminate. In showing that causal usage was focused more narrowly than 'but-for' factors, Hart and Honoré showed that some reasons for this selection *were* free of policy or value choices. On the other hand, as we saw in some of the examples in Chapter 6, under heading 2, some other grounds for the elevation of but-for factors to the status of a cause were not so neutral but were influenced by expectations drawn from past behaviour, morality and legal rules. The highly evaluative nature of some of these considerations drawn from the background context produces 'softness' or indeterminacy in the answer to the question 'Did X cause Y?' But why is this indeterminacy fatal to the workability of a strict liability regime hinging on a causation requirement? Why is the impossibility of eliminating *all* evaluative issues from causal usage so powerful an argument? Nearly all civil liabilities are 'flawed' by the 'soft-centre' of a causal requirement. A fault-based rule such as negligence also incorporates a causal element, and it is not immediately obvious how the indeterminacy generated by the fluidity of causal determinations is avoided or reduced by the presence of an extra requirement such as carelessness (see also under heading 4(c), below). In negligence might not added requirements, such as the 'duty' concept

10 Borgo, op cit 442.

(which is often imposed restrictively in just those cases where the indeterminacy of causation is a problem, such as omissions to control a third party) merely serve to mask this indeterminacy by reducing the class of potential defendants with regard to whom the causal enquiry need be made?[11]

Some commentators do reserve their complaints about the workability of causation as a criterion of liability for *general* theories of strict liability such as Epstein originally claimed his was. Thus Perry says:

> It should be emphasised that the conclusion applies only to a *general* standard of strict liability. The coherence of what might be called localized standards in which liability can only be said to be 'strict' relative to certain specified preconditions having been met, for example the defendant's having manufactured a defective product, is not called into question.[12]

This is a revealing concession. Does it mean that if a cause-based regime was limited in its scope – for example, to certain types of loss, such as personal injuries, caused by certain defendants, such as pharmaceutical firms – it would be as workable and manageable as negligence, with its filters relating to type of loss, duty, and so on? If so, the indeterminacy criticism of the *causal* requirement in a strict liability regime collapses. In short, the indeterminacy objection does not show that fault regimes are necessarily workable and that causally-based strict liabilities are not. Rather it shows that *limited* rules – such as negligence or the strict implied warranty of merchantability or the full strict liability imposed on operators of activities dangerous to the environment by the 1992 Council of Europe's Convention on Waste Liability – work best because they apply only to a limited class of defendants. This should lead to the conclusion that in choosing between, say, a rule that drug manufacturers be liable for drug-related risks only if such risks were reasonably foreseeable, and a rule that they be liable whether or not the risk was foreseeable, we cannot dismiss the latter simply by asserting that it is less workable because it hinges on indeterminate causation. A reason must still, of course, be found for limiting the class of defendants in the first place.

(c)   The need for an antecedent independent theory of 'rights'

The central flaw in Epstein's strict liability theory was the initial absence of a theory of *why* causing harm should result in compensation, and the inadequacy of the reasons he later produced to fill this gap. To say, as Epstein did initially, that causing harm *should* result in compensation is simply an assertion that this is the appropriate limit of liberty. It gives no independent theory of rights, specifically of why rights should be limited in this way. Indeed, just as efficiency theory is flawed because it

---

11 Why does particularization of defendants need to be done by the negligence devices of duty and fault to be respectable? Might some other requirement under a *limited* strict liability serve the same restraining function? There is an associated complaint that a general strict liability based on cause would be unable to rank or apportion in cases where many factors are identified as causes. (See, Borgo op cit 450 and the attempt to do so by M Rizzo and F Arnold 'Causal Apportionment in the Law of Torts: An Economics Theory' (1980) 80 Columb LR 1399.) But this problem also has a parallel in fault systems, where apportionment based on relative blameworthiness often seems, at least in practice, as indeterminate as pure causal apportionment based on relative causal 'importance' would be.

12 S Perry 'The Impossibility of General Strict Liability' (1988) 1 Can JL Juris 147, 158.

fails to accommodate the social value attached to being free to act without penalty even if the conduct is inefficient and causes loss to others (see Chapter 6, under heading 6(ii)), so too Epstein's libertarianism is one-sided because it is overly concerned with the right of victims to be free of injury at the expense of the freedom of action of injurers who, it *might* be thought, deserve greater *exemption* than he allows from the obligation to pay compensation for harm produced as a by-product of the exercise of their freedom. Eminent critics noted that merely couching his later theory in the terminology of 'rights' or 'corrective justice' did not generate the necessary independent theory of rights. While the Aristotelian idea of 'corrective justice' is that 'wrongs' caused by A to B should be corrected (for example, by the payment of money compensation), it does not provide a justification for saying that all physical harms caused to the person or property of B are such 'wrongs'. It does not exclude, for example, the possibility that the social value of A's conduct may be regarded as a factor which prevents the causing of the injury from being regarded as a 'wrong'.

It is important to understand how Epstein was led astray by his incomplete reading of Hart and Honoré. It was incomplete in two principal ways. For a general theory of strict liability based on causation, Epstein had to maintain that causation was a *necessary* condition of liability. While Hart and Honoré showed that this was generally true, they were sensitive to those cases of tort liability such as vicarious liability which were not based on causation of loss.[13] They showed, in other words, that not all moral concerns reflected in tort law are embedded in common-sense notions of cause. This will prove highly relevant to the search for a rationale for the specific rules of the Directive which includes analogues of vicarious liability.

Epstein also had to argue that causation was a *sufficient* basis of liability. Now it is true that Hart and Honoré used examples similar to my one of the Thalidomide children's presence in the womb to show that only certain 'but-for' factors are isolated by ordinary usage as 'causes'. They eloquently showed that this selection process *could* on occasion be free of value-choices or 'policy', as the Thalidomide example confirms. However, their purpose was not to *advocate* a liability regime based merely on causation, but to refute the causal 'minimalists' who regarded the 'but-for' step as the only value-free step in the causal analysis. Epstein, however, seems to have extracted from Hart and Honoré's proposition that *sometimes* we can determine causation issues without appeal to policy choices or separate contingent moral values, the proposition that there are embedded in the ordinary usage of causal language *only* such neutral policy-free considerations: that causal judgments were always free of policy considerations. The paradigms are constructed in a way to highlight such cases. Yet, as we have seen (see Chapter 6, under heading 2), sometimes the reason we elevate a but-for factor to a 'cause' is because of our expectations arising from past behaviour, moral expectations or legal duties. Once it is conceded that the ordinary usage of causal language can sometimes be dependent on evaluations drawn from, and dependent on, the changing social context, the argument that it reflects some *independent* unitary principle of responsibility collapses. Just as there is no reason to suppose that *all* relevant moral concerns are embedded in ordinary causal usage, nor is there reason to suppose that all causal usage rests on some single principle of responsibility.

---

13 Hart and Honoré op cit lxxvii (unless seen in an attenuated sense, see Chapter 8, under heading 1(b)(i)).

(d)   Boundaries and the complexity of 'rights'

Despite its rhetoric, Epstein's theory never was in fact a general theory of strict liability. Even in the early writings it is clear that Epstein did not envisage all harms A
caused B giving rise to a right to compensation. Quite apart from an elaborate theory
of defences, it was clear, for example, that Epstein was only focusing on the easy
cases of *physical* injury to the person or property of B. Yet he gave no explanation
for this limitation on his theory and its attendant set of 'rights'. When later pressed
to enunciate his theory of rights,[14] Epstein's fierce belief in freedom of contract and
the importance of markets led him first to curtail, in terms of types of compensatable
harm, the spheres his theory was appropriate to, and then to lose faith in the very
strictness of the standard which had formed the core of his theory.

To elaborate on the types of harm issue: a key problem for Epstein's theory, as it
is for other general theorists of tort, is that without qualification this would apply to
the economic harm a more efficient business (A) causes competitors (B). Yet the
very profitability of free markets depends on the absence of any obligation to compensate in such cases. Without reaching outside his theory Epstein was unable to
explain the difference he was implicitly drawing between physical aggression and
economic aggression. Nor could he retreat behind a bright line rule such as 'no
recovery for economic loss in tort' because – given his market preferences – he
maintained that the right to enter into a contract 'is a property right just like the right
to be free of the invasion of harms from others' and should be protected by tort.[15]

Epstein eventually conceded that to differentiate economic aggression he had to
build into his theory of rights limitations resting on consequentialist arguments
about impact on the market.[16] But once Epstein was willing to fine-tune his theory in
regard to the types of injury according to utilitarian considerations derived from the
principles perceived as inherent in a free market system, why could not other economic principles – say, of efficiency and wealth maximization – be admitted to
restrain or qualify the standard of behaviour applied to the defendant?

Moreover, Epstein could not escape the problem by resort to the Coasian line of
argument that freedom of contract could be vindicated by allowing parties to contract around an initial set of entitlements based on a strict liability. Posner[17] used the
following powerful example to show why this is so: suppose that the application of
strict liability to road accidents increased the costs of driving; but suppose too that,
but for transaction costs, drivers would prefer to form bargains with each other
whereby compensation would only be payable in cases of fault. Since, because of
the transaction costs, such contracts will not be formed, what is objectionable about
tort itself arranging for that preferred risk-distribution? What is wrong in using tort
to try to 'mimic' these bargains? Surely in autonomy terms such an arrangement is
actually preferable to the imposition of an arrangement (strict liability) which drivers

---

14 Critics included J Coleman 'Moral Theories of Torts: Their Scope and Limits: Part 1' (1982) 1 Law
& Phil 371, 379–380 and 'Property, Wrongfulness and the Duty to Compensate' (1987) 63 Chi-Kent
LR 451, 453–4; R Posner 'The Concept of Corrective Justice in Recent Theories of Tort Law'
(1981) 10 J Legal Studies 187. More recently see N Simmonds 'Epstein's Theory of Strict Tort Liability' (1992) Camb LJ 113.

15 R Epstein 'Causation and Corrective Justice: A Reply to Two Critics' (1979) 8 J Legal Studies 477,
479, n 9.

16 R Epstein 'Causation in Context: An Afterword' (1987) 63 Chi-Kent LR 653, 654–6.

17 R Posner 'Epstein's Tort Theory: A Critique' (1979) 8 J Legal Studies 457, 463.

do not want and which they cannot bargain around. To impose strict liability in such cases would be to reduce freedom by pre-judging preferences. In this example, a principle of negligence better vindicates principles of liberty and choice, and Epstein's application of these to contractual relationships led him to a strong, non-interventionist, sanctity of contract position. Even if we could deduce from causal usage ideas about the prima facie boundaries on autonomy, people may freely choose different boundaries. Once Epstein had conceded that toleration of invasions of the person or property of another may better vindicate autonomy, he was led inexorably by his pro-market ideas towards an agnostic approach to liability rules in tort, a heavy reliance on contract and exemption clauses, and a deepening neglect of the dilemma of bystander injuries for which the existence and form of tort protection is vital. He now attacks others for attempting, as he had earlier, to argue on formal grounds in favour of one general principle of liability, and resorts inter alia to an incentive analysis in evaluating the choice between negligence and a strict liability.[18]

4   A CORRECTIVE JUSTICE ARGUMENT FOR NEGLIGENCE

If the nature of Epstein's defeat *had* supported the contention that general strict liability over a broad area would be somehow unworkable or indefinable, it would clearly have major significance for the search for a theoretical foundation for stricter product liability. But it does not. It does highlight that a *completely* unbounded strict liability has practical problems – not least the possibly multiple 'causes' of a single car accident – and conflicts with fundamental values of modern Western societies, such as that of a competitive market (see also under heading 5, below, and Chapter 8, under heading 1). But just because causation per se does not seem acceptable as the sole principle of responsibility, this does not mean it is impossible to imagine and impracticable to operate a *limited* causally-based strict liability regime, the other boundaries of which are based on some coherent moral principle. As we will see, there may well be a reason why, in certain limited sectors a strict liability idea of, say, 'paying one's way' is morally sound (see Chapter 8).

Certainly the most glaring gap in Epstein's theory – its inability to explain which types of loss should not be subject to the liability and why – should alert us to a common flaw in general theories of civil liability. At present these tend to focus primarily on the defendant's standard of behaviour rather than other profound concerns such as the forms of loss which are actionable, and therefore such theories will be unable to capture the diversity of societal values which are, or should be, reflected in tort rules. Specifically, the nature of Epstein's defeat should lead to greater attention by theorists to understanding and integrating into their theory the remaining principal boundaries of civil liabilities, both common law and statutory. The moral values reflected therein are no less important than those reflected in the causal requirement and in the issue of whether or not the defendant is held liable for unforeseeable losses.

So far theorists have not given the necessary attention to the boundaries of civil liability. The occasional superficial attempt has been made to tackle the separate

18 R Epstein 'Causation in Context: An Afterword' (1987) 63 Chi-Kent LR 653, 657, 661. On Epstein's later writings see below Chapter 8, under heading 5.

rules of tort. Jules Coleman, for example, attempted to separate out product liability and argue that it – unlike other areas of tort – is not incompatible with corrective justice, but his analysis was built on crude assumptions about the alleged quasi-contractual basis of products relationships which are simply untenable[19] – bystanders being central to the phenomenon theory is called upon to address here. Much more commonly, modern moral theorists continue to produce theories of justice to underpin tort law which are too general. Typical of these is the negligence theory of Weinrib, which, because it provides a provocative defence of the old regime, provides the best foil in this discussion of possible justifications to a move to stricter product liability.[20] Weinrib's idea is, like Epstein's, seductively simple, albeit considerably more mystical: that private law is to be understood as an 'ordering that makes explicit the immanent rationality of the transactions it governs',[21] that the transactions relevant to private litigation are bilateral, and that the relevant rationality is what Aristotle called 'corrective justice'. Specifically this leads to assertions that inherent in this principle of corrective justice is a substantive requirement that tort liability be based on negligence.

Before looking at the theory in detail, it is useful to say a few words about corrective justice. Aristotle divided problems of justice into problems of *distributive* justice – that is, problems relating to the allocation of divisible common stock – and problems of *corrective* justice – that is, 'the justice that rectifies or remedies inequalities which arise in dealings between individuals ... either voluntary (dealings) as in sale ... or involuntary as where one man 'deals with' another by ... defaming him'.[22] Often corrective justice is expressed in terms of the correction of *wrongs*, a mechanism by which a prior distribution of rights is protected from disturbance; and the conventional view is therefore that 'corrective justice' depends on a prior external determination of what is a 'wrong' or, in the law of torts, a 'tort'.[23] The problem with this Aristotelian division which is relevant here, is that 'corrective justice' may not comfortably capture all notions of justice which are not distributive. Take the tort of trespass to goods. Distributive justice supports my ownership of goods, but when X commits trespass to them, my claim may not be easily expressed in terms of *corrective* justice, since there is no obvious inequality after the goods' return. This means that for torts actionable per se, that is without proof of damage (eg defamation in the UK), a strict narrow view of corrective justice turning on

19 J Coleman *Risks and Wrongs* (Cambridge, Cambridge University Press, 1992) 419, 428.
20 Even though he inexplicably asserts that American product liability is solely instrumentalist (how does he know?) and therefore outside his Kantian model: E Weinrib *The Morality of Tort Law* (Address to the Tort Law Section, Association of American Law Schools Annual Meeting, Miami Beach, Fla, 9 Jan 1988). On the same basic theory see E Weinrib 'The Special Morality of Tort' (1989) 34 McGill LJ 403; 'Understanding Tort Law' (1989) 23 Val ULR 485. Compare the strict liability theory of V Palmer equally marred by its unsatisfactory treatment of boundaries: 'A General Theory of the Inner Structure of Strict Liability: Common Law, Civil Law and Comparative Law' (1988) 62 Tul LR 1303.
21 E Weinrib 'The Insurance Justification and Private Law' (1985) 14 J Legal Studies 681, 686. Note this ignores (1) the argument that distributive and corrective justice are not fundamentally different concepts of justice, merely different perspectives (see J Finnis *Natural Law and Rights* (Oxford, Clarendon Press, 1980) 179), (2) that corrective justice rationales can link many defendants to one plaintiff.
22 Finnis, op cit 178.
23 J Lucas *On Justice* (Oxford, Clarendon Press, 1980) 102; Finnis, op cit 178–9. The content of the 'economic efficiency' strategy depends similarly on a prior definition of starting points and goals, see Chapter 6, under heading 6(c).

correction may prove inadequate. (There may also be awkwardness in accommodating strict liabilities such as defamation, trespass and conversion within a notion of 'wrongs'.) As John Finnis notes, it was to fill this sort of gap that Thomas Aquinas coined the wider term of 'commutative justice', which was not limited to the idea of 'correction' and which dealt, quite apart from the issue of distributive justice, with 'what dealings are proper between persons'.[24] As we will see, one of the unsatisfying aspects of Weinrib's theory is that he fails adequately to consider the possibility that even if a tort rule, in particular a strict liability rule, cannot comfortably be accommodated within narrow versions of 'corrective justice' and 'wrongs', it may yet be supported by a version of commutative justice.

(a) Weinrib's theory

Weinrib starts by asserting that tort law is a mode of legal ordering which possesses two distinctive, general, pervasive and indispensable characteristics.[25] The first is the bipolar remedial procedure that links the plaintiff and defendant: the plaintiff sues the defendant and, if successful, it is the defendant who pays and the plaintiff receives exactly what the defendant pays. The second is causation: Weinrib asserts that 'liability in tort law depends on the defendant's having inflicted harm on the plaintiff',[26] which the damages are to repair. (Oddly, given his later conclusion that strict liability is disqualified as a tort standard, Weinrib states that since strict liability and fault are competing regimes for tort law, the underlying issue of the standard of the defendant's conduct is not such a key characteristic of tort law.)

Even apart from Weinrib's erroneous simplification of the phenomenon of tort liability by seeming to deny that it embraces liability for omissions, this statement is very odd. Only in some torts is harm necessary. A number of torts are actionable per se. In the UK, defamation is an example: the plaintiff need not prove any injury to reputation in order to succeed, nor is affirmative proof that no injury was done a defence. It is simply not accurate to say that 'a doing that results in no suffering ... (falls) beyond the concern of tort law'.[27] Similarly, vicarious liability is a well settled feature of tort law, yet it is a liability imposed on the employer in the absence of causal connection between the conduct of the employer and the plaintiff's loss (see Chapter 8, under heading 1(b)(i)).

Having ignored these and other inconvenient aspects of tort law, Weinrib goes on to build from his two distinctive features a unified 'internal ordering' of tort law that he alleges explains why, for example, the plaintiff receives exactly what the defendant pays. This is certainly a characteristic of the civil remedy of damages which instrumentalists find difficult to justify – after all, a rule aimed at the goal of compensation cannot explain why the defendant should pay, and a deterrence-justified rule cannot, as we have seen (see Chapter 6, under heading 5(a)), easily explain why the plaintiff should receive. It is also a problem for moralists who focus solely on the defendant's conduct as the potential 'wrong', relative to which the plaintiff and the

24 Finnis, op cit 179.
25 Weinrib 'Understanding Tort Law', op cit 493.
26 Weinrib 'Understanding Tort Law', op cit 494; 'Causation and Wrongdoing' (1987) 63 Chi-Kent LR 407, 415; 'The Special Morality of Tort Law', op cit 406. On omissions see 'Understanding Tort Law', op cit 516.
27 Weinrib 'Understanding Tort Law', op cit 512.

occurrence of damage to her, seem irrelevant. Weinrib correctly identifies this error of failing to recognize the composite nature of tort 'wrongs': the 'wrong' constituted by, say, the tort of negligence is an amalgam of factors, only one of which is the defendant's carelessness. Carelessness is sufficient to make the defendant's conduct wrongful, but not sufficient to constitute the *wrong* of the tort of negligence. The tort is multi-dimensional. What Weinrib fails himself to see is that defendant careless-ness and plaintiff damage are not the only requirements of the tort of negligence. Nor does he appreciate adequately that other tortious wrongs such as defamation and nui-sance are constituted by the fusion of *other* requirements: sometimes requiring defendant wrongdoing in the form of fault (nuisance), sometimes not (defamation); sometimes requiring proof of actual damage (*Rylands* v *Fletcher*), sometimes not (defamation). Even if confined to one tort, a theory is incomplete if it simply acknowledges that the relevant 'wrong' is an amalgam of factors. Without more, the theory becomes circular, spelling out the requirement of the 'wrong' from the boundaries of the particular tort. This leaves us with the question of where these boundaries came from: *why* is the victim of negligence only able to recover when the defendant has been careless, while the victim of defamation need not prove this; *why* is the victim of negligence only able to recover, in general, when the defendant has caused physical harm to the victim's person or property, while damage is irrelevant in defamation? *Why* cannot the victim threatened by negligent conduct claim the protection of an injunction when such a remedy is available for certain other torts?

Weinrib's purported general theory does not tackle these dimensions, for he is keen to concentrate on defendant behaviour and to establish that there is one unify-ing normative principle underlying tort law, that it is negligence, and that strict lia-bility is 'disqualified' from being a proper standard in tort law. Clearly this idea, if sound, would have serious implications for the moral defence of the rule initially proposed for products law reform and of the final Directive. How does he defend this idea?

(b)   The immanence of negligence

Having isolated the bipolar remedial relationship and causation as the two distinc-tive features of tort law, Weinrib concludes that the 'causation that pertains to an intrinsically ordered tort law has been described in general terms as the doing and suffering of harm', and asserts that a requirement that the actor exercise reasonable care is 'the norm implicit in the doing and suffering of harm'.[28] Yet the origin of this conclusion is obscure. Weinrib identifies liability to pay damages as reflecting the impermissibility of action and asserts that tort law is concerned with the *propriety* of activity.[29] Thus, he says, it follows that general strict liability is disqualified as a standard of justice in tort because it 'implicitly denies the legitimacy of action'.[30] But is tort law confined to 'illegitimate' action? The crudest origin for this idea may be that since 'torts' means 'wrongs', all tort law is an expression of the Aristotelian notion of the correction of 'wrongs', so that to be held tortiously liable for certain conduct necessarily implies that it is wrongful *and* impermissible. Since, the argu-

28 Weinrib 'Understanding Tort Law', op cit 514, 517–8.
29 Weinrib 'Understanding Tort Law', op cit 519; 'The Special Morality of Tort Law', op cit 404.
30 Weinrib 'Understanding Tort Law', op cit 519–20.

ment continues, it is not sensible to apply the term 'wrong' to behaviour that is innocent, the law of torts requires negligence and tortious strict liability is inappropriate.

But however we may play with words, this is simply not a representation of how
the law of torts operates. For example, defamation is a tort, and as such has been traditionally described as a civil 'wrong', but, as we have seen, it can be committed
innocently, at least in the UK. It is a strict tort: the defendant can be liable despite
the use of all reasonable care. The fact that – as with all strict torts – it may be awkward or impossible to describe the tort in terms of breach of a 'duty' does not prevent defamation being a central part of tort law. If we want to, we can accommodate
this state of affairs within an Aristotelian vision of corrective justice by construing
the notion of 'wrong' in the latter as broadly as it is in the classic statement that 'defamation is a civil wrong'. Alternatively, one could reserve the Aristotelian notion of
'wrong' to cases of defendant wrongfulness, impropriety, lack of virtue,[31] etc, and
attempt to justify strict torts such as defamation in the wider terms of commutative
justice (for it hardly makes sense to see the only remaining potential justification of
defamation and other strict torts as distributive justice). What one cannot do is simply equate tort wrongs and Aristotelian wrongs, and assert that the latter must
involve defendant fault so that the former must.

Of course, *negligence* will emerge as the norm 'immanent' in *tort* law and seem
to do so naturally and 'internally' if one has already made the assumption that civil
liability should only arise when it carries with it moral blame and a judgment that
the conduct is illegitimate. This assumption is consistent with the standard conclusion of legal philosophers 'that "strict liability" is generally speaking unjust'[32]
because it holds defendants liable for mischances about which there is nothing he or
she could have done, for how can conduct be described as 'illegitimate' if the actor
could not have avoided it? However, the assertion that only illegitimate conduct
should attract civil liability needs more support than a mere assumption that this is
so. Nor can strict liability be rejected simply on the basis of this assumption. But
Weinrib offers no argument to support the assumption.

Strict liability cannot be rejected or 'disqualified' merely because of some *internal* moral logic based on the allegation that it renders all conduct impermissible.
That liability for conduct need not imply that the relevant conduct is illegitimate can
be illustrated simply. Say a society had a civil liability rule which stated that an accident victim has to pay the full cost of the emergency services he/she uses such as
fire, ambulance and blood transfusions. Such a rule makes internal sense and does
not imply that because we have later to pay for the service, resort to them was morally wrong, illegitimate or impermissible. To hold someone strictly liable is not necessarily to blame him for what he has done. Nor can Weinrib extract from the
phenomenon of the damages remedy an implication of the impermissibility or otherwise of the relevant conduct, and thereby of the internal inevitability of negligence
as the tortious norm of conduct. One could argue, for example, that the absence of
injunctive relief in the tort of negligence itself supports the opposite conclusion: that
even here the defendant is free to conduct himself negligently as before, so long as
after the event of negligently causing certain forms of damage, he is willing to pay
the price. Obligation to pay under a strict liability rule need carry no other moral
implication than that one should 'pay one's way' in certain cases even in the absence

31 See eg D Lyon *Ethics and the Rule of Law* (Cambridge, Camb University Press, 1984) 127.
32 Lucas, op cit 117.

of negligent conduct; in particular, it need not imply that one's act is necessarily per-missible or impermissible.[33] Of course, *if you had started out* with the assumption that civil liability must extend only so far as occasions of moral blame, payment of damages *would* signal more than this, and it would follow that strict liability would be 'disqualified'. But this assumption cannot be generated simply by the phenome-non of payment of damages. It needs independent support.

The reason a general strict liability rule neither exists nor is attractive is not because strict liability renders action impermissible, but because there are many contexts in which (for specific reasons) we clearly do not want the person who causes a loss to pay for it (see under heading 5, below, and Chapter 8, under heading 1). The classic example is economic loss caused non-fraudulently in a competitive market, but there are others. Not insignificantly, this is also an area which the tort of negligence does not cover.

(c)   Boundaries

Weinrib's two 'distinctive features' of tort law neither in practice nor in theory render negligence the inevitable norm of tortfeasor behaviour. Moreover, they do not provide the explanation of the selective incidence of tort liability – both as between torts and within a tort such as negligence. Indeed, he is particularly weak on the boundaries point. His criticism of Epstein's general theory of strict liability can be turned back on him, for in his attack Weinrib not only raises the standard, but misguided, causal minimalists' complaint against strict liability that causation as the principal criterion of liability is 'excessively general', and 'fails to single out a defendant' because 'the causal sequence can stretch back endlessly'; but also when confronted by examples of existing and workable pockets of strict liability he alleges that their boundaries are merely 'artificial' limitations which 'confirms that strict liability is not theoretically viable'.[34] But, as we have seen (see under heading 3(b), above), it is also only its boundaries which make the tort of negligence viable. Firstly, if we look at the boundary line drawn by causation itself, there are in the tort of negligence the very sort of causal truncations of liability which would operate in a strict liability regime. For example, whether a defendant had faultlessly or care-lessly run a pedestrian down, he or she would not be held to have caused the death of the pedestrian when the latter's ambulance was struck by lightning en route to hospital. Why is the causal truncation 'artificial' when occurring under a strict liabil-ity rule and not when under the tort of negligence?

Secondly, and more generally, negligence case law is replete with judicial pro-nouncements that a 'duty of care' is not owed to the whole world, but must in every case be owed to the plaintiff. A careless defendant is *not* liable for all the foreseeable damage he or she causes, nor could it sensibly be so, as the example of negligently inflicted pure loss of profits in a free market illustrates. Why are not the duty requirements of claims in the tort of negligence – requirements which are

---

33 One needs more and cannot simply assert, as Coleman does, that in certain cases strict liability implies the activity is permissible so long as compensation is paid (giving strict liability for blasting in the US as an example), while in other cases such as product liability (which he takes as strict), it cannot have this meaning: 'Moral Theories of Torts: Their Scope and Limits' (1983) 2 Law & Phil 5, 27–8.

34 Weinrib 'Causation and Wrongdoing', op cit 418–9.

particularly severe in the area of economic loss – also similarly 'artificial'? Weinrib does not give an adequate account of these crucial boundaries, dismissing the duty issue as something necessary 'satisfactorily' to capture the 'nuances' of every possible occasion.[35] But what does 'satisfactorily' depend on, and how can issues as large as whether a person owes a duty of care with respect to whole fields of harm, such as economic loss and nervous shock, be described as mere 'nuances'? Similarly, the definition of what is a 'harm' is also hardly a 'nuance': why in the tort of negligence is it not yet (as it is to some extent in contract) sufficient for the plaintiff to prove merely that the defendant's negligent conduct exposed her to a risk and thereby caused the plaintiff to lose a chance of avoiding a deleterious outcome such as cancer?[36] Why is not the mere exposure to an increased threat of a deleterious outcome enough, as it is in defamation? Why, in other words, is the actual outcome of physical damage nearly always required in the tort of negligence? In short, neither Weinrib's two distinctive features of tort law nor the Aristotelian concept of 'wrong' help us decide whether or not negligently increasing a person's risk of cancer should be a 'wrong'. Nor can they tell us when a defendant's careless omission to control a third party should be a 'wrong' or when causing 'ulterior harm' should be. Weinrib deals with both areas by denying that the tort of negligence recognizes liability in such cases.[37] It does, and it does so for reasons which, like the reasons for *confining* liability by the device of duty requirements of relationship, are not mere 'artificial' limitations to make the tort of negligence workable, but provide the complex substance of this particular tortious 'wrong' which theory needs to explain.

To sum up: a tort of negligence bounded only by requirements of carelessness and 'damage' is open to the same criticism of unworkability as Epstein's early unbounded general strict liability. But the tort of negligence *is* confined within intricate limitations,[38] all of which are necessary elements in defining the 'wrong' in the particular case. In just such a way, the boundaries of a strict liability rule (other than causation) may produce a rationally fine-tuned conception of a 'wrong'. Thus, the strict tort of defamation is coherent, even though there is neither a damage requirement nor a carelessness requirement. Its other detailed requirements limit the ambit of the tort not artificially, but to that particular sphere where, for specific and describable reasons, a remedy is thought just: the publication of a defamatory statement about a living person to a third party (not the publisher's spouse or the defamed) which is neither true, fair comment nor privileged. In short, the non-causal boundaries of a strict liability regime cannot simply be dismissed as 'artificial', although they may be!

5   A MORAL RATIONALE FOR LIMITED STRICT LIABILITY

General theorists such as Epstein and Weinrib err in their apparent assumption that intellectual 'coherence requires that tort law be the expression of a single normative

---

35 Weinrib 'Understanding Tort Law', op cit 523.

36 J Stapleton 'The Gist of Negligence, Part 2' (1988) 104 LQR 389.

37 Weinrib 'Understanding Tort Law', op cit 516 (omissions), 520 (ulterior harm: ie where the prospect of the harm that resulted was not what made the defendant's conduct wrongful, see Hart & Honoré, op cit 263).

38 See eg the distillation of four major considerations in J Stapleton 'Duty of Care and Economic Loss: A Wider Agenda' (1991) 107 LQR 249.

idea'.[39] Weinrib asserts that 'tort law is a distinctive and coherent mode of legal reasoning only inasmuch as it actualizes corrective justice',[40] a term, as we have seen, Weinrib takes as reflecting a narrow fault-related notion of a 'wrong'. But why does coherence require a unitary principle? Certainly life can be made simpler by narrowing our search to one principle, and we may even be able to claim for the one we select internal consistency without reference to any extrinsic goals; but is it for that reason a more coherent view? Certainly a *descriptive* theory could only coherently present the law of tort as diverse pockets of 'legal ordering', each with its own internal logic and fusion of factors necessary to constitute the 'wrong' which the particular 'tort' reflected. Even within a pocket, liability may be multi-layered with respect to any one parameter. Thus, in the tort of negligence the standard of conduct embraces not only the fault standard but the strict liability implicit in an objective standard of care and the strict liability of vicarious liability. This is important because only if we appreciate the diversity of and within pockets of civil liability can we see why it is possible that a fault-based rule and a strict liability *can* be almost indistinguishable in practice, so flexible is the standard of care and so rare the truly unforeseeable risk cases which would force a court to rely on the formal distinction based on defendant conduct. This point is supported by studies showing the loose ambiguous usage of the term 'strict liability' in nineteenth-century tort law; by the time gap before cases unequivocally involving unforeseeable risks arose and forced courts to decide that the implied warranty of merchantability was strict; and by the same gap in the history of s 402A before it was shown that there was no liability for unforeseeable design defects.[41] Descriptive theories which focus on defendants' conduct exaggerate the importance of the fault/strict liability divide and fail to explain these historical phenomena.

What advance is made by a *normative* theory which seeks only one norm immanent in tort law? At the very least such a theory has to ignore and/or positively reject as unjust many settled and important areas of tort law. Even if the goal is simply to see which torts can be supported by a narrow view of corrective justice based on the assumption that a legal 'wrong' requires as a necessary, if not a sufficient, condition moral blame, wrongdoing or fault, the deduction that these torts are only fault-based torts such as negligence is circular. The interesting question in the products context is whether non-instrumental versions of justice, be they called moral theories or fairness notions, can be found to support *limited strict* tortious liability, since both the full strict liability of Calabresi and the hindsight cost-benefit rule of the initial proposals of European reformers rest on such a principle, and the small real increase of liability under the actual 1985 Directive was achieved primarily by a form of limited strict liability. How could a strict tort be couched in terms of a 'wrong' which reflected a moral notion wider than one necessarily implying blame to the defendant? Is there an ethical reason for sometimes imposing liability on a defendant, even if a reasonable person acting reasonably would have done the same thing? If we abandon the attempt to squeeze such a strict liability within the 'corrective justice'/'wrong' formula, the question becomes, could a strict tort be justified in terms

---

39 Weinrib 'Understanding Tort Law', op cit 504.
40 Weinrib 'The Special Morality of Tort Law', op cit 412.
41 On usage see G Schwartz 'The Character of Early American Tort Law' (1989) 36 UCLA Law Rev 641, 644 and S Stoljar 'Concerning Strict Liability' in *Essays on Torts*, ed P Finn (Sydney, Law Book Co, 1989) 267; on time gaps see respectively dates of relevant case law (Chapter 9, footnote 13) and discussion in Chapter 6 under heading 4.

of a broader concept of fairness between litigants, that is of commutative justice? How in the circumstances could we argue that it is fair that the defendant pay damages to the plaintiff?

Certainly moral and legal philosophers who regard it as generally unjust to hold someone strictly liable for results which the defendant could not help, and therefore could not be blamed for, concede that there may be occasions in which 'justice' requires exceptions to be made and where limited strict liability *is* fair. In commutative justice terms it is a recognition that there may be areas in which such a principle requires the correction, not of morally blameworthy 'wrongs', but of merely innocently caused 'changes'.[42] One possible example, as we will see, might be where an enterprise causes physical damage (albeit innocently) in pursuit of profit. Lucas, for example, concedes that:

> Up to a point it is fair to hold the manufacturer of explosives liable for any explosion whether or not it was the result of some fault of his: after all he did not have to engage in that business, and if he chooses to it is fair that he should carry the risk and not passing bystanders ... [the manufacturers] are not blameworthy but have incurred a duty to indemnify others against loss.[43]

Vicarious liability is also defended by Lucas, although on the more instrumental basis that 'by making (employers) strictly liable we give them added incentive to keep their employees up to the mark'.

Two related moral complaints about civil strict liability must first be overcome before we can launch a moral argument for a limited strict liability regime: that strict liability stigmatises the innocent; and that it is unfair to hold a person legally responsible for outcomes they could not help. The stigma allegation rests on the dubious assumption that civil liability necessarily taints the defendant. For example, one reason Lucas gives for saying that while criminal strict liability 'cannot be automatically affixed without injustice', civil strict liability may sometimes be fair, is because the former, being criminal, carries some stigma.[44] This suggests that civil strict liability does not stigmatize, or at least not in the same way as criminal strict liability. It may even be that civil strict liability does not necessarily carry *any* moral taint. Certainly in discussing the possible basis in justice of criminal strict liability, David Lyons contemplates the feasibility of a strict liability system which eliminates the condemnatory function of conviction, while Jules Coleman has simply concluded that to hold someone strictly liable is not necessarily to blame him.[45] We have seen that if one *assumes* liability carries with it moral blame, guilt or fault, strict liability *is* unjust, but it is equally possible, indeed more reasonable to expect that a strict liability which is openly imposed without defendant fault would carry no such stigma.

The second moral complaint is that, regardless of moral stigma in the eyes of others, the fact that strict liability burdens a defendant with outcomes he could not help is unfair. A partial response to this could be that in cases where the victim of the defendant's activity is similarly innocent, being unable to help the outcome is not a

---

42 See Finnis, op cit 179, that the Aquinas term is restricted neither to correction nor to voluntary transactions, but is almost as extensive as the notion of 'change'.
43 Lucas, op cit 117. See also 140.
44 Lucas, op cit 140.
45 D Lyons *Ethics and the Rule of Law*, op cit 164; J Coleman 'The Morality of Strict Tort Liability' (1976) 18 Wm & Mary LR 259, 280.

positive argument for preferring the defendant to the plaintiff. A more complete response has recently been provided by Tony Honoré whose new theory of the moral basis of strict liability also contains the seeds of a coherent limitation of strict liability.[46] Honoré notes that the objective standard of care in negligence imposes a form of strict liability on that minority of 'shortcomers' who cannot, because, for example, of physical, emotional or intellectual incompetence, attain it. He shows that if we set aside consequentialist rationales such as those of the wealth maximization school, and the pragmatic rationale of the easing of the burden of proof, the objective standard of care in negligence, no less than an overt strict liability rule, itself requires a moral rationale. Honoré then argues that it is a necessary part of our having a personal history, identity and character – of being a choosing person – that we are held responsible in the sense of given credit or discredit for the outcomes we cause, even when they are simply due to bad luck. Since this 'outcome-responsibility' is inseparable from our status as choosing persons, it is more fundamental than moral and legal responsibilities, which are simply species of it, with strict liability and negligence being sub-species of the latter.[47]

Honoré notes that, to be fair, allocation of this fundamental moral or pre-moral responsibility for outcomes must entail that a person should not only bear the risk of bad luck, but that he or she is also entitled to benefit if the luck is good. Under a system of outcome responsibility, in effect we *bet* on the outcome of our conduct, receiving and being entitled to receive credit and esteem for successful outcomes, and discredit (and resentment if third parties are affected adversely) for bad outcomes, even if the bad outcome was not our fault. Honoré also notes that, to be fair, outcome responsibility must also over a period be beneficial. That is, it must work so as to entitle each person to potential benefits which are likely on the whole to outweigh the detriments to which it subjects him. This then specifies the minimum necessary *capacity* a party must have before it is fair to subject him to outcome reponsibility, namely, the general capacity to profit from the system of outcome responsibility most of the time. Since most people win more than they lose from a system of outcome responsibility because they generally succeed in doing what they set out to do and get credit for it, for most people outcome responsibility is not only a necessary recognition of their being choosing human individuals, but it is fair.

Honoré argues that while 'capacity to act otherwise' *is* a condition of responsibility, so long as we adhere to an objective standard of care in negligence it is not, and cannot be, a capacity exercisable in *all* the particular circumstances in which the person found themselves. Some characteristics, such as the person's temperamental impatience, are *not* taken into account in evaluating his capacity; he is responsible for these, while others, such as insanity, are taken into account in his favour. Which characteristics are regarded as relevant to judging capacity is a normative question as the differing attitudes between legal systems to the issue of inexperience illustrate. The point is, however, that not *all* circumstances are taken into account when capacity to act is evaluated. It is therefore coherent to argue that outcome responsibility is fair so long as the person had a general capacity for decision and action

---

46 T Honoré 'Responsibility and Luck: The Moral Basis of Strict Liability' (1988) 104 LQR 530.

47 Note: not all social discredit is due to bad outcomes caused by the person discredited. For example, a person who carelessly or callously fails to take easy steps to rescue a dying stranger is not a 'cause' of the death in the ordinary usage of that term, nor does legal liability attach, but the conduct *does* attract social discredit. The same point can be made for causal connections falling short of causing harm, eg creating opportunities for others to do harm.

such that the person stands over a span of time to win more than they lose. Honoré notes:

> On this view the capacity to remain alert when alertness would have avoided the accident does not refer to the possibility of someone's remaining in a steady state of alertness for an indefinite period but rather to the ability to remain alert in normal conditions most of the time.[48]

Here there is a small but relevant weakness in the Honoré discussion of capacity, which seems only to revolve around the issue of individual failures to reach an *achievable* standard of care. The discussion and the way its conclusions are reached fail adequately to address the issue of capacity in the clearest test case for strict liability, namely that of the unforeseeable, and hence unavoidable, risk. Thus, when Honoré concludes that the required capacity is a 'general ability to perform the sort of action which would in the instance case have led to a different outcome',[49] it is difficult to apply this conclusion to the issue of what capacity is necessary before a defendant-manufacturer can be held strictly liable for unforeseeable adverse drug reactions. Presumably it is simply the capacity to make a decision not to engage in an activity where liability for unforeseeable outcomes attaches, and although the Honoré analysis can accommodate this, it necessitates some distortion of his language in order to do so.

To return to Honoré's theme: outcome responsibility is a necessary part of being human. It is more fundamental than that 'narrow view of morality' called moral desert. This can be illustrated by the phenomenon that while the moral desert, blame or fault associated with conduct constituting murder is identical to that associated with conduct constituting attempted murder, yet the social and legal discredit associated with these are different. Outcome responsibility, which attaches only to the former, can explain this, while theories of moral desert cannot. But outcome responsibility does not lack a moral basis, for the person knows that the outcomes of his conduct will be credited or debited to him according to how they turn out, and so long as he has the general capacity to win credit more often than not, it is not only the more fundamental form of responsibility, but it is one rooted in a broad morality of fairness.

Finally, before turning to Honoré's analysis of legal responsibility, an important lacuna in his central notion of a 'bad outcome' should be examined. Honoré does not expressly acknowledge that not all outcomes which are bad from the viewpoint of their victims and which those victims resent, are the sort of bad outcomes which attract social discredit, let alone legal sanction. Being put out of business by a new, more efficient competitor is no doubt a bad outcome for the collapsed business, which those involved in the latter would resent, but the successful competitor attracts no social discredit for causing this injury – indeed, the outcome may well attract social credit. For outcome responsibility, therefore, the badness of an outcome must be being judged not by the harm it causes victims, but on a broader view informed by basic social values – in the example given, by the value of free competition. As we see later (Chapter 9, under heading 3) this is an important level missing from the Honoré thesis: of all injuries caused to individuals ('bad outcomes', if viewed subjectively), only some are bad outcomes attracting social

48 Honoré 'Responsibility and Luck', op cit 550.
49 Honoré 'Responsibility and Luck', op cit 550.

discredit under outcome responsibility, and only some of the latter attract the added sanctions of legal responsibility.

Just as there are principles which explain why not all injuries are bad outcomes for the purpose of outcome responsibility, there are, as we saw earlier, reasons both pragmatic and principled why a person is not held *legally* responsible for all bad outcomes which receive social discredit. Liability for all bad outcomes – strict liability for them – would both swamp the courts and, since the threat of legal liability inhibits action, hamper an unacceptably wide field of human activity (see Chapter 8, under heading 1). Viewed from the perspective of defendant behaviour, what more then has to be proved before the production of a bad outcome attracts not only social discredit but legal liability? Different extra requirements in relation to defendant behaviour create two sub-species of liability: negligence and strict liability, but since both forms of liability are predicated on the party already having incurred social discredit for the bad outcome, both can be seen as acting to reinforce and enhance outcome responsibility.

Honoré argues that under a fault-based rule of law the extra element (in addition to outcome responsibility) needed before a competent person is held liable relates to moral desert: he or she is held liable because of a 'bad' or 'uncooperative' disposition. This is an unhappy choice of terms since by them Honoré seems only to mean that, while he or she has the ability to succeed most of the time in doing the sort of thing which would on this occasion have averted the harm, on the actual occasion he failed to do so – he was objectively and subjectively careless. Yet the notion of 'uncooperativeness' does not seem to capture this idea accurately, and indeed is somewhat misleading. Shortcomers, that is incompetent persons who, due to the bad luck of circumstances, such as temperamental impatience or clumsiness, are incapable of reaching the objective standard of care, lack this element. Yet a moral defence of their liability in negligence and that of those (both competent and shortcomers) subjected to an overtly strict liability regime *can* still be made, because we can fall back on to the broad morality of outcome responsibility for bad luck.

The value of Honoré's idea is that it convincingly meets the philosopher's objection to strict liability, that it is unfair to hold someone liable for an outcome they could not help. By showing that one way people are held responsible in ordinary life is the credit and discredit which attaches to outcomes they cause, he showed that being responsible in ordinary life need not involve being at fault or to blame. Being responsible for bad outcomes in this way is fair so long as the individual stands to succeed more often than fail in the relevant activity. The remaining problem for Honoré is how to pinpoint the extra element justifying a rule of limited strict liability.

CHAPTER 8

A new theory of strict moral enterprise liability

1   THE PROFIT MOTIVE AS A MORAL DISTINCTION

Although in his theory of outcome responsibility Tony Honoré gives a convincing account of why strict liability may not be immoral, he is less successful in positively accounting for the boundaries of the tort of negligence, and where and why there are only limited pockets of strict liability. We have seen that criticism of a causally-based full strict liability regime on the basis of the unworkability of the causal requirement (Chapter 6, under heading 4, Chapter 7, under heading 3(b)) or that such liability 'implicitly denies the legitimacy of action' (Chapter 7, under heading 4(b)) is not convincing or well-founded. But it is clear that such a *general* liability *is* regarded as unacceptable, being too oppressive and in conflict with basic values of our society such as a free competitive market (see Chapter 7, under headings 4 and 5). Honoré accepts the standard arguments against a *general* principle of strict liability for harm caused: that it would be resented as unduly inhibitive and place an intolerably heavy burden on human activity. It is important, he notes, that we sometimes have the right to do something without the risk of penalty even if the exercise of the right causes harm or net social loss.[1] To be held strictly liable, something extra is needed. But what is this?

Honoré characterizes the existing pockets of strict liability in terms governing activities which are specially dangerous to others. For strict liability he sees the extra element needed, in addition to outcome responsibility, as conduct carrying with it a special risk of harm. Here society not only ascribes discredit and requires regret and apology, it also demands compensation for damage:

> It falls typically on those who pursue permissible but dangerous activities: storing explosives, running nuclear power stations, keeping wild animals, marketing drugs or other dangerous products, and in France and Germany, driving a car.[2]

But even though it is a common *assertion* that the common feature of existing pockets of strict liability is 'special risk' or 'extra-hazardous activity', this argument is unconvincing both descriptively and normatively. Firstly, many areas of apparently high risk activity are not subjected to strict liability; examples include surgery, rail transport, and the industrial use and dissemination, especially in the form of pollution, of toxic chemicals. Secondly, and more importantly, it is difficult to see how one major source of strict liability, namely vicarious liability, could come within the

---

1   H Hart and T Honoré *Causation in the Law*, 2nd edn (Oxford, Clarendon Press, 1985) lxxvi–ii. The harm requirement also helps secure a sphere of freedom of action (even if eg careless): lxxix.

2   T Honoré 'Responsibility and Luck: The Moral Basis of Strict Liability' (1988) 104 LQR 530, 537. See also 541–2, 546.

(admittedly slippery) bounds of the 'extra-hazardous activity' concept. Finally, if Honoré's theory of strict liability is normative, it is the concept of 'special risk' which does the work, yet we are not told in detail what its moral force is.

(a)   Moral enterprise liability

But there *is* a coherent theme which does link most existing pockets of tortious strict liability, including those aspects of the product rules in the US and EC which are strict. It is the taking of risks *in pursuit of financial profit*. A non-consequentialist basis of these liabilities might be expressed in terms of a moral argument that if, in seeking to secure financial profit, an enterprise causes certain types of loss, it should be legally obliged to pay compensation to the victim. This I will call the '*moral* enterprise liability' argument to distinguish it from the diffuse concept of 'enterprise liability', which has been used in many different and loose ways.[3] Since strict liabilities may cover unforeseeable losses, it may be difficult to accommodate such a rationale within the narrower definition of 'corrective justice', but there is room within the broader notion of commutative justice for requiring the payment of compensation in such circumstances (see Chapter 7, under heading 4). In the following discussion developing the moral enterprise liability argument I am not necessarily promoting it in preference to other rationales but using it to show that, by providing a basis for the limitation of product rules to activities 'in the course of the defendant's business', it provides a considerably better fit with those rules than economic theories, although still not a completely satisfactory fit.

Communal response to the profit motive has not been well-explored by those seeking a moral understanding of common law and statute. In *The Concept of Law* Hart noted that a law may be unjust because it does not provide a remedy where compensation would be thought morally due. Significantly, he gave as his example 'the failure of English law to provide compensation for invasions of privacy, often found *profitable* by advertisers' (emphasis added),[4] but he did not pursue the issue of how and why the profit motive may be morally relevant. Everyday experience, however, suggests that it is. It is true that research has shown how ordinary people's ascription of responsibility for compensation for injuries can be dependent on their perceptions of existing legal obligations to compensate.[5] But it does seem that the wave of public concern in the UK and Europe following the emergence of the Thalidomide injuries and the victims' unsuccessful struggle to win compensation under existing fault rules, reflected a moral outrage consistent with the principle of 'moral enterprise liability'. Nor is it is insignificant that the Pearson Commission, Law Commissions and EC reform bodies took as self-evident that it was *commercial* activity which warranted heightened liability. Public reactions to events such as the

---

3 On the vagueness of the concept see F Kessler 'The Protection of the Consumer under Modern Sales Law' (1964) 74 Yale LJ 262. G Priest's allegedly 'single coherent concept' is in reality an indeterminate shifting amalgam of vague loss-spreading, deterrence and moral elements: 'The Intellectual Foundations of Modern Tort Law' (1985) 14 J Legal Studies 461, 463, 466. (On Priest see also G Schwartz 'The Beginning and the Possible End of the Rise of American Tort Law' (1992) 26 Georgia LR 601.) So, too, is that of H Klemme 'The Enterprise Liability Theory of Torts' (1976) 57 U Colo LR 153.

4 H Hart *The Concept of Law* (Oxford, Clarendon Press, 1961) 160.

5 S Lloyd-Bostock [1980] Ins LJ 331.

Thalidomide tragedy suggest that, although hitherto obscure, there has developed a moral response to the profit motive in modern mass markets. The content of this response seems to be that quite apart from any collective interest in the incentives liability might be able or unable to generate for future deterrence, and quite apart from the lure of plundering deep pockets, the individual victim is entitled to compensation from the individual profit seeker, even when the latter has not been careless.

This can be framed as an extension of Honoré's thesis. There does seem to be strong anecdotal evidence that when a bad outcome is seen as due to *commercial* operations, the resultant resentment and social discredit is often greater than it might otherwise be. This reaction (perhaps, but not necessarily, expressible in the language of exploitation)[6] in turn goes to support an elevated legal responsibility for such outcomes in moral enterprise liability. Moreover, and more specifically, Honoré's notion of betting on outcomes strongly supports moral enterprise liability. While not *every* activity must 'pay its way' in terms of legal liability for attendant losses, nor every risk taken bear 'the burden' as well as 'the benefit' of the risk-taking, the pursuit of commercial profit does provide that extra element on which to base the additional responsibility represented by legal liability. The notion of betting on outcomes has a strong and direct analogy in the operation of free markets. Enterprises gamble on whether their activity, product or service will make a profit or not. In the process, risks, both foreseeable and unforeseeable, are taken. This gamble is the raison d'être of the enterprise and the market. The free market prospers because more often than not such gambles pay off. More often than not profit is made. If a new product succeeds, the manufacturer not only acquires social credit – a point explicitly relied on by the Pearson Commission in recommending strict liability for products[7] – but this is reinforced in terms of the hard cash of financial profit. If the product causes personal injury, a bad outcome, the manufacturer suffers social discredit, but it has already pocketed the price and there is no direct penalty for that outcome. Legal liability for bad outcomes in such cases may, therefore, be justified in order to ensure the sort of rough symmetry Honoré points to in his theory of outcome responsibility. Just as there is the trade-off of social discredit for bad outcomes given the social credit for the more common good outcomes, there may be a justified trade-off of a manufacturer's obligation to pay for the bad outcomes when its product causes injury, given the entitlement of manufacturers to retain the financial profits it can realize if a product is successful. In other words, there may be a moral quid pro quo: if X is to be 'allowed' to charge above cost for a good or service and thereby derive profit, those injured by a good or service must be compensated. A product line may be unforeseeably profitable: if an enterprise is allowed to internalize unforeseen benefits of the risk-taking, why not require it to internalize losses, even if unforeseeable? Access to the market and its potential advantages, including the possibility of limited liability through incorporation, may have an entrance fee, namely that of strict liability for certain losses to others.

As we saw earlier (Chapter 7, under heading 4(b)), the imposition of strict liability on an activity does not *necessarily* entail fault, guilt, blame or shame, or any

---

6 See eg the rejection by the drafters of the Strasbourg Convention that a consumer be used as the 'guinea-pig' of development risks: Law Coms p 66.

7 Pearson Com para 1233. See also G Calabresi 'Product Liability: Curse or Bulwark of Free Enterprise' (1978) 27 Clev St LR 313, 324.

other version of moral condemnation of the activity; and, after all, profit-making *is* approved of in Western economies.[8] Yet although society does not condemn nor seek to penalize it, the pursuit of profit can provide the potential distinguishing ground for a level of responsibility – strict liability – which activities lacking this element would not attract. In the tone of the public debate concerning recent product (and other) disasters, a thread of moral expectation can clearly be heard that business should 'pay its way' by the payment of compensation, and it is not fanciful to suggest that long-term confidence in a profit-based economy may rest on the better vindication of these ideas.

(b)   Historical examples from the common law

Even though 'the validity of a moral ... does not depend on fashion or favour',[9] it is important to note that concerns consistent with the 'moral enterprise liability' argument have already surfaced in some areas of civil liability. First and most obviously, the common-law warranties created for sales contracts by nineteenth-century judges were only applied to those selling in the course of a business. Indeed, the whole edifice of modern statutory sales law is limited in this way. Secondly, in the US there is a settled common law rule, set out in s 519 of the Second Restatement of Torts, that one who carries on an abnormally dangerous activity, such as storing dynamite, is liable for the injuries an explosion causes, even if the person took all reasonable care to avoid the explosion. While in commenting on the rule, the drafters of the Restatement evaded the problems in defining 'abnormally dangerous', they did assert that the rule had been based on the idea of an enterprise being 'required to pay its way' (Comment d). It may well be that the 'extra-hazardous' activities given as examples (explosions, etc) are simply ones in which the social costs of commercial risk-taking were historically the first to be made apparent and the first, therefore, to trigger general notions of moral enterprise liability. Thus in *Bamford* v *Turnley* (1862) Baron Bramwell noted that, although the risk-taking involved in the enterprise of railways was beneficial for society, this was not so unless 'they pay their expenses'; and so, were sparks from a train to ignite a neighbouring wood, the railway enterprise 'obviously ought to compensate the owner of such wood ... *if they burn it down in making their gains*'[10] (emphasis added). Similarly, recent thorough examinations of US tort law in the nineteenth century found that, while indifference to precision about certain terminology makes it difficult to pin down the standard of liability being applied, it is clear that pursuit of private profit was seen by courts as a reason for being sceptical rather than appreciative of the activities of enterprises.[11]

Recently John Fleming suggested that the 'spectacular retreat' by the House of Lords on the issue of local authority liability may lie in the distinction between

---

8 Nor does it necessarily involve moral approval – after all, even if a manufacturer is held strictly liable for the injuries caused when its car explodes, this would not mean selling cars that explode is approved of so long as the damages are paid for.

9 C Fried *Contract as Promise* (Cambridge, Harvard University Press, 1981) 2.

10 *Bamford* v *Turnley* (1862) 3 B & S 66, 85; 122 ER 27, 33. Similarly, strict liability for animals may nearly always in practice have concerned commercial activities such as zoos, circuses and farming.

11 G Schwartz 'Tort Law and the Economy in Nineteenth Century America – A Reinterpretation' (1981) 90 Yale 1717, 1757, 1774; 'The Character of Early American Tort Law' (1989) 36 UCLA Law Rev 641.

commercial undertakings for private profit and public projects.[12] Similarly, another area in which the values underlying moral enterprise liability may have surfaced is that of injuries caused by manufacturing errors. Even under the ostensibly fault-based regime of the tort of negligence, courts effectively impose strict liability on manufacturers for such injuries. This generates virtually no judicial or academic concern. Perhaps this can be accounted for solely by the pragmatic interest in ease of adjudication which is achieved by adopting the (impossible) target of a perfect production-line norm across all units, but it seems more likely that such a wide-spread consensus also has a moral dimension – a view that the enterprise should pay its way for this bad luck, even if unavoidable.

The development of s 402A itself in the US is littered with important references to the profit motive. In proposing strict liability for manufacturers in *Escola* (1944), Traynor saw its burden being imposed 'as a cost of doing business'.[13] After the rule had been adopted in relation to product sales, some courts, in extending it to non-sale transactions of supply, explicitly noted that in these situations the profit motive of the manufacturer was apparent whether or not a 'sale' in the strict sense took place.[14] Similarly, in determining the classes of defendant to whom the rule in s 402A was to apply, US courts have referred to the profit motive as a key factor and have, on this basis, extended the rule, for example, to blood banks who operate in pursuit of commercial profit, and have exempted hospitals not regarded as in the business of generating profit.[15] When a US cigarette company unwisely tried to defend a product liability claim on the basis that liability would damage its profits (and thereby the economic well-being of a wider community dependent on its profit-ability) the court roundly rejected the idea. It stressed that a fundamental purpose behind the imposition of strict liability is to require that a product 'pay its way', and to permit defendants to argue their interest in making a profit would turn the liability on its head, since 'strict liability is, if anything, intended to temper the profit motive' with responsibility for the costs the activity may inflict.[16] Finally, in the landmark case of *Grimshaw* (1981) the court repeatedly referred to the defendant's pursuit of corporate profits at the expense of safety, and it is believed that public distaste for cold calculation of risks and benefits *in order to maximize profits* lay behind this and other record awards of punitive damages.[17]

Another example might be market-share liability. This is the doctrine US courts have developed to deal with the dilemma facing plaintiffs who have been injured by

---

12 J Fleming 'The Economic Factor in Negligence' (1992) 108 LQR 9, 11.

13 *Escola* v *Coca-Cola Bottling Co of Fresno* 150 P 2d 436, 441 (1944).

14 W Keeton, D Owen & J Montgomery *Product Liability and Safety* (Mineola, Foundation Press, 1980) 752.

15 S Brook 'Sales-Service Hybrid Transactions: A Policy Approach' (1974) 28 Southwestern LJ 575, 591; W Russell, 'Products and the Professional: Strict Liability in the Sales-Service Hybrid Transaction' (1972) 24 Hastings LJ 111, 131–2. See also *Suvada* v *White Motor Co* 210 NE 2d 182 (1965); *Liberty Mutual Insurance Co* v *Williams Machine and Tool Co* 338 NE 2d 857, 860 (1975); *Keen* v *Dominicks Finer Foods Inc* 364 NE 2d 502, 504 (1977); *Niffenegger* v *Lakeland Const Co* 420 NE 2d 262, 265 (1981); *Connor* v *Great Western Savings and Loans Assoc* 417 P 2d 609, 621–2 (1969). Conversely, lack of profit in non-commercial supply is a reason for exclusion: J Henderson, 'Extending the Boundaries of Strict Product Liability: Implications of the Theory of the Second Best' (1980) 128 U Penn LR 1037, 1048.

16 *Cipollone* v *Liggett Group Inc* 644 F Supp 283, 288–9 (1986).

17 *Grimshaw* v *Ford Motor Co* 174 Cal Rptr 348, 384, 388 (1981). See also G Schwartz 'The Myth of the Ford Pinto Case' (1991) 43 Rutgers Law Rev 1013, 1044.

a generic product risk and who cannot identify which producer of the generic product produced the actual item which caused his or her injury. The doctrine, which can be applied in the products, employment, pollution and other contexts, dispensates the plaintiff from proving that the defendant caused the injury. Thus if P was injured by a generic product X (eg diethylstilbestrol) P can sue any of the manufacturers of X without having to show that it produced the specific unit which caused the injury and can recover damages from the individual defendant proportional to its market-share. To abandon the causal requirement in tort is a radical strategy for fixing liability on an enterprise. While not on all fours with the moral enterprise liability argument, the market-share device broadly shares the ethos of such liability, at least where 'enterprise' is seen as broadly as a generic industry.

Next consider the vicarious liability of employers for the torts of their employees in the course of their employment. This liability, which is strict because it attaches even where the employer has used all reasonable care, could be taken to represent the common law's most dramatic, if only partial, expression of the moral enterprise liability argument. Scholars have described vicarious liability as something of an aberration within the law, the stability and purposes of which are not yet fully understood.[18] But although leading modern torts scholars conclude that its most convincing explanation lies in a combination of policy considerations, none of which on its own would be sufficient to justify it,[19] the financial profit idea may provide a single basis which is at least as coherent as any other idea or combination of ideas.

It is true that vicarious liability is superficially odd. Unlike most, but not all, tort principles it requires neither that the defendant-employer's conduct caused the relevant harm nor that it be independently tortious. But neither of these features necessarily shows vicarious liability to be unjust. Among the ideas traditionally suggested to explain the doctrine was a crude version of moral enterprise liability: that since the master obtains the benefit of the servant's work, he should also bear the burdens caused by his servant's torts in the course of employment.[20] The idea is often too quickly dismissed as an unsatisfying rationale for the doctrine on the basis that there are a host of occasions where deriving a benefit from another's action is not sufficient to trigger vicarious liability. If, however, the notion of 'benefit' is given the tighter meaning of 'financial profit', then it does successfully explain nearly all the key features of the doctrine – the course of employment requirement, the general absence of vicarious liability for independent contractors,[21] its application to partnerships, the absence of a requirement that the employer's conduct cause the harm, and the strictness of the employer's liability. Thus, for example, it can be seen that while the benefit derived from an independent contractor's services is fixed and

---

18 R Pound 'The Economic Interpretation and the Law of Torts' (1940) 53 Harv LR 365, 375–6; G Schwartz, 'Tort Law and the Economy in Nineteenth Century America - A Reinterpretation' (1981) 90 Yale LJ 1717, 1770, n 396. See also *Imperial Chemical Industries Ltd* v *Shatwell* [1965] AC 656, 686 (per Lord Pearce).

19 J Fleming *The Law of Torts*, 7th edn (Sydney, Law Book Co, 1987) 340; P Atiyah *Vicarious Liability in the Law of Torts* (London, Butterworths, 1967) 15.

20 Atiyah *Vicarious Liability*, op cit 17–8; Y Smith 'Frolic and Detour' (1923) 23 Columb LR 444, 718; T Smith 'Scope of the Business: The Borrowed Servant Problem' (1940) 38 Mich LR 1222, 1223; C Robert Morris, 'Enterprise Liability and the Actuarial Process – the Insignificance of Foresight' (1961) 70 Yale LJ 554, 599.

21 Note one key difference between the employee and independent contractor is that the latter has a chance of profit: *Montreal* v *Montreal Locomotive Works Ltd* [1947] 1 DLR 161, 169, PC.

predetermined, the benefit from the services of employees is open-ended, for after paying the employee's fixed wages, the employer takes the 'surplus', the residual profit of the activity as determined by the market.[22] Similarly, the profit idea may well help link many of the otherwise mysterious exceptions where vicarious liability for the torts of independent contractors is imposed, at least in the modern precedents where there tends to be close *economic* integration between employer and contractor.[23] Unlike the other traditional rationales for the doctrine, the idea of the profit-seeker paying his way also well explains why sharing in the net profits of a business is powerful evidence that the person is a partner and, as such, to be burdened with vicarious liability for the torts of others.[24] Finally, moral enterprise liability on profit seekers also well explains (i) the causal point, (ii) the strictness of the liability in vicarious liability and (iii) the industry practice towards the doctrine.

(i)   Causation and vicarious liability

Unlike most cases of civil liability where causing harm is the centrally important (albeit not necessarily sufficient) ground for responsibility, under vicarious liability the employer is held liable even though in ordinary language he probably would not be said to have 'caused' the relevant harm.[25] Of course, since usage of language is not uniform, some may say an employer was 'a cause' in such circumstances, but probably most would not, and this is because in view of the employee's carelessness, the role of the employer appears relatively trivial in explaining the result. The carelessness tends to 'swamp' other factors which might otherwise be candidates for 'a cause' (Chapter 6, under heading 2(a)). But even for those who would baulk at describing the employer as a 'cause', it is quite clear that its activities are a but-for factor in relation to the harm since, but for the enterprise, the employee would not have had the opportunity of acting in the context he was acting in. Hart and Honoré have shown that we do accept in other contexts that legal responsibility may attach in special circumstances to behaviour which, while not fitting within a uniform usage of 'causing harm', provides the opportunity for another to do harm.[26] What I am arguing here is that the special circumstances which may justify the imposition of vicarious liability on the employer even in the absence of uniform agreement that the employer's conduct was a 'cause' of the harm, is the profit motive of the employer in creating the opportunity for the employee to act in this way.

It must be remembered that the moral enterprise liability argument resting on the profit motive – the 'profit idea' for short – does not completely justify vicarious liability because the latter doctrine has other boundaries which require explanation. For example, it is only triggered by losses caused in the course of employment by the employee's *torts* (usually negligence), while the profit rationale of moral enterprise liability could be used to support a strict liability on the employer which was

---

22 Atiyah *Vicarious Liability*, op cit 18.
23 H Collins 'Ascription of Legal Responsibility to Groups in Complex Patterns of Economic Integration' (1990) 53 MLR 731, 734–5.
24 Atiyah *Vicarious Liability*, op cit 18. In the broader context of alleged joint ventures see the discussion of the profit-sharing point by Mosk J (dissenting) in *Connor* (1969) op cit.
25 Hart & Honoré op cit lxvii, lxxix.
26 Acceptable perhaps under an attenuated notino of 'causal connection', Hart & Honoré op cit lxxix, 59–61, 194–204 (although they do seem principally concerned here with the *careless* creation of opportunities).

original, that is, personal and not dependent on the liability of an employee. Its imperfect reflection in vicarious liability is still useful, however, when searching for moral analogues of the liabilities set out in the Directive on Product Liability. This is because, for example, under the terms of the Directive, the plaintiff need not show that the defendant *caused* the defect in the product, and although it is a defence for the defendant to show that the defect did not exist when the product left his control, it is no defence to prove that the defendant did not cause it. This is important because although the conduct of all defendants under the Directive will bear a but-for relation to the injury (since all must have at least 'supplied' the product), there will be some for whom it cannot be said that in common usage *everyone* would select their behaviour as 'a cause' of the plaintiff's injury. For example, in earlier discussion of the manufacturer's marketing of a drug which causes an unforeseeable adverse drug reaction, it was noted that while some might say that the manufacturer's conduct was a cause of the injury, others might baulk at using the term in that context (Chapter 6, under heading 2(b), n 11). A similar disagreement on usage may arise where the manufacturer's omission of, say, child-proof lids provides the opportunity for another to be careless. In both cases some may say that the manufacturer's conduct was a 'cause' of injury, but others might argue that it merely provided the opportunity for another to cause harm.

Nonetheless, the Directive's reach, like that of vicarious liability, overcomes this problem by not being limited to those defendants whose conduct satisfies a requirement of being 'a cause'. What is it about the conduct of those defendants (which clearly has at least provided the opportunity for the product to harm the plaintiff) which justifies legal responsibility? The argument here is that the profit idea reflected in the Directive's requirement that the defendants have been acting 'in the course of a business', provides the sort of special circumstances needed to justify the absence of a causal requirement, just as it can be seen to do in vicarious liability.

(ii)   The strictness of vicarious liability

The profit motive underlying moral enterprise liability can also justify the imposition of a strict liability which is not dependent on another's liability. It is clear from the Directive (and s 402A) that some defendants may be liable even though they personally exercised all reasonable care with respect to the condition of the product. A simple example is that the manufacturer of a final product is liable for a design defect in a component which was caused by an up-stream designer and component manufacturer, but which was not reasonably discoverable by the final manufacturer given the state of quality control technology at the time. For such defendants, liability under the Directive (or s 402A) is strict. But is it merely vicarious liability for the carelessness of others? I will later argue that the notion of 'defect' adopted in the Directive (and in the US) will in practice implicate some party in carelessness in nearly all cases (see Chapter 10, under heading 4). This would mean that the liability of some defendants could very nearly be regarded as a form of vicarious liability, and could be justified in a similar way to mainstream vicarious liability. But the argument here is that even if liability could be imposed under the Directive (and s 402A) when no-one had been careless, the strict liability which the Directive (and s 402A) would impose on parties such as the manufacturer of the final product in the above example could be justified. The justifying principle would be that an adequate moral balance in the marketplace requires enterprises which, in pursuit of financial profit, create the opportunity for defective products to cause loss, to pay compensation to those injured by such products.

The moral enterprise liability argument also justifies the strictness of vicarious liability. But although vicarious liability is strict, it is also *vicarious*, ie limited to injuries caused by the *torts* of employees in the course of their employment. Even though successful in explaining other boundaries of the doctrine, the moral enterprise liability argument cannot justify this limitation. Yet none of the other modern suggested bases of vicarious liability, singly or in combination, provide a justification for this limitation either. The deep pocket potential of many employers, their ability to distribute or spread losses by insurance or otherwise, are all attributes which would apply as strongly to losses associated with the non-tortious conduct of employees in the course of business.

(iii) Industry practice and vicarious liability

Finally, the profit idea provides a satisfying explanation for the modern position of employees. UK courts are hostile to employers enforcing their common law entitlement to seek an indemnity from the tortfeasor-employee, and such enforcement is now rare. So settled in some countries is the consensus that this is a just arrangement, that there is a growing momentum to remove formally the personal liability of the employee in line with this practice.[27] The puzzle this state of affairs appears to present is that one of the principal beneficiaries of the vicarious liability doctrine in practice is the original tortfeasor. But this is resolved if that doctrine is seen, not in terms of some identification of employer with employee, but in terms of a moral enterprise liability which distinguishes the profit-seeker paying its way from the employee who does not participate in profits.

(c) Statutory illustrations: workers' compensation

The discussion of vicarious liability leads on naturally to the most important area of statutory liability which can be rationalized as a (partial) expression of the profit idea – workers' compensation. In the UK, workers' compensation was the political compromise between late nineteenth century employees agitating for the right to sue their employers on the basis of vicarious liability for the torts of fellow servants, and the resistance of employers to this threatened expansion of their vicarious liability (which was eventually accomplished by the abolition of the common employment defence). Employers hoped that by accepting the workers' compensation proposals – liability for all accidents to employees in the course of employment but with financial ceilings – they would halt the movement toward total abrogation of the common employment defence and a subsequent flood of employee claims in tort which would have been subject to no fixed financial limit. Organized labour shared the employers' perception that workers' compensation would be less in their interests than the abrogation of the common employment defence, and while not actively hostile to workers' compensation, their energy was focused on the abrogation of the defence and the good promise of safety incentives it seemed to present.[28]

27 Fleming *The Law of Torts*, 7th edn op cit 340–1.
28 R Bartrip and S Burman *The Wounded Soldiers of Industry* (Oxford, Clarendon Press, 1983) 164. See also 201, 206, 221 and generally.

The actual proponents of workers' compensation were motivated by a combination of economic deterrence[29] and moral justice goals, summed up in the campaign slogan: 'the cost of the product should bear the blood of the workman'.[30] The notion of justice embodied in this slogan and relevant here can be traced back as early as 1846 when one of the most influential figures in the reform process, Edwin Chadwick, had argued that since a 'labourer ... produces a *surplus* on a return to make it profitable and worthwhile to employ him' (emphasis added), it was unjust that the social costs of industrial accidents – even unavoidable accidents – should fall on ratepayers, and that liability rules should be used to internalize the cost to the enterprise.[31] The complex debate about industrial safety and compensation reached a turning point in the 1893 parliamentary debate on a Bill designed to abolish the doctrine of common employment completely, and thereby expose employers to employee claims based on vicarious liability. A prominent campaigner for a no-fault system of compensation, Joseph Chamberlain MP, seized on the fact that an employer's vicarious liability, being a strict liability, did not depend on the employer's fault, and argued that the principle on which it was based would not find a 'final or satisfactory' vindication until it provided compensation for *all* injuries in the course of employment, not just those attributable to the *torts* of fellow-servants.[32] This argument about the moral incoherence of the underlying principle of vicarious liability was politically 'devastating'.[33] Thereafter reform pressures in favour of the more coherent workers' compensation compromise snowballed, and the appropriate Bill was successfully introduced in 1897, albeit in the form of a no-fault statutory scheme imposing on employers an obligation to pay compensation rather than in the form of a strict civil liability to pay damages. The employee could elect to pursue his or her tort remedies instead of the workers' compensation remedy.

The key anomaly on which Chamberlain relied for the impact of his 1893 speech was the one alluded to in the previous section: that there is no coherent reason why an employer's strict liability ought to be confined to a liability dependent on the torts of his employees. We could confine liability on the basis of personal fault. But once we embrace an employer's strict liability for losses attendant on his enterprise, we are embracing a wider principle, one relating to responsibility for the enterprise which should cover all such risks. My argument is that this principle to which logic points is equivalent to the idea of moral enterprise liability developed earlier; that vicarious liability was a stage on the route to its full expression; and that workers' compensation moved closer to this by shearing vicarious liability of its anomalous limitation to injuries caused by employees' torts. Given the industrial context of the debate, it is understandable that Chamberlain overlooked the remaining anomaly: that the employer's strict liability to third parties should also – and for identical reasons – be shorn of its dependence on an employee's tort. Once we pursue the logic this far we arrive at a consistent principle by which enterprises would be strictly

---

29 Clearly set out in both the form of prevention incentives and price deterrence. On the evolution of these goals, see Bartrip and Burman op cit 3, 16–7, 62, 67–72, 83, 93–6, 113, 134, 189, 202, 213.

30 Quoted by W Prosser *Handbook of the Law of Torts*, 5th edn (St Paul, West Publishing Co, 1984) 573.

31 Quoted by Bartrip and Burman op cit 72. In general see 69–72.

32 8 Official Report 4th Series (21 Jan–20 Feb 1893) cols 1961–5.

33 D Hanes *The First British Workmen's Compensation Act 1897* (New Haven, Yale University Press, 1968) 63. See also 104.

liable for injuries, both foreseeable and unforeseeable, caused by the enterprise in the course of its pursuit of profit, ie we arrive at a full version of moral enterprise liability.

I am not arguing that this moral idea was the sole, or even dominant, principle actually at work in the emergence of vicarious liability and later of workers' compensation. But it is certainly a perceptible theme and one explicitly linked to the profit motive of enterprise. It is relevant that in introducing the 1893 Bill to expand the reach of vicarious liability, the Home Secretary (Asquith) had stated that the move was to be justified on the principle that

> where a person on his own responsibility, and for his own *profit*, sets in motion agencies which create risk for others, he ought to be civilly responsible for the consequences of what he does.[34] (emphasis added)

The same principle, word for word, was cited as the basis for the Workmen (Compensation for Accidents) Bill 1897 by the then Home Secretary (Sir Matthew White Ridley),who drew on what he saw as a growing moral sentiment:

> ... if you look at what is going on elsewhere not less than at the growth of public opinion in this country, and at what has passed in Parliament itself, you will see that there is a growing feeling that it is proper ... to make trades responsible for the risks they create.[35]

And Joseph Chamberlain saw the emergent principle as a cross-border phenomenon:

> In foreign countries this risk of compensation for *all* accidents is described as a risk *professionnaire* – that is to say, a risk which is one of the charges upon the trade in which it is incurred; and it is supposed to be as much a part of the cost of producing the article as, for instance, insurance against fire, or even the cost of materials.[36]

Although the relative historical importance of the idea of moral enterprise liability cannot easily be determined, at the very least we can say that the immediate and almost unanimous acceptance of the workers' compensation reform of 1897[37] is consistent with a widespread moral idea that it is not unjust to impose a strict liability on those who cause loss while taking risks in pursuit of commercial profit, even where the risk is unforeseeable or cost-justified. In 1916 in the US, for example, Thayer wrote that 'a community which accepts the principle of [a workers' compensation statute] ... cannot be expected to find anything intrinsically unreasonable in the doctrine which seeks to throw upon the undertaker the full responsibility for harm arising from his enterprise, on the theory that the business should bear its losses in the first instance regardless of fault ...'[38] To put it more strongly: if workers' compensation (and vicarious liability) are to be justified on the basis of a principle of individual responsibility and justice between individuals – and it is noteworthy that in 1897 the UK Parliament explicitly preferred the system of individual employer liability to the collective insurance model of workers' compensation then operating in Germany – then it seems to be the principle I have been describing: moral enterprise liability.

---

34 8 Official Report (4th Series) (21 Jan–20 Feb 1893) col 1948.
35 See respectively, 48 Official Report (4th Series) (3 May 1897) cols 1427 and 1432–3.
36 48 Official Report (4th Series) (3 May 1897) col 1469.
37 Hanes op cit 103.
38 E Thayer 'Liability without Fault' (1916) 28 Harv LR 801, 802–3.

(d)   Other statutory examples

The workers' compensation system can be seen as a principal forerunner of modern collectivist reforms. In practice, employers responded to the new liability by insuring. Claims began to bypass employers and to be dealt with by their insurance companies. Compensation was paid and more and more *seen* to be paid directly out of insurance pools. It came to be seen as a simple rationalization, in tune with collectivisit moral sentiments about 'community responsibility'[39] that the concept of an individual employer's responsibility to pay compensation be replaced by a central fund collected from risk-creating employers to which claims were directly made by an injured employee. The wider these sentiments about rationalization and responsibility, the wider the 'no-fault' 'non-tort' pool which was set up. It is not insignificant that the radical New Zealand scheme of no-fault compensation for personal injuries, which replaced tort to the extent of overlap, was recommended by a Royal Commission whose reference was limited to finding a coherent reform to the workers' compensation system in that country, but which could find no satisfactory moral justification for limiting a compensation scheme to work accidents.

But inasmuch as workers' compensation could be seen as (and in its historical context certainly was) a statutory imposition of a liability on an *individual* enterprise in order to protect, and therefore create rights in, those it deals with, it links up with later twentieth century legislation aimed directly at the liability of individual businesses to private individuals. There is, of course, all the legislation on the supply of goods (see above). Nuclear enterprises in the UK were subjected to strict liability by the Nuclear Installations Act 1969. In the Employer's Liability (Defective Equipment) Act 1969, the UK Parliament created for the benefit of injured workers a statutory extension to the doctrine of vicarious liability under which employers are strictly liable for injuries caused to their workforce by machine tools (etc) manufactured negligently by an independent supplier, even where the latter was reputable and selected carefully. Although not imposing strict liability, other UK legislation, including the important Unfair Contract Terms Act 1977, has placed those who act in the course of a business in a more demanding position in terms of civil liability than those who do not, and EC measures have followed this pattern.[40] The argument I am putting here is that although, apart from vicarious liability and sales warranties, the common law has failed to give special status to losses produced in the course of business – at least explicitly – modern Parliaments have. This legislative activity is consistent with a developing moral consensus concerning the special status of losses generated by the pursuit of financial profits. Sometimes, as in the original workers' compensation legislation, this surfaces in the strictness of a new liability imposed on activities which are in the course of business.

In short, although moralists have had little to say in explanation of common law and statutory pockets of limited strict liability – perhaps in the latter case because it is so easy to dismiss Parliamentary action as being in pursuit of distributional aims – it does seem that a satisfying basis can be found in the profit idea justifying 'moral

---

39 This was, for example, the moral basis of the New Zealand accident compensation scheme: *Compensation for Personal Injury in New Zealand: Report of the Royal Commission of Inquiry* (Woodhouse J, Chairman) (Wellington, Govt Printer, 1967) para 56.

40 See the Directives on unfair terms in consumer contracts (OJ No 95/29, 21 4 93) and product safety (OJ No L 228/24, 11.8.1992). Also draft Directives on liability for services (OJ No C 12/8, 18.1.91) and waste (OJ No C 251, 4.10.89), amended proposal (OJ No C 192, 23.7.91).

enterprise liability', even if no existing strict liability regime is an exact reflection of the idea.

2 THE MORAL ENTERPRISE LIABILITY ARGUMENT AND THE JUSTIFICATION OF BOUNDARIES OTHER THAN THE STRICTNESS OF THE LIABILITY AND ITS LIMITATION TO ACTIVITIES IN THE COURSE OF BUSINESS

How closely do the liability regimes in the initial European reform proposals (hindsight cost-benefit) and in the final Directive coincide with this profit idea justifying a moral enterprise liability? We saw earlier that every civil liability is multi-dimensional. While some dimensions of the proposed and the final regimes are supported by the profit idea, some are not.

(a) Mass production

The profit idea could be used to justify the imposition by the Directive of liability which is strict and limited to activities in the course of the defendant's business. It also justifies the fact that no distinction is made between mass-produced and bespoke goods since both can be produced in pursuit of profit.

(b) Types of loss

The types of compensatable loss may at first appear more problematic. First of all, there has been throughout the twentieth century a developing special concern with personal injuries. Although common law judges – along with efficiency and other tort theorists – have again failed adequately to reflect this major development, Parliament has on many occasions acknowledged it, particularly in the context of civil liability. Revolutionary changes to the limitation laws were prompted by the plight of victims of latent diseases. Although a similar reform followed some decades later in the context of non-personal injury claims, it is only in relation to personal injury claims that the court has an overriding discretion to waive limitation rules[41] – a phenomenon of compassion to the personal injury victim which appears extraordinary in the context of traditional limitation law, but which creates no controversy in the present day. The codification of occupiers' liability to trespassers in the Occupiers' Liability Act 1984 made it clear that personal injuries and personal injuries alone were to be covered. There are special discovery rules for medical records. Exclusion and limitation of liability by contractual terms is more severely regulated by the Unfair Contract Terms Act 1977 when the relevant risk is one of personal injuries. It was the priority given to the compensation of personal injuries which led to the radical New Zealand scheme of replacing tort law in much of that field. Similarly, we have seen that it was the Thalidomide injuries which not only dominated the 1977 Law Commissions' report on product liability, but which led to a huge Royal Com-

---

41 Limitation Act 1980, s 33, discussed in J Stapleton *Disease and the Compensation Debate* (Oxford, Clarendon Press, 1987). See also *Halford* v *Brookes* [1991] 3 All ER 559 (CA).

mission enquiry into the issue of civil liability for personal injuries (see Chapter 3, under heading 3). Unsurprisingly, both these reports recommended new product rules specifically limited to personal injury claims, as did the roughly contemporaneous report on product liability published by the Council of Europe, the Strasbourg Convention. Recently the American Law Institute also instigated a massive study of liability for personal injuries.[42]

In legal literature there are few attempts to develop a moral rationale for this differential.[43] But moral concerns vary in intensity according to many criteria, and it is not difficult to imagine that the type of loss suffered may be one such criterion. The law can reflect these differences in intensity of moral concern in an additive way. While we may have such a strong moral concern with intentional conduct that we impose sanctions on it across a wide range of situations and types of deleterious outcome, we may have a less strong concern about merely negligent conduct and not provide a remedy for some types of loss which, had they been intentionally caused, would have given rise to a remedy. We may only want to impose strict liability in a very few contexts selected on grounds such as the defendant's pursuit of profit, and then only in respect of personal injuries. In Honoré's terms it certainly would seem intuitively correct that of all losses, personal injuries give rise to the most social discredit. This perspective allows an adequate account of the earlier priority given in product liability reform to personal injuries. We might rationally, and for reasons to do with autonomy and the dignity of the person, regard it as immoral for an enterprise not to compensate the 'guinea pigs' it maims in taking risks for profit, and reinforce this moral discredit with a legal obligation to pay, while being less outraged by damage to property. Whether or not we include the latter in the legal rule depends on the relative importance we attach to such arguments about the sanctity of the person. That is, while there may be a general moral principle that he who stands to make a financial profit from risk taking should pay for the financial losses of those injured in the process, when this principle is elevated to a legal rule we may (or may not) want only to cover those types of loss giving rise to the most social discredit. Thus some reform proposals are limited to personal injuries, while the Directive covers damage to private property.

Where the 'victim' is another enterprise whose property has been damaged in the course of its own pursuit of profit, the argument about profit-seekers starts to cut both ways, and this may provide a sound justification for the failure of the Directive to provide a remedy in such cases. Similarly, in those cases of pure economic loss I have called 'quality claims' (see Chapter 6, under heading 5(d)(iv), and Chapter 11, under heading 2(b)), one could argue that even private victims have rarely the need of the protection of tort since quality claims are adequately handled by the law of sales, which itself imposes a strict liability for quality on those who supply goods in the course of a business. Finally, the exclusion from the Directive of those pure economic loss cases involving loss of profits may be justified on the same basis on which damage to commercial property may be excluded: that the profit argument begins to cut both ways.

---

42 American Law Institute *Reporters' Study: Enterprise Responsibility for Personal Injuries* (Philadelphia, ALI, 1991).

43 Two rare examples are: R Abel 'Should Tort Law Protect Property Against Accidental Loss?' (1986) 23 San Diego LR 79; I Schwenzer 'Product Liability and Property Damages' (1989) 9 Tel Aviv Studies in Law 127.

It is not impossible, then, to justify the pattern of recoverable losses under the Directive in terms of a moral version of enterprise liability. It is the remaining boundaries of the Directive which may not be justified by this or perhaps *any* moral principle.

(c) Unforeseeable risks, 'put in circulation', products

The profit idea would seem to justify liability for all unforeseeable risks and yet the development risk defence in the Directive (whatever its construction) excludes at least some of them (see Chapter 10, under heading 3). It would also justify liability for injuries caused by products not put into circulation or commercial supply, and yet such injuries, which include injuries to the producer's workforce and neighbours, are excluded from the Directive. The profit idea would also justify liability for injuries due to the provision of services or the production of realty in pursuit of profit, and yet these are both excluded from the Directive by its definition of 'product'.

From a moral perspective, what is special about being injured by a product which has been put into commercial supply rather than, for example, discharged as commercial effluent? What is special morally about being run down by a defectively manufactured bus as opposed to a defectively operated bus? There *is* no moral principle which can ground these vitally important limitations on the scope of the Directive. As we see in more detail in Chapter 12, the current instability and random breakdown of the boundaries of the s 402A rule in the US are directly related to the absence of coherent justifications, either moral or economic, for those boundaries.

(d) Defendants

The final parameter of liability under the Directive which needs a moral rationale is who can be made liable. The Directive does not require that the defendant cause the plaintiff's injury or cause the defect in the product (Chapter 6, under heading 2(c)). For example, even if the defective condition of a component is due to the behaviour of an upstream component producer or its out-of-house designer, the producer of the final conglomerate product is liable. In some cases mere suppliers of finished products will be liable. But lack of a causal requirement does not mean that the selection of possible defendants cannot be justified by the moral enterprise liability argument. As with the doctrine of vicarious liability, the profit idea can justify a suitably limited strict liability on a defendant even though the defendant did not 'cause' the injury so long as the defendant could be said, in the pursuit of profit, to have 'created the opportunity for the event to occur' (under heading 1(b)(i), above).

This line of reasoning can be used to justify the producer of the final product being made liable: production and manufacture of the final product for profit created, or helped create, the opportunity for the risk to eventuate. In Honoré's terms, it is not unfair to hold him responsible, even for undiscoverable risks he could not have found or avoided, since he possesses general capacity and has instigated the relevant risk-taking for his financial profit. Moreover, this approach is supported by common sense for, unless the law recognises the economic integration of legal units in this way, evasion of the liability is encouraged. In his major study of vicarious liability Atiyah noted not only that a manufacturer could escape the threat of res ipsa loquitur and therefore of liability in a *Donoghue* v *Stevenson* type of case by delegating the washing and checking of the bottles to an independent contractor, but that since the same applies to the use of components, the canny manufacturer of final products will be tempted to contract out the risky side of the component business to an independent contractor for whom he is not vicariously liable.[44] The common law could have dealt with such evasive tactics by declaring that the legal unit of the entrepreneur who had initiated the risk-taking for profit had a strict non-delegable duty to see that care was taken in the risk-taking. It is a step the common law has not taken. The point here is that at least vis-à-vis the final product manufacturer, sound moral and practical reasons *could* be adduced for liability even in the absence of full causal responsibility for the defect. Comparable arguments can be used to support the liability of own-brand suppliers.

But if a causal connection is not essential to finding a moral basis for the enterprise liability, what are its limits? If in 'moral enterprise liability' the 'enterprise' can comprise more than one legal unit, as in the above example, where *both* the component manufacturer and the manufacturer of the final product are liable, what are the outer bounds of this concept of 'enterprise'? Which legal units fall inside it?

Let us take the other chain–members, wholesalers and retailers. Does the profit idea behind the moral enterprise liability argument apply with equal force to them and so equally justify imposition on them of strict liability? It is true that these businesses mark up the price of the goods and thereby make a profit in return for taking the risk of releasing the goods through the chain of supply. So, as stated so far, the moral enterprise liability argument would apply to these parties. But there may be moral reasons which would lead us to modify such a form of the moral enterprise liability argument. We might want to distinguish among profit makers between the initiator of the risk-taking and others who profit from dealing with the goods and impose strict liability only on the initiator of the risk. Assuming we have grounds for drawing this distinction, it could be applied either to actions by victims – so that the risk initiator alone would be strictly liable to them; or it could be applied just to recourse actions between members of the chain – so that any of the chain members could be held strictly liable to victims but the initiator of the risk-taking would be liable to indemnify profiting suppliers. The Directive is consistent with the former approach while s 402A adopts the latter 'blunderbuss' approach by making any supplier who profits from dealing with the goods strictly liable to the victim.

To sum up: this and the previous section have argued that a moral defence of a limited strict liability for losses resulting from risk-taking for profit not only could be found, but has roots in important areas of the common law and, in particular, in modern statutes. As with the efficiency rationales, however, it fails to justify many boundaries of the liability set out in s 402A and the Directive.

But whereas theories of efficiency and morality provide arguments against the *boundaries* of existing product regimes, the arguments of some of the most vigorous US analysts proceed on the basis that the rules themselves (or at least the non-excludability of the liability) are open to attack and condemnation on the basis that they are distributionally unjust and paternalistic. It is to the background of these arguments that we next turn.

---

44 Atiyah *Vicarious Liability*, op cit; Collins op cit.

3   LOSS DISTRIBUTION AND DISTRIBUTIVE JUSTICE

Loss spreading is the argument that we want to spread losses across many parties in order to dissipate their impact. As we have seen, it fails to justify a liability rule since it fails to identify what would be a more appropriate loss-spreading device than the tax pool. A *loss distribution* goal, on the other hand, is best defined as a goal which seeks, for specified reasons, to distribute particular losses over classes of *particular* individuals.[45] Both s 402A and the Directive have the *effect* of distributing losses in this way, but to what extent can we assert such effects are a goal? It is important to emphasise that reasons for loss distribution can be found both within a commutative justice perspective and within a distributive justice perspective. The argument developed in the preceding section is that a 'moral enterprise liability' argument based on the profit idea provides a good moral explanation for a limited strict liability on those acting in the course of business and that such an argument could be extended to provide a moral justification for distributing the burden of product losses across more than just the producer of the product. So far I have presented this moral idea as one which seeks to secure *commutative* justice, but we must now ask whether the loss distribution form of the profit idea can be and is better seen as an argument about *distributive* justice, and why it would matter if it were to be described in this way.

We saw earlier that corrective justice is a perspective which sees a rule in tort law in terms of the correction of a wrong done by one individual (the defendant) to another (the plaintiff), that is to the re-establishment of the status quo as far as possible between two individuals. It is a perspective which is dependent on a theory of 'wrongs' and hence on a theory of distributive justice. Distributive justice relates to where burdens should, in fairness, be allocated. Where, for example, the gains of a common enterprise are shared between parties, then as a matter of distributive justice, it is said,[46] the burdens of that enterprise should be shared in the same way. Clearly the application of this idea depends on one's social and ideological perspective with regard to the issue of how to define 'enterprise' or 'activity'. On one hand there is the idea that, since we are all involved and collaborate in a common society, running common risks from which we all benefit in some (even if attenuated) way, we should collectively, as a matter of distributive justice, bear the risks and pay compensation to the injured. This idea of collective responsibility underlay the shift from the system of individual employers paying workers' compensation to the collective insurance of the Beveridge plan, and the shift in New Zealand from workers' compensation to the radical non-tort scheme of compensation for personal injuries (see Chapter 3, under heading 3). But it is a vision which cannot logically be used to support a civil liability rule which burdens only a specific defendant or group of defendants. Even if we approve this perspective in general, we may still have *specific reasons* for separating out certain risk-taking enterprises for special treatment. The moral coherence of no-fault non-tort schemes of compensation limited to certain activities depends on the soundness of these specific reasons. But what interests us here is the possibility of seeing *tort liability* rules, such as those in s 402A and the Directive, as designed to secure a form of distributive justice among

---

45 Insurance seeks to spread losses across like insureds, so it is *not* a system of loss distribution in the sense used here.

46 Finnis, op cit 180.

those benefiting from a defined collective activity (such as the production and marketing of products) and the soundness of the reasons for separating out these risks from others.

A civil liability can be viewed both from a corrective justice perspective – that an individual has been 'wronged' by another individual – and from a distributive justice perspective, which looks to the distribution of burdens the rule produces and seeks justifications for it. The more defendants a plaintiff is able to sue with respect to her injury, the more convenient a distributive justice perspective becomes, if it is possible to treat all those defendant units as engaged on a common enterprise. Similarly, where a civil liability rule imposes a *strict* liability, interpreting it in terms of a moral 'wrong' is awkward for moral philosophers wedded to the idea that a wrong requires fault, so that the distributive justice perspective which does not suffer from this problem becomes more convenient. It comes as no surprise, then, to find that much of the discussion of product liability rules has portrayed the law in terms of distributive values. But before we look to see the impact this choice of treatment has had, it is important to emphasise in detail that in the context of civil liability these two concepts are not fundamentally different ideas of justice but merely different perspectives from which conveniently to evaluate the reasons for complex legal rules.[47] They differ in their starting point both in terms of an historical reference point and in terms of how widely we allow a law's actual impact and effects to inform our understanding of why the law was made.

The temporal point can be illustrated by the change in the law brought about by *Donoghue* v *Stevenson. Viewed from today*, and with only the impact on the individual plaintiff and defendant in our chosen field of view, we can portray this rule as a rule of corrective justice. We can define the relevant 'wrong' done by the manufacturer to the product user and the consequent entitlement of the latter to have the damage done to her interests corrected (insofar as money damages are able). We can do this without resort to distributive language. But *viewed from the perspective of the manufacturer just before trial*, enjoying the entitlement to injure third parties carelessly without exposure to tort damages, the creation of the rule in *Donoghue* v *Stevenson* was re-distributional: it shifted the burden of the relevant risk off the initial victim and on to the manufacturer. It rearranged wealth. If we choose to focus on the individual's existing cause of action against an individual defendant, we can describe it in terms of securing corrective or commutative justice. If we choose to focus on who (*as individual(s) or as a class*) is enriched by the legal change that established this cause of action, we can represent the change as *intended* to secure this redistribution of risks, ie intended to secure distributional justice, and our reasons for the law must establish why it is fair to make this redistribution.

Thus we can represent the legal changes achieved by s 402A and the Directive as either intended to secure corrective/commutative justice or distributive justice. If we choose to see them in the former light, then we need to express the rule in terms of a 'wrong' and see if we can find a moral justification for why this is a wrong. The discussion so far in this chapter proceeded from this perspective. But alternatively we could choose to emphasise that the burden of risk has been *shifted* by the rules on to the shoulders of the defendants, and ask whether, if this was the intended goal of the legal change, the rationale for the redistribution is morally sound. At one level this could simply mean restating our justification for imposing liability on the particular

47 Finnis, op cit 179.

defendants in terms of explaining why the risks of an enterprise should be treated specially and shifted on to its shoulders by a limited strict liability rule. The moral enterprise liability argument successfully supplies this explanation showing why we might create an added layer of strict responsibility for risks associated with profit-making.

But the distributional perspective also raises the issue of how widely we cast the notion of 'enterprise'. How reasonable is it to assume certain parties are engaged in a common enterprise which distributive justice would say calls for the sharing inter se of burdens? Answering this question illuminates many interesting issues. Take vicarious liability and assume it is based, albeit imperfectly, on moral enterprise liability values. We have already seen (under heading 1(b)(iii), above) that although an employer is vicariously liable for the torts of its employees, it is widely regarded as inappropriate or improper that the former should extract an indemnity from the latter, and this is consistent with a concept of 'enterprise' which is linked to commercial profit making: to be included in the 'enterprise' which attracts special treatment a party must not merely benefit from it as employees do, but share in its profits which, qua employees, they do not.

But what are the outer limits of our concept of 'enterprise'? Is it the boundary of the capital and legal unit of the producer? Or do we aggregate the activities of all who, in supplying the product down the chain, take a profit, and use the earlier distributive justice argument to require them to share the burden?[48] Should we distinguish amongst those who, for example, did (manufacturers, designers, etc) and those who did not initiate the risk taking, and treat, say, manufacturers differently from mere suppliers of a finished product? Or should we define the enterprise for the purposes of initial liability to the victim to include all those taking a profit on the product; but for the purposes of recourse actions between tortfeasors take the view that each acted in their own commercial interests at arm's length, not as units in a single enterprise, and allow recourse only against risk initiators? If we are simply considering the legal entities represented by those defendants which a legal rule selects, the questions we have arrived at in terms of the appropriate degree of aggregation are ideological. When a component supplier is to be regarded as sufficiently 'integrated' into the enterprise of manufacture of the final product cannot be resolved by legal analysis. What we can say is that whichever approach is chosen, a revision of the moral enterprise argument could comfortably be found to accommodate it.

But there are other distributional issues here besides who to select as the defendants. For if the distributive justice perspective involves looking at the distributional *effects* of the adoption of a legal rule in order to test how well our moral rationale justifies them, then we could choose to cast our eyes beyond the defendants and look at the wider distributional impact. How convincing our rationale – in this context, the moral enterprise liability argument – then remains will depend on how wide a field of vision we choose and which effects we take into account. For example, in the real world, when a commercial defendant is exposed to a new liability it is routine for it to seek liability insurance. To the extent that the burden of liability in individual cases is borne by the pool of like insureds, the liability could be portrayed *as intended to have the effect* of generating a 'trade expense'. We would then need to ask whether our rationale could justify a liability intended to achieve this effect. The

---

48 Compare N Simmonds *Central Issues in Jurisprudence* (London, Sweet & Maxwell, 1986) 74; Fried, op cit 181–2.

moral enterprise liability argument could do this only if the profit-seeking 'enterprise' for the purposes of the argument was defined in terms of the relevant insurance pool.

Similarly, we might choose to notice that a producer held liable under a product liability rule may distribute some of the burden to its shareholders. This result is easily justified by the moral enterprise liability argument because shareholders are profit-sharers. If, however, we choose to look even wider and note the potential depressive impact of liability on the wages of employees of defendants, a rule which achieves this effect cannot claim much support from this moral rationale, since employees do not share in profits. The same applies to the distributional effect on customers when prices are raised in response to the imposition of liability: while they 'benefit' from the enterprise, they do not take a commercial profit, and it is the idea of commercial profit which has enabled us to justify rules limited to commercial defendants acting in the course of business. This illustrates a general point: that the wider the distributional *effects* of a civil liability one takes into account and seeks to justify, the less likely a coherent distributional *rationale* will be found for burdening the ever more disparate parties involved.

To sum up: to the extent that the moral enterprise liability argument *justifies* distribution of losses associated with defective products, it can only justify some of the distributional *effects* of product liability rules. This is inevitable: any rationale which can successfully justify a *limited* rule of civil liability will fail once the rule's wider impact is taken into account. In the real world there will be effects – particularly of insurance – which no rationale could accommodate while successfully justifying a *limited* class of defendants. Just as with efficiency incentives, the moral force supporting a liability regime tends to weaken the further one investigates the effects of the regime. In the particular context of product liability this can be illustrated by the slogan[49] that the new tort rules can be justified in terms of the distribution of product losses to all who benefit from their manufacture and supply, producers, retailers, buyers, shareholders, etc. If 'benefit' is to be attenuated in this way – in order to be wide enough to justify distribution to all these parties – then why stop short of adopting some notion of 'community responsibility' for product-caused losses? Indeed, why stop short of a New Zealand-type scheme for personal injuries? The special advantage of the *profit* idea is that it justifies the limited scope of a strict enterprise liability consistently with rejection of universal strict liability, while coherently defining that scope in terms of conduct 'in the course of business'. Once we look beyond the boundaries of the regime to observe the loss-distributional impact on parties not within its boundaries, our rationale for the limited nature of the regime loses force.

This is important because one of the principal tactics of critics of s 402A and the Directive has been to take this wider view of the distributional *effects* of the rules and to assert that loss distribution to parties remote from the production process is *intended*; and on this basis they can mount apparently very damaging attacks on the distributional fairness of the rules.

---

49 See eg *Beshada* v *Johns-Manville Products Corpn* 447 A 2d 539, 547 (1982).

4   DISTRIBUTIVE JUSTICE AND THE INSURANCE JUSTIFICATION

All change to civil liability rules is in some way redistributional, so criticism of the adoption of s 402A or the Directive based solely on the fact that it is redistributional, is unpersuasive. What is more, it is self-defeating, because judged from today, repeal of those rules would also be redistributional. What we must ask is whether the nature and degree of redistributional impact is the *goal*; whether it should be; if so, why; and, if not, whether it is a tolerable side effect of pursuit of other goals.

One major thread in the product liability debate in the US, which produced echoes in the European reform process,[50] concerned the redistributional impact the new product rules would have *on customers*. In a zero transaction cost world, it would not matter on whom the initial burden lay, as in any given seller-buyer relationship perfect readjustment could be made via the price mechanism (see Chapter 5). If it lay on the buyer, she could take out exactly the correct first party insurance to cover the risk both in terms of the possibility of the outcome occurring and in terms of the nature and size of loss she would, as a result, suffer. If the seller bears the loss, it could choose to take cost-justified precautions (the prevention response). Alternatively it could choose to do nothing at all about prevention and reflect the burden in its prices (the pure price deterrence response). In the latter case it could reflect exactly the level of risk in the price charged to the particular customer. Since the projected losses of each individual customer vary according to her characteristics – eg the level of wages she may lose – the price charged would vary with each buyer. In this sense the supplier who bears the risk could be said to be providing the customer with a form of insurance. Since no product can be made absolutely risk-free, some element of the price can always be *represented* in this way (see above Chapter 5, under heading 6).

Unlike the distributional effects a business's liability may have on its employees or shareholders, the impact it may have on its customers presents the possibility that where the customer is also a potential victim of the product (typically, but not always, as a user of it), the price increment which he or she bears as a result of the burden of product risks being thrown on to the chain of supply *can be portrayed* as an intended form of insurance; compulsory insurance if sales clauses excluding the liability are banned. Although Karl Llewellyn had noted the insurance perspective of quality warranties in 1925, the insurance representation of s 402A is usually traced to the statement of Justice Traynor in *Escola* (1944) that:

> the cost of an injury and the loss of time and health may be an overwhelming misfortune to the person injured and a needless one, for the risk of injury can be insured by the manufacturer and distributed among the public as a cost of doing business.[51]

Both Llewellyn and Traynor could be read as merely describing the acceptable *side effects* of a legal regime set up on, and justified by, independent grounds but the later

---

50 See eg Pearson Com para 1235; Law Coms para 38(c).

51 *Escola* v *Coca-Cola Bottling Co of Fresno* 150 P 2d 236, 441 (1944); K Llewellyn 'The Effect of Legal Institutions upon Economics' (1925) 15 Am Econ Rev 665, 680. See also the echoes of this argument in Pearson Com para 1235 and Law Coms para 38(c). Note that this 'insurance – through liability' argument is different to the argument that liability should fall on the party who is best able to insure (see Chapter 5, under heading 2(c)).

representation that insurance was the, or an, *intended* goal of s 402A has had a profound effect on the products debate.[52] This is because it is based on the large assumption that the loss is initially to lie on the victim who is therefore in need of insurance to shift it. It ignores the economic argument that where the victim is not the cheapest cost avoider (cca) and transaction costs are high, the loss (even if unforeseeable) should be shifted by a legal *entitlement* to compensation from the cca. Where this applies the victim is in no need of insurance. The mere portrayal of insurance as a goal of tort, therefore, involves an important choice about initial entitlements and distributive justice. Moreover, by definition it undermines any moral justification of the liability of individual defendants because it is, in effect, an argument that losses should be shifted off the victim and then redistributed back via defendants' prices to victims. While the exploitation of individual defendants in this way may have pragmatic justifications in terms of convenience for buyers, it has no *moral* basis.

It is very important to stress that other types of loss distribution rationales for civil liability *can* be defended on moral grounds: we have seen, for example, that a pattern of loss distribution to certain targets such as producers (and perhaps suppliers) of products and via them to their shareholders can be justified on the basis of a theory of moral enterprise liability linked to profit-seeking (see under headings 1–2, above). However, to impose a liability on individual defendants so that it can be distributed back to victims has no moral justification. Not only is there no justification for using the product manufacturer in this way, but the goal of insurance provides no basis for constructing a liability regime limited to products. Moreover, in practice the system works unjustly *as a insurance* mechanism being, as we will see, open to charges of paternalism and allegedly perverse redistributional effects, in particular, that it is fiscally regressive.

Not surprisingly, then, a very popular tactic for those unhappy with the new liability has been to seize on the Traynor quote, assume insurance is the principal justification given for s 402A (and the Directive), then to detail its inconsistency with deterrence and compensation goals, and in particular to expose its injustices. Opponents claim the principal injustice inherent in product liability, assuming a insurance rationale, is that where clauses excluding the liability are banned or not enforced, the effect is to *force* customers to pay for this insurance element in the price. Customers cannot choose to go without the insurance cover for the relevant product risk (say, that a new generator is faulty) on the basis that they already have first-party cover or want to buy it elsewhere or because, given their own circumstances, they do not see the risk as relevant to them. Customers will know more than the supplier about their needs (maybe they do not need cover because they have a reliable back-up generator) and more about their prospective losses (only the customer will know the *level* of threatened losses such as loss of wages, loss of profits consequent on damage caused by the defective product to the property of the

---

52 For examples on the 'right' of the debate see P Danzon 'Tort Reform and the Role of Government in Private Insurance Markets' (1984) 13 J Legal Studies 517; R Epstein 'Product Liability as an Insurance Market' (1985) 14 J Legal Studies 645; G Priest 'The Current Insurance Crisis and Modern Tort Law' (1987) 96 Yale LJ 1521, 1524, 1535–6, 'Modern Tort Law and its Reform' (1987) 22 Val ULR 1; L Brenza 'Asbestos in Schools and the Economic Loss Doctrine' (1987) 54 U Chi LR 277, 293. For an example from the 'left' see R Abel 'Should Tort Law Protect Property Against Accidental Loss?' op cit 97–8. Surprisingly Jules Coleman also seems to adopt this perspective without question: *Risks and Wrongs* (Cambridge, Camb Univ Press, 1993) Chapter 20.

customer, and so on). By buying first-party cover directly from an insurer, so the critics claim, the insured gets a policy more geared to its needs than the crude average 'premium' represented by the compulsory component of the price resulting from the imposition of product liability which is the best an imperfect market can provide. When a buyer who already has first-party cover for those risks he chooses to cover is forced to pay a price including an insurance element, he not only gets cover which he may not want (perhaps covering heads of damage such as non-economic loss) and would not pay for by way of a first-party policy; but also he is forced to pay for those heads of loss for which he already has first-party cover. A person with first-party health care cover does not need it provided via an increment in the product price.

Such arguments are couched not only in libertarian terms of unjustified invasions of autonomy but also in terms of redistributional injustice, because those customers who do not need or want the type of insurance cover (said to be) represented by the product price element reflecting potential liability are in effect subsidizing those who do. The most poignant presentation of the redistributional point is in relation to the poor. First, since in imperfect markets all customers pay the same price increment and yet some (eg those who earn more) can expect higher payouts from the liability insurer since tort damages are meant to restore the victim's standard of living, insurance via product pricing is regressive against the poor. By contrast, direct first-party insurance pools could more easily consist, it is argued, of equivalent earners, and thereby be distributionally neutral. Secondly, it is argued that as the imposition of product liability forces prices up to provide insurance to potential buyer-victims, it hits the poor worst because they are less able to afford the increase, are the most likely to have preferred lower levels of cover (or none at all), and are therefore the most disserved by a rule that forces them to spend their scarce resources in an unwanted way.

This critique rests on major assumptions about the availability and sensitivity of first-party insurance, in particular that it could more cheaply be tailored to the potential losses of the buyer. In theory it is true that the buyer has a far superior knowledge of his own needs in terms of heads of loss for which cover is thought by him worthwhile and of the levels of projected loss of, say, loss of wages. But it is not at all clear that first-party insurers will find it economically worthwhile to set up and review first-party insurance categories all that finely,[53] and this is particularly so when the premium level is low and the risk profile of the insured is volatile: both of which are especially true in the case of many of the poor who have an unstable stream of wages (usually the head of loss of most importance). If anything, one might guess that risk-averse insurers, not convinced that the poor would be a lucrative separate target, might lump them together in pools with the higher paid in a similarly regressive manner as liability insurance in effect does.

But there is another counter-argument: the efficiency of first-party insurance cover depends not only on the accuracy of determining the quantum of the individual insured's loss but also on the accident propensity of the insured. Even if we assume this is a constant among all buyers, rich or poor, it is the case that the product manufacturer and its liability insurer, because of their relatively focused

---

53 Those who doubt the availability and sensitivity of first-party insurance include C Wilson 'A Model of Insurance Markets with Incomplete Information' (1977) 16 J Econ Theory 167; H Latin 'Problem-Solving Behaviour and Theories of Tort Liability' (1985) 73 Calif LR 677, 689, n 71.

attention on the issue, are more likely to be able to *gauge* accurately the likelihood of their product causing injury than the buyer or her insurer. They are therefore more likely to set *this element* of the insurance premium accurately. Even so, it is probably a good guess that *insurance* via liability is a less efficient, more regressive and paternalistic regime than first-party insurance. But where does that conclusion get us and the critics of product rules?

5   THE 'BACK TO CONTRACT' SCHOOL

For many on the 'right', representing product liability as being based on the insurance justification is a simple device to lead us 'back' to their favoured freedom of contract regime. The allegedly oppressive impact on the poor of s 402A, viewed as a insurance mechanism, is used by the most extreme member of this group, Huber, to argue passionately for a reform which vindicates the right of the poor to be 'free' to buy tainted yoghurt.[54] In his somewhat notorious *Liability: The Legal Revolution and its Consequences* (1988),[55] he advocates a return to a caveat emptor regime under which buyers would be left free to take out as much or as little first-party insurance against product risks as they choose.

Less extreme 'back to contract' analyses are the work of Priest, Alan Schwartz and (the later writings) of Epstein who sweepingly asserts that 'the adverse consequences of the modern American (tort) system can be traced to one central theme: the decline of freedom of contract and the rise of direct judicial regulation'.[56] Epstein accepts, however, following Posner this far, that it may be preferable in a context of imperfect information to impose a liability which reflects (what we guess is) the average bargain, the 'consensual norm', which fully-informed buyers would be willing and able to pay for. Protection of the autonomy of potential victims, ironically, may require a liability rule to mimic agreements they and defendants would want to make if fully informed. This could well involve, for example, making producers strictly liable for manufacturing defects, but with coverage only for physical losses and not pure loss of profit claims. Then, however, Epstein and his group insist on the protection of the autonomy of the non-average buyer who wants a different division of risks by the enforcement of express warranties and of exclusion clauses. Exclusion clauses are important because, through their deployment, the buyer can take on more risks than average and enjoy a resultant discount in price. A buyer of a product who knows that, since he has already retired, he does not face potential loss of earnings should the product injure him, can put his personal knowledge to his financial advantage by seeking and agreeing to a clause excluding liability for this type of loss – even though the average buyer might not want such a clause.

The idea of imposing a certain liability arrangement to get around information

---

54 P Huber 'Symposium Discussion' (1989) 10 Cardozo LR 2329, 2337.

55 P Huber *Liability: The Legal Revolution and its Consequences* (New York Basic Books, 1988). On which see M Hager 'Civil Compensation and Its Discontents: A Response to Huber' (1990) 42 Stan LR 539.

56 R Epstein 'Product Liability: From Contract to Regulation in the US and Europe' (1989) 9 Tel Aviv University Studies in Law 49, 53; see also eg 'The Risks of Risk/Utility' (1987) 48 Ohio LJ 469, 474. See also A Schwartz 'Proposals for Product Liability Reform: A Theoretical Synthesis' (1988) 97 Yale LJ 353 and 'The Case Against Strict Liability' (1992) 60 Fordham LR 819.

barriers, while vindicating the autonomy of the parties by allowing them to contract around it, is a classic strategy and one which, significantly, is reflected in the original nineteenth-century Sale of Goods legislation (see Chapter 3, under heading 2). The strength the approach has over Huber's is that it recognizes and accommodates the fact that buyers may not only have an interest in insurance, but in avoiding the injury altogether. In imperfect conditions buyers may not be confident that the mere threat of eventual loss of business, which is the only form of deterrence generated under a rule of caveat emptor, will generate an optimal incentive to prevention. If buyers believe that by the imposition of liability sellers will be given a greater incentive to take precautions than merely to adjust prices upwards, then on balance they may prefer a liability regime rather than the cheapest first party insurance. For example, I may well be able to get the cheapest insurance cover against the risk of poisoning from eggs directly from a (first-party) insurer because I am able to specify what heads of loss and what total loss I want to buy cover for; and it *may* then be worth the insurer's while to offer me better rates than other egg eaters. But where I am not the cheapest cost *avoider* of the particular loss, I might prefer safety to savings and prefer a liability regime, if I believe it gives the cheapest cost avoider (directly or indirectly) a better incentive to take precautions. In other words, even if our touchstone *is* 'autonomy' for buyers – or the 'consumer sovereignty norm' – this may well best be served by a liability regime.

(a) Ideological sidewinds in the search for the 'consensual norm'

While the less extreme 'back to contract' strategy just discussed seems to accommodate buyers' interest in safety, it has two dangers. First, the strategy's success depends on how well we can guess what would be the 'consensual norm' in conditions of full information. Yet there is a dearth of reliable data on this. One cannot legitimately use the pattern of agreements, warranties, and so on, which *actually* occur since it is possible, perhaps even likely, that any informationally stronger party will have been able to extract bargains more favourable to it than could have been obtained were there informational equality. The phenomenon of sellers offering 'warranties' which buyers do not appreciate are already required by law is a good example here. The best we can do is guess what the parties' preferences are; for example, the extent to which the average buyer prefers to pursue freedom from, rather than financial security in the event of, a risk eventuating.

Take heads of damage. It is generally agreed that the majority of consumer plaintiffs in product claims would not choose to shift the risk of loss of profits on to the seller because, not being businesses, they are not vulnerable to such loss and so will not want the product price to reflect liability for such loss. The reflection of this 'consensual norm' is the rule that loss of profits is not recoverable under s 402A in most jurisdictions or under the Directive.[57]

But there are some trickier questions than heads of damage. For example, what

---

57 See *Seely* v *White Motor Co* 403 P 2d 145, 151 (1965) and Chapter 11, under heading 2(c). This example also illustrates that inequality of bargaining power may be a necessary but not a sufficient ground for legal intervention since, unless we intend to act paternalistically (ie against the wishes, but in what we claim are the interests, of some group), we need to determine what people would have chosen had they been free to do so.

standard of obligation, if any, would the consensual norm impose in relation to the various classes of product injury? Indeed, would the bargains which buyers and sellers would make, but for informational barriers, reflect our academic classifications of 'foreseeable' versus 'unforeseeable', manufacturing versus design defects, latent versus patent dangers? Would we expect, for example, a separate deal according to each parameter, ie one agreement putting the risk of foreseeable patent manufacturing errors on one party, foreseeable latent manufacturing errors on the other, and so on? Or would the parties be indifferent to some or all of these distinctions on the basis that, quite apart from informational barriers, it is too expensive to fine-tune bargains in this way, or because one side is willing to concede in other areas (such as heads of damage) so long as the other accepts liability across these distinctions (see below)?

Most importantly, the necessity of using intuition[58] about the content of the consensual norm makes the process vulnerable to ideological bias. For example, those who particularly fear government control of the individual and who see adjudication by courts of open-ended standards as a form of 'government' control may characterize the adoption by courts of standards of reasonableness or cost/benefit ('risk/utility' in US terminology) as a lamentable move in the direction of 'a rejection of markets in favour of explicit government control'.[59] It is a short step from finding such adjudications distasteful to assuming that contracting parties for some reason share the same conclusion: 'reasonableness rules are too complicated to be attractive in any consensual situation'.[60] Such an ideological stance then forces the analyst, when faced with clear examples where contracting parties *have* apparently adopted a reasonableness standard – contracts of service, contracts for services, etc – to read down the agreement[61] to refer to an 'industry standard' version of reasonableness which reduces the courts' adjudicative discretion (while favouring business). The application of such thinking requires that where there is differential access to knowledge about risk among the parties, the standard of the liability will not be open-ended but mechanical. To this end the back-to-contract analyst such as Epstein asserts that under the consensual norm in product liability, liability is imposed for manufacturing errors and latent design conditions as a result of which a product does 'not perform in accordance with its own performance standards when put into ordinary use'; and as a corollary there should be no liability for patent defects (the patent/latent distinction being treated as relatively clear and unproblematic).[62] But while this consensual norm certainly selects for liability those cases where the consumer is likely to be less knowledgeable about the risk, is it true that it reduces the open-endedness of the enquiry? The strength of a chair or the crashworthiness of a car are presumably latent factors. If a chair collapses under the weight of a feather, it comes within the concept of a product design failing in ordinary use. But what if a

---

58 As conceded by Alan Schwartz 'Proposals for Product Liability Reform' op cit 366.

59 R Epstein 'The Unintended Revolution in Product Liability Law' (1989) 10 Cardozo LR 2193, 2206. See also A Schwartz 'Proposals for Product Liability Reform' op cit 383 ff.

60 R Epstein 'The Historical Origins and Economic Structure of Workers' Compensation Law' (1982) 16 Ga LR 775, 802.

61 And case law (often boldly against the evidence, see eg R Epstein 'The Risks of Risk/Utility' (1987) 48 Ohio St LJ 469, 472, n 13, which presents evidence directly in opposition to the assertion in the text that traditionally 'compliance with custom was virtually a safe harbor'.)

62 R Epstein 'Product Liability: The Search for the Middle Ground' (1978) 56 NCL Rev 643, 648; 'The Risks of Risk/Utility' (1987) 48 Ohio St LJ 469, 474.

chair collapses with a 5-stone person, a 10-stone person, a 40-stone person? What is 'ordinary use', and who is to decide? And what about 'performance standards'? How many and how serious must a drug's side effects be before it falls below its performance standards, and who is to decide?

The search for the consensual norm can also be distorted by the searcher's selective sensitivity to other issues. Take unforeseeable losses. Epstein, for example, notes that while strict liability is appropriate for manufacturing errors, it would be wholly inappropriate for unforeseeable losses.[63] The reasoning seems to be that a strict liability regime in the design field might inhibit research and development. Yet a searcher for the consensual norm *who had a victim's sensitivities* might stress the buyer's possible belief that, in terms of her amalgam of interests in both safety from and insurance against the occurrence of the injurious event, *she* would be better off if liability here were imposed on the seller. We might even guess that the consensual norm at which such opposing interests might arrive was one in which (i) the buyer succeeded in throwing on to the seller the risk of all foreseeable and unforeseeable physical injuries due to the manufacture and design of the product (the liability rule thereby escaping at least some of the uncertainty attendant on a defect-based rule) with allowances for contributory negligence and volenti, and (ii) the seller succeeded in imposing limitations on the heads of damage recoverable, for example, excluding claims for loss of profit consequential on the product injuring property already owned by the buyer, and excluding claims for non-economic losses. In other words, both sides might prefer to treat *all* product risks in the same way and accept full strict liability limited in terms of types of loss. Of course, we cannot know for sure what the consensual norm would be, but to the extent that Epstein's evident bias towards suppliers' concerns, such as the inhibition of R & D, lead him to a consensual norm probably different from that which the parties would actually prefer, he is himself open to the charge of paternalism with which he berates the drafters of s 402A and the Directive – in his case, a paternalism which favours business.

(b) Exclusion clauses and barriers to 'voluntary' bargains by a fully-informed buyer and paternalism

The second problem with the less extreme 'back to contract' approach is that, while based on sensitivity to one form of inequality of bargaining power (the informational difficulties of buyers), it is insensitive – perhaps wilfully blind – to those remaining forms of inequality of bargaining power which legal economists have shown can prevent even a fully informed buyer extracting the bargain she wants and is willing to pay for (see Chapter 5, under heading 7). Whether 'freedom of contract', particularly with respect to exclusion clauses, really is the preferable route to protecting the autonomy of buyers, or whether it is the guise under which they are oppressed and sellers enriched, depends on a number of factors including how close to the consensual norm the distribution of risk between the parties achieved by the initial liability is, and how 'voluntary' any acceptance of exclusion clauses would be in the particular market conditions.[64]

---

63 R Epstein *Modern Product Liability Law* (Westport, Quorum Books, 1980) 150; 'Legal Liability for Medical Innovation' (1987) 8 Cardozo LR 1139, 1157–8.
64 It should now be clear just how rhetorically useful the insurance justification has been to the back-

In a perfect product market it would be irrelevant as between buyer and seller where the product risk lay, since whatever readjustment of the risk around the initial legal entitlements the parties agreed on, if any, it could be taken account of in the price mechanism. Thus, if we shifted to a caveat emptor regime, we would in theory expect prices to fall an appropriate amount, and where an individual buyer wanted to shift the risk on to the seller, he could offer to pay for a suitable warranty. In a shift from caveat emptor to a regime of (disclaimable) warranty we would expect prices to rise, and where an individual buyer in such a regime wanted to bear the risk she could accept an exclusion clause along with an appropriate discount from the price (see Figure 5.2). We saw, however, that in the real world there are market phenomena which may inhibit individual buyers securing the deal they want and are able to pay for. The difficulty buyers have in shopping around, especially in concentrated mass-markets, can prevent the market mechanism producing the variety of offers theory suggests and achieving the full price fall or rise appropriate to the arrangement.[65] In particular, there was widespread post-war concern that warranties of quality in goods were so widely disclaimed by sellers that those buyers who wanted them often found it impossible to contract on that basis, while those who did not were not securing an appropriate discount for the exclusion (see Chapter 3, under heading 2). The effect of such market conditions is not only to infringe the autonomy of many buyers, but to make sellers *richer* at the expense of buyers relative to what would be the case if buyers could, for example, extract the appropriate discount for accepting the exclusion clause.

The back-to-contract school tend to ignore or downplay these market phenomena. By simply asserting that 'someone must have an incentive to break the logjam'[66] the conclusion is reached that this distortion is not a significant factor in the market, and so long as initial rules deal with the risk informational issue, whatever business is able to get away with in terms of clauses excluding that liability must be the 'ideal' or consensual norm. The irony is that what we witness business getting away with are *uniform* inflexible limitations or disclaimers of goods warranties in mass-markets. Yet with bootstrap logic, pro-contract theorists then see this uniformity and inflexibility as proof of business having competitively adjusted to the consensual norm[67] (set by the brave breaker of the logjam) (see Chapter 5, under heading 7) rather than as evidence that businesses need make no such readjustment to consumer pressure, given the degree of concentration in the mass market.

---

to-contract analysts, because it enables them to portray the product rules of s 402A and the Directive as oppressive, paternalistic and regressive. This usefully disguises the possibility that a return to more freedom of contract, specifically in relation to exclusion clauses, in certain markets would have both a greater paternalistic element, since arguably more buyers would be forced into arrangements they do not want, and would have a pronounced re-distributional impact in favour of business. I do not doubt there are sound distributional arguments which might be made against the product rules in terms of squeezing of profit margins with the result that business shifts production out of the jurisdiction or into a socially less useful line of business (see Chapter 9, under heading 5). But such arguments should be made openly without the beguiling rhetoric of autonomy and paternalism which in fact can cut both ways.

65 A point noted by UK judges, see eg 'Consumers who have need of manufactured articles and services are not in a position to bargain', *Smith* v *Eric S Bush* [1989] 2 All ER 514, 520 (Lord Templeman). For a philosophical treatment of such unjust 'exploitation' within 'free' bargains, see J Lucas *On Justice* (Oxford, Clarendon Press, 1980) 211–2, 216 ff.

66 R Epstein 'Beyond Foreseeability: Consequential Damages in the Law of Contract' (1989) 18 J Legal Studies 105, 116. See also Fried op cit 104, although compare 107.

67 G Priest 'A Theory of the Consumer Product Warranty' (1987) 90 Yale LJ 1297, 1317.

Moreover, where does this put the argument about autonomy? Pro-contract commentators such as Huber start out by showing how, under s 402A, a standard price increment reflecting liability insurance acts regressively against poor buyers seen from the perspective of the alleged insurance goal of liability. But his result only follows because it is not economic for suppliers to tailor the price increments attributable to undisclaimable liability according to the risk level of the individual buyer. Nonetheless, Huber ends by proposing 'free contract' regimes in which vindication of the buyer's autonomy depends on her being able to extract just this sort of tailor-made arrangements either from first-party insurers (in Huber's scheme) or suppliers (in Epstein's). And yet what evidence there is seems to suggest great uniformity of contract terms, especially in supply contracts.

If, in Epstein's regime of liability reflecting the consensual norm with freedom to exclude liability, at least some non-average buyers were free to obtain their preferred bargain by accepting appropriate finely-tuned exclusion clauses, it would no doubt be, in terms of protection of autonomy, superior to a liability regime which banned exclusion clauses. If, however, market conditions are such that suppliers respond to a freedom to use exclusion clauses by offering a uniform exclusion clause, buyers must take it or leave it and have no greater freedom than in a regime which bans exclusion clauses. In neither regime is it meaningful to say that individual autonomy is respected. At best we can compare the regimes in terms of which better reflects the wishes of the majority.[68] If in Epstein's regime uniform exclusion clauses reflect a distribution of risks between buyers and sellers which is further away from the true consensual norm (eg, by purporting to exclude any liability for personal injuries) than the initial liability, then a regime which banned such exclusion clauses would be better at protecting the autonomous wishes of the majority. Even though it forces non-average buyers into deals they do not want, these buyers would be fewer in number than those oppressed by the Epstein regime. If paternalistic motives are ones which seek to set up a legal rule in order to improve someone's welfare by getting them to behave in their 'own real interests', even though those who are supposedly to benefit would choose different behaviour,[69] then, in certain market conditions, adoption of Epstein's regime could be portrayed as more paternalistic than adoption of one which banned exclusion clauses.

What this means is that one cannot simply portray any regime which bans exclusion clauses as more paternalistic than one which does not. In imperfect market conditions, either regime forces some parties to accept deals they would not freely choose to accept. If the dynamics of the market force people to be treated as groups, then the evaluation, in terms of vindication of 'autonomy', of the legal order operating in that market must take this into account. So the question should be, which regime forces more parties to accept unwanted deals and is therefore more paternalistic? The answer to this question depends on how large a market one is looking at (eg all buyers of all goods or only commercial buyers of vehicles, etc) because the consensual norm will vary with the size of the market. The answer also depends on the power of sellers in the market to impose uniform exclusion clauses which shift

---

68 Compare J Attanasio 'The Principle of Aggregate Autonomy and the Calabresian Approach to Product Liability' (1988) 74 Virg LR 677.

69 The distinction, according to Kennedy, between paternalistic and distributive motives: D Kennedy 'Distributive and Paternalistic Motives in Contract and Tort Law, With Special Reference to Compulsory Terms and Unequal Bargaining Power' (1982) 41 Maryland LR 563, 570, 572.

the distribution of risk away from the consensual norm. When dealing with sweeping legal rules, such as s 402A, which cover many different market types, answers to these questions must be crude 'averages'. Even so, it is (at least to European eyes) a sound guess that in the narrower market covered by the Directive (the market of goods supplied commercially for private purposes) most buyers cannot resist exclusion clauses, so that the safer, less paternalistic, course is that they should be banned. Of course, the validity of this conclusion also requires that the liability initially imposed reflects the consensual norm, and in particular that it does not shift on to suppliers risks which the majority of private buyers would choose to bear themselves. While arguments about autonomy may be a sound basis for criticism of the fine detail of the content of product rules (especially concerning, for example, heads of loss), where the rules are limited in operation to markets in which power to resist exclusion clauses is uncommon, the autonomy argument provides *support* for the ban on exclusion clauses, *not* their permission.

A mirror can also be held up to the attack by the back-to-contract theorists on s 402A (and the Directive) as being, from an insurance perspective, redistributional and in particular regressive against the poor. A 'move back to contract', such as allowing exclusions of all liability for personal injuries, would result in lower prices, but in only an *averaged* lowered price; and this would redistribute *to the poor* (relative to today). Yet using civil liability to redistribute to the poor is widely regarded – *especially by the 'right'* – as an inappropriate technique for alleviating poverty. Does this mean we should – simply because of its possible redistributive impact in practice – reject out of hand arguments for a return to freer contracting?

We have now come full circle because the answer to this question depends, of course, on which effects of a legal rule you choose to look at. Every change of civil liability rules is redistributive, and is therefore prone to the objection that *if* this redistribution was its goal, this was an inappropriate avenue to use to achieve it. More generally, how well our rationales will appear to work depends on how far we follow the ripple effects of a legal rule. Of course, if we pursue the ripples of tort liability into the insurance pools we will find it operating regressively against *someone*. Insurance *by its nature* does this for, whether of the first party or third party kind, it acts regressively against any member of the pool who presents a lower than average risk. Indeed, whenever any element of liability insurance is passed on to any group of potential plaintiffs it can be portrayed as regressive if damages are linked to the plaintiff's standard of living. This applies, for example, to tort damages in personal injury cases: if a British Rail fare contains a flat rate element to take account of third-party liability insurance premiums, it operates regressively against the poor because, if a rich and a poor passenger are injured by the carelessness of a driver, the rich tort plaintiff will receive more from the relevant liability insurance pool than the poor person, even though they had earlier paid the same amount in 'cover'. What 'back-to-contract' analysts downplay is that the same applies to contract liability as well, as is illustrated by the same British Rail example, assuming that the rich and poor passengers sue in contract. It is also shown by an example involving claims on the implied warranty of merchantability, or even on express warranties. The fact is that it is not worth while for the insurer (in a first-party insurance contract) or the potential defendant (in the liability context) to sub-divide his dealings with potential victims in order to avoid large regressive effects.

Obsession with insurance pools and regressiveness leads people to suggest either a ban on insurance or the cutting back of the liability itself in order to reduce its regressive impact. The latter tactic seems to be that favoured by the back-to-contract scholars in their campaign against tort liability. But so long as we are content to retain civil liability we could, in our search for a moral justification for a particular legal rule such as the Directive, choose to ignore the possibility that defendants may be insured, with its distributional implications. We could then concentrate on explaining why particular parties are held liable, producing rationales couched in either corrective or distributive justice terminology, to test against the many dimensions of the rule. The principal attraction of doing this and ignoring the insurance dimension is that it prevents us overlooking the vital class of bystanders and thereby guides us towards the values which tort laws are more probably attempting to vindicate. The insurance rationale and the back-to-contract theorists' 'solutions' to it depend on ignoring, or at least side-lining, bystanders (see Chapter 6, under heading 3). If we allowed bystander injuries the central place they deserve in tort we would clearly see that rules such as the special products rules in tort could not sensibly have been based on a goal of insurance. Bystanders are strangers to the defendant and have paid and will pay no element which could be construed as an insurance premium. Were insurance a *goal* of the product rules – and along with others it *is* one of the rationales used by European reformers[70] – they would not cover claims by bystanders because, seen from this perspective, such claims allow injured bystanders to freeload off defendants and premium-paying buyers. But the very raison d'être of European reform was to allow such claims.

6   COLLECTIVISM

The centrality of bystanders in tort law in general and in the European reform of product liability in particular contradicts the claim that a coherent and important goal of such law is insurance. At most such rules can be presented as having insurance *effects* where the 'freeloading' of bystanders off those other potential victims who had had to pay an element in price to cover liability costs – while not coherent as a *goal* of civil liability – is yet a tolerable side effect of the pursuit of other goals. Put more generally, the acceptance of the proposition that distributive goals are not appropriately pursued via civil liability does not mean that the redistributive side-effects of the pursuit of other goals is intolerable – indeed, we have seen that such side-effects are inevitable in changes to and the operation of liability rules (see Chapter 6, under heading 6).

The reason a distributive goal such as insurance cannot be a goal of civil liability is that it does not explain the boundaries of tort law: why, for example, some injured people are not given a claim by tort. One value which could be used to generate boundaries for civil liability is autonomy – not merely a respect for the autonomy of defendants/injurers, because this leads to a 'no-liability' position, nor an absolute respect for the autonomy of the injured for this leads, as we have seen, to the open-ended compensation goal. But civil liability such as tort is best seen as reflecting the compromise between the freedom of defendants to act in a way that injures others and the freedom of others not to be injured. The boundaries of tort liability could be seen, for example, as guesses as to the trade-offs in autonomy between potential

70 Pearson Com para 1235; Law Coms para 38(c).

defendants and potential victims which these parties would have reached had they been able to arrange it. Such guesses have to deal with the parties at the most general level, ie that of social groups. *This 'collectivist' guess need not be paternalistic* in the sense of the law seeking what is 'best' for the individual or society, but may simply be an attempt to mimic what individuals, necessarily dealt with as a social aggregate, would have regarded as the correct balance of interest, autonomy, risk, etc. One way of putting this is that at the level of civil obligations between certain parties, the best way individual autonomy can be vindicated is by a concern with *social values*. These may then include factors such as a concern with the social costs of opening the 'floodgates' of litigation to which an individual might not advert.

On this view of tort law, the spheres in which such collectivist guesses would fall to be made include not only those of bystander injuries but cases where there is reason to believe that, although the injured and injurer were in some formal bargaining relationship, their overt bargain does not reflect the bargain free individuals would reach if forced to compromise. In the twentieth century we have come to realize how often transaction costs are so high that legal rules are needed to establish the consensual norm. If the parties are in contractual privity then we may be inclined to call such rules rules of contract law and speak of terms implied by law; if they are not, we will call them rules of tort law. But in either case these rules perform the same juristic function and it matters little in the former case whether we call them rules of contract law or tort law. The back-to-contract theorists fail to recognize the role of this form of intervention in protecting autonomy by failing to accommodate rules implied by law in their theories (see Chapter 6, under heading 3, and Chapter 13, under heading 5).

7   PATERNALISM

What does it mean to say that product rules, like much 'consumer protection', is motivated by paternalism? We have just seen that in real markets a fully informed buyer may still not be able to get the deal he/she wants because of the nature of the market, and this led us to the possibility that autonomy arguments could support a liability rule reflecting the trade-off, the 'consensual norm', and a ban on exclusion clauses. But even in the absence of such market forces, a buyer may not *choose* what is regarded as best for her. Imposition of a legal regime motivated by a desire to improve someone's welfare, even though they would not choose that arrangement, is paternalistic.

A paternalist might well defend compulsory contract terms and imposed obligations such as the irrebuttable warranty of merchantability and the Directive (with its ban on exclusion clauses) regardless of how weak or strong the parallel efficiency or distributional rationales may be. The law's setting of minimum levels of quality and/ or safety could be rationalized on the basis that, for example, we estimate that fully informed buyers, users and bystanders would at least have sought such a level had it not been for factors such as irrationality and bounded rationality. It would be argued that the civil law is an appropriate instrument to protect citizens from their own folly and here, unusually, paternalism and efficiency strategies coincide.[71] A paternalist

---

71 A Kronman 'Paternalism and the Law of Contracts' (1983) 92 Yale LJ 763, 766.

might, alternatively or in addition, be keen to increase the reach of liability in order to promote the 'goal' of insurance of victims[72] while conveniently turning a blind eye to the distributional consequences – favourable to bystanders and unfavourable to others such as poor buyers. Similarly, paternalists might regard certain values such as a basic level of safety in goods as so important to the 'decency' or 'humanity' of the community that it should be mandated by civil law even though it sets a standard in goods which the poor would not be able to afford in direct dealings, and even though its indirect effect might be to price some of the poor out of the relevant market.

This argument, which combines a paternalistic level of safety with a positive embrace of the social insurance effects of civil liability, is amorphous. Yet it did seem to form a theme in the products reform debate in Europe. The tenor of the Thalidomide debate, for example, suggests that many think it the 'decent' thing for the unforeseeable losses caused by drugs to be borne by the manufacturer, even if the economically more efficient position would be to let them rest where they initially fall, on the victim. To put an emotionally charged example: suppose that the 'back-to-contract' school tolerates a manufacturer or retailer being held prima facie liable for supplying tainted yoghurt, but insists that the autonomy of the poor be protected by enabling the poor purchaser to bargain for a lower price by the acceptance of an exclusion clause relating to the risk of personal injuries of which she has (let us say) been adequately warned. The idea that the poor should be put in this position may seem distasteful to the community at large. We might speculate that the setting of minimum (non-negotiable) standards of safety in goods by the imposition of civil liability assists, and is perhaps necessary for, the market system to maintain its high level of community support in the modern age. It is not too fanciful to suggest that a market system which sold tainted yoghurt or very risky children's toys to the poor and let the loss lie where it fell would lose public confidence. That is, the very sort of reasons which support public regulation of a bare level of safety in goods can also be used to support the paternalist's defence of product liability. Nonetheless, though attractive and probably an important rhetorical theme in reform, paternalism is so vague it can be tailored to fit any of the relevant forms of legal intervention, whether full strict liability, hindsight-cost-benefit or negligence, depending on the desired result. It supports rather than dictates specific reform options.

72 Kennedy op cit 626.

CHAPTER 9

Gaps in the theoretical basis of the Directive

1 OVERVIEW

At this point we can draw together and summarize the foregoing search through modern theories of civil liability for a basis to the stricter liability created in the products field. We found that while there are sound reasons why a general strict liability has no moral foundation, a coherent moral theory of limited strict liability can be constructed (the 'moral enterprise liability' argument) which helps to explain certain types of civil and statutory liability, such as vicarious liability and workers' compensation. We saw how the 'back-to-contract' school argued that moral respect for autonomy demanded a liability regime of substantially different content to the full strict liability which could be supported by a version of the moral enterprise liability argument and a liability which was excludable. Such a strategy was found to hinge, just as more overtly collectivist and paternalist strategies do, on ideologically vulnerable guesses as to what people would want. Once account was taken of bystanders and of others who are similarly unable to bargain, it was found that the existence of tort and terms implied by law necessarily required a broader vision either of what people wanted (Chapter 8, under heading 6) or what was paternalistically thought good for them (Chapter 8, under heading 7). In other words, it was not possible merely to construct a coherent theory of civil obligation out of a concern for autonomy since the line at which the law should intervene to ensure the correct balance of interests between plaintiff and defendant was crucially dependent on guesses as to what people want or should want. It is, for example, wholly possible to present moral enterprise liability as that form of intervention by the law which best vindicates the autonomy of the relevant parties as well as reflecting, or perhaps because it reflects, the weight given by individuals and society to outcome responsibility in the context of business activity. The arguments of the back-to-contract theorists do not, therefore, damage the claim that a moral enterprise liability argument can provide a coherent robust theory on which to base limited stricter liability.

2 REFORMERS' INITIAL POSITION: HINDSIGHT COST-BENEFIT AND THE MORAL BASIS OF 'DEFECT'

The regime actually proposed by the initial European reformers (and the regime which s 402A had seemed to reflect in the US until *Beshada* (1982)) is one of hindsight cost-benefit liability (see Figure 5.1 and Chapter 6, under heading 4). Under this regime the enterprise bears risks or 'bad luck' only in cases where the costs of the product outweigh its benefits or, in other words, where the product is 'defective'. It would cover the allegedly unforeseeable losses of the Thalidomide children, but not the losses caused by aspirin to those few who suffer severe side effects, because the social benefits of aspirin clearly outweigh these costs. Where did this cost/benefit, or 'defect' boundary, come from, and can a moral defence of it be made? After all, if it is to be no defence for the defendant to show she used all reasonable care, and that she could not have foreseen the risk, why should the utility of her conduct be an exculpatory factor? Where is the moral rationale for allowing those who benefit from the aspirin enterprise to do so at the expense of (exploiting?) those who suffer ill effects? The version of moral enterprise liability developed in the earlier discussion is not an adequate or complete answer, for that version suggested that all losses of specified types due to product condition be borne by the enterprise and not just those generated by risks which, with hindsight, appear too costly to have been run. It provided a sound reason for imposing strict liability on business activity, but can it be coherently modified to explain the defect requirement?

This search for a moral rationale for the defect requirement is important for two reasons. First, policing this boundary is particularly expensive, often requiring costly expert evidence. Secondly, since, as I have argued elsewhere, a judicious manipulation of the foreseeability concept allows all but a very few cases to be portrayed as 'foreseeable' risks, it is the defect requirement which drags back the move to stricter liability to something comparable to a negligence regime (see Chapter 6, under heading 4, and Chapter 10, under heading 3). It is the inclusion of utility as an exculpatory factor in the formulation of the new rules which most dulls their impact, at least from a doctrinal point of view.

(a) The reform as super-negligence

A factor said to have influenced reformers on both sides of the Atlantic was the pragmatic goal of easing the plaintiff's task of proving breach of a standard of care ('negligence-in-fact') against complex commercial concerns.[1] There was a view that most product-related injuries were probably due to manufacturer negligence, but that they arose in circumstances which made this difficult and costly for plaintiffs to prove. The possibility, therefore, arises that the reform was really intended as a form of super-negligence from which the inclusion of the defect requirement would naturally follow, and that the elements of strict liability were nothing more than inevitable side effects of overcoming the particular proof problems allegedly suffered by product victims, rather than the outcome of a new moral vision of civil liability.

It is undeniable that a concern with difficulties of proof has played a significant role in the development of certain spheres of civil obligation; Chamberlain used such concern to support his call for the introduction of workers' compensation; it has been argued that the rule in *Rylands* v *Fletcher*, far from being an independent strict liability, is simply a covert pocket of super-negligence in which the fault principle is not displaced, but where the defendant bears the virtually impossible burden of disproving negligence; and evidentiary problems facing plaintiffs in certain types

---

1 See eg Law Coms para 23(e), 38(e). G Schwartz 'The Vitality of Negligence and the Ethics of Strict Liability' (1981) 15 Georgia LR 963; 'New Products, Old Products, Evolving Law, Retroactive Law' (1983) 58 NYULR 796, 809–910.

of negligence case have led the courts to invent remarkably imaginative routes around traditional causal requirements with the effect of creating what could be called strict liability.[2]

But were the initial product reform proposals simply designed to alleviate proof problems? The flaw in this suggestion is that, if this had been the aim, the least disruptive strategy would have been simply to reverse, within a retained negligence system, the burden of proof on the issue of fault in roughly the sort of way the 1991 draft Directive on liability for defective services did.[3] Yet despite shifting the burden of proof on a number of other significant issues, UK and European reformers explicitly rejected this strategy because of the centrality in European eyes of the need for the new liability to cover unforeseeable losses, such as those allegedly involved in the Thalidomide[4] case.

(b)   Representational theories

Another candidate for the origin of the 'defect' boundary in reform proposals is the manufacturer's representations of the safety of a particular product and/or the consumer's expectations of it. Concern with these runs as a strong theme through early US case law on the modern products rule and surfaces as one of the plethora of 'policies' by which the Law Commission and other European reformers claim to have been guided.[5] Whatever its merits as a rationale of the merchantability requirement in the law of sales (see (d) below), in the tort context, where bystanders are central to any moral rationale, the representations of the defendant must be irrelevant, given that bystander injuries are not triggered by reliance on such representations, except in a most attenuated way.

(c)   The fallacy about 'but-for' liability

Law reformers in Europe and the US gave little thought to possible justifications of the 'defect' requirement. Those who did advert to the possibility of the shift to a 'defect-free' strict liability regime (such as 'full strict liability', see Figure 5.1) confused such strict liability with a liability in which a product manufacturer would be held liable for any injury which, but for the condition of his product, would not have been suffered. I took pains earlier to show that this unacceptable result which would, for example, render a gun manufacturer liable (in effect an 'insurer') for every victim killed or injured by it would not follow from the adoption of a full strict liability regime (Chapter 6, under heading 4, Chapter 7, under heading 3(b)). This is

---

2 See respectively: 8 Official Report, 4th Series (21 Jan–20 Feb 1893) cols 1967, 1969; S Stoljar 'Concerning Strict Liability' in *Essays on Torts* ed P Finn (Sydney, Law Book Co, 1989); *McGhee* v *National Coal Board* [1973] 1 WLR 1; *Cook* v *Lewis* [1951] SCR 830; *Sindell* v *Abbott Laboratories* 607 P 2d 924 (1980). On the 'justice' of such moves see H Hart *The Concept of Law* (Oxford, Clarendon Press, 1961) 162.

3 OJ No C 12/8, 18.1.91, see 12.08.

4 Law Coms para 34.

5 See eg *Restatement of Torts* (2nd) s 402A, comment g; *Henningsen* v *Bloomfield Motors Inc* 161 A 2d 69, 82–4 (1960); W Prosser 'The Assault Upon the Citadel (Strict Liability to the Consumer)' (1960) 69 Yale LJ 1099, 1123; M Shapo 'A Representational Theory of Consumer Protection: Doctrine, Function and Legal Liability' (1974) 60 Virg LR 1109; Law Coms para 23(d), 38(d).

because the latter would require more than a mere 'but-for' relation to the harm: the condition of the product would actually have to *cause* the injury. Nevertheless, the misguided association of 'defect-free' strict liabilities with a bizarre 'but-for' liability persisted, and was indirectly supported by the academic dominance of Posner and his argument that a cost/benefit, or 'defect', limitation was normal, efficient and justifiable.

(d)   Origin in warranty: moral basis of unmerchantability requirement in warranty claims

The assumption that a defect requirement was needed in any new products rule was also supported, indeed probably determined, by the warranty context in which the products rules evolved. As we saw in Chapter 2, the modern products reform movement originated in the simplistic belief that the benefits of warranty law could be spread to those non-privy victims who had been injured by products. The relevant warranty claims required the plaintiff to prove the product was unmerchantable, and the assumption that the parallel new tort rule would be comparably limited was easily made. This suggests that a search for a moral basis for the defect limitation in the Directive and in s 402A would be illuminated by an examination of the moral justifications developed for the unmerchantability requirement in warranty claims. Yet surprisingly little attention has been paid by contract theorists to this issue of unmerchantability – the 'very heart of the law of sale'[6], so we must speculate. The implied warranty of merchantability cannot be rationalized as a mere recognition by the nineteenth-century judges who developed it of terms implied *in fact*, ie terms which, had the parties been asked at the time of agreement, they would have acknowledged as underlying their understanding. After all, some sellers were no doubt relying on the caveat emptor principle which had been vindicated in other nineteenth-century cases in order to protect them from liability in the event of the goods they sold proving unmerchantable. In their eyes there would have been no 'gap' to be filled in the agreement, and so moral theories about how to fill gaps in a set of express terms – for example, by relying on the idea of promise – fail to justify the merchantability requirement. To deal with the issue by simply asserting that it is a 'fair implication' that sellers/manufacturers make a strict promise of merchantability, a promise that the good will 'do the job', is unconvincing.[7]

On the other hand, one could argue that where parties disagree about a contractual issue – here, about where the risks of lack of product quality lie – then it is morally sound to guess what the parties would have agreed had they been *forced* to a compromise. Working backwards, one could then assert that such a compromise would be one which divided the risks according to a concept of merchantability, drawing some support from the fact that nineteenth-century cotton traders chose to conduct business on the basis of an express standard term of merchantability.[8] But even if this *is* the compromise a buyer and seller linked by the price mechanism would

---

6 P Atiyah *The Sale of Goods*, 8th edn (London, Pitman, 1990) 142.

7 Compare C Fried *Contract as Promise* (Cambridge, Harvard University Press, 1981) 22–3 and J Gordley *The Philosophical Origins of Modern Contract Doctrine* (Oxford, Clarendon Press, 1991) 242–3.

8 A W B Simpson 'The Origins of Futures Trading in the Liverpool Cotton Market' in *Essays for Patrick Atiyah*, ed P Cane & J Stapleton (Oxford, Clarendon Press, 1991) 179, 185, n 35.

reach, it does not mean that it is an appropriate standard to apply in claims by bystanders. Here the fiction of a forced compromise collapses into the most abstract collectivist guess about what a society of individuals (not necessarily linked by the price mechanism) would agree to (see Chapter 8, under heading 6). It is not self evident that strangers would arrive at a compromise based on the hindsight cost-benefit distinction reflected in the initial European reform proposals.

3   UTILITY, BAD LUCK AND A MODIFIED DEFECT-LIMITED VERSION OF MORAL ENTERPRISE LIABILITY

Even if the foregoing arguments are conceded, that is, (1) that the commitment to stricter product liability did not necessitate a defect requirement, (2) that a 'defect-free' regime, such as full strict liability based on causation and other boundaries, is workable and morally coherent (Chapter 7, under heading 3(b), Chapter 8), and (3) that adoption of a defect requirement by law reformers was ill-informed, we may still be able to construct a moral defence of its inclusion. This involves looking at the issue of utility.

There are two relevant 'defect-free' standards of strict liability: the full strict liability described in detail earlier; and a strict liability based on foresight (see Figure 5.1). Some moralists, while adhering to the traditional philosophical view that responsibility for unforeseeable risks is unjust (see Chapter 7, under heading 5), reject a limitation of liability based on cost/benefit notions. They argue that tort law should be based on a system of rights and that the introduction of utility considerations in this way prevents this.[9] Under such 'foresight strict liability', defendants ought to be liable for causing foreseeable harm regardless of the utility of their conduct. The idea that a party should be liable for running a known risk at another's expense is not an odd one. The famous outcry over the failure of the injured woman to recover in *Bolton* v *Stone* is testament to this, as is the community's punitive distaste for a manufacturer calculating whether it is cheaper to remedy a known risk or to run it, thereby injuring innocent users of his product.[10] The consensus behind the covert imposition of strict liability for manufacturing errors could be said to reflect a similar moral sentiment. A problem with this moral idea, however, is that if rights are linked to the causation of harm, then utility considerations will sometimes creep in anyway, since judgments about causation can turn on issues of moral expectations themselves linked to notions of utility (see Chapter 6, under heading 2). Could it not be that the mother is said to 'cause' the death of her child by neglect, whereas the stranger is not, because we expect the mother to act, and we do this because it is the more useful arrangement from a society's point of view? There is, in other words, a countervailing theme in civil liability, in particular surfacing in elements of the

9 See eg J Steiner 'Putting Fault Back into Products Liability: A Modest Reconstruction of Tort Theory' (1982) 1 Law & Phil 419; G Fletcher 'Fairness and Utility in Tort Theory' (1972) 85 Harvard LR 537, 169; S Perry 'The Impossibility of General Strict Liability' (1988) 1 Can JL Juris 147; A Harari, *The Place of Negligence in the Law of Torts* (Sydney, Law Book Co, 1962); early Epstein's writings.
10 See respectively R Epstein 'A Theory of Strict Liability' (1973) 2 J Legal Studies 151, 170; *Grimshaw* v *Ford Motor Co* 174 Cal Rptr 348 (1981), on which see G Schwartz 'The Myth of the Ford Pinto Case' (1991) 43 Rutgers LR 1013.

causal determination, which we cannot ignore: that individual rights need be integrated with community interests.

A parallel conclusion can be reached if we ask the question whether a modified version of the moral enterprise liability argument could be devised to support the 'defect-free' regime of 'foresight strict liability'. In the earlier discussion (see Chapter 7, under heading 5), we found that an important gap in Honoré's scheme of a strict liability based on outcome responsibility was the ambiguity of 'bad outcomes': did he mean 'bad' from the victim's point of view or from society's? The economic loss suffered in a free market when an entrant begins to compete successfully is a bad outcome for the individual loser but, far from attracting social discredit for causing this loss, the entrant often wins social credit. If only some of the outcomes which are viewed as 'bad' by the individual victim are viewed as bad outcomes attracting the social discredit underpinning outcome responsibility, the form of strict liability supported by the 'moral enterprise liability' argument (which is an application of outcome responsibility theory) hinges on the nature of those extra factors which filter out certain subjectively bad outcomes in this way. If these factors relate *only* to matters such as the type of loss suffered (eg that inflicting physical loss was a bad outcome both subjectively and socially but inflicting economic loss was not), then the previous assertion that full strict liability is supported by moral enterprise liability holds. Another possibility might be that the moral enterprise liability argument supports only 'foresight strict liability' on the basis that one of the prerequisites of society seeing something as a 'bad outcome' is that the risk of it was foreseeable to the actor. This, however, does not seem a tenable argument – for it suggests society would not view the Thalidomide victim's injuries as bad outcomes simply because they were unforeseeable.

Could it be argued that a version of the moral enterprise liability argument supports a hindsight cost-benefit liability, that is a strict liability which involves the extra limitation of a 'defect' requirement? The answer is yes, if we accept the plausible argument that one prerequisite of our seeing something as a 'bad outcome' for the purposes of outcome responsibility is that overall the conduct of the defendant (whether known to the defendant at the time or not) involved a surplus of social costs loosely defined. This would explain a position in which, for example, a pharmaceutical company was held responsible and incurred social discredit for social disasters such as the Thalidomide injuries (even if unforeseeable), but was not held responsible nor incurred social discredit for aspirin side effects, despite these being foreseeable. In this respect it is noteworthy that the connection between social credit and defect is itself made at places in the European reform documents. The Pearson Commission noted that

> If his product range is a success, the producer will no doubt claim public credit; if a product within that range is *dangerously defective*, he should be prepared to accept a claim for compensation[11] (emphasis added).

So this does seem to provide a coherent moral basis for the defect requirement in the product reforms in Europe and the US.

11 Pearson Com para 1233. See also Law Coms paras 23(a), 38(d).

4   THE STRICTNESS OF WARRANTY

The ability of this version of the moral enterprise liability argument to explain both the defect limitation and the strictness of the hindsight cost-benefit rule initially proposed by European reformers is unmatched by any alternative moral theory. In particular, there has not only been no relevant *moral* defence of the merchantability requirement of the warranty cause of action, out of which grew the movement towards a stricter tort duty with respect to products, but there has been no convincing moral defence of the crucial *strictness* of the implied warranty of merchantability. The modern moral philosopher's argument that strict liability is unjust because it holds a party liable for risks he or she could not foresee and therefore could not avoid (see Chapter 7, under heading 5) is, strangely, not directed at those contractual obligations which are strict. While this is surprising enough in the area of general contract analysis, it is astonishing in the products context[12] because it was the alleged anomaly between those able to sue under the strict warranty and those relegated to proof of negligence in tort which provided the engine for products reform. Without an explanation of why the strict standard is more appropriate and just in the sale of products context (while it is not in the context, say, of the supply of services), this 'anomaly' could just as easily have been resolved by a reduction of the quality standard in the law of sales to one of reasonable care (see Chapter 13, under heading 7). The caselaw in which the strictness of the warranty of merchantability was established provides no clue to such a rationale (see Chapter 2, under heading 2). If anything, it supports the speculation that the strictness of this warranty was simply a side effect of its original association with the warranty of description,[13] which in turn may have owed its strictness to its association with the warranty relating to title which, being vital to property rights, is understandably strict.

But the really interesting issue is whether there exists a moral rationale for the strictness of the warranty of merchantability. The preceding discussion suggests that, were a rationale to be sought, a version of the moral enterprise liability argument could not only support the strictness of the warranty but also its offspring, the hindsight cost-benefit strict liability initially proposed in Europe. The theory justifies the imposition on those acting in the course of business (profit-seeking) of stricter liability. It explains why liability wide enough to encompass unforeseeable bad outcomes should be imposed on those seeking financial profit. And it can be adapted to explain why this should only occur where outcomes are adjudged 'bad' by an objective, social criterion. This leaves us a final set of questions concerning the degree to which the final inclusion of the development risk defence shifted the new regime from this hindsight cost-benefit regime back towards negligence.

---

12 See eg Fried, op cit. Even proponents of negligence standard in tort seem inexplicably to accept the strict standard in contract: see the writings of Weinrib and Posner.

13 *Randall* v *Newsom* (1877) 2 QBD 102, 109. See also *Frost* v *Aylesbury Dairy Co* [1905] 1 KB 608, 610; *H Parsons (Livestock) Ltd* v *Uttley Ingham & Co Ltd* [1978] 1 QB 791, 800; *Raineri* v *Miles* [1981] AC 1050, 1086.

5   THE DEVELOPMENT RISK DEFENCE

The moral complexity of the final Directive stems partly from the inclusion of a 'development risk defence', by which a defendant can escape liability if he proves that 'the state of scientific and technical knowledge at the time when he put the product into circulation was not such as to enable the existence of the defect to be discovered' (Article 7(e)). This can best be discussed here not just in terms of a defence, but as a boundary of the basic liability, since it relates not to the behaviour of any individual defendant, but to the type of risks covered by the Directive. At this point the task is to understand why, and specifically on what possible moral basis, a reform which was initially fuelled by a concern to compensate victims of unforeseeable risks associated with products, ultimately produced a law which provides a defence for just such occurrences.

The key arguments centred on the width of business profit margins, research and development (R & D) and the availability and affordability of risky or new products – arguments which have less to do with the 'correct' or 'just' relationship of injurer to injured and more to do with long-term social good. The demands of inter-party justice may conflict with these other values, as Hart noted,[14] and the general good may require, for example, that no remedy be made available for some moral wrong because the social consequences are unacceptable. Here the argument would be that, although stricter liability for products can be supported by wealth maximization theory and by versions of the moral enterprise liability argument, real world considerations of the risk averseness of producers and insurers, and the relationship of this to R & D and the availability of useful products, are judged to outweigh the efficiency or justice arguments and support the inclusion of a development risk defence so that unforeseeable losses are not borne by enterprise but by victims.

The debate here therefore links up with the earlier discussion of wealth maximization where we found that reform of civil liability is re-distributional and that, whatever goals we may want to pursue in law reform, the strategy in pursuit of them must be tempered by any counteracting sensitivity we have to those who are inevitably, if unintentionally, made poorer by the proposed legal changes (Chapter 6, under heading 6(iv)). We saw, for example, that while single-minded wealth maximizers dispute whether strict liability has any significant efficiency advantages over negligence, the two regimes have dramatically different distributional consequences. Relative to negligence, the initial European proposals would have made consumers better off, while full strict liability would have made them even better off. Thus, a reformer embracing both deterrence and compensation goals might not be convinced by Calabresi's arguments that full strict liability is the more efficient strategy of the two, but embrace it for its redistributional impact.

Here, conversely, pro-market critics of the initial reform proposals in the UK and Europe attacked the proposed shift to stricter liability of producers, and in particular their exposure to liability for unforeseeable losses suffered by non-privy victims, because it would have cut into profit margins of defendants. For these critics the long-term health of a market economy depends less on the dubious fine-tuning of competition which attempts to make prices reflect true social costs purports to achieve, and more on ensuring an adequate and predictable return on capital. The argument was put most emotively in the area of drugs. If profit-margins are

---

14 Hart *The Concept of Law*, op cit 161–2.

squeezed sufficiently a drug company may withdraw a useful product or raise its price above the reach of the poor; or vital R & D might be inhibited or prolonged (the phenomenon of 'drug-lag'). Such phenomena are now well-known in the US across a wide range of industries, and some of the most striking examples of spiralling defence and insurance costs come from the fields of drugs and vaccines where some product lines have been withdrawn, R & D on others terminated, and the price of many of those remaining on the market has been raised dramatically.[15] For example, the increase in the volume of, and cost of defending, tort claims against manufacturers resulted in a sharp fall in the availability of vaccines used for the compulsory childhood immunization programme , so sharp that in 1986 the US government created a mandatory no-fault non-tort compensation scheme in an attempt to stabilize supplies.[16] Society should, therefore, decide – so the argument goes – that even if a negligence regime has a substantially lower deterrent effect on potential defendants relative to a regime of full or hindsight cost-benefit strict liability, and no matter how strong the moral defence of such versions of strict liability could be, preserving the regime of negligence rather than moving to a strict form of producer liability is a price worth paying for the development and affordability of drugs and other useful products.

The initial European reformers, proponents of a hindsight cost-benefit regime covering development risks, *had* considered claims that a move to strict liability for manufacturers would unduly hamper enterprise. Indeed, they included such concerns within their many 'main policy considerations'; but they rejected them.[17] This was understandable. After all, once reformers had assumed that the new liability would be 'defect-bounded', the potential new burden imposed by the shift to strict liability for product manufacturers was substantially reduced. At most producers would face a new liability in those very few cases where, firstly, the relevant risks of a product could not be said, by any stretch of the judicial imagination, to be foreseeable at the time of supply (see Chapter 10, under heading 3); secondly, the risks outweighed the benefits; and, thirdly, where the victim would not have had a remedy in the law of sales already. EC producers already faced exposure for unforeseeable risks in the law of sales, and insurance was obtainable at levels which were neither crippling nor unduly inhibitive of R & D. Such steep rises in insurance costs and resultant squeezing of profit margins as had been observed in the US in the mid-1970s were thought by many to be more probably attributable to insurance cycles and local phenomena, including the use of juries, contingency fees, punitive damages and a general increase in claims consciousness and civil litigation.

Countervailing arguments support the initial position of the European reformers. For example, in those rare cases where a particularly valuable product line is threatened in the way described, government intervention and protection is arguably a

15 See eg *Brown v Superior Court* 751 P 2d 479, 479–480 (Cal Sc, 1988); C Siggins 'Strict Liability for Prescription Drugs: Which Shall Govern – Comment K or Strict Liability Applicable to Ordinary Products?' (1986) 16 Golden Gate ULR 309, 325–6.

16 M Nerars 'The National Childhood Vaccine Injury Act of 1986' (1988) 63 Wash LR 149; V Schwartz and L Mahshigian, 'National Childhood Vaccine Injury Act of 1986: An Ad Hoc Remedy or a Window for the Future?' (1978) 48 Ohio State LJ 387. See also earlier example discussed in M Franklin and J Mais 'Tort Law and Mass Immunization Programs: Lessons from the Polio and Flu Episodes' (1977) 65 Calif LR 754.

17 Pearson Com paras 1258–60, 1273–6; Law Coms paras 23(i), 38(i), 39–42, 55–65 (pharmaceuticals), 104–5, but see paras 62–5 (Scottish Law Com whose caution echoed many of the concerns of US courts: insurability, fear of unknown impact on R & D).

better focused and more legitimate derogation from the main reform strategy than the inclusion of a general development risk defence.[18] It is not self-evident that in an entrepreneurial society the risk and uncertainty of unforeseeable losses should fall on the victim. Some, such as Calabresi,[19] would on the contrary, argue that in such a society those who choose to be entrepreneurs and who expect to reap high returns for innovative risky new products should shoulder such costly uncertainties. He goes as far as to suggest that since the free market system is predicated on the value of allowing entrepreneurs to reap the unforeseeable profits of risk-taking when they guess rightly that the product's benefits will outweigh its costs, then the entrepreneur should be called upon to shoulder the corresponding costs of unforeseeable risks in their activity lest confidence in the fairness of the free enterprise system be compromised. This view – broadly in line with the moral enterprise liability argument without the detailed philosophical underpinnings – is also applicable to insurers who should be willing to offer insurance against unforeseeable losses even though appropriate premium rates cannot be assessed actuarially because they themselves reap profits where, unforeseeably, no claim is made on a policy. If those in either the actual enterprise or the parallel insurance markets are risk-averse and unwilling to fulfil the complete entrepreneurial role the free enterprise system assigns them – a role which includes the management of risk, uncertainty and innovation – they should, according to Calabresi, get out of the market. The more enterprises and insurers are willing only to take quantifiable risks while seeking unlimited profits, the greater the risk that public opinion will shift towards reliance on government control of risk, and the more undermined will be the key principle of the free enterprise system – that such management of risk is best left to the private sector. Liability for unforeseeable losses may thus be, in Calabresi's words, a 'bulwark' of the free enterprise system, while narrower regimes such as negligence may prove eventually to be its 'curse'.

Proponents of the development risk defence, on the other hand, concentrated on pragmatic arguments. The best of these was that the issue was not so much simply one of the risk-averseness of business but their desire for stable profit margins – a goal which also has attractive social benefits such as stability of employment for the workforce. Although perfect economic models might suggest that business could carefully respond to liability for unforeseeable losses associated with products with a fine mix of delicate price increases and/or lowered activity (product volume), most businesses and insurers respond much more crudely to changes in liability, claims rates and success rates. They are less likely to persevere in notoriously risky (because innovative) lines of business, but to diversify productive investment into product lines with more stable profit margins. The argument is that squeezed profit margins result less in the inhibiting of R & D than in its redirection into less useful areas. It is, after all, arguable that this phenomenon is observable even under a negligence regime when pharmaceutical companies prefer to develop 'me too' drugs which cleverly copy the therapeutic effect of existing drugs rather than attempt to develop entirely new drugs, or when they sit on patents of new drugs which would

---

18 Compare the Californian protective legislation of 1986 relating to an AIDS vaccine discussed by R McKenna 'The Impact of Product Liability Law on the Development of a Vaccine Against the AIDS Virus' (1988) 55 U Chi LR 943, 943–4, 956, 962.

19 G Calabresi 'Commentary' (1983) 58 NYULR 939, 941; 'Products Liability: Curse or Bulwark of Free Enterprise?' (1978) 27 Clev St LR 313, 321–7.

have improved therapeutic effect but at lower profit margins than those achieved by an existing product line; or when they fail to develop 'orphan drugs' to treat rare diseases because at most, such drugs can only command small profit margins because of the small markets involved. Like the compensation goal, however, the profit-margin argument is one-dimensional. It points to narrower and narrower liability burdens on profit-seekers and at its most robust supports a caveat emptor regime. In effect, then, what the proponents of the development risk defence argued was that while the inroads into profits generated by, say, the negligence regime are tolerable, those generated by a liability which burdens producers with the unforeseeable risks of their products would not be.

By 1985 those holding this view – such as the British government – were able to insist on the inclusion of the development risk defence in the final Directive, a compromise which, as we have seen, is redistributive towards product suppliers relative to the initial proposals. This development was helped by a general lack of knowledge of, or at least faith in, the price deterrence mechanism so relevant to unforeseeable losses, and a consequent belief that most deterrent impact of liability resulted from liability for foreseeable risks. At the same time the moral confidence of the earlier law reformers that producers should be liable for unforeseeable losses was replaced by the fears of those (politicians, bureaucrats) involved in the later stages of reform negotiation that the market results said to be threatened by such a move would eventuate. Not that these results were guaranteed. At most the evidence of inhibition of R & D in the US was anecdotal. What evidence there is of inhibition could be ascribed to the insurance cycle and to the psychologically irrational response to the wave of civil litigation *in general* in the US, which is unlikely to be repeated in Europe. This reading of the US experience draws support from the fact that the deterioration in the US drugs and vaccines markets had also been observed in State jurisdictions which had never exposed those products to the new liability in s 402A (because of their reading of Comment K – see Chapter 10, under heading 7). Since most of the relevant empirical data is unavailable and probably unattainable, however, this last vital issue of the weight to be put on the risk of R & D inhibition had to turn on intuition.

How appropriately to make the trade-off between the values represented by efficiency or a moral enterprise liability argument and these real-world concerns about R & D etc, is necessarily an ideological one. It depends on the weight to be given to desiderata such as the protection of choice, the security of supply of certain products, minimum levels of physical security and the long-term protection of a free enterprise culture. These are not susceptible to further legal analysis. What can be said is that with the triumph of those demanding the inclusion of the development risk defence, the theoretical rationales for reform – patchy and inadequate as they were – collapsed. As we will see in the next chapter, the inclusion of the development risk defence in effect reduces the liability of manufacturers to that of negligence (albeit potentially with a 'super-negligence' standard): in virtually all cases where a product will be held 'defective', it will be possible to say that a party (not necessarily the defendant) has been careless with respect to a foreseeable risk. Either the careless party will be held liable, or someone else will be liable, but only because carelessness has occurred. Liability in these latter situations is a form of vicarious liability. Liability will, in other words, be predicated directly or indirectly on negligence. The doctrinal novelty of the Directive is, therefore, not that it imposes a stricter core liability than it would have if the initial proposals for full strict liability or hindsight/cost-benefit liability had been adopted. The novelty is just the peripheral extension to otherwise innocent suppliers of a form of vicarious liability – a liability which, from a moral point of view, we have found to be an unsatisfactory halfway house en route to a coherent strict liability (see Chapter 8, under heading (1)(b)(ii)). This, along with the reversal of the burden of proof on many, but not all, key issues, is all that remains of novelty in the reform package which *as a whole* no longer rests on a coherent economic or moral foundation.

6   CONCLUSION TO PART 2

The diverse set of policies which reformers in the US and EC gave to support product liability reform are vague, malleable, unranked and sometimes contradictory. Their manipulation can be used to support a range of options. Critics have discovered that vague legal policies are useful tools for distortion and have been able to attack the movement towards stricter liability from within its own professed parameters. Reformers on both sides of the Atlantic did not seek sound theoretical supports for their proposed reform. They saw it fundamentally as a limited rationalization of civil obligations by the extension of the strictness of warranty to accommodate injured non-privy victims, yet failed to note the obscure basis and origin of the warranty. But when the ECJ is confronted with borderline cases, it will need some principles on which its purposive approach can operate. The conclusion that the law reform process here was ill thought out and ultimately a result of pragmatism and political compromise, although true, will not be of any use in providing the necessary doctrinal guidance for the court.

A search for a rationale for the initial impetus towards stricter liability in tort requires a focus on unforeseeable losses and on bystanders, since any rationale of tort needs to explain why a stranger has a right against another stranger. Yet the theoretical debates – nearly all in the US – about tort law in general, and in product liability in particular, substantially neglect both issues. Nonetheless, we have found it possible to construct both efficiency and moral rationales for imposing stricter liability on 'enterprise', rationales which can justify a civil obligation limited to parties (rather than pointing to a fund) that is strict, that has a 'defect' requirement, that relates only to certain types of loss, and that does not require proof that the defendant 'caused' the loss in a narrow sense. Furthermore, we were able to construct a moral argument to justify a limitation of the new strict liability to activities in the course of business.

Nevertheless, although it is possible to construct rationales which support rules narrower than a form of social insurance and expressible in corrective and distributive justice terms, there are limitations to such rationales. As we will see in following chapters, they fail to explain other boundaries of the Directive – eg the limitation to 'products' and to products 'supplied'. In the reform process such boundaries were simply assumed to be self-evident by reformers who, being chiefly interested in what seemed like the natural extension of warranty law, remained complacent about defining the principles on which the reform was to be based. We will see that to the extent that the notion of 'defect' imposes a form of 'super-negligence' or vicarious liability on product suppliers, and to the extent that increased claims consciousness may eventually increase the products claims rate, such suppliers will become more attractive targets for claims than others whose activities overlapped with those of the suppliers in the context in which injury occurred (see bus example in Chapter 6, under heading 5(f)). Theories of efficiency and moral enterprise liability as well as the consensual norm approach of the 'back-to-contract' school cannot justify specific doctrinal boundaries such as the limitation to 'products' because they are unable to justify why the liability of product enterprises should be more swingeing than that imposed on other commercial enterprises. This raises a question about the long-term stability of the point of doctrinal development so far reached by product reform. One can envisage product manufacturers lobbying for change if they resent bearing losses which they regard as more appropriately the responsibility of other enterprises. Aeroplane manufacturers might complain about being sued in cases they allege are due to pilot error; car-ferry designers might object to being sued in cases where crewmen fail to close hull doors; river dredger manufacturers might not like being sued for failing to provide optimal field of vision in cases where they claim crew negligence (see Chapter 13, under heading 1). If we reach a stage where product manufacturers argue for an extension of the Directive to cases of defective services, their attacks on the current doctrinal position will be substantially assisted by the incoherence of its stated rationales. The anomalies and uncertainties generated by the present law may be tolerable in the short and medium term, but the clash of this pragmatically developed law with 'the need for an overall view of an area of law, built on a sound theoretical basis',[20] is likely eventually to require a major rethinking of the justification for its existence.

---

20 P Atiyah *Pragmatism and Theory in English Law* (London, Stevens, 1987) 101.

PART THREE

Stability of the new products doctrine

CHAPTER 10

The 'defect' requirement

1 INTRODUCTION TO PART 3

Two principal criticisms are made of the product rule reflected in s 402A of the US Restatement of Torts and these have been echoed in the analytical criticism of the 1985 Directive. First, there is the complaint that the imposition of strict liability on product manufacturers is unfair because here it involves exposure to the indeterminate and potentially crippling loss associated with unforeseeable risks. As the following discussion shows (under headings 3–6, below) this is a misguided attack. Under both the US and EC rules manufacturer liability for unforeseeable losses is, despite the 'strict liability' rhetoric, rare, if not completely non-existent. The second and dominant complaint about the product rules relates to their operation in relation to complaints about the design of a product for which the rules provide, it is said, too open-ended and vague a standard of liability. This attack, too, is misguided, not because liability for design defects is not uncertain in its operation from case to case – it is – but because the characteristic which makes it so infects not only the new product rules but also the traditional principles operating in the tort of negligence and in contractual warranty. The latter part of this chapter explains why these sources of uncertainty are not, as is widely believed, a specific evil of s 402A and the Directive, but are inherent in any regime which relies on reasonableness standards, causal requirements, defences linked to behavioural standards and ill-defined rules of recourse. To the extent that the uncertainty of these elements of the product rules generate instability, it is an instability which also infects the realistic alternative rules of liability. Similarly important for a debate about the product rules themselves are those sources of instability which are unique to that regime. These are the boundaries to the rules in which theorists show such little interest: the limitation to products; to products supplied, and so on. Chapter 12 argues that, far from being self-evident, these boundaries are without justification and generate anomalies which neither economic nor moral theories can resolve.

2 FROM ENTITLED EXPECTATIONS TO COST/BENEFIT OR RISK/UTILITY

In order to determine whether a product is defective the courts of the EC Member States will have to inject content into the definition given in the Directive:

A product is defective when it does not provide the safety which a person is entitled to expect, taking all circumstances into account, including:

(a) the presentation of the product;
(b) the use to which it could reasonably be expected that the product would be put;
(c) the time when the product was put into circulation. [Article 6(1)]

In many cases the definition will not be problematic in application. For example, the court can clearly take account of the use to which the product was to be put: Thalidomide is not defective in its beneficial application to leprosy and AIDS.[1] The court can also look to the expected circumstances of use of the product and this would include any further post-supply preparation before use which could be expected: pork is not defective because it needs cooking to be safe (the risk here is notorious), while producers of clothing cannot rely on it being washed before use.[2] In other cases, more specific questions will need to be resolved by case law: does 'presentation of the product' include claims, instructions or warnings carried in separate advertising, and must the 'presentation', to be relevant, emanate from the manufacturer rather than, say, the retailer?

The core theoretical problem with the definition, however, is that it is circular. This is because what a person is entitled to expect is the very question a definition of defect should be answering. The Directive's wording echoes the consumer 'expectations' terminology found in some of the Comments accompanying s 402A – wording itself derived from the criterion of liability in the implied warranty of merchantability out of which the product rules had emerged both in the US and EC.[3] But while a buyer's 'expectations' *may* be a coherent form in which to set the contractual standard,[4] it is neither coherent nor appropriate for the tort standard. In sales legislation and case law the 'expectations' relevant to 'merchantability'[5] are explicitly linked to the nature of the market in which the particular goods were actually sold, their description in that sale, their price, etc. In the contractual context if statute *is* going to impose a minimum level of quality and safety, it is understandable that the level is tied to the particular type of market transaction involved. In other words, it makes sense that it is the characteristics of the transaction which govern what the buyer is entitled to expect or entitled 'to think he was buying'.[6] Most of the relevant UK sales case law in recent years relates to the necessary elaboration of

---

1 [October 1989] Prod Liab Internat 164.

2 Compare respectively *Heubner* v *Hunter Packing Co* 375 NE 2d 873 (1978) and *Grant* v *Australian Knitting Mills Ltd* [1936] AC 85.

3 G Schwartz 'Foreword: Understanding Product Liability' (1979) 67 Calif LR 435, 448–9. Since 1973 the term 'merchantability' in UK sales law has been the subject of statutory definition, see now s 14(6) of the Sale of Goods Act 1979.

4 And there is concern at the Law Commissions that it may inappropriately favour suppliers in a market of low customary standards: the Law Commission and the Scottish Law Commission *Sale and Supply of Goods* (HMSO, May 1987) Cm 137, para 3.26. In any case it can hardly hope to provide detailed guidance – the standard would still need to be fleshed out over the diverse cases to which it applies: P Atiyah *The Sale of Goods*, 8th edn (Pitman, London, 1990) 143 ff.

5 Or, to use the term now favoured by the Law Commissions in the consumer context and the EC itself in the General Product Safety Directive, 'acceptability': Law Commission and the Scottish Law Commission, *Sale and Supply of Goods* (Law Com No 160) (HMSO, May 1987) Cm 137; Council Directive on General Product Safety OJ No L 228/24, 11.8.1992 (Article 2) defining 'safe product' in terms of minimum acceptable risk.

6 *Shine* v *General Guarantee Corpn* [1988] 1 All ER 911, 915 (Bush J). Even if the courts decide the

what the standard means in relation to conditions in goods which are either not dangerous or which, in the event, did not cause injury. As a consequence, debate has centred on the awkwardness of applying a 'merchantability' concept of quality, which was developed in the context of primary commodities to a consumer context of manufactured goods of complex design; and on the importance of including non-fundamental quality defects (durability, finish, etc) within the idea of 'non-merchantability'. Nonetheless, the application of the standard to safety issues can be illustrated: a new luxury car might be regarded as unmerchantable because of the low crashworthiness of its side panels, while a comparable characteristic might not render a modest new car unmerchantable.

Outside that contractual context, however, the characteristics of the particular transaction and the legitimate 'expectations' of buyers they may be judged to support are irrelevant. This realization is the necessary starting point of a tort standard which at its centre seeks to protect mere bystanders – ie complete strangers to any prior consensual transaction. Given the central concern of tort with bystanders, it would be bizarre and unworkable to require a tort standard to be linked to some prior transaction with another party, such as the sale of a particular good. Sometimes the contractual standard would be too high as would be the case of buyer expectations generated in a luxury market. Sometimes it would be too low, as if a contractual standard were held not to address certain issues of safety (such as fitness for non-ordinary uses) which tort law may seek to do. A bottle of drugs without a child-proof lid may, for example, be judged merchantable and yet fall foul of a tort standard which tolerates liability for foreseeable misuses of a product. Similarly, the contractual standard may be linked to a minimum level of safety which is customary in the market and yet tort may seek to apply a standard higher than that of the relevant custom. Defectiveness in tort must first be evaluated from the perspective of the bystander taking account of intervening causes or co-causes (eg what precautions an intermediary such as the user is expected to take) and only then readjusted if necessary for cases where the plaintiff is the buyer (see below under heading 9). If tort were only concerned with obvious cases – manufacturing errors such as snails in ginger beer or a new product's failure to perform its most basic function as when new brakes simply fail – and with imposing strict liability for them, a general 'expectations' test would be appropriate and achieve the desired result: no-one expects snails in ginger beer or new brakes to fail completely. But in those more complex situations where modern tort liability also operates – eg cases of foreseeable misuse or complex design systems where the standard is neither agreed nor obvious – the 'expectations' test is misleading and inadequate.

In time these problems with linking a tortious standard of liability for defective products to 'expectations' became recognized in the US. During the 1960s and 1970s US courts grappled with the 'consumer expectations' test for 'defect' suggested in the Restatement. The 'test', shorn of its contractual basis between plaintiff and defendant, became meaningless and its forced application either generated a vastly increased manufacturer's liability on the basis that consumers never actually *expect* to be injured by a particular product, or a dramatic narrowing of liability to

---

standard need be only fitness for *ordinary* purposes, there is the added question of whether the buyer should be entitled to a good fit for all or only some such purposes. At present UK law adopts the former idea of entitlements under 'merchantability' but strong arguments can be mounted for the latter standard, see *Henry Kendall & Sons* v *William Lillico & Sons Ltd* [1969] 2 AC 31, and Atiyah, op cit 156–7.

exclude situations where product risks were patent or where consumers had a low opinion of the level of safety offered by a particular product type.[7] In some cases the test simply bewildered courts faced with complex products about which consumers have little or no sophisticated expectations of safety at all. By the early 1980s the inappropriate and unsupportable 'consumer expectations' test had been been supplanted in most US jurisdictions by an approach openly based on balancing a product's costs and benefits – in other words, the balance between its risks and its utility.[8] This confirms the view that, despite the Directive's adoption of the language of 'expectations', the only coherent approach to a *tortious* standard of 'defect' in the area of product liability is one based on a general view as to what a reasonable level of *minimum* safety should be *quite apart* from the contractual history of the product in question. As a reasonableness standard can be portrayed in terms of a trade-off between the risks and the utility of the product, this conclusion sits comfortably with the cost/benefit analysis of 'defect' described with such inflated precision by the lawyer-economists. At least one Law Lord – Lord Griffiths – has suggested that while English judges may not overtly adopt the cost/benefit approach to the notion of 'defect' in the Directive, 'they would as an educated response to the facts of a particular case undertake a balancing exercise of an analogous kind'.[9] In other words the core of the 'defect' enquiry will substantially parallel the issue which underlies the negligence standard – the trade-off between risk-taking and social cost as reflected in the magnitude and gravity of risk balanced against the cost of precautions and social utility. Practitioner handbooks fleshing out the standard in the Directive will therefore look remarkably like current handbooks on the substance of the duty in negligence. The only really important question to which manufacturers will need an answer concerns the strictness of the behavioural standard.

3   DISCOVERABILITY OF DEFECT, THE DEVELOPMENT RISK DEFENCE: MANUFACTURERS

Despite the 'strict liability' rhetoric in its Preamble, the Directive rarely imposes more than a negligence regime on manufacturers. The origin of this surprising and not obvious result is worth pursuing in detail because of the widespread assumption in business and the legal profession that the Directive imposes strict liability on manufacturers. It follows from three factors: the adoption of a defect-limited regime under which the evaluation of a product's relative benefits necessitates consideration of any available substitutes; Article 6(2) of the Directive; and the wording of the defence in Article 7(e) of the Directive. Article 7(e) states that it is a defence if the defendant proves 'that the state of scientific and technical knowledge at the time when he put the product into circulation was not such as to enable the

---

7 It is noteworthy that Lord Griffiths has attacked the test on these grounds: Lord Griffiths, P de Val and R Dormer 'Developments in English Product Liability Law: A Comparison With the American System' (1988) 62 Tulane LR 353, 381.

8 G Priest 'The Modern Irony of Civil Law: A Memoir of Strict Product Liability in the United States' (1989) 9 Tel Aviv University Studies in Law 93, 116–7, 119; Aaron Twerski 'A Moderate and Restrained Federal Product Liability Bill: Targeting the Crisis Areas for Resolution' (1985) 18 J Law Reform 575, 606.

9 Lord Griffiths, P de Val and R Dormer, op cit 382.

existence of the defect to be discovered.' The first thing to notice about this defence in Article 7(e) is that it refers to the discoverability of the *defect* not of a product *risk*. This suggests that it is considerably wider than its popular name – the 'development risk' defence – might imply. Development risks are those risks which only become apparent as a new product is used. The risks of Thalidomide to the unborn foetus is a classic example. The defence seems wider because it also seems to shield a defendant in situations in which the risks of a product are well-known at the relevant time (such as the risk of hepatitis infection in donated blood, or the risk that a car's steering wheel might crush a driver's rib cage in an accident, or that a food product might be criminally tampered with on supermarket shelves), but where, given available substitutes, it is regarded as not defective at the relevant time. Later, once the state of the art has developed in a way which enables the product cheaply to be made safer (for example by the development of purification processes for blood, or air-bags or seat belts for cars, or tamper-resistant or tamper-apparent packaging for food) the benefits of untreated blood, etc, would decline because these are necessarily assessed in the light of available feasible substitutes; and they may then (although not necessarily) be regarded as less than the product's costs. Article 7(e) makes clear that defendants will not be liable before such state of the art developments occur. The defence is, in fact, redundant in virtually all such cases: it should be held that there is no defect because, according to Article 6(2), 'a product shall not be considered defective for the sole reason that a better product is subsequently put into circulation.' In other words, the benefits of a product are to be assessed at the time of circulation (see under heading 5, below). If, as assessed then, they outweigh the product's costs, there is no defect and hence no need for the defence.[10]

There will be rare cases of known risks where the defence *may* still be necessary and these are worth description because they highlight the moral incoherence into which the Directive falls because of its ambivalence towards the imposition of strict liability. *Costs are, it seems, to be evaluated at the time of trial* (see below) *while benefits seem to be assessed at the time of supply* (Article 6(2), under heading 5, below). But it is unclear how a case will be handled when the *incidence* of a *known* risk increases over time. Take, for example, the case of refrigerators. Old style designs used external mechanical locking devices which posed a risk to anyone who might be caught inside. In the early decades of mass use of refrigerators this was no doubt seen as a very remote possibility of misuse which could legitimately be ignored in the design process. When, however, the first generations of refrigerators came to be discarded on to open rubbish tips on which trespassing children played, a number of children became trapped inside them and died. Magnet-based locks which could be released from the inside were then incorporated into latter designs. Now this case could be handled in the following way. The thrust of Article 6(2) suggests that, under the Directive, the old style designs would not be regarded as defective because at the time of supply the apparent benefits of the design seemed

10 Note: (1) It will still be possible to argue from the later appearance of a better product that it *had* been feasible at the earlier date, a problematic tactic in jury trials, see under heading 6(vi), below. (2) The line where the burden of proof is split: the plaintiff has the burden of showing 'defectiveness' – that the benefits as they appeared at the time of circulation did not outweigh the product's costs; the defence has the burden of establishing the 'state of the art' defence in Article 7(e). If the defendant adduces evidence that, at the time of circulation, there were no other feasible substitutes, this goes to the issue of 'defect' not to the defence in Article 7(e), as argued by A Clark *Product Liability* (London, Sweet & Maxwell, 1989) 184.

significant and were not reduced by comparison with a safer alternative (magnets not having yet been developed and deployed, at least in refrigerators) because the relevant risk appeared so remote. On this approach, sensitive to the producer's lack of fault, the defendant's product would be held not defective and so the defendant would have no need to call upon the defence in Article 7(e). Yet the Directive also displays an alternative philosophy. The very existence of the Article 7(e) defence suggests that, in determining defectiveness, the costs of a product which have become known at trial will be relevant even if undiscoverable earlier. If so, then in a case such as that of the old style fridge manufacturer defending the risk/benefit balance of his product, the defendant may be unable to argue that the benefits of his design outweighed the unforeseeable *increased* costs of his design which had become apparent by the time of trial, even though technically he is allowed to ignore the safer design developed later. He would then be forced to rely on the defence in Article 7(e) concerning an undiscoverable *defect*.[11]

In general, though, cases falling into such fact patterns are likely to be relatively few. This means that it is true to say that while formally the defence in Article 7(e) may be better termed a 'state of the art defence', its importance in the Directive seems to centre on its impact on liability for development risks, that is where the relevant risk only becomes apparent as the new product is used. With this caveat we can retain the loose but entrenched 'development risk defence' terminology.

The next important point to notice about the aim of this defence is that *no* party can be liable if the defect in the product was undiscoverable given the state of the art at the time of supply. Furthermore, a defendant can only be liable if the defect was discoverable at the time of supply *either by that defendant or by some other party*. That it need not be the defendant by whom the defect was discoverable seems clear from the wording of the Directive. Article 7(e) lays down that it is a defence if the defendant proves that the state of scientific and technical knowledge at the time he put the product into circulation was not such as to enable the existence of the defect to be discovered. It seems unlikely that this was intended to imply 'to be discovered *by him*'. As we will see in Chapter 11, the inclusion as defendants of mere suppliers, importers and own-brand suppliers was intended, respectively, to facilitate the plaintiff's search for the relevant manufacturer; to relieve him or her of the task of suing outside the EC; and to sheet home responsibility to the initiating enterprise. All these goals would be thwarted if such a defendant were allowed to show that the risk was not discoverable *by him* even though discoverable by the distant manufacturer.[12] It is considerably more consistent with these choices of non-manufacturing defendants that liability could fall on them whenever it could fall on the manufacturer. This approach produces the defence in Article 7(e) in exactly the form in which it appears, a form which in effect, as we will see, imposes generally a regime of fault liability on manufacturers and the equivalent of a vicarious liability on those other defendants despite their use of all reasonable care. If this is accurate, it is in the fact that the Article 7(e) defence only requires the defect to be discoverable by someone

---

11 An important point because it shows that the abolition of that defence (and the defence is due for EC review in 1995) would not merely affect those sectors associated with development risks such as pharmaceuticals. There may also be difficulty in such defendants fitting into the language of the defence: C Newdick 'The Development Risk Defence of the Consumer Protection Act 1987' (1988) 47 Camb LJ 455, 462–4.
12 Contrast S Whittaker 'The EEC Directive on Product Liability' (1985) 5 Yearbook of European Law 233, 270.

that the most novel aspect of the Directive lies, because in practice it is the only source of strict liability and it is a substantial liability for certain classes of defendant such as importers. Such parties who would, by no stretch of the standard of care in negligence, have been regarded as careless for not discovering the relevant defect may now be liable under the Directive (see under heading 4, below).

Looking first at the impact of the defence in Article 7(e) on the party whom the plaintiff would, if necessary, allege should have discovered the defect: the manufacturer will nearly always meet this description even if other parties do too. The effect of the defence in Article 7(e) is to contain that party's liability at least within the bounds of its parallel liability in negligence (and probably even more narrowly). This is because, despite the hopes of the Directive's drafters, *there is no workable half-way house between a defect which is absolutely undiscoverable and a risk which is reasonably discoverable.*[13] To explain why this is relevant we must first remember that in negligence both the costs and benefits of the defendant's conduct are evaluated as they appeared at the time of that conduct. A defendant is only judged in the light of reasonably foreseeable costs and benefits. Under the Directive the benefits of a manufacturer's product are also assessed at the time of circulation/conduct (see above and under heading 5, below), but the costs are technically evaluated in the notion of 'defect' as they appear at the time of trial (otherwise the drafters would not have needed to include the development risk defence at all). *If the development risk defence is so wide that it excludes liability for all except those defects which were reasonably foreseeable to the defendant-manufacturer, the latter's liability under the Directive is no greater than in negligence.*

Product defects may be characterized according to whether at the relevant time the defect was:

(a) undiscoverable given the state of the art
(b) discoverable but only by extraordinary means
(c) discoverable by ordinary or 'reasonable' means.

Under a fault rule the defendant is not liable for defects in classes (a) or (b) because there is no fault involved in failing to discover and take precautions against a defect which would not have been revealed by reasonable care. The defence in Article 7(e) clearly shields a defendant from liability in cases falling into class (a), that is defects which were undiscoverable by *any* means available at the relevant time. Examples of such *absolute* impossibility are very rare. Adverse side effects of drugs which *only* manifest themselves in humans *and* only affect the user's offspring or even later generations are one example: there is no way to detect the defect until the birth of the first affected member of that second generation. Virtually all other defects could, however, be described as discoverable by some means existing at the relevant time. The question is where does the Article 7(e) defence draw the line among these discoverable risks? This is a crucial question because the only way in which the Directive could involve a liability on manufacturers substantially wider than negligence would be if it imposes liability for defects falling into class (b), that it *refuses* the Article 7(e) defence for defects which could only be discovered by extraordinary means, *and* the number of cases in that category is significant.

The first problem with this interpretation is that it may be doubted whether a

---

13 J Stapleton 'Product Liability Reform – Real or Illusory?' (1986) 6 OJLS 392; C Newdick 'Risk, Uncertainty and "Knowledge" in the Development Risk Defence' [1991] Anglo-Amer LR 127.

meaningful line can be drawn between categories (b) and (c). Would a court be willing to impose liability under the Directive on the basis that the defect was 'scientifically discoverable' and yet have felt unable to manipulate the standard of reasonable care in negligence to achieve liability there too on the basis that the defect was 'reasonably discoverable'? Those who assert that this line is intelligible and workable, and that the Directive *will* therefore impose a liability on manufacturers which is wider than the liability achievable in negligence[14] must argue along the lines that the defence of Article 7(e) will be refused if the technical tools and processes for discovery exist. The time and cost of applying them to the product in order to discover the defect must be ignored. The defence would be reserved for those rare cases of *absolute* impossibility of discovery. Take the example of Thalidomide. Once the tragic effects of Thalidomide on the human foetus became known, exhaustive testing on pregnant animals began, but it took considerable time and money to pinpoint a particular type of animal which would display the teratogenic effect. No-one at the time of Thalidomide's development would have thought of testing the drug on *that* animal, but the tools for discovery *did* exist. Those who argue that the Directive imposes a liability on manufacturers stricter than that possible under negligence must concede that the defect of Thalidomide was 'scientifically discoverable' under their interpretation of this term because the testing of pharmaceuticals on animals was known and the relevant species did in fact exist. All that was lacking was the idea of applying them to the task of screening Thalidomide for safety.

Not only is it unlikely that courts will reach such a strange result, but if supporters of the Directive are correct in reading the defence in this way, it becomes a nugatory defence because for virtually all product defects these bare tools of discoverability *would* have existed at the relevant time. Take, for example, a case where a person on a course of drugs for a certain eye condition cuts grass which has been treated with a particular pesticide and is made ill by the unexpected interaction of the two chemicals;[15] or take the deleterious effects of X-ray machines. Although *in practice* the problem in these types of cases only emerges slowly as evidence of an association accumulates and the data on a causal connection becomes sufficiently weighty to be statistically significant, in theory there was at the relevant time the technical potential for discovery: the synergistic effect of the two chemicals *could* have been tested on appropriate laboratory animals and the long-term risks of X-ray exposure *could* have been detected if the costly and lengthy process of carrying out the appropriate exposure experiments had been undertaken. But for some risks – such as bugs in complex software programmes or very low incidence latent physical reactions to chemicals – this full precirculation screening process would be astronomically expensive. The question is, once the liability is limited to *defective* products but a defence is provided for undiscoverable defects, should this technical ability to find and *eventually* characterize the risk be sufficient to justify liability for conduct before such determinations have in fact been widely accepted? Should those now supplying meat be held liable if eventually it is shown that the factor responsible for bovine spongiform encephalopathy ('mad cow disease') *has* been passed via that meat to humans to cause Creutzfeldt-Jakob disease – a risk which as yet is given

---

14   Such as the senior EC bureaucrat responsible for the progress of the draft and final product Directives, H-C Taschner 'La Future Responsabilité du Fait des Produits Défectueux dans la Communauté Européene', Revue du Marché Commun 257, 261 (1986).

15   See eg [Feb 1991] Prod Liab Internat 26.

little credence in scientific circles, but a risk for which the technical means of *eventual* detection do exist?

Manufacturers and pro-business governments such as the Thatcher administration in the UK clearly thought the defence had a wider ambit than this mere 'absolute absence of means of discovery' since it is hardly likely that the goal of their fervent lobbying was a defence which would cover only a few rare cases. To have a substantial value for defendants the defence must be wider and at the very least include, for example, a notion of scientific creativity. Such a notion would enable the defendant to argue that although the scientific means of discovery existed, no-one had yet thought to apply the means in a way which would have led to the discovery of the defect. For example, in the Thalidomide case no-one had yet suggested testing pregnancy drugs on pregnant animals from the species which would have manifested birth defects. Indeed, there had been a vague confidence that the placenta could always be relied upon to filter out most deleterious substances, so that research on the effects of drugs on the foetus was not regarded as useful. Moreover, if a drug was not toxic for the mother – and Thalidomide was not – this was taken as evidence of non-toxicity for the foetus.[16] Similarly in the chemical case, no-one had yet thought to test the interaction of eye drops and pesticides, and in the radiation case the actual safety concern was with the risk of immediate burns – no-one thought it worth while to spend decades testing for long-term radiation cancer in humans.

But the moment the defence is widened to shield defendants from liability for defects which were not yet the subject of scientific curiosity or creativity, a whole series of judgmental issues is introduced which can only be determined by some notion of what it is *reasonable* to expect of the defendant; in other words, by a fault criterion. For example, will the defence be defeated if the plaintiff can show that one person in Siberia had the relevant 'linking' idea even if that person did not publish the idea? Was the Thalidomide side effect 'discoverable' at the instant Dr McBride noted that the mother of a deformed baby had taken that drug during pregnancy? If the courts were to use the instant of a first tentative linking idea, it would be difficult to justify. Why is this point morally or instrumentally important? Manufacturers would only escape liability if they could show that the defect was absolutely impossible to discover – an extraordinarily difficult burden to discharge – but would be liable if a very obscure, unpublished scientist had had a relevant 'linking' idea. Why should this distinction be relevant to law or even morality?

Indeed, where is the distinction to be drawn? How specific must the discovery be to demolish the defence – would the idea of testing pharmaceuticals on animal X be sufficient or only the idea of testing it on pregnant animal X? And how certain must the Siberian be that the test result was statistically significant and reliable? Would it matter that there was not yet a consensus that the idea was sound? Scientific 'knowledge' accumulates slowly with a gradual solidification of a consensus that a particular association of factors is convincing. This is particularly the case with complex systems such as adverse but latent physical reactions to drugs and other chemicals. At what point is the law to make a distinction and why? Whose knowledge, whose judgment on the issue is important? It seems meaningless and absurd for the law to seize upon the instant when one particular individual might have the suspicion, speculation or 'hunch' of a connection which much later is shown to have had substance.

16 M Sherman and S Strauss 'Thalidomide: A Twenty-Five Year Perspective' (1986) 41 Food, Drug & Cos LJ 458, 461.

To give the defence substance it must cover not only cases where the defect was absolutely undiscoverable but cases where it had only been noted by an obscure Siberian scientist. There is no logical distinction between the bizarre latter case and a myriad of other cases where the defect was discoverable only by extraordinary means. To give the defence substance then it must protect in cases of defects which could only be discovered, if at all, by extraordinary means. The manufacturer would only be liable for reasonably discoverable defects. That a half-way house between 'reasonably discoverable' and 'absolutely undiscoverable' is not workable can also be demonstrated by the well-known phenomenon in the tort of negligence of the elastic notion of 'foreseeability' and the dependent 'standard of care'. If the court is minded to do so it can manipulate the concept of foreseeability to cover all but the most freakish risks and consequences of careless conduct.[17]

The UK implementation of the Article 7(e) defence illustrates the UK government's view that the 'only plausible' interpretation of the defence is one which gives it a non-negligible ambit.[18] The UK defence has been attacked for being in essence an industry standard which is potentially even lower than an objective reasonableness standard. It provides a defence where the defendant proves:

> that the state of scientific and technical knowledge at the relevant time was not such that a producer of products of the same description as the product in question might be expected to have discovered the defect if it had existed in his products while they were under his control. (s 4(1)(e) of the CPA)

The use of the words 'might be expected' suggests that this is not an industry standard but more likely a 'reasonable discoverability' standard, although in a sense even an 'objective' state of the art standard is industry-related because the state of the art depends on the level of investment. In any case, even if the UK capitulates to pressure from the European Commission and adopts the exact wording of Article 7(e), the defence will still hinge on what 'discoverability' means and can only be given substance as a defence by an interpretation based on notions of reasonableness. The result will be that, for manufacturers, the defence in Article 7(e) will provide no less a protection than is available in the tort of negligence, save that the relevant burden of proof lies on the defendant.

4   THE STRICT LIABILITY OF CAREFUL SUPPLIERS

The conclusion that every defendant sued under the Directive has a defence where the risk was not reasonably discoverable allows a characterization of the nature of the liability imposed on the different classes of defendant. For those in the chain of supply on whom the tort of negligence imposes the highest duty of discovering defects (ie for whom the reasonableness standard is most demanding) the liability imposed by the Directive need be no more demanding. Indeed, if the development

17 The duty in negligence to carry out safety tests and quality control on products is itself an example of that attenuated concept, relying as it does on the very general assumption that manufacturing activity carries with it the *possibility* of danger even though there may be no indication of where that danger may arise.

18 487 HL Official Report (6th series) cols (14.5.87, per Lord Lucas). See also 483 HL Official Report (6th series) cols 840 ff (20.1.87) and cols 851–3 (9.3.87).

risk defence *is* given a reasonableness basis it would be odd if the parallel standard in negligence was regarded as a different one. The tort of negligence generally requires most effort in safety investigations and monitoring to be done by manufacturers, imposes very much lower obligations on retailers and virtually no duty of inspection, let alone safety testing, on other intermediaries such as importers and wholesalers. When seen alongside the Directive, then, the manufacturer's liability in negligence is, in this respect, at least as wide: there is potential liability for those defects present in the goods supplied by the manufacturer which his reasonable care would have discovered. But the potential liability of other suppliers is greater under the Directive, for they can be liable, it seems, for defects present in the products they supply if the defect was reasonably discoverable *by someone* (see under heading 3, above). This includes cases where the laws of negligence would regard the defendant's failure to discover the defect as reasonable given the defendant's position in the relevant distribution chain. In other words, under the Directive, as in the US,[19] a non-manufacturing party can be held liable for a risk in regard to which *he* has used, in the eyes of the tort of negligence, all reasonable care.

A strict liability is defined as one which can apply to a party despite its use of all reasonable care, so there is no doubt that these non-manufacturing suppliers are exposed by the Directive to a *new* and a *strict* liability. This is not the case for manufacturers. Those occasions on which a product will be held defective under Article 6, and the defect held reasonably discoverable under Article 7(e), will nearly always be occasions on which the law of negligence would have regarded it as the *manufacturer's* role to discover the defect present in the good when he supplied it.[20] This suggests that virtually all the cases in which non-manufacturing defendants will be held liable under the Directive will involve fact situations in which the manufacturer would have been liable in negligence. In other words, the only substantially new liability imposed by the Directive – that on non-manufacturing suppliers – is analogous to vicarious liability[21] under which innocent suppliers are held strictly liable for the carelessness of others in the distribution chain. In setting up such a multi-layered system of liability – imposing no more than a fault-based liability on manufacturers but a strict liability on other suppliers who would escape personal liability in negligence – the Directive certainly ensures for the plaintiff practical advantages parallel to those which are familiar from the field of the vicarious liability of employers: the trigger to liability remains the phenomenon of carelessness, but the plaintiff no longer has to pinpoint and sue that particular party who should have discovered the danger and handled it carefully.

What the Directive's multi-layered package lacks is a satisfying theoretical basis for the strict liability of some, but only some, suppliers in the chain. The analogy with the theoretical dilemma of employer's vicarious liability – discussed earlier in

---

19 *Thiele* v *Chick* 631 SW 2d 526 (1982) (innocent truck distributor).

20 These include cases of manufacturing errors and other pre-supply product alterations which the law in effect takes to be foreseeable (see below under heading 5), as well as cases where the manufacturer of a final product is held negligent for failing to review the design of a component supplied by a reputable component part manufacturer, eg see *Winward* v *TVR Engineering Ltd* [1986] BTLC 366, CA.

21 Significantly a term used by the senior EC bureaucrat responsible for product liability when he described the planned liability on mere suppliers: Hans-Claudius Taschner 'Product Liability – Actual Legislation and Law Reform in Europe' in *Consumer Law in the EEC*, ed G Woodroffe (London, Sweet & Maxwell, 1984) 113, 121.

Chapter 8, under heading 1 – should now be apparent; inasmuch as an economic or moral basis for strict liability *is* available, it is one which justifies a strict liability without dependence on another's carelessness. If strict liability under the Directive *is* justified by a modified version of the moral enterprise liability argument, for example, there is no justification for narrowing its scope to only those occasions on which another has been careless. Alternatively, if the relevant moral principle of the Directive is that apparently underlying the development risk defence, it is a principle of fault; and is it not unjust for some defendants effectively to be able to use a defence based on reasonable care while others are unable to do so and are consequently exposed under the Directive to a strict liability? There *may* be pragmatic arguments for such vicarious liability – and part of Chapter 11 investigates these troublesome issues – but the European reformers scarcely adverted to them, leaving careful suppliers to be aggrieved by the results of the reform process.

5   BENEFITS, TIME OF EVALUATION AND THE STATE OF THE ART

General negligence case law provides a reasonable indication of what is relevant to the cost/benefit criterion. The likelihood and severity of a risk is weighed against the utility of the activity and cost of any precaution available, including – at least in theory – cessation of production of that product. More importantly for the current discussion, in negligence the advantages and disadvantages, the 'costs and benefits', of the defendant-manufacturer's activity are both evaluated as they appeared at the time of the relevant conduct. We have just seen that under the Directive the costs of the product are, by virtue of the defence in Article 7(e), also likely to be evaluated without hindsight – that is, they will be assessed only in the light of what was reasonably discoverable when the defendant supplied the product. *If the benefits of the product were to be assessed with hindsight, ie as known at the time of trial, there would be room for the manufacturer's liability under the Directive to be strict.* In that case, if there had been, between the date of circulation and the date of trial, advances in the safety of substitutes on which the evaluation of a product's benefits necessarily depends, then at trial the benefits of the original product (blood unscreened for hepatitis, cars not fitted with airbags, food without tamper-resistant packaging) could appear less than its costs.[22] If benefits were assessed at trial the defendant would be held liable for supplying a defective product even though he had exercised all reasonable care at the time of supply, his conduct being reasonable because judged at that earlier time, the foreseeable benefits of the product seemed to outweigh its foreseeable costs.

The introduction of seat belts illustrates this: assume that the development of car seat belts can be dated at 1968. In 1967 a car was designed without belts. Assume that the merits of that design are being assessed in 1967. The benefits will be assessed, inter alia, on the basis of whether there are better alternative designs given the state

---

22 Stapleton, op cit. One could also imagine cases where the state of the art developments reveal that the original products had *greater* benefits than appeared at the time. On the problems of determining how 'feasible' alternative designs are see the careful discussion of the slow transitional introduction of car safety features in H-V v Hulsen, 'Design Liability and State of the Art: The United States and Europe at a Crossroads' (1981) 55 St John's LR 450, 458–460.

of the art in 1967. Suppose that the injury costs of the unbelted car design are 50 points and the benefits, given that there is no alternative feasible design incorporating belts, are 100 points. Then, in 1967, because the benefits outweighed the costs, the unbelted car (model X) would be adjudged non-defective. Now consider the situation if the same unbelted model is produced in 1986. The injury costs are the same (50 points) but because developments in the state of the art in the intervening years have provided a safer alternative design (ie a car with belts fitted), the benefits of the unbelted design are now relatively less. If they are assessed at less than the costs of the design then the 1986 unbelted model will be held to be defective. This illustrates that developments in the state of the art over time not only affect but can reverse the outcome of the cost-benefit assessment on a particular product design. Developments can change an earlier judgment from non-defective to defective; or they can change an earlier judgment from defective to non-defective if, for example, they reveal hitherto unknown benefits in the design which now outweigh its costs.[23]

Once it is recognized that changes in the state of the art over time can alter the assessment of the product which either implicitly or explicitly depends on a cost/benefit balance, a decision has to be made as to the point of time at which the benefits ought to be examined. Take the example of the development of seat belts again. There is clearly no problem where a person suffers injury in 1967 due to the lack of a seat belt in the 1967 model – the product will be declared non-defective. Similarly, if the person suffered the injury in 1986 while travelling in a 1986 model not fitted with belts, the result is clear: the car will be held defective. The question is what should happen if, after 1968, a person travelling in a 1967 unbelted car suffers injury as a result of the lack of a seat belt? If the development of seat belts between the date of circulation and the date of injury *is* taken into account, the cost-benefit assessment will be reversed and the defendant will be held strictly liable; the unforeseeable decline in the relative benefit of his product will be held against him. Should it be taken into account? If it is, then the time for assessing benefits will be the date of injury (or trial). The result is that the person injured in 1967 in the 1967 car will fail in his 1967 claim, but a person injured in the same 1967 car a year later in 1968 will succeed in showing that the vehicle was defective. Superficially, at least, this may seem objectionable, and it is certainly true that with minimal explanation (a mere comment that it would not be fair to apply the current safety standard to products put into circulation in 1967) and with no analysis, the initial European reformers chose the alternative solution: that post-circulation developments in the state of the art will not be taken into account and that the *defectiveness of the product should be assessed according to the safety standards prevailing when the producer put it into circulation* (see under heading 3, above).[24]

Although there *are* real problems with the alternate rule (see below, under headings 6 and 7(vi)), the important point here is that what this decision did was to remove any scope for the imposition on manufacturers of substantial strict liability

23 In certain situations developments in the state of the art will not affect the assessment: for example, where they merely reveal hitherto undiscoverable risk; where the earlier assessment was that the costs outweighed the benefits so that the development of a safer alternative design will simply make this imbalance greater; and in cases where the earlier assessment was that the benefits outweighed the costs, discovery of added benefits will simply reinforce this assessment.

24 See Law Coms para 49; Strasbourg Convention Expl Report para 42. For an example of the same rule operating in the US see *Bruce v Martin-Marietta Corpn* 544 F 2d 442 (1976) (held that passengers on an aircraft built in 1952 could not expect it to have the safety features of one built in 1970).

by the Directive. The Directive is now seen to provide that the benefits of a product are to be evaluated only with the foresight available at the date of supply – because 'a product shall not be considered defective for the sole reason that a better product is subsequently put into circulation' (Article 6(2)). Evidence of such later products is admissible but only, it seems, if they were feasible at the time of circulation and can thereby confirm that the product in issue was defective at that time. The liability imposed on manufacturers by the Directive is then no wider than the liability in negligence – indeed, as we will see, it is narrower.

The European reformers' decision to evaluate benefits only relative to the state of the art of substitutes available at the time of circulation by the manufacturer is not as self-evidently sensible as it may first appear. Only if our vision is informed by notions of fault does it seem objectionable that the manufacturer of a 1967 car could be later held liable for its relative lack of worth in 1968 because of subsequent developments such as seat belts. But if our vision *is* fault-based, why distinguish between such cases and undiscoverable risks? What has happened in the history of seat belts – as with other improvements in safety devices over time – is that the social minimum level of reasonable quality has risen, and it continues to do so (air bags are available but cost approximately £300 and, at least in the EC, are very probably not yet required by the minimum level of reasonable quality). As in the case of unforeseeable risks in a product, the question arises of who should carry the risk of being caught out by the increasing expectations of minimum safety generated by technological improvements and the phenomenon of 'product lag' (the delay between the time a new safety device or design is agreed in principle to be necessary for the minimum level of safety and the time when complex production lines can be 'tooled up' for the new design). A truly strict cost-benefit rule might seek to place such risks on those who profit from the enterprise of product supply rather than allowing them to remain on the innocent victims of product condition. But it might not because of the value, for example, of a business being able to 'close its books' on a past product line, or feeling uninhibited in introducing safety modifications in later models, or because it is thought more appropriate that the responsibility shift on to users not to continue using products which fall below the rising minimum standard of safety. But it is particularly odd that the initial reformers who provided a shield from liability in the case of post-supply developments in the state of the art of controlling known risks nevertheless, by their initial rejection of the development risk defence, rejected such a shield in the case of undiscoverable risks. This protective attitude to manufacturers is even more odd when compared to the attitude of the law of negligence to the manufacturer's post-sale behaviour. It is no longer regarded as reasonable that a manufacturer can always wash its hands of a product once it loses physical control over it by supplying it to another. The law of negligence has recently been developing post-marketing duties with respect to post-supply discoveries of a product's risky condition, amounting in some cases to an obligation to issue warnings to users, and in other cases to a duty to recall products such as drugs, cars and chemicals so that subsequent developments in safety design can be incorporated or to remove the items from circulation completely.[25] The effect of Article 6(2) seems to be to

---

25 See eg *Walton v British Leyland* (1978) Times 13 July, also reportd in [August 1980] Prod Liab Inter 156 (on car recall). National computerized registry of car ownership greatly facilitates recall of vehicles which have more than doubled since the 1980–4 period (now 700,000 annual average): [April 1991] *Prod Liab Internat* 50 and [Oct 1993] Prod Liab Internat 157.

prevent liability under the Directive in any such cases. If this is true, then the liability imposed on manufacturers by the Directive is not only not a strict liability, but is a liability even narrower than their current liability in negligence.

6   THE TIME DIMENSION IN THE US

The US products regime parallels this broad picture except in two important respects. First, the original rule reflected in s 402A imposed liability on any commercial supplier in the chain – leaving the ultimate allocation of liability costs to the dubious accuracy of rules of recourse. Relative to the channelled liability of the Directive, the US rule imposed a strict (vicarious-like) liability on many more innocent middle-parties, and as we saw under heading 4, above, this itself became a focus of concern precipitating statutory reform. More importantly, the US attitude to the time dimension is different in one unexpected way, and this relates to the 'relevant time' to assess defectiveness.

The issue of whether a product supplier would be liable for product risks which were not reasonably foreseeable at the relevant time tended to be overlooked at first in the US (Chapter 6, under heading 4). Given that the original proponents of the new rule in the US focused on manufacturing errors, this was understandable. The way the courts have been able in negligence to impose what is effectively a strict liability on manufacturers for manufacturing errors assumes that manufacturing errors are by their nature foreseeable because no industrial process is foolproof. Aided by the fiction of the perfectability of technology, the standard of care is raised with respect to such 'foreseeable' risks in such a way that the manufacturer can be found negligent by reason of having an inadequate quality control system or vicariously liable for the negligence of his employees in operating the manufacturer's production and quality control system.[26] Deviations from the production line norm are taken, without more, as evidence of carelessness. This device – tantamount to assuming negligence in manufacturing error cases – ignores the fact that variations from the production line norm often occur as an inevitable result of production and that it is not feasible to inspect *all* items if adequate inspection requires destructive testing of the product (but even if it does not, testing all products would often be astronomically expensive). The strategy also depends on the courts being willing to treat as foreseeable a very unspecific risk of 'manufacturing error' involved in the production process.

It is true that the presence of the state of the art defence in Article 7(e) might prompt some EC defendants to try to avoid liability for manufacturing errors under the Directive by arguing that, given the state of quality control technology the particular bad apple in a production batch was undiscoverable. But this argument would very probably be rejected by courts. Apart from the exceptional cases of unavoidable impurities in vital health products such as blood and vaccines (which courts have been reluctant to treat as ordinary manufacturing errors attracting covert strict liability treatment in negligence), it would be bizarre if courts continued to be willing to impose covert strict liability for manufacturing errors in the tort of negligence but not under the Directive, particularly given the clear indication in its Preamble that, if

---

26 See *Hill* v *James Crowe (Cases) Ltd* [1978] 1 All ER 812.

anything, the Directive's liability was to cover 'the risks inherent in modern technological production' (Second Recital). It is likely, then, that under the Directive, as in
negligence, manufacturing errors will be assumed to be both discoverable and
'defects'.

Lack of specificity in the definition of the relevant risk seems more difficult to tolerate in the case of design conditions which cause injury. We all appreciate life is
risky and that even the most seemingly innocuous process or product could harbour
risks. In this sense even design injuries are foreseeable. The question is, need we
foresee precisely what they are in order to be liable for them? In manufacturing error
cases courts do not seem to require the plaintiff to show that the defendant should
have foreseen the risk of the *particular* production line error. In design cases, in contrast, courts seem to require considerably more specificity so that the possibility
arises of the law regarding the relevant design risk in the product as unforeseeable.
The initial advocates of the rule in s 402A focused on manufacturing errors, and the
issue of unforeseeable manufacturing risks was and still is ignored. Once design
cases came to be brought in volume the issue of foreseeability of risk eventually
arose. In negligence, should those injured by asbestos, or diethylstilbestrol (DES)
have to prove not only the well-known fact that chemicals can cause deleterious side
effects but that a particular chemical might cause a particular side effect? Similarly,
although it is widely known that otherwise benign chemicals can interact causing
deleterious synergistic effects, should a plaintiff complaining about a *particular*
interaction of products be called upon to show that the defendant should have foreseen this particular link? In negligence the answer given by courts to these questions
was yes, so the question then became – should a plaintiff claiming in relation to
defective design under the rule reflected in s 402A have to show the design risk, narrowly specified, was foreseeable? Clearly where the claim is framed in terms of failure to warn this would seem to be a logical necessity, as Comment j to s 402A itself
implies and recent important US cases confirm,[27] but it does not necessarily follow if
the claim is simply one of defective design (eg if the rule was one of *hindsight* cost/
benefit – see Chapter 5). Yet even here the response of US courts has been to require
the plaintiff to show foreseeability of risk and to allow defendants the state of the art
defence both as to product risks and availability of safer designs – that, *at the relevant time*, the state of the art was not such as to allow the product defect to be discovered. Despite the 'strict liability' rhetoric of s 402A and the occasional brave
court which takes it sufficiently seriously to impose liability for unforeseeable
defects,[28] this has overwhelmingly remained the majority view: *the liability of manufacturers for design conditions under s 402A is, as under the Directive, fault-
based.*[29] Despite the rhetoric of some courts, the focus is on the reasonableness of

27　See eg decisions of the Californian Supreme Court in: *Brown* v *Superior Court* (1988) 751 P 2d 470;
　　and *Anderson* v *Owens-Corning Fiberglass Corpn* 810 P 2d 549 (1991) (no liability for failure to
　　warn of foreseeable risks).
28　See eg *Halphen* v *Johns-Manville Sales Corpn* 484 So 2d 110, 114 (1986) (La); *Dart* v *Wiebe Manu-
　　facturing Inc* 709 P 2d 876, 881 (1985) (Ariz); *Elmore* v *Owens-Illinois Inc* 673 SW 2d 434, 438
　　(1984) (Missouri) ... but note strong dissent of Welliner J and Donnelly J; *Beshada* v *Johns-Manville
　　Corpn* 447 A 2d 539 (1982); *Cunningham* v *MacNeal Memorial Hospital* 266 NE 2d 897, 903
　　(1970). Academic interest in liability for unforeseeable risks has been slightly greater: J Fleming 'Of
　　Dangerous and Defective Products' (1980) 9 Tel Aviv Studies in Law 11, 27–8.
29　G Schwartz 'The Beginning and the Possible End of the Rise of Modern American Tort Law' (1992)
　　26 Georgia LR 601, 625–7; J Henderson and A Twerski 'A Proposed Revision of Section 402A of
　　the Restatement (Second) of Torts' (1992) 77 Cornell LR 1512, 1531–2.

the manufacturer's *conduct* in design, which allows into consideration by analogy the considerable negligence case law detailing what is reasonable in this context.

What is 'the relevant time' in the US for the purposes of the state of the art defence? We have seen that by the extension of a supplier's obligations into the post-supply period, its potential liability in negligence has been widened considerably. In the US this development has not only occurred in the tort of negligence, but also in some cases brought under the rule reflected in s 402A where products have been held defective because the manufacturer has failed to warn or recall the product when post-supply developments revealed safety risks or better alternative designs.[30] In *Kozlowski's* case (1979), for example, a duty to warn 30 years after sale was recognized.[31] It is true that setting fair boundaries in liability in this area is problematic: for how long should a manufacturer have to concern itself with these matters, and to what degree is it desirable for resources to be diverted from ensuring new products are safe to conducting post-supply surveillance on old products? How accurately would a manufacturer be able to anticipate the extent to which it needs to adjust price structures to cover future costs of indefinite post-sale duties relating to discoveries and developments in the state of the art? Nor could a fair approach fail to take into account the degree to which the burden involved would vary with the type of product. For instance, even in the US, a 1952 aeroplane is not expected to be kept up to the latest standards of aviation safety.[32] On the other hand, as we have seen, there are some products for which post-circulation surveillance is the only way certain risks may be reasonably discovered. The principal examples have been the low-incidence long-latent adverse human reactions to certain chemicals and drugs. The point of interest here, however, is that the manufacturer's liability for design conditions under the Directive is actually narrower not only than that in negligence but also than the equivalent fault-based liability of US manufacturers in some US jurisdictions under the rule in s 402A. It is therefore not a valid criticism of the Directive that it imposes a significant new strict liability on manufacturers. Inasmuch as a strict liability may be imposed covertly on them under the Directive, it is in respect of manufacturing errors for which they already face a covert strict liability in the tort of negligence.

---

30 In the US the principle which dates from *Comstock* v *General Motors Corpn* 99 NW 2d 627 (1959) is well settled: V Schwartz 'The Post-Sale Duty to Warn: Two Unfortunate Forks in the Road to a Reasonable Doctrine' (1983) 58 NYULR 892; J Lamken 'Efficient Accident Prevention as a Continuing Obligation: The Duty to Recall Defective Products' (1989) 42 Stan LR 103. US examples include in 1991 the electronics manufacturer Phillips recalled 1.7 million faulty resistors and the following year in one recall programme alone General Motors recalled 1.5 million cars for modification, and there is a possibility that GM will soon recall up to 4.7 million trucks (for fuel tank modification) at a cost of up to $1 billion, see [July 1991], [Jan 1992] and [March 1993] Prod Liab Internat respectively. European examples: 1993 recall of 3.5 m bottles of Heineken beer; recall of Perrier water in 1990 which cost £45m: [Sept 1993] [May 1990] Prod Liab Internat.
31 *Kozlowski* v *John E Smith's Co* 275 NW 2d 915 (1979).
32 *Bruce* v *Martin-Marietta* 544 F 2d 442 (1976), contrast *Turner* v *General Motors Corpn* 514 SW 2d 497 (1974).

7   THE DEMANDING DESIGN STANDARD AS A ROBUST NEGLIGENCE STANDARD

The second group of complaints about the product rules in the US and EC relates to the standard to be applied in the context of injuries caused by the *design* of products. Critics argue that the available standards are too demanding and too vague. The flaw in these criticisms is that they apply not only to the product rules but equally to the well-settled fields of warranty and negligence as well as to the unitary products rule some US reformers argue should replace all three existing rules. Let us first take the allegation about the design standard being too demanding. On the one hand this relates simply to the general post-war elaboration of and rise in the standards expected of manufacturers, in terms, for example, of the extent of R & D. More importantly, the criticism focuses on doctrine. It is true that over the decades since the rule in s 402A was adopted, it has provoked US courts into significant doctrinal developments of help to plaintiffs. In every case, however, the same development could have been adopted in a negligence (and sometimes a warranty) claim.

(a)   Design defect

The very existence of design claims and the application of a cost/benefit or, to use to more common US terminology, risk/utility standard to them appeared to many to be somewhat startling when such claims began to be made in significant numbers during the late 1960s (Chapter 2, under heading 5), and especially from the early 1970s when the first challenges were made to drug designs (one of the most fruitful sources of design litigation – see Chapter 2, under heading 6). Yet Californian courts had quietly been processing equivalent design claims for some decades and the eventual acceptance of the propriety of design claims under s 402A can simply be seen as that regime taking on the form of what Schwartz describes as a 'mature negligence regime' in which the reasonableness standard is robustly generalized into this particular field of human activity.[33]

One particular form of a design claim has caused considerable concern – that of alleged inadequate '*crashworthiness*' or, more generally, of a design's inadequacy resulting in '*enhanced injury*' suffered following an accident caused by a factor external to the product. Such claims alleged that due to the design of the product, often a car, the victim of an accident suffered injuries greater than they would have done but for the particular condition of the product of which they complain (eg inadequate thickness of car doors, absence of air-bags, etc). Examples from recent transport accidents in the UK and Europe show the power of the argument, which has provided a particularly useful way of avoiding the statutory limitations on the liability of the sea and air carriers (flowing from international conventions) by establishing a claim against the vehicle's manufacturer: could passengers injured when crew negligently failed to close the bow doors on a Channel ferry argue that their

---

33 Schwartz, op cit 438. See also G Schwartz 'New Products, Old Products, Evolving Law, Retroactive Law' (1983) 58 NYULR 796, 802. As to why judges took this route, see G Schwartz 'The Beginning and the Possible End of the Rise of Modern American Tort Law' (1992) 26 Georgia LR 601. *Pike v Frank G Hough Co* 467 P 2d 229 (1970) is a clear example of a US court allowing negligent design claims.

resultant injuries were caused or exacerbated by the designer's failure to include longitudinal or lateral bulkheads or at least a warning system on the ship's bridge, and that this aspect of the ship's design took it below the minimum level of safety required under a cost/benefit criterion? When an aircraft crashed at Manchester in 1985 all 54 deaths were caused by inhalation of fumes; and the central allegation against the aircraft manufacturers was that the aircraft was defectively designed because its interior was upholstered with a material which, if burned, was known to give off poisonous gases, even though alternative fire-resistant upholstery was available. While at the time of the *Evans* case (1966) the US courts were still refusing to consider such claims, two years later such a claim was allowed in *Larsen* (1968), and within a decade this had become a universally accepted and very fruitful source of complaint.[34]

The very adoption of an overt cost/benefit criterion may carry with it a pro-plaintiff dynamic in the US. Gary Schwartz has convincingly argued that the average US jury-person has an ambivalent attitude to corporate risk-taking and probably a hostile attitude to the corporate defendant defending itself by arguing that it had carefully balanced a product's risks (especially if they relate to the risk of death) and its benefits, so that US defendants often refrain from using this, their best formal argument.[35] But again, claims relating to the inadequate design of products can be made in negligence. There may well be practical reasons why such claims were in the past less often made than were claims for manufacturing errors but the propriety of such claims in negligence is without doubt. Many past negligence cases rested on a plaintiff's complaint that her predicament was made worse by the negligence of the defendant in relation to design. For example, the basis of a large number of negligence claims by injured employees in the US and UK is that the design of a production line machine failed adequately to protect against the risks of accident inherent in the relevant process. Similarly, the highly publicized Thalidomide litigation of the late 1960s and early 1970s was a classic example in the UK of a negligent design and R & D allegation, yet it was never challenged as being outside the realm of *Donoghue* v *Stevenson* negligence liability. A number of other UK design cases can be found, typically focusing on the inadequacy of R & D or failure to warn.[36] Moreover, in recent years UK appellate courts have clearly confirmed manufacturer liability in negligence for the design condition of products. Although the issues raised on appeal in *Lambert* v *Lewis* (1982)[37] did not focus on the trial judge's finding of liability against the manufacturer of a towing hitch on the basis of negligent design, both the Court of Appeal and House of Lords expressly accepted that finding. Similarly, in *Winward* v *TVR Engineering Ltd* (1986)[38] the Court of Appeal had no

34 *Evans* v *General Motors Corpn* 359 F 2d 822 (7th cir, 1966), cert denied, 385 US 836; *Larsen* v *General Motors Corpn* 391 F 2d 495 (8th cir, 1968). *Evans* was eventually overruled in *Huff* v *White Motor Co* 565 F 2d 104 (7th cir, 1977).

35 G Schwartz 'The Myth of the Ford Pinto Case' (1991) 43 Rutgers LR 1013, 1040, 1042.

36 *Hindustan Steam Shipping Co Ltd* v *Siemans Bros & Co Ltd* [1955] 1 Lloyds Rep 167; *Williams* v *Trim Rock Quarries Ltd* (1965) 109 Sol Jo 454; *Wyngrove's Executrix* v *Scottish Omnibuses* 1966 SC (HL) 47; *Vacwell Engineering Co Ltd* v *BDH Chemicals* [1971] 1 QB 88; *Wright* v *Dunlop Rubber Co* (1972) 13 KIR 255; *Independent Broadcasting Authority* v *EMI Electronics & BICC Construction Ltd* (1980) 14 BLR 1 HL. From the Commonwealth see also *O'Dwyer* v *Leo Buring Pty Ltd* [1966] WAR 67; *Suosaari* v *Steinhardt* [1989] 2 Qd R 477.

37 *Lexmead (Basingstoke) Ltd* v *Lewis* [1982] AC 225. Compare the (defective tug) claim behind the interlocutory appeal in *Esso Petroleum Co Ltd* v *Hall Russell & Co Ltd* [1989] 1 All ER 37 HL.

38 *Winward* v *TVR Engineering Ltd* [1986] BTLC 366, CA.

difficulty in finding the manufacturer of specialised motor cars liable in negligence for its failure to review the design of component carburettors, even though supplied to it by a reputable firm (Ford Motor Co). Although design claims first appeared in volume in the US in the form of s 402A claims, there is no doubt that they could equally well have been developed first in negligence or warranty, had a sufficiently aggressive approach been adopted by courts and plaintiffs' lawyers.

(b)   Failure to warn

This conclusion applies a fortiori to that subset of design claims which allege that the product defect is constituted not by the physical attributes of the product but by the supplier's failure adequately to warn of the risks of those attributes. The potential of this tactic lies in its flexibility: a plaintiff could argue, for example, that the defendant failed adequately to warn about the necessary level of maintenance of the product or to warn of its length of useful or safe life. Failure-to-warn claims are now the most common form of litigated product case in the US. This is understandable. The outcome of the common manufacturing error cases is usually easy to predict, because of the courts' adoption of the production line norm, so that such claims are typically settled out of court. A direct allegation that the physical design of a product is defective is often a very costly one to prove. It is also one which courts may well be reluctant to uphold if grave socio-economic dislocations are thereby threatened because a firm, an industry or a community is dependent on that product line. Grave dislocations do not *necessarily* follow a finding of defective design: the courts' determination of costs and benefits may be wildly out of line so that it is worth a manufacturer's while to 'tough it out', to stand by its product by continuing to market it and pay damages for any claims that are made, making a relevant adjustment to product price. But sometimes the dynamics of the market (including consumer confidence) do not allow this, and grave consequences follow. The most notorious US examples here involve whole product categories where the defect is in the generic nature of the thing: asbestos and intra-uterine contraceptive devices. Tobacco may be the next. It is not surprising, then, that plaintiffs' lawyers in the US rapidly adjusted to the possibility of bringing design-related claims by framing them in the apparently more modest form of a failure-to-warn claim where a finding of liability only appears to involve the defendant in a one-off judgment cost and the minor cost of appropriately labelling the product-line. There are also practical advantages of this format. Where the product is so badly damaged in an accident that evidence of physical defectiveness is difficult to find, or where, as in the US, it is the plaintiff who must show defectiveness at the time the product was put into circulation, a failure to warn claim overcomes the relevant evidentiary gap. It can also be useful as an aggressive move to outflank a defence of contributory negligence.

Warnings might be divided into two types: warnings that instruct on how to use the product safely (eg 'maximum load: 2 stone'); and warnings that focus on risks which may arise in intended use (eg 'smoking can cause cancer'). While it is usually feasible to write down the former instructions adequately, it is often not feasible to list all the 'informed choice warnings' which a complex product's risks might require.[39] In either case the causal issue should, in theory, be central to the claim.

39 Schwartz 'The Myths of the Ford Pinto Case' op cit 1050.

The plaintiff should have to prove not only that a warning was feasible but that it would have attracted the attention of a relevant party so that the injury could and would have been avoided. Sometimes courts have been assiduous in insisting on this causal relation. The so-called *'learned intermediary'* doctrine in the US, for example, rests on this approach. Under this doctrine manufacturers, typically of health care products, are able to escape liability by showing that they gave adequate information about the relevant risk to an intermediary, such as a general practitioner, who will direct or supervise its use. Its main field of operation is prescription drugs.[40] This doctrine seems to rest on the sound assumption that as between a manufacturer's warning and the attitude of a GP, what predominantly influences a patient in whether or not to take a drug is the latter. In other words, a manufacturer's package insert is highly unlikely to override a GP's assurance, advice and warnings about the medication, so that channelling claims to the GP seems justified. An inventive way around the doctrine is for plaintiffs to argue that the manufacturer so over-promoted the product that hard-pressed intermediaries were unable adequately to exercise the judgment on which their client's 'informed consent' depends. In general, however, this tactic has failed to convince courts, which tend to be particularly protective of drug manufacturers.

Faced with a court insisting on proof of the requisite causal link between her injury and the inadequacy of warnings, a plaintiff would find little comfort in the modern psychological studies about the efficacy of warnings. These reveal not only that excessive warnings, particularly of obvious hazards, are counterproductive because people can be lulled into a false sense of security by their limitations or learn to see warnings as superfluous, but that warnings in general are ineffective in most circumstances because behaviour is dominated by factors such as past experience and the example of others' behaviour.[41] Similarly for large classes of victims, warnings are not a feasible way of making products safer because, for example, they cannot read or at least cannot read the language in which the warning is cast. So defendants will often be able to argue that even had they given a warning it would have been useless. This consideration should lead most plaintiffs to rely more on allegations of defective design, and courts should insist that they do so. In some cases even an arch-paternalist would not require a warning – for example, that glass bottles can shatter and cut if dropped, that tyres wear out, etc. But there may be some product contexts, perhaps the majority,[42] in which an adequate warning cannot

---

40 Although the doctrine has also sometimes been used in claims of employees injured by production machinery where the defendant-manufacturer argues it adequately warned the employer-intermediary. In many US jurisdictions exception is made for both oral contraceptives and cases involving mass immunization on the basis that, where the intervention is so much more elective, the manufacturer should warn the patient directly. The thinness of UK drug case law (no case has yet reached favourable judgment for the plaintiff) means that it is unclear if the doctrine applies in the UK; compare P Ferguson 'Liability for Pharmaceutical Products: A Critique of the "Learned Intermediary" Rule' (1992) 12 Oxf JLS 60. See also Law Coms paras 56, 58–9.

41 N Robinson and B Brickle 'Warning Labels: Science and the Law' Jan 24 1992, NLJ 83,84. On cigarette warnings see W Kip Viscusi *Smoking: Making the Risky Decision* (Oxford, OUP, 1993). See also, *Vacwell Engineering* v *BDH Chemicals* [1971] 1 QB 88, 110; *Wright* v *Dunlop Rubber Co* (1972) 13 KIR 255, CA; *Thomas* v *Hoffman-La Roche Inc* 949 F 2d 806 (5th Cir, 1992) (re warning in Accutane acne treatment case).

42 P Schlechtriem 'Presentation of a Product and Product Liability Under the EC Directive' (1989) 9 Tel Aviv University Studies in Law 33, 45–6 who argues that only in the 'extreme exception' where potential users are likely to notice the warning/instructions should a 'defect' be cured by a warning.

be conveyed sufficiently effectively to users anyway; and in such cases a failure-to-warn complaint will fail the causal test.

Take, as an example, the recent problem with an acne treatment: suppose that such a treatment causes severe birth defects to the subsequent children of certain women who take it. Should the issue be one of warnings at all? If a plaintiff alleges failure to warn, this implies that an adequate warning is possible and would have been heeded. But this in turn implies that a producer of such a product which *does* carry a warning should be allowed to argue that its well displayed, detailed and accurate warning was adequate and would have been heeded. But would this be acceptable? The risk that some women may, even so, not notice the warning, or appreciate its message, or be able to read it is a real one which, given the extreme risk, the community's standard of minimum safety might regard as not outweighed by the benefits of the drug. This issue lies at the heart of the current US claims concerning cigarettes, nearly all of which presently take the form of failure-to-warn claims. In the US, as in the UK and EC, public regulations require cigarette packages to carry warnings. Even if we make the large assumption that the *form* of these warnings is optimal in terms of their prominence, detailing of risk (eg of pulmonary disorders, of addiction, of hazard to passive smokers) etc, should their presence pre-empt an action for damages which challenges the *adequacy* of these warnings, as defendant cigarette manufacturers succeeded in convincing the US Supreme Court in 1992?[43] The court confirmed that plaintiffs could still formulate claims in terms of fraud or misrepresentation, and perhaps in retrospect this will emerge as a decision which implicitly took the view that the issue in such cases as tobacco claims should not be one of warnings at all, given the extreme risks involved, but should be whether such risky product designs should be marketed without liability attaching for injuries caused. This will not always be easy for courts to acknowledge: where the design is this dangerous *and* where a finding of liability would clearly threaten to precipitate major socio-economic dislocations, as it would in the product-category cases where the defect is generic and not remediable by modification to an alternative design, courts face a serious separation of powers dilemma.

In practice, EC courts may well choose to resolve such cases in defendants' favour, as most US courts now do, and the Californian legislature attempted to do, but this would not be because 'there is no intellectually respectable way to accomplish the imposition of product-category liability'[44] but because the potential impact of civil liability reveals itself here as too embarrassing from a constitutional point of view.

One would also expect problems for non-users employing a failure to warn formulation. Of course, technically they could challenge the adequacy of warnings to the relevant intermediary or user, but the adequacy of warnings issue here should then become linked to the wider, much more complex issue of overlapping enterprises (see Chapter 13, under heading 1), joint tortfeasors and, specifically, to the attitude taken to the responsibility of users for the care of non-users and bystanders.

---

43 *Cipollone* v *Liggett Group Inc* 112 S Ct 2608 (1992).
44 J Henderson and A Twerski 'Stargazing: The Future of American Product Liability Law' (1991) 66 NYULR 1332, 1336. On the Californian statute see D O'Leary Aitken 'The Product Liability Provision of the Civil Liability Reform Act of 1987: An Evaluation of its Impact and Scope' (1989) 62 S Calif LR 1449. The asbestos and Thalidomide disasters show that it is quite intelligible to describe a product as so dangerous that with or without a warning it is 'defective as designed', and this is just as intellectually feasible with large volume generic designs such as cigarettes as it is with low volume specific designs such as Thalidomide or a specific model of vehicle.

So for a number of reasons the formulation of a claim as one of failure to warn should itself be problematic. Yet such claims continue to dominate US products litigation. This is because, despite the theoretical problems of claims focusing on adequacy of warnings – especially that of establishing the causal issue – in practice such claims tend to produce a powerful pro-plaintiff dynamic, especially where judges are not sufficiently assiduous in their handling of the issue before the jury. As one court put it:

> Failure to warn cases have the curious property that, when the episode is examined with hindsight, it appears as though addition of warnings keyed to a particular accident would be virtually cost-free. What could be simpler than for the manufacturer to add the few simple items noted above ... The primary cost is, in fact, the increase in time and effort required for the user to grasp the message. The inclusion of each extra item dilutes the punch of every other item ... Unlike plaintiffs we must review the record in the light of these obvious information costs.[45]

The relatively poor control over juries in many cases, particularly with regard to the causation issue, has produced strikingly pro-plaintiff verdicts and generated much of the criticism of the current product rules.[46] On the other hand, it must be noted that the concentration on the issue of warnings has had some pro-defendant side-effects. The tacit presumption that, had warnings been given, they would have been heeded might, as we have seen, be turned to advantage by a manufacturer who *has* given warnings. If the defendant succeeds in convincing the jury that the warning was clear and detailed, it will then be up to the plaintiff to urge on juries the psychological evidence of the inefficacy of warnings – bad tactics if the initial complaint had been a failure-to-warn claim. The problem for plaintiffs is especially acute in the case of patent dangers where, once a warning is given, it will be especially difficult to argue that the product fell below reasonable expectations of safety if it is assumed that warnings are heeded. The use of warnings or their equivalent also provides potential defendants with a strategy around regulation of exclusions. It has been claimed, for example, that warnings and instructions for use have become popular with suppliers since the Unfair Contract Terms Act 1977 limited suppliers' ability to exclude the statutory obligations relating to quality. The aim has been to specify the ordinary uses to which the product should be put.[47] A similar strategy might be attempted in an effort to evade the liability set out in the Directive which, by virtue of Article 12, cannot be 'limited or excluded'.

Finally, despite the identification of failure-to-warn claims and their attendant problems with the product rules, such claims are equally viable in warranty and especially in negligence, where their clear connection to fault in human behaviour seems best accommodated.

---

45 *Cotton* v *Buckeye Gas Prods Co* 840 F 2d 935, 937–8 (1988).
46 See eg J Henderson and A Twerski 'Doctrinal Collapse in Product Liability: The Empty Shell of Failure to Warn' (1990) 65 NYULR 265 who refer to the 'inherent lawlessness' of failure to warn litigation (271); G Schwartz 'The Myths of the Ford Pinto Case' (1991) 43 Rutgers LR 1013, 1053 who argues that the causation requirement rarely troubles the plaintiff in a 'failure to give instructions' claim.
47 J Macleod 'Instructions as to the Use of Consumer Goods' (1981) 97 LQR 550, 558–560. On the current unsatisfactory treatment of these issues by the courts see E Macdonald 'Exclusion Clauses: The Ambit of s 13(1) of the Unfair Contract Terms Act 1977' (1992) 12 Legal Studies 277.

(c)   Manufacturers' liability for foreseeable acts of third parties or victims (such as misuse); victim behaviour

In the US, manufacturers' liability was seen to expand considerably when courts began to entertain claims under the new product rule that sought to make them liable when the product injury was due to material alteration of the product's condition or misuse of it by another party.[48] Where such alteration occurred before the manufacturer supplied the product, liability had not been seen as problematic. Pre-supply alteration by third parties such as criminal tampering or by Act-of-God could be treated as a defect for which the manufacturer was rightly held responsible, given the unstated fiction that modern quality control should be able to identify products whose condition departs from the production line norm (see Chapter 6, under heading 2(b), headings 4 and 6 above and Chapter 11, under heading 7). In other words, the 'state of the art' defence would not shield a manufacturer because departures from the norm, howsoever and by whomever caused, were assumed to be discernible by the manufacturer.

But US courts have also countenanced liability in cases where the alteration of the product occurred after the manufacturer loses physical control of the product by supplying it. As under the Directive (see Article 7(b), CPA, ss 4(1)(d), 4(2)), there is no liability under s 402A unless the product was defective at the time of supply. Nevertheless, the US and EC notions of 'defect' can be used to cover cases of post-supply alteration: for example, in the case of criminal tampering with products on supermarket shelves[49] the product might be alleged to be 'defective' at the time of supply because it lacked packaging that was adequately tamper-resistant or tamper-apparent. Another such case is modification by a user (not necessarily the victim) where the product is allegedly defective either because it allowed or encouraged such dangerous alterations or because there was no warning of the foreseeable risks which might be created if the user made the relevant modification; a classic example is where an employer removes guards from production machinery to increase productivity.[50] A related allegation is that a product was defective at the time of supply because it allowed, facilitated or encouraged negligent installation or maintenance. This is a route by which manufacturers can in effect be held vicariously liable for the carelessness of suppliers further down the distribution chain.[51] Yet another allegation is that a product is defective because its design or lack of warnings allowed, facilitated or encouraged foreseeable misuse of the product. It is on this basis, for example, that cheap, highly inaccurate handguns ('Saturday night specials') have been controversially held defective, and their manufacturers held

---

48 See eg M Gallub 'Limiting the Manufacturer's Duty for Subsequent Product Alteration: Three Steps to a Rational Approach' (1988) 16 Hofstra LR 361.

49 In the most notorious recent case in the US – where seven people died in 1982 having ingested the over-the-counter drug Tylenol laced with cyanide – the manufacturer settled out of court with 21 claimants: [June 1991] Prod Liab Internat 88 and 95. Note the offence created by s 38 of the Public Order Act 1986 (1986, c 64) (contamination of or interference with goods with intention of causing public alarm or anxiety, etc).

50 See eg *Germann v F L Smithe Machine Co* 395 NW 2d 922 (1986). It has been estimated that 39% of product alterations result from the conduct of employers, Gallab, op cit 366 n 15.

51 Or to use the parallel but needlessly cryptic terminology of the landmark case of *Vandermark v Ford Motor Co* 391 P 2d 168 (Cal, 1964), it imposes a 'non-delegable duty' on manufacturers to ensure such carelessness does not occur.

liable to injured victims.[52] Relevant here, too, are cases dealing with the difficult issue of when a product should be accompanied by a warning as to the time after which continued use would be unsafe.

These routes to manufacturer's liability under the rule in s 402A generate much criticism in the US, especially the cases where liability is imposed in cases of foreseeable product misuse *by the victim*. The propounders of the rule such as Prosser had thought such cases would fall outside the new rule, just as they had fallen outside the warranty of merchantability, which was linked to fitness for *ordinary* uses.[53] An extensive, often critical, literature has developed tracing the twists and turns of the sometimes bizarre case law in each of these different types of design defect case. In contrast to its 1979 draft (Article 4), the final Directive also seems to tolerate claims that a product may be defective when it injures while being misused – for example, where a child is injured by eating pharmaceuticals supplied in a container which is not child-proof – because the definition of 'defect' includes consideration of 'the use to which it could reasonably be expected that the product would be put' (Article 6(1)). In this way 'defectiveness' can be linked to plaintiff (mis)conduct.

But identical allegations can be and are made in the tort of negligence where defendants are routinely held liable for the conduct of others. Where the relevant act or omission is that of a third party, the question can be handled in negligence under any of a number of different analytical categories: duty, cause or remoteness (or 'proximate cause' in the US). Thus a defendant may be held to owe or not to owe a *duty* to avoid damage likely to be caused by a third party according to whether, for example, the defendant has control over that third party. Alternatively, the issue might be said to turn on whether the act of the third party broke the chain of *causation* (so that the defendant could not be said to have caused the damage), or, even if it did not, that in the circumstances its consequences should be regarded as too *remote* for policy reasons.[54] When the relevant act was that not of a third party but of the plaintiff herself, the court hearing a negligence claim has further doctrinal alternatives for presenting the desired result, namely the defences of volenti and contributory negligence. Take the case of a person who attempts to climb a ladder in high heels, or a child who is allowed by its parents to play with a power mower as a toy. There is no doubt that a court would not impose negligence liability on the ladder or mower manufacturer, but the court would have a choice as to how to reach that result: that there was no breach of the standard of care, that the ladder did not cause the injury, that the user was contributorily negligent or even, in some circumstances, that the user was volens to the risk.

In many cases where the conduct of someone other than the defendant caused the relevant harm the facts allow these analytical devices to be used interchangeably, and this can present problems for the organization of doctrinal analysis, which US judges have often eschewed by allowing the relevant issues to proceed to the jury as

---

52 *Kelley v R G Indus Inc* 497 A 2d 1143 (1985). See Anon 'The Manufacture and Distribution of Handguns as an Abnormally Dangerous Activity' (1987) 54 U Chi LR 369. Although criticism centres on the alleged preemption of the political process, note that in 1991 a law allowing such claims was approved by residents of the District of Columbia: [Dec 1991] Prod Liab Internat 187, [Jan 1992] 5.

53 W Prosser 'The Assault upon the Citadel (Strict Liability to the Consumer)' (1960) 69 Yale LJ 1099, 1144.

54 See eg the varying analyses of the Law Lords in *Home Office v Dorset Yacht Co Ltd* [1970] AC 1004.

questions of fact.[55] It may be true that the particularly complex problems raised by third party or victim behaviour first became the subject of substantial litigation and academic analysis under the product rules, but again, identical cases and problems arise where claims are couched in negligence. A return to a simple negligence cause of action would not eliminate them or their problems, as the notorious case of *Moran* v *Faberge Inc* (1975) shows:[56] a perfume manufacturer was held liable *in negligence* to a child injured when the plaintiff's friend poured it on a candle. The best example of this parallelism of negligence with the product rule is the issue of plaintiff fault. Until the 1970s the US common law rule was that contributory negligence was a complete defence to claims in negligence. Comment n to s 402A limited defences based on plaintiff behaviour under that rule (probably because the drafters only had manufacturing errors in mind)[57] to cases where the victim knew of the defect and yet voluntarily proceeded to use the product, and since most product cases fall outside this fact situation, this meant that under that rule a plaintiff's contributory negligence usually had no adverse effect on his recovery.[58] Then, beginning in the late 1960s, most courts faced with negligence claims began to apply an apportionment rule (called 'comparative negligence') – a sensible response to the recognition that the plaintiff had some causal relevance to the injury.[59] After the landmark case of *Daly* (1978)[60] apportionment has been carried over in many (but not all) jurisdictions to claims under s 402A where the plaintiff's behaviour can now reduce recovery on the basis of an apportionment rule. A separate defence of misuse operates in some jurisdictions to bar recovery completely.

(d)   Patent dangers (the 'open and obvious' rule)

When the pressure of design defect claims brought under the rule reflected in s 402A forced courts to enunciate more clearly what could constitute an unacceptable product condition, there came a dramatic change in judicial attitudes to patent (ie 'open and obvious') dangers. In earlier negligence case law in the US such as *Campo* v *Scofield* (1950)[61] there had been a strong reluctance to uphold complaints about patent risks, courts often rejecting them under the doctrine of volenti. But from the early 1970s many US courts have accepted the legitimacy of complaints that a product risk, albeit patent, was 'unreasonably dangerous' and that the product was defective under s 402A. The irrelevance to bystanders of the fact that the risk may have been patent to users was one factor at work here, as well as an appreciation that some users (such as employees working on assembly lines and children) may be inadvertent. Where a manufacturer could at low cost make the product safe it was thought reasonable to expect the manufacturer to do so. The flexibility apportionment for plaintiff's fault afforded courts was probably also a substantial factor in the acceptance of patent danger claims. Nonetheless, this was a common law development equally available in s 402A and negligence claims. This is confirmed by the

55 Gallub, op cit 366–7.
56 332 A 2d 11 (1975).
57 G Priest 'The Modern Irony of Civil Law' op cit 113.
58 G Schwartz 'Foreword: Understanding Product Liability' op cit 455–6.
59 *Li* v *Yellow Cab Co* 532 P 2d 1226 (1975).
60 *Daly* v *General Motors Corpn* 575 P 2d 1162 (1978).
61 95 NE 2d 802 (1950).

fact that the change in attitude is usually dated from a negligence case, *Pike v Frank G Hough Co* (1970),[62] and in particular associated with the influence of *Micallef v Miehle Co* (1976),[63] another case handled in negligence.

(e) Assessment of benefits of design/'feasible alternative designs'/'unavoidably unsafe'

It has generally been agreed that in evaluating the benefits or utility of a product design under s 402A the availability of a substitute product which would meet the same need and not be as unsafe is relevant. It was, for example, one of the highly influential list of relevant factors formulated by Wade in 1973,[64] and comparisons of this sort are a popular tactic with plaintiffs as it enables the discussion to be more closely focused than would otherwise be the case. One of the more dramatically pro-plaintiff shifts of s 402A doctrine over the decades since its adoption has been the much increased weight courts have given to this factor. While the absence of an alternative design is often wrongly treated as conclusive of the product's non-defectiveness and thereby helps defendants (see below), the more common phenomenon in the past has been for courts to allow evidence of an alternative design to go to the jury in a way which suggests that its existence alone justifies a verdict for the plaintiff. The flaw in this apparent linkage between the existence of a feasible alternative design and defectiveness is that the standard of defectiveness no longer remains a *minimum*, even though this is the nature of the standard suggested by a cost/benefit, risk/utility, consumer expectations or reasonableness approach which should allow the conclusion that a design was not defective even though the manufacturer 'could have done better' in terms of safety. Indeed, *if*, for example, a car with seat belts is non-defective, the fact that its additional safety device (eg air-bags) failed to inflate, should not *necessarily* render the *car* defective.

The linkage is understandable. In designing, say, a car, the designer has to take into consideration a large range of issues relating to safety and risk: the strength of front, side and rear panels; brake and steering efficiency; rear-vision field; passenger restraints; dash-board configuration, etc. Each of these features relevant to safety must then be traded off against other factors which can also relate to safety. For example, automatic car door locks reduce the risk of child passengers accidentally opening the door but increase the risk of entrapment in the event of a crash. More often the trade-off is with factors not related to safety such as fuel economy – thicker door panels reduce fuel efficiency – and product price. Every extra safety feature may itself be relatively modestly priced but cumulatively may raise the total price of the product substantially. In the notorious Ford Pinto case, the relevant hypothetical alternative design was one in which a $10 safety precaution had been taken. As Huber points out, '$10 is not much but full-force rear-end collisions aren't common either and there are innumerable equally rare hazards that could be averted for $10'.[65] Had the designer taken all such precautions the price of a Pinto ($2000)

---

62 467 P 2d 229 (1970), where a vehicle's blindspot caused by the absence of a rear-view mirror was obvious but was held not to preclude per se the defendant's liability.
63 348 NE 2d 571 (1976).
64 J Wade 'On the Nature of Strict Tort Liability for Products' (1973) 44 Miss LJ 825, 837.
65 P Huber *Liability: The Legal Revolution and Its Consequences* (Basic Books, New York, 1988) 42.

would have multiplied, placing it out of the reach of many low-income households. In retrospect, however, these other safety risks, trade-offs and precautions inevitably tend to be under-emphasized in a trial focused on the particular hazard which *did* eventuate. In such cases the fact that an alternative design existed, cost only $10 and would have avoided the injury complained of, exerts tremendous force on the mind, at least of the average juror, when inadequately reminded of the dilemmas facing the designer of complex products.

In this light, the much touted concept that the focus of s 402A and the Directive should be on the product not the defendant's conduct is revealed as both misleading and prejudicial. The product's design must be seen as a whole, as a calculated human compromise, and judged against a minimum standard. US courts have found it hard to capture this minimum nature of the tort standard, yet it is essential to the logic of a defect or cost/benefit based regime that the standard is one a product could meet even though it has in fact caused the relevant injury, and even though a feasible alternative safer design existed. Glass doors are a good example here. Perhaps 'one-touch' electric car windows are another. The failure of many US courts to impress on juries this characteristic of their adjudication task has led to strongly pro-plaintiff outcomes in cases decided under s 402A. It is, however, a failure which has also infected the handling of claims brought in negligence and could undermine any of the rules suggested as replacements for s 402A.

The mirror image of this problem is one which – if Henderson and Eisenberg are correct in their perception of a retrenchment in US judicial sympathy for product plaintiffs[66] – is likely to become more important. This is the widely accepted fallacy that where there is no feasible alternative design, the product is *necessarily* not defective. The eminent US tort scholar, Gary Schwartz, has written, for example, that:

> one simply cannot talk meaningfully about a risk-benefit defect in a product design until and unless one has identified some design alternative ... that can serve as the basis for the risk-benefit analysis.[67]

Reflecting this thinking a 1992 draft proposal for s 402A of a 3rd Restatement of Torts requires plaintiffs at least to show that a safer alternative design exists.[68] The flaw in this approach is that while it is true that a product's utility can only be assessed in the light of any available substitutes and that the absence of such a substitute will tend to enhance the utility rating of a product, such an absence still does not *necessarily* imply that the product's risks are outweighed by its utility. Take an innovative new cosmetic contact lens that changes colour in sunlight but which is found to blind 10% of users after five years of use near sea air. Surely we do not need to ask the question about feasible alternative designs here? At least by the time the risk is known, would we not all agree the product was 'unreasonably unsafe' etc, even if there was no substitute? All-terrain vehicles are a recent example of this: their inherent instability could not be reduced by modification of their design and yet they were widely regarded as defective (and are now banned in the US[69]).

---

66 J Henderson and T Eisenberg 'The Quiet Revolution in Product Liability: An Empirical Study of Legal Change' (1990) 37 UCLA LR 479.

67 G Schwartz, op cit 'Foreword: Understanding Product Liability' 468.

68 Henderson and Twerskii, op cit. See also the 1987 New Jersey statute: D Fischer and W Powers *Product Liability* (West Publishing, St Paul, 1988) 181.

69 [1989] Prod Liab Internat 97 (banned in 1988).

Of course, the degree of incoherence in this 'no feasible substitute/no defect' fallacy depends on what is meant by 'substitute'. For some few products, typically health-related products such as transfusion blood, there is clearly as yet no substitute, howsoever defined. But for most products, its function, if defined widely, can be fulfilled by other products. The above draft s 402A(2)(b) of the 3rd Restatement applies to design defect cases 'only if the foreseeable risks of harm presented by the product, when and as marketed, could have been reduced at reasonable cost by the seller's adoption of a safer design'. The force of this provision, then, will depend not only on what 'reasonable cost' means, but on the class of products courts regard as the relevant pool of potential substitutes. After all, a bicycle may be a safer, cheaper, alternate means of transport than the Pinto car, but is it a relevant 'substitute'? On the other hand, is it a reasonable rule to allow a defendant to escape liability simply by the plaintiff's inability to prove that that *particular* product genus – such as tobacco, silicone breast implants or all-terrain vehicles – could be made safer?

This last point is of particular relevance to Comment K to s 402A of the 2nd Restatement. This Comment simply noted that some products, particularly useful drugs, may be incapable of being made safe for their ordinary use (the known but unavoidable adverse reactions associated with the rabies vaccine were cited as an example) but are nevertheless not defective so long as they carry an adequate warning.[70] From this truism that even useful drugs can be seen as poisons, there has developed an incoherent reverence for design conditions which can be fitted into the class of *'unavoidably unsafe'* products. Recent case law and suggested reform statutes reflect this idea that such products are worthy of separate, preferential treatment.[71] Thus, for example, in *Brown v Superior Court* (1988)[72] the Californian Supreme Court held that claims with respect to products which fell into the Comment K class could not proceed under s 402A but only under a rule of negligent failure to warn. This leads to bizarre results: if a product design can be portrayed as being unavoidably unsafe, liability under the product liability rule is denied and the plaintiff is relegated to a cause of action for negligent failure to warn. But the known unavoidability of at least *some* manufacturing errors is not handled in the same way, except where the product happens to be in the health care field; eg donated blood contaminated with hepatitis is given preferential treatment. This irrational attitude to unavoidable dangers in products is not supported by the text of Comment K itself, which merely notes that *some* such products are not defective because they are so useful.

Had the effect of Comment K been to force claims in respect of certain classes of products to be brought in negligence, it would only have had peripheral advantages for manufacturer-defendants (on issues such as burden of proof) because the design evaluation in both s 402A and negligence turns on a comparable foresight balance of costs and benefits. Under either, unavoidably unsafe products should be treated as other products are. For some – such as aspirin and the illustrations used in Comment K such as rabies vaccine – the benefits of the product carrying adequate warnings

70 J Page 'Generic Product Risks: The Case Against Comment K and For Strict Tort Liability' (1983) 58 NYULR 853. There is a parallel problem with the separate treatment of products such as sugar and tobacco in Comment I, see D O'Leary Aitken 'The Product Liability Provision of the Civil Liability Reform Act of 1987: An Evaluation of its Impact and Scope' (1989) 62 S Calif LR 1449.
71 See eg the 1987 New Jersey statute: Fischer and Powers, op cit 181; Priest 'The Modern Irony of Civil Law' op cit 122–3.
72 *Brown v Superior Court* 751 P 2d 470 (Cal SC, 1988).

will be discovered clearly to outweigh the known but unavoidable risks. Yet for others it must be the case that the benefit of the product, *even with optimal warnings*, will not be outweighed by its costs. Tobacco, asbestos, intra uterine devices, all-terrain vehicles and sub-compact cars such as the Pinto, might all be examples of such products. Certainly the earlier example of innovative cosmetic contact lenses is one, as would be a new drug with inherent risks like those of the rabies vaccine, but which had a merely cosmetic goal (eg inducing darker skin colour), or merely replicated the therapeutic benefit of existing and safer drugs (a 'me too drug'). Perhaps the likeliest example at present is cosmetic silicone breast implants, the risks of which may be regarded (at present) as unavoidable, and yet the benefits of which might be regarded as low. But this is not the 'consensus' reading of Comment K adopted by the Californian Supreme Court in *Brown*: in their view, it protects the relevant product not only from claims under s 402A but also from claims of negligent design, leaving the plaintiff with only the possible allegation that the manufacturer had negligently failed to warn adequately of the unavoidable risk of which it knew or should have known.[73] This is a drastically pro-defendant reading of the Comment.

What, in fact, underlies such bizarre case law on the words of Comment K is a special protectionism towards the pharmaceutical industry. Defendants have rarely succeeded in arguing that non-drug products which were unavoidably dangerous were intended to or should be covered by the protective interpretation of Comment K. Indeed, while some courts evaluate the issue of the unavoidability of danger within the drug class on a case-by-case basis, some courts, such as that in *Brown*, are so protective of this industry that they declare a whole class of drug products *by definition* unavoidably unsafe and therefore protected from allegations arising under s 402A and from claims for negligent design. Manufacturers of products in such a class (such as prescription drugs) need then only defend themselves against negligent failure-to-warn claims, even if the particular prescription drug was not unavoidably dangerous.

While in the US the desire of the drafters of the Restatement to make it clear that manufacturers were not liable for supplying useful drugs such as penicillin, even though they carried unavoidable risks, has led to this incoherent and unnecessary exception to the rule in s 402A, the formal terms of the Directive have fortuitously avoided this trap by making no such exception for risks which are unavoidable. If a product's utility outweighs its costs, it will be non-defective even if the risk is unavoidable, but the unavoidability of a risk attracts no other special protection per se.

Of course, the 'defect' evaluation under the Directive is necessarily so impressionistic that it may well admit an unconscious systematic advantage to certain defendants. The particularly likely case here is that of pharmaceuticals and other medical products towards which an ambivalent social attitude is evident within the modern history of product liability. On the one hand, in some jurisdictions the Thalidomide legacy produced more oppressive rules for this industry: West Germany enacted legislation in 1976 to impose on the pharmaceutical industry strict liability with no development risk defence; special compensation schemes for drug-related

---

73 The position favoured (albeit in the alternate) by J Henderson and A Twerski's 'A Proposed Revision of Section 402A of the Restatement (Second) of Torts' (1992) 77 Cornell LR 1512, 1522–3, 1536–7.

injuries were imposed on the industry in Finland, Sweden (via voluntary group insurance) and Japan and Norway (via a statutory scheme);[74] and the Law Commission and Pearson Commission both regarded the full application of any new strict liability to the pharmaceutical industry as the very hallmark of the integrity and success of product liability reform.[75] On the other hand, as we have seen, special protection (via the reading of Comment K) is given to such defendants under the US products regime, and the inclusion in the final Directive of a development risk defence owed much to the success of the pharmaceutical industry in convincing governments, such as the Thatcher administration, that this protection was vitally important for the public welfare.

The root of this protectionism cannot simply be the exceptional potential social benefits of this class of products – fertilizers and insecticides could claim the same degree of social value. A more likely cause is that because their direct and specific goal is to benefit (by improving or protecting) the health of the community, the cost to health of the victims can be weighed in the 'defectiveness' evaluation *directly* against a commensurate benefit in a way that cannot be done in the case of, say, insecticides. Powerful general assertions can then be made, for example, that all the toxicity that has occurred in the history of modern drug development would be outweighed if only one new drug of the therapeutic impact of penicillin was developed and marketed.[76] In the reform process, such comparisons were used to suggest that even if only on a very few occasions drug and vaccine innovation produces products of such great effect, this justifies protecting the whole industry from the further disincentives to availability which exposure to strict liability for development risks might involve.[77] What is more, in the medical field the issue of a product's *affordability* becomes a great deal more emotionally powerful because it is in the public interest that such products should be *affordable*.[78]

The economic strategy of price deterrence requires that, where the price of a non-substitutable commodity rises, those who, because of unwillingness or inability to pay, are at the margin will be priced out of the market. The result is tolerable where the commodity is, say, overseas package holidays, but may appear distasteful when the effect is due to inability to pay and the product is, say, a medicine, vaccine or blood transfusion needed to save or protect life. Some economists have conveniently sidestepped this moral issue in calling for the price deterrence strategy to be applied to medical contexts.[79] However, rightly or wrongly,[80] but predictably, many

---

74 J Fleming 'Drug Injury Compensation Plans' (1982) 30 Amer J Comp Law 297; M Brahams 'No-fault' in Finland: Paying Patients and Drug Victims' (1988) 138 NLJ 678.

75 Pearson paras 1259, 1273–5; Law Commissions paras 61, 105. Note the compromise draft Directive discussed in December 1984 which would have allowed a development risk defence for all *except* the pharmaceutical industry; J Searles 'Report from Brussels' [Jan 1985] Prod Liab Internat 6.

76 W Wardell and L Lasagna *Regulation and Drug Development* (Washington, Amer Enterprise Inst for Public Policy Research, 1975) 138.

77 *Brown* v *Superior Court* supra 481; *Kearl* v *Lederle Laboratories* 218 Cal Rept 453, 459–460 (1985); 483 Official Report (HL), cols 826, 828, 832–3, 839.

78 *Brown* v *Superior Court* supra 477–9, 482; *Kearl* v *Lederle Laboratories* supra 459; *Feldman* v *Lederle Laboratories* 460 A 2d 203, 209 (1983).

79 Eg R Kessel 'Transfused Blood, Serum Hepatitis and the Coase Theorem' (1974) 17 J Law & Econ 265, who argues that the fact that strict tort liability would increase the price of blood should not determine policy (278).

80 For it is probably more satisfactory to ensure the poor have access to the perceived necessities of life (here, affordable health care) via state programmes.

US courts and commentators have cited this issue as an important subsidiary argument supporting preferential treatment of drugs, vaccines and related products. As Justice Mosk of the Supreme Court of California said in *Brown* (1989), 'the additional expense of insuring against such [strict] liability ... could place the cost of medication beyond the reach of those who need it most'.[81] It is not fanciful to suggest, therefore, that just as the general availability and affordability of medical products have been powerful forces in the history of US and EC product liability reform, it is likely that these considerations will act as powerful (albeit covert) pro-defendant influences in the evaluation of defectiveness in individual cases in these market sectors, even though no overt preference for, say, 'unavoidably dangerous' products appears in the formal wording of the Directive's definition of 'defectiveness'.

(f)   Evidence admissibility and burden of proof

Another source of pro-plaintiff influence on product cases are issues of admissibility of evidence and burden of proof. Courts, faced with claims under the rule reflected in s 402A, constructed novel approaches to these issues. Probably the best illustration of this is the attitude taken to evidence that the defendant-manufacturer had taken *post-incident remedial measures*, that is, had taken precautions against the relevant risk after the plaintiff had been injured. Until the early 1970s such evidence had generally been excluded from claims arising out of the incident on the basis that such safety improvements would be inhibited if their adoption would help plaintiff in pending cases. But in *Ault* (1974)[82] the Californian Supreme Court allowed such evidence to help the plaintiff establish the issue of 'defect' in a product claim based on the rule in *Greenman* (the Californian version of the rule in s 402A). In other words, the court allowed the emergence of a later better product design to support the plaintiff's argument that it had been a feasible alternative at the time of circulation and in that light that the relevant product had been defective at that earlier time (see under heading 3, above). The court argued that the admission of such evidence would give a counteracting incentive to potential defendants to adopt such measures in order to reduce the risk of liability for *future* incidents. This new rule – followed in 22 states[83] – runs counter to the existing common law rule in negligence claims (set out in Federal Rule of Evidence 407), and is one which may tempt pro-plaintiff juries to raise the standard of liability so high that the state of the art defensive argument becomes nugatory in its force. But it is, nonetheless, one which a robust and demanding doctrine of negligence could and might choose to tolerate.

A second pro-plaintiff shift in matters of evidence concerned the issue of public

---

81 *Brown v Superior Court* supra 479. T Blandchard 'Strict Liability for Blood Derivative Manufacturers: Statutory Shield Incompatible with Public Health Responsibility' (1984) 28 St Louis ULJ 443, 464 argues that increases in price of blood products and perhaps other drugs would not significantly reduce consumer access to such products since most patients are covered by some type of third-party reimbursement plan, but this does not meet Bosk's moral argument about those who fall outside this protected group.

82 *Ault v International Havester Co* 528 P 2d 1148 (1974).

83 T Stewart and S Andreas 'Subsequent Remedial Measures: An Analytical Model for Product Liability Cases' (1990) 26 Tort & Insur LJ 74, 79. See also J Cartun 'Admissibility of Remedial Measures Evidence in Product Liability Actions: Towards a Balancing Test' (1988) 38 Hastings LJ 1171.

regulation (eg licensing) of certain products, especially the weight to be given to Federal Drug Administration (FDA) approval of drugs. Pro-defendant critics of modern products law have identified and decried the general trend of courts to allow cases on defective design to get to the jury even though the drug had FDA approval. But again, this is an approach open to the law of negligence. Indeed, it has long been settled in the UK's law of negligence, for example, that an employer's compliance with statutory regulation was merely evidence, not conclusive evidence, of reasonable care, and this also applies to the licensing of pharmaceuticals.[84] A comparable approach is likely in the application of the Directive which is silent on the issue save in those rare cases where the defect is *itself* an inevitable consequence of compliance with 'mandatory regulations issued by the public authorities' in which case the defendant has a defence (Article 7(d)).

The most dramatic development in relation to evidence in product cases came with *Barker* v *Lull Engineering Co* (1978)[85] where the Californian Supreme Court laid down a two-limb test of design defect: the product is defective either because it fails to perform as safely as an ordinary consumer would expect when used in an intended or reasonably foreseeable manner (the consumer expectations limb) *or* because the risks inherent in that design are not justified by the design's intrinsic benefits (the risk/utility limb). Along with this doctrinal test came a dramatic reallocation of the burden of proof: once the plaintiff shows the product's design proximately caused the injury, this creates a rebuttable presumption that the design is defective in the risk/utility sense, and it is then up to the defendant to prove on the balance of probabilities that the product was not defective. The fairness arguments in favour of shifting burdens of proof on to business defendants are well known and relate to their relatively superior access to the relevant information on costs and benefits (see Chapter 3, under heading 3). They underlie, for example,[86] certain provisions of the Directive: once the plaintiff proves that a defect in the product caused the injury, it is up to the defendant to prove, for example, that he did not supply it or that the state of the art was not such at the date of supply so as to allow the defect to be discovered. But under *Barker* the plaintiff did not even have to adduce evidence on 'defect'. Coupled with the defendant's difficulty in proving a negative and the reluctance of many courts to give defendants a directed verdict even after they have adduced overwhelming evidence supporting their case, the result has been significantly to enhance the prospect of success for complaints about alleged design-related defects.

Under the Directive the plaintiff still bears the often onerous burden of proof that the product was, given the state of the art at the relevant time, defective and caused his or her injury – burdens especially difficult to discharge in cases of old products

---

84 C Newdick 'The Impact of Licensing Authority Approval on Pharmaceutical Product Liability: A Survey of American and UK Law' (1992) 47 Food & Drug LJ 41, 52.

85 *Barker* v *Lull Engineering Co* 573 P 2d 443 (1978), on which see G Schwartz 'Foreword: Understanding Product Liability' (1979) 67 Calif LR 435. Yet another pro-plaintiff approach to evidence is shown by *Farmer* v *International Harvester Co* 553 P 2d 1306 (1976), where the court allowed an inference to be drawn after a crash that it was due to a vehicle defect.

86 They also underlay recent radical government proposals in Australia which would have placed the burden of proof on the issues of 'defect' and causation on the defendant: J Kellam 'The Trade Practices Amendment Bill (No 2) 1991' [Feb 1992] Prod Liab Internat 18. The proposal was amended and the resultant law closely mimics the Directive: Trade Practices Amendment Act 1992 which added Part VA to the Trade Practices Act 1974 (Cth) on which see J Kellam *A Practical Guide to Australian Product Liability* (Sydney, CCH, 1992).

and latent manifestation of injury. But the plaintiff does not have to establish who created the defect nor is it a defence for the defendant to prove he did not create it. Even more unusually in a civil liability, the Directive places significant burdens of proof on the defendant (see Article 7) and this will carry with it a similar pro-plaintiff tendency as in the US. Under the Directive, for example, the burden on the defendant to show that he did not put the product into circulation will be very difficult to discharge in cases where the injury has been caused by counterfeit or stolen products. Similarly, in cases where the product is damaged or in some altered state, the burden of proof on the defendant to show that the product was not defective when the defendant put it into circulation (Article 7(b)) may be impossible to discharge even on the balance of probabilities. For example, salmonella in food is notoriously difficult to discover, and producers of the tainted food will face great difficulties in establishing that, given their quality control, the food left their control free of that infection. The defendant must prove that the defect came about by an event further down in the chain of distribution and supply (for which he was not responsible),[87] by, for example, deliberate tampering, inadequate storage conditions in the distribution chain (a significant risk in the food sector generally) or a relevant alteration of the product, such as supply of the product by the retailer without its instructions and warnings. In many cases this could prove an impossible burden to discharge. Yet, as with all the doctrinal developments in the US which have been attacked as imposing too demanding a standard of liability on defendants, they are developments which a mature law of negligence could achieve. Even the much less innovative House of Lords has, at least in one noteworthy personal injuries case, effectively shifted a critical (because immovable) burden of proof to a commercial defendant.[88] These criticisms are not, therefore, uniquely applicable to s 402A or the Directive.

8   THE DESIGN STANDARD AS TOO OPEN-ENDED: WHEN REASONABLE MINDS DIFFER

Even if the product rules, such as those in s 402A and the Directive, were shorn of these pro-plaintiff doctrinal developments there would still remain the complaint that, in contrast to the simple production line norm adopted in manufacturing error cases, the design standard is too open-ended and vague.[89] Part of this problem is that scientific risk assessment may be difficult and risk perception can also be unreliable. Psychological evidence suggests, for example, that people routinely under-perceive common risks while over-perceiving rare or mysterious risks. Similarly, the evaluation of societal benefits can be problematic: we can all see some benefit in chemical food preservatives, even chemical food colours, but are we (or our judges)

87 And of course he may still be responsible on the basis that the defect was constituted by the design being vulnerable to such changes – see above.
88 *McGhee* v *National Coal Board* [1973] 1 WLR 1 on which see J Stapleton, 'The Gist of Negligence: Part II' (1988) 104 LQR 389.
89 It is important to distinguish the fallacious argument put here by P Danzon 'Medical Malpractice Liability' in *Liability: Perspectives and Policy* ed R Litan and C Winston (Washington DC, Brookings Instit, 1988) 101, 118 that 'under an efficient negligence system, claims can only be explained if standards of due care are continually changing'. A standard or rule may be clear (eg 'the exam begins at 9.30 am') and yet be broken by shortcomers for a variety of reasons.

competent sensibly to weigh this vague utility against, say, a certain cost in health to a subset of those who ingest these chemicals? Should we measure, say, medical 'benefits' in absolute terms relating to efficacy or, in contrast, in relation to any therapeutic advance over existing and otherwise comparable drugs (a major difference of approach between, for example, the drug licensing authorities of the UK and Norway). A third problem is that in litigation involving complex designs, we have seen that there is a tendency for the post-accident trial discussion to focus on the risk which eventuated and to underplay, and thereby under-assess, the other risks which a designer needs to balance in arriving at the design compromise (see under heading 7(e), above).

There is a fourth and even more important problem revealed by the design standard than these systematic distortions of the cost/benefit assessment, and it relates to genuine differences of opinion. The well-instructed person who must determine 'defectiveness' will try to balance the costs and benefits of the product (as perceived by him or her), albeit at a very general level. The era of economic analysis of law has helped sharpen our understanding of why cost/benefit issues may be relevant to legal standards, but has been unsuccessful in translating this in the real world beyond the balancing of broad impressions that has long underlain the reasonableness standard in negligence. While we may agree with Lord Griffiths that underlying a standard of 'expectations' lurks a foresight cost/benefit standard,[90] in practice it can be operated no more precisely than a 'reasonableness' standard. In practice, the terminology of 'costs and benefits' will collapse into the idea of reasonable expectations of safety. What, then, is the design standard?

In some design cases there is no dilemma: where the relevant aspect of the design prevents the product performing the task (or the range of tasks) which all would agree such a product is expected to perform. Here the clear and agreed minimum-performance standard can resolve the case. Examples include a chair not being able to support the weight of a ten-stone adult and a television not being able to be used without short-circuiting. It *is* true that even here design claims can have a particular ramification which manufacturing errors do not. A finding of defectiveness against a *mass-produced* design condemns not just the item involved but the whole line, and this can produce severe economic consequences beyond the individual case. But in this group of design cases this is not regarded as a problem. The fact that a producer of chairs which cannot hold a ten-stone person may, as the result of one lawsuit, decide that it must endure the costs of abandoning an entire product line and (perhaps) of recalling identical items already sold does not generate criticism.

The problem lies in other design claims where there is no clear or agreed performance standard against which to judge the product. Significantly, but not surprisingly, many of the flood of product complaints in the late 1970s and 1980s were of this type. How 'crashworthy' must a car design be? That a car's design should, in general, withstand a very mild collision (2 mph?) without crushing its occupants is agreed, but at significantly higher speeds there is no agreement. In designing a car, the design-engineer must trade off certain characteristics: more metal in the car doors to withstand crashes means higher fuel consumption, lower brake efficiency, and so on. Different designers might compromise these factors in different ways. Even the technical basis of these trade-offs may be questionable because of variations in opinion: technical experts may differ about, say, the inferences to be

90 See fn 9 above.

drawn from experimental data about the stress coefficient of a particular metal. How can the law set a standard by which to evaluate complex design choices such as this? In an important article in 1973 James Henderson argued that the conscious design choices of manufacturers typically pose 'polycentric issues' for adjudication; that is, they require the resolution of an issue (defectiveness of design) on which many factors bear, the weight of any one of which may vary according to the weight ascribed to any one other factor.[91] Even if we ignore juries and assume the judiciary possess the necessary scientific competence to assess such factors,[92] it is difficult, if not impossible, to reduce polycentric questions to the sort of step-by-step analysis of discreet questions to which the adjudication process is best suited. The more polycentric the question, the less the opportunity available for litigants to participate meaningfully in the decision-making process because of the absence of sufficiently specific rules upon which to focus their arguments. This, Henderson argues, offends the rule of law so that the greater the commitment to adjudicating such issues, the greater the threat to the integrity of the adjudication process itself. He argued that, unless more specific and discreet issues relating to product standards were focused upon, outcomes would remain unpredictable.[93]

Inconsistency and unpredictability of outcome in design-defect cases has certainly emerged as the key criticism of product laws. Clearly, inconsistency and unpredictability generate confused deterrence incentives, because potential defendants receive conflicting signals about what value to put on design variables in the future. Potential defendants would also find it hard to gauge their need for insurance cover. It is widely feared that this unpredictability is having an unduly chilling effect on research and development of new product designs. It is not surprising, then, that although most commentators and courts seem to reject Henderson's pessimism, their confidence that the jury system could 'adequately and responsibly perform the necessary balancing test required'[94] by the evaluation of design choices has begun to be conditional on the formulation of standards 'which identify the proper variables, which are capable of being administered in the civil trial context and which provide the jury with effective, intelligent guidance'.[95] The pressure for reform has become focused, inter alia, on setting such guide-lines for design cases.

91 J Henderson 'Judicial Review of Manufacturers' Conscious Design Choices: The Limits of Adjudication' (1973) 73 Columb LR 1531. Henderson misleadingly confined his analysis to *advertent* choices. It is possible that the relevant design behaviour being evaluated was inadvertent (for example failing to appreciate the known and agreed stress coefficient of a car door-panel). But, *as in negligence*, the performance standard of the behaviour should in theory be assessed regardless of the advertence or inadvertence of the defendant. Nor does every inadvertent design-choice necessarily bring the design below the legal standard: contrast 1548, 1550–1.

92 And this is not self-evident; see S Jasanoff and D Nelkin 'Science, Technology and the Limits of Judicial Competence' (1981) 214 Science 1211, and in *Texaco Ltd* v *Mulberry Filling Station Ltd* [1972] 1 WLR 814, 847 (a case turning on the 'reasonableness' of a restrictive covenant) Ungoed-Thomas J noted the necessary problem of 'balancing a mass of conflicting economic, social and other interests which a court of law might be ill-adapted to achieve'. On jury competence see J Fleming *The American Torts Process* (Oxford, OUP, 1988) 113, 116.

93 Henderson, op cit 1539; J Henderson 'Renewed Judicial Controversy Over Defective Product Design: Toward the Preservation of an Emerging Consensus' (1979) 63 Minn LR 773, 780. For examples of contrasting case law outcomes see Huber, op cit 110.

94 S Birnbaum 'Unmasking the Test for Design Defect: From Negligence [to Warranty] to Strict Liability to Negligence' (1980) 33 Vand LR 593, 638. See also 648–9 on random and unpredictable outcomes in design cases.

95 G Schwartz 'Foreword: Understanding Product Liability' (1979) 67 Calif LR 435, 450–1.

Yet, while nearly all reform proposals are successful in making explicit the reasonableness standard by which design defects are to be judged, these proposals fail successfully to address the polycentric potential of the design cases. Even Henderson's own recommended sequence of distinct issues requires the plaintiff to prove that an alternative design was technologically feasible at the time of manufacture, and then that 'it would have enhanced overall product safety and been cost-effective to adopt'.[96] But cost-effectiveness of a design rests on its social costs, and even crude estimates of such figures are generally unavailable to designers and courts. More importantly here, while certain factors related to social costs can appear objective (for example, the anticipated incidence of accidents due to the design and the physical cost of each accident), others are subjective. For example, if value is to be measured by willingness to pay, cosmetic values must enter into the equation. The degree to which a buyer values cosmetic elements of design varies between buyers, but might it not also vary in relation to other design features: for example, might not a buyer's assessment of the value of cosmetic appeal vary according to fuel consumption? If judgments of cost-effectiveness themselves raise polycentric issues, then even with the benefit of full information different courts could arrive at different outcomes in evaluating complex design trade-offs.

In any case, this and related attempts to control the problem of design standards are misguided, because there is a more fundamental phenomenon they do not address. This phenomenon *is not confined to the evaluation of polycentric questions* (although, as we will see, it may well be compounded in such cases), nor to cases arising under the post-war product-liability rules, nor to design-of-product complaints in general. It is not even confined to cases turning upon a reasonable-care standard. The fact that the phenomenon first caused concern in certain defective-design cases arising under the US product-liability rule is an historical accident. The challenge thrown out by this phenomenon, therefore, is not one which can be met by reform directed solely at defective-design cases or even at product cases in general. The phenomenon has two parts, the first of which is that reasonable minds may differ on how to apply a relevant standard to particular facts. We have seen that in a large number of product-defect cases this characteristic is absent because the standard being applied is clear and attracts widespread support.[97] The same is true in a large number of non-product cases: throwing bricks into a crowded street for fun would clearly be agreed to be a breach of the reasonable-care standard in negligence. But in many other situations reasonable minds may differ about the application of a standard such as reasonable care, concepts such as causation and defences based on behaviour, and the appropriate apportionment in cases of contributory negligence and multiple tortfeasors.[98] Even here, though, problems of confidence in the legal system often do not arise because the fact that reasonable minds can differ is masked by the actual or apparent uniqueness of the fact situation. Thus, a road accident can be portrayed at some level as unlike any other road accident, so that the fact that the defendant in case A was held negligent but the defendant in (the factually similar) case B was not, will not necessarily be perceived as a failure of consistency

---

96 J Henderson 'Why Creative Judging Won't Save the Product Liability System' (1983) 11 Hofstra LR 845, 849 and n 17a therein.

97 The manufacturing-error cases and the 'below agreed minimum performance cases' of defective design.

98 Of course the argument applies not only when conduct is being evaluated under a standard but also where, for example, the adjudicator has to decide if a scenario presented a 'foreseeable' risk.

in the system. An equivalent emphasis on the particular factual context of a nuisance claim can similarly prevent it operating as an inhibiting precedent in later like cases. In this way confidence in the system is maintained; so is the pretence that coherent deterrence incentives are possible under the relevant standard.

But greater problems arise across cases where the behaviour being evaluated is perceived as identical and is likely to occur frequently. Here, the possibility that reasonable minds may differ in applying the relevant evaluative standard threatens to produce different results on admittedly identical facts. One of the most common examples of such cases is the creation of *mass-produced* goods. Here the finding that one item's condition falls below the required standard may have implications in later cases involving the identical condition in an identical item. Often, as we have seen, this potential multiple flow-on effect poses no threat to confidence in the system, either because the relevant condition was in fact a manufacturing error or because there is an agreed design standard which will be applied consistently (for example, repeat manufacturing errors and 'below agreed minimum-performance design defects'). However, in that subset of design complaints where reasonable minds differ, confidence in the adjudicatory system will be shaken as apparently identical design-defect cases are decided differently at different times. The problem is most apparent in the US because of the jury system and absence of a unitary common law appellate structure. In the UK and EC, where courts will give reasoned judgments on these issues and appellate courts provide some discipline, the phenomenon will to some extent be masked by a facade of principle.[99]

It is important to stress that this problem is not confined to cases raising complex or polycentric issues. It can arise in a simple case. Take the example of the strength of a chair design. While there is no doubt a consensus that a dining-chair should withstand the weight of a ten-stone person, consensus becomes less likely the greater the weight the chair is required to withstand. Reasonable minds might well differ about whether the chair should reasonably be expected to bear a thirty-stone person. This example shows that the problem of inconsistent outcomes in design cases is not solvable by more finely tuned guidelines for the fact-finders. What guidelines could produce consistent answers to the question of whether a chair which fails to hold a thirty-stone adult is defective? How could an answer to the question be rationally defended, and would any answer to it operate as a binding precedent? Answering the defectiveness question is not fact-finding but opinion-giving. Nor is the problem limited to the special product-liability rules set out in s 402A of the Second Restatement of Torts and the Directive. It arises equally in common law claims of negligent design. More importantly, it could *also* arise outside the goods area altogether; for example, in claims which called for the evaluation of the condition of mass-produced services such as software packages and mass-produced realty such as playground structures. It also arises outside tort law, for example in the test of merchantable quality in sales law.

To sum up: where reasonable minds can differ on an issue *and* that identical issue can be raised in court again and again, the potential inconsistency of outcomes, particularly across the various cultures of the EC, may threaten both the common assumption that justice requires identical issues to be resolved identically[100] and the

99 Contrast the argument of P Atiyah and R Summers that the formality of English judicial reasoning leads to more transparent adjudication *Form and Substance in Anglo-American Law* (Oxford, Clarendon Press, 1987) 86–7.

100 In other words, fairness may *require* inconsistency of results, on which note: J Lucas *On Justice*

assumption of economists that legal standards can – at least in theory – provide coherent economic incentives for future behaviour.[101] Put in this wider context, design defect cases are not a special problem. They simply reveal the tip of a larger dilemma for courts and theorists, a dilemma which will persist as long as, for example, the design of products can be challenged, be it in the modern law of warranty based on standards of merchantability or acceptability, in the law of negligence or under the special product rules of s 402A or the Directive. Repeal of the special product rules would not remove the dilemma presented by the design defect claim.

What we should do about this dilemma is a separate and an ideological issue. Some, who regard the apparently 'standardless adjudication' of modern product design litigation in the US as an objectionable game of chance,[102] argue for the replacement of liability rules relating to product design which incorporate balancing tests by 'bright lines' rules. There is an implicit rejection of any notion that a substantive norm which produces inconsistent outcomes could be just. Typical of these critics is Epstein, who now argues for the replacement of the reasonableness and other balancing tests by the adoption, firstly, of an industry custom norm (at least cases concerned with dealings he regards as 'consensual'); and secondly, of a set of rules (albeit incomplete) for strangers.[103] There are internal problems with this proposal. After all, what *is* the industry custom on a car's crashworthiness? But the real objection to this line of analysis is that while the standard of industry custom may be administratively more workable, its adoption would redistribute wealth to business. We may not be indifferent to this, or we may be cautious about the increased reliance such a regime seems to place on regulatory authorities to deter industry from lowering 'customary' safety levels. To some it may seem plausible that advertent designers would be more sensitive to the threat of liability than most potential tort defendants, and certainly more sensitive to its incentives than to those said to be provided by regulatory surveillance. Indeed, pursuit of administrative workability might more logically lead to a rule of full strict liability where only the uncertainty surrounding the causal issue would generate substantive instability, there being no additional relevant standard of conduct to compound the problem.

9 CONCLUSION

Analysis of the core idea of 'defect' in the EC product rule shows, first, that contrary to the common description of those rules as imposing 'strict liability' on manufacturers of products, the 'defect' notion in combination with Article 6(2) and

---

(Oxford, Clarendon Press, 1980) 104: 'It may be ... justice itself is indeterminate'; T Honoré 'The Dependence of Morality on Law' (1993) 13 OJLS 1, re the necessity of law for a cooperative morality (ie one in which reasonable minds may differ on vital moral issues).

101 In this sense the central political argument alleging the 'chilling effect that the current ambiguously stated [products] doctrine must have on socially beneficial activity' (H Perlman 'Interference with Contract and Other Economic Expectancies: A Clash of Tort and Contract Doctrine' (1982) 49 U Chi LR 61, 129) is threatened.

102 R Epstein 'Product Liability: The Search for the Middle Ground' (1978) 56 NCL Rev 643, 652.

103 Epstein, op cit 651; R Epstein 'The Risks of Risk/Utility' (1987) 48 Ohio St LJ 469, 470 ignoring central hard issues such as liability for omissions and crashworthiness.

the defence in Article 7(e) of the Directive generates a liability on manufacturers rarely, if ever, greater than the liability in negligence and one that is often narrower. The liability of other suppliers under the Directive seems, on the other hand, to be a form of vicarious liability. Such an analysis also shows that the most substantial criticism of the parallel US product rule – that the 'defect' notion is too uncertain in operation in the design field to provide a workable and acceptable standard – is a criticism which can be made in relation to all civil obligations resting on standards on which reasonable minds may differ. Reduction of this source of uncertainty would not be secured even by the complete repeal of the special products rule. It would require a radical redesign of other forms of complaint such as the law of negligence and perhaps of warranty – replacing balancing standards such as 'reasonableness' with more mechanical ones. In the UK and the rest of the EC lower levels of litigation and less volatile (jury-free) trial systems make it likely that inconsistencies of outcome in design defect cases will be less common than in the US. But the instability which such inconsistencies exemplify is important because its source is general and inescapable, affecting not only the sort of standards already mentioned but also causal determinations, defences linked to behavioural standards and rules of recourse. Critics of defective design standards who assume that mechanical certainty is possible neglect this. These general matters are discussed in Chapter 13. Similarly, the embarrassment claims in respect of generic designs can cause from a separation of powers perspective is hard for the law to avoid convincingly because they simply lie at one end of a spectrum of design claims stretching from the cosmetic which scars to the cigarette which kills (see under heading 7(b), above). The only distinctions here are ones relating to the size of the market and the consequent size of the socio-economic impact of upholding the individual plaintiff's complaint. So courts may find it invidious and awkward to distinguish plaintiffs' claims on such bases.

Before leaving the 'defect' issue, we must note that its role in product rules raises another issue of general importance. Earlier (under heading 2, above), in explaining why the warranty legacy of 'expectations' was an inappropriate form in which to couch the tortious 'defect' notion, it was noted that a tort standard for products such as that in the Directive must be prima facie applicable to claims by bystanders injured by the product, and so must be relatively independent of the content of any prior transaction of sale or supply. But its exact relationship, if any, to such transactions raises one of the most troublesome problems for the modern law of civil obligations, namely that of determining the appropriate relationship of contractual and tortious obligations, their boundary and possible concurrent operation. In the product liability rules of the Directive and s 402A in the US this difficulty is compounded because the very core notion is that of 'defect' rather than behaviour or causation. This can be explained by the following example. Say S offers to sell pet food on the explicit basis that it is of low or damaged quality and presents a 1 in 10 risk of being contaminated in a way dangerous to dogs (but not cats). B, fully understanding these facts and extracting a favourable price reduction, buys the product and then gives some to his friend X without referring to its unusually low quality. Subsequently both B's dog and X's dog die from eating the pet food. We would probably want the explicit agreement between S and B to be binding inter se, so long as there was no evidence of misrepresentation or oppression. Markets in used or substandard quality goods have an important economic role. For example, such goods are often bought in order to be repaired or reconditioned, perhaps for resale. Similarly, products such as tyres which are substandard and are sold 'as is', 'with all faults', may be put by buyers to uses (eg buffering the sides of boats) which are not rendered dangerous by the substandard quality of the tyre tread. These examples illustrate the powerful reasons why, prima facie, a law of contract should enforce the agreement between S and B and allow S to undertake obligations of quality to B lower than the ordinary expectations in a sale of goods of a particular type. In the above example, then, there would be no breach of contract even though B's dog died.

There is more controversy about the appropriate rights of X against S. It would resurrect the privity fallacy to say that where there was a breach of contract between S and B (it always barred X's tort claim against S, but a more limited principle might sometimes be adopted by a legal system to limit the civil obligations of S (and any other member of the chain of supply causally responsible for the injury, such as the manufacturer) to those contractually undertaken. If it were, X would be relegated to any claim she might have against B in tort. This would mean that, so long as S had adequately warned B of the dangers of the product, S's obligations would be discharged and responsibility for the product would pass completely to the intermediary, B. The learned intermediary doctrine (see under heading 7(b), above) is one example of this channelled approach to civil obligations. The immunity from suit of the pure vendor of realty is another (see Chapter 12, under heading 1(b)). Of course, S's obligations to B would be linked to what *the buyer* could expect in terms of product safety, having received such information, not what a bystander would or was entitled to expect of a product of that general type.

In contrast, a legal system might draw the relationship of contractual and tortious obligations differently. It might allow the quality obligations of S to B to be lower than for the standard pet food sale but still impose on S higher obligations relating to quality for the benefit of X. Under such a regime S might (depending on the facts of the case) be liable to X even though S had discharged its obligations to the intermediary B, and even if B had independent obligations of care to X. The fact that the Directive predicates the bystander's claim on a notion of 'defect' linked to a 'person's' legitimate expectations of safety (rather than the buyer's) suggests that it is the latter relationship of contract and tort obligations which is intended;[104] so that even though the supplier's obligations to B might be discharged, yet there could still be obligations under the Directive to a bystander in certain circumstances. This could catch, for example, the case when oil sold as industrial oil is later resold and used as cooking oil. While the informed intermediary, here the first buyer, could hardly complain, the injured bystander might claim against the original supplier on the basis that an industrial oil can and should be coloured in a way to prevent it being mistaken as fit for human consumption. Such an approach could also catch the case of a dangerous medicine or chemical being supplied to a parent who was fully warned of the absence of a child-proof seal, but whose child was subsequently injured by ingesting the contents. It would, in other words, recognize the principle reflected in modern negligence law that sometimes a party may not only be causally responsible for the results of the carelessness or other misconduct of another party, but also that legal responsibility is appropriate where, for example, preventative action by that first party would have been easy.[105]

This relationship of contract and tort which seems implicit in the Directive is

---

104 Schlectriem, op cit 36 ff.
105 For example, by a direct warning to users such as adding colour to industrial oil; or otherwise such as adding child-proof seals to medicine containers.

obscured by being accommodated within the notion of 'defect'. In the above examples B must be denied recovery, but how is this to be explained? One approach is
to regard the product as defective under the Directive. B's inability to sue thereun-
der[106] could then be explained in terms of there being no causal relationship between
the defect and B's damage because, given the presentation of the product, B's use
was the sole cause of his dog's death. Even volenti might have a place here – though
not contributory negligence which would not completely bar B's claim. The problem with this approach is that, in the light of the explicit agreement between S and B
as to the quality of the product, to call it 'defective' in the context of the S-to-B
transaction seems very odd.

Alternatively, one could argue that defectiveness is relative: that, vis-à-vis B, S
supplied a non-defective product but vis-à-vis X the same product was defective.
But this is an even more awkward approach. The root of the conceptual strain is that
the liability in the Directive is centred on an abstract notion of 'defect' rather than
(as coherent civil obligations need to be) on the relevant relationship between the
plaintiff and defendant, and the appropriate allocation of risk between them taking
into consideration all the facts including any causally relevant conduct of intermediaries. The 'defect' notion prevents this necessary flexibility. The awkwardness of
trying to adjudicate the liability of human beings in terms of some abstract characteristic of a product becomes even greater when more complicated fact situations are
considered; for example, when the 'presentation of the product' includes some
information given by a retailer and some by the manufacturer. It is noteworthy that
the Directive gives no clue as to what sources of a product's 'presentation' will be
relevant to 'defectiveness' and hence to liability. This suggests that bright-line rules
will not be used and that each case will be determined on its facts. If so, the strain of
condensing a complex judgment about the relative responsibilities of the parties into
a bald determination of 'defect' will be extreme. This is not only a theoretical matter
of conceptual strain. The focus on 'defect' also has an effect of channelling liability
towards those responsible for creating the conditions of and supplying the product,
and away from those such as careless intermediaries whose conduct may be just as
causally relevant, if not more so. This distortion of the practical impact of liability
rules in cases of 'overlapping enterprises' is a major source of instability in the
product rules (see Chapter 13, under heading 1).

---

106 B could be refused a duty of care in negligence on the basis that it would allow his circumvention of
   the agreement: J Stapleton 'Duty of Care and Economic Loss' (1991) 107 LQR 249.

CHAPTER 11

Relatively stable boundaries

1   INTRODUCTION

In addition to the notion of 'defect', the liability rule in the Directive is bounded by special requirements relating, for example, to types of actionable loss (including financial thresholds and, potentially, financial ceilings) and to types of defendants. It is also bounded by the notion of 'product' and by notions relating to what defendants must have done with the product to bring themselves within the reach of the liability. Most of the former group of boundaries, dealt with in this chapter, are less problematic than the latter group, discussed in Chapter 12, for two reasons. Firstly, although the trend towards expansion of liability in the US has been reflected in a relaxation of traditional rules concerning causation, the nature of actionable damage and identification of defendants, the contexts in which these developments occurred are considerably wider than product cases. So even if pressure in these directions were to occur in Europe, the resultant instability would not be identified with the product rules specifically. Secondly, the US rule, by rendering all suppliers equally liable, openly exposes the regime to the expansionary pressures that arise in the absence of a coherent rationale for a rule limited to products, etc. The results are artificial devices of control and the infection of surrounding areas of law when these fail to convince courts. In contrast, the channelling of the Directive's liability to producers masks these problems in a superficially sensible way, effectively submerging into the vagueness of recourse rules the fundamental issues concerning the competing bases of civil liability.

2   DAMAGE FORMING THE GIST OF THE CLAIM

Damage is the gist of the claim under the Directive. The plaintiff has no claim unless he or she has suffered an appropriate class of damage due to the defective product. First, it must be clear what types of injury can form the gist of the claim.[1] Then it has to be shown that the plaintiff has suffered an injury falling into this class of 'gist damage'. Only then can the causation question be addressed because the damage forming the gist of the complaint is the subject matter of that question. The sequence

---

1 The list of types of such 'gist damage' is usually shorter than the list of injuries which are recoverable under a rule because the latter includes injuries 'consequential' on a type of injury which falls within the former class of actionable damage – see in general J Stapleton 'The Gist of Negligence' (1988) 104 LQR 213 (Part 1), 389 (Part 2).

is: can a broken leg form the gist of a complaint? Did the plaintiff suffer a broken leg? Was the plaintiff's broken leg caused by the relevant product condition?

Article 9 sets out the types of injury which can form the gist of a complaint. It reads:

> For the purpose of Article 1, 'damage' means:
> (a) damage caused by death or by personal injuries;
> (b) damage to, or destruction of, any item of property other than the defective product itself, with a lower threshold of 500 ECU,[2] provided that the item of property:
>   (i) is of a type ordinarily intended for private use or consumption, and
>   (ii) was used by the injured person mainly for his own private use or consumption.
> This article shall be without prejudice to national provisions relating to non-material damage.

Firstly, it seems clear from this that certain harms such as the irritation caused by a very noisy heart valve, are not actionable under the Directive. Secondly, there are some interesting technical questions raised by Article 9. For example, will pure nervous shock be recoverable generally, or will domestic courts read in the sort of limitations on the class of claimants as they do at common law, or will they exclude it altogether?[3] Does 'damage to, or destruction of ...' include *loss* of property already owned by the plaintiff as when, for example, a defective security device fails to perform allowing burglars to steal the property of the houseowner's guest?[4] Does it cover the situation where a farmer paints a vehicle with a defective paint which fails to protect it from rust? What if a defective lawn-food renders the soil unable to grow bulbs successfully? In the UK, physical 'damage' has been held to mean 'physical changes'[5] but it is unclear whether such admixture of chemicals falls comfortably within this idea. In 1990,[6] for example, a High Court judge was called upon to rule whether radioactive fallout contaminating a house near Sellafield nuclear plant was 'damage to property', and after initial doubts held that it was not. Borderline cases like this highlight the force in the argument that virtually all damage, including physical damage, is in one sense economic damage and that consequently a line between physical and economic damage is often unconvincing.[7] This fact has bedevilled UK negligence law for the past two decades, no more so than in respect of 'quality claims' – those arising merely from the condition of acquired property. As these are mostly handled efficiently by the Directive (see below), this problem should be relatively unimportant in this context.

---

2 Discussed in Chapter 3, under heading 6(a)(ii).

3 Compare CPA, s 45(1). On how pure nervous shock might arise in a product context see *Barnette* v *Dickens* 135 SE 2d 109 (1964). The similar failure of the Occupiers' Liability Acts 1957 and 1984 to echo these restrictions is less productive of anomalies because its liability is only owed to a small group (entrants on the premises).

4 Note if the houseowner were to sue a suitable defendant in warranty there would be no problem because pure economic loss is as recoverable there as physical damage. See also Chapter 6, under heading 5(d)(ii).

5 *Pirelli General Cable Works Ltd* v *Oscar Faber & Partners* [1983] 2 AC 1, HL.

6 *Merlin* v *British Nuclear Fuels plc* [1990] 2 QB 557.

7 See *Junior Books Ltd* v *Veitchi Co Ltd* [1983] 1 AC 520, 545 (per Lord Roskill). For other cases on this borderline and on preferable principles for distinguishing cases, see J Stapleton 'Duty of Care and Economic Loss: A Wider Agenda' (1991) 107 LQR 249, 266 fn 74 and generally.

(a) Personal injuries; damage to private property

We saw earlier that recovery for both the direct 'repair/replacement' cost of personal injuries and the consequential wages lost to the individual were supported by the wealth maximization strategy because in such cases the victim was often not the cheapest cost avoider (Chapter 6, under headings 5(d)(i) and (ii) respectively). Where he or she is the cca, other doctrines such as contributory negligence can be used to limit or prevent recovery. Although economic theory does not discriminate between types of injury (Chapter 6, under heading 5(d)), we have seen (Chapter 3, under heading 4) that the initial UK and European reformers focused on personal injuries as worthy of separate and preferential treatment. Substantial moral arguments can be found to support this preference, which is widely echoed in popular feeling (see Chapter 8, under heading 2). Given the history of UK and continental European products reform, it is therefore most striking that the definition of gist damage in Article 9 extends beyond personal injuries to include damage to a person's already owned private property (including immoveables). It is not clear why, of all the initial reform bodies, only the EC included more than personal injuries. There is certainly no evidence that this was the result of a sophisticated understanding of economic theory. Most likely it was due to a combination of an uncritical reliance on the crude conceptualism of the common law (and its equivalents in other member states) which tends to deal with all physical damage in an undifferentiated way; a desire to follow the US model where possible;[8] and a desire to render the harmonization arguments stronger by enlarging the area to be affected by the Directive. Accordingly, the substantial arguments for the separate treatment of personal injuries were simply submerged under the expressed rationale:

> The express object of the preliminary programme for a consumer protection and information policy ... is to protect the economic interests of consumers as well as their health. The scope of the Directive therefore also extends to damage to property insofar as this is necessary to protect the interests of consumers ...[9]

(b) Exclusion of consumers' quality claims

If a consumer's economic interests are to be the focus, there might at first seem to be an anomaly in Article 9. A consumer's economic interests lie both in the physical protection of property he or she already owns – the repair or replacement of which is a head of injury covered by the Directive, as economic theory suggests it should be (see Chapter 6 under heading 5(d)(i)) – and in the quality of a product which the

---

8 Despite the reservations of some judges (see eg J Holman: *Brown v Western Farmers Association* 521 P 2d 537, 544 (1974)), strict tort liability in the US was extended to claims for injury to property already owned by the plaintiff on the unimaginative basis that there was no reason for distinguishing them – *Seely v White Motor Co* 403 P 2d 145, 152 (1965) (per Traynor C J).

9 EEC Memo para 18. Note (1) under the Directive it is strictly necessary that the property 'was used by' the victim (Article 9(b)(ii)) while the CPA covers cases where he/she had not yet begun to use it (s 5(3)(b)) – on which see 483 Official Report cols 888–9, per Lord Cameron of Lochbroom a relevant 'promoter' for the purposes of *Pepper (Inspector of Taxes) v Hart* [1993] 1 All ER 42; (2) the Directive is silent on when, if ever, the victim needs to have owned the property whereas the CPA resolves the issue of who has suffered the loss and when it occurred by deeming the loss to have occurred at the time an owner of the property first has material facts concerning the damage, s 5(5). Contrast the different solution in Latent Damage Act 1986, s 3.

consumer acquires. Yet complaints about economic loss associated with the latter (ie pure quality claims) are excluded, regardless of whether the defective product injured itself by, for example, exploding. Nonetheless, this distinction does, in fact, make good general sense, not because quality claims should not be allowed but because sales law already provides an adequate route to internalization where the product supplied is a 'good'.[10] The person to whom a good is supplied in the course of a business can sue the supplier under the latter's statutory obligations with respect to merchantability and fitness for purpose, regardless of whether it has been physically 'damaged' or 'changed' by its condition. Purported exclusions of the obligation are both void against consumer-buyers and a criminal offence.[11] The result is formidable protection for such buyers – protection which, although contractual in form, is comparable and in some ways (for example, as regards the strictness of the duty) superior to the type of forced risk allocation imposed in the name of public policy which a tort duty would have represented. It is true that the goal of internalization of the loss to the appropriate party – principally the negligent creator of the defect – is reached only indirectly, relying on the domino effect of warranty litigation up the chain, and that this is vulnerable to chain breakage (eg by an intermediate supplier going out of business or losing its supplier records[12]). But it is a preferable solution to the abandonment of the privity requirement in warranty actions – the option followed with unhappy results by a small minority of US jurisdictions faced with simple quality (repair/replacement) claims by private individuals[13] – or to the duplication and resultant complexity which the recognition of a direct tort claim in negligence[14] or under the Directive would have represented. UK judges are, therefore, fully justified in refusing to recognize a duty of care in negligence in such cases, as were the majority of US jurisdictions; and the drafters of the Directive were justified in excluding all quality claims in tort from its scope.

In this light it is important to note a possible divergence of the Consumer Protection Act and the Directive with respect to conglomerate property. Article 9(b) would seem to allow recovery to a buyer of such property for physical damage to the conglomerate property into which the defective property had been incorporated – eg a new car ruined in a crash due to its defective brakes – but section 5(2) of the CPA prevents such claims by buyers.[15] The CPA's position at first seems the more consistent position given the availability of a warranty action for the conglomerate product – so long as it is a 'good'. But where the conglomerate property is realty no general

---

10 Stapleton (1991) op cit 273; *6.05 (d)(iv)*.
11 Supply of Goods (Implied Terms) Act 1973; see now Unfair Contract Terms Act 1977, s 6(2), (3). The Consumer Transactions (Restrictions on Statements) Order 1976, SI 1976 No 1813.
12 Eg *Lexmead (Basingstoke) Ltd* v *Lewis* [1982] AC 225.
13 *Uniform Commercial Code* (3rd edn), Vol 1 at pp 537–538. See eg *Santor* v *A and M Karagheusian Inc* 207 A 2d 305 (1965) (private plaintiff). Contrast the majority rule against quality claims: *Seely* v *White Motor Co* 403 P 2d 145 (1965); *East River SS Corpn* v *Transamerica Delaval* 106 S Ct 2295 (1986).
14 Stapleton (1991) op cit. A well-known recent case in which the adequacy of this type of protection was used to support the denial of a negligence claim which would have leapfrogged up the claim is *Simaan General Contracting Co* v *Pilkington Glass Ltd (No 2)* [1988] QB 758 at p 782 (per Bingham LJ).
15 Compare Article 9(b) with *Aswan Engineering Establishment Co* v *Lupdine Ltd* [1987] 1 WLR 1, 21 (per Lloyd LJ), 28–9 (per Nicholls LJ). The Parliamentary promoters of the Consumer Protection Bill themselves cited a European Commission Memo on the 1976 draft Directive to support their interpretation of the Directive's words: 483 Official Report (HL), col 879 (per Lord Cameron) and col 868–70 (per Lord Cameron).

warranty of quality exists[16] (see Chapter 12, under heading 1(b)), so there is something to be said for the Directive's allowance of such claims, for example by the buyer of a new house which was destroyed by an explosion caused by an installed defective heater.

It is at this point that the tension noted earlier which arises from the separation of physical damage and economic loss claims comes closest to the surface in the Directive, because one need not go further than the heater case to find one where the defective product has rendered the premises of much lower value (because, for example, great expense will be required to render them safe). Here, it might be thought, there is an equivalent need for the law to provide a tortious claim to leap-frog the builder/vendor, particularly given the infrequency with which purchases of new housing are accompanied by independent surveys and the frequency with which the main contractor in home extensions is not good for judgment. Certainly some US courts have been sympathetic to claims against distant product manufacturers to recover the cost of abatement of asbestos risks in buildings.[17] The complex policy issues involved in the realty field are not confined, however, to cases where the conglomerate property is adversely affected (physically or merely economically) by the incorporation of a defective product. There are parallel and even more troublesome issues relating, for example, to the negligent services of sub-contractors, surveyors, etc. Given the much wider general ambit of the negligence claim, it is a much more likely site of any future pressure to expand the avenues of redress in the realty field than the Directive.

A second class of quality claim which falls outside the protection of sales law comprises claims for 'latent' quality defects in a product where it is not until the original buyer has sold the now-used item on to a subsequent purchaser that the defect becomes reasonably discoverable. The new owner has no claim based on the implied warranty of merchantability unless the original buyer sold the goods to him in the course of business, nor is the new owner likely to have been able to negotiate an equivalent express warranty from his seller, sellers of used products being more likely simply to lower the price to effect a sale. In the typical situation here, then, there is no warranty claim. This means that the denial of a tort remedy to either the original buyer or the subsequent owner forces the latter to bear the risk of the defect in quality. There are two possible reasons why it is unlikely that this state of affairs will generate much concern. First, it may not commonly happen that *both* the existence of latent defects in the quality of goods due to manufacture or design only emerges after a significant period of time *and* that adequate proof is then available to show the defect was present at the time of its last commercial supply.[18] Secondly, we may have more intuitive confidence that prices in second-hand goods markets adequately signal the fact that the buyer bears risks relating to defects in quality, including those generated by manufacture and design.

16 Note, eg, the limitations to the liability in the Defective Premises Act 1972 (eg it does not apply to extensions).

17 See, eg, *Board of Education of City of Chicago* v *A, C and S, Inc* 131 Ill 2d 428, 137 Ill Dec 635 (1989).

18 An important example of this uncommon class is the economic loss suffered when a subsequent purchaser of, say, a motorbike discovers that a material used therein (eg asbestos) poses a health risk which must be abated by costly replacement. A different but important type of claim (claims of poor durability) is often frustrated by evidentiary difficulties.

(c)   Exclusion of claims by commercial entities

Commercial entities cannot sue under the Directive. This follows from the limited types of damage which can form the gist of the action. Commercial entities cannot suffer personal injuries, and arguments roughly parallel to those applying to consumers justify the inability of commercial entities to sue in negligence or under the Directive for the repair or replacement of poor quality property which they have acquired in the course of business (Chapter 6, under heading 5(d)(iv)): sales law provides an adequate remedy. But this leaves the exclusion of a number of types of claim to justify. Firstly, and unlike in negligence and in contrast to the approach in most US jurisdictions to the liability in s 402A, commercial entities cannot sue under the Directive for the repair/replacement costs of property they already own which has been physically damaged by the defective product. If a defective car explodes and damages the parked delivery van of a fish shop and the facade of that shop, the fish business has no claim under the Directive. There is no economic justification for this exclusion (Chapter 6, under heading 5(d)(i)). The car manufacturer, not the fish business, is clearly the cheapest cost avoider. Nor can the fish business hope to contract in advance with all the relevant distant parties whose activities might injure its own.

Secondly, commercial entities cannot sue for loss of profit, be it consequential on physical damage to the already-owned property of the commercial entity (Chapter 6, under heading 5(d)(ii));[19] consequential on physical damage to property owned by a third party (Chapter 6, under heading 5(d)(iii)) or due to the acquisition of property (Chapter 6, under heading 5(d)(v)).[20] Here the economic analysis did not yield a clear strategy because only sometimes will the commercial victim be the cca or have been able at low cost to bargain with the cca. In other cases wealth maximization would demand that any net social loss be internalized by liability being imposed on an appropriate party. If justification for the Directive's total exclusion of injury to the economic interests of commercial victims of defective products cannot be provided by wealth maximization, can it be provided by the moral enterprise liability argument? The idea, prima facie, that those who take risks in the course of the business of profit-seeking should pay for damage caused, might have a counterpart: the idea that where the injurer and injured are *both* seeking profits, the basis of any tort liability inter se should be no more than negligence with its flexible attitude to the duty of care and exclusion clauses. In any case, there are even fewer contexts in which a commercial plaintiff would be better off suing under the Directive than in the case of private plaintiffs, so in practice the failure of the regime to cover the claims we have been discussing is unlikely to produce controversy and instability.

3   PROOF OF CAUSATION

Under the Directive the plaintiff must prove that the relevant product caused the injury. This can be problematic. For example, if a car's brakes fail, it may be difficult to determine whether this was due to the condition of the brakes as supplied or

---

19 An injury for which damages are prima facie recoverable in negligence.
20 Neither of which are recoverable in negligence.

to later defective servicing. More generally, establishing causation is especially problematic in the area of non-traumatic injuries such as toxic chemical effects, as is illustrated by the assertion made at one time that Thalidomide did not cause deformity but acted to preserve pregnancies of already deformed foetuses which would otherwise have been aborted naturally. In relation to non-traumatic injuries isolated medical opinion may seem little more than guesswork. One large study by the Californian Heart Association,[21] for example, found that when a panel of five cardiologists examined the files of 319 employee heart attack victims, there was a 3:2 division of opinion in most cases (215) on causality and agreement in only 47. More startling was the finding that when 101 of these files were resubmitted to the panel without their knowing that they had already been submitted, in 30% of the cases the cardiologists' previous verdict was reversed. Statistical evidence can be more reliable. For example, some hazards can be discovered by the specificity of the causal link (eg asbestos and mesothelioma) or by the local concentration of certain adverse effects. The employment context is the most obvious example of the latter, but environmental hazards can also be discovered that way, as when doctors in a Welsh town were challenged by the Welsh Office for their abnormally high prescription costs for asthma, and this was found to be linked to local open-cast mining.[22] But more often environmental effects, such as that of lead in petrol on exposed childrens' intelligence, and product injuries are dispersed across a wide geographical area, making causal connections hard to discover and prove.

Animal studies are one way of establishing a cause and effect link, but it is well known that there is a poor correlation between animal test results and effects experienced in humans. Human clinical trials avoid this problem but can involve ethical problems (eg with the denial of protection to the control group where a drug or vaccine protects against a life-threatening disease). Also, to be statistically significant, the number of subjects needed in order to pick up even quite high rates of adverse reactions is very large, and the problem is magnified if the effect is latent. In theory, the best way around this – massive focused epidemiological studies – is only feasible for a very few products. Even armed with epidemiological data, many plaintiffs would still not have sufficient evidence to discharge the burden of proof because typically such data cannot be sufficiently focused to eliminate related factors. Thus, while it is now known that the use of pressurized aerosols caused a substantial increase in asthma deaths in the 1960s,[23] it is not clear to what extent this was due to the chemical formulation of the product or to what extent it may have been due to the way in which GPs and patients misapplied the therapy. More recently a 300-page Court of Appeal judgment in *Loveday*'s case[24] weighed complex epidemiological evidence concerning alleged adverse reactions to the DTP (diphtheria, tetanus and

21 P Barth and H Hunt *Workers' Compensation and Work-Related Illnesses and Diseases* (Cambridge, MIT press, 1980) 109–110.
22 The Times (1988) 6 June, p 6.
23 W Inman and A Adelstein 'Rise and Fall of Asthma Mortality in England and Wales in Relation to Use of Pressurized Aerosols' [1969] 2 *Lancet* 279.
24 See *Loveday* v *Renton* Times, 31 March (CA), [1990] 1 Med LR 117. On which see R Lee 'Vaccine Damage: Adjudicating Scientific Dispute' in *Product Liability Insurance and the Pharmaceutical Industry: An Anglo-American Comparison* ed G Howells (Manchester, Manchester Univ Press, 1991) 52. Contrast *Best* v *Wellcome Foundation*, Irish Supreme Court, June 1992; Prod Liab Internat [May 1993] 76.

pertussis) vaccine but concluded that the plaintiff had failed to establish on the balance of probabilities that her severe permanent brain damage had been caused by the vaccine rather than some other cause. The asthma and vaccine examples illustrate the general problem in medical causation cases that more than one culprit may be implicated in adverse reactions. For example, vast sums of money have been spent trying to determine the medical cause of the so-called 'Spanish cooking oil' disaster (836 dead, 25,000 disabled), yet it is still not even certain whether the undoubted side-effects were generated by the adulteration of the oil or by the pesticide residues remaining in the vegetable products to which the oil was applied.

Some, perhaps most, deleterious physical side-effects of products are by their nature virtually undiscoverable because of these factors: low incidence effects, latency, indirect effects, such as when a product which lowers resistance to infection or causes hyperactivity and loss of concentration, especially in children.[25] Here private law cannot assist. Such risks lie outside any regime predicated on causation. The costs the victims bear cannot be internalized efficiently nor can those morally responsible be brought to book.[26]

But in some other cases legal rules and practice can have a marked impact on the plaintiff's problems in proving causation. Sometimes these can be exacerbated – for example, where earlier settlements of identical claims are buried by enforceable confidentiality agreements, or where the discovery of the often vast medical and research documentation necessary for a claim is rendered difficult and costly by the legal machinery and practice which govern it. Often many claims rest on closely similar medical issues of causation, yet the rules governing the legal aid available to plaintiffs in lead cases can present an additional barrier to claimants.[27] But although these and related procedural and management problems in handling toxic and/or mass tort litigation here and in the US have often been associated with product claims – asbestos, DES, Opren, Thalidomide, the Dalkon Shield, etc – they are not confined to them. Causation in environmental claims is just as problematic, as are the coordination issues of the sort of multi-party claims now common after mass transport accidents. This means that the pressure which increasing medical information and suspicions about causal connections puts on the legal system will be widespread, and the resultant controversies will not become so identified with the liability under the Directive that its stability will thereby be undermined.

---

25 *Low incidence effects*: eg a pregnancy drug which results in a very small increase in club feet. Contrast the usefulness of the general rareness of the effect itself, a factor aiding the identification of causation in the case of DES (rare vaginal cancer) and asbestos (rare form of cancer called mesothelioma). *On lower resistance* compare: *Beavis* v *Apthorpe* (1962) 80 WN NSW 852; *Smith* v *Leech Brain & Co Ltd* [1962] 2 QB 405. *On hyperactivity, etc*: see the recent case where sweet colourings were implicated in the death of a child who walked in front of a car, allegedly due to his total incapacity to concentrate after ingesting tartrazine: Express and Star (1989) 19 September, p 19.

26 J Stapleton *Disease and the Compensation Debate* (Oxford, Clarendon Press, 1986).

27 The problems of strategy and funding associated with multi-party litigation are well explored by G Dehn 'Opren – Problems, Solutions and More Problems' (1989) 12 J Consumer Policy 397 and M Mildred 'Representing the Plaintiff in Drug Product Liability Cases' in *Product Liability, Insurance and the Pharmaceutical Industry: An Anglo-American Comparison*, op cit 24.

4 'GIST DAMAGE': POTENTIAL PRESSURE POINTS

(a) Redefining 'damage' to circumvent problems of causation in cases of past outcome

Sometimes, as we saw, a plaintiff has clearly suffered an appropriately actionable type of injury such as cancer, but has difficulty proving a causal link between it and the defective product. This requires proof that 'on the balance of probabilities, but for the relevant condition of the product, the plaintiff would not have suffered the [damage] of which s/he complains'. One strategy for such a plaintiff is to argue that the types of injury which can constitute the necessary 'damage' forming the gist of the claim should be expanded or reformulated in terms of loss of a chance.[28] Suppose the plaintiff suffers from a particular type of cancer which he alleges is due to exposure to a chemical product. If there is a background risk that a person in the plaintiff's relevant section of the population would have suffered from that cancer anyway, and the risk from the product is estimated by expert evidence to be slightly lower than this background risk, no plaintiff will be able to prove, on the balance of probabilities, that the cancer was due to the product. Conversely, if the risk from the product is slightly higher, all exposed plaintiffs will be able to prove that their cancer was caused by it even though *in fact* almost half will have been due to the background risk. In 1992–3 just such a dilemma was presented to the High Court in London when a test case was brought by two leukaemia victims who claimed their father's sperm had been affected by radiation when working at Sellafield Nuclear Plant. They lost.[29] The fact that the case turned on a battle of expert evidence as to whether the natural background radiation was marginally greater or marginally lower than that emitted by the plant reveals how much of a lottery both the plaintiff and defendant face in such circumstances.

One way around these problems for both sides would be for the law to allow the 'damage' forming the gist of the complaint to be redefined in terms of the 'loss of the chance of avoiding cancer' which the product's exposure had clearly caused. Now the proposition a plaintiff would have to prove would become: 'that on the balance of probabilities, but for the relevant condition of the product, the plaintiff would not have suffered the [damage] of which s/he complains', where 'damage' is 'the loss of the chance of avoiding the cancer'. In this way the traditional form of the causation test, including the balance of probabilities requirement, is left unaltered – except that the subject-matter of the test has been changed from the outcome (cancer) to the lost chance of avoiding it. The plaintiff who faced, say, a background risk of 2%, which was increased by 1% by the defective product, would then be able to prove, on the balance of probabilities, that but for the defective product he would certainly not have suffered the loss (of some of his remaining chance to avoid the cancer) of which he complains. The cancerous plaintiff would not be complaining about the cancer but about the lost chance of avoiding it, and the *full* value of *that* loss would then be recoverable; although in monetary terms this sum would be identical to a sum representing a proportion of the full value of a claim where the cancer formed the gist of the complaint.

The common law is already familiar with lost chance claims. It is well settled that

---

28 For more detail see J Stapleton 'The Gist of Negligence' (1988) 104 LQR 213 (Part I), 389 (Part II).
29 The Independent (1993) 9 Oct, p 5 (40 other claims awaited the outcome of this case which cost £8.5m).

a plaintiff who has established that he or she has suffered a type of actionable harm (eg a broken leg) can recover in tort or contract for *consequential* lost chances; for example, the 5% increase in the chance that the leg will develop cancer is equivalent to a loss of 5% of the chance of avoiding that outcome. Moreover, the UK courts allow plaintiffs to complain about a *pure* lost chance in contract, and in many claims against negligent professionals for economic loss the damage which is identified as actionable – eg the production of a defective legal document which merely has the potential later to prejudice the plaintiff's interests – is indistinguishable from a lost chance.[30] In the personal injuries field the Court of Appeal has also addressed the question carefully and held that damage formulated in this way should now be actionable in tort, but on appeal the House of Lords, although clearly hostile to the idea, failed to rule coherently on it.[31]

Substantial deterrence and fairness arguments can be launched in favour of allowing victims (of personal injuries at least) to formulate their claims in terms of lost chances, and a wave of interest in these ideas has already swept through North American tort scholarship.[32] Moreover, the popular counter-arguments in Britain are false. It is claimed that lost chance claims abandon the balance of probabilities test or fail to decide the necessary issues of past fact, but these assertions are false because the 'lost chance' formulation still requires the plaintiff to prove, on the balance of probabilities, the past fact that the defendant caused her to lose the chance. It is true that in lost chance claims it might appear that the standard of proof of past facts is being lowered. Certainly this is how it appears if one fails to shift one's focus from the outcome suffered by the cancerous plaintiff; but not if the perspective is allowed to shift to lost chances.

Nevertheless, sound and forceful counter-arguments do exist. If the law were to allow claims for lost chances then, for example, every leukaemia victim resident nearby would be able to sue the operators of Sellafield Nuclear Plant on the basis that its operations, by increasing the risk of that cancer, had caused the victim to lose some of the chance he or she had of avoiding that disease, of which there is admittedly a natural background risk. Similarly, epidemiologists estimate that 1000 non-smokers a year in the UK die from the effects of cigarettes, of whom 300 die from lung cancer.[33] Yet in the UK a total of 40,000 people die of lung cancer each year. Were lost chances to be actionable, for which of these 40,000 deaths would evidence about the domestic and work environments endured by the victim allow a passive smoking claim to be made? Courts could easily be swamped with such claims, case-by-case adjudication of which would be an extremely costly exercise and one which might well be as much a lottery of expert evidence as the current regime. Indeed, whereas the current approach to claims based on outcome is taken to require simply a determination of whether the risk created by the defendant's relevant conduct was

30 See, eg, *Bell* v *Peter Browne & Co* [1990] 3 All ER 124, CA; *D W Moore & Co Ltd* v *Ferrier* [1988] 1 All ER 400, CA. On this point and the general arguments in the text see J Stapleton (1988) op cit 235.

31 *Hotson* v *East Berks Area Health Authority* [1987] AC 750. See J Stapleton (1988) op cit 389 ff.

32 See, eg, D Gerecke 'Risk Exposure as Injury: Alleviating the Injustice of Tort Causation Rules' (1990) 35 McGill LJ 797; C Schroeder 'Corrective Justice and Liability for Increasing Risks' (1990) 37 UCLA Law Rev 439; J Fleming 'Probabilistic Causation in Tort Law' (1989) 68 Can Bar Rev 661; W Landes and R Posner 'Tort Law as a Regulatory Regime for Catastrophic Personal Injuries' (1984) 13 J Legal Studies 417.

33 *Passive Smoking: A Health Hazard* (London, Imperial Cancer Research Fund and the Cancer Research Campaign, 1991); Independent on Sunday (1993) 31 January, p 1.

greater than the background risk,[34] a claim based on lost chances would require experts to put a percentage figure on the relative risks. The scope for disagreement and controversy here is very great, as is the scope for consequential embarrassment for the legal process.

(b)   Lost chance claims in the absence of the outcome

By far the most troublesome danger of allowing the gist of a tort claim to be constituted by notions of a 'lost chance' is that it would be difficult to confine that form of claim to those plaintiffs who had already actually suffered the adverse consequences, the risk of which the defendant's relevant conduct had increased. Once the lost chance formulation is allowed in this field the counter-arguments become much more powerful. In contract, privity can maintain a tight limit on pure lost chance claims, but in tort, if ever the requirement that the plaintiff has already suffered the outcome is abandoned, the potential volume of claims would become enormous. For example, suppose it is discovered that a defective X-ray machine has given dangerously high doses of radiation, or that a medicine can cause sterility, or that a paint or insulation material can cause cancer, or that the dust emitted from a nuclear plant which settles on surrounding properties is radioactive. Every exposed individual has lost a chance of avoiding the deleterious outcome, yet if each were allowed to claim now for that loss their claims would swamp the courts with nakedly speculative claims involving very great difficulty. If every *healthy* resident nearby could sue Sellafield for exposure to increased radiation it would threaten to bring the whole system of civil compensation for damage into public ridicule. Certainly such 'floodgates' concerns weighed with the judge in the recent case of *Merlin* v *British Nuclear Fuels* (1990)[35] when he decided against homeowners complaining about radioactive fallout from Sellafield contaminating their properties. In extreme cases, allowing the compensation of all those exposed to a risk on the basis of lost chances may so deplete the available funds that it would prejudice the chances of recovery of those patient or cautious enough to wait to see if the outcome did eventuate and only then sue for compensation for that outcome. In the US this is exactly what is now threatened in the asbestos field,[36] and were claims by exposed passive smokers to be allowed, a similar result could be predicted. The patient exposed victim who waits to see if the outcome occurs may also face limitation problems because he or she may have had all the material facts *about the exposure claim* many years before.

Arguments can be found for allowing some such claims, however, especially where the risk can be mitigated by the expenditure of money. Courts may become more tolerant of speculative claims where, for example, the early detection of the onset of the threatened disease is beneficial in terms of treatment, and where this

---

34 Though this is objectionable even under traditional theory which should require an accurate valuation of the plaintiff's loss: Stapleton (1988) op cit 399. In *Malec* v *J C Hutton Pty Ltd* (1990) 65 ALJR 316, the High Court of Australia seemed to perceive this error and avoided it by taking into acocunt the percentage chance that a post-tort supervising event which had occurred before trial would have resulted in the plaintiff suffering the outcome anyway.

35 *Merlin* v *British Nuclear Fuels* [1990] 2 QB 557. See also *Stephen* v *Riverside Health Authority* [1990] 1 Med LR 261, QBD (anxiety after negligent exposure to radiation, not knowledge of 'injury').

36 L Brenza 'Asbestos in Schools and the Economic Loss Doctrine' (1987) 54 U Chi LR 277, 279.

may require costly forms of medical surveillance. Similarly, the kernel of the now disgraced House of Lords decision in *Anns v Merton London Borough Council*[37] may in time be resuscitated when more liberal courts are faced with the sort of pressing personal security issues involved when a homeowner discovers, for example, that an insulation product can cause serious disease and that avoidance requires costly removal. Even more dramatic will be cases – now surfacing in the US – where implanted medical appliances, such as Bjork-Shiley heart valves,[38] are found to carry a risk of catastrophic malfunction, where avoidance requires full scale surgery, and where medical opinion is that the risk involved in the latter outweighs the risk of breakage. Although virtually all US courts so far refuse overtly to recognize claims based solely on a lost chance resulting from exposure to risk, a few courts have responded by allowing plaintiffs to claim for the emotional distress caused by *fear* of personal injuries (the so-called 'cancerphobia' etc cases); or for the cost of avoidance and mitigation measures such as medical surveillance and the removal of material such as lead paint, asbestos and urea formaldehyde insulation from buildings.[39] Even now there are reports in the UK press that pure 'phobia' claims of this sort are entering the litigation pipeline,[40] one involving fear of HIV infection brought by a woman whose haemophiliac husband died of the disease after receiving infected blood. Others are mooted in respect of pituitary gland-derived drugs which have been discovered to cause the equivalent of mad cow disease in recipients some of whom, as a consequence of this risk, have now found that mortgages are more difficult to secure and that life insurance premiums have doubled. Already 95 Bjork-Shiley valve recipients in the UK (415 worldwide) have secured out-of-court settlements from the manufacturer for the fear that its potential failure has generated – a settlement which preserves claimants' rights to substantial compensation if the valve eventually breaks.[41]

But even if recovery for mere exposure to risk is only allowed in the form of phobia claims, for example, the danger of opening the floodgates too wide is still very great. After all, the boundaries of 'phobia' are substantially wider than those of the unsatisfactory concept of 'nervous shock'. Similarly, once the cost of mitigation and avoidance measures was allowed, it would be inevitable that state and local government bodies would become major tort plaintiffs. In the US some of the biggest claims for such costs have been made by public plaintiffs: in 1990, for example, 29 states filed a $16 billion claim against asbestos manufacturers for the cost of removing that product from their public buildings; and in 1991 the city of Philadelphia filed a class action on behalf of all US cities with a population greater than 100,000 against former makers of lead-based paints, claiming reimbursement of money the

---

37 *Anns v Merton London Borough Council* [1978] AC 728, reversed in *Murphy v Brentwood District Council* [1991] 1 AC 398.

38 The manufacturer has settled with over 51,000 of the heart valve recipients Prod Liab Internat [Feb 1993] 25. There have been 470 recorded failures of this heart valve (43 in the UK) with fatal results in two-thirds of cases (33 in the UK): Prod Liab Internat [March 1992] 38. See also The Guardian (1992) 3 December and Prod Liab Internat [Oct 1993] 156.

39 See E Elliott 'Why Courts? Comment on Robinson' (1985) 14 J Legal Studies 799; V Levit and A Maskin 'Recovery for Medical Surveillance' [April 1989] Prod Liab Internat 54; *Dartez v Fibreboard Corpn* 765 F 2d 456 (5th Circ, 1985); *Re Moorenovich* 634 F Supp 634 (D Me, 1986).

40 See, on the HIV-phobia claim, The Times (1989) 10 November; human growth hormone, The Guardian (1992) 6 July; heart valve failure, [May 1990] 69, [Dec 1992] 181 Prod Liab Internat and NLJ 14.9.90, p 1259.

41 The Guardian, (1992) 3 December and Prod Liab Internat [Oct 1993] 156.

cities are required to spend to abate the threat of lead poisoning in public housing.[42] For many reasons, such claims are not likely to be as common in the EC as in the US, but they *are* possible and neatly raise in exactly mirror image the argument which was recently used by the House of Lords to reject the preventative *Anns*-type claim, namely that where local authorities end up bearing the burden of negligent activities of others, it is the local taxpayer who suffers. In future might courts be persuaded by this argument to *allow* tort claims of such a preventative nature?

The Directive's strict terms do not seem readily amenable to all such developments. The notion of 'personal injuries' might stretch to the phobia claims, however, and so this may become a pressure point in the new regime. But there is no reason to believe that such radical arguments would first arise in the EC in the products context at all. The landmark phobia case in the US, *Ayers* v *Jackson Township* (1987), arose out of the fears of 339 town residents exposed to risks from a toxic waste dump, while the most notorious case involved Rock Hudson's lover's fears of having contracted AIDS from him.[43] The dilemma such cases raise would not, therefore, necessarily be identified with the product rule nor present a special threat to its integrity.

5 IDENTIFICATION OF DEFENDANTS

A similar conclusion can be reached concerning cases involving 'indeterminate defendants', where a victim who can indisputably prove his injury was due to a particular type of product is unable, because of lapse of time or generic labelling, to identify which of the manufacturers of that type of product had made the particular product unit(s) which had caused that injury. In such situations the manufacturers represent multiple possible causes, and traditional law provides no simple technique to assist the plaintiff over the evidentiary gap.[44] In North America, some courts have been willing to accept evidence of concerted action in the way the product type was marketed. But as this leads to a joint and several liability, it is harsh on the particular manufacturers who are before the court. This acts as a brake on the courts' keenness to help plaintiffs by this technique. The creation by the California Supreme Court in 1980 of the extraordinary 'market-share' doctrine[45] can be seen as a device to help plaintiffs in those many cases where evidence of concerted action is weak or absent, without at the same time imposing joint and several liability. In effect, the doctrine allows recovery but only to the extent that the particular defendant created the risk in the market: a 50% market share obliges the defendant to pay 50% of the claim. In a sense it is like a lost chance claim at one remove, because in any particular case the defendant either did or did not expose the plaintiff to its product and yet is obliged to pay in all. Allowing recovery on such a basis is like allowing the plaintiff to recover to the extent that it was likely to have been this manufacturer who made

---

42 See Prod Liab Internat [March 1990] 46; [Oct 1991] 155 but see [June 1993] 92.
43 *Ayers* v *Jackson Township* 525 A 2d 287 (NJSC, 1987); on the successful claim against the Hudson estate, see NLJ 21.7.89.
44 See Stapleton (1988) op cit on these points see J Fleming 'Probabilistic Causation in Tort Law' (1989) 68 Can Bar Rev 661.
45 Created in *Sindell* v *Abbott Laboratories* 607 P 2d 924 (1980). See also the more radical decision in *Hymowitz* v *Eli Lilly & Co* 539 NE 2d 1069 (1989).

the relevant product unit. There are, however, very many problems with the doctrine, and although a number of US states now accept it, only one has applied it outside the DES (diethylstilbestrol) context.[46]

These problems suggest that few European courts are likely to be tempted to adopt the doctrine.[47] Even if they were, under the Directive the risk of the relevant evidentiary gap is shifted in most cases on to suppliers under Article 3(3), so that the opportunity for a market-share type of argument would only arise at the recourse stage where, say, a dispensing chemist seeks indemnity from those who had supplied it with generic goods. Since recourse actions arising out of the Directive are to be governed by the local rules of Member States, should a party seek to relax the rules of identification by a market-share argument, the pressure on orthodoxy and the threat of instability would be associated with such local rules, not with the Directive.

6   LIMITATION PERIODS AND FINANCIAL CEILINGS

The Directive sets a three-year limitation period to run from the time the plaintiff became or should reasonably have become aware of the actionable damage, the defect and the identity of the producer, leaving Member States to continue to apply any special rules regulating the suspension or interruption of the limitation period (Article 10). In implementation of this provision the UK has set up a separate system of rules, roughly parallel to the existing limitation provisions governing latent personal and property damage, but in an unnecessarily awkward way which has attracted sound criticism.[48] The problems associated with these rules are not unique to product liability but are endemic to any limited regime attempting to grapple with the conflicting fairness and efficiency issues raised by latent injury and long-tail liability.[49] What is special about the limitation regime in the Directive is that it also includes a bar against the commencement of claims more than ten years after the producer put the product into circulation. This rule may well preclude a significant number of claims. In a study of US appellate decisions on product liability 10% were found to involve cases of injury occurring more than ten years after supply.[50] It would certainly eliminate, for example, most asbestos, DES and tobacco claims, plus other severe latent disease cases where plaintiffs already typically face substantial problems proving medical causation. It would also eliminate many claims relating to con-

---

46 Prod Liab Internat [Sept 1990] 138, [Nov 1992] 170; *Smith* v *Cutter Biologicals Inc* (1992, Hawaii Supreme Court) HIV-contaminated blood products.

47 When the Netherlands Supreme Court recently allowed plaintiffs to sue any of the relevant suppliers of the generic good (who are then jointly liable to the plaintiff and can only limit their liability by the market-share doctrine in recourse actions against other suppliers: HR 9-10-1992, Case No 14667, Rvdw 219 – a DES case arising from facts which occurred before the Directive became law), it emphasised that the new rule did not extend to claims derived from the products Directive. (I am grateful to Jasper Teulings for details of this case in English).

48 CPA, ss 5(5), (6), (7), s 6(6), Schedule 1.

49 Stapleton op cit, 'Gist of Negligence'; see also Chapter 6, under heading 5(h).

50 G Schwartz 'New Products, Old Products, Evolving Law, Retroactive Law' (1983) 58 NYULR 796, 813. On the comparable rules in the US (half of whose States have an equivalent provision – ranging from 6–12 years) see L Merlo 'Status and Trends in State Product Liability Law: Statutes of Limitation and of Repose' (1987) 14 Journal of Legislation 233.

sumer durables such as cars, fridges, etc, where the safety a person is entitled to expect might otherwise have been thought to include durability beyond ten years. Reform alternatives more favourable to plaintiffs were available. For example, in claims made after, say, ten years, there could have been a reversal of the burden of proof on the issue of whether the defect was present when the defendant put the product into circulation. The current rule places this burden, which is a more onerous one the older the product is (see Chapter 12, under heading 2), on the defendant.

The availability of less draconian alternatives leads to a suspicion that the ten-year ban was based not only on a policy of protecting defendants from the worst cases of evidentiary difficulty but also, as with the option of financial ceilings for personal injuries claims (Article 16(1)), on a simple policy of limiting the liability of producers under the rule. One reason for this latter goal, as applied to long-tail liability, may have been to reduce the risks of commercial disruption which manufacturer bankruptcy and successor corporation liability can have. Although not limited to product claims, the most dramatic examples of the phenomenon of mass latent injury claims (mass 'toxic' tort claims) in the US have been in the product field where it has caused a number of manufacturers of asbestos and intra-uterine device (IUD) to seek protection under the bankruptcy laws. There is also concern in the US that uncertain future long-tail liability of a company will inhibit efficient takeovers when the predator fears that the corporate veil will be lifted sufficiently for the liability of the victim company for its past defective products to flow on and disturb its future cost structures in an open-ended way. The ten-year bar may also have been thought a useful way to reduce the chance for the embarrassment of the law which occurred when the injuries resulting from a company's defective products only become evident long after the company had been wound up. Here the legal position in the UK had been that the injured plaintiff could not sue his or her liquidated defendant's insurer even though the latter had insured the risk at the relevant time and was itself financially sound.[51]

Perhaps the ten-year bar was also designed to reduce and mask the troublesome phenomenon of overlapping activities and enterprises. Once a product is supplied and used it becomes more obvious how many other causal factors may be at work in producing an injury related to that product. Many products need substantial maintenance and repair to remain safe, and this can apply to quite mundane articles: the non-skid soles of shoes will eventually wear out, as will tyres. Even if some responsibility should be on the producer to warn of the degree of maintenance required and of a product's 'useful life', some responsibility must eventually shift to users, whom victims should therefore be encouraged at least to join in the action. As the product becomes older, this reality becomes more pressing, and the blinkered special products rule channelled to only one of these causal factors becomes more patently inefficient and unfair. Perhaps the ten-year ban was designed in part to reduce the risk of this embarrassment to the rule. But the ban will not in practice be severely prejudicial to many plaintiffs. Against purchasers we know that the Directive only provides the marginal advantage to plaintiffs that they do not have to prove matters such as that the product was defective when it left the defendant's control. Since in many

---

51 *Bradley* v *Eagle Star Insurance Co Ltd* [1989] AC 957 HL. But now see Companies Act 1989, s 141. On related injustices caused by the 'capital boundary problem' see H Collins 'Ascription of Legal Responsibility to Groups in Complex Patterns of Economic Integration' (1990) 53 MLR 731, 736–8.

long-tail liability situations – eg those involving asbestos, DES – it is not in dispute that the product remained in substantially the same condition as when it left the producer's control, the plaintiff is no worse off being denied a claim under the Directive after ten years. But the presence of the ban does suggest that the analysis which went into the Directive was fairly crude.

7   THE CLASS OF DEFENDANTS

The most obvious difference between the Directive and s 402A is that while in neither case is it necessary to prove the individual defendant was at fault or caused the relevant condition in the product, s 402A (comment f) applies to any and every commercial seller in the chain of manufacture and distribution of the relevant product including wholesalers and distributors, while the Directive channels liability to a subset of product suppliers. The EC approach better reflects theoretical justifications for liability but, as we will see, still suffers from some of the instability which the wide US approach generates.

In designing a new liability there is always a conflict between the simple pragmatic goal of providing plaintiffs with a wide class of potential defendants from which to select at least one who will not be judgment-proof,[52] and targeting the primary liability narrowly on those parties indicated by theoretical goals. Under the Directive (Article 3, CPA, s 2(2)) there are two tiers of defendants.[53] The primary group consists of *producers*, *importers* into the EC (if applicable) and *own-brand suppliers* who, while not actually manufacturing the product, adopt it as their own in a particular way. If the injured party cannot identify any of these primarily liable defendants, there is a procedure whereby any *suppliers* of the product may also be rendered liable (Article 3(3), CPA, s 2(3)). The imposition of liability on manufacturers strongly reflects the direct targeting strategy, while to some extent the targeting of own-brand suppliers, and certainly of importers and mere suppliers, reflects a subsidiary interest in the pragmatic goal.

In the vast majority of cases there will be no importer or own-brand supplier and any mere supplier will be able to escape liability by naming its own supplier, so the main target of liability will be the manufacturer. This result is strongly supported by economic theory. By channelling to a specific link in the chain the goal of price deterrence may be enhanced because the recording of liability costs associated with a particular product, which is necessary in order for the price to be properly calculated, will be administratively cheaper and more accurate, especially if the product in question represents a large part of the business of the liable party. Any particular product is typically a larger part of the business of its producer than of those lower in the chain such as distributors and retailers. For example, the costs of drugs liability could be channelled to the retail chemist, but in the real world it would be costly (perhaps prohibitively so) for the retail chemist and its insurer to keep the sort of records which would enable them to adjust accurately the price of drugs and

---

52 Relying on the smoothness of contractual and recourse processes to ensure that losses ultimately get located on the party/parties which are most appropriate in the light of theoretical goals.

53 Although the four reports of the initial UK and European reformers scarcely explain their strategy: Law Coms paras 69–70, 98; EEC Memo para 6; Strasbourg Expl Rep para 27.

premiums (respectively) across the large range of drugs sold. By contrast, the producer will manufacture a smaller number of products and so the costs to it of keeping records and adjusting prices should be lower.

In a world of transaction costs, the prevention goal is enhanced if liability is channelled to the cheapest cost avoider. Economic theory seems to suggest that prevention is most cheaply done by the actions of *one* party in the chain. In Chapter 6, under heading 2(c) we saw that (ignoring user behaviour) the cheapest cost avoider is nearly always the party who caused the defective condition in the product (or where it is an inherent characteristic of a raw material, the party who selected the raw material for processing). This is usually the manufacturer.[54] There are obvious cases where the product is defective because of a condition created by the manufacturer as a result of a manufacturing error or design choice. But a party may be a cause even if not the creator of the condition. It is true that under the Directive liability will attach only when a defendant supplies a product which was defective *at the time*. Our expectations of detection by parties lower down the chain than the manufacturer are usually low. For example, we do not expect Sainsbury's to detect a dead bee in a can of soup it sells. So the omission by a mere supplier to detect defects is not usually isolated as a cause of that defect. But considerable (and perhaps unrealistic) reliance tends to be put on the quality control systems of the manufacturer of the final product. Even in respect of defects originating by an Act of God or higher up-stream, the manufacturer is likely to be regarded as at least *a* cause of its presence, even if the defect is undiscoverable (see Chapter 6, under heading 2(b) and Chapter 10, under heading 7(iii)). Similarly, we saw in Chapter 8, under heading 2 that the moral enterprise liability argument becomes most forceful in cases where the defendant has most directly profited from the risk-taking – eg by initiating the product line. This is nearly always the manufacturer.

In the US the attenuated notion of 'enterprise' is seen as the whole process of production and marketing of the product.[55] While this certainly has the practical advantage of facilitating claims by victims, especially where one or more of the chain members is untraceable, bankrupt or otherwise difficult to sue, it does so at the price of diluting the substantive arguments which can be used to defend the boundaries of the rule, especially the moral argument about risk and profit. Taken to extremes, for example, the US approach would render liable every party who derives business from commercial risk-taking, including financiers (of any party including the ultimate purchaser[56]), endorsers, trademark licensors and advertisers. Technically the Restatement avoids such a wide catchment of liability by being restricted to 'sellers of products'. But it is not clear why a line should be drawn at this particular point. For example, US courts hold distributors liable even though the relevant product was never in their physical possession.[57] What distinguishes the profiting role of such parties who at a distance arrange the necessary shipment between the manufacturer and retailer and those who arrange the necessary finance for the

---

54 See Law Coms paras 72–4.
55 See, eg, *Vandermack* v *Ford Motor Co* 391 P 2d 168, 171 (1964). Pearson used the term in this broad sense, see para 1239.
56 See, eg, R Reiter 'Bank Credit Cards and Enterprise Liability' (1973) 21 UCLA Law Rev 278; compare J Henderson and A Twerski *Products Liability* 2nd edn (Boston, Little Brown and Co, 1992) 138–9.
57 *Canifax* v *Hercules Powder Co* 237 Cal App 2d 44 (1965); B Leete, 'Products Liability for Non-Manufacturer Product Sellers: Is It Time to Draw the Line?' [1982] Forum 1250, 1254.

manufacturing process? This question is raised directly by the practice in the pharmaceutical area where a company which has designed and developed a drug then licenses another company simply to manufacture it.

The result in the US has been considerable instability as some courts acquiesce in plaintiff pressure to enlarge the defendant class by allowing s 402A claims against parties other than sellers or suppliers such as mere designers. Meanwhile, many commentators have noted the weakness of the economic and moral arguments available to explain the liability under s 402A of 'innocent' middle-parties such as wholesalers. They argue that the unfairness to such parties, whom plaintiffs typically join along with manufacturer-defendants, is compounded by the American costs rule because, even if exonerated at trial, they are forced to bear their own costs. In anticipation of this threat innocent middle-parties are forced to carry costly insurance in situations where it is clear they will not ultimately be held liable.[58] As a result, in many US jurisdictions the politically powerful middle-party lobby has successfully fought for a *contraction* of the class of defendants. In one of the very few significant statutory reforms of products doctrine to have occurred since its emergence in 1960, many state legislators have enacted laws to remove altogether the joint liability of such 'innocent' defendants or, more commonly, to limit it to contexts where the more appropriate defendant is judgment-proof. Such limitation provides some confirmation that the original basis of the joint liability of these defendants was a desire to ensure that the plaintiff was compensated.[59]

The US rule clearly must rely heavily on the efficiency and accuracy of recourse rules to relocate losses on to the most appropriate parties in policy terms. An injured party might well choose to sue a chain member which is not the appropriate one in terms of, say, the prevention goal; and the party sued can only protect itself either by contractual arrangements made before the incident or by contribution or indemnity (ie recourse) proceedings afterwards to shift the liability costs on to a more appropriate party. The more parties initially exposed to liability, the more common will resort to recourse claims be. Recourse claims are expensive and dilute economic incentives. Also they may not succeed as, for example, when a retailer is unable to identify from its stock records the relevant supplier of stock, the '*Lambert* v *Lewis* problem'.[60] More importantly, there are also major problems with the content of recourse rules which are an important source of instability associated with the class of defendants in US products law (see below under heading 8).

Much of this instability was avoided by the European decision to channel liability to a narrower class of defendants; although the explicit justification for this in the European reform documents consists merely of a few scanty references to better focused prevention and insurance cover.[61] But potential for instability still exists. Take first the consequence of imposing liability on mere suppliers, the most novel provision in the Directive. The origin of Article 3(3) is understandably pragmatic.

---

58 Leete, op cit 1255–8; J Henderson and A Twerski, *op cit* 170.

59 Leete, op cit; Henderson and Twerski, op cit 170–3. See also Chapter 2, under heading 6 and s 105 of the Model Uniform Product Liability Act (1979) 44 Fed Reg 62714.

60 *Lambert* v *Lewis* [1980] 1 All ER 978, CA; [1981] 1 All ER 1185, HL; T Hervey 'Winner Takes All' (1981) 44 Mod Law Rev 575, 576.

61 The latter to avoid the 'pyramiding' of insurance which occurs in the US as chain members exposed to s 402A overestimate the risk of being sued and the success rate of claims, and take out excessive insurance, inflating product prices unnecessarily: Law Coms para 38(h), 77–8; Strasbourg Expl Rep para 28; EEC Memo para 6; Pearson paras 1240, 1242.

European reformers wanted to help plaintiffs to trace producers and importers, to provide incentives for suppliers to keep records of their suppliers, and to provide incentives for producers to label otherwise 'anonymous' products.[62] As a result Article 3(3) states that any commercial supplier of the product will be liable if the plaintiff requests him to identify the parties primarily liable with respect to that product provided that the request is made within a reasonable time after damage occurs and at a time when it is not reasonably practicable for the person making the request to identify those persons, and provided the supplier fails within a reasonable time to comply with the request or identify the person who supplied the product to him. It has been noted earlier (Chapter 10, under heading 4) that it is rare for suppliers as such to be held liable for negligence with respect to defective products because of the (usual) impracticality of quality control at the supply stage, and that this provision therefore imposes a significant potential strict liability on suppliers reflecting obligations not simply to the buyer (as are the suppliers' existing warranty obligations) but to bystanders as well.

The principal incentive created by the liability of suppliers is for them to keep as accurate stock records as possible about the origin of the goods they handle. In theory, suppliers might also be given an incentive to put pressure on manufacturers to take preventative action or at least to label their products. In reality, it will nearly always be cheapest for suppliers simply to maintain adequate records of their own suppliers and thereby avoid the liability. Sometimes where goods reach the user only under a generic description, this will be a very expensive task. For example, as a result of government encouragement, 40% of prescriptions within the National Health Service are for generic drugs, vaccines, etc.[63] This means that NHS suppliers (Area Health Authorities, pharmacists, GPs, etc) will need to maintain careful records of the source of each product. In some cases, such as emergencies and GP home visits, this will be awkward. In others, and in many non-medical contexts, it will not even be feasible because, for example, it is uneconomic not to bulk products such as refined sugar, petrol, processed minerals, or even blood for transfusion, which have come from different sources.[64]

The liability is in practice vicarious and, as we have seen (Chapter 8, under heading 1, Chapter 10, under heading 4), vicarious liability is, however pragmatically sound, an incoherent doctrine from a moral viewpoint. If the manufacturer's liability is not to be strict, why should that of mere suppliers be? If a supplier's liability is to be strict, why should the undiscoverability of defects be relevant? When such suppliers are sued despite their use of all reasonable care, they will probably have no-one to sue in turn because their records are, by definition, insufficient to identify anyone against whom to launch a Sale of Goods claim. As in the US, resultant discontent will put strain on the legitimacy of the liability regime under the Directive.

Consider next the joint liability of the manufacturer of the final product and others involved in the design, manufacture and supply of the product. The assumption of reformers[65] that the producer of the finished product is the source of the defect and

---

62 A highly publicized problem in the field of pharmaceuticals in the US. See in general, eg, Law Coms para 101; Pearson paras 1245–6.
63 P Ferguson 'Pharmaceutical Products Liability: 30 Years of Law Reform?' [1992] Jur Rev 226, 236.
64 Contrast Strasbourg Expl Rep para 49 (rejected by Pearson paras 1245–6). The same applies to the manufacturer of products containing such items as components, eg the manufacturer of fruit pies who bulks its fruit pulp from many sources before incorporation into the pies it then cooks.
65 EEC Memo paras 6, 15; Strasbourg Expl Rep para 61.

initiator of the risk-taking, breaks down where, for example, a High Street retailer or mail order firm is sufficiently powerful to initiate product lines and retail them under its own brand name, presenting itself as its producer. Here the Directive imposes primary liability not just on the actual producer but on any person who, by putting his name on the product or using a trade mark or other distinguishing mark, has held himself out to be the producer of the product (Article 3(1), CPA, s 2(2)(b)), although this liability can be simply avoided by a sufficient indication that the supplier did not so hold himself out, for example, by indicating that the goods were manufactured for the retailer by another company.[66]

Where the defect is due to an up-stream out-of-house component part manufacturer, the Directive also imposes liability on both parties (by enabling the 'product' to be defined as either the finished product or as the component). There are pragmatic advantages to such joint liability: if the final producer is liable along with the producer of the defective component, he acts as a back-up in cases where the latter is not good for judgment. Similarly, there might, for example, be difficulty in proving whether the defect lay in the subsequent finished product or its defective components, eg was it the egg filling, the pie crust or the way it was assembled and cooked which caused the victim's food poisoning? In such cases rendering the producer of the finished product jointly liable shifts these evidentiary problems off the shoulders of the victim and into the recourse claims between that producer and the component manufacturer.[67] But even where it is clear which component was defective, the four initial European reform reports give no guidance as to the *respective* responsibility of the producer of the final product and component manufacturer (or own-brand supplier). A similar point could be made about the relative responsibility of importers. There was some discussion of the type of case where the finished product is attributable to the defective condition of a component part; but the reports simply start with the assumption that the producer of the subsequent finished product should be liable. They then go on to address what is seen as the issue of controversy: whether the producer of the component part should be liable at all once the component has become incorporated into the subsequent product. In line with the current consensus in the US, the European reformers answered this question in the affirmative, citing prevention arguments and the practical advantages of having more than one party to sue.[68] Even if the final producer could be held liable in negligence,[69] this does not help determine the appropriate division of liability *between* chain members. The most the Directive tells us is that a component manufacturer will have a full defence if 'the defect is attributable to the design of the product in which the component has been fitted or to the instructions given by the manufacturer of the product' (Article 7(f), see CPA, s 4(1)(f)), but that does not touch the more common problem discussed here.

---

66 The retail pharmacist who merely adds his own label to a prescription medicine will probably be held not to have held himself out as being the producer of the drug but one who had mixed ingredients may well be.

67 This shifting of evidentiary burdens parallels that which happens in ordinary vicarious liability cases and that which operates where the importer is held (vicariously) liable. But where the final manufacturer is sued, fault may virtually always be implied from his failure to detect the defect.

68 Law Coms paras 66–82; EEC Memo para 7. On the US position see Henderson and Twerski, op cit 137.

69 And we saw in *Winward* v *TVR Engineering Ltd* [1986] BTLC 366 (see Chapter 10, under heading 7(i)) where such a producer was held negligent with respect to a design error in an out-of-house component.

Even more problems will arise when the defect is found to have been created by a party wholly outside the reach of the Directive, as when a defect in a product is due to the activities of a trademark licensor, an out-of-house designer or to buyer specification (all of whom seem to have the defence in Article 7(a) of not having 'put the product into circulation' ... see Chapter 12, under heading 6). Even manufacturing defects may be traceable to immovable defective machines which were designed by out-of-house enterprises. Because the designers did not put the relevant injury-causing defective product into circulation, they would have the defence under Article 7(a) and would not be liable under the Directive. What will a court hearing a recourse action against such a party make of its omission from the Directive? What was the legislators' intention?

8 JOINT AND SEVERAL LIABILITY; RELOCATION OF LOSSES

Where two or more parties are liable to the plaintiff in relation to the relevant harm two questions need to be asked. Firstly, should the parties be jointly and severally liable so that the plaintiff can sue either party for all the loss; and secondly, if so, what rules should then govern any recourse action brought by a party held liable for the whole loss against the other guilty party or parties?

(a) Joint and several liability

Under the Directive liability is joint and several (Article 5). Yet in the US one of the few areas in which tort law has undergone substantial statutory reform in the past quarter century is that of joint and several liability. In the last decade 35 states have limited joint and several liability to a greater or lesser extent in response to the anomalies thought to have been produced by the adoption of comparative fault and in response to the insurance crisis it is said to have fed. In fact, whether joint and several liability seems anomalous or unfair depends on the perspective from which it is viewed. To the innocent plaintiff, it no doubt seems fair that the risk that a joint tortfeasor will prove to be judgment-proof should not fall on her but on the other solvent tortfeasor. Joint and several liability relieves the plaintiff of the cost of identifying and suing all or most possibly liable parties. From the solvent defendant's point of view, however, it can be argued that if tortfeasors can claim a reduction in the damages they have to pay because the plaintiff was contributorily negligent, they should also be allowed to use the same argument with respect to guilty judgment-proof third-party tortfeasors. It is a sign of the ideological climate in the US that this argument has tended to prevail recently, despite the absence of convincing evidence that there was a liability-driven insurance 'crisis', let alone one attributable to the doctrine of joint and several liability. Nevertheless, the case for abolition has some plausibility in the US context where the volume of litigation is high and defendants bear their own costs even if successful. Insurers complain that the uncertain risk of their insureds being held liable for the full judgment because joint tortfeasors are judgment-proof presents them with a dilemma: a choice of mounting a much more vigorous and costly defence in court to try to defeat the claim, or settling at a higher level than the facts merit because of the fear that, if the case goes to trial, the insured will be held liable for all of the large verdict the jury is likely to award when it sees the deep pocket of an insurer behind the defendant. Either way premiums have to rise.

The argument used to support joint and several liability – that it allows the plaintiff to pick and choose the defendant who is best to sue[70] – leads in practice, it is said, to a choice of the defendant with the deepest pocket even if only marginally responsible for the injury, and it is then up to the defendant to try to join as many other defendants as possible in the hope some will be solvent. Suppose a person buys a tin of peas for a dinner party. On opening it he notices it has foreign objects in it (small, sharp metallic strips), but he ignores them and feeds the peas to his guests. The host dies and the guests suffer serious injury due to the metal. When confronted by the paucity of their host's estate, the guests are most likely to sue the manufacturer who, if held jointly liable, will have to pay the entire verdict even if only, say, 5% 'responsible' relative to the deceased's carelessness. The more willing courts are to hold defendants liable for the acts of third parties (especially private individuals) by means, for example, of expansion of duties on manufacturers to warn users of unsafe handling practices, the more numerous such problematic situations will be (see Chapter 10, under heading 3).

In the US the debate about the justice of joint and several liability is fierce[71] and fuelled by local factors such as important immunities from suit, the wide availability of punitive damages and the volatility of juries, especially in relation to intangible loss such as pain and suffering. In EC countries these factors are absent. Moreover, abolition of joint and several liability would tend to cause plaintiffs to join as many joint tortfeasors as possible,[72] and this could raise the cost of litigation sufficiently to place it out of the reach of some plaintiffs who, of course, do not yet have the option, as US plaintiffs do, of employing a contingency fee arrangement with their legal representatives. It is highly unlikely, therefore, that the provision for joint and several liability in the Directive would be the target for destabilizing criticism.[73]

(b)   Relocation of losses

Under the Directive there is the possibility that the plaintiff will sue and succeed against a party on whom it is inappropriate in policy terms for the loss to remain. Indeed, there is no guarantee that the victim will even select the party which *he* regards as responsible, especially if another potential defendant is easier to sue or

---

70 T Weir *Torts*, Vol XI of *International Encyclopedia of Comparative Law* (Mouton, The Hague, 1976) 58–9.

71 J Phillips 'Comments on the Wright-Twerski Colloquy Concerning the Joint Liability Debate' (1990) 57 Tenn LR 321.

72 Although the costs rule (ie plaintiff pays costs of defendant not held liable) adds a brake to this strategy.

73 Even though as in negligence, there are some sectors in which the problem of the insolvent joint tortfeasor will remain endemic, eg, often in the construction field, it is only the professional advisers (designers, architects, engineers) who are good for judgment by the trial date, so that claims surface as failure to warn cases against these vulnerable parties. See, eg, *Eckersley* v *Binnie & Partners* (unreported case dealing with the Abbeystead pumping station disaster, leave to appeal refused by House of Lords 9.6.88, see Independent (1988) 10 June and *Pirelli General Cable Works Ltd* v *Oscar Faber & Partners* [1983] 2 AC 1, HL.

has a deeper pocket. This situation arises both despite channelling – for example, the plaintiff may choose to sue the importer rather than the manufacturer, or the producer of the final product rather than the component producer – and because of channelling – for example, when the plaintiff sues the final producer but where the defect is due to the designer who cannot be sued under the Directive because liability is channelled elsewhere.

One problem here is that an initial target of a claim may decide for a variety of reasons, such as a desire to preserve a continuing commercial relationship, or because of the small amount involved per claim, not to seek recourse against the other parties who were jointly liable to the plaintiff. But this is an inevitable price which has to be paid for a system of joint and several liability. In fact it is impossible to fashion a rule which will always ensure that the correct party bears the liability. The success of a rule in terms of the attainment of its substantive policy goals depends on how often people are willing to 'correct' the initial location of liability and on how expensive it is for them to do so. Relocation of loss by prior contractual arrangement with all relevant potential defendants is a possibility, but in practice this is only considered if it can form part of existing relationships (eg of sale) so that, for example, a retailer typically secures no direct contractual rights of contribution or indemnity against a distant component or final manufacturer, but only against its immediate supplier. Leaving aside, then, the possibility that relocation of loss might be achieved via contract, the simplest way in which this could be done would be if the new regime included a suitable rule of allowing contribution or indemnity between parties. At the recourse stage the interests of plaintiffs can be ignored in favour of achieving the economic and moral goals of the product liability regime.

What should the recourse rule be in the case of a bystander injured by a manufacturing defect? Superficially the answer seems relatively straightforward with respect to the economic goals. If we assume that prevention is most cheaply achieved by *one* party (rather than the combined efforts of two or more), on a crude first order approximation economic theory suggests prevention is optimised if the entire loss is focused on the cheapest cost avoider.[74] Economists do acknowledge reasons for holding other chain members primarily (ie jointly) liable *to the victim*: where the cheapest cost avoider is judgment-proof, holding the next cheapest cost avoider jointly liable is the second-best solution in efficiency terms; and in some

---

74 On such 'alternative care situations' see W Landes and R Posner 'Joint and Multiple Tortfeasors: An Economic Analysis' (1980) 9 J Legal Studies 517, 518. It is feasible (i) for one party to be the cheapest cost avoider which is nearly always the defect creator, say the producer of a defective component, (ii) but another further down the line to be the cheapest defect detector, say the producer of the finished product, and (iii) the sum of detection and warning costs of the latter plus the prevention costs of the former to be less than the detection and prevention costs of either. In such so-called 'joint care' cases, if the basis of liability is strict, economic analysis does not seem to provide a simple recourse rule to govern the allocation of liability costs between them. See, eg, R Cunningham 'Apportionment Between Partmakers and Assemblers in Strict Liability' (1982) 49 U of Chi LR 544, 554–6. Indeed, there seems to be a certain circularity to economic analysis here because detection and prevention costs to some extent reflect current legal rules. Currently little is required by the negligence regime of parties downstream of the creation of the defective condition in the product and, as a result, such parties have relatively under-developed detection and prevention systems. Hence their detection and avoidance costs would be high. It may be a reasonable generalisation to make, then, that 'joint care' cases are relatively rare in the products field and a recourse rule is better fashioned in response to the characteristics of the more central 'alternative care' cases.

cases the market power of a party (eg an own-brand supplier) held jointly liable could generate secondary incentives if it pressured the cheapest cost avoider to take action.[75] However, first order economic analysis dictates a recourse rule which allows a full indemnity to be recovered from the cheapest cost avoider directly (leap-frogging other links in the chain, if necessary). Since the cheapest cost avoider will almost invariably be the party directly responsible for creating the defective condition of the product, the prevention goal would require a rule under which any party held liable under the product liability rule could then directly recover a full indemnity from the party responsible for creating the defect. Similarly, price deterrence is optimized by liability being focused on the party of whose total activity the product forms the largest part, and this is usually the party responsible for creating the defect.

Such a recourse rule would mean that although plaintiffs are relieved of the requirement to identify who created the defective condition of the product (see Chapter 10, under heading 7(vi)), a defendant could shift his loss only if he could identify that party. Sometimes this would not be difficult. For example, in a clear manufacturing error case an importer or own-brand supplier could be indemnified by the producer, and the producer of a finished product containing a defective component could be indemnified by the producer of the component. But if the failure of the importer, for instance, to detect the defect could, in the circumstances of the case, be regarded as a co-cause (see Chapter 6, under heading 2), economic theory gives no clear answer as to where the loss should eventually rest. Nor does reference to the moral enterprise liability argument give much more guidance.

One way to rationalize the joint liability of certain chain members *to the victim* is that, given their market power, they are appropriately regarded as initiators of the risk-taking associated with the manufacture of the product, even though the physical creation of the defective product is due to the activities of its producer. The liability of own-brand suppliers and that of producers of the finished product for defective components must rest on this reasoning.[76] If this is the *only* basis of their liability to the victim, their liability to the manufacturer might be thought to support a contribution rather than indemnity rule. But even so, how would a court compare the role of instigator against perpetrator of risk-taking in order to determine the degree of contribution?

On the other hand, perhaps at the recourse level, where the conflict is no longer between the profit maker(s) and the victim but between various profit makers, a court might emphasise the role of the actual producer in making the defective product – a strategy which would satisfy economic theory. On this basis, in the simple manufacturing defect case, the own-brand supplier and importer would be entitled to extract a full indemnity from the producer; and, in a defective component case, the producer would be entitled to an indemnity from the component producer,[77] unless their failure to detect the defect could be said to be a co-cause of

---

75 In general see Landes and Posner, op cit 526, 528. The latter argument was used by the Californian Supreme Court in *Vandermack v Ford Motor Co* (1964) supra 171, but see discussion by Leete, op cit 1253, 1256–7.

76 Misrepresentation theories for their liability, for example, are unconvincing in the sales context and are inapplicable to other claimants. Buyers of Ford cars are not duped into believing Ford made every component, and few are misled by a St Michael wine label into thinking that Marks and Spencer runs vineyards.

77 A rough but not exact analogy here is the joint liability of the vicariously liable employer the ration-

the injury. Some support for this interpretation of the fairness goal of product liability reform is found in the fact that the Law Commissions seemed to see nothing objectionable in a powerful own-brand supplier being able to shift his loss in this way by prior express contractual terms, which suggests the outcome accords with the policies they were pursuing.[78] In this context the moral enterprise idea which can be used to justify the original liability of the parties *to the victim* provides little guidance as to whether the rule should be one of contribution or indemnity.

The European reform

The European reformers did not analyse the problems raised by their choice of defendants to whom liability is to be channelled, nor was the possible need for or the suitable form of a recourse rule considered. Neither the 1985 Directive nor the CPA includes any rule on the matter. European reformers were content to rely on each jurisdiction's existing rules of recourse governing the apportionment of civil liability.[79] The US experience would not have been of much assistance here even had it been analysed. The large number of potential defendants there under the various rules relevant to products has generated much recourse litigation. In some US jurisdictions which model their contribution statute on one of the two versions of the Uniform Contribution Among Tortfeasors Act, liability is divided per capita. In others an 'equitable contribution' approach is used to apportion on the basis of hazy notions of 'fault' and 'responsibility'. But although a consensus has been reached that when held strictly liable in tort under the rule in s 402A a middle-party can extract a full indemnity from the manufacturer or other party responsible for the creation of the product defect, the judicial reasoning used to reach this position has tended to be implicit and limited to the facts of the specific case. There appears to be no judicial attempt to analyse or even state *general* principles of recourse which would govern the more complex issues raised by, say, a recourse action by a retailer against a (non-privy) wholesaler or, more importantly, by a party held liable under the product liability tort rule and a party whose liability in respect of the damage was based on another legal rule. US theorists have not taken a great deal of interest in these complex issues.

The Directive leaves the issue to domestic rules (see Articles 5 and 8), but these are notoriously vague. The relevant UK statute is the Civil Liability (Contribution) Act 1978, s 1(1) of which states that any person liable in respect of damage may recover contribution from any other person liable in respect of the same damage. The amount of the contribution 'shall be as may be found by the court to be just and equitable having regard to the extent of the person's responsibility for the damage' (s 2(1)) and so can range from zero to a full indemnity (s 2(2)). The problems in

---

ale of which is both substantive (eg the burden and benefit argument) and pragmatic (providing a financial guarantor behind the tortfeasor for the benefit of the victim) – see respectively G Williams *Joint Torts and Contributory Negligence* (London, Stevens & Sons, 1951) 433; P S Atiyah *Vicarious Liability in the Law of Torts* (London, Butterworths, 1967) 26; but where once the plaintiff is paid the law in theory (but not in practice) allows the innocent defendant to claim a complete indemnity (on which see Chapter 8, under heading 1(b)).

78 Law Coms para 99.
79 Law Coms paras 44, 99, 124. See also EEC Memo paras 6, 12; Pearson para 1249; EEC Directive 1985 Article 5; CPA s 2(5), s 2(6).

applying these provisions in the products field can be illustrated by looking first at the case where two parties are liable for the relevant damage under the CPA and only under the CPA. Since under the CPA some parties can be liable to the victim despite having taken all reasonable care and having no causal responsibility (in the usual sense) for the damage, how will courts apportion the loss between two such parties? They will need to develop a notion of responsibility not explicit in the terms of the CPA and with little guidance from the reform documents (even assuming courts would look at these). Of course, there will be some easy cases. Using notions of causal responsibility for the creation of the defect would allow the innocent retailer to obtain a full indemnity from a distant manufacturer who had created, say, a product with an undiscoverable manufacturing defect, and would allow causal apportionment between two equally innocent middle-parties, such as a retailer and wholesaler. Such an approach draws support from the fact that in the sale of goods legislation Parliament imposed implied warranties on every party in the commercial supply chain back to the party who created the relevant defective condition.[80]

But what happens when it is clear that one of the parties held liable under the CPA was careless? Of what relevance to the recourse action is the fact that one party is also liable in negligence? Certainly, the Civil Liability (Contribution) Act contemplates contribution or indemnity between parties whose liability is based on breaches of different legal duties (see s 6(1)). But on what basis the liability should be apportioned in such cases – causation, blameworthiness, a combination of both these or on some other basis? – is an area of great uncertainty both in the UK and in the US.[81] Does the negligence of a party justify allowing a non-negligent party to recover a full indemnity from the former?[82] While this would accord with the rule that a vicariously liable employer is entitled to a full indemnity from its negligent tortfeasor-employee, there is no general clear authority for this approach. Indeed, many commentators argue that there are cases running the other way, showing that blameworthiness is not the sole criterion under the 1978 Act.[83] Of course, refusal to award an indemnity in such cases might be explained on the basis that the court impliedly found some fault or carelessness on the part of the 'strictly liable' party. On the other hand, it may arise from a desire not to neutralize the original imposition of strict liability.[84] After all, the Directive allows completely innocent suppliers to be held liable while excluding from liability certain parties, such as out-of-house designers, even if they have been negligent. So the task of apportionment of liability

---

80 See also *Young and Marten Ltd* v *McManus Childs Ltd* [1969] 1 AC 454, 475 (Lord Upjohn); *Simaan Co* v *Pilkington Glass Ltd (No 2)* [1988] 1 All ER 791, 804 (Bingham LJ).

81 T Hervey '"Responsibility" under the Civil Liability (Contribution) Act 1978' [1979] N L J 509; Williams, op cit 160.

82 Certainly Glanville Williams thought this should be the case, op cit 160. See also Landes and Posner, op cit 553, but contrast J Phillips 'Contribution and Indemnity in Products Liability' (1974) 42 Tenn LR 85, 102–3.

83 Hervey (1979), op cit 510; M Brazier *Street on Torts*, 8th edn (London, Butterworths, 1988) 532, citing cases which appear to hold that the negligence of a co-tortfeasor does not necessarily relieve a strictly liable defendant of liability completely. Compare *Tennant Radiant Heat Ltd* v *Warrington Development Corpn* [1988] 1 EGLR 41, CA discussed below. The general point is supported by the devices some modern courts have used to prevent employers (actually their insurers) from obtaining indemnity from their careless employees, eg *Morris* v *Ford Motor Co Ltd* [1973] QB 792.

84 Certainly, as between a strictly liable landlord and careless tenant, the Court of Appeal recently preferred to deal with their claim and counterclaim (not a recourse claim) as 'a problem of causation' alone: *Tennant Radiant Heat Ltd* v *Warrington Development Corpn* [1988] 1 EGLR 41, CA, 44 (Dillon LJ).

under the Directive inevitably requires the court to elaborate on the notion of 'responsibility' and, in so doing, to decide the relative importance of the various policy objectives thought to justify different aspects of the regime under the Directive.[85]

It may be, of course, that in recourse actions most courts *will* simply always give sole weight to the negligence principle, allowing full indemnity against a negligent party. But if so, this would have profound implications for the theoretical basis of civil obligations. It would mean that whatever mix of moral, economic or pragmatic ideas was used to justify the initial imposition of strict liability *to victims*, it would be eclipsed at the recourse stage by the fault principle. Thus, whatever the stated rationale of imposing strict liability on, say, an own-brand supplier to a product victim, in practice the purpose of such liability would be seen to be that of facilitating recovery by the plaintiff because strictly liable defendants would be entitled to shift responsibility on to any negligent party. The only type of case in which strict liability would serve any other goal would be that in which no human negligence could be said to have been involved in the relevant injury, yet such cases would be rare. Modern theories of civil obligation have yet to tackle this fundamental dilemma.

Resolution of the problem requires a clear statement of underlying ideas. Twenty years ago[86] Tony Weir argued provocatively against allowing a right of recourse between strangers at all, or at least at the suit of insurance companies (and perhaps 'other excellent loss spreaders'). His argument was that it was perfectly acceptable for the victim to choose from among available tortfeasors the one who was 'strictly liable, rich and institutional' and for this choice to remain undisturbed by a recourse action. Provided the plaintiff was compensated and the loss was likely to be well spread, the plaintiff's preference for the institutional defendant rather than a 'poor friend whose carelessness he must prove' was admirably humane. By allowing the initial institutional target to sue the other tortfeasors, 'the recourse action represents a defeat of the human by the institutional'. The argument is flawed by its assumption that the goals of tort law are compensation and loss-spreading – ideas which cannot justify *any* limits to liability (see Chapter 5, under heading 2). But Weir's general sympathies suggest a way forward in the task of ranking the principles on which common law liabilities must be based. Once we take seriously the need to identify the boundaries of civil liabilities and their economic or moral goals and the need, for recourse purposes, to rank these goals, we might choose to elevate the concern which underlies the moral enterprise liability argument. In other words, just as between the private victim and the tortfeasor acting in the course of profit-making we might be able to make a moral case for more onerous standards of liability, so too when it came to recourse actions we might apply harsher rules, eg that a defendant who was responsible for the victim's harm could *only* seek recourse against another tortfeasor if the latter was acting in the course of profit-seeking. We would thereby protect the negligent private tortfeasor from the onslaught of a well-funded recourse action in the way Weir would prefer, but on a sounder moral basis than he chose.

85 Just how problematic this type of comparison and speculation is, is illustrated by the controversy in the United States about the inter-relationship and priority of policies underlying product liability in tort and the statutory regime governing no-fault workers' compensation payments. The problem can sometimes emerge in simple claims by a plaintiff against a defendant (see *Cambridge Water Co v Eastern Counties Leather plc* [1992] EGCS 142, CA (but now see (1993) Times, 10 December, HL) on the ranking of natural rights incident to ownership and nuisance).

86 Weir, op cit 58–9, 78.

Certainly this idea is supported by the attitudes of some courts to an employer's insurer who seeks indemnity from a careless employee. But in adopting this approach one would need also to address a legitimate concern about access to justice for victims. When a plaintiff sues a particular defendant, the latter may well choose to join other tortfeasors then rather than delay pursuit of recourse to a separate action.[87] This process of joinder can have severe implications for the plaintiff in impeding settlement, delaying litigation and adding to the cost of adjudication. As the law recognizes more and more parties to be implicated in responsibility for damage, especially where parties are held liable for the conduct of third parties, these adverse consequences for plaintiffs grow. Were the law to allow defendants recourse only against commercial joint tortfeasors in order to give priority to a moral attitude to profit-seeking over the negligence principle, it would also have to restrict circumvention of this rule by restricting the right of such defendants to join non-commercial parties as defendants to the original action of the plaintiff. There might also be something to be said for refusing to commercial defendants any right to join other parties in order to simplify and smooth the path of the victim's claim. The consequences of such suggested developments are hard to see, but they do suggest the possibility that recourse rules could be reformed in a principled way.

To sum up: the application of the Civil Liability (Contribution) Act to the sort of multi-party situations likely to arise under the CPA is not clear. It will no doubt be a source of costly settlement negotiation and litigation. Ideally this litigation would quickly answer the hard questions about how to rank liabilities resting on different grounds; otherwise the theoretical underpinning of different liability regimes might become confused. Of course, this would be hardest where one of the relevant liabilities was based on the common law, for who can say what are the goals of a rule such as negligence, and the weight it should give vis-à-vis other liabilities? But the problem is scarcely easier in the case of statutory liabilities such as that in Part I of the CPA, because the background discussion of its goals was so sketchy and inconsistent and, moreover, intertwined with the pragmatic desire to facilitate recovery by victims which would no longer be relevant at the recourse stage. In practice, the whole field of contribution and indemnity is conveniently shrouded in mystery by the tendency for out-of-court settlements on the issue to be subject to secrecy clauses;[88] by the failure of past courts to attempt to address these issues, their omission to set out clear reasons for their decisions and the virtual absence of appellate litigation on the issues. Ideally, a liability regime should establish clear rules of recourse in addition to clear rules of primary liability.

---

87 Again, the costs rule adds a brake on the joinder strategy.
88 As in the case of the Hillsborough football disaster: (1990) The Independent, 9 October.

CHAPTER 12

Specific sources of instability

1 THE LIMITATION TO 'PRODUCTS': CLEAR EXCLUSIONS

The liability under the Directive is limited to defects in a 'product', the latter being defined as 'electricity' and 'all movables' even though incorporated into another movable or into an immovable (Article 2). The corresponding definition in the CPA defines 'product' in terms of 'goods', but to the degree that the two definitions differ, the former will prevail by virtue of s 1 of the CPA. The full relevance of this may not strike most UK practitioners because in the Treaty of Rome 'movables' and 'goods' are treated as interchangeable concepts, and it may therefore be thought that the Directive's concept of 'movables' is synonymous with the notion of 'goods' thus allowing the considerable case law on the term 'goods' in UK sales law to be used here. But this would be wrong. Already the ECJ has given the notion of 'goods' a wider meaning: something capable of money valuation and of being an object of commercial transactions (see Chapter 4, under heading 11). The first question, therefore, is what is meant by 'product'? Some things are clearly caught by the Directive (and by s 402A which does not attempt to define the term): food for human or animal consumption, food additives, water, gas, minerals such as asbestos, alcohol, tobacco, guns, motor vehicles, aircraft, ships, train door locks, chemicals, drugs, vaccines and insecticides. Some things are clearly excluded and the first question is, can a coherent explanation for these be found?

(a) Game and unprocessed agricultural products

Under the Directive a special exemption was granted for game and primary agricultural products (ie products of the soil, of stock-farming and of fisheries) which have not undergone initial processing (Article 2). Although Member States can opt to include such products, very few have done so (see Figure 3.1). Given that there are more than a million cases of food poisoning and several hundred deaths a year resulting from salmonella infections in Europe,[1] it is relevant to ask whether this exemption owed more to political expediency than to substantive policy arguments. One argument in favour of it was that agricultural produce is particularly prone to hidden defects caused by environmental factors beyond the control of the producer, and that the arguments for strict liability are weaker where the producer did not create the risk and was not in a position to exercise much quality control over the

---

1 (1989) Times, 28 April, p 6 (World Health Organization 'conservative' estimates).

product.[2] Three objections can be made to this. Firstly, the final Directive contains a defence in the case of undiscoverable defects. Secondly, from the consumer's point of view it could be argued that the producer creates the risk by exposing others for his financial profit to defective produce (even if the defect was contamination from an uncontrollable and undiscoverable source such as a damaged nuclear reactor). Thirdly, the assertion that 'the risks involved in agricultural or fishery production may usually be laid at the door of nature or of a polluter rather than of the producer'[3] is unsubstantiated, and recent health scares concerning contamination with salmonella, residues of pesticides, hormones and stock-food additives, and other risks associated with factory farming strongly suggest that many defects in such goods are man-made.

The two remaining arguments in favour of the exemption relate to practical issues of proof. The first runs that because such produce is typically bulked at trade markets, identification of the source of the defective item would be difficult, if not impossible.[4] The second points to the perishability of such goods and argues that the Directive's rebuttable presumption that the defect existed at the time it left the producer's hands would often be irrebuttable in practice by the primary producer because, for example, of the impracticality of attaching 'eat by' labels to produce which is bulked.[5] Again the weight of these arguments depends on where sympathies lie. Problems of identifying the source of a defect are used elsewhere to justify *extension* of liability (to importers and mere suppliers) not its restriction. Similarly, a special rule about the burden of proof could have been used to deal with the unusual proneness of agricultural products to develop post-production defects due to later inadequate handling. As it is, the producer of, say, salmonella-infected eggs, is granted a complete exemption from liability under the Directive, even if he was clearly identifiable and there is no doubt that the defect arose in his production process.

The exemption included in the CPA seems to extend beyond initial processing to 'industrial' processing. If this provision is challenged, it will have to be read down to the 'initial processing' as in the Directive (whatever this is held to to mean).[6] More dramatic still is how the CPA deals with the situation when a product which has undergone the relevant processing causes injury. Under the Directive the primary producer would be liable, but under the CPA the liability attaches *only* to the processor (s 1(1)(c)) and, if applicable, to the producer of the finished product: to the fruit pulp producer and fruit pie maker but not the fruit grower; to the delicatessen which makes its own mayonnaise from unprocessed salmonella-infected eggs but not the egg producer, even if identifiable. The rationale given is 'that those involved in processing should be expected to conduct the appropriate tests to ensure that hidden defects, howsoever caused, are detected'.[7] The irony of this justification is that the difficulty in screening primary agricultural produce for certain risks is used to exempt the previous producer. Needless to say, the unrealistic burden such a

2 Law Commissions para 90 (Scottish Law Com): 483 Official Report (HL), cols 718, 734–5; DTI *Implementation of EEC Directive on Product Liability* (DTI, Nov 1985) para 32.

3 Law Commissions para 90 (Scottish Law Com). But see para 86–7.

4 DTI, op cit para 32; 483 Official Report (HL), col 718.

5 DTI, op cit para 32; Law Coms paras 93–4 (Scottish Law Com); 483 Official Report (HL), col 718.

6 See Chapter 4, under heading 11 and fn 43 for the Parliamentary statements on meaning of these terms.

7 DTI, op cit para 29.

rule places on the processors was vigorously opposed by the relevant processor industries as unfair,[8] and this aspect of the CPA is bound to be challenged in the courts at some point.

The exemption of game and unprocessed agricultural produce cannot be supported by any moral, economic or legitimate pragmatic argument, and rests on two false assumptions. First, in justifying the requirement that agricultural products have passed through an industrial process, the British government argued that the new 'regime (had been) designed for industrial goods'[9] and the Directive itself also reflects concern with the 'risks inherent in modern technical production' (Second Recital). Yet the new liability is not limited to defects produced by the intervention of industrial and mechanical processes. Even in the case of agricultural produce which *has* passed through the necessary processing, the liability which then attaches is not limited to defects arising out of that process, hence the liability of the delicatessen for the salmonella-infected mayonnaise. The second assumption is that the activity of farming is itself not a technological process. Yet, as the English Law Commission rightly noted in rejecting the exemption, examples of 'natural' products are hard to come by in the modern era when typical farming techniques include the application of pesticides and fertilizers to crops, or the ingestion by stock animals of hormones, antibiotics and other chemical foodstuffs and additives.[10] But such processes were clearly not intended to come within the Directive's idea of processing. The successful political pressure of EC primary producers has therefore ensured that those injured by residues of these substances have no remedy under the Directive unless, of course, the product subsequently underwent an appropriate 'process'. This creates a bizarre lottery for the injured and perhaps a point of considerable future strain within the product regime.

(b)   Immovables (realty)

On some occasions the Directive allows a person to sue when they have been injured by the state of premises. Under the Directive a product remains a product even if it is incorporated into an immovable (realty), for example by being affixed to a building.[11] Here, however, the victim does not have the option she would have in the case, say, of defective brakes in a car, of defining the product as either the component or the conglomerate finished product. In such cases the 'product' complained of can only be defined as the component since the conglomerate, being an immovable, falls outside the definition of a 'product'. This means that if the damage complained of was caused by, say, a defective light fitting, affixed fridge or building materials (which cause injury by their nature rather than method of use, eg defective wood, cement, etc) the person who suffered the damage can sue the manufacturer, importer or mere supplier of the thing which caused the damage but not the manufacturer (ie the builder) or mere supplier of the house into which it has been incorporated qua manufacturer or mere supplier *of the house*. However, the

---

8 482 Official Report (HL), cols 1028–9.
9 483 Official Report (HL), col 737; see also cols 734, 759–60.
10 See Law Commissions paras 85–6.
11 Directive Article 2; CPA, ss 1(2), 45(1). For background, see Law Commission paras 52–3; Pearson para 1277.

Directive[12] does seem to allow the plaintiff to argue that a party who puts the conglomerate into circulation has thereby also put the component product into circulation. So it allows the plaintiff who cannot identify the manufacturer of the relevant
fixture to sue the mere supplier of the conglomerate which incorporates the component product (Article 3(3)) so long, of course, as he had done so in the course of
business (Article 7(c)) and so long as the court holds that supply of (or otherwise
giving access to) premises amounts to 'putting them into circulation' under Article
7(a). This suggests that the Directive would allow a victim of a defective fixture or
building material to sue the commercial vendor or lessor of premises; and this party
could only avoid liability by naming the party which had supplied it with the
defective product.

But a person might suffer personal injuries due to the design or construction of
the building *itself*. For example, office blocks can suffer from 'sick building syn-
drome' caused by air-conditioning and lighting conditions. Yet the Directive does
not cover defective buildings because it restricts the definition of 'product' to movables. Thus, if a building collapses and injures X, X cannot sue under the CPA if the
cause of the collapse is determined to be the design of the building or the way it was
constructed. Some interesting anomalies will be created by this boundary, eg the
possibility that certain large but pre-fabricated structures (such as oil platforms) may
qualify as 'a product' before being affixed to land and so be caught by the Act. But
the most interesting question is why this boundary exists. The only reason given by
European reformers for the exclusion of defective buildings was the existence in
several countries of a local system of liability specific to immovables.[13] But
although this is true, it is of only limited relevance, at least in Britain, because the
relevant differences in liability rules relate principally to pure vendors, a group only
peripherally affected by the Directive.

Pure vendors

Claims relating to the acquisition of realty fall outside the protection of sales legislation. In the nineteenth century it was the marketing of new goods which underwent revolutionary changes (see Chapter 2, under heading 2). In the realty sector
no dramatic technological developments or market changes were taking place. The
property was inspectable as it always had been, and patterns of actual inspection
did not change.[14] Buyers of realty may initially have suffered from the same sort of
lack of information about quality as did buyers of goods, but the logistical barriers
to their acquisition of such information (at least with respect to defects discernible
by expert inspection) were nowhere near as severe as those often facing buyers of

12 Unlike the CPA which terminates the chain of recognized 'supply' of such a good at the point it is
   incorporated into the realty, so that the plaintiff cannot sue a party on the basis of his later supply of
   the conglomerate into which the good has been supplied (see CPA, ss 46(3), 46(4), 1(3)), the rationale being that the supplier should only have to name the producer of the finished conglomerate
   property not all producers of all components in that thing: see 483 Official Report (HL), col 750 per
   Lord Cameron.
13 See Strasbourg Expl Memo para 23; EEC Memo para 3.
14 Supporting evidence that inspectability and expectations of inspection were a significant factor here
   is provided by short leases of furnished dwellings where, exceptionally, warranties of habitability
   were implied. Here, as Atiyah notes, it was not uncommon for people to enter leases for a short
   period (a 'season') without examining them: *The Rise and Fall of Freedom of Contract* (1979) at
   p 454, n 21.

goods. Implied warranties of quality were not, therefore, recognized generally in such sales. Caveat emptor was allowed to survive, and this led to a refusal to allow the buyer to circumvent the supposed bargain by suing the vendor in tort, not only for pure economic loss but also for physical injuries caused by the state of the property.[15] Third parties injured by realty were also met with this 'immunity' of the pure vendor. So entrenched became this rule of law that it survived *Donoghue* v *Stevenson* and a pure vendor remains immune from negligence claims for physical loss arising out of his non-feasance, such as failure to warn of dangers not created by his own positive conduct.[16] This immunity has some bizarre effects. A building owner owes a duty of care to mere casual visitors to the premises, even to trespassers, but none to the person to whom he sells it nor to those who live in it after the sale with whom he would seem to have a much more proximate relation. But there are special considerations which might, on balance, support it. For example, in the typical (and very common) case of sales of dwellings subsequent to the first sale where neither seller nor buyer acts in the course of a business, both will nearly always be legally advised, so that the rule of caveat emptor may not be unfair to either party.[17]

Builders

But even if the gap which has developed between the liability of mere suppliers of goods and pure vendors of realty could be justified on some grounds, it should be of only secondary relevance to the question of whether realty should be included within the scope of the Directive. This is because the primary focus of the new regime is on the manufacturer of the product not the mere supplier, and as regards the manufacturer of goods or realty there is no significant difference between contractual and tortious liability for defects due to defective manufacture. Thus in contract, although the starting point of the manufacturer's liability may have been caveat emptor, this has been ousted in the case of goods by implied warranties and, in some cases of builders of realty, by statutory obligations as to habitability.[18]

15 On this general principle see J Stapleton 'Duty of Care and Economic Loss: A Wider Agenda' (1991) 107 LQR 249. Recent doubts about whether other classes of realty buyers do actually contract on this understanding have led paternalist US courts to imply warranties of habitability into sales of dwellings and led the Law Commission to take the unusual step of suggesting the alternative of tortious protection despite the fact that this would expose the vendor to a wider duty in tort than in contract (*Civil Liability of Vendors and Lessors for Defective Premises*, Law Commission No 40 (1970), para 53).

16 See, eg, *McNerny* v *Lambeth London Borough Council* (1988) 21 HLR 188 (bare landlord). The technical basis of the rule in precedent has been rightly attacked: see G Williams 'The Duties of Non-Occupiers in Respect of Dangerous Premises' (1942) 5 MLR 194 at pp 202–203. See also P North *Occupiers' Liability* (1971) at pp 204–205. Glanville Williams argued that case law authority does not prevent the imposition of liability in both tort and contract on a vendor with respect to known latent defects, op cit 202–3. Similarly the Law Commission recommended the vendor be liable in tort in cases of failure to warn of known risks, but this was not adopted: Law Commission No 40, para 51–55.

17 Compare Law Commission *Caveat Emptor in Sales of Land* (Law Com Consultation Paper) (November 1988) with Law Commission, *Let the Buyer be Well-Informed* (Law Com Rec Paper) (December 1989) and S Waddams 'Non-Disclosure in Sales of Land' (1989) 105 LQR 377. The treatment of third parties is not so outrageous as it first appears: she would almost always have a claim against the occupier because the dangers of which the vendor knew would often be reasonably discoverable by the occupier. In general see Stapleton op cit 275–6 and the dominant concern in this debate with recovery for pure economic loss.

18 Defective Premises Act 1972, s 1.

Similarly in tort the manufacturer owes a duty of care with respect to those physically injured whether by goods *or realty*.[19] In addition, by the time the British and other European reformers considered the issue, the earlier view that a vendor who was also the builder could escape such contractual and tortious liability by claiming his vendor status had been soundly rejected by both courts and Parliament.[20] There seems, then, to be no relevant special law of immovables sufficiently important to justify the exclusion of defective buildings from the class of 'defective products' in the Directive. Were they to be included (and the concept of 'put into circulation' adjusted appropriately), the person injured by a badly constructed staircase which collapsed would have an equivalent remedy to that of the rider of a badly made bicycle which collapses, both under the Directive as well as at common law.

Those peripheral areas where there *are* special rules could easily be excluded. First, many realty transactions are private sales of used dwellings and in such cases a pure vendor could claim the defence in Article 7(c) that the product was neither manufactured by him for sale or any form of distribution for economic purpose, nor manufactured or distributed by him in the course of his business. If it were thought necessary explicitly and comprehensively to establish the immunity of *all* pure vendors of realty, this could have been achieved by restricting claims with respect to defective realty to those against their manufacturers, and by barring secondary claims against mere suppliers. This would also have taken care of the other possible distortion involved in allowing claims for defective realty: its impact on the liability of occupiers and landlords. If an occupier or landlord who allowed access to his premises were to be regarded as 'putting them into circulation', and he did so in the course of business, then the recognition that premises were 'products' under the Directive would allow claims by such entrants against the occupier or landlord. This would create a parallel liability to the well-settled rules on occupiers' and landlords' liability, the stability of which would thereby be threatened. But by barring claims against mere suppliers of defective realty, this distortion would be prevented.[21]

US courts, keen to provide consumers with better remedies for harm caused by defective premises, have principally preferred to do this by implying into contracts with builder-vendors and developers for the sale of new dwellings common law warranties of quality or habitability, and a similar initiative has been taken by some courts with regard to landlords.[22] Only a few courts have yet overtly applied s 402A-derived liability to builders, perhaps because in only a few cases has it been necessary to escape the privity requirement of the warranty claim, as where a distant

---

19 See respectively *Donoghue* v *Stevenson* [1932] AC 562; *Sharpe* v *E T Sweeting & Son Ltd* [1963] 1WLR 665 and *AC Billings & Sons Ltd* v *Riden* [1958] AC 240.
20 See Defective Premises Act 1972, s 3, and *Targett* v *Torfaen Borough Council* [1992] 3 All ER 27 CA.
21 The Directive threatens distortion, however, in another way: courts may hold, for example, that a commercial occupier 'supplies' certain goods on its premises (affixed or not) for the use of entrants (eg washing machines in a laundromat) thus imposing a strict liability on occupiers in such cases (see below under heading 4(b)).
22 T Dworkin and J Mallor 'Liability for Formaldehyde-Contaminated Housing Materials: Toxic Torts in the Home' (1983) 21 Am Bus LJ 307, 323–4, who note the courts are divided on whether to relax the privity requirements with respect to such warranties. On landlords' implied warranties (which are of reasonable care only) see D Fischer and W Powers *Product Liability* (West Publishing Co St Paul, 1988) 648; J Early, 'Let the Landlord Beware: California Imposes Strict Liability on Lessors of Rental Housing' (1986) 51 Missouri LR 899, 905 fn 59.

purchaser sues the builder[23] or where occupants sue the builder-vendor. But this move recognized that policy justified classifying premises as a 'product', and since cases had already settled that s 402A liability could apply to the supply of used products and that it attaches to mere suppliers of products, the way was open for the application of s 402A to mere landlords and vendors of used premises. Since the Supreme Court of California duly took this step in 1985 in *Becker* v *IRM Corp.*[24] there has been considerable consternation in the US at the resultant disruption this extension of the s 402A liability causes to the law of landlord's liability and occupier's liability (both hitherto at most negligence-based) by the introduction of stricter obligations with respect to certain classes of risk. To sum up: to the extent that the sole reason given for the exclusion of realty from the Directive – the potential disruption of settled areas of law – is valid, it is one which could easily have been addressed. Moreover, since the economic and moral arguments justifying the new liability on manufacturers of dangerously defective goods seem to apply equally well to realty, its exclusion provides yet another major point of anomaly and perhaps long-term instability within the regime under the Directive.

2   THE MEANING OF PRODUCT: SOME ILLUSTRATIVE BORDERLINE CASES

As we have seen, the Directive applies to 'movables', a vague term to which the ECJ may give a construction as wide as 'anything capable of money valuation and of being an object of commercial transactions' (see under heading 1, above). On the one hand – as we see later (under heading 6, below) – this may extend the reach of the Directive dramatically beyond the expectations of UK practitioners. On the other hand, it raises important questions about whether certain articles which seem clearly to be 'goods' fall outside the reach of the Directive.

(a)   Human body products

The most important examples here are articles derived from the human body. As recent UK litigation has shown, there is no dispute that suppliers of infected blood, etc, can be sued in negligence and for breach of statutory duty.[25] The Pearson Commission also specifically recommended that articles from the human body should be regarded as 'products' under the separate new liability in tort,[26] and certainly they fall within the notion of tangible property, just as animal body products do. But in the context of UK sales law, Patrick Atiyah has argued that they may not be

---

23 See, eg, *Schipper* v *Levitt & Sons* 207 A 2d 314 (1965) (child of purchaser's lessee suing builder-vendor); *Kreigler* v *Eichler Homes Inc* 74 Cal Rptr 749 (1969) (subsequent purchaser suing builder-vendor); D Zipser 'Builders' Liability for Latent Defects in Used Homes' (1980) 32 Stan LR 607, 613. See also *Avner* v *Longridge Estates* 77 Cal Rptr 633 (1969) (defective house lots). Contrast *Lowrie* v *Evanston* 365 NE 2d 923 (1977); *Cox* v *Shaffer* 302 A 2d 456 (1973).
24 698 P 2d 116 (1985). See Early, op cit. But contrast *Armstrong* v *Cione* 738 P 2d 79 (1987).
25 *Re HIV Haemophiliac Litigation* [1990] NLJR 1349, CA.
26 Pearson para 1276.

regarded as 'goods' because not ordinarily thought to be the subject of commerce.[27] Since this is the very criterion the ECJ may well apply in setting the boundaries of 'product' in the Directive, it is an important argument. In practice, however, it has weight only in the case of items such as human semen and organs; the mere suggestion that they might be the subject of sale precipitated controversy and legislation in Britain.[28] It is very much weaker in the case of whole blood and blood-products which have long been the subject of a vigorous market. Thus, for example, it was Factor VIII clotting agent supplied commercially from the United States which infected 1,200 of the 5,000 British haemophiliacs with HIV in the early 1980s (prompting a government compensation scheme later extended to non-haemophiliacs infected by transfusions and tissue transplants). Indeed, in the US most blood derivatives such as this are, in fact, collected and supplied commercially by major pharmaceutical companies.[29]

On the other hand, blood and its derivatives have had a special place in the history of product liability. It was in this context US courts and commentators first recognized that strict liability for unavoidable risks could have an impact on availability and affordability of products; and in the case of these products, this was very much against the public interest. Thus, as early as 1954 in the landmark case of *Perlmutter* v *Beth David Hospital*,[30] the New York Court of Appeals refused to impose strict liability on a hospital which had given the plaintiff a blood transfusion tainted with jaundice virus. This, like the more common hepatitis contamination, was an unavoidable risk of transfusions.[31] Although some commentators and the occasional court have supported strict liability for the supply of blood and its products,[32] most states (46) have now adopted statutes which eliminate strict liability for blood and its products, both under a theory of warranty and tort liability derived from s 402A.

Under the Directive, even if blood donors were to be held to be 'producers' of their blood, etc, on the basis that they had 'manufactured' it (see Article 3(1),

27 P Atiyah *The Sale of Goods*, 8th edn (London, Pitman, 1990) 24–5, 51.
28 See Human Organ Transplants Act 1989 (1989, c 31). They have also been explicitly excluded from the product liability regime by statute in one US jurisdiction (Idaho), see J Wunch 'The Definition of Product for the Purposes of Section 402A' [1983] Ins CJ 344, 363. Although see L Styron 'Artificial Insemination: A New Frontier for Medical Malpractice and Medical Products Liability' (1986) 32 Loyola LR 411.
29 T Blanchard 'Strict Liability for Blood Derivative Manufacturers: Statutory Shield Incompatible with Public Health Responsibility' (1984) 28 St Louis ULJ 885–6.
30 123 NE 2d 792 (1954) (the strict liability relevant here was that derived from implied warranty). See also generally R Grief 'Hospital and Blood Bank Liability to Patients Who Contract AIDS Through Blood Transfusions' (1986) 23 San Diego LR 875, 882, 885–6; Blanchard, op cit 444.
31 In the present discussion it is important to note that the decision rested, not on a denial that blood was a 'good' or a 'product', but on a characterization of the hospital-patient transaction as predominantly one of service not sale. Since, in the US, strict warranty liability is thought only to attach to transactions of a predominantly 'sales' character (see below under heading 4(c)), it was held not to apply. Later, courts in the US took the same evasive route when faced with transfusion claims based on strict tort liability derived from s 402A, which is also construed as not applying to predominantly 'services' contexts.
32 R Kessell 'Transfused Blood, Serum Hepatitis and the Coase Theorem' (1974) 17 J Law & Econ 265, 288; G Calabresi and K Bass 'Right Approach, Wrong Implication: A Critique of McKeen on Products Liability' (1970) 38 U Chi LR 74, 86; M Franklin 'Tort Liability for Hepatitis: An Analysis and a Proposal' (1972) 24 Stan LR 439; Blanchard, op cit; A Baker 'Liability Without Fault and the AIDS Plague Compel a New Approach to Cases of Transfusion-Transmitted Disease' (1990) 61 U Col LR 81; *Cunningham* v *MacNeal Memorial Hospital* 266 NE 2d 897 (1970) (accepting whole blood could be a 'product', strict liability under s 402A applied); *Brody* v *Overlook Hospital* 299 A 2d 668 (1972).

s 1(2)), they would have a full defence because they do not supply it in the course of a business (Article 7(c), s 4(1)(c)).[33] But later suppliers of whole blood, such as hospitals who transfuse it in the course of their business, would be caught by the supplier's liability under Article 3(3) and s 2(3) and, unless donors could be identified, that liability could not be avoided. Similarly, those who process blood into its derivatives and then supply it in the course of a business, would be caught as the producer of the derivative. Although in both cases considerable protection would be afforded by the development risk defence in cases where the contamination was undiscoverable at the time of transfusion, this might not be regarded as sufficient protection; and the ECJ might be persuaded to develop some technique by which this class of article could be taken completely outside the reach of the Directive. Given the terms of the Directive, characterizing the supply transaction as one predominantly of service would not achieve this and the court may be forced to add some qualification to the notion of 'product'. Whether this would extend to all human body articles and whether it could be couched in coherent terms is unclear. More importantly, if an exception was made to ensure the availability and affordability of blood and its products, the question of whether pharmaceuticals and other medical products should be covered by the Directive would inevitably arise. We have noted (Chapter 9, under heading 5) the importance attached both in the US and in Europe to avoiding the excessive deterrence of R & D into drugs, etc, and to maintaining their affordability. Although an explicit exemption for such products was eventually rejected by the EC reformers, sensitivity to these issues remains; and if special treatment of body products was developed by the ECJ, a more generously pro-defendant application of the concept of defect in the drug and medical device field (Chapter 10, under heading 7) would be encouraged.

(b)   The second-hand market

Another major question which the ECJ will have to determine is whether there should be implied into the definition of 'product' in the Directive the requirement that the product be defective when *new*. The dilemma for the court is that, while the explicit assumption behind the reform process is that compensation should be imposed on producers for 'the risks inherent in modern technological production' (2nd Recital), the Directive seems to go further than this. The relevant distinction is not between goods which are new or used at the time of injury. If a new product was supplied in a defective state, the Directive clearly allows claims to be made in respect of that supply even if the product was subsequently resold as used. Suppose, for example, that B buys a new car from retailer R and a year later sells it privately to V who is then injured by a defect in the car. So long as it can be shown that the defect existed at the relevant time – and if V sues the manufacturer that is the time when the latter supplied it – V can recover under Part I of the CPA, even though the product alleged to be defective is second-hand. Of course, the older a product is, the easier it will be for, say, a defendant manufacturer to argue that, on the balance of

---

33 On possible donor liability in US see Styron, op cit 443. Pearson's suggestion (para 1276) that the 'producer' of human blood and organs should be deemed to be the authority responsible for distributing them, has not been implemented.

probability, it was not defective when he put it into circulation (Article 7(e)), but that it had subsequently become defective by misuse, normal wear and tear or inadequate servicing. Resale itself often makes these assertions more difficult to refute because the history of the product becomes less clear.

The interesting issue concerns the liability of the mere supplier of second-hand products. Of course, under Article 3(3) (and s 2(3)) this will only attach where that supplier had supplied the product in the course of his business.[34] So in the earlier car example the retailer R is caught by Article 3(3) but B is not. If B had sold the car to a second-hand dealer S, who then resold to V, both R and S would be caught by Article 3(3). But both R and S could avoid liability by the maintenance of adequate records. This may be thought unjust in some cases. In respect of some types of product, records identifying the producer are readily available. In the case of used cars the identity of the producer is obvious even without records. Yet in respect of other products, such as certain used toys sold by a charity shop,[35] it may be impossible to identify the manufacturer and so the mere supplier will bear the full liability costs associated with products supplied by them, both when the defect arose out of original design or manufacture and when it arose in the period of use before it was acquired by the second-hand dealer.

The effect of the Directive contrasts with the position in the US where, somewhat controversially, most courts refuse to impose s 402A liability on commercial sellers of used products,[36] even in cases where the manufacturer and first retailer are liable under the rule. Although at first this seems an odd line to draw, given that the liability had early on been extended to commercial lessors of what are necessarily nearly always second-hand products, it suggests sensitivity to the fact that it would usually be impossible to ensure that second-hand dealers were subject to liability for defects of manufacture or design but not for defects arising after first retail supply and before acquisition by the second-hand dealer. If adequate records of origin did not exist, the dealer would be liable because he had supplied a defective product. Even if they did exist, the liability under s 402A could not be avoided,[37] and the shifting of loss on to the producer in a recourse action would depend on the *second-hand dealer's* ability to prove that the product had been defective when the producer supplied it. Here the age and past history of the product work *against* such defendants and in many cases they would fail to shift the loss, even though in some cases the defect *had* arisen after the first retail supply.

Of course, no problem arises from this result, if it is thought proper that the liability in s 402A should attach to such defects, that is if the Directive was to apply in some *original* way to the enterprise of second-hand markets. However, very few US courts

---

34 Under CPA the defendant need only be acting in the course of his business – thus an isolated sale of used equipment by a commercial entity is sufficient to come within this requirement. Contrast the requirement under s 402A of the Restatement that the defendant be in the business of selling *such* products. How regular the selling off of a company's vehicle fleet would need to be to qualify under such a test is treated as a question of fact.

35 A charity may also be *primarily* liable as an importer of a new product into the EC. On whether it acts in the course of a business, see under heading 3, below.

36 See eg *Tillman* v *Vance Equipment Co* 596 P 2d 1299 (1979). See also J Henderson 'Extending the Boundaries of Strict Products Liability: Implications of the Theory of the Second Best' (1980) 126 U Penn LR 1036, 1052–3, 1081–5; J Henderson and A Twerski *Products Liability* 2nd edn (Boston, Little Brown & Co, 1992) 146–7; Fischer and Powers, *op cit* 636. Re claims against the manufacturer and retailer here see *Gibbs* v *General Motors Corpn* 450 SW 2d 827 (1970).

37 As it could under Article 3(3) of the Directive.

have been willing to impose liability in this way.[38] Coherent arguments *do* exist to support this outcome. The commercial re-seller may bear moral responsibility, since he is in the business of creating and profiting from a market in second-hand products. Again, in the absence of a feasible claim against, say, the first owner whose misuse caused the defect, placing s 402A liability on the second-hand dealer might be the 'second-best' strategy to achieve prevention goals. It could also be argued that the complexities of second-hand markets – lower expectations of durability and even of safety which used products generate, and the correspondingly greater expectation that buyers will inspect for defects – can be adequately dealt with under the notion of 'defect', and that strict liability on suppliers should apply.

But it cannot have been intended to impose such liability on dealers in used products under the Directive. At present, the child injured by an EC or used defective toy bought from Oxfam could sue Oxfam *only* if Oxfam was unable to name the producer or its supplier (eg a donor). This suggests that making a profit out of selling defective toys was not per se seen as sufficient to justify the imposition of liability. Similarly, a person injured by a hire car will not be able to maintain a claim against the car lessor because it will invariably be able to name the vehicle's manufacturer. This suggests that the ECJ is likely to confine the Directive to defects arising out of the process of manufacture and distribution of new products. This is the position explicitly adopted in the CPA, which does not catch defects arising after supply by those primarily liable (the manufacturer, importer and own-brand supplier) (s 4(1)(d), (2)). Arguments do exist in favour of this restriction on the scope of liability. It could be argued[39] that the more appropriate party to bear losses arising after initial supply is the person who by misuse, for example, created the defect which caused the losses; and that later buyers in second-hand markets – often poorer sections of society – should not have to pay increased prices attributable to increased exposure of second-hand dealers to tort liability. But there is no evidence that such ideas were considered by EC reformers, making more difficult the court's task in reading in limits to the Directive against its express terms.

Another difficult issue is whether a commercial seller outside the original commercial chain who works on, reconditions or reasssembles a product can be liable under the Directive.[40] The 1992 Directive on General Product Safety (under which no civil liability to injured individuals arises) applies to new, used or reconditioned consumer[41] products, although it does 'not apply to second-hand products supplied as antiques or as products to be repaired or reconditioned prior to being used, provided that the supplier clearly informs the person to whom he supplies the product to that effect' (Article 2(a)). The products Directive is silent on this issue and it fails to extend the definition of 'producer', as the Product Safety Directive does, beyond the manufacturer to 'the person who reconditions the product' (General

---

38 P Hahn 'Consumer Protection: Should it Mandate Extension of Section 402A to Used Products Dealers?' (1985) 50 Missouri LR 186, 189–90; D Goodwin 'Protecting the Buyer of Used Products: Is Strict Liability for Commercial Sellers Desirable?' (1981) 33 Stan LR 535, 548.

39 Especially if, as the express terms of the Directive suggest, the second-hand dealer would lose the state of the art defence if the defect was discoverable by someone such as the prior user.

40 On reconditioning: would the sterilization for reuse of recyclable syringes by a hospital make it a 'manufacturer'? On the problem such cases cause under the Restatement, see *Crandell* v *Larkin and Jones Appliance Co* 334 NW 2d 31 (1983); *Young* v *Aro Corpn* 111 Cal Rptr 535 (1974); cases cited in J Kats, 'Used Products and Strict Liability: Where Public Safety and Caveat Emptor Intersect' (1983) 19 Cal West LR 330, 331, fn 6.

41 Only products intended for or likely to be used by consumers. OJ No L 227, 11.8.92.

Product Safety Directive, Article 2(d)). But even under the narrower terms of the products Directive, there must come a point where such activities constitute 'manufacture' for the purposes of the definition of 'producer' in the Directive, as in the case of a car built out of parts from a number of discarded cars. In such cases the seller would be primarily liable as producer of a finished product, and nice questions of degree, in particular concerning the application of the 'defect' requirement, will be raised in such circumstances.

Similarly, products which have been supplied and used are often then regarded as scrap to be discarded or recycled, for example as fuel. These include scrap metal, paper, glass and used lubricants.[42] Technically, such articles remain 'products' covered by the Directive and Part I of the CPA,[43] and interesting problems in establishing 'defectiveness' will also arise in respect of them.[44] Of course, in most cases those involved in the *original* production of, say, metal machinery which is much later melted down for recycling, will escape liability on the basis that the metal substance itself was not defective in the light of the use to which it could reasonably be expected to be put (Article 6(1)(b), CPA, ss 3(1), (2)(b)), and that the defect in the subsequent product was attributable to its designer's choice of substance (Article 7(f), CPA, s 4(1)(f)). But those involved in the industrial bulking and processing of scrap for re-use might qualify as suppliers under Article 3(3), s 2(3). Their liability would, admittedly, be only secondary, but such liability would be difficult to avoid in the case of bulked anonymous products. Moreover, they might be subject to primary liability as 'producers' of, say, 'scrap metal ingots'. In both recycling and dumping cases the adequacy of packaging, instructions and warnings by the relevant producer will be vital to the issue of 'defectiveness'. Is a refrigerator defective because it carries no instructions on how safely to dispose of its CFC coolants after it is dumped? What labelling is required of a pesticide producer to avoid liability for contamination by the pesticide after use of groundwater and subsequently of food?

3   THE RELEVANT PRODUCT HISTORY: A TRANSACTION 'IN THE COURSE OF A BUSINESS'

As in the case of the exclusion of realty and the second-hand market from the Directive, the most interesting issue reconditioned, reassembled or scrap products raise is how to justify in policy terms a line between defective products and defective services, and how sensibly to make such a line work in practice. To explore this issue we need first to consider the limitation of liability under the Directive to defendants acting in the course of a business. Under the Directive it is a defence for the defendant to show that the product was neither manufactured by him for sale or any form of distribution for economic purpose, nor manufactured or distributed by him in the course of his business (Article 7(c)).[45] This defence clearly excludes from the reach of the Directive a 'one-off' personal sale of a used car, for example, or the private

---

42 These are not unimportant products: scrap metal, for example, provides most of the raw materials for the steel industry, among others: 115 Official Report (HC), col 65.

43 Contrast Strasbourg Expl Rep para 25.

44 R Kidner 'Toxic Waste and Strict Liability for Products' (1988) 138 New LJ 379.

45 Under s 402A there is a corresponding limitation to defendants engaged in the 'business' of selling the product.

individual who occasionally makes jam and gives it to Oxfam for sale in its shops. Conversely, it probably catches a large manufacturing concern which donates some of its products to be sold by Oxfam shops. But does the notion of 'economic purpose' in the first limb of Article 7(c) mean that even if a person who builds a garden seat for her neighbour does not supply it in the course of an existing business, if she made it with a view to charging a profit-making price, she is caught by the Directive?[46] Similarly, and more importantly, if an Oxfam shop is a mere 'supplier' under Article 3(3) is it liable only if it supplied 'in the course of business' (Article 7(c)); but what does this phrase mean?

The statutory definition of 'business' in the CPA explicitly includes certain activities which overall are non-profit-making, such as those 'of a local authority or other public authority',[47] so that, for example, the activities of the NHS are caught even though they escape the provisions of other important legislation regulating sale of goods and provision of services, because the latter rules are predicated on there being a contractual base to the relevant activity. British courts are also likely to accept that the activities of non-government bodies such as private charitable hospitals, schools, research institutions and charity shops are capable of being a 'business',[48] even if such bodies do not seek to make a profit for investors: risk-taking in the marketplace is sufficient. But will the ECJ interpret 'business' in the Directive in this way? Certainly the economic strategies of prevention and price-deterrence would seem to be applicable to such cases. An environmental charity is set up, say, to manufacture and supply *at cost* de-leading filters for car exhausts. Its aim is to promote the use of such a product so it should be motivated by and sensitive to the same sort of economic incentives to achieve this end as would an ordinary commercial firm. Indeed, it may be more sensitive as it lacks the buffer of profits which can, at least in the short run, dilute economic incentives. But what if the moral enterprise liability rationale only justifies imposing the special liability on defendants whose risk-taking was in pursuit of an *overall financial profit for investors*? Oxfam shops and NHS hospital canteens charge above cost price for their products, and in that sense take a financial profit from the individual transaction, but do not as organizations seek to make profit for investors. Might the ECJ want to exclude them from the reach of the Directive on these grounds? This would be close to the approach in the US,[49] but there is no firm indication whether this is the route which will be taken.

---

46 Does the notion of 'course of business' require some sort of regularity of transaction, or can a single transaction yet come within that term if carried out with a view to profit? On which see *Davies* v *Sumner* [1984] 1 WLR 1301; D Price 'When is a Consumer Not a Consumer?' (1989) 52 Mod LR 245.

47 CPA, s 45(1). Comparable definitions exist in the Unfair Contract Terms Act 1977 (s 14), Sale of Goods Act 1979 (s 61(1)) and Supply of Goods and Services Act 1982 (s 18(1)).

48 See *Customs and Excise Comrs* v *Lord Fisher* [1981] 2 All ER 147 at 157, per Gibson J; *Town Investments Ltd* v *Dept of the Environment* [1976] 3 All ER 479 at 496, per Buckley LJ (on appeal [1978] AC 359); *Chitty on Contracts* Vol 1, 25th edn, ed A G Guest (London, Sweet & Maxwell, 1983) para 914; A G Guest); Law Commission No 156 *Implied Terms in Contracts for the Supply of Services* (HMSO, 1986) para 2.27.

49 Henderson, (1980) op cit 1047–8. See also S Brook 'Sales-Service Hybrid Transactions: A Policy Approach' (1974) 28 Southwestern LJ 575, 591–2. Even if the activities *are* commercially profit-making, some US courts will accept the nature of the defendant's activities as grounds for refusing to apply strict liability, eg commercial blood banks (see *Evans* v *Northern Ill. Blood Bank Inc* 298 NE 2d 732 (1973)). But contrast *Cunningham* v *MacNeal Memorial Hospital* 266 NE 2d 897 (1970) at 904 where the Supreme Court of Illinois imposed strict liability under s 402A on a non-profit hospital for the supply of contaminated blood.

It is worth noting that EC drafters still do not provide clear guidance on such issues. In the proposed Directive of 1991 on the liability of suppliers of services, the liability was directed to parties who are described variously as 'traders' or 'suppliers' when engaged in their 'professional activities' or transacting 'on a commercial basis', yet none of these terms is defined.[50]

4   THE RELEVANT PRODUCT HISTORY: 'PUT INTO CIRCULATION' ... BY WHOM AND HOW?

Under the Directive, a defendant has a defence if 'he did not put the product into circulation' (Article 7(a)). The corresponding terminology in the CPA is 'supply' (s 4(1)(b), s 46), but this must be read subject to the meaning the ECJ will attach to the notion of 'circulation'. But what *will* the ECJ decide has to have happened to the product to qualify it as having been 'put into circulation' by the defendant? The US experience here should be treated with great caution.

(a)   The US experience

In order to find some justification for the imposition of primary liability under s 402A on each and every member of the chain of manufacture and distribution, the drafters of the Restatement were under great pressure to give the concept in s 402A comparable to 'put into circulation' – 'put into the stream of commerce' – a narrow meaning. A narrow meaning would help narrow the class of those caught by s 402A and make more plausible the claim that those in that class were engaged in the same 'enterprise'. The drafters attempted this by adding the requirement that the defendant be in the business, although not necessarily the sole business, of supplying the relevant product (s 402A (1)(a)). As Comment f states, for example, regular if incidental sales of ice cream by a cinema are caught, but the isolated sale by a company of its outmoded production machinery is not. Considerable complex case law now exists on the question of how incidental the product transaction can be and still be regarded as part of the defendant's business.

Even so, the requirement that the product transaction be at least incidental to the defendant's business has proved inadequate to provide s 402A with principled boundaries, because courts and commentators have been able to find no good policy reason to restrict the liability to 'sellers' and to prevent it applying to other instances of 'putting into the stream of commerce', such as the giving away of free product samples and certain bailments of products either for consideration (eg car rental) or gratuitously (eg loan of demonstration models). It was recognized that some types of product only ever reach the consumer by transactions falling short of sale. This has led US courts no longer to require that the defective product was 'sold' or even that its ownership was transferred, but only that it was put into or kept in 'the stream of commerce' by the defendant. It is now accepted, for example, that s 402A should

---

50 OJ No C 12/8, 18.1.91, now being reconsidered by the Commission in deference to 'subsidiarity'.

apply to the commercial hire of chattels by vehicle rental firms.[51] There are also several cases where s 402A has been applied to free samples, loans of demonstration models and returnable reusable product containers, all of which intuitively seem justified applications of the rule.[52] But having abandoned the requirement of 'sale', US courts have found it difficult to draw the new boundary clearly and sufficiently narrowly to preserve the coherence of the liability within its theoretical underpinnings. For example, should the rule set out in s 402A apply to situations where what has happened is that the defendant has granted a contractual licence to use a chattel, eg a washing machine in a laundromat? If so, what about *gratuitous* licences to use products not ultimately for sale or hire, eg the access given by a supermarket to use a trolley or a water fountain in the store?

(b) The contrasting position under the Directive

In the Directive liability is channelled to the manufacturer (and the importer and own-brand supplier, if relevant). Mere supply of the product in the course of a business, even where it clearly assists the business in terms of goodwill, for instance, does not give rise to *primary* liability. The secondary liability of mere 'suppliers' who 'put the product into circulation' was designed merely to help the plaintiff: it can be avoided simply by naming the party primarily liable or the defendant's own supplier. So whatever the moral or economic justifications for the Directive, they will not be put under strain by the notion of 'putting into circulation' catching mere 'suppliers' (even if they are completely outside the ordinary contractual chain of manufacture, distribution and retail of the relevant product) because nearly always such defendants will be able to avoid liability. In other words, because it elsewhere channels primary liability to a very narrow class, the Directive can afford to have a very wide concept of 'put into circulation'. The absence from the Directive of any requirement that a defendant be in the business of supplying the relevant product type seems to ensure that 'put into circulation' not only covers cases excluded by the US rule – eg gifts or prizes of free chocolates by a book shop or a one-off sale of outmoded production machinery – but also many cases troublesome in the US context – eg free nappies available in the baby change room of a children's department store, inclusion of which in the US seems to depend on whether the store sold nappies of that type. Also by not requiring the 'putting into circulation' to be in pursuance of a contract, the Directive clearly allows the notion to encompass the supply of drugs, etc, in the important non-contractual context of the NHS.[53]

---

51 The landmark case is *Cintrone* v *Hertz Truck Leasing and Rental Service* 212 A 2d 769 (1965). See also *Brescia* v *Great Road Realty Trust* 373 A 2d 1310 (1977) (strict tort liability not applicable to private hire where defendant not in business of hiring them out). Some jurisdictions have explicitly adopted the extension of 'seller' to 'lessor' in their strict tort regimes for products, see eg Oregon Products Liability Act: (Or Rev Stat, s 30 900 (1985)) See also R Ausness 'Strict Liability for Chattel Leasing' (1987) 48 U Pitt LR 273.

52 See eg *McKisson* v *Sales Affiliates Inc* 416 SW 2d 787 (1967) (free sample); *First National Bank* v *Cessna Aircraft Co* 365 So 2d 966 (1978) (aircraft demonstration); *Bainton* v *Lamoire LP Gas Co* 321 NE 2d 744 (1974) (reusable returnable container).

53 Contrast the sales legislation such as the Sale of Goods Act 1979 and the Supply of Goods and Services Act 1982 which are predicated on contractual transactions. NHS transactions are pursuant to the fulfilment of a statutory duty not to a contract of sale, *Pfizer Corpn* v *Ministry of Health* [1965] 1 All ER 450, 455 (per Lord Reid).

The channelled nature of the liability under the Directive will also avoid the major danger, inherent in the US regime, that the product liability rule will indirectly destabilize the settled areas of occupiers' and landlords' liability. This danger arises from cases where the relevant transaction transfers neither ownership nor temporary possession of the product but merely involves the defendant giving, gratuitously or for consideration, access to or a licence to use the product. Take the examples of a supermarket trolley or a water fountain provided by the store, or the sports equipment provided in a school, or the ladder supplied in a 'pick-your-own' orchard.[54] Regardless of whether the case falls on the bailment side of the vague bailment/licence distinction important to our domestic laws on 'supply',[55] and even if the giving of access to the product might otherwise be thought closely incidental to the selling or hiring business of the defendant, because the product is on the defendant's premises, these cases raise the problem of overlap with occupiers' liability. The defendant in such cases could argue that occupiers' liability law required no more than reasonable care with respect to the state of its premises, that there have been no reasons advanced for a substantial reform of this area of the law and that any application of strict liability to occupiers' liability law on the basis that the occupier is a mere supplier of a product would have serious implications for occupiers and their insurers.

Not unexpectedly confusion reigns in this area in the US: different courts have, for example, held the loan of or licence to use a supermarket trolley to fall on opposite sides of the line![56] The defendant's case looks strongest where the product is merely provided gratuitously for the convenience of potential customers. But what if the product is more centrally involved in the principal transaction: for example, laundromat washing machines or static exercise bikes in a gymnasium? In such cases under a regime of unchannelled liability it may seem odd that a defendant-occupier should escape strict liability for these products in respect of which he seems to be in a position comparable to that of the retailer of *portable* products, but be strictly liable for hiring out take-home irons or road bikes, for instance. While this anomaly can be avoided by the application of strict liability to all such cases, as it was in the Californian laundromat washing machine case of *Garcia* v *Halsett* (1970),[57] this result can only be achieved at the cost of throwing the state of occupiers' liability into confusion. Here, as in the case of the Californian Supreme Court's application of strict liability in tort to landlords engaged in the business of leasing dwellings[58] (see above under heading 1(b)), the destabilization of occupiers' and landlords' liability is the inevitable consequence of the lack of a coherent basis for special liability rules limited to products. In a parallel way one might have thought that the creation of a separate new EC law on product liability might have posed a

---

54 The latter held to be a 'bailment' in *Gabbard* v *Stephenson's Orchard Inc* 565 SW 2d 753 (1978). For corresponding examples in the hybrid transaction context see cases cited below in fn 60.

55 This distinction, drawn in CPA, s 46 from the definition of 'supply', turns on whether a right to temporary possession has been given, but note that 'possession' has proved a concept sensitive to the policy considerations perceived by courts in the individual case: D R Harris 'The Concept of Possession in English Law' in *Oxford Essays in Jurisprudence* (First Series) ed A Guest (Oxford, Clarendon Press, 1961) 69, 71–2.

56 See *Keen* v *Dominick's Finer Foods Inc* 364 NE 2d 502 (1977); *Safeway Stores Inc* v *Nest-Kart* 579 P 2d 441 (1978). Whether the transaction is a form of gratuitous bailment (ie a loan) rather than a gratuitous licence is unclear (see preceding footnote).

57 (1970) 82 Cal Rptr 420.

58 See *Becker* v *IRM Corpn* 698 P 2d 116 (1985) for injuries resulting from a latent defect in the premises (a glass door) when the defect existed at the time the premises were let.

particularly tricky problem in England and Wales where the Occupiers' Liability Acts 1957 and 1984 suggest a Parliamentary intention to lay down an exhaustive code ('in place of the rules of the common law') relating to the duty an occupier owes entrants with respect to the state of the premises.

But the Directive masks these problems by channelling liability to the manufacturer. The notion of 'putting into circulation' can be allowed an ambit wide enough to catch cases where a business occupier exposes entrants to defective products on or attached to its premises such as cases of the provision of a supermarket trolley or laundromat machine, regardless of whether the transaction is classified as gratuitous bailment of a good or a gratuitous licence or even the provision of a 'facility', because liability can be shifted back in nearly all cases to the manufacturer. The implementation of the Directive by the CPA in terms of 'supply' may, therefore, be considerably too narrow. Indeed, might the notion of 'put into circulation' even cover the risk a mere carrier creates by transporting some dangerous substance or an employer's provision of movable work equipment to employees.

(c) Hybrid transactions in the US

Perhaps the most important area, however, in which the channelling of liability has masked the lack of a theoretical basis for the boundaries of the Directive is that of so-called 'hybrid transactions', that is, transactions in which provision of a defective product is accompanied by the performance of a service. This is the second area in which US courts were forced, by the failure in the early formulation of the common law products rule to channel liability, to introduce narrower boundaries. The term 'hybrid transactions' covers a wide and important range of situations. It includes cases where, in the course of rendering services, the defendant transfers property in a product; for example where, during the delivery of health services, medical substances and devices, drugs, optical glasses, bandages, plaster casts, intra-uterine devices, pacemakers, artificial hip joints, dental fillings and so on, are given or affixed to or inserted in a patient; or where, during car repairs, a defective spare part is installed; or the provision of food in a restaurant. Also included are cases in which the defendant has, in the course of rendering a service, only transferred temporary possession in the product (eg the loan of a replacement car while the defendant repairs the client's car[59]), or merely exposed someone to or given access to the product without transfer of ownership or temporary possession (eg where a doctor uses defective non-disposable needles or a plumber uses a defective machine or other tool; or where a dentist provides defective facilities such as chairs in her waiting room[60]). Finally, there is the important group of cases where the

---

59 Depending on the vague line between bailment and licence (ie on the meaning given to 'temporary possession') this might also include: hotel bath mats (see *Wagner* v *Coronet Hotel* 458 P 2d 399 (1969)), a hospital gown (see *Thomas* v *St Joseph's Hospital* 618 SW 2d 791 (1981)), a golf buggy on a golf course (see *Katz* v *Slade* 460 SW 2d 608 (1970) and *Sipari* v *Villa Olivia Country Club* 380 NE 2d 819 (1978)), a glass in a restaurant (see *Shaffer* v *Victoria Station Inc* 588 P 2d 233 (1978)), a bowling ball in a bowling alley (see *Dixon* v *Four Seasons Bowling Alley* 424 A 2d 428 (1980)).

60 For health care examples see *Ethicon Inc* v *Parten* 520 SW 2d 527 (1975); *Magrine* v *Krasnica* 227 A 2d 539 (1967). Other examples of defective facilities include hospital and hotel beds. Were one of the borderline cases suggested in the preceding footnote to be held to be mere licences rather than bailments, it would transfer to the list in this footnote.

defective product is provided by but consumed in the course of the provision of services by the defendant (eg where a hairdresser uses a defective permanent wave solution; or a health worker uses defective anaesthetic or disposable antiseptic tools such as swabs, needles, etc; or a fumigator uses defective fumigating chemicals). In certain of these cases, the type of product involved only ever reaches the consumer as an incident of the provision of a service, eg some anaesthetics.

The diversity and multiplicity of hybrid transactions present a considerable challenge to the coherence of the rule in s 402A. It is clear that the product manufacturer can be sued, but what about the service-giver? It could hardly be said, for example, that there was any economic or moral sense in rendering the dentist *primarily* liable under the product rule when a needle she is using shatters due to a latent manufacturing defect. It would put enormous strain on the concept to assert that the dentist and manufacturer were both engaged in a common 'enterprise'. US courts, therefore, introduced a further boundary to the rule: it was only to apply to cases where the transaction relating to the defendant was *predominantly* concerned with putting the good 'into the stream of commerce'.[61] This means, remarkably, that a court might well hold that the gratuitous loan of a car by a car retailer to a *prospective* client is within the rule, but that a comparable loan by a car repairer to an *actual* client while repairs are done would be a transaction dominated by the repair services and therefore outside s 402A. Technically the device by which this control was achieved is also weak. At the same time as courts were relaxing the notion of 'seller' in s 402A to embrace 'lessor' and the supply of free samples, they were reading into the very same word the 'predominance' requirement. This requirement may be coherent in the sales field as a way of distinguishing contracts for the sale of goods from other sorts of contract, but its deployment in the tortious context of s 402A can hardly rely on this. Here an independent reason is needed to explain why it is relevant to the claim of an injured bystander that the transaction by which the defendant put the product into circulation was predominantly one of sale. Had this been attempted, there would have been a clear conflict between the aim of shielding innocent incidental suppliers of products such as the dentist and the wide version of 'enterprise' which imposes liability on all suppliers (including innocent ones) and does not channel it to manufacturers. The distortions caused by this strategy show what can happen when a purposive approach to the interpretation of a rule is unsupported by coherent policies.

Nor is the test for predominance even clear. In Britain, where the characterization of the transaction has been important under sale of goods legislation and where courts favour formal reasoning to tackle the question, the analytical test of the 'essence of the transaction' often proves unhelpful.[62] But many US courts have added considerably to these difficulties by eschewing a formal analytical approach and by deciding more or less on a case-by-case basis, whether 'policy' seems to support the application of s 402A liability to the defendant. Many courts then reason backwards from this decision to the appropriate characterization to the transaction. Because of this and a concern to shield service-givers in general and

---

61   Reflected in Comment d of J Henderson and A Twerski's 'A Proposed Revision of Section 402A of the Restatement (Second) of Torts' (1992) 77 Cornell LR 1512, 1517.

62   P S Atiyah *The Sale of Goods* 8th edn (London, Pitman, 1990) 20–7; R M Goode *Commercial Law* (London, Penguin, 1982) 155–6. The situations in which such characterization is necessary were much reduced by the Supply of Goods and Services Act 1982, which implied terms of quality and fitness into all contracts involving the 'transfer of goods' not yet dealt with by previous enactments.

professionals in particular, the case law on the characterization of hybrid transactions as predominantly of sale or not often appears capricious.[63] The complexities of the necessary analysis are compounded where there is doubt whether what was done to the product by the defendant in the hybrid transaction amounts to its having been put into the 'stream of commerce' at all (12.04(c)). This added complexity arises in cases ranging from the loan of a replacement car while the owner's is being repaired, through those cases on the vague borderline between bailment and licence (such as defective hotel bathmats[64]), to cases where the service-giver merely used or gave access to the product (such as the use of tools or provision of waiting room chairs). Interestingly, most US courts who admit the similarity in moral and economic terms between innocent hybrid transactions and innocent transactions of retail sale have reacted by abandoning any predominance requirement and applying the s 402A rule in hybrid contexts even where the service element predominates, such as when a hairdresser applies a permanent wave solution to a client's hair.[65] This is an indication of how unwilling US courts are to resolve a doctrinal anomaly in favour of no-liability, which they could have done here by developing a rule to exclude all innocent non-manufacturing parties and the unavailability of a clear theoretical justification for confining the rule in s 402A.

Predictably the impact of the latter is also manifested in the disrespect shown to the basic boundary concepts of the s 402A rule. This 'disrespect' is not constituted by courts extending the concept of 'seller' to 'lessor', for example. The terms of the Restatement are not binding. Rather it consists in distorting the express terms of the Restatement to give effect to policies not implicit in those terms. Instead of stating ancillary rules, such as the predominance rule with justification, US courts often hide behind a distorted interpretation of the explicit terms of s 402A. For example in relation to hybrid transactions, courts have often rationalized a refusal to impose strict liability on mere suppliers by denying that a 'sale' has taken place or that the article is a 'product'. An absurd result is, for example, that something may be regarded as a 'product' in certain transactions but not in others. As Maloney puts it, 'the social policy underlying the [separate tort rule for products] doctrine has become the definition of a "product" and "sale".'[66] Thus in *Schriner* v *Pennsylvania Power and Light Co* (1985) the court held that:

---

63 J Riper 'Strict Liability in Hybrid Cases' (1980) 32 Stan LR 391, 400–2; O Reynolds 'Strict Liability for Commercial Services – Will Another Citadel Crumble?' (1977) 30 Okla LR 298, 311. In an illustrative case on professionals, a chemist who simply supplied a defective pharmaceutical was held not to be the 'seller' of a product but a 'service-giver', even though the transaction outwardly seemed predominantly a sale of goods, *Murphy* v *E R Squibb & Sons Ltd* 710 P 2d 247 (1985); *McLeod* v *Merrell Co* 174 So 2d 736 (1965). Contrast the result under the rule-of-thumb in *Benjamin's Sale of Goods* 4th edn, general editor A G Guest (London, Sweet & Maxwell, 1992), s 1–046 (L Sealy) 'a chemist who makes up a prescription sells it, since his work and skill goes entirely into the product'.

64 See fns 55, 59–60.

65 *Newmark* v *Gimbel's Inc* 258 A 2d 697 (1969) (ratio explicitly limited to non-professionals). See also Bottler J's dissent in *Magrine* v *Krasnica* 227 A 2d 539 (1967) (L Dir 1967), affd per curiam sub nom *Magrine* v *Spector* 241 A 2d 637 (1968) (App Dir 1968) 644; see also *Nowakowski* v *Hoppe Fire Co* 349 NE 2d 578, 584–5 (1976) (repairer strictly liable in tort for defective spare part). An even more striking example is *Niffenegger* v *Lakeland Construction Co* 420 NE 2d 262 (1981), where an asphalt-spreading machine 'leased' but still operated by the defendant caused injury and strict liability was imposed, even though the service element appears central.

66 J Malony 'What is or is not a Product Within the Meaning of Section 402A?' (1974) 57 Marquette

while still in the distribution system, electricity is a service, not a product; electricity only becomes a product, for the purposes of strict liability, once it passes through a customer's meter and into the stream of commerce.[67]

Even in relation to non-hybrid transactions, US courts have been known to use such distortion. The Illinois court in *Anderson* v *Farmers Hybrid Cos* (1980) gave effect to its disapproval of the application of s 402A to transactions involving living animals for a variety of policy reasons, by holding that live gilts (immature female swine) sold for breeding purposes are not 'products' within the meaning of s 402A.[68] This is 'substantive reasoning' at its most unconvincing and should sound a warning to courts in the EC keen to give a 'purposive' interpretation to the Directive.

(d)   Hybrid transactions under the Directive

Because primary liability under the Directive is channelled, it is not necessary in hybrid transactions to restrict the ambit of 'putting into circulation' to those transactions in which the product element predominates. As a result the phrase should not only be held clearly to cover a transaction which is a pure sale (supermarket food sales), predominantly a sale (provision of food by restaurant), pure hire (car rental) or predominantly a hire (long-term vehicle rental with back-up repair service), but should also be held to cover hybrid transactions such as the insertion of a heart pacemaker, the hire of opera-glasses, the loan of a hospital wheelchair, or the supply of free toothbrushes in a dental surgery. The accompanying service and the professional or non-professional status of the defendant can both be ignored.

It should be noted here that in place of 'put into circulation' the CPA uses the apparently narrower notion of 'supply' which requires (according to UK case law on that term) that ownership or a right to temporary possession has passed. So interpreted, the term would probably not catch the important sub-class of transactions in which, although products are provided in association with the supply of other products (the supermarket trolley or water fountain examples) or the performance of services (where the service-giver uses a defective tool or provides access to defective facilities such as waiting room chairs, hospital beds, etc), neither ownership nor a right to temporary possession of the defective product passes. It might also exclude the giving of access to laundromat machines or static gymnasium equipment, even though no service accompanies that transaction[69] and even though such products can only reach the ultimate consumer via transactions falling short of transfer of ownership or a right to temporary possession. In theory litigation of such issues might clarify the policy bases of the Directive because in interpreting the term

---

LR 625, 627. See also *Lowrie* v *City of Evanston* 365 NE 2d 923, 928 (1977) 'the policy reasons underlying the strict products liability concept should be considered in determining whether something is a product within the meaning of its use in the Restatement ...'; *Heller* v *Cadral Corpn* 406 NE 2d 88, 89 (1980); G Walker 'The Expanding Applicability of Strict Liability Principles: How is a "Product' Defined?" [1986] Tort & Ins LJ 1, 4; Wunsch, op cit 344–5; S Brook 'Sales-Service Hybrid Transactions: A Policy Approach' (1974) 28 SWLJ 575 ('if the "product" carrying the potential risks from defects was a service ...').

67 *Schriner* v *Pennsylvania Power & Light Co* 501 A 2d 1128, 1134 (1985).

68 *Anderson* v *Farmers Hybrid Cos* 408 NE 2d 1194, 1199 (1980). See criticism by D Harvey 'The Applicability of Strict Products Liability to Sales of Live Animals' [1982] Iowa LR 803.

69 Although compare *Blakemore* v *Bristol & Exeter Rly Co* (1858) 8 E & B 1035 120 ER 385, where

'possession' in domestic law, UK courts have taken into account the perceived social functions of the legal rule in issue.[70] But, in practice, the fact that primary liability is channelled to product manufacturers means that relevant litigation is unlikely to occur either in domestic courts or the ECJ; for instance, the laundromat owner would simply name the manufacturer of the machine, and the issue of whether he himself had 'supplied' the product for the purposes of the CPA or had 'put the product into circulation' for the purposes of the Directive would never come to be determined by a court.

To sum up: US courts have attempted to use the nature of the transaction in which the defendant was involved as a device to maintain coherent and workable boundaries to the product rule. The strategy stems from two underlying dilemmas in the product rules: firstly, it is not clear why those 'putting products into circulation', etc, should be singled out for special liability; and secondly, even if it were clear, how could we identify from amongst all those who have had some dealing with the product which party or parties constitute the product 'enterprise' for the purposes of imposing liability? The Directive *assumes* that liability should be channelled to the product manufacturer, but it does so at the cost of masking the more fundamental question of why injuries from defective products should be subject to a different legal regime from that governing liability for services. But this question is less easy to evade if the injury is unarguably attributable to a service. If a careful dentist's needle shatters due to a manufacturing defect we might agree that the liability should be channelled to the needle manufacturer. But what if the source of the injury was the service of the dentist, for example, defective use or installation of a perfectly sound product? Should the dentist be liable under the special rule? Should the notion of 'product' encompass a service?

5   THE DEFECTIVE PRODUCTS/DEFECTIVE SERVICES BOUNDARY: IS IT JUSTIFIED?

It is widely assumed that it is possible to distinguish the defective condition of products as a cause of injury from the quality of services; and that both US and European product rules should not apply to injuries due to defective services. In other words, it is widely thought that the concept of a 'product' does not encompass any 'service', and the publication of the European Commission in 1991 of a proposal for a separate Directive on liability for services tends to confirm this approach.[71] Superficially, this distinction appears workable. So, for example, invention, repair, engineering and architectural and other designs would escape liability under the product liability Directive, as would the mere provision of information, even – if the distinction was strictly applied – if it is in the hard-copy form of, say, a survey, map, will, cookbook or software-encoded disc because what is defective here is the information and this

---

the defendant-railway maintained a crane at its station to assist its customers to unload their goods, the court held the transaction constituted by its use was a gratuitous bailment. (The defendant was the 'mere lender of a chattel', 391.) For other examples at the borderline, see fns 59–60.

70 See D R Harris 'The Concept of Possession in English Law' in *Oxford Essays in Jurisprudence* (First Series) ed A G Guest (Oxford, Clarendon Press, 1961) 69, 71–2, 78–9.

71 Proposal for a Council Directive on the Liability of Suppliers of Services, OJ No C 12/8, 18.1.91. In

is a service. A fortiori, the provision of medical diagnosis or accountant's advice would lie outside the rule. There are two problems with this boundary. First, are there convincing reasons *for the law of tort* to distinguish between injurious products and injurious services? Secondly, could such a line be maintained in practice? In my view, both of these questions should be answered in the negative; and this fact imposes considerable and perhaps intolerable expansionary pressure on the concept of 'product'.

Underlying substantive policies do not support the exclusion of defective services. The economic policies of prevention and price deterrence and many of the pragmatic subordinate rationales of the rules such as risk-spreading, facilitating claims and compensation, apply equally to defective services.[72] Even the moral enterprise liability idea would not seem to distinguish between defective goods and defective services, and certainly its earlier weak manifestation in an employer's strict vicarious liability to compensate for injuries due to employee torts was not limited to injuries caused by or through equipment but also encompassed injuries caused by the defective services of employees. Indeed, it was concern about compensating fellow-employees for the latter type of injury which led to the introduction of workers' compensation (see Chapter 8, under heading 1(c)). It is not self-evident why the commercial operations of, say, dry cleaners and car repairers are not subject to the same moral considerations as those of goods manufacturers.

One argument used to support the exclusion of defective services from the rules is the alleged difficulty in operating a strict standard for services. For example, in the US case of *Lewis v Big Powderhorn Mountain Ski Co* (1976), it was argued that evaluating services meant evaluating conduct, and that this could only be done by applying a negligence standard.[73] But this is not so. A talisman of strict liability is the treatment of unknowable risks, and it is feasible to judge a service-giver's performance according to the state of knowledge existing at the time of trial. Although the common law and statutory presumption that a service-giver only undertakes to use reasonable skill and care is well-known and especially strong in the case of professionals, it is rebuttable.[74] In a series of cases where the service involved the design of a product or structure, British judges have been willing to accept that the service-giver had implicitly promised that the design would be fit to do what it was

---

the US see, eg, *La Rossa v Scientific Design Co* 402 F 2d 937 (1968) (design of manufacturing plant); *Chubb Group v C F Murphy and Associates* 656 SW 2d 766 (1983) (design of Kemper Arena); *Castaldo v Pittsburgh Des Moins Steel Co* 376 A 2d 88 (1977) (design of storage tank); *Laukkanen v Jewel Tea Co* 222 NE 2d 584 (1966) (design of supermarket pylon); *Hunt v Guarantee Electric Co* 667 SW 2d 9 (1984) (design of industrial process); *Lemley v J & B Tire Co* 426 F Supp 1378 (1977) (repair of brakes); *Hoffman v Simplot Aviation Inc* 539 P 2d 584 (1975) (repair of airplane); *Hoover v Montgomery Ward & Co* 528 P 2d 76 (1974) (installation of new tyre); *Gagne v Bertran* 275 P 2d 15 (1954) (soil engineering report); *Cardozo v True* 342 So 2d 1053 (1977) (cookbook recipe: implied warranty case). On software see J Stapleton 'Software, Information and the Concept of Product' (1989) 9 Tel Aviv U Studies in Law 147.

72 *Peterson v Lou Backrodt Chevrolet Co* 329 NE 2d 785, 788 (1975); *Lewis v Big Powderhorn Mountain Ski Corpn* 245 NW 2d 81, 83 (1976); M Greenfield 'Consumer Protection in Service Transactions – Implied Warranties and Strict Liability in Tort' (1974) Utah LR 661; Comment 'Guidelines for Extending Implied Warranties to Service Markets' (1976) 125 U Penn LR 365; J Chait 'Continuing the Common Law Response to the New Industrial State: The Extension of Enterprise Liability to Consumer Services' (1974) 22 UCLA LR 401; W Powers, 'Distinguishing Between Products and Services in Strict Liability' (1984) 62 NC LR 415, 434.

73 *Lewis v Big Powderhorn Mountain Ski Corpn* 245 NW 2d 81, 82 (1976).

74 Supply of Goods and Services Act 1982, ss 13, 16. On professionals see G Treitel *The Law of Con-*

expected to do, and was liable for failing to achieve it despite the exercise of due care.[75] Even in cases where the condition of goods is not involved, there are classes of services where the application of a strict standard is quite straightforward. For example, where the service is the giving of objective information (eg in maps) the information would be required to be accurate or at least not dangerously misleading. A number of the relatively rare US cases where strict tort liability has been imposed for the provision of services concern aerial navigation charts and illustrate the workability of such a strict standard in this class of services case.[76] Even in advice cases, a strict standard might be held to be discharged by adequate warnings of, say, the volatility of financial markets or the inadequacy of medical knowledge on a point, and this would reduce the areas in which a strict standard for advice appears unworkable. Finally, support for the argument that a strict standard is workable comes from the EC moves towards a Directive on liability for services: the European Commission had first envisaged a no-fault liability, and although the proposal published in 1991 imposes only fault-based liability with a reversal of the burden of proof on the issue of fault, consumer organizations continued to lobby for strict liability based on the quality and safety of the service provided as judged at the time of trial, that is hindsight cost/benefit strict liability (see Figure 5.1, page 97).[77]

A second argument used to support the distinction is that while proof of negligence-in-fact typically presents severe problems in the case of goods, these are said to be much less severe in the case of services.[78] Typically goods are mass-produced at a time and place distant from the involvement of the plaintiff so that proof of fault is said to be more difficult than in the case of services, where the defendant's activity is likely to be more accessible to the plaintiff's investigation. Even if this intuition were correct, it would be odd that one of the most important boundaries of the new tort rule depended heavily on such a pragmatic argument as ease of proof because the more important this factor is regarded, the stronger becomes the argument for a reform based simply on the reversal of the burden of proof in negligence. But is the intuition itself correct? Many goods are not mass-produced, but US courts and Euro-

---

tract 8th edn (London, Stevens, 1991) 739–740. On the corresponding presumption of strict obligations as to quality in contracts relating to goods (where bailor, seller, etc, acts in course of a business) see Sale of Goods Act 1979, s 14; Supply of Goods and Services Act 1982, ss 4 and 9; now irrebuttable as against a person acting as a 'consumer': Unfair Contract Terms Act 1977, ss 6(2) and 7.

75 *Samuels* v *Davis* [1943] KB 526 (dentist's supply of false teeth), contrast *Barbie* v *Rogers* 425 SW 2d 342 (1968); *Independent Broadcasting Authority* v *EMI Electronics Ltd* (1980) 14 B LR 1, 47–8 (design of television mast); *Greaves & Co (Contractors) Ltd* v *Baynham, Meikle & Partners* [1975] 1 WLR 1095, 1101 (design of warehouse). See Treitel, op cit. As to excludability of such implied terms, see Unfair Contract Terms Act 1977, s 3(2)(b) and Law Commission *Implied Terms in Contracts for the Supply of Services* (Law Com No 156) (Cmnd 9773)(1986) para 3.28. See below fn 82 and accompanying text.

76 *Fluor Corpn* v *Jeppesen & Co* 216 Cal Rptr 68 (1985); *Salooney* v *Jeppesen & Co* 707 F 2d 671 (1983); *Times Mirror Co* v *Sisk* 593 P 2d 924 (1978); D Abney, 'Liability for Defective Aeronautical Charts' (1986) 52 J Air Law & Commerce 323. See also *O'Laughlin* v *Minnesota Natural Gas Co* 253 NW 2d 836 (1977) (installation of furnace in home); *Kopet* v *Klein* 148 NW 2d 385 (1967) (installation of water softener); *Worrell* v *Barnes* 484 P 2d 573 (1971) (installation of gas fitting during house remodelling).

77 OJ No C 12/8, 18.1.91. National Consumer Council *Response to the Draft Directive on Liability for Services* (PD 48/D4/91, November 1991). The Commission withdrew the draft Directive for reconsideration after the Edinburgh Summit of December 1992 in light of the subsidiarity doctrine.

78 W Powers 'Distinguishing Between Products and Services in Strict Liability' (1984) 62 NC LR 415.

pean reformers have explicitly rejected this as a reason not to apply the new liability to the supply of those goods.[79] Moreover, some services are mass-produced or carried out at a distant time and place (or both) – eg nappy-cleaning and production of standard software packages, maps, etc, – and this has led some US courts to conclude, atypically, that certain examples of services should qualify as 'products' to which s 402A should apply. Even if it were an acceptable generalization that goods are mass-produced and services are not, surely it is at least arguable that negligence coped better with the manufacturing defects flowing from the mass-production of goods than it ever did with defective services; so if there had been a primary concern with ease of proof, manufacturing errors would have come lower on the reform agenda than services. But, as we have seen, manufacturing errors were the predominant concern, at least in the US. Even in the area of defective quality and design, is it so clear that proof of lack of reasonable care is easier in the case of services than of goods? Certainly, in the case of professional services the difficulties of providing negligence-in-fact are notorious.

The roots of the distinction may lie in the implied warranties of contract law which draw a similar distinction between goods and services. If warranty law *is* the source of the distinction, many criticisms could be made. Firstly, as we have seen (Chapter 10, under headings 2 and 9), it does not follow that a distinction derived from contract law and the allegedly different actual or 'legitimate' expectations of contracting consumers should be allowed to influence what an injured bystander is entitled to expect from the defendant. Secondly, even if the distinction did once reflect the assumptions of contracting parties, does it reflect contractual or consumer expectations today? Do buyers and users really have expectations about the safety and quality of services which are lower than the minimum standards set down for goods in sales law? There is a misleading argument to this effect based on the alleged nature of the service-provider's activity. Thus, in refusing to apply the s 402A tort standard to services, US courts routinely rely on a statement of Judge Traynor:

> The services of experts are sought because of their special skill. They have a duty to exercise the ordinary skill and competence of members of their profession ... Those who hire such persons are not justified in expecting infallibility, but can expect only reasonable care and competence. They purchase service, not insurance.[80]

This is assertion, not justification. It could equally well be asserted that those who buy and use goods are not justified in expecting infallibility; that they purchase products not insurance. But the passage is typical of influential US precedents involving service-providers perceived as 'professionals'[81] in which reference is made to the need to give skilled judgment on issues of intrinsic complexity, to uncertainty of results, the greater likelihood of undiscoverable risks in this context, individualized service and, particularly in the case of medical services, the public interest in the availability and affordability of such services. Even if these factors apply to all *professional* services (and even if this class could be clearly defined), their force as a justification for the exemption of *all* services from s 402A and the Directive is dramatically weakened by the existence of a diverse non-professional service sector to which they have little, if any, application.

---

79 Law Commission para 51.
80 *Gagne* v *Bertran* 275 P 2d 15, 21 (1954).
81 A vague concept at the margin because it depends on institutional factors (see fn 83 below).

Many non-professional services (eg dry-cleaning) are not characterized by judgments on complex issues. Some are 'mass-produced' and to the public appear indistinguishable from goods: what evidence is there that expectations of reliability of air navigational charts are not comparable to those of aircraft brakes? Comparable expectations are most likely where the defective service manifests itself in a dangerous good. Is the public likely to have significantly different expectations according to whether the chemical residues in clothing which cause dermatitis are due to defective dry-cleaning or to defective manufacture? And if expectations are comparable, why should buyers, users or bystanders not be *entitled* to the same protection, regardless of the source of injury? The strength of this argument is particularly clear where the service results in the production of dangerous goods or realty, and it appears to underlie some modern British case law on warranties where the courts have been willing to recognize strict implied warranties of fitness in contracts for the design and supply of things such as a warehouse. Professor Treitel suggests these cases might support a more general principle. Using the example of an architect, he states that 'there is considerable support for the view that, where he designs a structure, he gives an 'absolute warranty' that it will be fit for his client's purposes'.[82] This approach seems equally applicable to other services affecting the condition of goods such as installation, repair and servicing. Even if there is some relationship between the scope of the tort liability in the Directive and the expectations or entitlements reflected in warranty law, if warranties implied into some service contracts can be strict, there is no reason why the Directive should not apply at least to services of those types even if its liability is strict.

Importantly, these British cases and Professor Treitel's argument concern services rendered by professionals, suggesting that many activities of professionals do not have those characteristics which have been said to distinguish services from the supply of defective goods. On this basis the boundary line should be drawn, if at all, between certain professional activities and the supply of goods, and all other services. Nonetheless, under the actual boundary both professional and non-professional service-givers, their insurers and perhaps courts will find it difficult to justify applying different forms of liability to different aspects of their activities, fault liability in relation to the quality of service and strict liability under Article 3(3) if the injury was caused by defectiveness in a product supplied in the course of provision of a service. The fear is that imposition of strict liability on professionals – in particular health care providers – might lead them to practise defensively and increase the cost of their services to cover increased insurance premiums. This may have unacceptable effects on the availability and affordability of these services. But the more rational response to this concern would be to exempt only some[83] professional groups from the strict liability rather than to exempt all service-givers.

Finally, in the nineteenth century there was judicial concern with inequality of bargaining power in cases in which the original seller was in a better position than the buyer to gauge quality. Concern about such inequality between commercial entities

---

82 See above fn 75; G Treitel *Remedies for Breach of Contract* (Oxford, Clarendon Press, 1988) 29; N Palmer 'The Supply of Goods and Services Act 1982' (1983) 46 Camb LJ 619, 629–630. The italicized term was used by Lord Denning MR in Greaves, op cit at 1101. Contrast *City of Mounds View* v *Walijarvi* 263 NW 2d 420 (1978).

83 Separate defined exemptions being necessary because the notion of 'professional' is notoriously vague and in Europe is sometimes even used synonymously with 'commercial' (see under heading 3, above).

and the economic loss it could cause buyers led to the special treatment of *contracts* for the sale of goods (see Chapter 2, under heading 2). But it was the inequality which justified special treatment, not the fact that the transaction was one concerning *goods*. In the twentieth century substantial concern developed about another form of inequality of bargaining power, namely the inability of individual purchasers of mass-produced goods and mass services (such as carriage by rail, and so on) to rene-gotiate the terms of standard contracts, in particular standard exemption clauses. The resultant controls gave no extra protection to the consumer-buyer of mass-produced goods over the consumer-buyer of mass services.[84] Similarly, concern that private individuals had difficulty appreciating and resisting attempts to exclude business lia-bility for negligence, the increasing incidence of such attempts, and the particular importance now attached to keeping open avenues of compensation for personal injury, led to legislation to control contract terms and notices purporting to exclude or restrict such liability.[85] But once again the nature of the control does not vary according to whether the relevant transaction involved goods or services.[86]

So although the doctrinal origin of the product rules in the warranty is clear, they do not possess the coherence of the warranty rules because the evil allegedly being addressed by the product rules is quite different from the perceived evil which determined the sphere of operation of the warranty. Reformers of products law were not concerned, as had been the nineteenth century reformist judges, with economic loss caused by inequality of bargaining power in certain transactions (sale of goods), but with physical loss to plaintiffs who often could not sue in contract. Therefore, the central limitation of the new product liability rules to defective products seems inappropriate. References to the warranty origin of the new rules do not explain why it is sensible to treat product injuries preferentially. Indeed, judged from the perspec-tive of improving the position of strangers in respect of physical losses, the goods retailer's strict obligations to buyers for physical injuries should have been seen as an anomaly. Protection of strangers is the province of tort, and in response to claims for physical injury, tort had not found it justified to distinguish between the victims of defective goods and defective services.

6   THE DEFECTIVE PRODUCTS/DEFECTIVE SERVICES BOUNDARY: IS IT WORKABLE?

Is the distinction between products and services workable in the context of a consumer remedy for physical loss? The answer is: not very convincingly. If we ignore whether the distinction is justified, we will see that while it makes sense to speak separately of goods and services,[87] and to speak separately of contracts

---

84 Unfair Contract Terms Act 1977, s 3.

85 Ibid, s 2(1). See also s 2(2).

86 Where modern statutory controls do vary according to the subject-matter of the transaction, the explanations given relate not to the subject-matter per se but to other considerations. For example, while purported exclusions of the statutory implied terms as to quality and fitness for purpose in consumer transactions were invalidated, the parallel warranty as to the quality of a service is only subject to a requirement of reasonableness, because inter alia the Law Commission was not con-vinced that the latter practice was common: *Implied Terms in Contracts for the Supply of Services* (Law Com No 156, 1986) para 3.21.

87 Although there can be tricky issues here: if electricity had not been expressly included in the defini-tion of 'product' in the Directive and CPA, would it be a 'good'?

(predominantly) for the sale of goods and contracts (predominantly) for the supply of services, the concepts of defective goods and defective services are not easily separable. One illustration of this is the set of cases in which information is provided in a hard copy form. Earlier (under heading 5), we noted that if services are intended to be excluded, this should strictly require the exclusion of the mere provision of (defective) information even if it is in hard-copy form of, say, a survey, map, cookbook or a software encoded disc, because what is defective here is the defective information – and information is a service. Yet in promoting the Consumer Protection Bill, Lord Lucas of Chilworth thought that an incorrectly calibrated ruler would be caught by the Directive and CPA;[88] no-one is quite sure what side of the line software will be held to fall; while it is assumed by many that a dangerous error in a cookbook would not be caught. The ruler problem cannot even superficially be accommodated by noting that the Directive is expressed in terms of defective 'products' (not 'goods') and arguing that the concept of 'product' can be sufficiently wider than 'goods' to catch defective rulers. This sort of bootstraps logic could, after all, apply to other cases such as software and the cookbook example. The important conceptual question is how is it that such cases seem confusingly to straddle the line between defective services and defective goods/products so that, until a court makes a rule, we cannot be sure what their classification is. The key to this problem is that no such clear line exists. This is because the concepts overlap: indeed, in *most* legal claims the alleged 'defect' in the good, that is the condition in it which is the cause of the injury, will itself be the result of a human act or omission, or, in other words, a service. This means that attempts to restrict a liability rule to defective products will fail to eliminate claims more accurately described as arising from defective services.

Almost all defects in goods can at some level be more accurately described as attributable to human agency. Often this is not immediately apparent. For example, it may not be obvious that manufacturing defects (such as an incorrectly calibrated ruler) are traceable to the human design or human operation of the manufacturing process or of its machinery. Similarly, design defects in goods can be traced to the activities of the designer of the goods or the party responsible for the accompanying warnings, instructions, packaging, and the like, neither party necessarily being the producer of the finished product.[89] In some cases the human origin of the defect appearing in a good is clearer to see – as, perhaps, in the case of a dangerous recipe published in a cookbook. But in both the ruler and cookbook cases what is defective is the idea or information conveyed, and the origin of the defect is human conduct. This means that attempts to draw an explicit, coherent line between such cases are doomed to failure.[90] In this light, even arguments in favour of special protection for

88 Lord Lucas of Chilworth (a relevant 'promoter of the Bill' for the purposes of *Pepper* (*Inspector of Taxes*) v *Hart* [1993] 1 All ER 42), 483 Official Report (HL), col 800.

89 In which case, the latter's activity can be seen merely as the non-defective *service* of assembly: see this argument used unsuccessfully to resist imposition of strict liability in *Challonor* v *Day & Zimmerman & Co* 512 F 2d 77 (1975). For example, the producer of the finished product may have followed the explicit instructions or design of an out-of-house designer who may, for example, be a buyer who gives his/her own specifications (see Pearson para 1248 – although here volenti would presumably prevent successful claims by the buyer) or where a pharmacist simply follows a formula dictated by a GP. There will also come a point where the activities of a repairer or re-conditioner cause such a major reconstruction that such a person qualifies as the 'assembler' or 'producer' of a new product and becomes liable for the workmanship of design which he has built into the object.

90 Such as that of the parliamentary drafters in Clause 3(3) and 3(4) Consumer Protection Bill, rejected with uncomprehending disdain by the House of Lords: 483 Official Report (HL), cols 797–802; 485 Official Report (HL), cols 847–8.

the communication of ideas – on the basis of which US courts refuse to impose s402A liability for dangerous errors in publications – seem somewhat incoherent.[91] What is more, the general point being made here about underlying human conduct applies to virtually all manufacturing errors and defective designs even where the defect has nothing to do with the provision of information: the snail in the ginger-beer and the drug which causes birth defects are both usually traceable to human conduct.

An important illustration of the point is provided by public utilities such as gas and water. Here the alleged 'defect' may be contamination which raises the sort of issues familiar from *Donoghue* v *Stevenson*.[92] But alternatively the 'defect' in the utility supplied may be that it was supplied at dangerously high or low or fluctuating levels of pressure or voltage. Here the hand of human agency becomes clearer. Indeed, in the case of electricity – explicitly included within the definition of a 'product' by the Directive (Article 2) – a little reflection on its nature highlights how artificial it is to describe the utility in such cases as 'defective'. It is a much more accurate description to say that on those occasions when it might be said that the supply was 'defective',[93] what in fact is 'defective' is the form or way in which it was generated or the way it was delivered.[94] This in turn may be due directly to human agency or indirectly via the design of generating, transmitting or delivery equipment. The fact that it is quite evident that services underlie defective electricity, has created substantial confusion in the United States as courts try to decide if they should describe electricity as a defective product falling within s 402A. Without directly acknowledging the categorization problem, US courts have resolved cases on other, arbitrary grounds such as that the electricity caused injury at a place after the point of supply (usually held to be the local meter), in which case electricity tends to be deemed a 'product', and the liability rule of s 402A is imposed.

That defective services underlie defects in products means that it is quite misleading to argue, as is often done,[95] that the product rule shifted the analytical focus from

91 *Cardozo* v *True* 342 So 2d 1053, 1056–7 (1977).
92 See eg *AB* v *South West Water Services Ltd* [1993] QB 507, CA, the first reported case involving Part I of the CPA.
93 Although in this context there may be many occasions on which voltage fluctuations are due to such complex factors that they could not reasonably be guarded against, given current technology, and therefore would not fall below the safety a person was entitled to expect; see R Bragg 'Liability for Voltage Variations and the CPA 1987' (1987) 84 Law Soc Gaz 3008, who also notes the problem of determining the 'producer' if electricity is to be the 'defective product'.
94 Under the CPA such defects are excluded by the definition of 'relevant time' at which the defect must exist (time of generation), s 4(2). *Query*, will the relevant time under the Directive (the time the defendant 'put the product into circulation', Article 7(a)), be interpreted to mean a later time, eg the time of supply through a local meter? *Query*, also whether, if electricity had not been *expressly* included in the definition of 'product' in the Directive and CPA, would it qualify? What about that form of delivered electricity which drives telephone receivers to provide the 'service' of telephones? Will there be liability under the CPA for power-surges along telephone lines which cause injury to hearing? Another illustration of the point from the spectrum of electromagnetic radiation would be X-rays (on which the Directive is silent) supplied at too high a wavelength, see *Dubin* v *Michael Reese Hospital* 393 NE 2d 588 (1979).
95 See eg *Sutkowski* v *Universal Marian Corpn* 281 NE 2d 749 (1972); *Barker* v *Lull Engineering Co* 573 P 2d 443, 447 (1978); P Keeton 'Product Liability and the Meaning of Defect' (1973) 4 St Mary's LJ 30, 33; S Birnbaum 'Unmasking the Test for Design Defect: From Negligence [to Warranty] to Strict Liability to Negligence' (1980) 33 Vand LR 593, 601.

a defendant-producer's behaviour (on which the tort of negligence explicitly focuses) to the quality and safety of the product and thus removed evaluation of human conduct from adjudication. All it does is to require evaluation of the conduct by evaluating its end product rather than by directly evaluating the conduct itself. By focusing on defective products the rules necessarily involve liability for the results of those defective services which result in the defective condition of goods, while drawing an odd distinction between different forms of human conduct: 'pure services', that is human conduct which injures other than by the route of the condition of property is *not* covered by the US rule or the Directive; but other conduct, or 'services', which does result in a relevant condition in a product, *may* be covered.

Not even all human conduct which results in a relevant condition in a product is covered. Firstly, there are cases where the condition was introduced by a 'downstream service-giver', such as a garage mechanic who misaligns the brakes he is substituting or repairing in the plaintiff's already-bought car. None of such cases is covered either by the US rule or the Directive. These rules only cover product injuries arising from conditions already present when the product was put into circulation. Secondly, the focus of the rules on the production (and supply) of defective products can obscure, and indeed pervert, at least one alleged objective of the reform, which is to deter the creation of certain dangerous conditions in goods. For such deterrence to occur, liability must usually be directed to the person to whose conduct the injury is principally attributable. Very often, of course, this responsible party also happens to be a party who can be held liable under s 402A of the Restatement under the Directive, for example, the producer who has used in-house designers or process engineers or who is vicariously liable for its employees' acts in the course of manufacture, or in drafting the accompanying instructions or warnings, and so on. But where the party principally responsible is, for example, an 'upstream out-of-house' designer, that person will escape liability under the regimes contained in the Directive and the Restatement. This is because neither regime imposes liability on the person to whose conduct the injury was principally attributable unless this conduct produces a defective condition in a good *and* that person supplied it. Pure services such as medical advice and taxi-driving are, as we have seen, excluded by the first condition; and trade-mark licensors, up-stream out-of-house designers and downstream servicers would seem to be excluded by the second. In the former group of cases no remedy is available under the new rule. In the latter a remedy *will* lie against the producer of the product if the defect existed in the product when it left his hands. Whatever the arguments for holding the producer jointly liable with, say, the up-stream out-of-house designer in such cases, producers will no doubt wonder why their activities are vulnerable to liability under the rules while those of the party principally responsible for the defect are not liable at all. Since the regime under the Directive and CPA lacks clear recourse rules, the proper relocation of liability costs on to the service-giver in order to promote prevention is effectively left to turn on the efficiency of private contractual arrangements.

The point here is that if prevention is a goal, its achievement requires that all human behaviour which produces dangerous conditions in products should be the focus of liability. But the focus on defective products per se detracts from that goal by obscuring the human origin of the relevant condition and allowing inappropriate parties to be designated the responsible parties. Of course, the more obvious the source of the defect in a service, the more difficult it becomes to explain and justify drawing a line between defective products and defective services. In the case of defective premises, defects in design are often clearly due to the services of a party higher up the chain, such as architects, structural engineers and surveyors of whom it may be difficult to say that they had put the relevant property 'into circulation', and not to the conduct of parties on whom the Directive would focus liability: the manufacturer (the builder) or supplier (vendor). Similarly, the human origin of manufacturing (construction) defects in realty is often patently obvious. In operation the exclusion of realty from the Directive certainly helps to obscure the human origin of defects in property, and perhaps the fact that the human origin of defects in realty is often more obvious than the human origin of defects in products may even have been a submerged factor in that exclusion.

Concentration on the concept of a 'defective product' not only obscures the human source of defective conditions but thereby hinders realization of the policy goals of reformers. Even where the relevant condition of the product arose under the control of the manufacturer, the factors relevant to whether a product is defective, under both the US rule and under the Directive, such as the availability of safer substitutes, and the development-risk defence, demand an evaluation of the quality choices of the producer. Except in the case of manufacturing errors, the need for such an evaluation has emerged in the US as the centre of dispute in litigation, particularly in the 'failure to warn' form of complaint; and it will be similarly central in litigation under the Directive, which explicitly links the notion of defectiveness to warnings.[96]

So the question is: if the separation out for special treatment of injuries caused by defective products cannot be justified by reference to the warranty origin of the product-liability rules, nor because it is possible in this way to shift the enquiry away from human conduct, how did the concept of the defective product become the focus for reform? Apart from the possibility that this was merely the result of an inappropriate development of the warranty idea, could it also be the result of the illogical way in which cases of product-caused injury are perceived? Where human conduct results in the defective condition of a good it is possible *to pretend* that we are judging a product rather than human conduct, at least until the realities of the law in operation make the pretence impossible. This would help explain why, for example, the new liability is directed at the producer of the product and not *also* at the author of the defect (such as an upstream designer). More importantly, it might also help to explain why, initially at least, a truly strict standard for product cases was acceptable to European reformers.

Strict liability looks at results and ignores the reasonableness of the defendant's conduct. The form of strict liability which UK and European reformers initially recommended was one which judged the costs of the product with hindsight and did not allow a defence of unforeseeable risk. Was it that reformers were able initially to

---

96 A corresponding problem exists in sales law where the human source of most poor quality goods is superficially masked by the notion of 'unmerchantability'. Again it is in the warnings context that the inadequacy of the goods/services boundary is exposed. Already this has led one commentator to doubt whether s 14 of the Sale of Goods Act 1979 ('unmerchantability') went beyond physical shortcomings in goods themselves and also encompassed misinformation such as misleading attached instructions, because he could see this was indistinguishable from the type of information provided in an inaccurate textbook or map (see A Tettenborn 'Wild Oats and the Sale of Goods' (1986) 45 Camb LJ 389, 391, a casenote on *Wormell v RHM Agriculture (East) Ltd* [1986] 1 WLR 336). But this suggested tightening of the sales boundary would still fail to eliminate the problem, since the physical shortcomings of goods can also usually be attributable to human acts or omissions.

recommend strict liability for manufacturers, despite the general modern hostility of their legal systems to strict liability for physical losses, because in the case of goods (movables), the underlying involvement of human conduct can be masked by concentration on the object and on the concept of 'defect' which is superficially devoid of any reference to human conduct? Certainly in the early development of the US rule, manufacturing errors were the central concern, and here human failing is easily masked: the availability of the production-line norm can be allowed to pre-empt an evaluation of the defendant's safety choices.

On the other hand, when faced with the question of whether to impose strict lia bility, including liability for risks not reasonably discoverable, on defendants for conduct such as taxi-driving, engineering, surveying, and so on, US courts and European reformers have baulked. Is this because the connection between the plaintiff's injury and the human conduct which caused it is obvious? Once this connection is out in the open, the commitment to strict liability is severely and directly tested. Compare the following examples of unforeseeable risks. Suppose that a producer, after exhaustive testing, markets a cosmetic consisting of a simple blend of naturally occurring substances (for example, milk and grass) which carries an unforeseeable risk to users of developing cancer ten years after use. According to the initial European reform recommendations, such risks of a defective product were to be borne by the producer as a 'cost of the enterprise'. But reformers baulked at imposing strict liability in the equivalent situation of a business selling the 'health tip' that such and such a home-made blend of milk and grass was a useful cosmetic. The commitment to strict liability based on 'enterprise liability' never extended to pure services. So too it eventually crumbled when industry opponents of the new law emphasized the human face of the liability and the perceived unreasonableness of holding liable producers who had acted with all reasonable care but had failed to discover an undiscoverable risk.[97]

This suggestion that the reform focus on defective products may have been strengthened by a doomed attempt to shift attention away from human conduct and make the imposition of strict liability more palatable, gains some support from the attitude of reformers to computer software. Software, being mere information, is not a 'good' for the purposes of the UK law of supply of goods.[98] Were defective software to cause a plane or car to crash or a heart-lung machine to cut out, those thereby injured could of course use the Directive/CPA to sue the manufacturer of the

97 Although there was no equivalent initial commitment to a strict liability regime for producers in the US – that is, a commitment for the liability to cover undiscoverable risks – it is significant that the odd attempt by the New Jersey Supreme Court at consistency in the application of its enterprise-lia-bility rationalized product rule by holding a producer liable for (failing to warn of) an unforeseeable risk was denounced and successfully side-lined by an argument that emphasized the human limita-tions of producers, the injustice of a law requiring 'omniscience' from defendant-producers. (*Beshada* v *Johns-Manville Products Corpn* (1982) 447 A 2d 539. Comment 'Requiring Omnis-cience: The Duty to Warn of Scientifically Undiscoverable Product Defects' (1983) 71 Geo LJ 1635.) After three decades of litigation concerning the US rule, not only is the central concern with the reasonableness of the defendants' conduct now evident, but it is highlighted by the phenomenon that litigated cases (virtually all of which relate to alleged design defects) often include failure-to-warn allegations, complaints clearly directed at human behaviour.
98 J Stapleton 'Software, Information and the Concept of Product' (1989) 9 Tel Aviv U Studies in Law 147. The fact that information like this can be, and usually is, reduced to hard-copy form for com-mercial purposes is doctrinally irrelevant. Contrast *Advent Systems Ltd* v *Unisys Corpn* 925 F 2d 670 (1991) (software a 'good' within UCC on the basis of policy arguments). See also S Singleton 'Product Liability and Computer Software' Prod Liab Internat [Aug 1992] 114.

conglomerate product which had malfunctioned because of the defective software component in the same way that a manufacturer of a finished product can be sued in respect of defective accompanying instructions even though these originated, say, from an up-stream designer. But could the injured choose to sue the manufacturer of the software itself, as they would want to do if the tangible product (eg plane) had been supplied before the relevant software was incorporated? At first they would seem to have problems establishing a cause of action under the CPA which defines 'product' in terms of 'goods'. But in the market place, software is widely described as a 'product'[99] and some commentators suggest that defective software may be held to fall under the wider term 'movables' used in the Directive. The European Court of Justice might, it is widely argued, take a 'flexible' attitude to the notion of 'product' which will allow it to be expanded more widely than 'goods' to allow in phenomena which, in policy terms, are 'like' defective goods.[100]

But what is it about defective software that suggests it might be like defective goods? Is it like goods because, although it is a service, the human origin of errors in a program is less obvious than the human origin of most pure services? Is their human origin masked in a way that facilitates imposition of liability? Perhaps. Certainly the ECJ might catch software if it continued to use a very general objectified formula of 'product' such as 'something capable of money valuation and of being an *object* of commercial transactions' (see Chapter 11, under heading 3) – a wide formula consistent with current European Commission usage which describes the activities of life insurers as the provision of a range of 'products'.[101] But it should be noted that the success of the term 'product' as a way of masking the involvement of human conduct is variable. Suppose that the designer (A) of a navigational software program incorrectly enters the height of a mountain, causing a plane to crash. If the software package is a 'product' for the purposes of the Directive, is a map incorrectly drawn by B, which carries the same incorrect information to the pilot, also a product?[102] If so, suppose that the same information is conveyed to the pilot orally by an on-board navigator (C); is he the supplier of a 'product'? In all cases, of course, it is the same piece of incorrect information produced by human error which causes the crash; all that changes is the form in which the information is delivered and the degree to which the human error is masked.

In deciding whether 'defective software' is a 'defective product' within the Directive, the ECJ will have to identify what it is about defective products which makes claims arising out of the injuries they cause special. The warranty origin of the focus on defective goods does not provide the answer. Nor does the fact that many goods are mass-produced, because liability under the Directive is not confined to mass-produced goods and, in any case, non-goods such as software and maps can be mass-produced and cause physical injury. For the same reasons, the complexity of

---

99 IBM has routinely referred to their programs as 'products'; see R Freed 'Products Liability in the Computer Age' [1977] Jurimetries J 270, 277.

100 S Whittaker 'European Product Liability and Intellectual Products' (1989) 105 LQR 125; E Hondius 'The Impact of the Products Liability Directive on Legal Development and Consumer Protection in Western Europe' (1989) 4 Canterbury LR 34.

101 See Commission of the European Community *The Week in Europe* WE/8/91, WE/26/92, WE/40/92.

102 Contrast US cases on advice-givers. Here a number of courts have been prepared to conclude that aeronautical charts are 'products': P McCowan 'Liability of the Chartmaker' (1980) Insurance Counsel J 359; D Abney 'Liability of Defective Aeronautical Charts' (1986) 52 J Air Law & Commerce 323.

some goods and their sophisticated production techniques do not provide the key. Nor can the reason be that the focus on defects in goods eliminates the necessity to evaluate conduct because it does not. Even if 'product' is confined to the traditional concept of 'good', it is hard to see what is special about defective products. The above discussion suggests that there is no reason for treating them differently. If the vague and often contradictory policy goals mentioned by reformers relating to deterrence, insurability and so on *are* all that is available to guide the ECJ in deciding what are 'products', the concept seems doomed, as in the US, to extend beyond the notion of goods, but in an unpredictable way.

Even now within the actual and proposed laws of the EC important anomalies are evident arising from the intractable problem of distinguishing or justifying the distinction between defective goods and defective services. For example, will the 1991 draft Directive on liability for services catch the up-stream designer in the chain of manufacture of goods since the relevant definition of 'service' is 'any transaction carried out on a commercial basis or by way of a public service ... which does not have as its direct and exclusive object the manufacture of movable property or the transfer of rights in rem or intellectual property rights' (draft Article 2). If it does not, this class responsible for consumer injuries will fall outside the net of EC liability. Conversely, the draft Directive will probably catch product accreditors, endorsers, certifiers and testing bodies. This presents a significant problem, because the draft Directive on services is significantly more attractive to plaintiffs. Under it the plaintiff merely has to prove damage and a causal relation between damage and the supply of the service, whereas under the product liability Directive the plaintiff must also prove defectiveness. Under the draft Directive on services it is the defendant who has the burden of proof to show it was not his or her fault that the service caused the injury. A plaintiff may prefer to sue a relevant service-giver (such as a certification body or an up-stream designer) involved in the production of a defective product under the services Directive rather than to sue the manufacturer under the products Directive. Such de facto channelling to service-givers and away from product manufacturers would not be of great concern if service-providers took sufficient legal advice to know of their right to seek recourse, and if clear recourse rules existed; but they do not. Moreover, as recent UK case law on local authorities' liability for building inspections shows,[103] there are sound arguments against requiring certain bodies to shoulder primary liability if they may be unable to obtain effective recourse against the party who would be the more appropriate party to bear the liability. Will trading standards officers be liable for the injuries caused by the products sold by fly-by-night market traders?

Perhaps the most important area in which inappropriate de facto channelling will occur is where the facts are unclear as to whether, in a hybrid transaction, the injury was caused by the service or the product. Take the example of repair of the brakes during a routine car service in July 1993. In August 1996 the brakes fail and the driver is severely injured. Under the draft services Directive the driver might be able to sue the repairer who will be unlikely to be able to prove lack of fault unless it exercised costly quality control and kept detailed records.[104] The very wide

---

103 *Murphy* v *Brentwood District Council* [1991] 1 AC 398.
104 See discussion in National Consumer Council *Response to the Draft Directive on Liability for Services* (PD 48/D4/91, November 1991) p 21. Note also that the 'defect' may be that the brakes' design encourages negligent installation or servicing.

definition of 'services' in the draft Directive on services increases the inherent problems in the overlap of defective goods and defective services. It not only covers the traditional areas of plumbing, hairdressing, financial advice and design, but also the provision of facilities including schools, nurseries, transportation, hotels, entertainment, playgrounds and other leisure facilities. The scope for the de facto channelling of claims towards service providers and away from manufacturers of goods is clear. It will often be more convenient and advantageous for the person injured by an allegedly defective chair in a hotel, theatre or playground to sue the service provider than the manufacturer. Furthermore, such actions would have a disruptive impact on the settled areas of occupiers' liability law, at least in its application to commercial and public premises.

The draft services Directive has met with great opposition and criticism, not least because it is now becoming apparent how reform of one pocket of liability can unfairly result in a de facto channelling of claims to only one of the parties responsible for the injury. The product liability Directive already does this to some extent, and its long-term stability seems substantially weakened by this flaw, as the following chapter describes in more detail.

7   THE INSTABILITY OF THE 'PUT INTO CIRCULATION' REQUIREMENT

(a)   Pre-circulation injuries by finished products

Earlier we noted, in the context of non-manufacturing defendants, certain problems in applying the concept of 'put into circulation' in Article 7(a) of the Directive; for example whether a bottle on a supermarket shelf has been 'put into circulation' by a retailer, and whether a garage giving away free drinking glasses has 'put them into circulation'. Of more practical relevance, however, is the question of why, even *in claims against the actual manufacturer*, the Directive excludes liability injuries caused by products which have never been 'put into circulation' (however widely interpreted this term is). This boundary excludes any claim by employees or members of the public injured by the defective product during its production and before it has left the producer's control.

The EEC Memo on the initial draft Directive notes that 'one of the conditions for the liability of the producer is that the defect should arise in the producer's production process ... Liability is therefore excluded where the article is put into circulation against the will of the producer, eg through theft'.[105] But the justification for the requirement could hardly rest simply on a desire to protect producers from injuries caused by defective products stolen before they reach the point of supply. Pre-supply criminal tampering with products rather than theft would seem to be a much more pressing problem for defendants, yet it is not one covered by this or any other defence (see Chapter 10, under heading 7(iii)). Nor is the requirement that the product has been put into circulation necessary to exclude from the regime cases where the defect in the product was created after the time it was supplied by the defendant. This is achieved by the defence in Article 7(b). Perhaps, as the EEC Memo on the

105 EEC Memo para 14.

initial draft of the Directive suggests,[106] the requirement is a convenient way of ensuring some proximate causal nexus between responsibility for the product's defect and responsibility for the injury, because it can be taken as showing some form of authorization by the defendant of the victim's exposure. Convenient it may be as a 'bright line rule', but it unnecessarily excludes large classes of otherwise justified claims. We could devise a causal rule which said, for example, that the producer of the defective product was liable (regardless of whether the product had 'entered the stream of commerce' or been 'put into circulation' or been 'supplied') for all injuries foreseeably or directly caused by its defects. The causal connection would be severed by, for example, the intervention of third parties such as thieves who supply defective products without the producer's authority.

Is the justification for the requirement to be found in notions of 'representations' about the safety and quality of the finished product on the market and on the reliance or expectations of consumers? But if mere bystanders injured after the product's entry into 'circulation' can recover under the rule, regardless of reliance or expectations based on representations of chain members, why not someone injured before it gets into circulation? Why should a passer-by injured by a defective chemical exploding when being packed in the producer's warehouse not have a claim, but another passer-by, injured by such an explosion after the supply of the product to a retailer, have one?

The requirement of the product being put into circulation is also unsupported by the moral and economic arguments for the Directive. Take the idea of moral enterprise liability. If the basis of this is responsibility for the initiation of risk-taking for profit, surely it does not provide a justification for this limitation? Similarly, both the economic goals of price deterrence and prevention require the internalization to the relevant defendant of *all* the costs associated with the creation and marketing of the defective product, regardless of which side of the point of supply they occur. It would even seem to support liability for injuries incurred during testing of the product before circulation or supply.[107]

(b) Raw materials, unfinished products, byproducts, hazardous waste

Nor can implicit limitation in both the rule reflected in s 402A and the Directive that the injury must be caused by a *finished* product be justified by moral or economic arguments. Examples of injuries which thereby fall outside the rules are: the asbestos diseases suffered by the neighbours of an asbestos product manufacturer, its employees and their co-habitees; the injuries suffered by employees in the process of manufacturing DES; and the deformities produced by the contamination of food chains by mercury-bearing effluent in Minamata, Japan. It could be argued that injuries due to defective products which have not been supplied, such as raw materials, unfinished products and by-products, are just as much the moral responsibility of the enterprise as those associated with defective finished products after

---

106 EEC Memo para 14.
107 But except in the context of drug trials (which by definition seem 'post-supply', and on which in general see Pearson para 1341), commentators and reformers have repeatedly asserted that such injuries should not be covered: Liebman, *op cit* 432, 437; DTI *Implementations of EC Directive on Product Liability* (1985) para 56(a); Strasbourg Expl Rep para 43.

circulation, and are just as much a cost of the enterprise which should be internalized to promote price deterrence and injury prevention. Recognition of this policy analogy between product liability and liability for toxic pollution has led one influential US jurisdiction (New Jersey) to uphold the imposition of strict liability for toxic pollution.[108]

On this basis, the ideal product rule should be amplified: the defendant would be liable for all injuries due to defective products produced by it whenever they occur and regardless of their purported destination, so long as the injury was a foreseeable or direct consequence of the product defect. The producer of hazardous waste, for example, would be liable, if it could be shown to be 'defective',[109] for all injuries foreseeably or directly caused by it, and it would be the producer's responsibility to ensure, say, by contract with disposal or storage companies or by insurance, that he could obtain indemnity for such losses caused by the waste once he had lost direct control over it. Ironically, the European Commission has reached this position regarding producers' liability for waste, but from the opposite direction. In its draft Directive on civil liability for damage caused by waste[110] liability is channelled to the 'producer' of the waste, ie 'any person who in the course of a commercial or industrial activity produces waste ...' (draft Article 2(1)(a)). The controller of waste at the time of the relevant damage is only subjected to the sort of secondary liability which product suppliers bear under Article 3(3) of the product liability Directive which can be avoided by the controller naming the producer of the waste. For the operator of a waste storage site, however, such avoidance will be very much more difficult because waste will often have been dumped on the site long before damage results, by unknown or unidentifiable persons or in a mixed dump which prevents individual identification,[111] but in any case a separate proposed Directive imposes liability without fault on such parties.[112]

It is also noteworthy that it is proposed that the producer of waste be liable not only for waste it dumps far away from its site of generation, say a factory, but for waste stored within the factory gate. In other words, there is no requirement that it be 'put into circulation' before liability for the injuries it causes will be incurred, unless that phrase is to be given the widest interpretation of 'put into environmental circulation'. The employee or bystander injured by dangerous waste on the factory's premises will be able to sue, but not if the source of injury is a raw material, or a partly completed or finished product, since these are not waste for the purposes of the proposed waste Directive nor within the ordinary meaning of a product 'put into circulation' for the purposes of the products Directive. This is an incoherent

---

108 *New Jersey* v *Ventron Corpn* 182 NJ Super 210 (1981); R Hall 'The Problem of Unending Liability for Hazardous Waste Management' (1982–3) 38 Bus Law 593, 609.

109 Especially relevant to, say, hazardous waste dumps would be adequacy of labelling of 'what might reasonably be expected to be done with ... the product': s 3(2)(b). See R Kidner 'Toxic Waste and Strict Liability for Products' (1988) 138 NLJ 379.

110 Proposal for a Council Directive on Civil Liability for Damage Caused by Waste, OJ No C 251, 4.10.89; Amended Proposal, OJ No C 192, 23.7.91 (presented by the Commission pursuant to Article 149(3) of the EEC Treaty). Now see also EC *Green Paper on Remedying Environmental Damage* COM (93) 47. Compare the 1993 Council of Europe's Convention on Civil Liability for Damage Resulting from Activities Dangerous to the Environment.

111 D Wheatley 'Greener than Green' [1991] NLJ 208, 209.

112 OJ No C 190, 22.7.91, amended proposal COM(93)275 (landfill of waste).

position, confusing to business, insurers and injured parties alike. The anomaly which becomes apparent once liability for waste is considered may force a much more generous interpretation of 'put into circulation' in the products Directive, perhaps to the point where it simply comes to mean exposing another, in the course of one's business, to a product risk.

(c) Workplace injuries to employees

Some employees injured at work will be able to claim under the Directive/CPA regime: many industrial injuries are due to defective products such as machine tools and inadequately labelled chemicals and raw materials. If the defective product causing injuries was supplied to the victim's employer by a third party manufacturer, the employee will at least be able to bring a claim against that third party, and the importance of such claims is confirmed by the volume and success rate of third party product claims by US employees in general: they account for roughly 30% of US product liability claims and half the consequent payments.[113] But where the employer is also the manufacturer of the relevant product, the situation is very different. The 'circulation' requirement under the Directive operates in the same way as the 'sole remedy rule' under US workers' compensation law.[114] It prevents claims by those very victims of defective products whose special role in enabling the enterprise to take risks and, accordingly, profit had earlier been recognized as justifying the introduction of (no-fault) workers' compensation. In view of the fact that of all injuries associated with the production and marketing of a product, a very large proportion are suffered by the producer's workforce, this seems a remarkable position to have reached.

How any special workplace injury scheme and the general common law should be fitted together is a complex question. In modern times the argument for a separate scheme may no longer be accepted, especially now that moral enterprise liability notions have infiltrated wider consumer and environmental fields. What is hard to justify is a separate but *inferior* treatment of employees. This is hardly what the union lobby would have thought the special status of employees under the Treaty of Rome[115] was to mean. The result may cause substantial political dissatisfaction with the new law, and specifically with the requirement that the product be 'put into circulation'.

---

113 A phenomenon fuelled by the bar against US employees suing their employers in tort. P Atiyah 'No-Fault Compensation: A Question That Will Not Go Away' (1980) 54 Tulane LR 271, 286; J Liebman 'Strict Tort Liability for Unfinished Products' (1982) 19 Am Bus LJ 407, 436. In the UK some employees will also have the benefit of the Employer's Liability (Defective Equipment) Act 1969 which, like the Directive, even covers defectively designed ships: *Coltman* v *Bibby Tankers* [1988] AC 276, HL; and defectively made flagstones, *Knowles* v *Liverpool City Council* [1993] 4 All ER 321, HL. Query: does an employer's provision of movable work equipment to employees amount to putting it into circulation under Article 7(a)? See above under heading 4(b).

114 There have been judicial attempts to circumvent the 'sole remedy' rule – see in particular *Bell* v *Industrial Vangas Inc* 637 P 2d 266 (1981) (the 'dual capacity' doctrine) – but they have been largely unsuccessful: S Birnbaum and B Wrubel 'Workers' Compensation and the Employers' Immunity Shield: Recent Exceptions to Exclusivity' (1982) 5 J Prod Liab 119.

115 See, eg, Article 118A(3) of the Treaty of Rome, noted above Chapter 3, fn 68.

8   CONCLUSION

In the United States courts have been forced to pervert notions such as that of 'product' in order to achieve, covertly, the channelling of liability which is necessary to give the rule in s 402A some appearance of coherence. The example of electricity being a 'product' on one side of a meter but not the other is a clear illustration of the problem and the future handling of software will probably also generate comparable anomalies. But if 'policy' is to determine what 'product' means, the inability of theory to produce convincing reasons for limiting the liability will lead to pressure to extend its meaning beyond the traditional idea of 'goods' and to certain services and to realty. This has happened in the US. The potential for instability in doctrine seems clear, especially if the defective services/defective product distinction is acknowledged to be unconvincing and unworkable. Furthermore, the requirement that the product was supplied or put into circulation is wholly inappropriate in the tort context where its relevance to a bystander is impossible to see, and it is a requirement which excludes workplace and environmental injuries for no obvious reason.

The draft Directives on services and waste liability confirm the conclusion that, quite apart from being hard to justify, piecemeal reform of torts liability may generate substantial instability because the particular rule will tend to impinge haphazardly on other settled areas of law. Most importantly, limited tort reform such as that in the products Directive de facto channels liability to particular defendants without convincing justification. While we found in Part 2 that there may be sound moral reasons for treating those engaged in business differently from other defendants, there is no reason why the liability to which they are subjected should have become so complex. Why should it be that the liability of a business for waste is to be strict (draft Waste Directive Article 3: 'irrespective of fault'), but that its liability for its services should be only in terms of 'fault'? Why should it have the burden of proof in relation to fault in respect of services but not in relation to the fault-based concept of 'defectiveness' under the products Directive? And what about injuries suffered in circumstances of overlapping enterprises? Take, for example, the case where, due to a defective service (a delivery person puts the wrong chemical into a water storage reservoir), a product (water) is rendered defective injuring consumers (people supplied with the water) and bystanders (surrounding residents injured indirectly by the seepage of the tainted reservoir water into nearby land and streams).[116] Does it make sense to have separate rules applying to services, products and waste? Even if it does, how do they relate to one another in respect of the victim's claim and in respect of recourse between tortfeasors? It is of no use to respond that the ECJ will look to the purpose not the letter of the relevant Directives if we are not clear about what these purposes are and how they relate to each other. In practice the ECJ will be tempted to avoid such issues by portraying troublesome concepts such as 'defect' and 'cause' as questions of fact to be determined by local courts. But business and insurers faced with these costly complexities may become significantly disgruntled. In short, apart from the limitation to defendants' activity in the course of a business, the limitations and separate rules of liability for products, services and waste do not have sufficiently convincing justification to defend them from the anger of those prejudiced by the lottery generated by their anomalous and intersecting boundaries.

---

116 Compare (1989) The Observer 2 July, p 11 on the poisoning of 20,000 people in the Camelford area of Cornwall which gave rise to a successful claim by 180 people under s 2(1) of the CPA and other causes of action: *AB* v *South West Water Services Ltd* [1993] QB 507, CA.

CHAPTER 13

Some conclusions

1 OVERLAPPING ENTERPRISES AND THE POTENTIAL INSTABILITY OF LIMITED (PRODUCT) RULES

It is time to draw together the major themes of this enquiry. The first relates to the phenomenon of overlapping activities and enterprises. The manner in which this presents a major threat to the stability of the new products rule raises general questions about the fairness, workability and stability of any special liability rule limited to specific classes of defendants or causal factors. In the real world an injury can be related to many factors, only one of which might be the condition of the product (see Chapter 6, under heading 5(f)). For example, even in what may seem to be a 'simple product case' where the injury is clearly due to the product's condition – say a new television explodes or a bottle of ginger beer contains a decomposing snail – the defectiveness of the product is nearly always traceable to human activity, often by several people: the designer, an assembly-line worker and so on (Chapter 12, under heading 6). Within the chain of manufacture and supply we found that, in any particular case, the activity of other chain members besides the manufacturer (for example, an upstream designer or a retailer) might be selected as causally relevant to the resultant injury (Chapter 11, under heading 7). The behaviour of the victim could also be causally relevant, and it may in fact be so relevant in explaining the result that it swamps other factors (Chapter 6, under heading 2). The victim's abnormal susceptibility to the injury could also be such a cause.

In some circumstances the expertise or conduct of some intermediary may be causally relevant: the user of the product; a general practitioner advising on drugs; teachers and parents supervising children playing with electronic car windows or dangerous substances; or an experienced service-provider such as a hairdresser applying permanent-wave solution (Chapter 10, under heading 7(ii)). The older the product becomes, the more likely it is that the conduct of some intermediary may be relevant to issues of durability, maintenance, and so on (Chapter 11, under heading 6). In a rail crash, for example, injuries which result from the outmoded carriage design of the train might be more appropriately attributed to the rail operator's continued use of such carriages rather than to the manufacturer's omission, say, to warn about the 'useful life' of the carriage.[1] Similarly, there will be occasions on which the nature of the risk will focus primary attention on the intermediary; for example, say a light bulb fails during an open heart operation resulting in injury to the patient. Would not the hospital's failure to ensure back-up lighting facilities be regarded as of primary significance? Very much the same argument about the expectations and

---

1 See report on the Cannon Street rail crash (1991), The Independent on Sunday, 13 January, p 4.

responsibilities of intermediaries are raised in cases of passive smoking injuries where the behaviour of the user (and in workplace injuries, his or her employer) seem at least equally as implicated in the injury as that of the tobacco manufacturer.

In more complex situations too factors other than the condition of the product may be causally relevant. When a bus driver carelessly brakes on a poorly banked road and a passenger, unable to reach one of the few handles, falls and breaks a leg (Chapter 6, under heading 5(f)), we may at first consider that the local authority, the driver, the bus company, the bus manufacturer and designer might all be possibly implicated in causal responsibility. What is more, because causal attribution can depend on a variety of factors involving past behaviour, moral and legal expectations, the state of the art and so on (see Chapter 6, under heading 2), the *final* attribution of causal responsibility between these factors cannot be determined in the abstract but only in the specific legal, moral and historical context of the individual case. If the local authority had no legal obligation to ensure correctly banked roads nor had ever undertaken such a protective role, its omission to ensure the road was correctly banked (although satisfying the but-for test in relation to the passenger's injuries) would not be selected as a *cause* of the injuries (Chapter 6, under heading 2). But if it had such a legal obligation or had undertaken this role in relation to some roads and had, say, repeatedly ignored the frequent accidents occurring on this stretch of road, it is much more likely to be selected as at least a contributory cause of the injuries. The same dependency of causal attribution on context operates in the simple product cases above where, for example, the relevance of warnings, instructions, the obviousness of the risk and the conduct of intermediaries varies according to the surrouding facts including whether the ultimate victim was a buyer, user or bystander.

The main problem raised by the phenomenon of overlapping activities and enterprises, both within simple product cases and within the more complex cases illustrated by the bus example, is not the problem of workability of a limited rule in the individual case. After all, similar litigated claims may be sufficiently few in practice that they may be handled in isolation. This is how the law of negligence works in practice: the plaintiff chooses which parties to sue, and although the defendant is allowed to join third parties, there is no attempt *by the law* to ensure that all possibly relevant parties are joined or that the claim is characterized in a particular way either as, in the above example, a 'bus' case or a 'road' case or a 'product design' case or a 'local authority' case. The important problem the phenomenon of overlapping enterprises *does* raise is the issue of the long-term stability of a limited rule. This is because where injuries are due to many factors, the treatment of one factor under a special rule can distort the consciousness of practitioners, parties and courts. Even if the special rule secures no substantive doctrinal advantage for the plaintiff, in practice claims could de facto become channelled to the parties chosen by that rule as defendants (Chapter 6, under heading 5(f), Chapter 12, under heading 6).

In the Directive there is no direct requirement that the defendant caused the plaintiff's injury.[2] This causal requirement, with all its obvious associations with human behaviour and its dependency on a fluid context, is replaced by the apparently more mechanical concept of supply of a 'defective' product. But the advantage of the traditional requirement of a causal link to injury is that it allows an initial

---

2 Or caused the defect in the product. The plaintiff must, however, prove a causal connection between his or her injury and the defective product.

focus on all factors which may have a relevance to the injury, be it a moral relevance, preventative relevance, etc.[3] In a product case this group of causally relevant factors can include a variety of human behaviour in relation to the product – its design, creation, handling, storage, use or disposal – not simply its commercial supply which the Directive selects to the exclusion of all other factors. Yet the Directive does not allow the plaintiff to sue everyone with a causal connection to the injury. The superficial attraction of the 'defect' concept lies in its apparent objectification of the central liability issue, but the supporting rhetoric that the focus shifts from the defendant's conduct to the product, merely masks what is an evaluation of conduct, as failure to warn claims and defences based on plaintiff conduct make manifest (Chapter 12, under heading 6). The defect concept is not a good vehicle for giving effect to the complex range of responses the law of tort might have even to a simple product case: the attitude to a particular buyer's claim might be wholly different to that of a bystander (Chapter 10, under heading 9). The larger the number of those who are perceived as causally relevant to an injury, the more glaring becomes the inappropriateness of the 'defect' concept. The more plaintiffs choose to sue under the product rules rather than in negligence the more claims will be channelled to parties who have supplied a relevant product, leaving to the vagaries of recourse rules the appropriate final sorting out of legal responsibility amongst all implicated parties.

In the US this channelling to product suppliers by the rule set out in s 402A has occurred and has been fuelled by the 'sole remedy' rule in the workers' compensation field. Workers now claim against the makers of machines such as computers, stenographs and electronic check-out equipment for the repetitive strain injuries they suffer, even though in such cases it is widely accepted that workplace conditions (eg furniture, lighting, ventilation and rest breaks) play a key role in the aetiology of these medical conditions.[4] Outside the employment field the channelling effect of s 402A is also evident. For example, US victims of diseases due to asbestos in buildings nearly always sue the asbestos producer even though others such as occupiers, builders and architects are often implicated in its use within a building. The temporal reach of the tactic of 'blaming the product' is illustrated by a 1992 case in the Florida Supreme Court: when a salvage worker was harmed by exposure to polychlorinated biphenyls in a *disused* transformer being scrapped for metal, the court ruled that the manufacturer should have warned of the dangerous contents of its product.[5] Similarly, the concentration on products can distort the law's approach to victim behaviour: in 1992 a Texan distiller was held 25% liable (on the basis of failure to warn) for the death of a college student who died from alcohol poisoning after drinking twenty shots of tequila.[6]

A specific products rule tends to imply that other causally relevant factors are to be given less weight by the law, because the rule does not encompass claims against mere users and other non-suppliers of products. Whereas in the law of negligence consideration can be given to the role of intermediaries such as parents, occupiers or users, their role is peripheral under a products rule aimed only at product suppliers.

---

3 The various avenues by which a factor may be perceived as a cause mirror these different forms of relevance (Chapter 6, under heading 2).
4 Prod Liab Internat [July 1992] 104; Prod Liab Internat [Aug 1990] 123.
5 Prod Liab Internat [Aug 1992] 126.
6 Prod Liab Internat [Oct 1992] 148; since 1987 such warnings are necessary under federal law.

The temptation for courts is then to require less of victims and third parties and more precautions in the product, including precautions against foreseeable behaviour of that intermediary, before that product will be found to be 'non-defective'. It can become the product manufacturer's job to guard against negligent installation, alteration by a third party, negligent maintenance, negligent use or negligent supervision while in use (Chapter 10, under heading 7(iii)). In future, will victims sue the builder of a cross-channel ferry on the basis that the ferry is of defective design because it allows the captain to put to sea without ensuring that the crew has shut the bow doors? Could the next strategy of those wanting to launch tobacco claims relating to passive smoking be to shift the focus away from, say, the victim's employer who allows smoke-filled working conditions,[7] and on to the tobacco manufacturer and in this way avoid defences based on victim behaviour? Sometimes consideration of the product condition will be useful and illuminating. For example, in recent years investigation of many aircraft crashes initially ascribed to 'pilot error'[8] has implicated the arrangement and complexity of new cockpit display systems which allegedly confuse pilots leading to mistakes or too heavy a reliance on automatic systems. But in general the special focus on the product element in injuries threatens to distort the legal analysis in a substantial way.

A catalyst to this channelling of claims is the asymmetry of rules relating to exclusion clauses. A user or bystander whose property is injured by a defective product may be able to sue a range of parties in negligence. Those defendants who act in the course of a business will be able to exclude the liability so long as notice requirements are fulfilled and the exclusion is reasonable under the Unfair Contract Terms Act 1977. Under the Directive (Article 12, CPA, s 7), however, the liability cannot be excluded at all even if the exclusion is brought to the victim's attention and is reasonable. This gives plaintiffs an added incentive to sue under the Directive/CPA. For example, under UCTA it may be held reasonable for a lock manufacturer to attempt to limit its liability to repair and replacement, given the buyer's superior knowledge of the extent of the risk of loss or damage involved in the event of the lock's non-performance; but the buyer could use a claim under the Directive/CPA to evade this.[9]

In theory it should not matter whom the victim chooses to sue. Liability is generally joint and several and defendants have recourse against others who would have been liable for the same damage. It may even be quite acceptable to render certain relatively innocent parties liable to a victim for the pragmatic reason of giving that victim someone convenient to sue, and to rely on that defendant's rights of recourse to achieve other policies. The liability of importers under the Directive is justifiable in this way. But current recourse rules cannot be relied upon to rectify the distortions and consequent grievances generated by the de facto channelling which results from special rules such as the product rules (Chapter 11, under heading 8). In time this state of affairs and the issues of fairness, workability and stability it raises will be likely to attract the criticism of aggrieved parties, and should attract the concern of all lawyers not simply in the product field but whenever actual or proposed limited rules of liability are considered.

---

7 Compare *Clay*'s case, Commissioner's File CF/364/1989, noted NLJ 3.5.91, p 596.

8 A useful publicity tactic for both aircraft operators and manufacturers. On the general point see Prod Liab Internat [March 1992] 39; (1991) The Independent 27 February; (1991) The Independent on Sunday 23 June, pp 1, 8.

9 *Lobianco* v *Property Protection Inc* 437 A 2d 417, 424–5 (1981). See also Chapter 6, under heading 5(d)(ii). This is still the position after the 1993 Directive on unfair terms in consumer contracts.

2 DISTRIBUTIVE JUSTICE AND THE CHALLENGE OF NO-FAULT

During the last fifty years civil litigation by private individuals has become more common. Society has become more collectivist and more sensitive to the interconnectedness of human activity. One result has been that the development of the negligence principle of liability has exposed an increasing number of potential defendants to a liability for an increasing sphere of their activities. It is now common for one accident to be treated as resulting from the behaviour of a number of parties. This is a result of both a genuine increase in the complexity of human relations in the twentieth century and a change in expectations and in the perception of social behaviour. In this context the introduction of a limited liability rule, such as that in the products Directive, which channels claims towards one party while other parties who are perceived to be as implicated are not targeted, is more likely to lead to disquiet, grievance and ultimately instability.

This feature of the products law in practice raises a larger issue concerning the stability of tort law in general. At present commentators on tort seem most concerned with the challenge of two particular forms of claim, mass torts and toxic torts. In the first form – exemplified in the US by the asbestos and DES claims and in the UK by the Zeebrugge and Piper Alpha cases – one piece of defendant conduct is implicated in similar injuries to many victims. Handling such claims individually within the traditional two-party model of civil adjudication can appear inefficient and inequitable. The latter – exemplified by industrial and environmental disease claims such as the childhood leukaemia claims against UK nuclear plants – provoke concern, inter alia, about the adequacy of the traditional tests of medical causation. But the more fundamental threat to the integrity of tort law, which underlies even the simplest of claims, is the growing perception of the many factors contributing to the occurrence of an injury and an awareness that the imposition of liability has an impact far beyond the named defendants. Increasing sensitivity to all these issues has resulted in a weakening of the moral and economic defence of a corrective justice model of legal redress for wrongs. This is not because such a model cannot accommodate the idea of multiple potential defendants – it can. Nor is it simply because the prevalence of liability insurance dilutes any moral or economic incentives initially generated by the liability. It is also that the selection of only some of the potential defendants as those to be sued increasingly appears an artificial choice which helps support the wider criticism that tort in operation is a costly lottery for both plaintiffs and defendants. Similarly, appreciation that the liability burden imposed on a particular defendant is passed on or flows on to affect a much wider class of parties – for example, the defendant's employees, shareholders, customers, suppliers and others in its liability insurance pool – can appear to raise normative questions: was this ultimate distribution of loss fair? If in practice the burden of liability is borne by a wide section of society why not formally acknowledge and introduce 'community responsibility'[10] for the compensation of the relevant loss?

Twenty years ago leading British and Commonwealth tort scholars joined this elision of the descriptive and the normative with criticism of how the tort system worked in practice in the field of personal injuries (see Chapter 3, under heading 3). Socio-legal research showed that a range of non-legal barriers prevented all but a

---

10 Report of the Royal Commission of Inquiry, Compensation for Personal Injury in New Zealand (ch Woodhouse J)(Wellington, NZGP, 1967) para 56.

few people making and pursuing tort claims. Psychologists exposed how highly attenuated the legal notion of fault was in practice, and once fault came under attack it became fashionable to argue that those within the increasingly benevolent reach of tort doctrine were scarcely 'more worthy'[11] than those suffering personal injuries who were not covered. These attacks generated calls for the individual defendant to be replaced by a public compensation fund to which all the injured would have access on the basis of need and for the pursuit of the deterrence goal through other mechanisms. The resultant movement to a non-tort no-fault comprehensive compensation system was largely halted in the 1970s (see Chapter 3, under heading 4), but the underlying unease which these perceptions generated found continued expression in proposals for limited no-fault schemes.

In a few areas limited no-fault schemes are attractive to both victims and payers of compensation. In the area of work accidents, adverse drug reactions and road injuries such schemes operate in various jurisdictions stably and well. Victims are assured swift compensation while the payers are saved the cost and embarrassment of civil claims. But such schemes work well because they relate to injuries which are not perceived as being caused by overlapping enterprises. For example, it is generally agreed that the moral and economic arguments for imposing the responsibility for and the cost of *all* work accidents (not just those due to fault) to employers in a workers' compensation scheme justify us in ignoring the dissatisfaction which one side may feel in a particular case – eg where a faulty machine tool which caused injury had been supplied by a third party. Similarly, adverse drug reactions are perceived as almost exclusively the responsibility of the manufacturer, while no-fault road schemes attract support because the incidents they cover are usually identified closely with driver behaviour.

But limited non-tort no-fault schemes are impractical in most other areas for reasons which the products field illustrates well (Chapter 6, under heading 5(f)). This is not simply for the reason Pearson gave in rejecting a no-fault proposal for the compensation of injuries caused by defective products, namely that there would be difficulty financing it.[12] The fundamental and intractable problem is that the boundary rules of any such scheme would be perceived as hopelessly undermined by the phenomenon of overlapping activities or enterprises. Phrases such as 'an accident arising in or out of employment' can achieve a clear and workable boundary to a no-fault scheme because injuries occurring during the activity of work for another are perceived as appropriately a cost of that enterprise. But many product injuries are not similarly perceived as a cost of one enterprise alone as the earlier examples of the work tool and bus show. In short, not only does the product rule show the unwiseness of limited liability rules, but it also illustrates the general untenability of most limited no-fault schemes.

The stagnation of comprehensive reform proposals during the late 1970s *might* have been due to the rise of a powerful counter-idea in support of tort law in general

---

11 P Atiyah 'No-Fault Compensation: A Question That Will Not Go Away' (1980) 54 Tulane LR 271, 276. See also P Atiyah *Pragmatism and Theory in English Law* (London, Stevens, 1987): 'we now know how unbelievably costly, wasteful, inefficient and even inequitable the system of tort compensation for accidents is in the mass', p 37; R Abel 'A Critique of Torts' (1990) 37 UCLA LR 785: 'tort liability is incoherent as a moral system', p 791; D Harris 'Tort Law Reform in the United States' (1991) 11 Oxf JL S 407; on judicial disquiet see *Wilsher* v *Essex Area Health Authority* [1988] 1 All ER 871, 883 (per Lord Bridge).

12 Pearson paras 1222–3.

and of the 'plaintiff versus defendant(s)' model in particular. After all, it is one thing to note that, say, the synergism of tobacco and asbestos reflects the complexity of life, that the operation of liability insurance to some extent undermines moral or economic incentives on those held liable, and that very few injured people are able to obtain tort damages. It is another thing to argue that the collectivist desire to set up a comprehensive compensation system requires the removal of parallel tort claims. There may be financial reasons why this would be useful, but the issues of compensation and of the future of tort are separate ones[13] and tort may yet have arguments in its defence. Noting the complexity of factors contributing to an accident does not necessarily mean that it is irrational to impose liability on all of them and, if necessary, to allow a plaintiff to choose which factor(s) to complain about. Noting the way liability burdens can in practice flow through defendants to other parties does not necessarily mean that the theoretical justifications for the basic rule should also support that ultimate distribution of loss. The fact that a legal rule has a particular effect does not necessarily mean that that effect was its goal (see Chapter 8). For example, commercial relations are complex and underpinned by insurance, yet there is still confidence in a system which distributes contractual entitlements narrowly on the basis of notions such as fairness, and backs them up by the corrective justice tool of a cause of action between named parties.

Nevertheless, before reviewing the impact the product rule has had on tort doctrine, how it helps us evaluate modern theories of entitlements in civil liability and how it prompts questions about the path of future doctrinal developments, we must consider a powerful argument against the tort system. Given that tort helps so few individuals, can it be justified? It is sometimes argued, for example, that the randomness of tort claims is an efficient way to 'ginger up' a much wider target class of potential defendants in much the same way that a poorly funded regulatory body might choose to allocate its thin enforcement resources. More generally it could be argued that the reporting of tort claims can give the *appearance* that it performs non-compensatory functions well. It can, for example, appear to act as a sort of 'ombudsman'[14] focusing the indignation of the injured, channelling their retributive impulses and giving shaming publicity to 'wrongdoing', while perhaps also appearing to serve an investigatory function. Even in its compensatory aspects tort may be seen as useful *symbolically* in its vaunted goal of full compensation, including complete restoration of standard of living and awards for non-pecuniary losses such as pain. But idealists attack this argument about tort's symbolic value as a 'pervasive hypocrisy'[15] by which it pretends to the public to be guided by high moral sentiments, to achieve consistent control and to impose useful sanctions, when in practice its impact is rare, avoidable, unpredictable and weak. In response to the idealist, the cynic could argue that civil liability has never been more than a symbolic valve for grievances anyway. For example, many claims have always been excluded from the system by the impecuniosity or risk averseness of the aggrieved party. In any case, the current legal and settlement system as we know it could not cope if, say, all occasions of negligence were to give rise to claims. The symbolism argument rests on the idea that *despite* recourse to law being in practice available only to a few, its

---

13 J Stapleton *Disease and the Compensation Debate* (Oxford, Clarendon Press, 1986) 151.
14 A Linden 'Tort Law as Ombudsman' (1973) 51 Can BR 155.
15 R Abel 'Should Tort Law Protect Property Against Accidental Loss?' (1986) 23 San Diego LR 79, 120.

appearance of wide availability, of achieving deterrence, vindication and so on provides an essential reassurance for the population, and its rules as to 'wrongdoing' a
necessary public manifestation of social morality.

It is still an open political question whether the advantages of tort's symbolism
outweigh the dangers of complacency bred by a false assurance that the system of
justice is so widely available. But so long as tort survives – even if its role *is* only
symbolic – it is important that its rules appear coherent and fair, reflecting sound
moral or economic principles (see under heading 4, below). Indeed, if its role is only
symbolic, theoretical justifications for liability rules can more easily choose to
ignore those phenomena which tend to undermine the two party model of liability,
such as appreciation that a liability burden can be passed on through the defendant
to others.

3   THE IMPACT OF THE DIRECTIVE ON DOCTRINE

The creation of a separate additional liability rule for certain product-related injuries
may have an impact on wider doctrine. Some possible effects are more apparent
than real. For example, it may seem to create an anomaly that the Directive does not
cover any claim for pure economic loss while the almost parallel tort of negligence
bars such claims in only some cases of the acquisition of defective property.[16] In
practice, however, nearly all those who acquire defective products have a superior
remedy under sales law, so this anomaly is unlikely to attract controversy.

In the field of defences based on plaintiff conduct, the special product regimes in
both the EC and US are more likely to have a noticeable impact, albeit perhaps
indirectly. While it has always been possible to sue product manufacturers in negligence for the supply of addictive products such as alcohol, tobacco and tranquilliz-
ers, the problems of establishing proximate causation and negligence-in-fact and of
defeating the potential defences of volenti and contributory negligence have inhibited virtually all claims on both sides of the Atlantic until recently. It was, however,
possible that the adoption of a special products rule – even one whose rhetoric of
increased manufacturer liability is false – would galvanize victims and their lawyers
into launching such claims. Certainly in the US, the earlier reluctance to sue cigarette manufacturers has lately been replaced by a wave of litigation. Some alcohol
and tranquillizer claims have also been made and some claims against addictive
products are now entering the British litigation process. Although in the UK such
claims have been taken in negligence rather than under the CPA (because they relate
to products supplied before the commencement date of that statute) the special product rule in the US and its offspring, the product Directive, have clearly been a major
force in the consciousness which led to these new claims.

If judged by the standards applied in other negligence claims against manufacturers, plaintiffs in tobacco claims should have little difficulty in establishing the inadequacy of the packet warning (see Chapter 10, under heading 7(ii)), particularly in
the light of the promotional strategy of manufacturers and of their apparently limited
research to monitor the risks inherent in tobacco use. The relevant proof of medical

---

16 Compare *D & F Estates Ltd* v *Church Comrs for England* [1989] AC 177 and *Smith* v *Eric S Bush*
    [1990] 1 AC 831.

causation is now considerably easier to obtain in some of these cases than it was a decade ago, and this is particularly so in the case of tobacco-related illnesses such as peripheral vascular disease, which are not otherwise common in the population. This means that the central issue in most tobacco claims is likely to be the proper ambit of the volenti and contributory negligence defences. It is difficult to judge how British courts will respond to such defences. Certainly the average smoker's knowledge of the relevant risks of tobacco seem less than that held necessary to establish that other plaintiffs were volens to a risk. It is difficult to see how an addict – especially one addicted since childhood – could be regarded as sufficiently volens on the current restrictive approach to that defence. Parallel arguments could be raised in respect of contributory negligence which, even if raised successfully, would only lead to apportionment of damages. Here courts will face further pressure for they will need to trade off the ill-informed smoker's recklessness with the conscious strategy of cigarette manufacturers to protect profits by, for example, associating their products with healthy pursuits and failing to publicize studies revealing the dangers of a product said by the British Medical Association to be implicated in more than 100,000 deaths in England and Wales each year. In this context it may not *at first* seem likely that a court would allow more than small account to be taken of the plaintiff's behaviour especially since manufacturers claim that tobacco is so dangerous that its mere use by the plaintiff establishes contributory negligence. Yet there are major countervailing pressures. Tobacco is a major industry. A finding of negligence or defective design could precipitate considerable socio-economic dislocations, the creation of which courts might regard as more properly the responsibility of Parliament (see Chapter 10, under heading 7(ii)). The result might be the distortion of defences or other aspects of doctrine in order to avoid a finding of liability against tobacco manufacturers.

The special product rule is likely to have a more subtle impact on expectations about behaviour, not only of the plaintiff but of the product manufacturer, intermediaries and others. The rule may raise expectations that product manufacturers will take steps to ensure safety and reduce expectations that others such as users and other intermediaries will take such steps (under heading 1, above). This change could influence the resolution of issues both of causation – eg seeing manufacturers' omissions implicated when formerly they would not have been considered (Chapter 6, under heading 2) – and 'defect' (Chapter 10, under heading 7). It could also affect the remoteness of damage concept, which the Directive leaves to local rules[17] and which is raised in important contexts such as used products, products distributed via learned intermediaries and products used or handled by experienced personnel such as waste disposal site managers (see Chapter 10, under heading 7(ii), Chapter 12, under headings 2 and 7). These changes in expectations of behaviour caused by the products rule may also affect negligence claims. In addition, the slogan of 'strict liability' may lead to pressure to include more risks within the Directive's notion of 'risks discoverable within the state of scientific and technical knowledge', and this too could feed back into negligence claims, increasing the demands of that liability in the same way s 402A has affected negligence liability in the US. Indeed, the dramatic surge of product litigation in the past three decades can be seen as principally a working through – albeit a highly aggressive working through – of the negligence idea in the context of the design of commercially supplied products. The more the

17 EC Memo para 21.

Directive familiarizes practitioners with such complaints the more likely that they will also be taken in the tort of negligence itself, and it may well be that this 'kick-starting' of design claims in negligence will be the principal contribution the Directive makes to the development of civil liability.

US commentators have criticized the Directive for being silent or uninstructive on the doctrinal issue that has provoked prolonged and heated controversy under s 402A, notably the problem of adjudicating claims of defective design consistently and predictably. Examination of that problem, however, shows the criticism to be misguided (see Chapter 10). Allegations about design may be new, but even under the general law of negligence they are simply a logical working through of the general principle in *Donoghue* v *Stevenson*. They do, however, raise two dangers for the image of the law and the perceived meaning of justice. First, in some cases design allegations, if successful, threaten a socio-economic impact which is both dramatic and obvious. That private litigation has power to trigger such results is embarrassing from a separation of powers perspective (Chapter 10, under heading 7(ii)). Secondly, the standard to be applied in design cases under the special products rule *is* intelligible, contrary to widely held opinion in the US. But reasonable people can differ about how the standard should be applied and this can put pressure on the assumption that the application of a standard should result in consistent outcomes in order to be just (Chapter 10, under heading 8). These dangers are not confined to design claims under the CPA/Directive; they can arise far more widely. For example, claims for the recognition of a duty of care in negligence can raise the former while certain design claims under *Donoghue* v *Stevenson* or the warranty of merchantability raise the latter. Inasmuch as the Directive generates new interest in design claims they may start being brought not only under the new products law but under negligence and warranty, and with the proliferation of such claims these two dangers would increase.

Addition of yet another separate but limited liability rule also puts further strain on inadequate recourse rules. Examination of these (Chapter 11, under heading 8) shows that in the past, judicial and academic effort has gone almost exclusively into analyzing the basis and form of initial entitlements. This gives support to the criticism that, so far as it affects defendants, tort theory ignores the accurate ultimate allocation of responsibilities and incentives. It raises the large and perhaps intractable question of how to rank various liability rules. The problem of inadequate recourse rules is exacerbated by the late twentieth century shift in perception towards seeing many defendants potentially implicated in one claim (Chapter 13, under heading 2), even, for example, where a defendant's involvement consisted merely of failing to control the conduct of a third party. The Directive pushes this development even further by implicating parties (eg importers) whose involvement was simply supply of a defective product. Combined with the doctrine of joint and several liability, this increases the likelihood that the plaintiff will be able to choose a high-profile deep pocket defendant with a relatively trivial share in the responsibility for the damage complained of, increasing the dependence on recourse rules to readjust the distribution of liability burden more appropriately. Dissatisfaction with both recourse rules and the doctrine of joint and several liability may then increase among aggrieved deep pocket defendants.

4   TORT THEORY

The European reformers did not pretend to follow a single ideal theory of civil liability. Instead they cited a list of policies which they asserted underpinned the products Directive. Yet these included ideas so vague, conflicting and sometimes even mutually exclusive that they fail to provide convincing boundaries for the new liability. This presents a danger to the future stability of the law. Fortuitously product liability has proved a popular subject, or at least rhetorical backdrop, for theorists of tortious liability, so it might be thought that alternative justifications for the Directive would be readily available to courts wanting to adopt a purposive approach to the application and development of the law. But examination of modern tort theory in this context shows its inadequacies (Part 2). Firstly, the theories concentrate almost exclusively on the standard of the defendant's behaviour – the fault versus strict liability issue. Secondly, terminology is not uniform: even key ideas such as 'strict liability' and 'enterprise liability' are often used in different ways without careful definition. A third problem is that the paradigm plaintiff in tort, the bystander, is often neglected in favour of those who are said to be in a bargaining or potential bargaining position with regard to the relevant risk. Associated with this is the fact that major ideological choices lie unacknowledged within the analysis of many North American theorists. An important example of this which provides an interesting parallel with the 1970s radical attack on tort in the UK and Commonwealth, is the way pro-business academics in the US elide the descriptive with the normative to attack the special products-related cause of action. This is how the argument goes: for a buyer-plaintiff product liability can be portrayed as having the *effect* of insurance (the premium being the increase of price which liability produces); this effect is the *goal* of the liability; the liability is an inefficient and regressive way of providing this insurance (Chapter 8, under headings 4 and 5). The parallel is close between this insurance argument against product liability and the earlier attack on tort where the sequence went: an *effect* of tort is to compensate plaintiffs; the *goal* of tort is compensation; there are more efficient techniques of compensation. In both disguised policy positions can be unmasked by taking each to its logical extreme – caveat emptor in the former, abolition of tort damages in the latter. Neither argument is useful in justifying a *liability* system.

Fourthly, there is virtually no attempt to derive from basic principles the major boundaries (other than the standard of defendant behaviour) of the various relevant causes of action. In the products context, for example, available theory is unable satisfactorily to explain, let alone justify, the exclusion of pure economic loss claims, the restriction of the rule to products, and to products which have been put into commercial circulation (Chapter 12). Even in the context of defendant behaviour there is as yet no satisfactory theoretical justification for the multilayered liability, such as the general phenomenon of vicarious liability which finds an important new manifestation in the liability of mere product suppliers under the Directive and s 402A (Chapter 8, under heading 1(ii)). Similarly, there is only thin and unsatisfactory treatment of why the rules contain a 'defect' requirement (Chapter 6, under headings 4 and 5(f), Chapter 9, under heading 2). Symptomatic of this general neglect of the need to justify boundaries, is the failure of any theorist adequately to consider the important problems overlapping enterprises generate for limited liability rules such as these (see Chapter 5, under heading 4(d), Chapter 6, under heading 5(f), Chapter 9, under heading 6). Only Calabresi substantially noted the problem, but even he failed to address it fully, preferring to demonstrate his 'cheapest cost avoider' approach in contexts where the overlapping enterprises problem was limited, such as that of adverse drug reactions (Chapter 6, under heading 5(f)).

Nonetheless, current theoretical models of tort liability do illuminate broad principles buried within the product rule. While many of the boundaries of the product rule are difficult to justify, the one requiring that the defendant be acting in the course of a business does seem to reflect a broad principle at work across a larger field. This principle, here loosely called the moral enterprise liability principle (Chapter 8), focuses on a concern to treat with especial protection the interests of private individuals in the physical security of themselves and their property against invasion by the activities of those acting in pursuit of profit. In the future identification of such principles will be needed for the rational development of the law.

Even though theory fails satisfactorily to support a separate product rule, what does an alternative appeal to pragmatism establish? Certainly the pragmatic approach taken to manufacturing errors meets with general approval. In effect, courts now impose strict liability for manufacturing errors in negligence claims, and presumably this is what they will do under the Directive/CPA (see Chapter 10, under heading 6). The standard applied – the production line norm – is predictable and generally acceptable to both sides. But this leaves design defects. In the US the prevailing substantive rationales which try to explain the contrasting treatment of manufacturing errors (strict liability) and design conditions (an unreasonableness or risk/utility standard) are selective and unconvincing.[18] The only sound justifications are pragmatic ones: that the applications of the defect-based strict liability used in manufacturing error cases to cases of design would result in some cases in intractable problems of adjudication, at least in terms of consistency of outcome and sometimes in terms of avoiding constitutional embarrassment (Chapter 10, under heading 8 and Chapter 10, under heading 7(ii)); and that, given the risk-averseness of many businesses, exposure to such liability, including liability for unforeseeable risks, could result in undesirable distortions in the market supply of products (Chapter 9, under heading 5). Yet far from supporting a new separate products rule these pragmatic arguments support the status quo which had operated in negligence anyway, namely covert strict liability on manufacturers for manufacturing errors and a reasonableness standard for other product-related claims.

In the short term what this dearth of sound substantive and pragmatic justifications for the products Directive means is that boundary questions such as whether software is a 'product' or whether a laundromat has been 'put into circulation' cannot be answered by reference to principle. Opposing answers can be arrived at depending on which items from the menu of 'policies' referred to by European reformers are chosen by the courts to support their reasoning. Judicial reasoning attracts respect where affected parties perceive a clear, agreed and consistent set of principles on which it operates. Where it does not – as here – doctrinal instability and political grievance may well result in the longer term.

18 J Henderson and A Twerski 'A Proposed Revision of Section 402A of the Restatement (Second) of Torts' (1992) 77 Cornell LR 1512, 1516–7.

5 THE FUTURE OF DOCTRINE

Separate product liability reform is merely a ripple of a 'tidal wave'[19] in legal thinking, and the way in which theory fails to justify such reform can be used to suggest the path forward in larger fields of civil liability. Examination of theory showed that any defence of a tortious rule of liability must begin with the paradigm of injury to a *bystander* who had not bargained with the defendant(s) (see Chapter 10, under headings 2 and 9). When tort law should protect such a bystander is tort's major threshold question. Many considerations or 'policies' impinge on this issue. Some, which are clearly discernible in modern social debates and in legislation, are as yet only poorly reflected in tort doctrine. There is, for example, clearly a greater concern in modern legislation and debates with personal injuries than with, say, property damage suffered by private individuals (Chapter 3, under heading 3, and Chapter 8, under heading 2(b)); with activities in the course of a business than with other conduct (Chapter 8, under heading 1); and with the condition of dwellings than with that of other buildings – yet the common law's crude conceptualism scarcely acknowledges these concerns. The reform debate leading to the special product rule and examination of its possible theoretical underpinnings confirms the influence of the first two concerns and suggests that one way in which civil liability may develop in the future is in a more explicit and generalized recognition of these ideas. For example, one of the few real advances for the plaintiff in the product rule is the reversal of the burden of proof on certain issues. Perhaps a future reform could be the general reversal of the burden of proof on, say, fault in claims concerning personal injuries against commercial defendants.

There seem to be more general influences covertly at work within the common law relevant to the initial question of whether the law should protect the plaintiff. Clearly one of these is the so far unexplained tension between a 'linear' approach to tortious responsibility, under which a defendant need only satisfy obligations to an intermediate party, and an approach which imposes liability on some defendants even when they have satisfied such obligations (Chapter 10, under headings 7(ii) and 9).[20] Principles are also at work. These include,[21] for example, caution about indeterminate numbers or extent of claims ('opening the floodgates') and, importantly, about whether the plaintiff could reasonably have protected itself by other appropriate means than by later claiming the protection of tort. The latter substantive consideration clashes with the formal tort/contract divide which in this light appears to provide an artificial and inadequate organizing principle for modern doctrine (see Chapter 2, under heading 2, Chapter 6, under heading 3, Chapter 8, under heading 6) because sometimes those not in privity could have easily secured such protection while those in privity could not have bargained for it themselves. In modern markets being in privity cannot be taken as proof that the transaction was voluntarily entered into by a fully informed party, just as lack of privity does not necessarily denote helplessness.

This problem is exemplified by the varying ways the law would want to treat a buyer-victim according to the extent to which that buyer's transaction with the seller is regarded as raising or lowering the degree of safety he is entitled to expect, and it

---

19 G Gilmore 'Products Liability: A Commentary' (1970) 38 U Chi LR 103, 116.
20 J Stapleton 'The Frontiers of Liability' SPTL Conference, All Souls College, Oxford, July 1993.
21 J Stapleton 'Duty of Care and Economic Loss: A Wider Agenda' (1991) 107 LQR 249.

is an issue which is presently handled awkwardly by the law in general and by the Directive in particular (see Chapter 10, under heading 9). In future there need to be more rigorous attempts to identify these pre-requisites to protection, be it protection in the form of entitlement to the benefit of a duty of care or to a term implied by law. There would need to be careful review of the associated problems of the unwillingness of UK courts to imply terms into contracts, of concurrent liability and of the contrasting rules with regard to exclusion clauses in tort and contract. Real doctrinal sophistication would also require theorists to address the need for a recourse regime based on a clear hierarchy of norms defined in terms of types of right (property versus contract versus tortious), types of wrongdoing (fault versus strict liability) and the policy objectives underlying them. If, for example, a property right is always to trump a tort right[22] or if a negligent tortfeasor must always indemnify a strictly liable co-tortfeasor (Chapter 11, under heading 8), there would be major implications for how we are to understand civil obligations.

What of the future of the special products doctrine itself? Whether there will ever be sufficient pressure from aggrieved parties alone for repealing the Directive or at least generalizing its provisions to, say, all activity in the course of a business, depends on how many claims are made under it. At the moment there do not seem to be an unusual number (see Chapter 13, under heading 6). In any case the progress of modern tort law provides a number of examples of delay in reforming anomalies and unsatisfactory laws where the delay is unlikely to have been due to lack of claims: for example, the persistence of the privity fallacy until *Donoghue* v *Stevenson* in 1932, and the failure of that case to generate significant changes to occupier's liability rules and the builder/vendor immunity until Parliamentary action decades later. These examples do, however, show that *in time* academic and judicial criticism of anomaly can precipitate change. So is eventual reform on the cards? Although examination of the theoretical basis of the Directive has shown that most of its boundaries are insupportable and should be removed, the path of broad-ranging domestic reform which subsumes the product field has been inhibited and perhaps, as the present French difficulties suggest, blocked by EC membership (Chapter 3, under heading 6). Optimists might hope that the EC reform channel would prove fruitful. The 1995 review of the Directive is technically limited to the development risk defence and financial limits (Articles 15(3) and 16(2)) but might give way to a wider examination of the limited rule and if not to its repeal,[23] at least to its generalization along broad principles. This might be done, for example, by the abandonment of its limitations to 'products' 'put into circulation' as well as amendment to render it explicitly that kind of a 'minimum' Directive which would allow a Member State to enact a more protective law applicable across the entire domestic market place (see Chapter 3, Postscript). Pessimists might query the likelihood of the European Commission ever conceding flaws in its Directive, and might also query the ease with which interested parties would be able to initiate and sustain pressure for reform of civil liability within the current EC framework (Chapter 3, under heading 5(a)).

---

22 See, eg, *Cambridge Water Co* v *Eastern Counties Leather plc* [1992] EGCS 142, CA (but now see Times, 10 December 1993, HL); Stapleton, op cit 1993.

23 For it is one thing for the European Commission to have apparantly shelved the draft Directive on liability for services in deference to pressure for 'subsidiarity' (see European Parliament, *The Week*, 18–23 Jan 1993, pp 10–11; on subsidiarity see Chapter 3, under heading 6(a)(ii)); it is quite another for it to face the embarrassment of proposing the repeal of one of its implemented Directives.

6 THE SHORT-TERM PRACTICAL IMPACT OF THE DIRECTIVE

The products Directive and other consumer measures still appear attractive to Member States as recent Directives on general product safety and unfair terms in consumer contracts show. They allow governments to appear active in fields such as consumer protection and to appear to establish substantially greater protection than before even when this is in fact not the case, while local regimes survive untarnished. The reform becomes even more of a facade the more often the ECJ is persuaded for legal or political reasons to see issues such as defectiveness, causation and remoteness as ones of fact to be decided at local level. But a facade of doctrinal change can still have an impact. First, far from harmonizing laws within the EC, the Directive has added a further layer of liability which will make more complex the practitioners' task of advising clients on, and pursuing all possible avenues of, redress and defence. Supporters of the Directive argue that although additive to other causes of action, it is of benefit because it will increase claims consciousness among victims and their legal advisers. With its enticing slogan of 'strict liability' it would provide an attractive basis for claims even in complex cases, and because of its marginal advantages in some cases it would be the preferable route for the victim to take, thereby simplifying the claim. But this argument in support of the Directive assumes the victim succeeds under that cause of action which, of course, she may not.[24] Certainly if plaintiffs who succeed under the Directive *had known in advance* that this claim would succeed, they could have afforded to make only a claim under the Directive. But plaintiffs do not have foresight, and so they will claim under any and all heads which offer some chance of success.

Practitioners will have to be alive to the fact that whenever a claim *could* be made under the Directive, there will usually also be a claim in negligence which does not have such limitations, and failure to advise on such back-up claims may amount to professional negligence. The result is that most future claims under the Directive should and probably will be made with whatever causes of action would previously have been used, pleaded in the alternative. This is illustrated by the Camelford water reservoir pollution case where from the start it was clear that the plaintiffs had the strongest of claims under s 2(1) of the CPA but where claims were also made for breach of statutory duty, strict liability under *Rylands* v *Fletcher*, breach of contract, nuisance and negligence![25] In more complex factual cases this means the Directive, far from simplifying the plaintiff's claim, will have added a costly new dimension to it. This is all the more true when the condition of the product is only one of a range of factors implicated in the injury. Of course, because of its new stricter liability on non-manufacturing product suppliers, the Directive may well prompt claims against defendants, such as product importers, who had previously not been considered by plaintiffs or their lawyers as targets for a claim. But for the plaintiff class *as a whole* the occasional advantage given by this and by the reversed burden of proof on some

---

24 Even in a case where the condition of the product is centrally implicated in the injury, the product may, for example, be held to be agricultural produce which has not yet undergone the form of 'processing' necessary to bring it within the Directive. Or what if the complaint is held more properly to relate to the defendant's post-supply behaviour which is not caught by the Directive? What if the court holds that the injury was suffered at a point when the product had not yet been 'put into circulation'?

25 *AB* v *South West Water Services Ltd* [1993] QB 507, CA

issues, may be more than outweighed by the costly duplication represented by the cause of action under the Directive.

On the defendant's side there are comparably increased pressures to join more parties, and there may also be greater interest in setting up defence alliances and so on. The Directive is also having a practical effect on the behaviour of potential defendants in the field of record-keeping. In the NHS there is evidence that suppliers of products such as vaccines and drugs – eg dentists, general practitioners and pharmacists – are now making substantial efforts to record the origin of products in order to avoid s 2(3) liability. It is more speculative just what impact the Directive is having on research and development. Some manufacturers have tightened up quality control measures and vehicle recalls have more than doubled since 1985. Similarly, it is unclear if there has been any effect on corporate strategy. Certainly practitioner texts[26] on the Directive advise on the possible 'prudence' of the use of shell companies and the splitting off of manufacturing from the company's asset base through use of a separate manufacturing company, to reduce the assets immediately available to a prospective claimant. But it is likely that any additional incentive for such a strategy generated by the Directive is marginal.

Next there is the question of the success rate of claims and the overall rate of claims. Under the Directive the novel liability of mere suppliers is easily avoided and that of importers into the EC and own-brand suppliers will not often arise, so the principal new advantage for plaintiffs is in the area of burden of proof, especially the burden which lies on the defendant to establish the development risk defence or that the product was not defective when it left his control. Against these possible advantages must be set the continuing problems of access to the legal system (availability of legal aid, etc) and of the plaintiff's burden of proof on issues such as medical causation and 'defect'. Even going by the 'law in books', therefore, it is hard to see to what extent, if any, the *success rate* of claims involving products might increase. The careful and wide-ranging socio-legal research needed to establish the trend of success rates is costly, perhaps prohibitively so (see Chapter 4, under heading 3). Even establishing the trend of *claims rates* is difficult: there is only anecdotal evidence about the Directive's impact on claims rates in the EC. In the UK, the first Member State to implement the Directive, only one claim (the Camelford claim) has so far appeared in the law reports in the first six years of operation of the CPA. This is not to say there have been few claims. The Consumers Association have evidence that claims are being made and there is also a perception that people are making somewhat more consumer claims in general than five years ago, although this could be more the result of the deepening recession in the UK economy, than a response to the new law.

When faced with CPA claims, it seems that insurers are choosing to settle them out of court rather than to incur the expense of the trailblazing cases needed to determine the boundaries of the new law. The aim of those settling claims for defendants might also be to prevent the boost to claims consciousness which the high profile nature of such novel litigation would threaten. There is also anecdotal evidence that defence interests are simply nervous of European law in general, and this Directive in particular, and so are more keen to settle than they would otherwise be. In any case the new law only relates to products supplied after March 1988, so some

26 See, eg, M Thornton and T Ellis 'United Kingdom' in *European Product Liability* ed P Kelly and R Attree (London, Butterworths, 1992) 429, 470–1.

current product injuries may not even be covered by the Directive. High Street practitioners may also simply be preferring the well-trodden, and probably almost as generous, rules of negligence law.

Contrary to earlier fears that a new wave of claims would follow the Directive, the general claims environment seems to have remained unchanged since the Directive:[27] and there are still relatively few reported cases relating to products.[28] Similarly, contrary to fears preceding the Directive, the evidence suggests that it has not prompted significant insurance premium increases, at least so far.[29] This parallels the only marginal increase in insurance premiums witnessed after the introduction of the Unfair Contract Terms Act 1977 in the UK, and the statutory introduction of strict liability for pharmaceuticals in Germany in 1976. In the early years this may simply be due to the fact that product liability cover is often embedded in a general insurance policy also containing, for example, employers' liability and occupiers' liability components. The new product liability cover may be a loss leader for the whole package. Another explanation is that the insurance industry well appreciates how little the Directive really increases product manufacturers' and suppliers' liability and has accurately predicted that no boom in claims will result. The simplest explanation is that despite the theoretical strategy of insurance – collecting appropriate premiums at the time the insured risk is being incurred – the reality of insurance practice is that premiums chase claims experience, and there simply has been no significant increase in product claims yet.

It may be attractive to ascribe this absence of a claims boom to the problems of bringing suit in the UK, but there are more convincing explanations, such as practitioners' wariness of new European law or their apathy towards it. The contrast with professional liability supports this. The absence of a product liability insurance crisis can be contrasted with the recent professional liability insurance crisis in the UK which seems to have had its origin not in doctrinal expansion but in heightened claims consciousness and hence increased claims.[30] This suggests that, although one of the predicted effects of the products Directive is increased claims consciousness, this has not yet occurred or has failed to produce more claims because of factors not present in the professional liability area. Experience in the latter area shows that, despite barriers to justice in the UK, sufficient new claims can result from increased claims consciousness to have an important effect. In time this may happen in the products field: claims may increase along with insurance premiums and perhaps pressure for reform by parties aggrieved by the anomalies, inconsistencies and inequities associated with the Directive.

The experience in other Member States parallels the UK experience in terms of impact on claims rates, the rate of success of those claims and on insurance premiums. In general, though, it is still early days. Perhaps the first sign of a

---

27 Even before the Directive, reported case law on products was so thin scholars used case law from other fields to illustrate basic propositions, see, eg, C Newdick 'The Development Risk Defence of the Consumer Protection Act 1987' (1988) 47 Camb LJ 455, 457–8. Pearson found that, relatively, very few claims were made in the area of product liability, para 1202.

28 Indirectly this might seem to support criticisms about the difficulty of access to justice in the UK.

29 J Kellam 'Australian Product Liability – An Update' [Sept 1992], Prod Liab Internat 130, 131.

30 P Cane 'Liability Rules and the Cost of Professional Indemnity Insurance' (1989) 53 Geneva Papers on Risk and Insurance 347. In general see M Trebilocock 'The Social Insurance-Deterrence Dilemma of Modern North American Tort Law: A Canadian Perspective on the Liability Insurance Crisis' (1987) 24 San Diego LR 929; G Priest 'The Current Insurance Crisis and Modern Tort Law' (1987) 96 Yale LJ 1521; J Fleming 'The Insurance Crisis' (1990) 24 UBC Law Rev 1.

significant impact by the Directive will be when a mass tort occurs and plaintiffs go forum shopping to escape jurisdictions with financial caps. So far its principal practical impact has, ironically, been outside the EC altogether where it has led to limited product reform in a number of jurisdictions (see Chapter 3, under heading 7).

7   CONCLUSION

The process which produced the US products rule and then the products Directive raises important questions about the origin and coherence of law reform. In Japan, by happenstance, the health disaster which galvanized modern public opinion concerned environmental pollution at Minamata. The result in 1973 was a separate no-fault scheme of compensation for victims of air or water pollution.[31] By chance the corresponding cause célèbre in the UK and EC was a product, Thalidomide, and by adaptation of the US model the resultant law attempted to create a corresponding liability for product-related injury. This response produced pockets of special law related to newspaper headlines rather than categories related to social phenomena and concern. Yet unlike special limited non-tort schemes such as workers' compensation, the criminal injuries compensation scheme and the vaccine damage payment scheme, where the underlying special pleading was conceded and patent, a special rule of tort law such as the Directive seems more in need of doctrinal legitimation.

One device to give adoption of the special products rule intellectual respectability was by reference to the alleged anomalies within existing remedies for those injured by products: the buyer had a product-related remedy linked to a strict standard of liability, while others had the task of establishing fault. Ignoring the possible argument that it was the strictness of the contractual remedy which was the anomaly, reformers proposed that the change needed was to raise the entitlement of non-buyers up to that of the buyer under sales law. In the face of severe pressures to compromise generated by the EC reform process, this aim was eventually abandoned. What was left was the almost empty shell of the special rule which itself generated many more anomalies than the one its proponents attacked, and generated virtually no consumer gain.

The theoretical debate does not lend respectability to the Directive either. Popular models of liability are so far removed from the complexity of real tort rules that their inability to justify the special product rules fails to concern EC reformers and other lawyers who may complacently argue that, even if the Directive does little for consumers, if it seems to be working why change it? The argument here must be that even if a defence of civil liability can only rely on its symbolic value, that value depends *in the long run* on the goals of rules of civil liability being relatively simple and transparent so that the rules can guide behaviour and be applied with a minimum of anomaly and grievance. The products Directive – the paradigm example of an ad-hoc limited rule of liability – fails to satisfy these requirements. By creating artificial distinctions which have no correspondence to meaningful social phenomena it disrupts and inhibits the development of civil liability along broad rational principles while threatening to have an unfair and haphazard impact on certain

---

31 Pollution-Related Health Damage Compensation Law, Law No 111, 5.10.73 (as amended) (Japan).

market sectors. The final question then raised is whether our processes of law reform are still 'capable of ... striking through forms of legal separateness to reality'[32] as they did once in *Donoghue* v *Stevenson* and the Occupiers' Liability Act 1957, and if so, how long might it now be before this happens?

32 Mr Justice Evatt to Lord Atkin in 1933: G Lewis *Lord Atkin* (London, Butterworths, 1983) 67.

The European Communities Directive

The Council of the European Communities Directive of 25 July 1985 on the approximation of the laws, regulations and administrative provisions of the Member States concerning liability for defective products

Article 1

The producer shall be liable for damage caused by a defect in his product.

Article 2

For the purpose of this Directive 'product' means all movables, with the exception of primary agricultural products and game, even though incorporated into another movable or into an immovable. 'Primary agricultural products' means the products of the soil, of stock-farming and of fisheries, excluding products which have undergone initial processing. 'Product' includes electricity.

Article 3

(1) 'Producer' means the manufacturer of a finished product, the producer of any raw material or the manufacturer of a component part and any person who, by putting his name, trade mark or other distinguishing feature on the product presents himself as its producer.

(2) Without prejudice to the liability of the producer, any person who imports into the Community a product for sale, hire, leasing or any form of distribution in the course of his business shall be deemed to be a producer within the meaning of this Directive and shall be responsible as a producer.

(3) Where the producer of the product cannot be identified, each supplier of the product shall be treated as its producer unless he informs the injured person, within a reasonable time, of the identity of the producer or of the person who supplied him with the product. The same shall apply, in the case of an imported product, if this product does not indicate the identity of the importer referred to in paragraph 2, even if the name of the producer is indicated.

Article 4

The injured person shall be required to prove the damage, the defect and the causal relationship between defect and damage.

Article 5

Where, as a result of the provisions of this Directive, two or more persons are liable for the same damage, they shall be liable jointly and severally, without prejudice to the provisions of national law concerning the rights of contribution or recourse.

Article 6

(1) A product is defective when it does not provide the safety which a person is entitled to expect, taking all circumstances into account, including:
   (a) the presentation of the product;
   (b) the use to which it could reasonably be expected that the product would be put;
   (c) the time when the product was put into circulation.
(2) A product shall not be considered defective for the sole reason that a better product is subsequently put into circulation.

Article 7

The producer shall not be liable as a result of this Directive if he proves:
   (a) that he did not put the product into circulation; or
   (b) that, having regard to the circumstances, it is probable that the defect which caused the damage did not exist at the time when the product was put into circulation by him or that this defect came into being afterwards; or
   (c) that the product was neither manufactured by him for sale or any form of distribution for economic purpose nor manufactured or distributed by him in the course of his business; or
   (d) that the defect is due to compliance of the product with mandatory regulations issued by the public authorities; or
   (e) that the state of scientific and technical knowledge at the time when he put the product into circulation was not such as to enable the existence of the defect to be discovered; or
   (f) in the case of a manufacturer of a component, that the defect is attributable to the design of the product in which the component has been fitted or to the instructions given by the manufacturer of the product.

Article 8

(1) Without prejudice to the provisions of national law concerning the right of contribution or recourse, the liability of the producer shall not be reduced when the damage is caused both by a defect in the product and by the act or omission of a third party.
(2) The liability of the producer may be reduced or disallowed when, having regard to all the circumstances, the damage is caused both by a defect in the product and by the fault of the injured person or any person for whom the injured person is responsible.

Article 9

For the purpose of Article 1, 'damage' means:
  (a) damage caused by death or by personal injuries;
  (b) damage to, or destruction of, any item of property other than the defective
       product itself, with a lower threshold of 500 ECU, provided that the item of
       property:
       (i)   is of a type ordinarily intended for private use or consumption,
             and
       (ii) was used by the injured person mainly for his own private use or
             consumption.
This Article shall be without prejudice to national provisions relating to non-
material damage.

Article 10

(1) Member States shall provide in their legislation that a limitation period of three
years shall apply to proceedings for the recovery of damages as provided for in this
Directive. The limitation period shall begin to run from the day on which the plaintiff became aware, or should reasonably have become aware, of the damage, the
defect and the identity of the producer.
(2) The laws of Member States regulating suspension or interruption of the limitation period shall not be affected by this Directive.

Article 11

Member States shall provide in their legislation that the rights conferred upon the
injured person pursuant to this Directive shall be extinguished upon the expiry of a
period of 10 years from the date on which the producer put into circulation the
actual product which caused the damage, unless the injured person has in the meantime instituted proceedings against the producer.

Article 12

The liability of the producer arising from the Directive may not, in relation to the
injured person, be limited or excluded by a provision limiting his liability or
exempting him from liability.

Article 13

This Directive shall not affect any rights which an injured person may have according to the rules of the law of contractual or non-contractual liability or a special
liability system existing at the moment when this Directive is notified.

Article 14

This Directive shall not apply to injury or damage arising from nuclear accidents
and covered by international conventions ratified by the Member States.

Article 15

(1) Each Member State may:
   (a) by way of derogation from Article 2, provide in its legislation that within the meaning of Article 1 of this Directive 'product' also means primary agricultural products and game;
   (b) by way of derogation from Article 7 (e), maintain or, subject to the procedure set out in paragraph 2 of this Article, provide in this legislation that the producer shall be liable even if he proves that the state of scientific and technical knowledge at the time when he put the product into circulation was not such as to enable the existence of a defect to be discovered.

(2) A Member State wishing to introduce the measure specified in paragraph 1(b) shall communicate the text of the proposed measure to the Commission. The Commission shall inform the other Member States thereof.

The Member State concerned shall hold the proposed measure in abeyance for nine months after the Commission is informed and provided that in the meantime the Commission has not submitted to the Council a proposal amending this Directive on the relevant matter. However, if within three months of receiving the said information, the Commission does not advise the Member State concerned that it intends submitting such a proposal to the Council, the Member State may take the proposed measure immediately.

If the Commission does submit to the Council such a proposal amending this Directive within the aforementioned nine months, the Member State concerned shall hold the proposed measure in abeyance for a further period of 18 months from the date on which the proposal is submitted.

(3) Ten years after the date of notification of this Directive, the Commission shall submit to the Council a report on the effect that rulings by the courts as to the application of Article 7(e) and of paragraph 1(b) of this Article have on consumer protection and the functioning of the common market. In the light of this report the Council, acting on a proposal from the Commission and pursuant to the terms of Article 100 of the Treaty, shall decide whether to repeal Article 7(e).

Article 16

(1) Any Member State may provide that a producer's total liability for damage resulting from a death or personal injury and caused by identical items with the same defect shall be limited to an amount which may not be less than 70 million ECU.

(2) Ten years after the date of notification of this Directive, the Commission shall submit to the Council a report on the effect on consumer protection and the functioning of the common market of the implementation of the financial limit on liability by those Member States which have used the option provided for in paragraph 1. In the light of this report the Council, acting on a proposal from the Commission and pursuant to the terms of Article 100 of the Treaty, shall decide whether to repeal paragraph 1.

Article 17

This Directive shall not apply to products put into circulation before the date on which the provisions referred to in Article 19 enter into force.

Article 18

(1) For the purposes of this Directive, the ECU shall be that defined by Regulation (EEC) No 3180/78 (OJ No L 379, 30.12.1978, p1), as amended by Regulation (EEC) No 2626/84 (OJ No L 247, 16.9.1984, p1). The equivalent in national currency shall initially be calculated at the rate obtaining on the date of adoption of this Directive.
(2) Every five years the Council, acting on a proposal from the Commission, shall examine and, if need be, revise the amounts in this Directive, in the light of economic and monetary trends in the Community.

Article 19

(1) Member States shall bring into force, not later than three years from the date of notification of this Directive [30 July 1985], the laws, regulations and administrative provisions necessary to comply with this Directive. They shall forthwith inform the Commission thereof.
(2) The procedure set out in Article 15(2) shall apply from the date of notification of this Directive.

Article 20

Member States shall communicate to the Commission the texts of the main provisions of national law which they subsequently adopt in the field governed by this Directive.

Article 21

Every five years the Commission shall present a report to the Council on the application of this Directive and, if necessary, shall submit appropriate proposals to it.

Article 22

This Directive is addressed to the Member States.

Done at Brussels, 25 July 1985.

Consumer Protection Act 1987

1987 CHAPTER 43

An Act to make provision with respect to the liability of persons for damage caused by defective products; to consolidate with amendments the Consumer Safety Act 1978 and the Consumer Safety (Amendment) Act 1986; to make provision with respect to the giving of price indications; to amend Part I of the Health and Safety at Work etc Act 1974 and sections 31 and 80 of the Explosives Act 1875; to repeal the Trade Descriptions Act 1972 and the Fabrics (Misdescription) Act 1913; and for connected purposes. [15th May 1987]

Be it enacted by the Queen's most Excellent Majesty, by and with the advice and consent of the Lords Spiritual and Temporal, and Commons, in this present Parliament assembled, and by the authority of the same, as follows:-

PART I

PRODUCT LIABILITY

1   **Purpose and construction of Part I**

(1) This Part shall have effect for the purpose of making such provision as is necessary in order to comply with the product liability Directive and shall be construed accordingly.

(2) In this Part, except in so far as the context otherwise requires–

'agricultural produce' means any produce of the soil, of stock-farming or of fisheries;

'dependant' and 'relative' have the same meaning as they have in, respectively, the Fatal Accidents Act 1976 and the Damages (Scotland) Act 1976;

   'producer', in relation to a product, means–

   (a) the person who manufactured it;

   (b) in the case of a substance which has not been manufactured but has been won or abstracted, the person who won or abstracted it;

   (c) in the case of a product which has not been manufactured, won or abstracted but essential characteristics of which are attributable to an industrial or other process having been carried out (for example, in relation to agricultural produce), the person who carried out that process;

'product' means any goods or electricity and (subject to subsection (3) below) includes a product which is comprised in another product, whether by virtue of being a component part or raw material or otherwise, and 'the product liability Directive' means the Directive of the Council of the European Communities, dated 25th July 1985, (No 85/374/EEC) on the approximation of the laws, regulations and administrative provisions of the member States concerning liability for defective products.

(3) For the purposes of this Part a person who supplies any product in which products are comprised, whether by virtue of being component parts or raw materials or otherwise, shall not be treated by reason only of his supply of that product as supplying any of the products so comprised.

2   Liability for defective products

(1) Subject to the following provisions of this Part, where any damage is caused wholly or partly by a defect in a product, every person to whom subsection (2) below applies shall be liable for the damage.

(2) This subsection applies to–
   (a) the producer of the product;
   (b) any person who, by putting his name on the product or using a trade mark or other distinguishing mark in relation to the product, has held himself out to be the producer of the product;
   (c) any person who has imported the product into a member State from a place outside the member States in order, in the course of any business of his, to supply it to another.

(3) Subject as aforesaid, where any damage is caused wholly or partly by a defect in a product, any person who supplied the product (whether to the person who suffered the damage, to the producer of any product in which the product in question is comprised or to any other person) shall be liable for the damage if–
   (a) the person who suffered the damage requests the supplier to identify one or more of the persons (whether still in existence or not) to whom subsection (2) above applies in relation to the product;
   (b) the request is made within a reasonable period after the damage occurs and at a time when it is not reasonably practicable for the person making the request to identify all those persons; and
   (c) the supplier fails, within a reasonable period after receiving the request, either to comply with the request or to identify the person who supplied the product to him.

(4) Neither subsection (2) nor subsection (3) above shall apply to a person in respect of any defect in any game or agricultural produce if the only supply of the game or produce by that person to another was at a time when it had not undergone an industrial process.

(5) Where two or more persons are liable by virtue of this Part for the same damage, their liability shall be joint and several.

(6) This section shall be without prejudice to any liability arising otherwise than by virtue of this Part.

3   Meaning of 'defect'

(1) Subject to the following provisions of this section, there is a defect in a product for the purposes of this Part if the safety of the product is not such as persons generally are entitled to expect; and for those purposes 'safety', in relation to a product, shall include safety with respect to products comprised in that product and safety in the context of risks of damage to property, as well as in the context of risks of death or personal injury.

(2) In determining for the purposes of subsection (1) above what persons generally are entitled to expect in relation to a product all the circumstances shall be taken into account, including–
(a) the manner in which, and purposes for which, the product has been marketed, its get-up, the use of any market in relation to the product and any instructions for, or warnings with respect to, doing or refraining from doing anything with or in relation to the product;
(b) what might reasonably be expected to be done with or in relation to the product; and
(c) the time when the product was supplied by its producer to another;
and nothing in this section shall require a defect to be inferred from the fact alone that the safety of a product which is supplied after that time is greater than the safety of the product in question.

4 Defences

(1) In any civil proceedings by virtue of this Part against any person ('the person proceeded against') in respect of a defect in a product it shall be a defence for him to show–
(a) that the defect is attributable to compliance with any requirement imposed by or under any enactment or with any Community obligation; or
(b) that the person proceeded against did not at any time supply the product to another; or
(c) that the following conditions are satisfied, that is to say–
(i) that the only supply of the product to another by the person proceeded against was otherwise than in the course of a business of that person's; and
(ii) that section 2(2) above does not apply to that person or applies to him by virtue only of things done otherwise than with a view to profit; or
(d) that the defect did not exist in the product at the relevant time; or
(e) that the state of scientific and technical knowledge at the relevant time was not such that a producer of products of the same description as the product in question might be expected to have discovered the defect if it had existed in his products while they were under his control; or
(f) that the defect–
(i) constituted a defect in a product ('the subsequent product') in which the product in question had been comprised; and
(ii) was wholly attributable to the design of the subsequent product or to compliance by the producer of the product in question with instructions given by the producer of the subsequent product.

(2) In this section 'the relevant time', in relation to electricity, means the time at which it was generated, being a time before it was transmitted or distributed, and in relation to any other product, means–
(a) if the person proceeded against is a person to whom subsection (2) of section 2 above applies in relation to the product, the time when he supplied the product to another;
(b) if that subsection does not apply to that person in relation to the product, the time when the product was last supplied by a person to whom that subsection does apply in relation to the product.

5 Damage giving rise to liability

(1) Subject to the following provisions of this section, in this Part 'damage' means death or personal injury or any loss of or damage to any property (including land).

(2) A person shall not be liable under section 2 above in respect of any defect in a product for the loss of or any damage to the product itself or for the loss of or any damage to the whole or any part of any product which has been supplied with the product in question comprised in it.

(3) A person shall not be liable under section 2 above for any loss of or damage to any property which, at the time it is lost or damaged, is not–

    (a) of a description of property ordinarily intended for private use, occupation or consumption; and

    (b) intended by the person suffering the loss or damage mainly for his own private use, occupation or consumption.

(4) No damages shall be awarded to any person by virtue of this Part in respect of any loss of or damage to any property if the amount which would fall to be so awarded to that person, apart from this subsection and any liability for interest, does not exceed £275.

(5) In determining for the purposes of this Part who has suffered any loss of or damage to property and when any such loss or damage occurred, the loss or damage shall be regarded as having occurred at the earliest time at which a person with an interest in the property had knowledge of the material facts about the loss or damage.

(6) For the purposes of subsection (5) above the material facts about any loss of or damage to any property are such facts about the loss or damage as would lead a reasonable person with an interest in the property to consider the loss or damage sufficiently serious to justify his instituting proceedings for damages against a defendant who did not dispute liability and was able to satisfy a judgment.

(7) For the purposes of subsection (5) above a person's knowledge includes knowledge which he might reasonably have been expected to acquire–

    (a) from facts observable or ascertainable by him; or

    (b) from facts ascertainable by him with the help of appropriate expert advice which it is reasonable for him to seek;

but a person shall not be taken by virtue of this subsection to have knowledge of a fact ascertainable by him only with the help of expert advice unless he has failed to take all reasonable steps to obtain (and, where appropriate, to act on) that advice.

(8) Subsections (5) to (7) above shall not extend to Scotland.

6 Application of certain enactments etc

(1) Any damage for which a person is liable under section 2 above shall be deemed to have been caused–

    (a) for the purposes of the Fatal Accidents Act 1976, by that person's wrongful act, neglect or default;

    (b) for the purposes of section 3 of the Law Reform (Miscellaneous Provisions) (Scotland) Act 1940 (contribution among joint wrongdoers), by that person's wrongful act or negligent act or omission;

    (c) for the purposes of section 1 of the Damages (Scotland) Act 1976 (rights of relatives of a deceased), by that person's act or omission; and

(d) for the purposes of Part II of the Administration of Justice Act 1982 (damages for personal injuries, etc – Scotland), by an act or omission giving rise to liability in that person to any damages.

(2) Where–

(a) a person's death is caused wholly or partly by a defect in a product, or a person dies after suffering damage which has been so caused;

(b) a request such as mentioned in paragraph (a) of subsection (3) of section 2 above is made to a supplier of the product by that person's personal representatives or, in the case of a person whose death is caused wholly or partly by the defect, by any dependant or relative of that person; and

(c) the conditions specified in paragraphs (b) and (c) of that subsection are satisfied in relation to that request,

this Part shall have effect for the purposes of the Law Reform (Miscellaneous Provisions) Act 1934, the Fatal Accidents Act 1976 and the Damages (Scotland) Act 1976 as if liability of the supplier to that person under that subsection did not depend on that person having requested the supplier to identify certain persons or on the said conditions having been satisfied in relation to a request made by that person.

(3) Section 1 of the Congenital Disabilities (Civil Liability) Act 1976 shall have effect for the purposes of this Part as if–

(a) a person were answerable to a child in respect of an occurrence caused wholly or partly by a defect in a product if he is or has been liable under section 2 above in respect of any effect of the occurrence on a parent of the child, or would be so liable if the occurrence caused a parent of the child to suffer damage;

(b) the provisions of this Part relating to liability under section 2 above applied in relation to liability by virtue of paragraph (a) above under the said section 1; and

(c) subsection (6) of the said section 1 (exclusion of liability) were omitted.

(4) Where any damage is caused partly by a defect in a product and partly by the fault of the person suffering the damage, the Law Reform (Contributory Negligence) Act 1945 and section 5 of the Fatal Accidents Act 1976 (contributory negligence) shall have effect as if the defect were the fault of every person liable by virtue of this Part for the damage caused by the defect.

(5) In subsection (4) above 'fault' has the same meaning as in the said Act of 1945.

(6) Schedule 1 to this Act shall have effect for the purpose of amending the Limitation Act 1980 and the Prescription and Limitation (Scotland) Act 1973 in their application in relation to the bringing of actions by virtue of this Part.

(7) It is hereby declared that liability by virtue of this Part is to be treated as liability in tort for the purposes of any enactment conferring jurisdiction on any court with respect to any matter.

(8) Nothing in this Part shall prejudice the operation of section 12 of the Nuclear Installations Act 1965 (rights to compensation for certain breaches of duties confined to rights under that Act).

7   Prohibition on exclusions from liability

The liability of a person by virtue of this Part to a person who has suffered damage caused wholly or partly by a defect in a product, or to a dependant or relative of such a person, shall not be limited or excluded by any contract term, by any notice or by any other provision.

8   Power to modify Part I

(1) Her Majesty may by Order in Council make such modifications of this Part and of any other enactment (including an enactment contained in the following Parts of this Act, or in an Act passed after this Act) as appear to Her Majesty in Council to be necessary or expedient in consequence of any modification of the product liability Directive which is made at any time after the passing of this Act.

(2) An Order in Council under subsection (1) above shall not be submitted to Her Majesty in Council unless a draft of the Order has been laid before, and approved by a resolution of, each House of Parliament.

9   Application of Part I to Crown

(1) Subject to subsection (2) below, this Part shall bind the Crown.

(2) The Crown shall not, as regards the Crown's liability by virtue of this Part, be bound by this Part further than the Crown is made liable in tort or in reparation under the Crown Proceedings Act 1947, as that Act has effect from time to time.

• • • • •

45   Interpretation

In this Act, except in so far as the context otherwise requires–

(1) 'aircraft' includes gliders, balloons and hovercraft;

'business' includes a trade or profession and the activities of a professional or trade association or of a local authority or other public authority;

'conditional sale agreement', 'credit-sale agreement' and 'hire-purchase agreement' have the same meanings as in the Consumer Credit Act 1974 but as if in the definitions in that Act 'goods' had the same meaning as in this Act;

'contravention' includes a failure to comply and cognate expressions shall be construed accordingly;

'enforcement authority' means the Secretary of State, any other Minister of the Crown in charge of a Government department, any such department and any authority, council or other person on whom functions under this Act are conferred by or under section 27 above;

'gas' has the same meaning as in Part I of the Gas Act 1986;

'goods' includes substances, growing crops and things comprised in land by virtue of being attached to it and any ship, aircraft or vehicle;

'information' includes accounts, estimates and returns;

'magistrates' court', in relation to Northern Ireland, means a court of summary jurisdiction;

'mark' and 'trade mark' have the same meanings as in the Trade Marks Act 1938;

'modifications' includes additions, alterations and omissions, and cognate expressions shall be construed accordingly;

'motor vehicle' has the same meaning as in the Road Traffic Act 1972;

'notice' means a notice in writing;

'notice to warn' means a notice under section 13(1)(b) above;

'officer', in relation to an enforcement authority, means a person authorised in writing to assist the authority in carrying out its functions under or for the purposes of the enforcement of any of the safety provisions or of any of the provisions made by or under Part III of this Act;

'personal injury' includes any disease and any other impairment of a person's physical or mental condition;

'premises' includes any place and any ship, aircraft or vehicle;

'prohibition notice' means a notice under section 13(1)(a) above;

'records' includes any books or documents and any records in non-documentary form;

'safety provision' means the general safety requirement in section 10 above or any provision of safety regulations, a prohibition notice or a suspension notice;

'safety regulations' means regulations under section 11 above;

'ship' includes any boat and any other description of vessel used in navigation;

'subordinate legislation' has the same meaning as in the Interpretation Act 1978;

'substance' means any natural or artificial substance, whether in solid, liquid or gaseous form or in the form of a vapour, and includes substances that are comprised in or mixed with other goods;

'supply' and cognate expressions shall be construed in accordance with section 46 below;

'suspension notice' means a notice under section 14 above.

(2) Except in so far as the context otherwise requires, references in this Act to a contravention of a safety provision shall, in relation to any goods, include references to anything which would constitute such a contravention if the goods were supplied to any person.

(3) References in this Act to any goods in relation to which any safety provision has been or may have been contravened shall include references to any goods which it is not reasonably practicable to separate from any such goods.

(4) Section 68(2) of the Trade Marks Act 1938 (construction of references to use of a mark) shall apply for the purposes of this Act as it applies for the purposes of that Act.

(5) In Scotland, any reference in this Act to things comprised in land by virtue of being attached to it is a reference to moveables which have become heritable by accession to heritable property.

46 (1) Subject to the following provisions of this section, references in this Act to supplying goods shall be construed as references to doing any of the following, whether as principal or agent, that is to say—

(a) selling, hiring out or lending the goods;

(b) entering into a hire-purchase agreement to furnish the goods;

(c) the performance of any contract for work and materials to furnish the goods;

(d) providing the goods in exchange for any consideration (including trading stamps) other than money;

(e) providing the goods in or in connection with the performance of any statutory function; or

(f) giving the goods as a prize or otherwise making a gift of the goods;

and, in relation to gas or water, those references shall be construed as including references to providing the service by which the gas or water is made available for use.

(2) For the purposes of any reference in this Act to supplying goods, where a person ('the ostensible supplier') supplies goods to another person ('the customer') under a hire-purchase agreement, conditional sale agreement or credit-sale agreement or under an agreement for the hiring of goods (other than a hire-purchase agreement) and the ostensible supplier–

(a) carries on the business of financing the provision of goods for others by means of such agreements; and

(b) in the course of that business acquired his interest in the goods supplied to the customer as a means of financing the provision of them for the customer by a further person ('the effective supplier'),

the effective supplier and not the ostensible supplier shall be treated as supplying the goods to the customer.

(3) Subject to subsection (4) below, the performance of any contract by the erection of any building or structure on any land or by the carrying out of any other building works shall be treated for the purposes of this Act as a supply of goods in so far as, but only in so far as, it involves the provision of any goods to any person by means of their incorporation into the building, structure or works.

(4) Except for the purposes of, and in relation to, notices to warn or any provision made by or under Part III of this Act, references in this Act to supplying goods shall not include references to supplying goods comprised in land where the supply is effected by the creation or disposal of an interest in the land.

(5) Except in Part I of this Act references in this Act to a person's supplying goods shall be confined to references to that person's supplying goods in the course of a business of his, but for the purposes of this subsection it shall be immaterial whether the business is a business of dealing in the goods.

(6) For the purposes of subsection (5) above goods shall not be treated as supplied in the course of a business if they are supplied, in pursuance of an obligation arising under or in connection with the insurance of the goods, to the person with whom they were insured.

(7) Except for the purposes of, and in relation to, prohibition notices or suspension notices, references in Parts II to IV of this Act to supplying goods shall not include–

(a) references to supplying goods where the person supplied carries on a business of buying goods of the same description as those goods and repairing or reconditioning them;

(b) references to supplying goods by a sale of articles as scrap (that is to say, for the value of materials included in the articles rather than for the value of the articles themselves).

(8) Where any goods have at any time been supplied by being hired out or lent to any person, neither a continuation or renewal of the hire or loan (whether on the same or different terms) nor any transaction for the transfer after that time of any interest in the goods to the person to whom they were hired or lent shall be treated for the purposes of this Act as a further supply of the goods to that person.

(9) A ship, aircraft or motor vehicle shall not be treated for the purposes of this Act

as supplied to any person by reason only that services consisting in the carriage of goods or passengers in that ship, aircraft or vehicle, or in its use for any other purpose, are provided to that person in pursuance of an agreement relating to the use of the ship, aircraft or vehicle for a particular period or for particular voyages, flights or journeys.

Index